Pennsylvania State Reports Containing Cases Decided by the Supreme Court of Pennsylvania
by Pennsylvania. Supreme Court

Copyright © 2019 by HardPress

Address:
HardPress
8345 NW 66TH ST #2561
MIAMI FL 33166-2626
USA
Email: info@hardpress.net

GEO. T. BISEL CO.
LAW PUBLISHERS
AND STATIONERS
724 SANSOM STREET
PHILADELPHIA

LIBRARY
OF
THE PENNSYLVANIA STATE COLLEGE

Class No. B345.42

Book No. P381

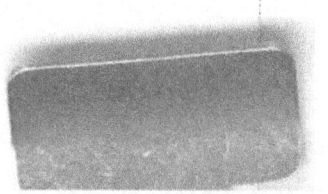

PENNSYLVANIA STATE REPORTS,

CONTAINING

REPORTS OF CASES ADJUDGED BY

THE SUPREME COURT

OF PENNSYLVANIA,

DURING

MARCH TERM, 1851, AT PHILADELPHIA, AND AT HARRISBURG IN 1851.

VOL. XVI.

BY GEORGE W. HARRIS,

OF HARRISBURG, STATE REPORTER.

VOL. IV.

PHILADELPHIA:
KAY & BROTHER,
LAW BOOKSELLERS, PUBLISHERS, AND IMPORTERS,
17 & 19 SOUTH FIFTH STREET, EAST SIDE,
FIRST STORE ABOVE CHESTNUT.
1856.

Entered according to Act of Congress, in the year 1852, by
GEORGE W. HARRIS,
in the Clerk's Office of the District Court of the Eastern District of Pennsylvania.

STEREOTYPED BY L. JOHNSON AND CO.
PHILADELPHIA.

Judges of the Supreme Court of Pennsylvania,

DURING THE DECISION OF THE CASES REPORTED IN THIS VOLUME.

Hon. JOHN BANNISTER GIBSON, *Chief Justice*.
Hon. MOLTON C. ROGERS.
Hon. RICHARD COULTER.
Hon. THOMAS S. BELL.
Hon. GEORGE CHAMBERS.

THOMAS E. FRANKLIN, ESQ., *Attorney-General*.

Judges of the Supreme Court of Pennsylvania,

ELECTED IN 1851.

Hon. JEREMIAH S. BLACK,
Since commissioned as Chief Justice for the term of three years, from the first Monday of December, 1851.

Hon. ELLIS LEWIS,
Commissioned for the term of six years.

Hon. JOHN BANNISTER GIBSON,
Commissioned for the term of nine years.

Hon. WALTER H. LOWRIE,
Commissioned for the term of twelve years.

Hon. RICHARD COULTER,
Commissioned for the term of fifteen years.

JAMES CAMPBELL, ESQ., *Attorney-General*,
Commissioned 21st January, 1852.

TABLE OF CASES.

	PAGE		PAGE
Afflick v. Thomas	14	Fitzwater v. Stout	22
Alexander v. Miller, Reed & Co.	215	Flory v. Hackman	196
Anthony v. Welsh	254	Forster v. Juniata Bridge Co.	393
		Fraim v. Commonwealth	163
Baldauf v. Camden and Amboy Railroad Co.	67	Franklin College v. Thurston	154
Baxley v. Linah	241	George v. Morgan	95
Bear v. Bitzer	175	Gilmore v. Beatty	463
Beatty v. Gilmore	463	Goldsmith v. Edwards	43
Beck v. Uhrich	499	Gordon v. Bowers	226
Bethel v. Railroad Co.	182	Gratz v. Hoover	232
Bitzer v. Bear	175	Groff v. Levan	179
Blythe v. Louden	532	Guthrie's Appeal	321
Bowers v. Gordon	226		
Brandon v. Meals	220	Hackman v. Flory	196
Brandt's Appeal	343	Hamilton v. Commonwealth	129
Bridenhart v. County	458	Harbold's Executors v. Kuntz	210
Brights v. McKinney & Heller	399	Haywood & Snyder v. Shell	523
Burke & Gonder v. Faunce	469	Heagy v. Trimmer	484
Bushey v. Dottarer	204	Heise v. Railroad Company	182
		Hennershotz's Estate	435
Camden and Amboy Railroad Co. v. Baldauf	67	Holliday v. Rheem	347
Commonwealth v. Fraim	163	Hoover v. Gratz	232
" v. Hamilton	129	Hubert v. Murphy	50
" v. Kidd	426	Jessup v. Smuck	327
" v. Quigley	353	Johns v. Davidson	512
" v. Stoner	387	Jones v. Wood	25
County v. Bridenhart	458	Juniata Bridge Co. v. Forster	393
Davidson v. Johns	512	Kelly's Appeal	59
Dottarer v. Bushey	204	Kelly v. Stewart	160
		Kidd v. Commonwealth	426
Edwards v. Goldsmith	43	Kirkpatrick v. Muirhead	117
Ermold v. Newkirk	417	Knouff v. Thompson	357
Ervine's Appeal	256	Kuntz v. Harbold's Executors	210
Eyster's Appeal	372		
		Lange v. Stouffer	251
Faunce v. Burke & Gonder	469	Lee v. Porter	412
Finney v. Finney	380	Levan v. Groff	179

TABLE OF CASES.

	PAGE
Lewis v. Rogers	18
Lex v Potters	295
Linah v. Baxley	241
Longnecker v. Oyster	269
Louden v. Blythe	532
Maish v. Weidman	504
Marberger v. Pott	9
Marshall v. Maurer	377
Maurer v. Marshall	377
Meals v. Brandon	220
McClellan's Appeal	110
McConnell v. Wenrich	365
McCulloch v. McKee	289
McGinnis's Appeal	445
McKee v. McCulloch	289
McKinney & Heller v. Brights	399
McKissick v. Pickle	140
Mifflin v. Railroad Company	182
Miller's Appeal	300
Miller, Reed & Co. v. Alexander	215
Miller v. Stone	450
Miller v. Zerbe	488
Moyer's Appeal	405
Morgan v. George	95
Morgan v. Worrall	95
Muirhead v. Kirkpatrick	117
Murphy v. Hubert	50
Newkirk v. Ermold	417
Northern Liberties v. The City of Philadelphia	79
Oyster v. Longnecker	269
Penny Pot Landing	79
Philadelphia v. The Northern Liberties	79
Pickle v. McKissick	140
Pocopson Road	15
Porter v. Lee	412
Pott v. Marberger	9
Potters v. Lex	295
Quigley v. Commonwealth	353
Railroad Company v. Bethel	182
" v. Heise	182
" v. Mifflin	182
Rheem v. Holliday	347
Robb v. Sample	305
Rogers v. Lewis	18
Sample v. Robb	305
Schneider's Appeal	407
Sheidle v. Weishlee	134
Shell v. Haywood & Snyder	523
Shore v. Haines	200
Short's Estate	63
Smuck v. Jessup	327
Staines v. Shore	200
Stewart v. Kelly	160
Stewart v. Walls	275
Stone v. Miller	450
Stoner v. Commonwealth	387
Stouffer v. Lange	251
Stout v. Fitzwater	22
Summers's Appeal	169
Thomas v. Afflick	14
Thompson v. Knouff	357
Thurston v. Franklin College	154
Trimmer v. Heagy	484
Uhrich v. Beck	499
Walls v. Stewart	275
Weidman v. Maish	504
Weishlee v. Sheidle	134
Welsh v. Anthony	254
Wenrich v. McConnell	365
Wither's Appeal	151
Wood v. Jones	25
Worrall v. Morgan	95
Zerbe v. Miller	488

In the Supreme Court of Pennsylvania in and for the Eastern District:

APRIL 22, 1848. *It is ordered by the Court:* That in the Eastern District, paper-books be prepared and printed by the plaintiffs in error for the use of each member of the court and the reporter; that they contain the names of the parties, the judgment of the court from which the appeal, certiorari, or writ of error is taken; a clear, succinct, and lucid statement or history of the case, noting particularly the matters in controversy between the parties; also that part of the evidence or charge or record on which the point turns. *It is also ordered*, that the errors on which the plaintiff in error relies be particularly set out, with such parts of the evidence, record, pleadings, or charge to which exception is taken; that there be a reference to the authorities appended to each point on which he relies, with an abstract of the principle ruled and its application to the point. *It is further ordered*, that the plaintiff in error, at least ten days before the argument, furnish the defendant in error with a copy of his paper-book; whereupon it shall be the duty of the defendant in error, or appellee, to furnish, within seven days thereafter, his counter-statement, if any he has, with his authorities bearing on the respective points; stating their application, and an abstract of the principles ruled.

It is also ordered, that from and after the present session of the court, no counsel in the Eastern District of the Supreme Court shall be permitted to occupy *more* than one hour in the argument of any cause in the Supreme Court, unless with the special permission of the court, and in such case only as may in their judgment imperatively require a relaxation of the rule. *Provided*, the counsel, if they think proper, be permitted to make such arrangement as that one counsel may occupy more than one hour of the allotted time, it being expressly understood that his colleague, if any he has, be restricted in his argument to the residue of the time: *And provided further*, that where there is but one counsel for the plaintiff or defendant in error, he may be permitted to occupy two hours in the argument of the case.

It is further ordered, that counsel be not at liberty to read any part of a report except the syllabus of the case, unless desired by a member of the court.
From the record.

J. SIMON COHEN,
Prothonotary.

In the Supreme Court of Pennsylvania in and for the Eastern District:

THE following general rules were adopted 5th January 1852:—

1. When a cause is reached in the order it stands on the list, and is called, it must be argued or in some other way finally disposed of, if not continued.
2. If the plaintiff in error or appellant is not ready, or is in such default that he cannot demand a hearing, a *non pros.* shall be entered.
3. If the defendant in error, or appellee, is not ready, the argument shall proceed *ex parte*.

4. No engagement elsewhere, on public or private business, shall be an excuse for non-attendance or want of preparation here.

5. If a cause be continued, no matter how or for what reason, it shall go to the foot of the list permanently, and shall never again precede any cause to which its continuance has once postponed it.

6. A cause more than two years old, counting from the return day of the writ or the time when the appeal ought to have been filed, shall not be continued by consent.

7. The counsel on each side may speak for one hour, and no more. Where two are concerned together, they may divide their hour between them as they please.

8. These rules shall take effect on the 12th day of January instant.

9. The prothonotary is charged with the duty of publishing these rules, so that all may have notice.

The members of the profession are respectfully requested, in preparing their paper-books, to state in them the Christian and surnames of the parties in the court below, and their position in the court of error; to state the kind of action, with a brief statement of the pleadings; also for which party the verdict was rendered, and its date and amount; and to furnish a brief history or statement of the case.

In the citation of authorities, counsel are requested to be careful to state correctly the names of the parties to the cases cited, and the book and page; and the principle or principles for which they are cited; and when the paper-books are not too extensive, that they be printed only on *one side* of the paper.

It is requested that paper-books for the reporter, in his absence, be left with the clerk. It is also respectfully requested that the names of the counsel concerned in each case be signed to the paper-book.

G. W. H.

CASES

IN

THE SUPREME COURT

OF

PENNSYLVANIA.

EASTERN DISTRICT—MARCH TERM 1851.
PHILADELPHIA.

Marberger et al. *versus* Pott.

An engagement endorsed on a bill or promissory note under seal, for $500, of the same date with the note, as follows: "I hereby acknowledge to be security for the within amount of five hundred dollars, until satisfactorily paid by W. A.:" *Held* to import the liability of a surety, and not that of a guaranty; that the surety was not discharged by mere forbearance to sue the principal, no notice having been given by the surety to the payees to proceed against the principal; that the plaintiffs were not bound to give notice to the surety of non-payment at the maturity of the note; and that it was not incumbent on plaintiffs to show that they had used due diligence to recover from the principal before suit against the surety.

ERROR to the Common Pleas of *Schuylkill county*.

This was an action brought by Samuel Marberger and Abraham Albright, against Benjamin Pott, as the security of William Audenried, on an obligation as follows:—

$500. POTTSVILLE, January 25, 1840.

Six months after date, I promise to pay to the order of Sam'l Marberger and Abraham Allbright, of West Brunswig township, five hundred dollars, without defalcation, for value received, with interest. Witness my hand and seal, date above written.

WILLIAM AUDENRIED. [SEAL.]

[Marberger et al. v. Pott.]

On the back of which said obligation, the following undertaking of defendant was endorsed:—

"Pottsville, January 25th, 1840.—I hereby acknowledge to be security for the within am't of five hundred dollars, until satisfactorily paid by Will'm Audenried. BEN. POTT."
Tested, WELLINGTON CLINE.

The summons was tested 18th August, 1845.

The bill or note and endorsement were given in evidence.

There was also given in evidence the following endorsements on the bill:—

"Paid the interest due to the 25th January, 1842. Say
"Sixty Dollars.
"$60. ABRAHAM ALBRIGHT."

"Received on account of this note, March 22, 1842.
"One Hundred Dollars of W. Audenreid.
"$100. ABRAHAM ALBRIGHT."

Showing that two years' interest, and one hundred dollars on the principal of the bill, was paid to the plaintiffs by Audenried long after the bill was payable.

On the part of defendant, Charles Frailey was called.

He said, *inter alia*, I am acquainted with William Audenried; as far as I know, in 1840, Audenried's circumstances were good. He then lived in Pottsville. I think the valuation of his real estate was after that about $30,000. In 1842, sold his personal property, as deputy sheriff. He had considerable personal property; the return of the sheriff was $1200 to $1400. I think up to some time in July, 1842, he was in business very largely, in the mill and lumbering business. I think there is no doubt Audenried had the ability to pay $500 in 1841 and the first six months of 1842; I think he was always able to pay double that amount in the fall of 1840, almost any hour. (On cross-examination.) I did not collect any of Audenried in the fall of 1840. I did not see him pay any debts in the fall of 1840. I recollect seeing him have money in the fall of 1840. I do not believe Audenried was worth a single dollar in the fall of 1840, after paying his debts. Within the last year Audenried was doing business, I don't think any one suspected him of being much in debt, although a general borrower; I loaned him about the middle of August, 1842. He broke up about that time.

The defendant further gave in evidence the judgments entered up against William Audenried, on which all his real and personal estate was sold. The first judgment was entered on the 11th July, 1842, for $500. The second, 25th July, 1842, for $3250. The personal property was sold at $1364.69. The real estate levied upon was condemned, and appraised at $33,341.

The list of judgments showed that Audenried was indebted far

[Marberger et al. v. Pott.]

beyond the value of his property. That they began to be entered up against him in July, 1842, about which time his insolvency became manifest. That all judgments entered up against him to the 23d August, 1842, were paid in full, and a balance was left from the proceeds of the sale of his property of $1041.14, applicable to subsequent judgments, which greatly exceeded that amount.

It did not appear that the plaintiffs had made any demand on Pott, or given him any notice of Audenried's default of payment, until the bringing of this suit.

KIDDER, President, after stating the facts of the case, charged the jury as follows:—The plaintiffs seek to recover the amount due upon the single bill in question from the defendant as guarantor.

The defendant contends he is not liable, upon the ground that the plaintiffs have not used that due and legal diligence to collect the amount from the principal, Audenried, which the law requires. This leads us to consider, first, the character of this guaranty, to wit, whether the same is absolute or qualified. From the terms of this guaranty, we cannot distinguish it from a common and ordinary undertaking of guaranty, and consequently the same rules are applied to it which are applicable to cases of this description, among which are, that the holder shall use due and reasonable diligence to obtain payment from the debtor, and, in case of non-payment, give reasonable notice to the guarantor, except in cases where the debtor is insolvent when the instrument becomes due. The single bill became due on the 25th of July, 1840. There is no evidence of any judgments against Audenried until about two years after the debt became due. There is no evidence that an effort was made to collect it from him, or that Pott had notice of its non-payment before the bringing of this suit on the 18th August, 1845. It is for you to determine whether Audenried was insolvent and unable to pay when this debt was due. If he was, the plaintiffs were not bound to pursue him or seek to obtain their claim; and, in this case, it would have been necessary for them to give the defendant notice of its non-payment. If he was not insolvent at that time, nor for some time afterwards, they should have used due and reasonable diligence to collect it from the debtor, and, on failure to obtain it, have given Pott reasonable notice of it.

It is for you to say, under the evidence, whether the plaintiffs have used due diligence in endeavoring to obtain it from Audenried. There is no evidence that Pott was notified of its non-payment before suit was brought. If you are satisfied that Audenried was insolvent when it became due, or that the plaintiffs have used due diligence, your verdict should be for plaintiffs for the amount of their claim. If you are not so satisfied, your verdict should be for the defendant. If you should be satisfied that Audenried was able to pay the debt for near two years after it became due, and the plaintiffs made no effort to collect it, we should think that the

[Marberger et al. v. Pott.]

due diligence which the law requires was hardly employed. It is, however, a question for you to decide, under all the evidence in this case.

It was assigned for error:
2. The court erred in assuming and calling the undertaking of Pott, a guaranty. His liability was that of a surety.
3. The court erred in charging the jury that "if he (Audenried) was not insolvent at the time the bill fell due, nor for a long time afterwards, they (the plaintiffs) should have used reasonable diligence to collect it from the debtor, and, on failure to obtain it, have given Pott reasonable notice of it."
4. The court erred in charging the jury that "if you are satisfied that Audenried was insolvent when it became due, or that the plaintiffs have used due diligence, your verdict should be for the plaintiffs. If you are not so satisfied, your verdict should be for the defendant."

Hughes, for Marberger and Albright, plaintiffs in error, contended that the undertaking of Pott was absolute and unconditional. He agreed to become security for the amount, "until satisfactorily paid by Will'm Audenried." The leading rule of interpretation, in such cases as this, is the intention of the parties.

When one endorsed, without date, upon a note, "I will see the within paid," signing it, the presumption is that it was done at the date of the note and as part of one transaction; consequently he is liable as an original promisor: Amsbaugh v. Gearhart, 1 *Jones* 482; see also White v. Howland, 9 *Mass.* 314.

A promissory note is made by A for a sum of money, payable to B on a day certain; C writes underneath, "I acknowledge myself holden as security for the payment of the amount of the above note. Witness my hand, C." In an action against C on this note, it was held to be a joint and several promise: Hunt v. Adams, 5 *Mass.* 358, and Same v. Same, 6 *Mass.* 522. See also Snevily v. Johnston, 1 *W. & Ser.* 309; Allen v. Rightmire, 20 *Johns. Rep.* 865; Leonard v. Sweetzer, 12 *Ohio Rep.* 1.

If Pott were a *surety*, and not a technical guarantor, then the forbearance of plaintiffs to sue until August, 1845, did not discharge him: see Dehuff v. Turbutt, 3 *Yeates* 157; Cope v. Smith, 8 *Ser. & R.* 112; U. States v. Simpson, 3 *Pa. Rep.* 439.

Loeser, for defendant, contended that the words of the engagement show that it was the intention of the parties that Audenried was to be looked to for the money in the first instance. That Pott's undertaking was that Audenried shall be of ability to pay when the bill became payable.

That Pott was not suable when the note became due.

[Marberger et al. v. Pott.]

That Pott was not suable immediately after the note became due: 14 *Wendell* 231. That Audenried was then able to pay.

That the charge was correct, he referred to *Story on Pro. Notes*, sec. 460, 479–80; 7 *Peters* 113; 9 *Ser. & R.* 198; 4 *Watts* 448; 3 *Pa. Rep.* 18; 2 *Watts* 128; 1 *Barr* 501; 1 *Jones* 460.

The opinion of the court was delivered April 21, by

COULTER, J.—A surety is not discharged by mere forbearance to sue. It is necessary that he should do some act to warn the holder of the instrument and put him on his guard. Such as giving him notice to proceed against the principal. Nothing of that kind is pretended here. The only feasible ground on which Pott can stand is that he was a technical guarantor and not a surety. The rule on that subject is that the intent of the parties, as collected from the language of the instrument, and the attending circumstances of the execution, furnish the true test and guide of interpretation as to the character of the obligation. The language of endorsement seems to be plain enough: "I hereby acknowledge to be security for the within amount of $500, until satisfactorily paid by Wm. Audenried." The word *security* has an established and well-known meaning in the minds of most people, and indicates an obligation to stand for the sum absolutely, unless discharged by the supine negligence of the obligor after notice. It is in broad contrast with the word guaranty, which imports a conditional liability, if due steps are taken against the principal. Beside, Pott agrees to be surety until the sum is satisfactorily paid by Audenried, which effectually excludes the conclusion that he was to be discharged by Audenried's inability to pay. The error of the court consisted in assuming that Audenried's liability was the common undertaking of guaranty, and that the plaintiff was bound to have shown that he used due diligence to recover the amount from Audenried before he could pursue Pott. We think his obligation imported the liability of a surety, that it was unqualified by the condition of a guaranty. That the plaintiff was not bound to give notice to Pott of the non-payment by Audenried at its maturity. And that Pott, to insure his own discharge from his obligation, was bound to show that he had given the plaintiff notice to proceed against Audenried. That mere delay to sue Audenried by the plaintiff did not discharge Pott.

Judgment reversed and *venire de novo* awarded.

Thomas *versus* Afflick.

The rule of the common law as to the computation of time is to include the first day and exclude the last: therefore, where notice to a justice of the peace of an intended suit, given in pursuance of the first section of the act of 21st March 1772, was served on the 19th of May, and suit brought on the 18th of June, it was held *that the notice was given thirty days before suit. The decision in Goswiler's Estate, 3* Pa. Rep. *200, was not well considered.*

ERROR to the Common Pleas of *Delaware county.*

The action was brought by Isaac Thomas, against John Afflick, who was a justice of the peace, to recover the panalty of $50 for taking illegal fees. It was alleged that the defendant took for a transcript twenty-five cents instead of eighteen and three-quarter cents. The notice of the intended suit was served on the justice on the 19th of May, 1845, and the suit was commenced on the 18th of June, 1845.

The first section of the act of 21st March, 1772, provides, that "No writ shall be sued out against, nor any copy of any process at the suit of a subject, shall be served on any justice of the peace, for any thing done by him in the execution of his office, until notice in writing of such intended writ or process shall have been delivered to him, or left at the usual place of his abode, by the party, his attorney or agent, who intends to sue, or cause the same to be sued out or served, at least *thirty days* before the suing out or serving the same," &c.

CHAPMAN, J., charged, *inter alia*:—The object of the provision requiring notice to be given to the justice, was that he might have an opportunity to tender amends. To do this, he was entitled to full thirty days before the suing out or serving the process. Had the defendant thirty days allowed him before the writ was served? It is the opinion of the court he had not, and, therefore, the action was brought too soon. It is said in Goswiler's Estate, 3 *Pa. Rep.* 200, whenever, by a rule of court, or act of the legislature, a given number of days is allowed to do an act, or when it is said an act may be done within a given number of days, the day on which the rule is taken, or the decision made, is excluded. If this rule be adopted in the computation of time, the day on which the notice was served must be excluded. It being the 19th of May when the notice was served, there would remain twelve days in that month. The suit was brought on the 18th day of June, the eighteen days in June added to the twelve in May make but thirty; and as the suit was thus brought before the expiration of the thirtieth day, defendant had not thirty full days in which to tender amends. You are, therefore, directed to render a verdict for the defendant.

[Thomas v Afflick.]

The direction as to the notice was excepted to, and was assigned for error.

W. Tilghman, for plaintiff in error.
J. W. Ashmead, for defendant.

April 21.
PER CURIAM.—The rule of computation is to include the first day and exclude the last; and applying it to this case, we find the action was not brought too soon. We might plausibly distinguish it from Goswiler's Appeal on the ground of a difference between an act to be done *before* the expiration of so many days, and an act to be done *after* it; but the distinction would be a shadowy one. The rule of the common law is the one just stated; and it would seem that the decision in Goswiler's Estate was not well considered.

Judgment reversed and *venire de novo* awarded.

Pocopson Road.

1. Viewers of a private road being required by act of Assembly of June 13, 1836, to report whether the same is *necessary;* a report that there is *occasion for the road* was held to be sufficient.
2. The act of June 13, 1836, authorizing the laying out of *private* roads, is constitutional.

CERTIORARI to the Court of Quarter Sessions of *Chester county*.
On the 2d day of February 1848, Stephen Darlington petitioned the court, setting forth that he laboured "under great inconvenience for want of a private road leading from the south-east side of his farm to the street road, near the west end of Painter's bridge, over Brandywine."

Viewers were appointed, who reported a private road as prayed for. To this report exceptions were filed, which were overruled, and the report confirmed.

At July term 1848, on the petition of Enos Painter, a jury of review was appointed, who reported that there was no occasion for the road.

At November term 1848, Stephen Darlington had reviewers appointed, whose report in favour of a road was set aside. Another jury of re-review was appointed, whose report in favour of a road was also set aside, September 14, 1849.

Same day, another jury of re-review was appointed, who reported a road on precisely the same ground as the original viewers and the viewers whose reports were set aside.

The jury reported that they "re-reviewed the said proposed

[Pocopson Road.]

road and parts adjacent; that after having so re-reviewed as aforesaid, and being of the opinion that *there is occasion* for the said road, we have laid out for the private use of the said Stephen Darlington a private road, commencing," &c., "being through improved lands of the said Enos Painter." October 29, 1849, report confirmed *nisi*, and ordered to be recorded, and the road opened twenty feet wide.

The 12th section of the act of June 13, 1836, relating to roads and highways, provides " if it shall appear by the report of viewers to the court directing the view, *that such road is necessary*, the said court shall direct what breadth the same shall be opened, and the proceedings in such case shall be entered on record, as before directed, and thenceforth such road shall be deemed and taken to be a lawful private road."

To this report exceptions were filed on the part of Painter:
1. The road reported by the re-reviewers is not "necessary," within the meaning of the act of Assembly, inasmuch as the petitioner's plantation, which said private road is intended to accommodate, adjoins a public road, &c.

The second and third were as to matters of fact; and
4. The law by virtue of which the proceedings have been had, is unconstitutional, because—
1st. The effect of the proceedings under it is to appropriate for the private use of one individual the property of another, without his consent, and without affording him any opportunity of negotiating for its price; and
2d. The obligation of the parties is not mutual, inasmuch as one party is bound to have the road opened through his property after its confirmation and assessment of damages, and the other party has the option whether to cause it to be opened and pay the damages or not.

December 12, 1849, the exceptions were overruled by the court, and the report confirmed.

Same day, a commissioner was appointed to take depositions in relation to the exceptions.

Depositions were taken by the commissioner on the 15th and 17th days of December, and "December 18, 1849, filed as of December 12, 1849, *nunc pro tunc*, by order of the court."

Several errors were assigned, one of which was that the court erred in overruling the exceptions and confirming the report. Another, that the court erred in confirming the report without hearing the testimony in support of the three first exceptions; and another, that the court erred in not setting aside the report, for the reasons set forth in the *fourth* exception.

The case was argued by *Smith*, for appellant.—He contended, *inter alia*, that the report does not show a *necessity* for a private

[Pocopson Road.]

road, as required by the act of Assembly of 13th June, 1836; that the 12th section requires that it should appear by the report that the road *is necessary*, but it alleges merely that there was "occasion for said road."

The Court of Quarter Sessions are bound to hear testimony outside of the report, to enable them to determine whether the proceedings of the jury were proper. 4 *Bin.* 174; 5 *Barr* 101.

That the provisions of the act of June 13, 1836, so far as they relate to roads, are *unconstitutional*, because they authorize the taking of the property of one man without his consent, and the transferring it to another: 4 *Hill* 142; 18 *Wendall* 9; 1 *Barr* 313; 6 *Barr* 90; *id.* 511; 11 *Wendall* 151; 18 *id.* 14, 50, 59; 5 *Paige* 159; 2 *Kent* 339—*note* c; 1 *Baldwin* 205.

Lewis, for appellee.—The objection to the *form* of the report was not made in the court below, and must be deemed to have been waived: 5 *Barr* 204–211; 5 *Whar.* 442.

The form of the report is sufficient, and is usual. The language of reports of this nature should not be nicely criticised. It is sufficient if it substantially appear that the viewers have performed their duty. TILGHMAN, J.—4 *Bin.* 177.

The facts of the case belong to the jury who are the judges both of the necessity for a road and the propriety of its location; and it is only where a disregard of duty is clearly proved, that the court can properly interfere upon exceptions involving those points.

The law is constitutional: 10 *Watts* 63, Harvey v. Thomas.

PER CURIAM.—None of the exceptions but one has an appearance of substance. Viewers of a private road are required by the road law to report whether it is necessary: the viewers of the road have reported that there is *occasion* for it, and hence it is argued they have not reported enough. Mere convenience is perhaps not so; but a report is never drawn with the precision of an indictment, and, in the apprehension of the mass, the terms are convertible. If this exception were to prevail, very few private roads would stand the test.

Proceedings affirmed.

Lewis *versus* Rogers.

1. Creditors can attack a judgment *collaterally* only *for collusion*, not for matter of defence, original or subsequent. A judgment creditor who objects to a prior judgment on the ground of failure of consideration, can do so only on the trial of an issue directed as to the prior judgment, to ascertain the amount due upon it; but while it stands as a debt of record, unabated in whole or in part, and unaffected by any such proceeding in relation to it, neither the sheriff nor a subsequent judgment creditor can resist the enforcement of it as a lien, and the sheriff cannot legally disregard it in the appropriation of the proceeds of sale of the real estate bound by it.

2. A sheriff who does not incur any risk of mispayment in the appropriation of the proceeds of sale of real estate, has no right to impose conditions or take a promise to refund from a judgment creditor, to whom he pays a part of the money arising from the sale of the real estate bound by the judgment, and to which the judgment was from the record apparently entitled.

ERROR to the Common Pleas of *Chester county*.

Dr. Coates, on the 9th day of December, 1836, executed a judgment bond and mortgage to George Brinton, to secure the payment of two thousand dollars.

This bond, with the accompanying mortgage, was assigned, in 1839, to George W. Pennock, who, on the 23d day of March of that year, entered judgment on the bond, in his own name, as assignee of George Brinton. On the 2d day of July, 1841, the mortgage was assigned to Joseph J. Lewis, the defendant, and the judgment marked to his use on the record. No money at this time appeared to have been paid on account of interest or principal, and it was alleged by the assignee that none had been.

On the same day a judgment was entered in favor of Joseph J. Lewis, against George W. Pennock, on single bill and warrant of attorney, for one thousand dollars; and on the 21st of August following, another judgment for three hundred dollars, was likewise entered in favor of the same plaintiff and against the same defendant.

These two judgments were stated to have been taken by Mr. L. to secure himself against any set-off which Dr. Coates might have against the bond and mortgage assigned, which at the time of the assignment were apparently worth about two thousand five hundred and twenty-seven dollars.

In the year 1842, George W. Pennock failed, and took the benefit of the insolvent laws, and his land was sold by the sheriff of Chester county, under sundry executions, returnable to the August and November terms. The proceeds of sale paid all liens prior to those of the last-mentioned two judgments for one thousand dollars, and three hundred dollars.

Mr. Lewis having sued out the judgment accompanying the mortgage assigned to him, Dr. Coates claimed a set-off of five hundred dollars, with interest from the 21st of January, 1837. He

[Lewis v. Rogers.]

also claimed to have paid to George W. Pennock two hundred and ninety-three dollars and ninety-four cents, of the interest on the judgment and mortgage.

On the 31st of January 1843, Mr. Smith received for Mr. Lewis three hundred and fifty-nine dollars and twenty cents of the proceeds of sale of G. W. Pennock's real estate. The rest of the money applicable to the payment of Mr. Lewis's judgments was retained for some time in the sheriff's hands, to await the result of the controversy in the scire facias on the judgment accompanying the mortgage. Mr. L. claiming only to be paid the money in case he failed to recover the principal and interest apparently due by the judgment and mortgage.

In the spring of 1843, money being in demand, the counsel for Dr. Coates suggested to Mr. Lewis that he might as well take the money from the hands of the sheriff and put it to interest, and he gave it as a reason that if the set-off prevailed against the judgment, he would be entitled to it, and might as well have the use of it—and if it did not prevail, he could pay it back with interest, which he would be getting in the mean time. The suggestion was adopted and the following paper signed:

George W. Pennock, } *In the Common Pleas of Chester county.*
  v.   Vend. Exp.
Jesse Coates.

March 29, 1843. It is agreed that the balance of the money in the sheriff's hands, detained in this execution, be paid to Joseph J. Lewis, without prejudice to the rights of any person—the same to be returned with interest, in case it shall be found, on the termination of the suit of George W. Pennock, assignee of George Brinton, for the use of Joseph J. Lewis, that the money has not been properly paid to the said Joseph, but belongs to other parties.

      WILLIAM DARLINGTON, Deft's Att'y.
      JOSEPH J. LEWIS.

The sheriff, on the next day, paid six hundred and twelve dollars and eighty-two cents to Mr. L., under agreement.

The two sums amounted to a few dollars less than the difference between the apparent value of the mortgage according to its face and the sum recovered against Dr. Coates.

On a trial of the issue on the *scire facias sur judgment* accompanying the mortgage, Dr. Coates succeeded in proving a considerable amount of interest paid to George W. Pennock prior to his assignment of it, and in establishing his set-off. The verdict rendered August 14, 1843, was for one thousand eight hundred and two dollars and thirty-eight cents.

The following statement shows the extent of the defalcation established by Dr. Coates against the mortgage, and also the sums

[Lewis v. Rogers.]

received by Mr. Lewis, calculated to the day of the verdict against Dr. Coates:

Mortgage, dated Dec. 9, 1836...............................		$2000.00
Interest to Aug. 15, 1843, date of verdict against Coates,		922.00
		$2922.00
Amount of verdict...		1802.38
Difference..		$1119.62
Paid Mr. Lewis by Sheriff—Jan. 1st, 1843.......	$364.20	
Interest, Aug. 15, '43, 7 mo. 14 days........	13.22	
March 30, '43, ...	612.82	
Interest, Aug. 15, '43, 4 mo. 16 days........	13.89	
		$994.13
		$125.49

   This suit was brought in the name of the late sheriff to recover from Mr. Lewis the sums which he had received from the said sheriff, with interest, on the allegation that he had not paid to George W. Pennock the consideration-money of the assignment.

   The plaintiff filed a declaration containing a single count—for money lent, for money paid to the use of the defendant, for money received by defendant for the use of the plaintiff—and on an account stated—and entered a rule of reference. The case was referred—award in favor of defendant. Plaintiff appealed, and on the 13th of December 1849, filed an additional count, founded on the agreement between the defendant and Mr. Darlington.

   The plaintiff, in order to sustain on the trial the allegation that the consideration-money had not been paid, produced George W. Pennock as a witness; but an objection being made to his competency, the court rejected him. The plaintiff then exhibited the witness's certificate of discharge as a bankrupt, dated 1843, and produced also from the records several unsatisfied judgments, sufficient to absorb the whole fund claimed. The witness was again offered, received, and exception taken.

   George W. Pennock being admitted as a witness, testified that he had received but $1287.80, in consideration of the assignment; and that the consideration agreed to be paid was the full value of the mortgage and judgment, without any credit for interest or set-off. He denied that Mr. L. had paid him any thing else, or any money for him.

   The defence on the facts was that the whole was paid. James B Wood, the deputy sheriff in 1843, testified to Mr. Lewis paying $50.14 at one time and $200 at another, for George W. Pennock.

   Joel Pennock testified that G. W. Pennock, between the first of

[Lewis v. Rogers.]

August court and the last of November, stated he was going to Mr. Lewis to get some money; that he returned, and said he had got it; could not tell the amount; it was hundreds of dollars.

T. C. Crowell, Esq., testified to repeated acknowledgments by G. W. Pennock that Mr. Lewis owed him nothing; but that he was indebted to Mr. L.

Mr. Lewis was returned by G. W. Pennock as a creditor, for $1300, in his statement annexed to his petition for the benefit of the insolvent law; and also in his statement of liabilities annexed to his bankrupt petition.

F. E. Hayes testified that G. W. Pennock told he had received the consideration of the mortgage.

The defendant requested the court to charge that if the jury believed that the judgments, Joseph J. Lewis v. George W. Pennock, were taken, as averred by the plaintiff, as collateral security for the payment of $1000 and $300, in case a set-off against the mortgage for these or any less amount should be established, the defendant had a right to receive the amount of these judgments at the time the same were paid to him; that if the jury believed that the defendant had received no more moneys by virtue of these judgments than the amount by which the mortgage was reduced by Dr. Coates's set-off the plaintiff cannot recover; that the sheriff, in whose hands were the proceeds of sale of G. W. Pennock's real estate, bound by the lien of this judgment, would have been justified in paying the money to the defendant at the termination of the suit of Pennock v. Coates, in which Dr. Coates established his set-off; the defendant therefore had a right to receive said money, at the time and under the circumstances he did, and the plaintiff cannot recover; and that there was no privity of contract between the late sheriff and defendant.

The judge in his charge decided that there was no legal impediment to the plaintiff's recovery, and a verdict was found in his favor.

There were several specifications of error filed, one of which was that the court below erred in sustaining the plaintiff's action.

The case was argued by *Smith*, for plaintiff in error; and by *Pennypacker* and *Hickman*, for defendant in error.

The opinion of the court was delivered April 21, by

GIBSON, C. J.—Creditors can attack a judgment collaterally only for collusion; not for matter of defence original or subsequent. A debtor, or his representative, may have a judgment against him opened on ground laid, and when let into a defence on the merits, reduce or discharge it; nor will I say that if he were to refuse to move for the benefit of his creditors, they would not be permitted to

[Lewis v. Rogers.]

move in his name. An insolvent man is not suffered to give away his property by means of a judgment, which, though proper at first, has become a security for less than the amount of it; but while it stands as a debt of record, unabated in whole or in part, neither the sheriff nor an antagonist creditor can resist the enforcement of it as a lien. Had there not been an agreement between the present defendant and the counsel of the debtor whose land was sold, there would not be a doubt that an action in the sheriff's name for a creditor's use could not be maintained to recover the payment back. The agreement was with a counsel who had no right to interfere further than to prevent his client's unappropriated money from lying idle in the sheriff's hands; but what were the terms of it? It was a promise to return the money to the sheriff with interest, if it should be found, on the termination of the suit with Doctor Coates, that it belonged to other judgment creditors. But it could not be thus found. An action may be maintained on a promise to a third person by the party beneficially interested in it; but a sheriff who does not incur the risk of a mispayment, has no right to impose conditions or take a promise to refund. He has no beneficial interest. He may pay the money into court or distribute it; but while a judgment remains a lien, unabated in the only way it can be abated, he cannot pass it by. Here the money was paid on a judgment entitled to it. Neither can a judgment creditor interfere collaterally. The ground of interference, in this case, was failure of consideration for the bills and warrants; and it could be taken only on the trial of an issue in the original suits to ascertain the amount due.

Judgment reversed.

Fitzwater *versus* Stout.

1. Where there is a spark of evidence of a fact, it should not be excluded from the jury.
2. Where the owner of grain takes up cattle trespassing upon it, in order to sell them he must proceed according to the act of Assembly, or he will be deemed a trespasser *ab initio*, and responsible in damages to the owner of the cattle.

ERROR to the Common Pleas of *Montgomery county*.

This was an action of trespass, brought by Christian D. Stout against George W. Fitzwater and John Fitzwater, Jr., for breaking and entering his close, at Upper Dublin township, Montgomery county, and taking and driving away five cows of the value of $——, and converting them to their own use.

Defendants pleaded not guilty, and also pleaded specially that under an execution issued upon a judgment againt Stout, the plaintiff, ten acres of grain in the ground (*inter alia*) was levied upon and sold by the sheriff to John Fitzwater, Sr., for a full consideration, which grain was the close mentioned in plaintiff's declaration; that said cattle were found upon said grain, treading down, depasturing, and destroying the same, and that said defendants, by command of said John Fitzwater, took up and drove away the said cattle.

Christian D. Stout, the plaintiff below, had in his possession on the last day of January 1848, five cows, in one of which he had an absolute, and in the other four a qualified property. These cattle on that day were found pasturing on a grain-field, which formed part of a farm then held by the plaintiff, under a lease from John Fitzwater, the father of the defendants,—John Fitzwater, Sr., being the owner of the grain, *having previously purchased it at sheriff's sale.* The defendants below, George W. Fitzwater and John Fitzwater, Jr., on the day referred to, at the instance of their father, entered upon the grain-field, and took and drove the cattle thence to a tavern occupied by one Robert Thompson, and locked them up in his stable. The plaintiff demanded the cows from Thompson, and he refused to deliver them up. He also demanded them of the Fitzwaters, and they refused to give them up.

On the 11th May following, the cows were sold by George Scheetz, upon a warrant of a justice of the peace, issued by order of John Fitzwater, Sr., for $102.05. George W. Fitzwater bought one of them at the sale.

KRAUSE, J., charged the jury, that if the defendants participated in the subsequent selling of the cattle and disposition of the proceeds, in violation or disregard of the act of Assembly relating to strays, or did other unlawful acts after the cattle were taken to Thompson's, they were trespassers *ab initio*, and liable as such in damages; and also, that there was evidence of a demand by plaintiff on defendants for the cattle on the 18th of February 1848, and submitted the fact or question for their determination.

"The jury may find against one or both defendants, if they find against them at all; and it is proper to say to them that the court recollects no testimony showing acts of *John* to implicate him in what was done after the cattle were taken to Thompson's. As before stated, however, the facts are for them, and not for the court; and if, in considering all the testimony, they find that John did participate in what was so done, and in disregard of the acts of Assembly, he is answerable as stated."

Verdict for plaintiff, for $134.

It was assigned for error:
1. The court erred in submitting as a question of fact for the jury, whether there was any subsequent participation in the sale of the cattle—there being no evidence of such fact in the cause.
2. The court erred in submitting as a question of fact for the

[Fitzwater v. Stout.]

jury, whether there were any acts done by defendants after the cattle were taken to Thompson's, which would render the defendants liable as trespassers *ab initio*—there being no evidence of such acts in the cause.

3. The court erred in charging the jury that there was evidence of a demand by plaintiff on defendants for the cattle on the 18th February 1848—there being no such evidence in the cause.

4. The court erred in not charging the jury, that there was no evidence in the cause of any acts done by defendants after the cattle were taken to Thompson's, which would in law render them liable as trespassers, and therefore, that plaintiff was not entitled to recover.

The case was argued by *Freedley*, for plaintiff in error.—He contended, *inter alia*, that in charging the jury, the court were in error, there being no evidence whatever in the cause, either of participation by defendants in the sale or proceeds of the cattle, or of any unlawful act or acts of any kind done by the defendants in relation to the cattle after they were left at Thompson's—nor was there any evidence of a demand by plaintiff of the defendants as stated by the court.

Mulvany, for defendant, contended, *inter alia*, that there was evidence that the defendants participated in the refusal to deliver up the cattle when they were demanded by the plaintiff, and in the illegal disposition of them which was made.

The opinion of the court was delivered April 21, by

COULTER, J.—The four errors assigned amount to this, that the court submitted to the jury the facts, whether George W. Fitzwater and John Fitzwater, the younger, participated in any acts after the cattle were taken to Thompson's, and whether they participated in the sale subsequently made, and whether a demand was made of the cattle; there being no evidence to implicate the defendants in these conclusions.

But the case was fairly enough submitted to the jury as to these matters of fact. There was undoubtedly some evidence, as to John, and it was distinct as to George W. The court told the jury that they might find against either of the defendants, if the testimony did not warrant a finding against both. It is unnecessary to go over the case, further than to say, that from the commencement to the closing scenes, John, the elder, and his two sons were actors in concert, and spoken of by the witnesses as the Fitzwaters who drove away the cows. And one of the witnesses testifies that he was present when cows were demanded of the Fitzwaters, when they were locked up in Thompson's stable. This evidence is not

[Fitzwater v. Stout.]

very distinct, but under the circumstances it ought not to have been excluded from the jury. It was at least a spark.

The proceedings under the stray law, were in no sense complied with, except in taking the cows and locking them up. Under what process or by what authority they were sold, does not appear. Even if Fitzwater, the elder, was right in taking the cows of Stout, his tenant, trespassing on his field, and locking them up by himself and his sons, they had no right to keep them during pleasure, sell them as they pleased, unless by some Brehon law not recognised by our courts. A poor man lost his property against law. We see nothing in the record which requires the judgment to be disturbed.

Judgment affirmed.

Jones *versus* Wood.

1. An article of agreement for the sale of land is merged in the deed made in pursuance of it, which is delivered and accepted.
2. Fraud will vitiate any contract. Where land is, by article of agreement, agreed to be sold by A. to W., and W. afterwards sells the same to J., *the deed to be made by A. to J.*, which is afterward made and delivered to J. in the presence of W.: in a suit by W. against J. for the value of a certain piece of land, alleged by W. to form a part of his original purchase, but which, by a subsequent deed, had been conveyed by A. to J. for an additional consideration, in order to affect J. with fraud in the transaction as between A. and J., it must be shown that J. participated in the fraud, or at least had knowledge of it.
3. It is error for the court to submit to the jury for their deliberation an alleged fact of which there was no evidence.
4. Where the donee of a power to sell land possesses also an interest in the subject of the power, a conveyance by him made without actual reference to the power will not be deemed an execution of the power, unless there be evidence of an intention to execute it, or at least in the face of evidence, disproving such an intention; but where the donee has *no estate in the premises*, and his conveyance can be made operative *only* by treating it as an execution of the power to sell, it will be so considered.
5. Notes of the testimony of deceased witnesses taken on a former trial between the same parties and bearing directly on the same subject of dispute, viz: the boundaries and extent of a certain tract of land, are admissible in evidence in a suit for the value of a piece of land adjoining that the extent of which was in dispute in the first suit.

ERROR to the Common Pleas of *Chester county*.

This was an action of covenant by Thomas Wood against John Jones, to recover the alleged value of 25 acres and 128 perches of land, at $25 per acre.

The Rev. Robert Annan owned a tract of land, situate partly in Lancaster and partly in Chester county, known as the "Annan Farm," containing 412 acres and allowance.

He died in 1819, leaving a will, directing his real estate to be sold by his executor, and appointing Dr. Samuel Annan and another his executors, of whom Dr. Annan is the survivor.

[Jones v. Wood.]

This tract of land was held by two deeds, both from Colonel James Taylor to Robert Annan, one of them dated October 22, 1799, for 412 acres and allowance, and the other of the same date, conveying " about 28 acres, being lately surveyed, upon a warrant to the said James Taylor, dated the 18th day of October, A. D. 1785."

The first of these deeds only, ever came to the possession of Dr. Annan, the executor, or was ever within his knowledge.

Along with this deed was a plot or draft of the land, drawn with *black* lines, corresponding precisely with the courses and distances in the deed for 412 acres, and exhibiting within *dotted* lines, outside of the black lines, the land supposed to be vacant, and now said to be covered by the deed for 28 acres.

On the 9th of August 1838, Dr. Samuel Annan, surviving executor of Robert Annan, deceased, entered into contract with Thomas Wood to convey to him the Annan farm, containing 412 acres and allowance, for $10,000, seven thousand of which was to lie in the land, secured by bond and mortgage to Dr. Annan as surviving executor.

At the time of entering into this contract, Dr. Annan told Wood, that the part marked on the plot by *dotted* lines was supposed to be vacant, and he could take it up if he thought proper—showed him the deed for 412 acres—told him it was all he had to sell—and gave him the plot to take home with him and run the lines by.

On the 11th of August 1838, Wood entered into contract with Jones to convey to him the Annan farm, " containing somewhere about 412 acres," for $25 per acre, " $7000 to lie in the land six years, if desired by the purchaser, to be secured by bond and mortgage at legal interest annually, to be executed to Samuel Annan, executor of Robert Annan, deceased, *by whom the deed will be executed to said Jones.*"

In the latter part of 1838, Wood called on Moses Whitson to survey the Annan tract, and gave him the draft above referred to. Whitson surveyed it, Wood pointing out the lines, and including the supposed vacant land, making 475 acres 38 perches in all. Sometime after, he was informed by Wood or Jones that no warrant for the vacant land could be found, and was requested to run the lines, leaving it out. He did so, in Wood's presence, who pointed out the lines again, and, as was supposed by all, excluded the vacant land, but in fact crossed it, and included near 10 acres of it.

In an interview between Annan and Wood, the same autumn, Wood demanded that Annan should convey to him the whole land, including the supposed vacancy, and Annan refused to do so, saying he had never sold him any but the 412 acre tract.

The same autumn, Wood took legal advice as to his rights under the contract with Annan.

[Jones v. Wood.]

The deed from Dr. Annan, surviving executor, to Jones, was prepared by Whitson, embracing the 412 acres, and about 10 acres of the vacant land, pursuant to the last survey of Whitson, and on the 2d of April 1839, was executed and delivered by Dr. Annan to Jones, *in the presence of Wood, who signed as a subscribing witness.*

At the same time, Jones executed a mortgage to Dr. Annan for $7000, of the same premises, conveyed to him—paid him $3000, and paid Wood the balance of the purchase-money. Wood was a subscribing witness also to the mortgage.

After the last survey of Whitson, finding there was more vacant land outside thereof than had been supposed, Dr. Annan took out a warrant, dated 8th November 1838, and had it surveyed and returned to the land-office. There were surveyed on it 33 acres 116 perches.

On the 3d of April 1839, Dr. Annan, as an individual, and not as executor of his father, conveyed this land to *Jones* for $400, "being the same tract of land surveyed by virtue of a warrant for the same, bearing date the 8th day of November 1838."

This action was brought by Wood against Jones to recover the value of the land conveyed by deed of April 3, 1839, at $25 per acre, and was founded on the agreement of August 11, 1838.

It was brought to July term 1848, after the decision of this court that Jones had a good title to the ten acres of supposed vacant land included in the deed of April 2, 1839. Wood v. Jones, see 7 *Barr* 473.

PLAINTIFF'S EVIDENCE.—*Paper marked* X.—This article of agreement, made and concluded this 9th day of August 1838, between S. Annan of the one part, and J. Wood of the other, witnesseth that the said Annan has sold unto said Wood, all that tract of land, known as Annan's farm, bounded by lands of S. Steele, J. Wood, and others, on the following conditions, viz: The said Wood is to pay or cause to be paid unto the said Annan, the sum of three thousand dollars, on the first (of) April 1839, at which time he is to get possession, and the said Wood is to pay the further sum of $7000 at the end of six years, in lawful money—for which latter sum he is to pay at the end of each and every year the sum of $420, being legal interest, at six per cent. per annum, until the whole is paid. The latter sum of seven thousand dollars is to be secured on the property by bond and mortgage which the said Wood binds himself to execute or cause to be executed, at the time of paying the first sum of three thousand dollars, at which time a deed, or full and sufficient title for the property, will be given by the said Annan—the farm is to be taken in a tract, be the same more or less—the lines to be run by the deeds and plot, and made out as nearly as possible, &c. * * * At the signing of the article of agreement, the sum of $100 is to be paid by the said Wood, which is to be deducted from the amount to be

[Jones v. Wood.]

paid the 1st of April 1839. Any variation of the lines, particularly along between the said farm and the land formerly owned by the Thompsons, the said Annan is not to be accounted for, &c.
Signed, SAMUEL ANNAN, [L. S.]
THOMAS WOOD, [L. S.]

Receipt given for the above hundred dollars August 9, 1838, and signed by Samuel Annan.

Article of agreement made and concluded this 11th day (of) August, A. D. 1838, between Thomas Wood, of Steeleville, Chester county, State of Pennsylvania, and John Jones, of East Bradford township, county of Chester, and state aforesaid, as follows, viz: The said Thomas doth sell all that plantation or tract of land known as the Annan farm—situate part in the county of Lancaster, Sadsbury township, and State of Pennsylvania, and part in West Fallowfield, Chester county, of said state—bounded by lands of James Steele, Joshua Lamborn, James Ross, A. Rokestron, and said Wood's other lands, and others—containing somewhere about four hundred and twelve acres, be the same more or less. For which said Jones agrees to pay the said Wood the sum of $25 per acre—the land to be surveyed at said Jones's expense —and the usual allowance of six per cent. to be made in payments as follows: five hundred dollars, part thereof, on the execution of this article—seven thousand dollars to lay in the land six years, if desired by the purchaser, to be secured by bond and mortgage at legal interest annually, to Samuel Annan, executor of Robert Annan, deceased, by whom the deed will be executed to said Jones—and possession given on the 1st day of April 1839, at which time the said Jones is to pay the balance, be the same more or less—to be paid to said Wood, who is herein bound to procure said deed and possession at the time above mentioned from said Annan. In witness whereof, said parties set their hands and seals the day and year above written.
THOS. WOOD, [L. S.]
JOHN JONES, [L. S.]

Deed from Samuel Annan, M. D., surviving executor of Robert Annan, deceased, to John Jones, dated April 2, 1839, duly acknowledged and recorded—consideration $10,000—reciting a deed from Colonel James Taylor to Robert Annan, for two tracts, containing together 449 acres 70 perches, in Sadsbury township, Lancaster county, and West Fallowfield, Chester county.

Thomas Wood, the plaintiff below, is a subscribing witness to this deed.

Deed from Samuel Annan, M. D., to John Jones, dated April 3, 1839, consideration $400, for 25 acres 128 perches, in West

[Jones v. Wood.]

Fallowfield, Chester county, bounded by lands of Joshua Wood, Abraham Rakestraw, and John Jones, being the same tract surveyed by virtue of a warrant, dated November 9, 1838.

Warrant to James Taylor, dated October 18, 1785, for 25 acres of land, partly in Sadsbury township, Lancaster county, and partly in West Fallowfield township, Chester county, adjoining his other land.

Receipt of receiver general, dated October 18, 1785, for £2 10s. paid by James Taylor, for said 25 acres.

Deed from James Taylor to Rev. Robert Annan, dated October 20, 1799, for about 28 acres in West Fallowfield, Chester county, lately surveyed on a warrant to James Taylor, dated October 18, 1785.

The plaintiff then proved by John Robb, Abraham Rakestraw, and Joshua Wood, that during the lifetime of Rev. Robert Annan, and after his death, eight or ten acres, part of the vacant land, had been enclosed and occupied with the Annan farm—that Dr. Samuel Annan was in Edinburgh at his father's death—was educated there, and was very seldom at the farm, and that they knew of no vacant land at that place.

The plaintiff's counsel then offered to read in evidence the notes of the testimony given by Moses Criswell and Andrew Thompson, on the trial of the case of Jones v. Wood, at February term 1847, the witnesses being since dead.

Defendant's counsel objected to its admission, on the ground that the controversy between the parties in that case was different from the present, and related to other land.

The court overruled the objection, admitted the evidence, and defendant's counsel excepted.

Those witnesses proved that the said field, part of the vacant land, had been farmed with the Annan farm, before and after the death of Robert Annan, and that timber was cut by Robert Annan on the vacant land outside of the field; and that they knew of no vacant land there.

The plaintiff here closed his case.

The defendant then read in evidence the deposition of Dr. Annan, taken in September 1849, on commission.

He testified, *inter alia*, that he was the executor of the will of his father.

I did, on the 9th of August, 1838, enter into a contract with Thomas Wood for the purchase and sale of a tract of land. The original contract between myself and Wood is now in Baltimore, Md. I herewith annex and refer to a printed copy (marked X) and make it a part of this my deposition, which said printed copy is a true one to the best of my knowledge and belief. I sold to Wood a tract of land containing 412 acres, with the allowance of

[Jones v. Wood.]

six per cent. The printed copy (marked X) will describe the land I sold to Wood. The original contract was in writing. I had a conversation with Wood, preparatory to the completion of the contract, which conversation was in Baltimore, Md., and I then told him that the tract contained 412 acres, with the allowance, and I showed him a plot or draft of a survey, which I believe now to be the one marked A, which was the one, and the only one, I delivered to Wood, August 9, 1838, to run the lines by, which was produced to me on my examination before arbitrators, in the case of Jones v. Wood, at West Chester, Pa., March 19, 1846, the courses and distances of the black lines on which corresponded with those of the deed from James Taylor to Robert Annan, dated October 22, 1799, under which the latter held the Annan farm. And I also told him that the part marked on the plot by dotted lines, outside of the black lines, on the Chester county side of the farm, was vacant land, which I had not thought it worth while to take up, but he (Wood) might take it up if he thought proper—that the 412 acres and allowances were all I had to sell. I showed him the deed, and told him the deed was made from the plot or draft I gave him. I also informed him that there had been an altercation between Thompson and my father about one of the lines, and that if I accepted of his offer of $10,000, he must make out the lines as nearly as he could by the plot, but that if he would give me $25 an acre I would be responsible for the lines.

I gave him the plot to take home to run the lines by, and told him expressly that the lines must be run by it; and I also told him that he must do the best he could with the lines marked on the plot, which I also gave him. The tract was sold to him for 412 acres, that he must take it at that with allowance, be the same more or less. Wood lived near the tract. The vacant land was never known as a part of the Annan farm; it was always known as vacant land.

By the request of Wood, I made the deed to Jones on April 2d or 3d, 1839, and received from Jones $3000 in cash, and took his bond secured by mortgage for $7000, payable at the end of six years, with interest to be paid annually.

In the autumn of 1838, I took out a warrant for 40 acres of vacant land, and had it laid on by the deputy county surveyor, adjoining the land which I had sold to Wood and conveyed to Jones, under which warrant I sold the piece of vacant land as surveyed, to Jones, in the beginning of April 1839, for $400, and made the deed to him for it.

Thomas Wood was fully aware of my taking up said vacant land, and selling and conveying it to Jones. He was aware of it in April 1839, because I refused to convey it in the deed of the large tract, and I supposed, at the time I executed the deed, that it did not include any part of the vacant land. * * * I suppose he must

[Jones v. Wood.]

have been aware of it in the fall of 1838. * * * I told Wood if he would give me $25 an acre, I would make out the lines by the 412 acre survey as nearly as possible, and would charge for no more than I could make a title for. * * * The dispute between my father and Thompson about one of the lines, which dispute, I believe, involved a part of the 412 acre survey, was the chief reason why I made the offer I did to Wood. I also thought that there possibly might be a difficulty with the Loves and Tweeds, and my intention was rather to give up small strips than go to law. * * * On the Chester county side is a road; a field is cut off running east and west; that field was farmed by my father. * * * That field must have had in it a portion of the vacant land. I did not know, when I lived with my father, that any portion of that field was vacant land, nor did I learn it at any time prior to the sale. * * * I know of no such deed from Colonel James Taylor to the Rev. Robert Annan, dated October 22, 1799, for 28 acres, and do not believe there ever was such a valid deed, because there never was a warrant or survey upon which to base it. There was but the one deed from Colonel Taylor for the 412 acres. * * * I don't think any part of the vacant land was enclosed, except so far as this field goes, (the field before spoken of.) * * * I did not know that my brothers had cut timber off the vacant land; neither did I know the vacant land ran down into the field, till Whitson surveyed it for Wood. * * * I lived on the farm (Annan's) about a couple of years. It was about 1814 or 1815. I went to Europe in 1817. * * * My father owned and lived on the farm at that time. * * * I handed the title-papers of the Annan farm over to Jones. There was no deed among them from Colonel James Taylor to the Rev. Robert Annan, for 28 acres, dated October 22, 1799. * * * There was but one deed from Colonel James Taylor to my father, among the papers of my father, for parts or the whole of the Annan farm, and there were not two deeds.

The defendant then proved the loss of the plot (marked A) referred to by Dr. Annan.

Moses Whitson was examined on the part of defendant, and proved that he was called on in the latter part of 1838, he thought by Wood, to survey the Annan tract, and that he surveyed it. That he made inquiry for the Annan papers, the old deeds, but was informed by Wood that he was not in possession of them. That all the draft he had was the draft marked A. That it was suggested by Wood and others, that certain land belonged to the Annan tract, but that he, witness, informed them that there were no courses and distances set forth in the plot to include the land in the survey. However, we ran round in accordance with the adjoining landmarks, and included within our survey all the land suggested as the Annan tract. That he included the vacant land, and made the quantity 475 acres 38 perches. That he was again called

[Jones v. Wood.]

on by Wood, to run the line or lines between the vacant land and the other, according to the old draft. * * * The contents of what was thought to be *vacant land* were 25 acres 3 roods and 8 perches. We ran that much out of the survey of the whole we had previously made. He afterwards said the draft was a draft of the 412 acres and allowance, and that draft was enclosed by black lines, with the exception of the part spoken of as *vacant*— that was enclosed by dotted lines. The black lines had courses and distances, the dotted lines had not. Thomas Wood remarked that the whole included in the dotted lines had been considered the Annan tract. The black lines of themselves, formed a plot— closed. The dotted lines were outside of it. * * * We found no marks on the ground on the dotted line, except the difference in the growth of the timber, &c.

Hagerty testified, *inter alia*, "that Wood contended that he had bought all that tract known as the Annan farm, and that the vacant land had been used as a part of the Annan farm, and he claimed it on that ground. In 1838 or 9, Wood demanded it— Annan refused to convey it. That Annan thought it had overrun too much, and he did not want to be speculated upon. After the deed from Annan to Jones, Wood told me he had witnessed the deed. He said he was in the squire's office, and they asked him to witness it, and he did not see how he could get out of doing so, and he didn't know what effect it would have, whether it would bar him from recovering or not."

Defendant's counsel gave in evidence a mortgage from John Jones to Dr. Samuel Annan, executor of the will of Robert Annan, deceased, dated April 2, 1839, for $7000, on 449 acres 70 perches of land, being the same premises that day conveyed by Dr. Samuel Annan, surviving executor, &c., to John Jones. *To this mortgage Thomas Wood, the plaintiff, was a subscribing witness*—the said mortgage being given for a part of the purchase-money mentioned in the article of agreement of August 9, 1838.

Also, a warrant to Dr. Samuel Annan, dated Nov. 8, 1838, for 40 acres of land, in West Fallowfield, Chester county, and a survey in pursuance thereof, of 33 acres 116 perches and allowance, being the same warrant recited in the deed from Dr. Samuel Annan to John Jones, dated April 3, 1839.

Also, the deed from Colonel James Taylor to Robert Annan, dated October 22, 1799, for 412 acres and allowance, being the deed recited in the deed from Dr. Samuel Annan, surviving executor, &c., to John Jones, dated April 2, 1839.

The defendant here closed his case.

Defendant requested the court to charge the jury as follows:

1. The deed of April 3, 1839, from Dr. Samuel Annan to John Jones, is not an execution of the power in the will of the Rev. Robert Annan, authorizing his executors to sell his real estate.

[Jones v. Wood.]

2. The deed of April 2, 1839, from Dr. Samuel Annan, surviving executor of the Rev. Robert Annan, to John Jones, closed all questions as to the quantity of land agreed to be sold by the agreement of August 9, 1838, between Dr. Samuel Annan and Thomas Wood, and also as to the amount of purchase-money, and the plaintiff cannot recover on the article of agreement.

3. The plaintiff, having been present when the deed of April 2, 1839, from Annan, as executor, to Jones, was executed, having witnessed that deed, and the mortgage for the $7000, which, according to the article of August 9, 1838, was to be given upon the premises covenanted to be conveyed by that article, not objecting to the deed and mortgage, and receiving the purchase-money, acquiesced in the conveyance as a completion of the contract, and cannot recover.

Charge of the court.—This is an action of covenant, brought by Thomas Wood, against John Jones, to recover about $600, with interest, the alleged price of 25 acres 128 perches of land. The action is brought on an article of agreement, under seal, executed by these parties on the 11th of August, 1838.

It is contended by the plaintiff, that he has complied with his covenants—that he has caused to be made to the defendant a deed by Dr. Annan for the "Annan farm," agreeably to the article, and although he has received a part of the consideration, there remains due him the price of 25 acres and 128 perches. Has the plaintiff established this position? It is not disputed but that the plaintiff complied with his covenant so far as relates to the tract of 449 acres 70 perches, but this does not embrace the whole "Annan farm." It seems that the Rev. Robert Annan acquired title to about 412 acres with allowance, in the year 1799, by deed from James Taylor. Another deed was also made to him by Taylor, of the same date, for a piece of 28 acres, for which Taylor had a warrant of the 28th of October 1785, which was stated in the deed to have been surveyed, but not returned, and which bounded on the larger tract. This latter tract has ever since been considered a part of the "Annan farm." It was enclosed, occupied, and farmed by Robert Annan, up to his death, in 1819, and has been treated as such to the time of the sale.

It is very clear the deed for 449 acres 70 perches did not convey it, and therefore the defendant alleges the plaintiff has no right to recover. Did the case stop here, his allegation would undoubtedly be correct. This brings us to the contract between Annan and Wood. The article of agreement stipulates that Annan was to convey the "Annan farm"—the lines to be run by the plot and deeds—"the farm to be taken in a tract, be the same more or less"—consideration, $10,000. By this agreement, Wood was entitled to have a deed for the whole "Annan farm." Notwithstanding the deeds and plot are referred to, still the general description

[Jones v. Wood.]

will prevail. Besides, the deed for the smaller tract ought not to be excluded from the reference. It appears by the evidence, that on the 3d of April 1839, Dr. Annan executed a deed to Jones for the 25 acre tract—omitting to name himself as executor. He had procured a warrant for 40 acres, which included the 25 acres, and had the same surveyed. The plaintiff contends this conveyance was an execution of the power conferred upon Annan by his father's will, and Jones having thus obtained title to the whole "Annan farm," he is liable to the plaintiff for the balance of the consideration, as stated in the article of agreement. To this the defendant replies that the deed of April 2, 1839, from Dr. Annan, executor of his father, to John Jones, closed all questions as to the quantity of the land agreed to be sold by the agreement of August 9, 1838, between Annan and Wood, and also as to the amount of purchase money, and that the deed of April 3, 1839, from Annan to Jones, is not an execution of the power in said will. Two questions are thus presented for solution. Did the deed of April 2, 1839, close all questions as to the quantity of land and amount of purchase-money? If such was its effect, there can be no recovery in this suit. It is a well-established rule of law, that as between vendor and vendee by the acceptance of a deed or payment of purchase-money, the article is merged, and the parties are precluded from alleging a deficiency of land or claim for a surplus. The execution of a conveyance is the consummation of the article, unless there be fraud or deceit; mutual misapprehension is not enough. The inquiry is merely this: *Was Wood deceived or defrauded?* It is contended that he was—that Dr. Annan had a right, and was bound by the article to convey the "Annan farm;" that he suppressed from Wood's knowledge material facts in relation to the title, and that his object was to secure to himself a private advantage out of his father's estate. *If you are satisfied there was fraud or deception practised by Annan upon Wood*, the deed of the 2d of April 1839 is not in the latter's way. But still, if there was a reasonable ground for doubt as to the title to the 25 acres, and that doubt was honestly entertained, there was nothing improper or fraudulent in excluding this tract from the conveyance. If Wood was not deceived by Annan, he cannot complain. If you shall decide he was not, your verdict must be for the defendant. If you come to a contrary conclusion, then the question arises whether the deed of April 3, 1839, was an execution of the power in the will of Dr. Annan. Has Jones obtained a title to the "Annan farm," or in other words, has the article of agreement between him and Wood been complied with by Wood? Certain rules are laid down in law which are to govern in a question such as this.

1. When there is a reference to the power, it will be deemed to be executed.

[Jones v. Wood.]

By this deed, 3d of April 1839, there is no reference to the power—reference is made to the warrant obtained in 1838.

2. Where there is a reference to the property.

Here the attempt was to convey, and there was a conveyance of the identical property.

3. When the instrument would have no operation excepting as an execution of the power.

Under the two last rules, the power may be deemed to have been executed.

But it is urged there was no intention to execute the power, and that the intention must govern. The intention to execute the power need not be expressed in the instrument; it will be inferred when the property itself is the subject-matter of conveyance, or where it would be void unless it be by virtue of the power. It is said by defendant's counsel, Dr. Annan did not know the tract belonged to his father's estate. He had sufficient evidence of the fact in his possession, and, under the circumstances, making to Jones the deed he did, he could not gainsay it, nor disturb Jones in his possession. The latter was put in the same position as if the whole 475 acres had been originally conveyed to him by Dr. Annan, as executor of his father's will. I therefore charge you that the deed of the 3d of April 1839, was an execution of the power under the will, and the plaintiff is entitled to recover, provided you are satisfied Wood was deceived or defrauded, as before stated.

The defendant's point (quoting first point) is answered in the general charge, to which answer, as well as that part of the charge where it is said, "Was Wood deceived or defrauded?"—if you are satisfied there was fraud or deception practised by Annan upon Wood, the deed of the 2d of April 1839 is not in the latter's way.

The defendant's counsel excepted to the charge of the court, and to their answers to the points submitted, or so much thereof as relates to the deed of April 3, 1839, being an execution of the power; and in referring it to the jury, to say whether fraud or deceit were practised on Wood at the time of the execution of the deed of April 2, 1839.

Verdict was rendered for the plaintiff.

Specifications of error:
1. The court erred in admitting the testimony mentioned in the first bill of exceptions.
2. They erred in their answer to the defendant's first point.
3. They erred in saying in their charge, "Was Wood deceived or defrauded?" If "you are satisfied there was fraud or deception practised by Annan upon Wood, the deed of the 2d of April 1839 is not in the latter's way."
4. They erred in referring it to the jury to say whether fraud

[Jones v. Wood.]

or deception were practised by Annan on Wood at the time of the execution of the deed of April 2, 1839, there being no evidence whatever of any such fraud or deception.

J. Hickman and *W. Darlington*, for plaintiff in error.

1. First error.—The evidence offered was notes of testimony taken on a former trial between the same parties, but about the price of another piece of land. The question then was as to the title to a part of the land conveyed by the deed of April 2, 1839. The present contest is about the price of other land. The same *subject-matter* is not in dispute.

2. The deed of April 3, 1839, was not an execution of the power contained in the will of Robert Annan.

The deed does not refer to the *will* nor to the *estate* held under it. It refers to the *warrant of* 1838.

Where a party has a *power*, and also an *interest*, the *intention* is the great object of inquiry: 4 *Kent's Com.* 335–6.

Here Dr. Annan had an *interest* as well as a *power*.

The intent must be so clear that no other reasonable intent can be imputed: 4 *Kent* 335.

The intent here is to convey the title he obtained by the warrant of 1838. It is clearly expressed in the deed.

If the words of the will (power by will) may be satisfied without supposing an intention to execute the power, then unless the intent to execute be clearly expressed, it is no execution of it: *Id.* 335.

If a man disposes of that over which he has a power *in such a manner that it is impossible to impute to him any other intention* but that of executing the power, the act done shall be an execution of the power: Andrews *v.* Emmot, 2 *B.C.R.* 303.

This is always a question of intention, whether the party meant to execute the power or not: Sir W. GRANT, Bennet *v.* Abunow, 8 *Ves.* 616.

The intention may be collected from circumstances, as that a part of the will would be inoperative unless applied to the power: *Id.* 616.

In Doe *v.* Roake, 2 *Bing.* 497, all the authorities are reviewed by Chief Justice BEST, and the case ruled on the authority of Andrews *v.* Emmot, 2 *B. C. R.* 303.

The *intention* to execute the power must be *apparent* and *clear*, so that the transaction is not fairly susceptible of any other interpretation: Judge STORY, in Blaggs *v.* Miles, 1 *Story's Rep.* 426, 446, cited in 1 *Russ. & Myl.* 525, (n.)

Intention, in these cases, governs. When it can be inferred that the power was not meant to be exercised, the court cannot consider it as executed: 1 *Sugden on Powers* 440. Same principle, Hay *v.* Mayer, 8 *Watts* 208–9. Allison *v.* Kurtz, 2 *Watts* 185.

No intention to execute the power can here be found. But on

[Jones v. Wood.]

the contrary a denial of the power, and a clear intent to convey as an individual, what he supposed he owned as such.

3 and 4. The judge laid down the law correctly, that the deed closes all questions as to quantity of land and purchase money in the articles, unless there be fraud or deceit; but he left it to the jury to infer fraud or deceit, without any evidence. This was erroneous. It is presumed he meant fraud or deception at the execution of the deed of April 2, 1839. We may search in vain for any evidence of it. The deed was drawn by Whitson, pursuant to a survey made under Wood's direction; it was executed by Annan to Jones, under the article between Wood and Jones of August 11, 1838, and in the presence of Wood, who signed it as a witness; the $3000 were paid to Annan in Wood's presence; the mortgage for $7000 was executed by Jones to Annan for the same property, and Wood signed as a witness, and not a word of dissatisfaction is heard. Wood settled with Haggerty for his share of the profits, and all was supposed to be at an end. Jones could have no idea but that all was closed. He then purchased of Annan the 25 acres, and paid him for it. *Nine years* elapsed, and Wood sued Jones, alleging he was deceived. But was Wood, at any time, deceived by Annan? Annan did not agree to convey the vacant land. He refused to convey it. Wood demanded that he should, and advised with counsel. It was an open question between Annan and Wood, whether Annan could be compelled to convey or not. Wood might have refused to accept the deed of Annan for any part of it, unless the whole were conveyed. But he chose to go on and complete the business upon Annan's terms, leaving out the vacant land. This he did with his eyes open. The deed of April 2, 1839, the payment of the money, and the mortgage closed all questions upon the articles. The defendant was entitled to an explicit direction to the jury to that effect.

The deed closes all questions as to the quantity of land and purchase-money in the articles: Cronister *v.* Cronister, *W. & Ser.* 443; Smith *v.* Evans, 6 *Bin.* 102; Baily *v.* Snyder, 13 *Ser. & R.* 162; Creigh *v.* Beelin, 1 *W. & Ser.* 83; Shurtz *v.* Thomas, 8 *Barr* 363; 10 *Watts* 427.

In this case the deed was accepted without a release of dower. The purchaser took the title, which he consented to take in satisfaction: 8 *Barr* 364.

The acceptance of the deed of April 2, 1839, by Jones, from Annan, having been in pursuance of the article of August 11, 1838, between Wood and Jones, and in Wood's presence, he not objecting, it was as if accepted by Wood—Jones merely standing in his shoes.

But even if Annan ought to have conveyed the whole to Jones, and refused, and Wood allowed the business to be so completed, how can Jones be affected by Annan's conduct so as to make him

[Jones v. Wood.]

liable to. Wood? There is no evidence of fraud in Jones. If Wood has any claim, it should be upon Annan for refusing to convey on the 2d of April 1839. There is not a tittle of evidence of any fraud on Jones's part at any time, nor on the part of Annan on the 2d of April 1839. Yet the judge says *if fraud or deception was practised by Annan on Wood*, the deed of the 2d of April 1839 is not in the latter's way. *This was leaving a question to the jury without any evidence whatever, and was error.*

Lewis, for defendant in error.—As to the first point taken by the plaintiff in error, the evidence of the deceased witnesses related to precisely the same question—and this would have been shown if the testimony had been exhibited by the paper-book. The paper-book of the former cause shows that the testimony then produced, as now, was to prove what constituted the Annan farm. On the first point the following cases were referred to: Hobart v. M'Coy, 3 *Barr* 419; Cooper v. Smith, 8 *Watts* 536; Ottinger v. Ottinger, 18 *Ser. & R.* 142.

If in a dispute respecting lands, any fact comes directly in issue, the testimony given to that fact is admissible to prove the same point or fact in another action between the same parties or their privies, though the last suit be for other lands: *Greenleaf on Evidence*, sec. 164; Foster v. Derby, 28 *Eng. C. L.* 213.

2. The deed of the 3d of April 1839 was an execution of the power.

Powers executed by deed or will need not recite or refer to the instrument creating the power, if the act done be such as cannot take effect but by virtue of the power. Hence, a conveyance by one who was executor, with full power to sell and convey, shall be construed to be an execution of the power contained in the will, although that power be not recited: Alison v. Kurtz, 2 *Watts* 185.

In Alison v. Kurtz the subject was fully considered, and the court below founded their charge on the doctrine of that case. See also Miller v. Meetch, 8 *Barr* 418.

It was the duty of Annan to convey the whole Annan farm: Wood v. Jones, 7 *Barr* 480.

The opinion of the court was delivered April 21, by

BELL, J.—It is conceded the court below was right in the instruction given, that acceptance of the deed of April 2, 1839, executed by Annan to Jones, was a consummation of the prior agreement, and operated to put an end to all questions concerning the quantity of the land to be conveyed, and the purchase-money to be paid, which might otherwise arise under the covenants of August 11, 1838. As a general rule, by such acceptance the parties to the transaction are absolutely precluded from looking behind the conveyance for subjects of strife, suggested by their pre-

[Jones v. Wood.]

vious negotiations and contracts; for the last step is esteemed as indisputably expressive of their final conclusions. In the present instance, this well-settled doctrine is as applicable to Wood, the vendor to Jones, as to the latter and his immediate grantor, Annan. The evidence is uncontradicted that the former was present and participated in the conveyance, as a discharge of his agreement with Jones to cause a deed to be executed by Annan for the premises before purchased. He was, undoubtedly, acquainted with its description of the tract to be granted, for he had caused the survey to be made by which that description was ascertained. He was, too, present at its execution and delivery, attesting it, as a subscribing witness, without, so far as appears, a word of complaint or remonstrance; though before that, he had unsuccessfully demanded from Annan a conveyance of the whole tract, including what has been called the vacant land. Under these circumstances, he was properly regarded, on the trial, as an actual party to the instrument, and subject to all the rules incident to that relation.

This view of his legal position must have precluded his recovery in this action, had not the court permitted him the choice of claiming the benefit of an exception to the rule which otherwise concluded him. The learned president correctly informed the jury that the practice of a fraud or any deceit by a vendor, misleading a purchaser, would absolve the latter from the conclusive effect of the conveyance, and open the door for inquiry under the original agreement. To this instruction no exception can be taken. As an abstract proposition, it is unquestionable. But the court went a step further, by referring to the triers of fact, as a legitimate subject for discussion and decision, whether Wood had been defrauded by the deceitful practices of Annan, or by concealment of material facts in relation to the title which the vendor was bound to disclose, but failed to do so in the hope of securing a private benefit to himself? "If," said the judge, "you are satisfied there was fraud or deception practised by Annan upon Wood, the deed of the 2d of April 1839 is not in the latter's way." This certainly was a most material inquiry, were there any proof upon which to found it. But we have looked in vain through the record, for evidence tending to fasten upon Annan the practice of a fraud. A recurrence to every lawyer's experience of the facility with which a jury is but too apt to yield itself to a reiterated suggestion of falsehood and malpractice, especially where an innocent party has suffered loss, though from his own neglect, strongly illustrates the value of our legal maxim, that fraud is not to be presumed, but must be proved. Was there any, the slightest, proof of it here? The insinuated fraud is said to consist in the undue concealment by Annan, of the extent of what was known as the Annan farm, and, by wilful misrepresentation, inducing Wood to accept a less quantity of land than by the terms of his purchase he was entitled

[Jones v. Wood.]

to. To determine whether this was so, we must look to the evidence of Annan's knowledge on this subject. The first fact which presents itself in this connection is that, at the time of the sale, he was not a resident on the farm, and had not been since boyhood, many years before; much of the intermediate period having been spent abroad. When first called on by Wood, and before the purchase, he expressly declared the tract contained but 412 acres, and he now swears—his statement standing wholly uncontradicted—that he knew of no muniment connected with the title of the estate, save the deed of 1799, from Colonel Taylor to his father, for 412 acres and allowance, and the draft (marked A) by which the land, the subject of that deed, was correctly delineated by black lines, laid down by course and distance, and exhibiting that portion of the tract he had always understood was vacant land, as enclosed by dotted lines, unmarked by course or distance, in such a way as to lead to the conclusion it formed no part of the conveyed land; that he never had possession of the second deed made by Taylor, and knew not of its existence; that when Wood first proposed to purchase, he distinctly informed him the extent of the tract he had to sell was included within the black lines of the draft, which was furnished to the buyer as a means of ascertaining the boundaries, at the same time telling him that the piece of land exhibited as enclosed within dotted lines was vacant, and he (Wood) might, if he saw proper, take it up; that he (Annan) disclaimed any title to it, and refused to bind himself to convey any exact number of acres, or to be responsible for the correctness of the apparent lines of the tract, but put upon Wood the duty of ascertaining them, from the *data* then furnished. This Wood undertook to effect, and accordingly actually caused new surveys to be made by an artist of his own selection; in the first of which he included the estimated 28 acres as part of the farm, but afterwards caused the greater portion of it to be left out of the second survey, under the conviction that his original impression was erroneous. The deed was prepared in accordance with this second survey; but before its execution Wood, for some reason, seems to have recurred to his first impression, and, therefore, insisted that Annan should convey both parcels of land. The latter refused, because, as he said, he owned the title of the original tract alone, and finally, after the lapse of months, the deed as prepared was executed and accepted with Wood's full assent; nay, by his procurement. Before the conveyance, however, Annan, acting upon what he swears was his conviction, procured a warrant for what he supposed was vacant land, and, after causing it to be surveyed, sold and conveyed it, as his own, to Jones, the day next succeeding his grant of the first tract. I have thus given a detail of the leading features of this transaction. They furnish, to our apprehension, no evidence, however inconsiderable, that from the beginning to the end of it, Dr.

[Jones v. Wood.]

Annan knew or suspected his deceased father had been the owner of the so-called vacant land; or that he practised any art, or used any device to blindfold Wood, or to prevent him from attaining to the truth. As evidence of practised deceit, our attention was called to the language of the original agreement between Annan and Wood, in which it is stipulated that the lines of the tract are to be run "by the *deeds* and plot;" to the answer returned by Annan to one of the plaintiff's cross-interrogatories, in which he is made to say he had *a deed* for the 28 acres; and to the fact that, after his sale to Wood, he procured a new warrant, under which he set up a title to the land mistaken as vacant. But these portions of the evidence, candidly treated, furnish no ground upon which to erect an hypothesis of actual fraud. As to the answer to the cross-interrogatory, it, beyond question, was made to assume an affirmative instead of a negative shape, by the blunder of the commissioner in using the article "a," instead of the word "no." In answer to the very next question, which asserts the existence of such a deed, and inquires of the witness's knowledge regarding it, he flatly denies all cognizance of it, and reiterates that he never had such a deed. Besides, the admission of such a document is in direct contradiction of all he had said before and says after. As to the fact of a new warrant, it is sufficient to observe that so far from evidencing knowledge of a previous warrant and survey constituting the title conveyed to his father, it indicates a belief that no such title had existence; or, at the very least, it proves nothing relating to the disputed point. We are thus reduced to the forced inference of knowledge, to be deduced from the use of the plural "*deeds*," in the article of agreement. But, surely, no sane man, looking with unprejudiced eyes, can conjure from this word the monster fraud charged upon the seller. If the jurors did found themselves upon ground so utterly insufficient to sustain a structure so weighty, it but proves the accuracy of the remark I made in the outset. Looking at the whole of the proofs dispassionately, we have failed to discover any thing which can properly give birth to even a suspicion of deceit and falsehood practised by Annan; and we are almost forced upon the conclusion that the verdict pronounced is to be ascribed to the simple fact that Annan received money which ought to have gone into Wood's purse. But, though it may be conceded that such a consideration would naturally operate with men unversed in, and therefore unimpressed by the force of merely professional reasoning, it affords no apology we can recognise as sufficient for the conclusion arrived at.

I have, hitherto, considered this contest as though it were an action between Wood and Annan. But, still more unfavourably for the plaintiff, it is an effort to compel Jones to pay a second time for a portion of his land. To compass this, proof of the grossest fraud, practised by Annan on Wood, would be ineffica-

[Jones v. Wood.]

cious. It would be necessary to go farther, by showing Jones's participation in, or, at least, knowledge of the imputed iniquity. This necessity seems to have been overlooked at the trial. The attention of the jury was confined to the averred malpractices of Annan. When the argument was first broached in this court, the existence of proof involving Jones was not hinted. Indeed, such a suggestion must, necessarily, fail of success. From the beginning, Wood seems to have been the active agent in perfecting the arrangements ending in the conveyance. Jones, for aught that appears, was the passive recipient of the title Wood and Annan caused to be prepared for him. It is not intimated he knew of or had reason to suspect the existence of Taylor's second conveyance, or that there was any thing to lead him to doubt the truth of Annan's assertions, except the demand made by Wood, afterwards at least tacitly abandoned. And had there been, mere doubt is insufficient to entail upon him a consequence which can flow only from actual fraud. He appears to have relied, as he had a right to do, upon Wood's undertaking to procure for him a sufficient conveyance of the "Annan farm." Wood recognised this as the obligation he had assumed, and was, therefore, active in settling the terms of that conveyance. Jones received it at his hands, and afterwards took from Annan a transfer of the remaining land. In all this, we cannot perceive the slightest shadow of blame, legal or moral, attaching upon the defendant. So clear is this, that, I repeat, no accusation of impropriety in him seems to have been indulged below, nor was it here, until a suggestion of its necessity drove the ingenious counsel, who argued for the defendant in error, upon an endeavour to point to proof of it. In this, however, he wholly failed.

It follows from what I have said, there is in that part of the charge under review, faults of commission and omission. Of commission, in putting the jury at liberty to find an asserted fact, without proof of it. Of omission, in, inadvertently, neglecting to point out to them that fraud practised or participated by Jones, is indispensable to the plaintiff's success in this action. For these errors the judgment must be reversed, and the cause remitted for another trial.

But the other objection to the charge is untenable. Under the authority of Allison v. Kurtz, 2 *Watts* 185, and the doctrine there recognised, repeated in Miller v. Meetch, 8 *Barr* 418, the deed of April 3, 1839, from Annan to Jones, may be accepted as a competent execution of the power to sell, conferred by the will of the Rev. Mr. Annan. The distinction settled by the decisions seems to be this: When the donee of a power to sell land possesses, also, an interest in the subject of the power, a conveyance by him, without actual reference to the power, will not be deemed an execution of it, except there be evidence of an intention to execute it, or, at

[Jones v. Wood.]

least, in the face of evidence, disproving such an intention; but where the donee has no estate in the premises, and his conveyance can only be made operative by treating it as an exertion of the power to sell, it will be so considered. It is upon this ground the authorities are to be reconciled, and, among them, our own cases of Allison v. Kurtz, and Hay v. Mayer, 8 *Watts* 208, particularly referred to on the argument. The principle stated embraces the conveyance in question, and justifies the opinion expressed by the court upon this point. Were it, however, erroneous, it would inflict no injury on the defendant, since, doubtless, the grantor, and those claiming the benefit of the sale, would not be permitted to question the validity of that conveyance, as a means of transferring the title of the testator. This remark is, of course, based upon the supposed acquiescence of the parties interested under the will, by participating in the avails of the sale.

The exception to the evidence received is unfounded. The former statements of the deceased witnesses were made on the trial of an action between the same parties, and bear directly upon the same subject of dispute, namely, the boundaries and extent of the tract known as the "Annan farm." This was a point of inquiry in both instances, material to the issue involved, and, therefore, opening to the parties plenary opportunity of interrogating the witnesses, in chief and by cross-examination. The question of the competency of the evidence consequently falls directly within the rule settled by our own cases, cited on the argument, and stated by Mr. Greenleaf, with his accustomed accuracy, in his work on evidence. (*Green. on Ev.* sec. 164.)

Judgment reversed and a *venire de novo* awarded.

Edwards *versus* Goldsmith.

1. One who was counsel for the plaintiff at the time of the admissions of defendant made before the institution of the suit, but not counsel in the suit, and having no interest in the result of it, was a competent witness for the plaintiff to prove admissions by defendant as to the contract on which the suit was founded, and which were made at an interview had in consequence of a note from the counsel.

2. In an action of *indebitatus assumpsit* by a broker, to recover compensation fixed by a special contract to sell certain real estate on ground-rent, it was not competent for defendant to prove the usual rates charged by brokers for services of a like character.

3. The evidence of a contract leaving it obscure, it consisting in part of a memorandum in writing by defendant made subsequent to the contract, the same with certain parol evidence, was submitted to the jury to decide what the contract was: *Held* to have been properly submitted.

4. Where a broker was to receive a definite commission for procuring a purchaser for certain lots of ground, and complied with his part of the contract, but the defendant, without good reason, failed to fulfil his part of the contract:

[Edwards v. Goldsmith.]

Held, that the broker could recover, in *indebitatus assumpsit*, the amount of compensation agreed upon.

ERROR to the District Court, *Philadelphia*.

This was an action of assumpsit, brought by Thomas O. Goldsmith against George W. Edwards, to recover the sum of $750, under an alleged contract with Edwards, contained in the following memorandum, which was admitted to be in *his* handwriting:—"15 lots, 250 each, on ground-rent, payable in ten years. Ground-rent deeds to be made at $300 and $250 cash advanced, in all $550 on each lot; each house to be of the cash value of $750. The profit to Mr. Goldsmith, $750, to be taken out in 3 of the lots, or a lot equal to $45 per annum, on some other part of the ground."

The narr. contained a special count on this alleged contract, and a count in *indebitatus assumpsit*, to which the defendant pleaded "Non assumpsit," and "Payment with leave," &c.

On the trial, the plaintiff gave the above-mentioned memorandum in evidence, and called one Charles Nece, who testified that Goldsmith had called on him to take some of the lots; that he had agreed to do so; that Edwards had seen him, and said he was satisfied with him; and that he had in consequence made certain preparations to build, but that he never could find Edwards to get a deed from him, and he finally desisted.

The counsel for plaintiff then offered to examine W. L. Brown, Esq., who, being examined on his *voir dire*, said—"I am not now the counsel in this case. I never was retained in the case. I was not the retained counsel. Dr. Goldsmith consulted me in regard to this matter. I have no connection at all with this suit. I have no interest direct or indirect. I do not expect to be paid as Mr. Goldsmith's attorney in case he recovers."

Whereupon the said witness was objected to as the former attorney of the plaintiff, and the objection was overruled, and the witness admitted, to which ruling the counsel for the defendant excepted, and his exception was duly noted by the judge, and the witness then testified—"I can't remember when I saw Mr. Edwards; it was before suit brought. Here is a memorandum, (the witness looks at the memorandum before given in evidence by the plaintiff,) he admitted it to be his. He said he was not satisfied with the purchaser. Edwards admitted his own obligation to carry it out, if a proper purchaser was brought, and refused to comply with it as regards Mr. Nece. He refused to pay Dr. Goldsmith, as he was not satisfied with Mr. Nece."

And being cross-examined, the witness said—"I sent Mr. Edwards a professional note. I presume it was in regard to this controversy. Mr. Edwards came to my office in consequence. The conversation took place there. I am not prepared to say that he used Nece's name, but said that the doctor had not produced a proper purchaser."

[Edwards v. Goldsmith.]

The plaintiff here closed his case, and the defendant's counsel asked the judge to direct a non-suit to be entered against the plaintiff, because he had not proved his case; which the judge declined to direct.

The counsel of the defendant then offered in evidence Andrew D. Cash, to prove the usual rates of commission charged on the sale of real estate in the city and county of Philadelphia, which testimony was objected to by the plaintiff, and the testimony overruled by the judge, to which decision the counsel of the defendant excepted, and the exception was duly noted.

And the jury having been addressed by the counsel on both sides, the counsel of the defendant requested the judge to charge as follows:—

Defendant's points.—1. Upon the proper construction of the agreement entered into by the defendant with the plaintiff, nothing was due or to be paid to the plaintiff by the defendant, until the houses of the cash value of $750 each should be erected upon each of the fifteen lots; as it was made the duty of the plaintiff, by this agreement, to see that this stipulation should be complied with on the part of the purchasers from the defendant, on ground-rent.

2. As the plaintiff has neither averred nor proved a compliance on his part with the agreement entered into by the defendant, as properly construed, and he has not averred or proved that he was prevented from complying therewith by the acts of the defendant, the verdict of the jury must be for the defendant.

3. Under the terms used in the memorandum of agreement between the parties, this was a joint speculation of the plaintiff and defendant; and until brought to a successful close, by the sale of the lots, the erection of the houses, &c., through the efforts of the plaintiff, he could not claim his share of the profit, to wit, $750; and as the matter is not concluded, the plaintiff cannot recover.

SHARSWOOD, J.—I decline charging as requested by the defendant. Upon the memorandum which has been read as the contract, in connection with the parol evidence which has been given, it is for you to say what the contract was.

If the contract was as stated in the memorandum, as to the mode plaintiff was to be compensated, the plaintiff, not having proved that he tendered or demanded a deed, is not entitled to recover, unless the defendant has dispensed with the necessity of so doing by an absolute refusal to comply. You have the evidence of Mr. Brown on this subject. If this was a contract with plaintiff as set forth in the contract, and a purchaser was procured with whom the defendant was satisfied, and afterwards refused without good reason to fulfil the contract, then the plaintiff is entitled to recover. If the contract was, however, that plaintiff was not to

[Edwards v. Goldsmith.]

be paid till the houses were finished, then the plaintiff cannot recover under the declaration.

Counsel of defendant excepted to that part of the charge, that the construction of the contract was not for the court; and to the refusal of the court to charge as requested.

It was assigned for error:
1. The judge erred in admitting W. Linn Brown to testify on behalf of the plaintiff below.
2. The judge erred in refusing to permit the defendant below to prove, by competent testimony, the usual rates of commission charged on the sale of real estate in the city and county of Philadelphia.
3. The judge erred, 1st. In declining to answer the defendant's points as requested by him. 2d. In leaving the construction of the contract to the jury. 3d. In not charging that the plaintiff could not recover.

The case was argued by *G. W. Biddle* and *Meredith*, for Edwards, plaintiff in error, who contended, *inter alia*:—That parol evidence was not admissible to explain even an imperfectly worded written contract: Halliley v. Nicholson, 1 *Price, Ex. Rep.* 404. Yet the judge, instead of expounding the contract correctly, or telling the jury there was no contract, left it to them to say what the contract was, in connection *with the parol testimony given*. This is clearly error, as is shown by the following authorities.

The construction of written instruments is the province of the court; and it is of the utmost importance that this province should not be invaded by the jury: Welsh v. Dusar, 3 *Bin.* 337; Denison v. Wertz, 7 *Ser. & R.* 372. It is error for the court to leave to the jury the construction of a deed or other writing: Moore v. Miller, 4 *Ser. & R.* 279; Vincent v. Huff, 8 *Ser. & R.* 381; Roth v. Miller, 15 *Ser. & R.* 100.

No doubt where the instrument cannot be understood without reference to facts *dehors* the writing, the jury are to judge of the whole; but here there were no facts to explain or modify the character of the instrument, and the plaintiff in his declaration puts his case upon the contract as evidenced by this memorandum.

The contract which the plaintiff went upon, being for the recovery of a lot upon the procuring of a purchaser, and the erection of the houses, &c., and he not having averred that he was prevented from a compliance by the acts of the defendant, he clearly could not recover: Alexander v. Hoffman, 5 *W. & Ser.* 382, in which it was held, that "in an action to recover compensation for work and labour under a special contract, the plaintiff cannot recover for part performance upon a declaration containing a general averment of performance, but must set out specially the defend-

[Edwards v. Goldsmith.]

ant's default as the ground of his failure to perform according to his contract." See also Algeo v. Algeo, 10 *Ser. & R.* 234.

And the plaintiff cannot help himself here by his count in *indebitatus assumpsit*. The rule, as laid down in Cutter v. Powell, and the subsequent authorities, is, that while a *special* contract remains unperformed, no action of *indebitatus assumpsit* can be brought for any thing done under it; though where a party has been prevented by the conduct of defendant from completing, and has done something, he may recover what his services were reasonably worth: 2 *Smith's Leading Cases*, Am. ed. 9, 17, *et seq.* And see also the cases cited in 1 *Whar. Dig.* Tit. *Assumpsit*, pl. 11 to 17, particularly Harris v. Ligget, 1 *W. & Ser.* 301; Martin v. Schœnberger, 8 *W. & Ser.* 367.

Kneass, for defendant.—It was not erroneous to allow William Linn Brown to testify on behalf of the plaintiff below. An attorney or counsel concerned in a case may be a witness, though his judgment-fee depends upon his success: Newman v. Bradley, 1 *Dal.* 241. So although he expects to receive a larger fee from his client if the latter succeeds: Miles v. O'Hara, 1 *Ser. & R.* 32. Mr. Brown had no sort of interest whatever in the suit; he never had been retained, and expected no compensation. It was of no consequence whether the interview at which the conversation occurred, was sought for by the one or the other, or was entirely accidental: whatever admissions are made by a party to the attorney of the other party, may by him be given in evidence.

There was no error in the rejection of Andrew D. Cash as a witness for the defendant below, to testify as to the usual rates of commissions on the sale of real estate. There was a contract between the parties;—all the plaintiff had to do was to procure a suitable purchaser, and the testimony of real-estate brokers could shed no light on the contract.

The answers to the defendant's points and the charge of the court were correct.

The contract was for a recovery upon the procuring of a purchaser. This is shown by the memorandum and parol testimony submitted, and the judge rightly left it to the jury to say what the contract was. No doubt the construction of a written instrument is the province of the court; but when this instrument cannot be understood without reference to facts, *dehors* the writing, the jury are to judge of the whole. Such was the case here, and the plaintiff in his narr. goes upon the contract as shown by the memorandum and parol testimony together.

The contract did not impose upon the plaintiff below the necessity of looking to the erection of the houses. He was simply required to procure a purchaser of the lots upon the terms stated. Such a purchaser was procured by him, and at once his right of

[Edwards v. Goldsmith.]

action accrued; for the agreement, so far as he could attend to it, was thus fully performed: Harris v. Ligget, 1 *W. & Ser.* 301. He who has performed a special agreement to do a particular thing, may recover the stipulated price of it by an action of *indebitatus assumpsit*, and use the agreement as evidence of the amount of compensation due. This has been held in Kelly v. Foster, 2 *Bin.* 4, on the authority of Alcorn v. Westbrook, 1 *Wils.* 117; Brook v. White, 4 *Bos. & Pul.* 330; and of Mr. Justice BULLER, *N. P.* 129. See also Snyder v. Caster, 4 *Yeates* 353; Filzell v. Mitchell, 3 *W. & Ser.* 331; 1 *Chit. Pl.* 249, 316; 7 *Cranch* 299; 4 *East* 147; 4 *Bos. & Pul.* 351; 6 *East* 564–9; 2 *Sand.* 350, note 2; 2 *Bin.* 4; 5 *Whar.* 405.

The opinion of the court was delivered May 2, by

CHAMBERS, J.—The first error assigned in the case was the admission of William Linn Brown, Esq., to testify in behalf of the plaintiff below, having been of counsel to the plaintiff at the time of the alleged admissions of the defendant made to him respecting the contract between the parties. Mr. Brown had no connection with the suit, had received no compensation, and expected none. He had no interest in the event of the suit. His competency and admission were in accordance with the law as ruled in the case of Newman v. Bradley, 1 *Dal.* 244, and Miles v. O'Hara, 1 *Ser. & R.* 32, which have not been departed from by the court.

The second error assigned is the rejection of Andrew D. Cash as a witness for defendant, to testify as to the usual rates of commission on the sale of real estate in this city. This action is founded on an alleged special contract between the parties, by which remuneration was fixed, and which the plaintiff below was bound to establish to the satisfaction of the court and jury, to enable him to recover. It was that contract which determined the amount of compensation for services rendered, and not the ordinary charges of commission on the sale of real estate in other cases and between other parties. The sum claimed and allowed by the jury, it is said, is disproportioned to the services; but the inducements which the plaintiff could offer and render in the way of activity, discernment, and influence, to enhance the property and procure a purchaser, which the defendant might think so advantageous to him as to promise the compensation stipulated for, might have been understood by the parties, though not disclosed by the evidence. In the rejection of the evidence offered there was no error.

The next error assigned is to the charge of the court, in not answering, as requested, the points presented in behalf of the plaintiff in error, in leaving the construction of the contract to the jury, and in not instructing the jury that the plaintiff could not recover. It is to be remarked, that there was some misapprehension with the court below, as well as with the counsel, in considering the writing called the "memorandum" as the contract between the parties, which it was not, but part of the evidence of the alleged contract. The evidence adduced to prove the contract was the admission of Edwards in this memorandum and the admissions made by him to Nece and Brown. This "memorandum" was made by Edwards some time after the contract, and after Nece had been procured as a purchaser and accepted; and was furnished by Edwards to the scrivener, who had been directed by Edwards to prepare the deeds from him to Nece. Goldsmith was no party to it, nor had he any participation in placing it with the scrivener.

The testimony of Nece went to prove a contract varying in some of its terms from that indicated by the memorandum. Nece is explicit that Edwards told him that he was to advance $300 on each lot, $50 of which was to go to Goldsmith—that Goldsmith was to get $50 for the sale of each lot, and that, as a purchaser, he had agreed to take the fifteen lots.

The evidence in the cause left the contract obscure, and as its construction was dependent on parol evidence, it was properly submitted by the court to the jury. The court did instruct the jury that if the contract was as stated in the memorandum as to mode, plaintiff was to be compensated; the plaintiff was not entitled to recover unless defendant had dispensed with the necessity of so doing, by an absolute refusal to comply; and if the contract was, however, that plaintiff was not to be paid till the houses were finished, the plaintiff could not recover under the declaration. This was answering the points of defendant's counsel as favourably as was warranted, so far as the memorandum was considered the evidence of the contract; and if there had been no other evidence of the contract, the plaintiff ought not to have recovered, according either to his allegation or proof.

But it was still a material question of fact for the jury, whether by the contract between the parties Goldsmith was to be paid $50 on each lot, out of the $300 to be advanced by Edwards, on procuring a purchaser, and which it was alleged was not dependent on the erection of houses, which were to be erected by Nece, with the aid of the advance from Edwards, and over which Goldsmith had no control. The testimony of Nece did conduce to prove this, and the admission of Edwards to Brown, that he was under an obligation to comply if a proper purchaser was brought, did support this construction of the contract. It was further testified by Nece that Goldsmith had procured him to become the purchaser of the lots—that with the references he gave Edwards, he was satisfied, and accepted him (Nece) as the purchaser of the fifteen lots; and in the prosecution of the sale, Edwards gave him a plan, requested him to get a surveyor, to have the lines marked, and make the necessary preparations for building.

[Edwards v. Goldsmith.]

To this part of the evidence the jury might apply the charge of the court, in which they were instructed that if this was the contract with the plaintiff, as set forth in the contract, and a purchaser was procured with whom defendant was satisfied, and afterwards refused without good reason to fulfil his contract, then the plaintiff is entitled to recover. The contract was thus submitted rightly to the jury on the testimony; and if the jury were satisfied that by its terms Goldsmith was only to procure a purchaser who was acceptable, for the fifteen lots, that he had done so, and performed his part of the contract, the plaintiff was entitled to a verdict which may be supported on the second count of *indebitatus assumpsit*. It is settled, by repeated adjudications of this court and others, that when the terms of a special agreement have been performed by the plaintiff, the law raises a duty, for which a general *indebitatus assumpsit* will lie: Kelly v. Foster, 2 *Bin.* 4; Bomeisler v. Dobson, 5 *Wh.* 398; Harris v. Ligget, 1 *W. & Ser.* 301; Filzell v. Mitchell, 3 *W. & Ser.* 331. The court did not err in refusing to answer the points as requested by defendant's counsel, and in their charge there was not error. The contract was left obscure by the conflicting evidence, yet this was for the jury and the consideration of the court before whom the cause was tried; and if there has been error, it has been with the jury on the facts which this court cannot undertake to correct.

Judgment affirmed.

Murphy *versus* Hubert.

1. A deed, whether voluntary and without consideration, or for a valuable consideration, made upon a parol trust, declared at the time of the execution of the deed, that the grantee would hold in trust for the children of the grantor, if intended as a fraud upon creditors of the grantor, is void as against the creditors, but it is valid as against the grantor and the children for whose benefit it was designed, and the grantee will be entitled to hold against the children or their vendee; whether the trust be by parol or in writing the rule is the same; and the circumstance of the grantee *of the children* being in possession will not vary the principle. See 7 *Barr* 420.

2. Acts by a trustee, a married woman, in relation to the trust property, made as agent of her husband, and her declarations accompanying such acts, are evidence against her husband.

3. If a deed be made in consideration of a bond executed by the grantee, and the bond was subsequently cancelled by the grantee, *then a married woman*, this would not revest the estate in the grantor, or defeat the estate of her husband.

Error to the District Court, *Philadelphia*.

This was an action of ejectment brought by Lyttleton Hubert, and Curtis Butler and Delia his wife, late Delia Chase, against Archibald Murphy, to recover possession of a lot, with the houses thereon erected, situate on Shippen street, extending to Bedford

[Murphy v. Hubert.]

street, Philadelphia, and being twenty feet in front. The plaintiffs claimed under a deed from Samuel Murray to Delia Chase, dated 13th January 1819, for the premises, and a deed from Butler and Delia his wife to Lyttleton Hubert, dated 20th October 1841, for one moiety of the premises; the consideration stated in the latter deed to be one dollar. Both these deeds were recorded.

The defendant Murphy claimed under the children of Samuel Murray, the grantor to Delia Chase. (See 7 *Barr* 420, for the report of a former trial between these parties.) Deed 9th March 1840.

On the part of the plaintiffs was given in evidence a deed from Richard Peters, Esq., and wife, and others, to Samuel Murray, dated 19th November 1804, not recorded. This deed was in the possession of Murphy. Deed from Samuel Murray to Delia Chase, dated 13th January 1819, recorded. The consideration expressed on the face of this deed was $800, and a further consideration of a certain yearly ground-rent of $33.33, subject to which the premises were conveyed to Delia Chase. She resided on the premises for a number of years.

Deed from Curtis Butler and Delia his wife, late Delia Chase, to Lyttleton Hubert, dated 20th October 1841, and recorded, for one undivided moiety of the same premises.

Certificate of the marriage, on 19th December 1822, of Curtis Butler and Delia Chase.

Plaintiff's counsel then closed.

Defendant's counsel gave in evidence the deposition of Loughead. He testified that he knew the property; knew Samuel Murray; he died in 1837 or 1838. Delia Chase was his sister. That he knew the children of Samuel Murray; their names were Nancy and Fanny. Nancy was the eldest. Some days after the death of Samuel Murray, Delia called on deponent, and brought with her a deed for the premises from Samuel Murray to her, and on being asked why she had not claimed the property before, she said that her brother had given this property to her when he was in difficulties, in debt, and about to take the benefit of the insolvent laws—that he thought she had a better right to it than his creditors, she being his sister. Deponent observed it was extraordinary, as Samuel Murray had left a will and left the property to his two daughters. She said that Fanny should have it, but Nancy should have none of it; and inquired the best course to pursue to enable her to hold the property, or have it for the youngest daughter. She said that she had not paid any thing for the property. She said there was a year and a half or two years' ground-rent due on the premises, at the time she called on me.

On another occasion she said that she had since paid a part of the ground-rent.

"To the best of my recollection, in the course of conversation with her, I think she observed that her brother had conveyed the property to her to save it for the benefit of himself and children. These may not be the identical words, but it is the substance of the conversation."

Charles Acres testified that Samuel Murray was living in his own property, between Shippen and Bedford streets, and died there. That he left two children; one was married to Peter Hercules. He said that Delia told him that the property was conveyed to her to secure it for the children. He further said that the substance of a conversation had with Murray and Delia was that Murray had made the deed, and that "she had given her brother a bond to pay $800, if any thing happened to the property before it came to the children."

J. Wortheym testified, *inter alia*, under objection:—"She (meaning Delia) stated to me that this property was her brother Samuel's; that he had been in difficulties, and the property was made over to her so that it might not be lost, and that his creditors might not get hold of it; that he had creditors at the time, and he was afraid they might get hold of it.

"That she had never paid a cent for it, and that Samuel had paid for the deed, and that he had always paid the taxes and ground-rent; that Samuel and the children ought to have the property again. I told her I thought it was impossible, as she had a husband, and it was impossible for her to do it, &c. This conversation took place in 1844 or '5, in the house where Samuel lived. * * * Samuel occupied the front on Small street, and had the rest in possession, except the part that Delia had. By possession, I mean that I collected rents for him, and took receipts in his name. I commenced business for him in 1831. He (Murray) was in possession at that time. He continued in possession to the time of his death. I think he died in the Bedford-street house, in 1837 or thereabouts—from 1836 to 1838. He said he was collecting for Murray some two or three years—collected from the house next door to where he lived in Bedford street, and from a room or two in Shippen street. Collected from verbal authority—was always the agent of Samuel Murray, and not of Delia; * * * He told me he had been in difficulties, and was afraid his creditors would get it. But he said he had got over his difficulties, and he said he ought to have it back, he and his children; that he had worked for the money, and it was no more than right that he should have the benefit of it, he and his children, as she had never paid any thing for it.

"I asked Murray why he was so foolish as not to make *a deed of trust* for it. He answered that the squire who had drawn up the deed, said it was all right and all the same." * * * "I meant, by a deed of trust, so that it might be kept for him and he could get it back from her."

[Murphy v. Hubert.]

Another witness, Richardson, testified:—" I heard Delia say that she had bought the property from her brother; that her brother had been in debt was the reason that she had paid him that money, and that after her brother was out of trouble he had refunded the money again.''

Defendant Murphy offered in evidence a deed for the premises, from Peter Hercules and Delia Anna to Thomas Donnelly, trustee for Margaret Murphy, wife of Archibald Murphy. Deed dated 9th March 1840, recorded in March 1840.

On the part of plaintiff, it was testified that Murray said the property in question was his sister's; that next day, Delia was present, and Murray said he had sold the property to his sister, the witness thought for $800.

It was proved that Fanny, the younger of Murray's children, was dead.

Other evidence was given on each side.

On the part of the plaintiff, points as follow were proposed:

1. The plaintiffs, by their evidence, consisting of the deed of Samuel Murray to Delia Chase, of January 13, 1819, and the certificate of marriage of Delia with Curtis Butler on the 19th December 1822, and the deed from Curtis Butler and wife to Lyttleton Hubert, dated October 20, 1841, have established a *prima facie* case entitling them to a verdict.

2. That no evidence has been given by the defendant Murphy to impair or destroy the title of both of the said plaintiffs under the deed and documents mentioned in the foregoing proposition.

3. If the jury believe from the evidence that the deed from Samuel Murray to Delia Chase, of January 13, 1819, was made by him to defraud, delay, or hinder his creditors, this circumstance, though it rendered the deed void as respects any creditor intended to be defrauded, delayed, or hindered, does not affect the validity of such deed as between the parties to it, but it is good as a voluntary deed against Murray and those claiming under and through him.

4. That the premises being subject to the payment of a ground-rent, to which Lyttleton Hubert would be liable, there was a valuable consideration in the conveyance to him from Curtis Butler and wife.

5. That the evidence to set aside a solemn instrument between parties, and convert it into a transaction of a different kind, must be what occurred at the execution of the instrument, and should be clear, precise, and indubitable.

6. That the evidence of the different witnesses for defendant, as to the meaning and intention of Samuel Murray, by the conveyance to his sister Delia Chase, is of so loose, uncertain, and contradictory character that the jury should attach no weight to it.

7. That any acts or declaration of Delia Chase after her mar-

[Murphy v. Hubert.]

riage with Curtis Butler, done or made by her without his knowledge and consent, do not affect the title of Curtis to the premises, nor that of his partner, Lyttleton Hubert.

And the counsel for the *defendant* requested his honor to charge the jury on the following points:

1. If this was an agreement by parol, that the plaintiff, Delia Chase, should hold the estate as a trustee for the children after Murray's death, it is a valid and effectual trust, and the defendants must have a verdict claiming under the children.

2. Such a trust is consistent with the deed, and may be proved by parol evidence.

3. If Delia Chase gave her bond as a consideration for the conveyance, and then agreed to or actually did destroy that bond before "*the squire*," this revested the equitable title in S. Murray, and made *her* a mere trustee for *him* and *his* heirs.

4. If the conveyance was made in consideration of a bond of $800—with an agreement that Delia might either pay the bond or give back the estate—and the parties afterwards destroyed the bond—she determined her election, and the equitable estate became the estate of S. Murray, as if no deed had been made.

5. If this conveyance was made to defraud and defeat creditors, and is held in consequence thereof to be binding upon the parties thereto, the conveyance, being in trust for the children, vests the equitable estate absolutely in those children, which estate could not be affected by any act of S. Murray during his life.

6. A settlement for the use of his children absolutely, made by a man indebted at the time, is a legal settlement binding upon all parties, *unless creditors* interfere.

SHARSWOOD, J., charged the jury as follows:—The prima facie title is in the plaintiff. The defendant Murphy shows title at least in one moiety, derived from Samuel Murray: that is enough to protect the possession of the whole.

The title was in Samuel Murray. The plaintiff claims through a deed from him to Delia Chase, dated 18th January 1819, recorded 14th March 1820. The consideration on its face is $800, and it is subject to a ground-rent.

This transaction is the nucleus of this lawsuit. The defendant claims under Samuel Murray, and he says that this deed was without valuable consideration, and upon a trust understood and declared at the time, that Delia Chase should hold the property for the use of Samuel Murray for his life, and after his death for his children, or some other such trust. Evidence has been given on this subject:—

1. The plaintiffs say that the deed was made for a valuable consideration, that there was a bond given for $800, followed by possession and exercise of ownership—that bond is not produced. Undoubtedly, if there was such a bond, unless it has been cancelled

by agreement of Murray and Delia Chase while *sui juris*, it is sufficient, even though there was an agreement that Delia Chase was to have the option either to pay the bond or restore the estate.

2. But plaintiffs say, that admitting the deed to have been voluntary, it was intended as a fraud on creditors.

Now, if the fact was so, I instruct you that it is not competent for any persons claiming under Samuel Murray to show a parol trust, either for himself or his children, said children being mere volunteers. Courts of justice do not sit to extricate a rogue from his toils. To enable the party to show a parol trust, in the face of an absolute deed, the purpose must have been an honest one. Else, by such fraudulent device, a dishonest man would be sure never to lose, and he has the chance of gaining. He may accomplish his fraudulent design, and then he is sure to get back his property, or, what is the same thing, keep it for his family: this would be affording encouragement to such frauds. On the contrary, it is the policy of common sense and common law, to environ a person with all possible perils, and to make it appear that honesty is always the best policy. Whether it was Murray's design to delay, hinder, or defraud creditors, is for you: if it was, then the defendant cannot set up a trust by parol evidence.

If, however, there was a declaration of trust by writing, which has been lost or mislaid, it would be different.

3. If there was no fraud, then there was an express trust. If yea, was it to be for Murray during his lifetime and then for his children; for his children after his death, or for his children after the death of Delia?

If Delia Chase was to have it for life, and after her death it was to go to his (Murray's) children, the plaintiffs are still entitled to recover the possession. If otherwise, and the trust was for Murray or for his children after his death, then your verdict should be for the defendant.

His honor answered the points of plaintiffs and defendant as follows:—The 1st point of the plaintiff affirmed. 2d, declines so to charge. 3d, affirmed. 4th and 5th, affirmed, but a trust may be shown by declarations and admissions subsequently made. The 6th point of the plaintiff, the court declines so to charge. 7th, affirmed, except so far as respects acts in regard to the property as his (Chase's) agent, and declarations accompanying such acts as part of the *res gestæ*.

The 1st point of defendant affirmed, if the purpose was honest. The 2d point of the defendant affirmed. 3d and 4th, affirmed, if Delia Chase was unmarried at the time. 5th, the court declined so to charge. 6th, affirmed.

The defendant's counsel excepted to the answers of the learned judge to the plaintiff's 1st, 3d, 4th, 5th, and 7th points; and to the defendant's 1st, 3d, 4th, 5th, and 6th points; and also excepted,

[Murphy v. Hubert.]

1. To that part of the charge which instructed the jury, that if the deed was in consideration of the bond, according to Blake's testimony, and if the bond was cancelled by Delia while she was a married woman, without her husband's authority, the plaintiff could recover, even though there was a parol agreement that Delia Chase was to have the option either to pay the bond or restore the estate.

2. The only evidence referred to of Delia having exercised her option or election is the evidence of cancellation of the bond, and that that is insufficient, if she was a married woman, and her husband did not authorize or consent to it.

3. The deed to Delia Chase being absolute on its face, that if it was made voluntarily by S. Murray, to hinder, delay, or defraud creditors, no parol trust for Murray or his children can be set up.

4. If the trust was for Delia during her life, and after her death for Murray's children, plaintiffs are entitled to recover possession.

5. If the trust was that Delia was at her death to pay $800, or will the estate to Murray's children, the plaintiffs were entitled to recover.

Verdict was rendered for the plaintiffs.

The case was argued by *Hirst*, for Murphy, plaintiff in error.
Hare, for defendants in error.
Todd, in reply.

The opinion of the court was delivered by

ROGERS, J.—This was an action of ejectment brought by Hubert and Butler and his wife, against Murphy, to recover possession of a lot with the houses thereon erected. The plaintiffs claim under a deed from Samuel Murphy (conceded to be the owner of the property) to Delia Chase, and a deed from Butler and wife, late Delia Chase, to Lyttleton Hubert, for one moiety thereof—consideration $1. On the written title, as exhibited in evidence, at law, it is beyond doubt plaintiffs are entitled to recover. A regular title to the premises is deduced to them. The defendant, however, insists that the deed of Samuel Murray, under whom plaintiffs claim, was without valuable consideration, and upon a trust understood as declared at the time, that Delia Chase should hold the property for the use of Samuel Murray for his life, and after his death for his children, &c. On this point evidence was given, the plaintiff, however, contending that the deed was made for a valuable consideration, that a bond was given as part of the purchase-money for $800. Whether the deed was given for a valuable consideration, or without consideration, or whether the evidence sustained the allegation of a parol trust, becomes a matter of minor importance, as, in a subsequent part of the charge, the court in substance instructed the jury that even admitting the deed to be voluntary

[Murphy v. Hubert.]

and without consideration, and that a parol trust was declared at the time the deed was executed, yet if it was intended as a fraud on creditors, the defendant is left without defence. Whether the instruction of the court in this particular be correct, is the only point in the case worthy of consideration.

After the verdict, we must take it as established that the deed was intended as a fraud on creditors, and also that there was a valid parol trust. Whether the evidence shows a trust does not enter into the consideration of this case. For the purposes of this point, that must be conceded, the charge proceeding on the concession that the trust is satisfactorily proved.

If there be a point settled on reason and authority, it is that a deed intended to defraud creditors, although void as against creditors, yet is valid as against the grantor, and those for whose benefit it is designed, whether it be the grantor himself, his child or children, or a stranger. The grantee holds the property as against the fraudulent grantor and his beneficiaries, the latter being considered in the light of volunteers, without consideration, and consequently placed in no better situation than the grantor, discharged from all secret trusts whether in writing or by parol. The distinction taken by the judge, I agree, is not sound, as, whether the declaration of trust be by parol or in writing, the rule is the same. That a trust cannot be enforced when it is designed to effect a fraud on creditors is settled by authority. The cases without exception decide that such a trust is void in itself, and therefore incapable of being made the foundation of a right in others: Carroll v. Boston Marine Insurance Co., 8 *Mass. Rep.* 517; The Dodman M. Co. v. The Worcester Fire Insurance Co., 11 *Met.* 429; Ellington v. Currie, 5 *Ired. Eq.* 21; Church's Lessee v. Church, 4 *Yeates* 280; Worrall's Accounts, 5 *W. & Ser.* 111, 113.

The case was put by the judge on the ground of fraud, nor is it designed to interfere with a class of cases where *bona fide* settlements are made on children, intended for their benefit, and without dishonest purpose as it regards creditors. They are supported on different principles, which it is not designed to disturb. They have no application whatever to this case.

The defendant, however, insists that it is the plaintiff who claims, through the medium of a fraud; that he invokes the aid of the court to turn the defendant out of possession of the premises. But this is a mistaken view of the situation of the parties. It would not hold a moment had we a court of chancery. But although we have no separate court for the administration of equity, yet we grant relief, not, it is true, in the same form, but on the same principles as courts of equity. Equity in this State is the same as in England, a principle acknowledged in repeated decisions. In the case in hand, the defence is not a legal, but an equitable defence, the defendant alleging that although the deed purports to be

[Murphy v. Hubert.]

an absolute deed in fee simple, yet it was intended in trust for the grantor and others. It is not the plaintiff that asks the aid of the court, but the defendant. The plaintiff's title is good. At law, the defendant has no defence whatever. Were the case in equity on bills for an injunction, by which mode only would the defendant be entitled to retain the possession, the chancellor would refuse relief when it appeared that defendant who asked the aid of the court had been guilty of a fraud in attempting to screen his property from the just claims of creditors. The chancellor would refuse to interfere. He would leave the party to his remedy at law, where the plaintiff would be entitled to recover on the well-settled principle that although the deed was void as to creditors, yet the title *is valid as between the parties.*

The defendant thinks that being in possession differs this from the cases ruled; but this is not so, as is shown in the cases cited, and on principle. If it were, it would nullify the rule. All that would be necessary would be for the fraudulent grantor either to retain the possession himself, or to give the possession to his children or other beneficiaries named in the parol or written trust.

The rule is founded in policy. The reason is extracted from one of the cases cited, which is correctly given by the judge. Courts of justice do not sit to extricate a rogue from his toils. To enable a party to show a secret trust in the face of an absolute deed, the purpose must have been an honest one, else, by secret fraudulent device, a dishonest man would be sure never to lose, and he has the chance of gaining. He may accomplish his fraudulent design, and then he is sure to get back his property, or what is the same thing, keep it for his family. This would be affording encouragement to such frauds. On the contrary, it is the policy of common sense and common law to environ a person with all possible perils, and to make it appear that honesty is the best policy. The court left the question of fraud to the jury, taking a distinction between a declaration of trust in writing or by parol, which, although erroneous, is an error in favor of the defendant, of which he cannot complain. That the deed from Samuel Murray to Delia Chase was intended to delay, hinder, and defraud creditors, was abundantly proved. Indeed it does not appear to be denied by the defendant. That the deed was executed under a mistaken apprehension that he would be made liable as bail, is nothing. That he was unwise may be admitted, but that is no reason for overruling the plain principles of law. Hard cases, appealing to the sympathy of a judge, make bad precedents.

The defendant also excepts to the answer to the seventh of plaintiff's points, and to the *third* of defendant's. As a general proposition the answer to the seventh point is correct, for undoubtedly the acts and declarations of a wife, without the knowledge and consent of the husband, do not affect his title. Had the defend-

[Murphy v. Hubert.]

ant desired a more particular direction, he might have had it by a prayer for that purpose, distinguishing between her declarations as to the trust and declarations as to the extent of the trust, the parol trust being established. To reverse now on that ground (supposing there is any thing in the distinction) would be to reverse for an error which the court did not commit, to which their attention was not directed.

That the answer to the third point is correct, cannot be matter of doubt, as an absolute deed cannot be annulled or discharged, nor the title impaired by parol. A deed in this State is equivalent to feoffment with livery and seisin, and cannot therefore be affected except by writing. That the parties intended to cancel the agreement, but failed to do so according to the forms prescribed by law, may be matter of regret, but it is a mistake which we cannot correct.

After a full examination of the case, we are of opinion, that as no error prejudicial to the defendant has been committed, the judgment must be affirmed.

Judgment affirmed.

Kelly's Appeal.

1. Horses purchased by A, B, and C, in partnership, were levied on under an execution against A for his private debt, and on an execution against B and C for the debt of B on a judgment confessed by B against himself and C; *after* the sale the judgment was on motion of C set aside as to him. *Held*, that the vacating of the judgment did not affect the validity of the previous sale under executions against all the partners, but that the proceeds of it represent the property, and the execution creditors occupy the place of the purchaser; that C can claim out of the proceeds only to the extent of the interest he had in the property; and if on the settlement of the account, under the direction of the court, in the course of the distribution of the proceeds of the sale, he appears to have been entitled to *no* interest *in the horses*, he is not entitled to any share of the proceeds of their sale.

2. The distribution of the proceeds of a sheriff's sale is, by the 86th section of the act of 16th June, 1836, to be made according *to law and equity;* and in the course of the distribution of the proceeds of the sale of property purchased in partnership, and sold on executions against the partners as individuals, for their separate debts, the court may direct an account to ascertain the respective rights of the partners to the proceeds in dispute.

In the matter of the appeal of Neil Kelly from the decree of the District Court for the city and county of *Philadelphia*, confirming the auditor's report in the cases of Lanigan v. McAfee, D. C., fi. fa., March term 1850, 192, and Patrick Kelly v. P. Earle and Neil Kelly, D. C., March term 1850, 278.

In 1848 and 1849, Neil Kelly and Peter Earle were engaged in several joint adventures to Ohio, &c., for the purchase and sale of cattle. About the summer or fall of 1849, Michael McAfee be-

[Kelly's Appeal.]

came connected with them in the business. In the spring of 1850, Kelly, Earle, and McAfee returned from Ohio to Philadelphia, with 20 horses, of which Kelly had bought 14, McAfee 4, and Earle 2. Earle had 5 of Kelly's 14 horses also transferred to him, so that on arriving in Philadelphia, 9 horses were under the exclusive control of Kelly, 7 under Earle, and 4 under McAfee, each to sell and receive the money for his lot. Earle and McAfee each sold his lot of horses at Philadelphia, and received the proceeds. Kelly's 9 horses were levied on soon after their arrival in Philadelphia, by virtue of a fi. fa. issued and put into the sheriff's hands February 25, 1850, in the case of Ann Lanigan v. Michael McAfee, D. C., March term 1849, No. 104. Judgment $350.

Fi. fa. returnable first Monday in March 1850. A levy was made under it, upon all the interest of McAfee in the 9 horses in Kelly's possession.

On March 9, 1850, *after the return day of the fi. fa. in Lanigan v. McAfee, Peter Earle*, without the knowledge or consent of Neil Kelly, executed a bond and warrant of attorney to Patrick Kelly for $1107, real debt, naming himself (Earle) and Neil Kelly obligors, and signing thus,

PETER EARLE and NEIL KELLY,   [L. S.]
by PETER EARLE,   [L. S.]

Judgment was entered on this bond and warrant against both Earle and Neil Kelly, viz. D. C., March term 1850, No. 35, and a fi. fa. issued against both, and put into the hands of the sheriff.

After the sale, delivery to the purchaser, payment of the money into court, and appointment of the auditor to distribute it, viz. in April 1850, a rule on plaintiff was granted to Neil Kelly to show cause why the judgment should not be set aside, which was afterwards, April 20, made absolute *as to Neil Kelly*.

The sheriff made returns to each fi. fa. in the cases of Lanigan v. McAfee, and Patrick Kelly v. Earle and Neil Kelly.

The return to Lanigan v. McAfee recites, that in obedience to that writ and to a fi. fa. in Patrick Kelly v. Earle and Neil Kelly, (March term 1850, 278,) I seized and took in execution, and sold 8 horses and a mare, as the property of the defendant within named, (viz. McAfee,) and the said Earle and Kelly, the proceeds whereof, less costs, amounting to the net sum of $440.65, I pay into court under both executions, &c.

The return to the fi. fa. in Patrick Kelly v. Earle and Neil Kelly, is similar to the return in Lanigan v. McAfee, excepting that it refers to the fi. fa. in the latter case, as this fi. fa. had been referred to in the former.

An auditor was appointed to distribute the fund, who reported

[Kelly's Appeal.]

that the $401.01, which after costs and charges remained for distribution, should be divided between Lanigan and Patrick Kelly; Lanigan to receive $282.89, and Patrick Kelly $118.12, and that Neil Kelly was not entitled to any of the fund.

The 86th section of the act of 16th June 1836 provides as follows:—In all cases of sale upon execution, as aforesaid, when there shall be disputes concerning the distribution of the money arising therefrom, the court from which the execution shall have issued shall have power, after reasonable notice given, either personally or by advertisement, to hear and determine the same, according to law and equity.

To this report the following exceptions were filed on the part of Neil Kelly:

1. The auditor erred in reporting that Neil Kelly could claim nothing from the fund in court.
2. In refusing to award the fund in court to Neil Kelly.
3. In reporting that the fund in court should be divided between McAfee and Earle.
4. In awarding $282.89 out of $401.01 to Ann McAfee, (Lanigan,) on her fi. fa., though against McAfee individually.
5. In awarding $118.12 to Patrick Kelly on his fi. fa., though the judgment on which it issued had been opened, and set aside as to Neil Kelly.
6. Because the distribution reported by the auditor is based on an attempt to trace and follow moneys, supposed once to have belonged to McAfee and Earle respectively, into the purchase by Neil Kelly of the 9 horses, the proceeds of which are now for distribution, although it was shown that Neil Kelly raised money himself which was applied for that purpose.
7. Because the auditor undertook to settle accounts between Kelly, Earle, and McAfee, in transactions prior to and unconnected with the purchase of the 9 horses by Neil Kelly, and the auditor based his distribution of the fund in court on said settlement.
8. In making the settlement in last (7th) exception mentioned, the auditor erred, 1st. In basing it on a statement of accounts furnished on the part of Earle alone, and Earle and McAfee, without any proof of its correctness or Neil Kelly's assent thereto. 2d. In not inquiring nor adverting at all to the state of accounts between Neil Kelly and Peter Earle in their joint transactions apart from McAfee, without which, the respective proportions of interests of Kelly and Earle in any partnership could not be correctly determined.

The report of the auditor was confirmed.

Exceptions were filed, alleging that the court erred,
1. In confirming the auditor's report.

[Kelly's Appeal.]

2. In confirming said report, whereby the fund in court was awarded to Ann Lanigan and Peter Earle.

3. In refusing to award the fund to Neil Kelly, or to direct the auditor to do so.

The case was argued by *S. Hood*, for Neil Kelly, the appellant. *A. H. Smith* and *W. L. Hirst*, for appellees.

The opinion of the court was delivered by

BELL, J.—The facts ascertained by the auditor show very clearly the existence of a partnership between McAfee, Kelly, and Earle, in prosecuting the two enterprises which gave birth to the present litigation. The horses, when levied in Kelly's hands and at the moment of sale, were, consequently, partnership property. What then was the effect of the judicial sale, as between the members of the firm and the separate creditors of some of them?

Had the chattels been sold by virtue of an execution or executions, at the same time in the hands of the sheriff, against McAfee and Earle alone, the purchaser would have stood in their shoes in respect of the things sold, and therefore entitled to call for a settlement of the partnership accounts; the extent of his interest being determinable by the result of that account. Being subrogated by operation of law to the place of the insolvent partners, he would have represented their rights. From this it would follow that, according to the account reported by the auditor, (the correctness of which has not been assailed here,) he would have taken the value of the horses remaining after payment of the executions. But, in fact, the property was sold under executions against all the parties; for it is scarcely necessary to say, that until the judgment rendered against Kelly was set aside, the process founded upon it was valid and effective to authorize the steps taken by the officer. Under the process, then, the interest of all the defendants in the goods sold passed to the purchaser, and the right thus acquired was in no degree affected by the subsequent action of the District Court. The money paid into court must therefore be taken as representing the subject of the sale, and the execution creditors occupy what would have been the place of the purchaser under the hypothesis before stated. Now, as the destruction of the judgment entered against Kelly can work no other result than to place him in the position, in respect to the avails of the sale, he would have occupied in respect to the horses themselves, had there been no execution against him in the hands of the sheriff, it follows that, as against the separate creditors of his fellows, he can claim no greater interest in the money in court than, on a settlement of accounts, he is found entitled to claim at the hands of his partners. The application of the principle brought in view to the case before us works no injustice, for it is shown the appellant had, in truth,

[Kelly's Appeal.]

no valuable interest in the horses when sold. A proper adjustment of the affairs of the partnership proves their whole worth resided in McAfee and Earle, in different proportions, and it is not to be doubted their individual creditors are entitled to the fund produced by the sale of them, in the same proportions. As the distribution was made below in accordance with the rights thus ascertained, there is no room for complaint by any of the parties.

The objection that the District Court, or its auditor, had no power to state an account between the partners, is met by the answer that by the 86th section of the act of 16th June 1836, the distribution of proceeds of sheriff's sales is to be determined according *to law and equity;* and it cannot be questioned that in a case like the present, a chancellor from necessity would direct an account to be taken.

Decree affirmed.

In re Short's Estate.

The third section of the act of 11th March 1850, relating to collateral inheritance taxes, which provides that the words "*being within this commonwealth,*" in the first section of the act of 7th April 1826, relating to collateral inheritances, "shall be so construed as to relate to all persons who have been at the time of their decease, or now may be, domiciled within this commonwealth, as well as to estates," is applicable to the estate of a person domiciled in Pennsylvania, who died *before the passage of the act,* viz. in December 1849, and is, as to such a case, constitutional, at least as to assets remaining in this State in the hands of the executors; and therefore stocks in corporations in other States, and bonds of such corporations, and cash in a bank in another State, belonging to such a decedent, are liable to the collateral inheritance tax for the use of this commonwealth, and the executors are chargeable with the amount of the said tax, out of the assets in their hands.

APPEAL from the decree of the Register's Court for the city and county of *Philadelphia.*

William Short, the deceased, was, at the time of his death, on 5th December 1849, domiciled in Philadelphia, where he died. He owned no real estate in Pennsylvania, but he owned a large personal estate. His personal estate *in Pennsylvania*, exceeding $70,000, was more than sufficient to pay the specific legacies in his will; but he owned a large amount invested in stock and corporations in other States, some bonds of the State of Kentucky, &c., in all exceeding half a million of dollars, and above $1000 of cash in a bank in New York. The register of wills for the city and county of Philadelphia decided that the collateral inheritance tax was to be charged and paid on the whole property left by the testator, as well on that which was not within the State of Pennsylvania, at the time of his death, as on that which was therein: amounting at its appraised value to $601,586.49; and making the

[In re Short's Estate.]

said tax, after allowance for commissions, expenses, and expected demands, $26,995.

From this decree an appeal was taken to the Register's Court for the city and county of Philadelphia, where it was affirmed. An appeal was entered by Samuel H. Carpenter, one of the executors of the will of deceased, to the Supreme Court.

The deceased was unmarried. On 11th September 1847 he made his will at Philadelphia. In this he bequeathed certain legacies, amounting in the aggregate to $25,000, to individuals, all of whom were citizens and residents of the State of Pennsylvania. He then devised the entire residue of the property which he might own at the time of his death to his two nephews, John Cleves Short, who was then a citizen and had been for many years a resident of the State of Ohio, and Charles Wilkins Short, who was then a citizen and had been for many years a resident of Kentucky; the income thereof to be received and enjoyed by them jointly, during their joint lives. On the death of either of them, the whole of the property was to be taken and enjoyed by the survivor, his heirs, executors, administrators, and assigns. He appointed these nephews, and Samuel H. Carpenter of Philadelphia, the executors of his will. Carpenter alone received letters testamentary.

It is provided in the first section of the act of 7th April 1826, entitled an "Act relating to collateral inheritances," "that from and after the first day of May next, all estates, real, personal, and mixed, of every kind whatsoever, passing from any person who may die seized or possessed of such estate, *being within this commonwealth*, either by will or under the intestate laws thereof, or any part of such estate or estates, or interest therein, transferred by deed, grant, bargain, or sale, made or intended to take effect in possession or enjoyment after the death of the grantor or bargainor, to any person or persons, or to bodies politic or corporate, in trust or otherwise, other than to or for the use of *father, mother, husband, wife, children, and lineal descendants born in lawful wedlock*, shall be and they are hereby made subject to a tax or duty of two dollars and fifty cents on every hundred dollars of the clear value of such estate or estates, and at and after the same rate for any less amount, to be paid to the use of the commonwealth," &c.

No estate which may be valued at less than $250 shall be subject to the duty or tax.

It was decided in 1847, in the case of the Commonwealth *v.* Smith, reported in 5 *Barr* 142, that it was not the *person*, but the *estate within this commonwealth*, on which the tax aforesaid was to be levied.

It was however enacted by the third section of an act passed on the 11th March 1850, (Acts of 1850, p. 170,) that "the words

[In re Short's Estate.]

'*being within this Commonwealth*,' in the first section of an act passed on the 7th of April 1826, entitled 'An act relative to collateral inheritances,' shall be so construed as to relate to all *persons* who have been, *at the time of their decease*, or now may be, domiciled within this commonwealth, as well as to estates; and this is declared to be the true intent and meaning of said act."

The case was argued, on the part of the appellant, by *H. D. Gilpin*.—It was contended that the decree of the register's court, now appealed from, ought to be reversed, because,

1. The law of Pennsylvania, as it existed at the time of the testator's death, when the estate liable to taxation passed from him to his collateral relatives, expressly limited the tax to property then within this commonwealth.

2. The act of Assembly passed on the 11th March 1850, and since the death of the testator, which has varied this law, does not, by its terms, apply to the case of a person who had died *before its enactment*.

3. If the language of that act were capable of such a construction, it will not be sanctioned by judicial tribunals, because it would make the law retrospective and destructive of vested interests.

4. If a construction of the language of that act could apply it retrospectively to the case of a *person* who had died before its enactment, still it has relation only to such of his *property* as was actually within this commonwealth when he died.

Reference was made to the case of Alexander's Estate, 4 *Pa. Law Journ.* 448; Commonwealth *v.* Smith, 5 *Barr* 142; Commonwealth *v.* Duffield, 2 *Am. Law Jour.* 86.

In relation to the second point or exception, that the act of March 1850 did not apply in its terms to a person who died, and whose estate had become vested in collateral relatives *before* its enactment; that it had not necessarily such a meaning; that its language appeared to be *prospective*—to relate to cases occurring *after its enactment;* that a construction which would give an operation to an act which would interfere with rights already accrued should not be adopted, unless its language was incapable of a different construction: 4 *Ser. & R.* 401; 7 *Johns.* 501; 5 *W. & Ser.* 199; 2 *Barr* 25.

But such a construction would violate those clauses of the constitution of Pennsylvania, which declare that "no one shall be deprived of his property unless by the judgment of his peers or the law of the land," and that "no law impairing contracts shall be made," and that clause of the constitution of the United States which declares that "no State shall pass any law impairing the obligation of contracts." That the transfer of property by will is subject to the laws and governed by the principles which are ap-

[In re Short's Estate.]

plicable to transfers effected by the acts of the parties. The judicial principles which would control and regulate this property, in case Mr. Short had sold it at the date of his will, must control it, though he devised it: 2 *Black. Com.* 294, 378; 4 *Ser. & R.* 364; 3 *Rawle* 132; 2 *Whar.* 396; 3 *id.* 15; 5 *W. & Ser.* 173; 8 *id.* 50; 5 *Barr* 149; 1 *Jones* 494; 2 *Cranch* 277; 7 *id.* 166; 4 *Whar.* 122; 12 *id.* 213; 1 *Howard* 311.

In this case, if the construction be that the property out of the State is taxable, it will require the appropriation of only about the one-half or two-thirds of the property left within the State and in the hands of the executor to discharge it on property out of the State, and paying to the legatees out of the State; but cases may occur where all the assets in Pennsylvania may be required to pay the tax on property abroad passing to legatees who are abroad.

Scott and *Hood*, contra.

The opinion of the court was delivered by
GIBSON, C. J.—That Mr. Short's property out of the State subjected him to personal liability for taxes assessed on it here in his lifetime, is not to be doubted. The general rule is that the *situs* of personal property follows the domicile of the owner of it, insomuch that even a creditor cannot reach it in a foreign country except by attachment or some other process provided by the local law; certainly not by a personal action without an appearance or something equivalent to it. But personal property may, for particular purposes, have an actual *situs* distinct from its legal one. At the death of the owner, however, he ceases to have a domicile, and all the incidents of it are at an end, except the title to the succession. For all besides, the title to the assets abroad devolves on a local administrator, whose business it becomes to collect them, sell them, and having satisfied the demand against them by creditors or the State, to remit the surplus of the proceeds to the executor or administrator at the place of the domicile, for distribution among the unpaid creditors and the next of kin. All this was shown on principle and authority, in Mothland *v.* Wireman, 3 *Pa. Rep.* 185, and in the case of Miller's Estate, 3 *Rawle* 312. The legislature acted on the principle of those cases in the act of 1826, by subjecting nothing to the collateral inheritance tax but property actually within the bounds of the States described as "passing from any person who may die seized or possessed of such estate, *being within this commonwealth.*" The position taken for the next of kin, in Smith *v.* The Commonwealth, was that the concluding words related to the person of the owner, and not to the property. But they are naturally referable to the subject of which the legislature was speaking, which was the thing to be taxed, and not to the person of the owner of it, which was beyond the legislative power. Any other interpreta-

[In re Short's Estate.]

tion would have tied up the hands of the State as to property within its grasp. Had we required both person and property to be here at the death, the right of the State would have been still further restricted; yet if the words are applicable to the person, they are at least as much applicable to the property. Indeed it is impossible to conceive how a tax could be assessed on the person of a dead man; and, as was held in Smith v. The Commonwealth, it must consequently be assessed on the property here, without regard to the domicile. Did the question therefore stand on the act of 1826 exclusively, we would hold the property in question to be free from the tax. But the legislature thought proper to enlarge its operation by assigning to it a more expanded meaning. By the supplemental act of 1850, it was declared that "the words 'being within this commonwealth,' shall be so construed as to relate to all persons who *have been* at the time of their decease, or *now* may be domiciled within this commonwealth, as well as to estates: and this is declared to be the true intent and meaning of said act." More pointed words to make the act retrospective, as well as prospective, could not have been chosen; and it will scarce be said the legislature had not power to make it so, at least as to assets remaining in the hands of the executor or administrator. No clause of the constitution forbids it to extend a tax already laid, or to tax assets not taxed before; and in establishing its peculiar interpretation, it has only done indirectly what it was competent to do directly. The argument has been that we ought not to give the act a retroactive effect, unless we are forced to do so by the stringency of its words. The principle is a sound one where retroaction would work injustice, as it would have done in Bedford v. Shilling. (4 *Ser. & R.* 401.) But certainly no injustice is done by increasing a tax to meet an increase of the public burden. Waving this consideration, the words of the act are too peremptory to be disregarded, or to leave room for construction.

Decree of the Register's Court affirmed.

Camden and Amboy Railroad Co. *versus* Baldauf.

1. Though in Pennsylvania a common carrier may *limit* his responsibility by a general notice, yet the terms of the notice must be clear and explicit, and the person with whom the carrier deals must be fully informed of the terms and effect of the notice: the limitation is to be confined to cases of special contract, express or implied; and where the notice is in the English language and the passenger a German, who did not understand the English language, it is incumbent on the carrier to prove the knowledge by the passenger of the limitation in the notice.

2. If tickets, without more, are evidence of a special contract, yet they must be printed in a language which the passenger understands, or their terms must be explained to him.

[Camden and Amboy Railroad Co. v. Baldauf.]

3. Where a trunk was lost, and no proof given as to when or how it was lost, the legal inference is that it was lost or mislaid in consequence of the negligence or fraud of the carrier or his agent.

4. Where a trunk of a passenger contains specie, it is not incumbent on him to inform the carrier of its contents, unless inquired of, notwithstanding the advertisement of the carrier that passengers are "prohibited from taking any thing as baggage but their wearing-apparel, which will be at the risk of the owner;" and where the extra weight of the passenger's baggage, including the trunk, was paid for, and the agents of the carrier took charge of it,—*Held*, that it was immaterial whether the trunk was to be viewed as baggage or freight, and that the carrier was responsible for its loss through the negligence or fraud of its agents.

5. Carriers cannot, even by a special agreement with the owner, discharge themselves from the ordinary care incumbent on a bailee for hire. Per ROGERS, J.

ERROR to the District Court, *Philadelphia*.

This was an action brought by Henry Baldauf against the Camden and Amboy Railroad and Transportation Company, as carriers of passengers and their baggage from New York to Philadelphia. The declaration contained three counts, charging the defendants below, 1. As carriers of passengers and their baggage. 2. As carriers of passengers and their luggage. 3. As bailees. The general issue was pleaded. The material facts appear in the special verdict.

February 16, 1849, jury called, and found a special verdict as follows:

That the defendants are carriers of passengers and their baggage, and not carriers of merchandise, from New York to Philadelphia. That the defendants had published in the public daily newspapers of New York and Philadelphia, from May to September 1846, an advertisement as follows, (prout copy of the same annexed, marked A.,) and delivered to the plaintiff, who is a German, and did not then understand the English language, as well as the other passengers, on the 22d August, 1846, a card or ticket as follows, (prout copy of the same annexed, marked B.) The plaintiff took passage in defendants' line upon the said 22d August 1846, and put on board the steamboat Independence, belonging to defendants, and forming part of defendants' means of conveyance, among other baggage, a trunk containing twenty-one hundred and one silver coins, commonly called French five-franc pieces, and also certain articles of wearing-apparel. The said trunk was delivered to the conductor or other agent of defendants on board of said boat. The extra weight of plaintiff's baggage, including the said trunk, was paid for, and the said agents did take charge thereof. The plaintiff did not notify the defendants or their agent that the said trunk contained coins or money, and no special agreement was made by them to accept or carry the same. The said trunk was lost, and not delivered to the plaintiff upon his arrival at Philadelphia, or at any time thereafter.

If the court shall be of opinion that the defendants are responsible for the injury arising from the loss of the money or silver coins aforesaid, then the jury find for the plaintiff, and assess the damage at twenty-two hundred and forty-five dollars ninety-five cents, ($2245.95.) If the court shall be of opinion that the defendants are not liable for the injury arising from the loss of the money or silver coins aforesaid, then the jury find for the plaintiff, and assess the damages at ten dollars. The $10 was for the wearing-apparel.

Advertisement (A).—The Camden and Amboy Railroad Line for Philadelphia and intermediate places, will leave Pier No. 2, North River, foot of Battery Place by steamboat, to South Amboy, every day, (Sundays excepted,) &c.

Fifty pounds of *baggage* will be allowed to each passenger in this line, and *passengers are expressly prohibited from taking any thing as baggage but their wearing-apparel*, which will be at the risk of the owner. I. BLISS, Agent.

Ticket (B).—Camden and Amboy Railroad Line. Received payment in full for passage to Philadelphia, from forward-deck passenger, No. — All *baggage* at the risk of the owner thereof. The proprietors binding themselves to no charge or care of the *same* whatever, either express or implied.

IRA BLISS, Agent.

Keep this receipt until called for.

February 20th, 1849, motion for rule for new trial, and to show cause why judgment shall not be entered for defendant on the special verdict, on reasons filed and points reserved.

June 30th, 1849, judgment for plaintiff for $2245.95.

The defendants then sued out their writ of error.

It was assigned for error:

The court erred in entering judgment for Henry Baldauf, the plaintiff below and the defendant in error, for the sum of two thousand two hundred and forty-five dollars and ninety-five cents.

The case was argued by *Read* and *Mallory*, for the Company.—Upon the special verdict in this case, two questions arise:

The first is, as to the special agreement imbodied in the passenger-ticket or receipt, by which "all baggage" is "at the risk of the owner thereof. The proprietors binding themselves to no charge or care of the same whatever, either express or implied."

The courts of this State have uniformly held that such an agreement is valid and discharged the carrier from all liability whatsoever, except in case of gross negligence or fraud.

This principle is distinctly recognised in Beekman *v.* Shouse, 5 *Rawle* 189, (1835,) in Bingham *v.* Rogers, 6 *W. & Ser.* 500, (1843,) and in Laing *v.* Colder, 8 *Barr* 484, (1848,) where it is said, "Since then, it has been expressly decided in Bingham *v.* Rogers, 6 *W. &*

[Camden and Amboy Railroad Co. *v.* Baldauf.]

Ser. 495, that a common carrier may limit his liability by notice to passengers, such as was given in this case, that the baggage is at their own risk. This must now be taken as the law of this State, and the court below asserted nothing beyond it."

The second question is whether, under the known course of the business of this company, in carrying passengers and their baggage, these defendants are liable for the loss of the very large amount of French silver coins placed in the trunk of the plaintiff without any information or notice whatever to the defendants or their agents, and contrary to their express prohibition.

The line was only a passenger line, and not in any manner a freight line, and the carrying of baggage was simply a consequence of the carrying of passengers. The question therefore is, what is meant by the term baggage of passengers; and this has been clearly and definitely settled in New York, not to include merchandise at all, nor bank-bills, nor gold or silver coins or money, particularly if the sums are large. Silver, which is carried in boxes of $1000 each, or in kegs of larger dimensions, is particularly a subject of freight, and liable not only to the ordinary charges for valuable articles, but is also often the subject of insurance by the carrier himself, and is very generally carried by the express lines, which are entirely unconnected with the steamboat and railroad companies.

As in Orange County Bank *v.* Brown, 9 *Wendell* 85, (1832,) a large sum of money in bank-bills, in an ordinary travelling-trunk, was not considered as included under the term baggage so as to render the carrier responsible for it. So in Pardee *v.* Drew, 25 *Wendell* 459, (1841,) NELSON, C. J., confirming his decision in 9 *Wendell*, extended the principle of non-liability to valuable merchandise placed in a trunk and carried as baggage; and in Hawkins *v.* Hoffman, 6 *Hill* 586, (1844,) the present chief justice of New York said, p. 589, 590, speaking of baggage, " It neither includes money nor merchandise. (Orange County Bank *v.* Brown, 9 *Wendell* 85; Pardee *v.* Drew, 25 *id.* 459.) It was suggested in the first case, that money to pay travelling expenses might perhaps be included. But that may, I think, be doubted. Men usually carry money to pay travelling expenses about their persons, and not in their trunks or boxes."

" It is undoubtedly difficult to define with accuracy what shall be deemed baggage within the rule of the carrier's liability. I do not intend to say, that the articles must be such as every man deems essential to his comfort; for some men carry nothing or very little with them when they travel while others consult their convenience by carrying many things Nor do I intend to say, that the rule is confined to wearing-apparel, brushes, razors, writing apparatus, and the like, which most persons deem indispensable. If one has books for his instruction or amusement by the way, or

[Camden and Amboy Railroad Co. v. Baldauf.]

carries his gun or fishing-tackle, they would undoubtedly fall within the term baggage, because they are usually carried as such. This is, I think, a good test for determining what things fall within the rule."

The same principle is stated by WILLARD, J., in Blanchard v. Isaacs, 3 *Barbour's S. C.* 389, (July 3, 1848,) "and by baggage, we are to understand such articles of necessity or personal convenience, as are usually carried by passengers for their personal use, and not merchandise or other valuables, although carried in the trunks of passengers, which are not designed for any such use, but for other purposes, such as sale and the like: Orange County Bank v. Brown, 9 *Wend.* 85; Pardee v. Drew, 25 *id.* 459; Hawkins v. Hoffman, 6 *Hill* 586."

The same principle is very clearly explained by Mr. Justice DANIEL, in The New Jersey Steam Navigation Company v. Merchants' Bank, 6 *Howard* 416, 417, (1848.) The learned judge says, "Whilst I am impressed with the strong necessity that exists for guarding against fraud or neglect in those who, by holding themselves forth as fitted to take charge of the lives, the health, or the property of the community, thereby invite the public trust and reliance, I am not prepared to say that there can be no limit or qualification to the responsibility of those who embark in these or similar undertakings—limits which may be implied from the inherent nature of the undertakings themselves, or which may result from express stipulation. It seems to me undeniable, that a carrier may select the particular line or description of business in which he engages, and that so long as he with good faith adheres to that description, he cannot be responsible for any thing beyond or inconsistent with it. The rule which makes him an insurer against every thing but the act of God or the public enemy, makes him an insurer as to performances only which are consistent with his undertaking as carrier. A common carrier of travellers is bound to the preservation of the *accustomed baggage of the traveller*, because of the known custom that travellers carry with them articles for their comfort and accommodation, and the price for which the transportation is undertaken is graduated on that presumption; but the carrier would not therefore be responsible for other articles of extraordinary value secretly transported upon his vehicle, because by this secresy he is defrauded of a compensation commensurate with the value of the subject transported, and with the increased hazards to which it is attempted to commit him without his knowledge or assent. But to render him liable, he must have received the article for transportation, and it must be a subject falling fairly within the scope of his engagement. Within this range he is an insurer, with the exceptions above stated. But a carrier may, in a given case, be exempted from liability for loss without fraud, by express agreement with the person for whom he

[Camden and Amboy Railroad Co. *v.* Baldauf.]

undertakes; for I cannot even imagine a principle creating a disability in a particular class of persons to enter into a contract fraught with no criminal or immoral element—a disability indeed extending injuriously to others, who might find it materially beneficial to make a contract with them."

The same rule prevails in Pennsylvania, McGill *v.* Rowand, 3 *Barr* 451, (1846,) and in a case decided by his honor Judge ROGERS, at Nisi Prius, (March 22, 1847,) of Levinson *v.* The Philadelphia and Trenton Railroad Company. See also Pudor *v.* Boston and Maine Railroad, 10 *Law Reporter* 117.

All baggage accompanying the traveller is governed by the same rules, whether it be the amount not exceeding 50 lbs., which is included in the regular fare, or the excess, for which additional fare is paid.

We submit, therefore, that the defendants are not liable for this very large amount of money carried in his trunk by a forward-deck passenger, without any notice or information whatever of its presence to the defendants or their agents.

G. Remak and *H. M. Phillips*, for Baldauf, the defendant in error. —The plaintiff was a German, ignorant of the English language, who went on board the steamboat Independence at New York, to take passage to Philadelphia. He had with him several trunks and other articles not in trunks, such as bedding, kettles, box, &c. &c.; and the agent of the company on board of the steamboat, after weighing out fifty pounds of baggage, received payment from the passenger for the surplus freight, including a large trunk with silver money in it, which was lost, and for the value of this the verdict was given. The whole testimony showed that it was the invariable custom of the company to allow passengers to take with them what and as much as they pleased, if the surplus, over fifty pounds, was paid for. By the advertisement (A) it will be seen that only "*fifty pounds of baggage will be allowed to each passenger*," and in this case, the trunk lost was not baggage, (*eo nomine*,) but freight, because the true construction of the notice is *prohibition* of excess to a passenger, and not a refusal to carry when paid for beyond the price of a personal passage. Up to fifty pounds, the luggage of a passenger is taken free of charge as baggage, but beyond that weight, it is taken upon payment of the freight.

The ticket (B) it is clear the plaintiff could not read nor understand, yet it is urged as protecting the company from liability for loss.

Upon the facts of the case, the defendant in error contends that the company is liable either as carriers or bailees, and that the receipt of money for the transportation of the trunk made them responsible for its safe and careful delivery. In this country *specie* is the only recognised money, and certainly a traveller may take

[Camden and Amboy Railroad Co. v. Baldauf.]

that with him as included within the necessaries, which, it is admitted, are protected by the law.

The plaintiff in error raises two questions: First, as to the special agreement imbodied in the passenger-ticket, or receipt, by which "all baggage is at the risk of the owner thereof; the proprietors binding themselves to no charge or care of the same whatever, either express or implied."

A passenger-ticket is a thing known to us all as a small piece of pasteboard with something printed on it, generally much defaced; but it is found in the verdict that the plaintiff *did not understand the English language;* and nothing is more settled by the law than that a carrier, to excuse himself from performance of the duty belonging to his calling, must prove notice to the passenger. The testimony in this case, and the finding, show this was pretty much an emigrant line, and to hold the doctrine contended for *contra*, would be to subject to impositions those who are least able to look out for themselves.

An agreement may be made, and when made, is undoubtedly valid, for a party may waive any thing for his own benefit; but the cases cited by the plaintiff in error do not establish the exemption of the carrier, excepting where there is direct evidence *of notice to the passenger*, and the consequent acceptance of the terms: Beekman v. Shouse, 5 *Rawle* 179; Laing v. Calder, 8 *Barr* 484; 9 *Watts* 89, Attwood v. Reliance Co.; 19 *Wend.* 234, Hollister v. Nowlen; *id.* 251, Cole v. Goodwin.

In the case of The N. J. Transportation Company v. The Merchants' Bank, 6 *Howard* 366, Mr. Justice NELSON says, "A question has been made whether it is competent for the carrier to restrict his obligation even by a special agreement. It was very fully considered in the case of Gould v. Hill, 2 *Hill* 623, and the conclusion is arrived at that he could not. See also Hollister v. Nowlen, and Cole v. Goodwin, 19 *Wend.*" He goes on to say of the carrier, "He is in the exercise of a sort of public office, and has public duties to perform, from which he should not be permitted to exonerate himself without the assent of the parties concerned. And this is not to be implied or inferred from a general notice to the public, limiting his obligation, which may or may not be assented to. He is bound to receive and carry all the goods offered for transportation, subject to all the responsibilities incident to his employment, and is liable to an action in case of a refusal. And we agree with the court in the case of Hollister v. Nowlen, that, if any implication is to be indulged from the delivery of the goods under the general notice, it is as strong that the owner intended to insist upon his rights and the duties of the carrier, as it is that he assented to their qualification.

"The burden of proof lies on the carrier, and nothing short of an express stipulation by parol or in writing should be permitted to

[Camden and Amboy Railroad Co. v. Baldauf.]

discharge him from duties which the law has annexed to his employment. The exemption from these duties should not depend upon implication or inference, founded on doubtful and conflicting evidence; but should be specific and certain, leaving no room for controversy between the parties."

Angell, in his Treatise on the Law of Carriers, assumes the law to be as settled in Hollister v. Nowlen, and The N. J. Trans. Co. v. The Merchants' Bank, sec. 237, 238, 239, referring to Gould v. Hill, 2 *Hill* (N. Y.) 623; and Mr. Angell adds, "The reasoning of Chief Justice GIBSON, in Atwood v. Reliance Co., 9 *Watts* 87, was to the same effect, though the question was not decided."

In Fish v. Ross, 2 *Kell.* 349, it was held that notices, receipts, and contracts, in restriction of the liability of a common carrier as known and enforced in 1776, are void, *because they contravene the policy of law.*

To the same effect are Bennett v. Dutton, *N. Hamp.* 187; Bean v. Green, 3 *Fair.* 422; Thomas v. Boston Co., 10 *Met.* 470.

In 2 *Greenleaf's Ev.* sec. 215, it is said, "The right of a common carrier by general notice to *limit, restrict or avoid* the liability devolved on him by the common law, on the most salutary grounds of public policy, has been denied in American courts, after the most elaborate consideration."

That the burden of proof is on the carrier to show that the person with whom he deals is fully informed of the terms and effect of the notice, is established in *Story on Bailments*, sec. 560, 558; *Angell on Carriers*, sec. 247; 2 *Green. Ev.* sec. 216; Brooke v. Pickwick, 4 *Bing. Rep.* 218; Kerr v. Willan, 2 *Starkie* 53; and Hollister v. Nowlen, and Cole v. Goodwin, already cited.

And where notice at the office has been generally held sufficient, it is not so, says Davis v. Willan, 2 *Stark. Rep.* 279, where the party who delivers the goods *cannot read.*

Now while it may be conceded that a carrier can in Pennsylvania restrict his liability, it is certain that this doctrine has been most reluctantly recognised, and will be confined to cases *of notice or agreement, express or implied.* In the present case, knowledge of the party is negatived by the verdict, and it would be an abuse of terms to call the ticket or advertisement notice *per se*, the verdict finding specially that it was otherwise.

The second point of the plaintiff in error *assumes* too much: neither the evidence nor the verdict justifies the assertion that "it was contrary to prohibition," or that it was "without notice:" it is a *petitio principii*, for it is a part of the very question for present decision. It is true that one of their witnesses said, "the instructions of the company to me as conductor were to carry passengers and baggage alone, merchandise excluded;" but it was also in proof that the hands weighing the trunk said "there must be money in it."

[Camden and Amboy Railroad Co. *v.* Baldauf.]

It has been already said that this was not baggage as such, because it was separated from the passenger by separate payment. All the books assert that a carrier is liable for care of baggage, although not paid for, because it is included in a passenger's fare; by a parity of reasoning, once separated from the passenger, its carriage paid for, and its control taken from its owner, does it not become something other than ordinary baggage, and does not the taking it make the party liable, either as carrier or bailee for hire? It is immaterial which, in this case.

The authorities relating to the first point show that a carrier's notice, to be available to him, must be express and unambiguous, as well as direct to the party. In the present case, it at best amounts to a *refusal* to carry more than fifty pounds, which was the foundation of the new contract, for which the plaintiff paid and the defendants received, as stated in the special verdict. The *weight* of money in the trunk, over 1700 ounces, sufficiently indicated that it was not *wearing-apparel*, and the jury have found that *its weight was paid for and the* (defendant's) *agents did take charge thereof*. We then assert the broad doctrine of a general liability for all they carry, (unless in cases of fraud or intended concealment amounting thereto,) and as the verdict finds that the trunk was *lost*, that is in itself evidence of gross negligence, which would overcome any notice or restriction.

Next, may not the *money* of a passenger be considered as baggage? The advertisement saying that wearing-apparel only is included in that term, is not set up, as so limiting it, nor ought it to be, in defiance of the express proof of plaintiff's ignorance of any such advertisement. Coin is the only recognised money; paper currency is an excrescence, which may at any time be lopped off, and therefore the case must be considered with reference to money known to the law, coin being exclusively such. To say that a passenger carrier is not liable for such, or that he may refuse to take it, is greatly to abridge the convenience and facilities for travelling, because, as was remarked by Justice BELL, in Laing *v.* Calder, "the carrier is one whom, in a vast majority of instances, he cannot but choose to employ;" and especially would this be the case in regard to emigrants, whom and whose money it is the policy of the country to invite.

The case of the Orange County Bank *v.* Brown was for the loss of eleven thousand dollars, in *bank-bills*, (which are not money, but promissory notes,) and they, it was held, were not included in the term *baggage;* but *money* for travelling expenses was included, though not a large sum, as in this case, taken for the mere purpose of transportation: the judge said that the conduct of the plaintiff's agent was a virtual concealment as to the money, that "his representation of his trunk and the contents as baggage was not

[Camden and Amboy Railroad Co. v. Baldauf.]

a fair one, and was calculated to deceive the captain." The plaintiff in that case was a *bank* and not a *passenger*.

Phillips v. Earle, 8 *Pick*. 182: the owner is not bound to disclose the nature or value of the goods; but if he is inquired of by the carrier, he must answer truly. So, too, 4 *Bing. Rep.* 218.

The cases cited by plaintiff in error fail to establish that the money of a passenger, carried for his own use, may not be included as baggage, and a contrary deduction may fairly be made from them. In the case of Hawkins v. Hoffman, the judge expressly says that *baggage* is not confined to wearing-apparel. So, too, in Blanchard v. Isaacs, baggage is considered as only that which is paid for by the passenger's fare, and it excludes, as such, things not carried for the passenger's personal use, but for other purposes, such as a sale.

In the N. J. Trans. Co. v. Merchants' Bank, Justice NELSON puts it upon the ground of fraud; while in the case cited by the plaintiff in error, McGill v. Rowland, 3 *Barr* 451, Mr. Justice ROGERS said, "Nor is it very obvious in what manner the court can restrict the quantity or value of the articles that may be deemed either proper or useful for their ordinary purposes. In the nature of things, it is susceptible of no precise or definite rule, and when there is an attempt to abuse the privilege, we must rely upon the integrity and intelligence of the jury to apply the proper corrective." In that case the plaintiff recovered for the loss of valuable jewelry, proved by the plaintiff's wife.

The case of Levinson v. The Phila. and Trenton Railroad Co. (N. P.; 1847,) was the case of a travelling jeweller, who carried his store-goods in his trunk.

The case of Tudor v. Boston and Maine Railroad Co. related to the admissibility of the plaintiff's testimony, and has no bearing on this point.

Beekman v. Shouse, and Atwood v. Reliance, are again cited in favour of the defendant in error upon this second point.

We submit, therefore, that the lost trunk was not baggage, or, even if it were so, that the defendants are liable; and that the judgment of the court below ought to be affirmed. A contrary doctrine, it is suggested, would be impolitic and promotive of carelessness or dishonesty, and would be withdrawing the wholesome protection of the law from travellers, the impositions upon whom, in all ages and countries, have become matters of by-word.

The opinion of the court, by ROGERS, J., was filed May 16.

ROGERS, J.—The general rule, according to the well-settled principles of the common law, is, that a common carrier is an insurer against every thing but the act of God or the public enemy. In Pennsylvania, however, it is ruled, not without great reluctance, that his common law responsibility may be limited or abridged by

[Camden and Amboy Railroad Co. *v.* Baldauf.]

the special terms of the acceptance of the goods. It is decided, it may be limited by a general notice that the baggage of a passenger is at the risk of the owner, provided the terms of the notice are clear and explicit, not liable to the charge of ambiguity or doubt; and provided further, which is indispensable, the notice is brought home to the employer. These principles are distinctly recognised in Beekman *v.* Shouse, 5 *Rawle* 189; in Bingham *v.* Rogers, 6 *W. & Ser.* 500; and Laing *v.* Calder, 8 *Barr* 484. On the ticket given to the plaintiff, as is found by the special verdict, notice is given that all baggage is at the risk of the owner, the proprietors binding themselves to no charge or care of the same whatever, either express or implied. It is truly said by BURROUGH, J., in Duff *v.* Budd, 3 *B. & B.* 177, that carriers are constantly endeavouring to narrow their responsibility, and to creep out of their duties, and that he is not singular in thinking that their endeavours ought not to be favoured. Of the soundness of this remark, this case affords a striking example. The company not only declare that the baggage is to be at the risk of the passenger, but they attempt to discharge themselves from all charge or care of it whatever. The proprietors say they bind themselves to no charge or care of the same whatever, either express or implied. There is a plain endeavour to shirk all responsibility whatever, even to the misconduct of their own agents, and to avoid the duty which the law casts upon them, to provide places for the safe custody of the goods, and persons whose business it is to take charge of such articles as are committed to their care. They undertake to carry for hire, and, by the very nature of their employment, to bestow, for the preservation of the goods, at least the ordinary care of a bailee for hire. From this duty I have no hesitation in saying they cannot discharge themselves, even by a special agreement with the owner. Such a stipulation would be void, being against the policy of the law. There is no principle in the law better settled than that whatever has an obvious tendency to encourage guilty negligence, fraud, or crime, is contrary to public policy. Such, in the very nature of things, would be the consequence of allowing the common carrier to throw off the obligation, which the law imposes upon him, of taking at least ordinary care of the baggage or other goods of a passenger. Under such a regulation no man's property would be safe, Cole *v.* Goodwin, 19 *Wend.* 251. The special verdict finds that the trunk containing the silver coins, five-franc pieces, and certain articles of wearing-apparel, was delivered to the conductor or other agent of defendants, on board of the boat; that the extra weight of plaintiff's baggage, including the trunk, was paid for, and the agents took charge of it; that the trunk was lost, and not delivered to the plaintiff on his arrival at Philadelphia, the place of destination, or at any time thereafter. The verdict omits to find when it was lost,

[Camden and Amboy Railroad Co. v. Baldauf.]

or how it was lost. As we are without proof on this point, the legal inference is, it was lost or mislaid in consequence of the negligence, or it may be fraud, of the defendants' agents. This would render the defendants liable, notwithstanding notice had been brought home to the plaintiffs. It is proper here to remark that neither concealment nor fraud can be imputed to the plaintiff. He was not bound to disclose the nature or value of the goods, unless inquired of by the carrier: in which case he must answer truly: Phillips *v.* Earle, 8 *Pick.* 182 ; 4 *Bing. R.* 218; Relf *v.* Rapp, 3 *W. & Ser.* 21.

Although he may limit the extent of his liability, yet the authorities are uniform that to discharge the carrier from responsibility, it is necessary to show clearly that the person with whom he deals is fully informed of the terms and effect of the notice. The exemption goes on the ground of a contract express or implied. *Angel on Carriers*, sec. 247; 2 *Green. Ev.* sec. 216 ; Brookes *v.* Pickwick, 4 *Bing. R.* 218 ; Kerr *v.* Miller, 2 *Starkie* 53 ; Cole *v.* Goodwin, 19 *Wend.* 251 ; Hollister *v.* Nowlen, 19 *Wend.* 234.

The facts found by the jury negative the idea of such a notice as amounts to a special contract. The plaintiff was a German, wholly ignorant of the English language. It is therefore a case of a passenger uninformed of the terms and conditions of the notice appended to the ticket on which the defendants rely for protection. The case of Davis *v.* Willan, 2 *Stark. R.* 279, rules that a notice at the office, when the party who delivers the goods cannot read, does not change the liability of the carrier. That case is in principle identical with this. It, in truth, would be absurd to hold, under the circumstances, the company exempted from their common law responsibilities, on the foot of a special or express contract, when he was ignorant of the terms of the proposed agreement. Granting that tickets in any case, without more, may be considered as evidence of a special agreement, it is surely not exacting too much to require the carrier to have his tickets printed and his advertisements made in a language which the passenger can understand, or that he should be required to explain to him the nature and effect of the proposed agreement. Although it may be granted that in this State a carrier may limit his responsibility, yet this principle has been reluctantly recognised, and must be confined to cases of special contract express or at least implied. The knowledge of the plaintiff of the contents of the notice, is negatived by the verdict. It is substantially found the plaintiff had no notice that his goods were carried at his own risk. In the absence of all proof of notice, the plaintiff had a right to rely on the common law responsibility of the carrier. The jury find that the extra weight of the plaintiff's baggage, including the trunk in which the specie was placed, was paid for by the plaintiff, and the agents of the company had charge of it.

[Camden and Amboy Railroad Co. v. Baldauf.]

Whether the specie is to be viewed as baggage or freight we conceive to be immaterial; for whether it be the one or the other, the defendants are clearly liable on two grounds; first, because they have failed to prove the nature and manner of the loss; and second, because they have also failed to bring home knowledge of the limitations and restrictions contained in their notice to the plaintiff. This renders them liable on the rule of the common law, as insurers against all losses except those occasioned by the act of God and the king's enemies.

Judgment affirmed.

Penny Pot Landing; or, Com'th ex rel. Northern Liberties *versus* The City of Philadelphia.

1. In 1690, Vine street, from Front street to the river Delaware, in the city of Philadelphia, was dedicated to public use, as a street of the increased width of 100 feet or more, by the act of the commissioners of property.
2. The proprietary, having granted this addition to Vine street for the public use and accommodation, could not revoke the grant by any subsequent act or deed. The rights of the adjacent lot-holders, as well as the public, to Vine street so enlarged, were vested rights, of which they could not be divested.
3. In addition to the right of the city of Philadelphia to the space annexed to and made part of Vine street in 1690, the same piece of ground was expressly granted to the city corporation by the charter of 1701, as Penny Pot landing.
4. Maps, ancient surveys, as well as reputation, are evidence to elucidate and ascertain a boundary, but not to impeach official grants on public record, control having been long exercised in conformity to the grants.
5. The dedication of a street or landing will be intended to be for the public, and not for part of the public in exclusion of any other part.
6. Street, in a town or city, signifies a public highway. No particular form or ceremony is necessary in the dedication of land to public uses.
7. Possession and use will not give an individual or a corporation a title to a franchise which is an encroachment on a public right.

This was a *quo warranto* to test the right of the city of Philadelphia to the franchise of taking toll and wharfage at the Penny Pot landing, alleged by the relators to be within the district of the Northern Liberties. This landing is an open space of ground on the east side of Front street, adjoining Vine street to the northward, containing 57 feet in breadth, and extending eastward to the river Delaware. It was alleged by the city to be a part of Vine street, which they aver is here 107 feet wide.

Two issues of facts were raised by the pleadings: 1. Is Penny Pot landing within the corporate limits of the city of Philadelphia? 2. Does the city charter of 1701 and the act of 11th March 1789 vest this landing in the respondents as their corporate property?

On the trial, at *Nisi Prius*, before Coulter, J., it was shown, on the part of the respondents, that William Penn, in 1683, laid out the town of Philadelphia, and established Vine street, of the width

[Penny Pot Landing; or, Com. ex rel. Nor. Liberties v. City of Philadelphia.]

of 50 feet, as its northern boundary. That on the 8th of 6th month 1689, there was surveyed to James West a lot of ground in the proprietary's lot, at the north side of Philadelphia, containing in breadth 60 feet, and in length 150 feet, bounded southward with a vacant lot, (said to be where the Penny Pot house stood,) eastward with Delaware River, northward with a vacant lot, and westward with a street. For this lot a patent was issued on the 30th of 6th month 1689. That on the 8th of 1st month 1689–90, James West presented a petition to the commissioners of property, "requesting 40 feet of the bank where the Penny Pot house stands, as an addition to 60 feet formerly laid out to him, he having bought the Penny Pot house of the widow." His request was granted, he complying with his promise, "to make a convenient slip with timber, and fill it up with earth, and pitch it with stone against the street, *which is to be left* 100 *feet wide.*" Accordingly, on the 24th of 1st month 1690, there was surveyed to him a lot of ground (including the lot of 60 feet granted to him on the 1st of 6th month 1689) containing in the whole breadth 100 feet and in length 250 feet, bounded northward with William Rakestraw's lot, eastward with the river Delaware, *southward with Vine street*, and to the westward with Front street. On the same day, eighteen other lots, extending northward along Front street, were surveyed to other persons, by virtue of the same warrant, and a survey of the same was returned into the secretary's office, wherein Vine street is laid down of the width of 120 feet east of Front street. On the 19th of 6th month 1690, the commissioners of property granted to James West a patent for the lot last surveyed to him, reserving thereout, during the term of fifty-one years, unto William Penn, his heirs and successors, the rent of ten English silver shillings; and at the expiration of the said term, the yearly value of the premises with the improvements thereon, to be valued and appraised, one-third of which valuation the said James West, his heirs and assigns, should thereafter pay unto the said William Penn, his heirs and successors; to be holden of the said William Penn, his heirs and successors, as of his manor of Springettsbury, in free and common socage, by fealty only, in lieu of other services. On the 25th of October 1701, William Penn erected the town of Philadelphia into a city, and by his charter established the boundaries thereof as the town was then laid out between Delaware and Schuylkill, and granted and ordained that the streets of the said city should for ever continue as they were then laid out and regulated, and that the end of each street extending into the river Delaware should be and continue free, for the use and service of the said city and the inhabitants thereof; and that the landing-places then and theretofore used at Penny Pot house and Blue Anchor should be left open and common for the use and service of the said city and all others. That on the 4th of July 1776, the said cor-

[Penny Pot Landing; or, Com. ex rel. Nor. Liberties *v.* City of Philadelphia.]

poration was dissolved, and by several acts of Assembly, passed between that date and 1789, its powers and duties were devolved upon the wardens of the city of Philadelphia, and upon commissioners for paving the streets, &c. The former body were, among other things, directed to let or demise the wharves and public landing-places in the city, and to appropriate the proceeds to watching and lighting the streets, &c. By act of 11th of March 1789, the present city corporation was erected, and all the rights of the late corporation in all wharves, landings, landing-places, &c. were vested in the corporation thereby created. And by the act of 2d April 1790, they were invested with all the powers of the wardens of the city. Since 1789, the landing has been used as a wood-wharf, and has been leased for that purpose by the respondents.

On the part of the Commonwealth it was shown that the northern boundary of Philadelphia, as originally laid out, was the north side of Vine street, of the width of 50 feet, extending in a direct line from Delaware to Schuylkill. And to show that there had been a charter of incorporation of the town of Philadelphia, as a borough, prior to the alleged widening of Vine street on the Delaware, and that the city of Philadelphia was incorporated with the same boundaries as the more ancient corporation, there were given in evidence the proceedings at a council held at Philadelphia, on the 26th of 5th month 1684, (present, William Penn, proprietor and governor, William Welsh, and others,) at which Thomas Lloyd, Thomas Holmes, and William Haigue were appointed to draw up a charter for Philadelphia, to be made a borough, consisting of a mayor and six aldermen, and to call to their assistance any of the council: Also, the petition of the inhabitants of Philadelphia, to the governor and council, in 1691, praying that the landing-place at the end of the street, near the Blue Anchor, might be regulated, &c.; signed by Humphrey Murrey, mayor, and others: The proceedings at the meeting of the governor and council on the 3d of 6th month 1691, at which it was ordered that, " in consequence of the application of the mayor, Humphrey Murrey, in behalf of the said city," praying, &c., that the said *mayor and aldermen* have notice to attend and view the same: Also, a protest on the 19th of 11th month 1691, by the commissioners of property, against these proceedings by the governor, Humphrey Murrey, mayor, and others: Also, the charter of 1701, whereby William Penn recites that " I *have*, by virtue of the king's letters patent, erected the said town into a borough; and by these presents *do* erect the said town and borough of Philadelphia into a city." By various ancient plans and surveys it appears that Vine street, up to the period of the revolution, was recognised as extending of an uniform width from Delaware to Schuylkill, and the landing in question was marked as "The Slip." At the expiration of the term mentioned in James West's patent, it was shown that his son,

[Penny Pot Landing, or, Com. ex rel. Nor. Liberties v. City of Philadelphia.]

Charles West, requested that the premises might be resurveyed, and that the proprietaries would release the third part of the yearly value, and accept in lieu thereof a rent-charge of fifteen pounds sterling. Accordingly, on the 30th of March 1747, the premises were resurveyed by William Parsons, surveyor-general, and found to be situate on the bank of Delaware River, *at the distance of 57 feet northward from Vine street, and bounded northward by the public landing-place, commonly called the Penny Pot landing.* On this resurvey a patent was issued to Charles West, on the 14th of May 1747, reserving an annual rent-charge of £15; and describing the premises as in the return of resurvey. By the act of 17th April 1795, the regulators of the Northern Liberties were directed to survey and regulate the streets thereof, to make correct drafts of the same, and to return the same, under their hands, to three justices of the peace, who should keep the same for public inspection for three months, after which the said justices, together with six resident freeholders, by them appointed, should give two weeks public notice that on a certain day they would examine the said drafts, and hear the objections of any persons thereby aggrieved; and that the justices and freeholders should have power to determine whether the same shall be finally established, or whether any or what alterations should be made therein; and should direct the same, with their adjudication thereon, and every necessary explanation, to be recorded in the office of the clerk of the Court of Quarter Sessions of Philadelphia county. On the plan of the first division of the Northern Liberties filed in the office of the clerk of the Court of Quarter Sessions in pursuance of this act, Vine street is laid down of the uniform width of 50 feet to the Delaware, and immediately north of it is the "public landing," of the width of 57 feet. The act of 4th April 1796 provided that the commissioners of the county of Philadelphia, in whom the public landings on the river Delaware, in the township of the Northern Liberties, were by law vested for the use of the public, might, with the approbation of three justices of the county, make rules for the government thereof, prescribe the rates of toll, and lease the same for any term not exceeding three years. And by the act of incorporation of the Northern Liberties, on the 16th March 1819, all landings, &c. held for the use of the inhabitants of the said district were vested in the corporation thereby created, and they were prohibited from altering the lines of any street which had been surveyed, regulated, and established under the act of 1795. It was also shown that in 1835 the city authorities reset the curbstone on the north side of the landing according to the city regulation, whereupon the commissioners of the Northern Liberties directed their superintendent to reset the same in accordance with the district regulations, which was done accordingly, and has so remained.

[Penny Pot Landing; or, Com. ex. rel. Nor. Liberties v. City of Philadelphia.]

COULTER, J., charged the jury that, by the charter of 1701, this landing, and the control thereof, were granted to the city corporation; that they had shown a lawful right to take toll at and to control the same; that the time elapsed was presumptive evidence of a grant from the Penns, and there was no evidence to the contrary; that the Penns having dedicated this landing to public use, subsequent surveys could not show that the city had not the right; that the act of 1819 did not vest the same in the district of the Northern Liberties; and that the fact that the district authorities entered and reset the curbstone in 1835 was a matter of small importance.

There was a verdict for the respondents; whereupon the relators' counsel moved for a new trial, and assigned as reasons for the same that the learned judge erred in charging the jury as above mentioned.

Brightly, for relator.—The City having in their pleadings relied on a title by prescription, could not set up another on the trial: *Chester Case* 548, 410–11; 1 *Burr.* 294: 4 *Burr.* 2143; *Cowp.* 505–7; *Will. Corp.* 2, sec. 486; 15 *Johns.* 358; 1 *Pike* 513; 3 *Pike* 570; *Moore* 297; 1 *Green. Ev.* sec. 58. No length of time will raise a presumption of right in favor of encroachments on the public; in such case the presumption is the contrary way: *Math. Pr. Ev.* 15; 1 *Green. Ev.* sec. 10; 4 *Burr.* 2164; 1 *Whar.* 469, 486; *Chester Case* 24, 44, 64; 2 *Watts* 23; 16 *Ser. & R.* 395; 3 *Penn. R.* 259; 7 *Pa. L. J.* 86; 1 *Jones* 447. And where admitted, the presumption only arises where the use or occupation would otherwise be unlawful: *Math. Pr. Ev.* 14, 15. Until the incorporation of the local authorities, the control of the city was not adverse: 1 *Whar.* 485; 6 *Peters* 439; 10 *Peters* 662, 712; 1 *Jones* 447. But there was abundant evidence to rebut any such presumption: 16 *Ser. & R.* 395; 1 *W. C. C.* 214. William Penn made a clear distinction between the rights of the city corporation to the ends of the streets and to the public landings. The ends of the streets are to continue free, for the use and service of the said city and inhabitants thereof; whilst the public landings are to be left open and common for the use and service of the said city and *all others*. Unless, then, this landing be a portion of the end of Vine street, and consequently within the corporate limits of the city, the respondents were not entitled to a verdict. Neither the charter of 1701 nor the act of 1789 mention the boundaries of the city: it is the town and borough of Philadelphia which is incorporated, as it is now laid out between the Delaware and Schuylkill. It is admitted in respondent's answer, that William Penn, in 1683, laid out the town of Philadelphia, and established Vine street, of the width of 50 feet, as its northern boundary; the

[Penny Pot Landing; or, Com. ex. rel. Nor. Liberties *v.* City of Philadelphia.]

landing was clearly excluded from this limit. In 1684, a committee was appointed to draw up a charter for Philadelphia to be made a borough, consisting of a mayor and six aldermen, 1 *Col. Rec.* 64; and although this borough charter is not now extant, there can be no doubt of its former existence, since, in 1691, we find Humphrey Murrey acting as mayor of Philadelphia, and recognised as such by the governor and council, and also by the commissioners of property. We also find by the document establishing this fact, that there were then aldermen of Philadelphia, as provided in the proposed charter : 1 *Watson's Annals* 336. And in the charter of 1701, William Penn recites that he *had* erected the said town into a borough, and did thereby erect the said town and borough into a city : 1 *Dal. Laws*, ap. 11. This is presumptive proof of the former existence of a borough charter : 1 *Spencer* 61. It was then the ancient borough, incorporated in 1684, which was erected into a city in 1701, and with the same boundaries, excluding the *locus in quo ; Reed's Explanation* 13 ; 1 *Whar.* 484. And if Vine street was widened in 1690, it by no means follows that the additional width was thereby thrown within the limits of the borough. It is true, the ancient plans, surveys, and documents given in evidence, cannot divest the right of the city; but they were strong evidence to rebut the presumption of a grant: 1 *Green. Ev.* sec. 129, 135, 138, 139, 145 ; 11 *Ser. & R.* 149; 6 *Bin.* 59 ; 2 *Ser. & R.* 50 ; 1 *Peters C. C.* 496 ; 2 *Litt.* 159 ; 3 *Rand.* 44. It is said the right to exact tolls may, on evidence of long and *undisputed* enjoyment, be presumed to have originated in a grant : *Calthrop* 122 ; but the antiquity of the usage must be very great, as, in the only cases on the subject, the tolls claimed had been received for centuries : *Math. Pr. Ev.* 303 ; 1 *Show.* 47 ; *Cowp.* 102 ; 6 *Cowen* 706 ; 10 *Shep.* 339. The whole difficulty, however, in this case was satisfactorily explained by the resurvey of West's lot, in 1747, when it was found to be 57 feet north of Vine street. The documents fixing the southern boundary of the Northern Liberties are also full of persuasive evidence to rebut all idea of this landing being within the city limits : 2 *Smith* 106 ; *Serg. Land Laws* 196, 224 ; *Gordon's Hist.* 78 ; 1 *Whar.* 412. The original survey of the Liberty lands has been lost for many years, 4 *Yeates* 144 ; the courses and distances, however, are given in *Reed's Exp.* 15. Out of these Liberty lands the manor of Springettsbury was laid out : 1 *W. C. C.* 262, the record of which is also lost ; but on the 12th of 8th month 1703, a warrant was issued to resurvey the manor, and a copy of an ancient plan, believed to be a return to this warrant, was given in evidence, on which the southern boundary of the manor is laid down as a direct line from river to river. The counsel also cited *Minutes of Common Council,* 17, 28, 498; 2 *Col. Rec.* 542, 563, 566, 587, 588 ; 3 *Col. Rec.* 618 ; 1 *Smith* 412 ; *id.* 318 ; 2 *Smith* 49 ; 3 *Smith* 224 ; 7 *Smith* 61 ; *id.* 177 ;

[Penny Pot Landing; or, Com. ex rel. Nor. Liberties v. City of Philadelphia.]
6 *Ser. & R.* 522 ; 3 *Smith* 274 ; 1 *Whar.* 46. He also contended, that the presumption of a grant arising from long-continued, uninterrupted enjoyment, is a presumption of *fact* to be drawn by the jury, *Math. Pr. Ev.* 3, 4 ; 1 *Green. Ev.* sec. 44–48, and not as here, by the *court.*

Olmsted, for the respondents.—The respondents did not endeavour to make out a title by prescription : they proved a *grant* of the right to tolls for the use of the landing. The respondents claim the right by the grant, in the charter of 1701, of the ends of the streets on the river Delaware, and of Penny Pot landing, by that name ; that is to say, they claim to take such toll because the *locus in quo* is either the end of Vine street, or because it is Penny Pot landing. The application of James West, in 1689, for an addition to his lot on the river Delaware, was granted by the commissioners of property, on his engagement to make a convenient slip, with timber, and fill it up with earth, and pitch it with stones against the street, "*which is to be left* 100 *feet wide.*" Here is the act of the proprietary officers to secure this landing for the use of the public ; it is thrown into the street, which is increased in width by this addition to 100 feet. The return of survey bounds the lot on the south by Vine street; the plan shows it so bounded, and also the patent. Then follows the address of the inhabitants of Philadelphia, through the intervention of the Assembly, that the ends of the streets be unlimited, and be left free to be extended in the river, and that the public landing-places at the Blue Anchor and Penny Pot house be confirmed free to the inhabitants. To which the proprietary answered : " About the ends of the streets and other public landings of this town, I am willing to grant the ends of the streets, when and where improved, and the other according to your request." 1 *Votes of Assembly,* 145, 148. Accordingly, a charter was granted to the city on the 25th October 1701, wherein it is ordained that the said city "shall extend the limits and bounds as it is laid out between the Delaware and Schuylkill," and that the " end of each street extending into the river Delaware shall be and continue free for the use and service of the said city and the inhabitants thereof." The streets, as there laid out and regulated, were to continue for ever; one of these was Vine street, as increased in width by the addition of Penny Pot landing. The fact of the former existence of a borough charter may be questioned : it is not now extant, and if it did exist, there is no reason to conclude that only those streets which were in existence during the time of the borough were to be provided for in the city charter.

But admitting that Penny Pot landing was not incorporated into Vine street at the date of the charter, but existed distinct from the street, as a public landing, then it was granted to the corporation

[Penny Pot Landing; or, Com. ex rel. Nor. Liberties v. City of Philadelphia.]

as Penny Pot landing by the charter: 1 *Whar.* 479, 484. The dedication of the street once made was irrevocable: 1 *Whar.* 469. No act of the proprietary or his officers could change it. The opinions of annalists and surveyors cannot counteract the positive act of the proprietary and his officers; but they made no effort to ascertain the true width of Vine street, nor was it necessary for them to do so. The respondents are not concluded by the acts of the regulators of the Northern Liberties, under the act of 1795. Their authority only extended to the regulation of the streets laid out in the Northern Liberties, *beginning at the northern bounds of the city of Philadelphia, on the river Delaware:* 3 *Smith* 224. The Penny Pot landing was not acquired by the application of public moneys, as was the case of the other landings granted to the corporation of the Northern Liberties by their charter, (1 *Whar.* 46;) it was the private property of the proprietary and by him granted to the respondents for the use of the public.

The opinion of the court was delivered by

CHAMBERS, J.—The corporation of the city of Philadelphia are called upon, by writ of *quo warranto*, issued by this court, to show by what right they exercise the franchise of taking toll and wharfage at a place called the Penny Pot landing, which is alleged by the relators to be within the district of the Northern Liberties. This landing is a space of ground on the Delaware river, and part of or adjoining Vine street, and which is claimed by the city as within her corporate limits. For the exercise of the franchise claimed by the city of taking toll and wharfage, it is incumbent on the city to show that she had and still possesses this right.

The case was tried at *Nisi Prius* before Justice COULTER, and on the merits, without regard to the pleadings, leaving the single and important question of right to be decided on the law and evidence by the court and jury. Being brought before this court, on a motion for a new trial, the whole case is presented for the revision and judgment of this court on the evidence and the charge of Judge COULTER to the jury.

The consideration of this case imposes on the court an inquiry into the early history of the location and plan of the city of Philadelphia by its eminent founder. For its elucidation, the court is indebted to the research and ability of the able counsel who have prepared the case and argued it for the parties. Penny Pot landing and that of the Blue Anchor were places of notoriety and importance when Philadelphia was first made a town and afterwards a city; the one being a landing at the foot of Vine street, and the other at the foot of Dock street, being for a long time the only places of landing on the Delaware for those who carried on trade, commerce, or intercourse with the city on the Delaware side. The high bank from Front street to the river presented, between Vine

[Penny Pot Landing; or, Com. ex rel. Nor. Liberties v. City of Philadelphia.]

and Dock streets, an obstacle to intercourse with the city, except at these openings and landings, which were deemed indispensable for access to the city, and were used as such. The importance of these landings, at that early day, would not be overlooked by the proprietary, the officers of his government, or the inhabitants or authorities of the city. On the part of the city it is alleged that her right to the occupancy of this piece of land, called Penny Pot landing, as a public street and landing, is by grant from the proprietary, and confirmed by his official agents to the inhabitants of the town of Philadelphia, within a few years after laying out the town, and before a charter had been granted them for a city. It is also alleged that the right of the city to the use and control of this piece of ground, either as a part of Vine street, or as Penny Pot landing, was further confirmed by the charter to the city from the proprietary. The control of the city is derived first by grant of this piece of ground known as the Penny Pot landing, by its being made a part of Vine street, by the proprietary, not as a transfer to the city of the absolute property in the soil, but as an appropriation and dedication of it for the public use as part of a street.

Vine street, as first laid out in the town plan of Philadelphia by William Penn, was but fifty feet wide, extending from the Delaware to the Schuylkill; but as he was the absolute owner of the landing and lands adjacent, not appropriated, it was competent to him to grant them and dispose of them, or any franchises and easements appurtenant to them, to whom he pleased, and on such terms and with such privileges and uses as he might deem proper.

In considering the evidence of a grant to the city, in this case of the public franchise and use claimed, reference must be had to the usages of the proprietary government, at that early period of its history, in the form and method of granting and appropriating the lands of the proprietary in his province. Whatever system of conveyance and grant was established, it was brief and informal, and was so much in the breast and will of the proprietary, that forms of grant and agreement were variable, according to the pleasure of the proprietary, the change of officers, or the expediency of the times.

It is in evidence from the books of the land-office, that by virtue of a warrant from the commissioners of property, dated 1st of 6th month 1689, there was surveyed, the 8th of same month, unto James West, shipwright, a certain lot of ground on the proprietary's lot, at the north side of Philadelphia, containing in breadth 60 feet, and in length 150 feet, bounded to the southward by a vacant lot, eastward by the Delaware river, northward by a vacant lot, and to the westward by a street.

This would appear to be the first appropriation by the proprietary at the north side of Philadelphia, and was either adjacent to

[Penny Pot Landing; or, Com. ex rel. Nor. Liberties v. City of Philadelphia.]

or in the vicinity of Penny Pot landing, being on Front street and the Delaware river. On the same day there was made for James West another survey of a lot at the same place, on the same warrant, being 150 feet by 160, bounded on the Delaware and a street. This last survey appears to have been experimental and not adopted as final; for from the minutes of the commissioners of property, it appears that "at a meeting of the commissioners, 6th of 1st month 1689–90, present, Markham, Turner, Goodson, and Carpenter, James West requesting 40 feet of the bank where the Penny Pot house stands, and in addition to 60 feet formerly laid out to him for a conveniency to build ships and vessels upon, for having bought the Penny Pot house of the widow, his request was granted, he complying with his promise, viz. to make a convenient slip with timber, and fill it up with earth, and pitch it with stones against the street, which is to be left 100 feet wide."

In conformity to this agreement, and under a warrant dated 22d of 1st month, 1690, there was surveyed and laid out on the 24th of the same month, unto James West, a lot of ground in the bank, of the proprietary's land, at the north-east part of Philadelphia, which said lot likewise included a lot of 60 feet, granted unto him by the commissioners, the 1st of 6th month 1689, containing the whole breadth, one hundred feet, and in length two hundred and fifty feet, bounded northward by William Rakestraw's lot, eastward with the river Delaware, of the said extent of 250 feet, southward with Vine street, and to the westward with Front street; which survey is entered in the surveyor-general's office.

On the day of this last survey, there were surveyed by the surveyor-general, eighteen other lots for other persons named, adjoining in the same vicinity on Front and Vine streets; a plot of which combined, representing their respective locations, and the streets on which they are bounded, is returned into the secretary's office on the next day, and there recorded and preserved. In that plot of the proprietary's appropriations or grants of lots, is the lot of James West, with its boundaries, as agreed by the commissioners, bounding it on "*Vine street*, 120 *feet broad*," from Front street to the Delaware, and describing Vine street as 60 feet broad west of Front street. And on the 19th of 6th month 1690, a patent issued from the commissioners of property, to James West, for his enlarged lot as described. It is to be observed in the agreement between West and the commissioners of property, his lot was to include part of the Penny Pot house landing, and to bound on the street which was to be left 100 feet wide. The survey of the proprietary officer, with the plot returned of it and the other lots, describe that part of Vine street adjacent to West's lot, as 120 feet broad.

Here are four official acts of the proper officers of the proprietary government for the granting, bounding, and recording appro-

[Penny Pot Landing; or, Com. ex rel. Nor. Liberties *v.* City of Philadelphia.]

priations of land, in conformity to the then existing regulations and usages of the land-office, and are preserved among the early records of that office, furnishing the highest evidence that Vine street was enlarged to 100 feet or more in width, from Front street to the Delaware; and that as so enlarged, it was, by grant from the proprietary, dedicated to the public use as a *street*, which signifies, in a town or city, a public highway. No particular form or ceremony is necessary in the dedication of land to public use. Cincinnati *v.* White, 6 *Peters's Rep.* 440. But in this dedication of the addition to Vine street by the proprietary, there is all the formality of grant which then characterized grants of land under his provincial government.

This enlargement of Vine street consisted of a part of the Penny Pot landing, adjacent to West's lot, and to which the widened street was appurtenant as a boundary; and as a public highway, it enured not only to his use and the other lot-holders in the vicinity, but to the use of the public. William Penn; having by his agents and accredited officers, granted this addition to Vine street for the public use and accommodation, in 1690, could not revoke that grant by any subsequent act or deed. In the case of Cincinnati *v.* White, 6 *Peters's Rep.* 431, in affirmance of this principle, it was ruled "that after land is set apart for public use, and enjoyed as such, and private and individual rights acquired with reference to it, the law considers it in the nature of an *estoppel in pais*, which precludes the original owner from revoking such dedication."

The rights of the adjacent and neighbouring lot-holders, as well as the public, to Vine street so enlarged, were vested rights, of which they could not be divested by William Penn; and if it were not competent to Penn, the proprietor and founder, to divest or impair his grant and dedication of this extended street, it cannot with any propriety be supposed that this could be done many years after his death, by acts on the part of some of the subordinate officers of the proprietary government. It is due to the high character and eminent integrity of William Penn, to say that, during his life, no act was done by him having any tendency to impair the grant and dedication of this street. It was consistent with the use of Vine street as a public highway, that the landing at the end of that widened street might be used by the public as a landing, under the government of the city authorities.

Every subsequent act by William Penn in relation to it was in confirmation of the previous grant. The Assembly of the province, in their address to the governor, presented on the 20th of 7th month 1701, in the tenth item says: "That the streets of the town be regulated and bounded, and that the ends of the streets on Delaware and Schuylkill be unlimited and left free to be extended on the river, as the inhabitants shall see meet; and that

[Penny Pot Landing; or, Com. ex rel. Nor. Liberties v. City of Philadelphia.]

public landing-places at the Blue Anchor and Penny Pot house be confirmed free to the inhabitants of this town, not infringing any man's property:" 1 *Votes As.* 145; 2 *Col. Rec.* 35. To this, the governor and proprietor replied, on the 29th of same month: "About the ends of streets, and other public landing-places of this town, I am willing to grant the ends of the streets, where and when improved, and the other according to your request:" 1 *Votes As.* 148; 2 *Col. Rec.* 39.

The charter of William Penn for the city of Philadelphia, dated 25th October, 1701, erects the said town and borough of Philadelphia into a city, "which said city shall extend the limits and bounds as it is laid out between the Delaware and Schuylkill."

"And I do for me, my heirs and assigns, grant and ordain that the streets of the said city shall for ever continue as they are now laid out and regulated, and that the end of each street extending into the river Delaware shall be and continue free for the use and service of said city and the inhabitants thereof, who may improve the same for the best advantage of the city, and build wharves so far out into the river there, as the mayor, aldermen, and common council, hereinafter mentioned, shall see meet.

"And I do also ordain, that the landing-places now and heretofore used at Penny Pot house and Blue Anchor, saving to all persons their just and legal rights and property in the land, so to be left open, as also the swamp between Budd's buildings and the Society hill, shall be left open and common for the use and service of the said city, and all others, with liberty to dig docks, and make harbors for ships and vessels, in all or any part of said swamp."

The addition to the width of Vine street, as stated, was made by the proprietary in 1690, and then dedicated to the public use as a street; and in 1701, by the charter from him to the city, it is ordained that *the streets of said city shall for ever continue as they are now laid out and regulated.* The acts of the proprietary, in his reply to the address of the Assembly, or in the charter granted to the city, were not in any way in derogation of his previous grants and concessions, but in confirmation of the same. The ends of the streets extending into the river Delaware were to be and continue free; and the landing-places before used at the Penny Pot house and the Blue Anchor, saving to persons their just rights, &c., were to be left open and common for the use of said city and all others. The control of the franchises for the public accommodation in the use of the streets and landings was necessarily and explicitly conferred on the authorities of the city.

If the city had not ample authority and control over Vine street as widened under the appropriation and dedication made as a grant from the proprietary, which the court is of opinion it had, it would be entitled to the control of the Penny Pot house landing under the concession of the proprietary to the Assembly, and the

[Penny Pot Landing; or, Com. ex rel. Nor. Liberties v. City of Philadelphia.]

express grant in the charter of 1701 to the city of that landing, which was to be left open and common for the use and service of said city and others, with liberty to dig docks, &c.

The occupancy of this landing and the control of the same by the city have been consistent with these grants as far back as the memory of witnesses will serve, and who testify that Vine street was of the width of 50 feet above Front street, and 107 from Front street to the Delaware.

Subsequent legislation has been in confirmation of the authority and right of the city. By act of 30th May 1780, (1 *Smith* 506,) the wardens of the city were authorized to let or demise the market-houses, ferries, wharves, and public landing-places; the moneys arising thereupon to be applied to the uses specified in the act of 9th March 1771, (1 *Smith* 370,) to wit, for watching and lighting the city, &c.

By the 40th section of act of 11th March 1789, to incorporate the city of Philadelphia, (2 *Smith* 462,) all the rights of the late corporation in all wharves, landings, and landing-places, &c. were vested in the corporation thereby created. By act of 2d April 1790, (2 *Smith* 526,) all the powers of the wardens of the city under former laws were vested in the present corporation.

What is alleged and proved by the relators to impair this right? It is said that, in the opinion of surveyors, map-makers, and historians, Vine street was of one uniform breadth of 50 feet, from the Delaware to the Schuylkill. The most ancient map of Holmes, made in 1683, when the town of Philadelphia was laid out, does so represent it, and rightly at that time; but it is to be observed that this map was made some seven years before the addition to Vine street was made by the proprietary. As it is conceded that Vine street was originally laid out only of the width of 50 feet, Holmes's map is not to be relied on as affording any evidence of any addition to this street as made in 1690. The subsequent maps and plots are but outlines to represent the ground boundaries and configuration of the city, without investigating with legal accuracy the rights of individuals or the public in every part, or defining them with a precision to be relied on. Whether these acts were those of the officers of the proprietary government or other citizens in making a map of the city, they could not divest the right of the city and public to streets and franchises before granted by the proprietary. The city of Philadelphia was not a party to the formation of these surveys and maps, and the city as well as the public and the lot-owners interested in the enlargement of Vine street, or in the landing on the river, extended for that width, were not to be prejudiced by them. Maps, ancient surveys, as well as reputation, are evidence to elucidate and ascertain boundary, as well as fix monuments; but in this case they are offered to impeach official grants on public record, and when on the landing control

[Penny Pot Landing; or, Com. ex rel. Nor. Liberties v. City of Philadelphia.]

has been exercised and tolls taken by the city authorities from time immemorial, in conformity to the official grants; against such evidence, such plots or surveys ought to have no weight.

The research of the relators' counsel has brought to our notice from the land office, a draft entitled "bank above the town," on which it is entered: James West, in the year 1690, had a patent for a lot 100 feet front, 250 long; bound northward by William Rakestraw, and southward by Vine street, both which cannot be true. There is no date to this entry, and it is presumed that it was made about 1747, the time of the resurvey in evidence, made for Charles West, son of James, and is to be accounted for by the omission to examine minutely the proceedings had in relation to the survey and return of James West's lot in 1689–90. The parties connected with that survey may be supposed to have been deceased, and the facts to explain it were only to be had by diligent search into the transaction, as it had been acted more than fifty years before. The survey and plot on file, and on record, exhibiting the lots and the names of the proprietors, their boundaries, and Vine street as widened in 1690, if seen as they ought to have been, would have relieved those investigating the matter of all doubt and uncertainty. The landing at Penny Pot house was no doubt of more extensive accommodation to the public and its importance in higher estimation to the city whilst it was one of the two great landings and avenues for the trade and intercourse with the growing city. But after Front street was opened, and wharves made at the foot of Market and other streets on the Delaware, and access had to the city from new landings and streets opened, the importance of Penny Pot landing may have declined, and the occasion to use Vine street as a highway would not probably then require more than the fifty feet in width, which would accommodate the public, without subjecting the city to the expense of paving and improving the extended way, which the public accommodation and necessities did not then require. But the extended growth and importance of this city and the Northern Liberties will make the act of the proprietary in widening Vine street from Front street to the river ever to be commended for its propriety, convenience, and utility.

It has been remarked in the argument, that while the proprietary granted that the ends of the streets extending into the river Delaware should be and continue free for the use and service of the said city and the inhabitants thereof, it was provided and granted that the Penny Pot and Blue Anchor landings (saving to all persons their just and legal rights and property in the land so to be left open, as also the swamp between Budd's buildings and Society hill) shall be left open and common for the use and service of said city, and *all others*, with liberty to dig docks and make harbors for ships and vessels in all or any part of the said swamp. We do not

[Penny Pot Landing; or, Com. ex rel. Nor. Liberties v. City of Philadelphia.]

consider the variation in the tenure as expressed by the terms used in the two cases as creating any difference of use. The use dedicated and transferred is public and indefinite, to be used and enjoyed according to its nature and circumstances, so as to afford to the *public* the accommodation intended. The dedication of a highway, street, or landing will be intended to be for the public, and not for part of the public in exclusion of any other part.

The city authorities must regulate the use of the street and landing for the accommodation of the inhabitants and strangers having occasion to use the privileges conferred. The erection and repair of wharves and landings and the improvement of the street would require, on the part of the city, expenditures of money, and it is just and proper that they should exact reasonable tolls or charges from those who found it convenient or advantageous to use the said wharves and landings. Without such expenditures, improvement, and repairs, they would be inconvenient, if not useless; and that the franchises should be enjoyed by the public, without annoyance or abuse, it is necessary that there should be established regulations for the government of the use. As it is the interest and policy of the city authorities to facilitate trade and commerce with the city, it is not to be supposed that they would be unreasonable in their exactions, or in their regulations for the common enjoyment of the public. If there were any such abuse of authority, which is not to be presumed, it might be a proper matter for legislative cognizance, reform, or control.

Vine street, from Front street to the Delaware, has a width from its south line to the boundary of what was James West's lot, and which is exceeding 100 feet. The variance in the reported width of that street, from Front street to the Delaware, at different early times, might have arisen from inaccuracy in commencing for mensuration at some distant point, or from inequalities of surface of the ground, which may have been variable at different periods. In 1690, the surveyor-general described it then as 120 feet wide, and now it is represented as 107 feet.

There is nothing to impair the rights of the city in the proceedings of the surveyors and regulators appointed under the act of 1795 to survey and regulate the streets laid out in the township of the Northern Liberties, beginning at the northern bounds of the city of Philadelphia on the river Delaware. If the northern boundary of the city was on the north side of Vine street 107 feet wide, the regulators were without authority when they attempted to do any act south of it, and neither by their opinion nor acts could take away any of the rights of the city to its franchises on Vine street and the landing on the same; and under the act which provided for paving the streets, there was no act done by the authority of the Northern Liberties in the way of paving and

[Penny Pot Landing; or, Com. ex rel. Nor. Liberties v. City of Philadelphia.]

curbing the part of the street now claimed on the part of the Northern Liberties, that could prejudice the rights of the city.

The right of the city to the control and regulation of Vine street and the landing on the Delaware at the foot of it, is, in the opinion of this court, derived from grants by the proprietary, as recited and commented on, and who was the absolute owner thereof. It is not a right depending on presumption or prescription. Possession and use alone would not give the city a title to the franchise claimed against the public. "It is well settled that lapse of time furnishes no defence to an encroachment on a public right." "If no grant be shown, presumption will not be made to support a nuisance by encroachment on a public right:" Commonwealth v. Alburger, 1 *Whar.* 486–8; and in the Commonwealth v. McDonald, 16 *Ser. & R.* 395, Justice DUNCAN says that "public rights cannot be destroyed by long-continued encroachment;" and in Barter v. Commonwealth, 3 *Pa. Rep.* 253, GIBSON, C. J., said, "that the government of every incorporated town has a right to improve the streets for public purposes, is a proposition about which there can be little dispute," and " no private occupancy, for whatever time, and whether adverse or by permission, can vest a title inconsistent with it." "The case of Commonwealth v. McDonald, by which this salutary principle has been established, is founded in the purest reason and fortified by the strongest authorities." And in accordance with this principle is the case of Rung v. Shoneberger, 2 *Watts* 23.

This opinion has been extended by the review of the many documents given in evidence and the points presented by the counsel; and in the opinion of the court, the learned judge before whom the cause was tried was warranted by the law and evidence in saying to the jury "that the city of Philadelphia had shown she had a lawful right to take toll and control this landing;" and as it is the opinion of the court that the mayor, aldermen, and citizens of Philadelphia, in behalf of the city, have shown by grant from the proprietary the right to exercise the franchise of taking toll and wharfage for the use of the piece of land formerly called Penny Pot landing, it is unnecessary to examine the claim of the Northern Liberties to the same franchise, as, if there is an existing right in the city of Philadelphia, which is prior, paramount, and exclusive, there can be no valid right in the incorporated district of the Northern Liberties. The whole case being by the court considered, the court overrule the motion for a new trial, being satisfied with the finding of the jury under Justice COULTER, and direct judgment to be entered for the Mayor, Aldermen, and Citizens of Philadelphia.

George *versus* Morgan.—Worrall *versus* Same.

1. The rule in Shelly's case is a settled rule of property in Pennsylvania; and in deciding whether a devise is within the rule, no influence is to be conceded to any supposed prohibition of the rule by the testator, or to the defeat of a particular intention. The leading inquiry is what is the great object of the devisor; but where the form of the disposition is constituted of terms of art, to which an ascertained meaning has been fixed by decision, the construction settled is binding on courts.

2. Where a testator devised as follows: "I give and bequeath unto my son Mordecai all that messuage or tenement situate, &c., with all its rights, members, privileges, and appurtenances, to hold to him for and during his natural life, and, after his decease, to the heirs of his body, lawfully begotten, and to their heirs for ever; and, in default of such issue, then to the heirs of my son Samuel, and their heirs for ever:" *Held*, that by the devise Mordecai took an estate-tail, under the rule in Shelly's case.

3. In a devise of lands a limitation of them in default of issue, means *an indefinite failure of issue*, unless there be something in the context to qualify the expressions, or the reference be expressly to persons then existing.

4. Superadded words, serving to limit a fee in the issue of the first taker, engrafted on words of procreation, will not operate to turn these into words of purchase, unless the superadded words denote a *different species of heirs* from that described in the first words, and showing an intent to break the ordinary line of descent from the first taker.

5. An intention to change the line of descent is not sufficiently manifested when the superadded words *import* eventual distribution of the estate; to have that effect, distribution must be expressly contemplated.

6. In Pennsylvania, a testator as to real estate, is to be regarded as speaking in reference to the common-law system of descent. Per BELL, J.

7. A deed from a tenant in tail purporting to bar the entail, but never entered on record and recorded, as required by law, and thus incompetent to bar the entail, was nevertheless held to be good to convey the grantor's right of possession, and was therefore admissible in evidence.

ERROR to the Common Pleas of *Delaware county*.

John Morgan, being seized in fee simple of the premises in dispute, made his last will on the 6th day of 8th month, called October, 1744, which will was proved on the 9th day of December 1744.

By this will, *inter alia*, the said testator devised in the following words:

"Also I give and bequeath unto my son Mordecai, all that messuage or tenement plantation situate in Radnor aforesaid, called by the name of the Hall of Nantmell, which I purchased of Richard Orme, deceased, with about thirty-eight acres of woodland, part of my other land adjoining, as, by a late survey appears, containing in the whole about two hundred acres, with all its rights, members, privileges, and appurtenances, *to hold to him for and during his natural life, and, after his decease,* to the heirs of his body, lawfully begotten, *and to their heirs for ever;* and, in default of *such issue*, then to the heirs of my son Samuel, and their heirs for ever."

[George v. Morgan.]

CHAPMAN, J., charged the jury that, by the above devise, Mordecai Morgan took an estate-tail, under what is called the rule in Shelly's case.

This instruction and charge was excepted to by the defendants below, and reduced to writing and filed at their request.

It forms the *first* error assigned, viz.: "That the judge erred in instructing the jury that Mordecai Morgan took an estate-tail under the devise made to him in the will of John Morgan, dated the 6th October 1744."

This was the main question in the cases.

The following plan will show the situation of this family, so far as connected with the present questions:

John Morgan, the testator, will and decease in 1744.

Mordecai Morgan 1st, born 1713, died 1804, son of John.

Mordecai Morgan 2d, only child of M. Morgan 1st, born in 1742, died July 1794, was in being at the date of will of John Morgan.

Mordecai Morgan 2d, left six children, of whom James was the eldest, viz.:

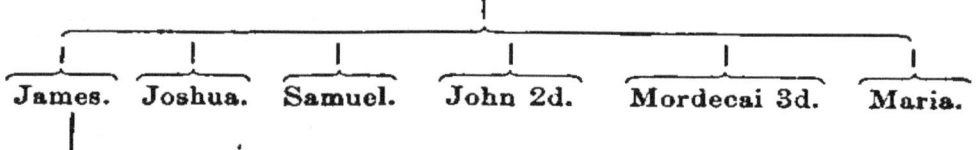

James. Joshua. Samuel. John 2d. Mordecai 3d. Maria.

James Morgan died about ten years ago, and left seven children, of whom Joshua, still alive, is eldest, viz.:

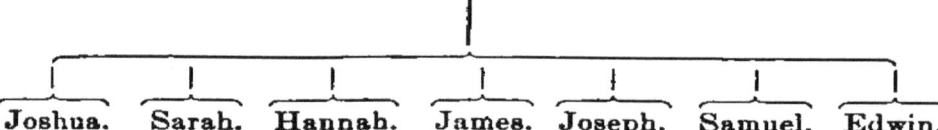

Joshua. Sarah. Hannah. James. Joseph. Samuel. Edwin.

Joseph Morgan and Samuel Morgan, younger children of James Morgan, were the plaintiffs.

The evidence showed that Mordecai Morgan 1st always lived on the two hundred acres thus devised to him, and died in possession in January 1804, aged about 94.

Mordecai Morgan 2d was the only son of Mordecai Morgan 1st. He also lived upon these two hundred acres, and died before his father, in July 1794, aged about 51 or 52 at the time of his death.

[George v. Morgan.]

He was consequently in being, and more than two years old, when the will of John Morgan, his grandfather, was made, in October 1744.

At the death of Mordecai Morgan the 1st, in January 1804, and from that time up to 1807, *all the six children of Mordecai Morgan the 2d* lived and made their homes on these two hundred acres.

In this interval, between 1804 and 1807, (about 1805 or 1806,) all the six children of Mordecai Morgan the 2d joined in building a barn, thirty-five by sixty feet, on these two hundred acres. Joseph, one of those children, was a mason; Samuel and John, two others, were carpenters. None of them got any thing for their labour. They all lived there together.

In 1807, the six children of Mordecai Morgan the 2d made an amicable division of these two hundred acres; James, the eldest, took sixty acres, with all the buildings, and *made a deed* for the residue, being about one hundred and thirty acres, to his four brothers and his sister Maria. They (the four brothers and sister) held their part in common, and afterwards divided among themselves, and released to each other. They divided after 1807.

After 1807, James never pretended to have possession. His brothers and sister had possession till they sold: when they sold, the parties to whom they sold went into possession.

The defendants below, and those under whom they claim, were, and since 1809 have been, in possession of the premises described in the several declarations in ejectment, being a part of the one hundred and thirty acres above mentioned, under title derived from the four brothers and sister of James Morgan, the other children of Mordecai Morgan the 2d.

The counsel of the plaintiff below offered in evidence a deed from *Joshua Morgan, the eldest son of James Morgan*, to Joseph Morgan and Samuel Morgan, two of his younger brothers, and the plaintiffs in these actions, dated January 20, 1848, purporting to bar an estate-tail, together with the record of the Court of Common Pleas of Delaware county, which was objected to as ineffectual for that purpose, not having been entered on record in the proper county, within *six* months, as required by law; but the same was admitted by the court, under an exception on part of the defendants, as evidence of the transfer of such title as was vested in Joshua Morgan. The effect and bearing of this deed is explained in the charge of the court delivered by CHAPMAN, President Judge, as follows:

The plaintiffs, in the first case, claim about thirty-six acres of land, now in the possession of Sarah George, and in the latter, they claim two acres, two roods, and twenty-two perches, now in the possession of Sarah Worrall. They have given in evidence a deed, dated the 20th of January, A. D. 1848, from Joshua Morgan

[George v. Morgan.]

to them, purporting to convey his interest in the property in dispute. Although the act of Assembly to facilitate the barring of entails has not been complied with, whereby the deed is ineffectual for such purpose, still it is the opinion of the court it is available in the claim to possession.

The question in these cases is, whether, under the will of John Morgan, dated the 6th of October 1744, Mordecai Morgan took an estate-tail? We charge you he did, and if you believe the evidence, the estate descended to the grantor of the plaintiffs. In such case, your verdicts must be for the plaintiffs.

To this charge, defendants' counsel excepted.

The jury returned a verdict for the defendants in each case, which verdicts were immediately set aside by the court. Whereupon, by agreements filed, verdicts were entered in each case for the plaintiffs, subject to the bills of exception taken to the admission of the evidence, the exception to the charge of the court, and the right to purchase writs of error, with the same effect as if verdicts for the plaintiffs had been originally rendered.

The defendants below, on the trial, gave in evidence a deed of release signed by James Morgan, father of Joshua Morgan, under whom the plaintiffs claim, of all interest in the land in dispute, to his brothers and sisters, including Mordecai Morgan, dated June 16, 1807, made for the purpose of effecting partition of the estate of John Morgan.

The will of John Morgan, before referred to, was in part as follows:

First, my will is, that all my just debts and funeral charges be fully paid by my executor. Also I give and bequeath unto my son Samuel, all that messuage or tenement, plantation, and tract of land thereunto belonging, commonly known or called by the name of Vainer, whereon I now live, containing about one hundred and sixty acres, (be it more or less,) with all its rights, members, privileges, and appurtenances, to hold to him for and during his natural life, and after his decease then to the heirs of his body lawfully begotten, if a son, and to his heirs for ever, and, if only daughters, then equally between them and their heirs for ever, provided always, and if his now wife survive him, then my will is, that she shall have and enjoy one-half of the rents and profits of my said plantation, for the benefit of her and my grand-children by her now husband, during such time as she remains his widow, but in case of her intermarriage with another person, then, my will is, that she shall have only five pounds a year paid her out of the rents and profits of the said plantation, during her natural life. Also, I give and bequeath to my said son, Samuel, all my messuage or tenement plantation, and one hundred acres of land thereunto belonging, situate in Radnor aforesaid, commonly known or called

[George v. Morgan.]

by the name of Brin-Sion, with all its rights, members, privileges, and appurtenances, to hold to him and his heirs for ever, out of which his wife is to have no dowry or inheritance whatsoever, if she survives her said husband.

Also, I give and bequeath unto my three grand-daughters, Sarah, Elinor, and Jane Morgan, daughters of my said son Samuel, one hundred and twenty pounds, lawful money of Pennsylvania, to be equally divided between them, each to have their respective share when they attain the full age of eighteen years, and in case either of them die before they attain that age, then the said sum to be to the survivors or survivor of them living to the age aforesaid.

Also, I give and bequeath unto my son Mordecai, all that messuage or tenement plantation situate in Radnor aforesaid, called by the name of the Hall of Nantmell, which I purchased of Richard Orme, deceased, with about thirty-eight acres of woodland, part of my other land adjoining, as by a late survey appears, containing in the whole about two hundred acres, with all its rights, members, privileges, and appurtenances, to hold to him, for and during his natural life, and after his decease to the heirs of his body lawfully begotten, *and to their heirs for ever*, and in default of such *issue*, then to the heirs of my son Samuel, and their heirs for ever.

* * * * * * * * * *

And I do hereby nominate and appoint my sons Samuel and Mordecai sole executors of this my last will and testament. To whom I give and bequeath all the rest and remainder of my estate, not hereinbefore given, of what kind, nature, and quality whatsoever and wheresoever to be found, to be equally divided between them. * * *

In testimony whereof, &c.

It was assigned for error:

1. That the judge erred in instructing the jury, that Mordecai Morgan took an estate-tail under the devise made to him in the will of John Morgan, dated the 6th of October 1744.

2. That the judge erred in admitting in evidence the deed from Joshua Morgan to Joseph Morgan and Samuel Morgan, dated January 20th, A. D. 1848, together with the record of the Court of Common Pleas of Delaware county, or either of them, as stated in the bill of exceptions.

3. That the court erred in instructing the jury, that "although the act of Assembly to facilitate the barring of entails has not been complied with—whereby the deed (of 20th January, A. D. 1848) is ineffectual for such purpose—still it is the opinion of the court it is available in the claim to possession."

4. The court erred in instructing the jury to find verdicts for the plaintiffs.

[George *v.* Morgan.]

5. The court erred in refusing and omitting to instruct the jury to find verdicts for the defendants.

Lewis, for plaintiff in error.—1st point. In construing this devise, effect is to be given to every word employed by the testator to manifest his intent, and no word or phrase is to be rejected to which effect can be legally given. In cases of wills, the governing rule of construction is the intent of the testator, which the court is to find out by his words, and to construe conformably thereto, as far as possible, consistent with the rules of law:" Lord HARDWICKE, in Browswood *v.* Edwards, 2 *Ves. Sr.* 247; Frogmorton *v.* Bramstone, 3 *Bur.* 1622. "Within a century past a more liberal construction of the words of a testator has prevailed:" Goodright *v.* White, 3 *Bl. Rep.* 1010. It is the cardinal rule in the construction of wills that the intention of testator to be collected from the whole instrument—or as is sometimes expressed, from the four corners—is to govern: per Justice ROGERS, in Johnson *v.* Morton, 10 *Barr* 247; *id.* 500, per COULTER, J.

The construction given to this devise below, requires that the words "for and during his natural life, and after his decease," as also the words "and to their heirs for ever," shall be expunged or disregarded as expressions indicative of the testator's intent. This liberty is taken with the will, on the ground that some *general intent* may be thus answered, to which any *particular intent* is to give way. But in this devise there is no conflict between a particular intent and a general intent. Mordecai the first, can take for life, remainder to his issue or children living at his death, in fee. This violates no rule of legal policy. Besides, these phrases are vague at best, and might well be exploded.

Powell, remarking on the case of Wright *v.* Leigh:—"The case cannot be considered as having any weight in producing a revival of the absurd, and, we have seen, discarded doctrine of general and particular intention, of which the writer will only further observe, that since it has long ceased to exist—if it ever existed—*in fact*, it were much to be wished that it were completely exploded in name." And calls it a doctrine vague and indefinite, "and fraught with absurdity and mischief:" 2 *Powell on Devises* 559.

The intention in this case, independent of any artificial rules of construction, is manifest.

At the time the will was made, Mordecai the first had a son, to whom the terms issue and heirs of his body might apply. He, Mordecai the first, was a young man, aged thirty-one at the date of the will, and might have other children; and if he should have, it was not intended to exclude them. They were the persons designated to take the remainder, and the words, "their heirs for ever," express the quantity of estate intended to be given, to wit, a fee simple: Goodright *v.* White, *Bl. Rep.* 1010.

[George v. Morgan.]

Our second point, therefore, is,—The words, "*heirs of the body*," and "*such issue*," as used by the testator, are to be understood as meaning *children or issue* living at the time of his decease. This construction gives effect to all the words of the devise: Archer's case, 1 *Coke's Rep.* 66; *Skin.* 430; Clerk v. Day, *Sir F. Moore* 593; 2 *Bl. Rep.* 1010; Long v. Beaumont, 1 *P. W.* 229. See also Henry v. Purcell, 2 *Bl. Rep.* 1002; Bagshaw v. Spencer, 1 *Ves. Sen.* 142; same case, 2 *Atk.* 570; 3 *East* 103; Table 2, 7 *Law. Lib.*; 2 *Burr* 1109; 7 *Taunton* 362; 5 *B. & C.* 866; 12 *Eng. C. L.* 392.

These are all English cases. It is not doubted that in England at the present day the devise now before the court would not be decided to give to Mordecai Morgan the first an estate-tail under the rule in Shelly's case; but, on the contrary, the plain intention of the testator would be allowed to prevail.

If among the decisions in the English books, some exist which cannot be reconciled, it may be lamented; but we are not to suffer for this. Pennsylvania has her own law on this subject, perfectly adapted to her own peculiar situation, settled by a long series of solemn adjudications; all of which are not now to be changed by the reappearance of the rule in Shelly's case. Long prior to the date of the will of John Morgan, (1744,) primogenitureship (if it ever had existed within her limits) had been renounced as inconsistent with both the feelings and prosperity of the people. This vital and wide difference between the descent of real estate in the two countries could not fail to have its effect upon the application of the rule in Shelly's case.

The "superadded words," as they are called, are admitted by every text writer (except, perhaps, Hargrave) to take a case out of the application of that rule, wherever "they break the line of descent." Why so? Because in such case they show the intention of the testator. In England, in nineteen instances out of twenty, the descent of the fee simple and the estate-tail are the same. In Pennsylvania, in nineteen instances out of twenty they vary. It follows, then, that the intention shown by the use of the superadded words is twenty times as strong in Pennsylvania as it would be in England. These superadded words exist in our case, although they were thrown out of it by the judge below without any reason assigned.

In *Pennsylvania*, where the word *heirs* is used, it is not applicable only to the heir at common law, but refers to our system of descent: 4 *Pa. L. J.* 193; 2 *Yeates* 54; 2 *Bin.* 20; 10 *Watts* 190; 3 *Barr* 158.

The leading case in Pennsylvania is that of Findley v. Riddle, 3 *Bin.* 139. This case was carefully argued three times. First, before Chief Justice TILGHMAN, at a circuit court for Franklin

[George v. Morgan.]

county, in June 1807, when he intimated an opinion that John took only an estate for life, but reserved the point.

2d. It was argued before him on a motion for a new trial, when he said, " Nothing can be more clear than that the testator meant to give his son John an estate for life only."

The case then came, by appeal, before the court in banc. In the opinions of the court, it is believed that almost every case upon the subject decided in either England or Pennsylvania up to that time was collected and investigated. See also Dunwoody v. Read, 3 *Ser. & R.* 435, where the same doctrine is held, so far as regards the estate-tail; Abbot v. Jenkins, 10 *Ser. & R.* 296.

In the case before us, there is the express estate for life to Mordecai Morgan the first, and the remainder is limited to all his issue, not successively, but to take all at the same time equally, and in fee simple. The time when they are so to take, is the death of Mordecai Morgan the first: 5 *Rawle* 231.

These cases are sufficient to establish the doctrine that at least in Pennsylvania the *plain intention* of the testator is at this day too strong for what was the rule in Shelly's case. Intention is paramount to all technical words: Miller v. Lynn, 7 *Barr* 443; Thompson v. Currin, 10 *Barr* 498.

If the rule in Shelly's case must be applied to this devise, the proper application of it will give to Mordecai Morgan the first *a fee simple*, and not an estate-tail.

3d. The bill of exceptions to the admission in evidence of the instrument dated 28th January 1848, and the proceedings to bar the estate-tail, may be considered in connection with the charge of the court that such instrument was sufficient to enable the plaintiff to recover. The court admitted that such instrument had no effect to bar the estate-tail. Then it was a mere nullity. The object for which alone it was made utterly failed. It had no legal existence until recorded within six months in the recorder's office of the proper county. It never has been so entered. If any estate-tail existed, it still remains in Joshua Morgan, the eldest son of James Morgan. The instrument was intended to convey, and did convey, an estate-tail or nothing. This is apparent on its face. There is no consideration for it, if it did not pass an estate in tail.

The deed of 16th June 1807, from James Morgan to Joseph Morgan and others, was a partition which these plaintiffs cannot dispute. No one but the owner of the estate-tail can do so or recover these premises.

E. and *W. Darlington*, for defendants in error.—1. Mordecai Morgan, the devisee, took an estate-tail in the premises in question under the will of his father, by virtue of the rule in Shelly's case. That rule is, " When the ancestor, by any gift or conveyance, takes an estate of freehold, and in the same gift or conveyance an

[George v. Morgan.]

estate is limited, either mediately or immediately, to his heirs in fee or in tail, always in such cases heirs are words of limitation of the estate, and not words of purchase:" 1 *Co.* 104 a; *Co. Litt.* 376. This is regarded as an unbending rule of property in England and in Pennsylvania, in all cases falling within its terms: Findley *v.* Riddle, 3 *Bin.* 159; Carter *v.* McMichael, 10 *Ser. & R.* 429; Paxson *v.* Lefferts, 3 *Rawle* 59. This case falls strictly within the rule—Devise "to M. for life"—"and after his decease to the heirs of his body lawfully begotten, and to their heirs for ever"—"and in default of such issue," over. The cases both in England and in this State show that the rule is maintained, and the question here presented has been again and again substantially decided: See 4 *D. & E.* 82; 2 *Strange* 729; Shelly's case, 1 *Coke* 104 a; *Hayes on Estate-tail*, 7 *Law Lib.* 106; 1 *Yeates* 332, 10 *Ser. & R.* 429, Carter *v.* McMichael; 1 *id.* 203; 17 *Ser. & R.* 444; 3 *Rawle* 59; Heilman *v.* Bouslaugh, 1 *Harris* 344.

2. The deed from Joshua Morgan to Joseph and Samuel Morgan, although not recorded so as to bar the entail, nevertheless conveyed the life estate of the tenant in tail, and in this possessory action is sufficient to entitle plaintiff below to recover. It was a fair sale for valuable consideration, $400. It was not its sole object to bar the entail. Even if it were, if it could not so operate; it might operate to pass the possessory right.

Tenant in tail may convey his life estate. It may be sold from him on execution: Armstrong *v.* Dornerger, 16 *Ser. & R.* 323; Elliot *v.* Pearsoll, 8 *W. & Ser.* 38.

A conveyance in fee of a life estate is no forfeiture of a remainder: McKee *v.* Pfout, 1 *Dal.* 486.

An agreement to convey a larger estate than the party has, is good for such estate as he might possess: Rohr *v.* Kindt, 3 *W. & Ser.* 567. A sale by the sheriff of a lot, when the defendant had but a ground-rent in it—the ground-rent passes: Streaper *v.* Fisher, 1 *Rawle* 155.

Lewis, in reply.—The word *heirs* is not used in its strict technical sense, but indiscriminately with the word *issue*, deemed by the testator equipollent; yet issue is a word of purchase, and not of limitation, and in wills may be construed to suit the intent of the testator; 3 *Rawle* 75; 1 *Ser. & R.* 155; *Hayes on Estates-tail*, table 4; 4 *D. & E.* 294. If issue of the body be substituted for heirs of the body, the testator's intent is preserved: 1 *Ld. Raym.* 203. The word *issue* is not to be blotted from the will; it explains testator's intent. Issue and heir used as synonymous in Clerk *v.* Day, *Sir F. Moore* 593. See also 4 *D. & E.* 294; Archer's case, 1 *Co.* 66; 3 *Keb.* 100.

This construction is not confined to cases in which the word *issue* occurs, but is applied where the word *heirs* is used in the same

[George v. Morgan.]

sense: 2 *Bl. Rep.* 1010; 1 *P. Wms.* 229; 1 *Ves. Sr.* 142. The word *heirs* is sometimes applied to *heir apparent.* See 2 *Lev.* 232. Here the words "heirs of his body" were used as equivalent *to issue or children.*

In Pennsylvania, where the word *heirs* is used, it is not alone applicable to the *heir* at common law, but refers to our system of descents: 4 *Pa. L. J.* 193; 2 *Yeates* 54; 2 *Bin.* 20; 10 *Watts* 190; *id.* 289; 3 *Bin.* 158; opinion of Judge GRIER, in the case of Packer *v.* Nixon, in the Circuit Court at Philadelphia.

W. M. Tilghman, also for plaintiffs in error.—Each case depends on its own circumstances. The grandfather, the testator, supposed that he was providing for all his children. The will was made 100 years ago. It was long acquiesced in. Our proposition is that the testator used the words "*heirs of his body* lawfully begotten," not in their strict legal sense, but as synonymous with *children.* The words, if construed as an estate-tail, would conflict with the estate *in fee* granted in the next clause. The rule is that where the *superadded words*, (that is, the words used after the terms "heirs of the body,") import distribution, the words "heirs of the body" are not to be construed strictly as meaning an estate-tail; and he contended that in this case the superadded words import distribution: Crosby *v.* Davis, 4 *Pa. L. J.* As to the case of Heilman *v.* Bouslaugh, 1 *Harris*, it was on a *deed*; and in a deed the term heirs of the body are terms of art, and the court did not go into other parts of the deed to ascertain *the actual intention.* But in a will the case is different, the actual intention is to be considered. It is not, however, admitted that the term "heirs of the body" means, in Pennsylvania, an estate-tail—but that the term "heirs" imply distribution. He referred to another part of the will to show in what sense the testator used the terms "heirs of the body." In this case the limitation over is *in fee*, and is to be considered as showing that the testator was not wedded to an estate-tail.

The opinion of the court was delivered April 21, by

BELL, J.—The rule in Shelly's case has been so repeatedly recognised as a feature of our law, that further discussion is precluded. In the recent case, Heilman *v.* Bouslaugh, 1 *Harris* 344, if not satisfactorily vindicated, it is, at least, shown to be a settled rule of property in Pennsylvania, not to be put aside but at the risk of unsettling titles, and the introduction of confusion and uncertainty. Indeed, our numerous concurring decisions on this point, if any effect is to be accorded to them, must terminate, in our courts, further speculation as to the original propriety of the rule, and confine us to the inquiry whether the terms used to express the disposition of an estate fall within its operation. In

[George v. Morgan.]

settling this question, when it springs from a last will, no influence is to be conceded to any supposed prohibition of the rule by the testator, or to the defeat of a particular intention by its interposition. Whether it shall be effective as a governing principle is not subject to his discretion where the form of testamentary direction invites it to action, and the frequent frustration of a partial design is one of its acknowledged consequences. In its application, the effort is to give effect to the leading intent, though at the sacrifice of a minor purpose, and, therefore, in this, as in other cases, the first inquiry is, what is the great object of the devisor. The ascertainment of this is, doubtless, subject to the ordinary rules of construction; but where well-considered and unimpeached adjudications have assigned to certain forms of disposition a determinate result, we are bound by it as an ascertained law of construction. In saying this, I am not unmindful of the oft-repeated remark that, as every testament is apt to present some feature peculiar to itself, the interpretation of one can render but little aid in assisting to the proper meaning of another. This is true; but it is equally so that where a particular manner of devise has become the subject of frequent adjudication, certainly without which there is no safety, public or private, it is requisite that the rule so settled shall be followed in all similar cases. This is peculiarly so, where the form of the disposition is constituted of terms of art, to which an ascertained meaning is commonly affixed.

The devise before us stands, I think, in this category. To say nothing of numerous English cases, it is impossible to distinguish it, in principle, from our own deliberate determinations in Carter v. McMichael, 10 *Ser. & R.* 429; Paxson v. Lefferts, 3 *Rawle* 59, and the prior decisions on which they are based. It is true, that, in the first of these, the limitation was to the *heirs male* of the body of the first taker, and the heirs and assigns of such heirs male; from whence Chief Justice TILGHMAN deduced an argument favoring the application of the rule in Shelly's case. But the conclusion was not made to rest solely on this. A very important part of the argument was drawn from the fact, that unless an estate of inheritance was given to the first taker, the remainder limited over in fee simple must be defeated. And the latter condition was the governing reason in Paxson v. Lefferts, with a reference to the precedent case. That devise was almost, if not altogether, identical with the present. The land was given to the testator's son Charles, during his natural life, and if he should leave lawful issue, then to them, their heirs and assigns for ever; but for want of such lawful issue, over in fee. It will be observed, the only difference is in the employment of the words "lawful issue," instead of "heirs of the body," used in the first part of our disposing clause. But if there be a distinction, this difference is in favor of the construction claimed by the plaintiffs below, since

[George v. Morgan.]

"heirs of the body" are, strictly, words of limitation, while the other terms operate, in a deed, as words of purchase, though they may be taken either way in a will. In our case, we may, consequently, accept, without further argument, what cost Mr. Justice KENNEDY some reasoning to prove in Paxson *v.* Lefferts, namely, that the terms employed imported limitation, and not purchase. On the argument before us, some stress was laid upon the substitution of "such issue" for "heirs of his body," as showing they were employed as expressive of the same meaning; and it was argued that as "issue of the body" are sometimes treated as terms of purchase, the court ought to lean towards that construction here. To this, a reference to the last case might be regarded a sufficient answer; but it may be added that, as a general rule, the words relied on, used in a will in reference to an estate in land, operate as a further limitation, unless there be something in the context to show the testator contemplated a failure of issue at a particular period, and not an indefinite failure. The question was made in Geering *v.* Shenton, 1 *Cowp.* 410, a case, in most of its features, very like the present. It was a devise to J. S. and the heirs of his body, lawfully begotten, and their heirs for ever; but in case the said J. S. should die without leaving *issue of his body*, then over in fee. It was held that the devisee took in tail, the words "shall die without issue of his body" qualifying the preceding general words. As adverse to this construction, it was urged that, by the superadded words of limitation, the testator evinced an intention to give to the issue of the first taker a fee as purchasers. But Lord MANSFIELD inquired of the counsel whether he knew of any case where, upon a limitation of lands upon a dying without issue, those words had been confined to a dying without issue living at the time of his death. The distinction, he added, is between a devise of lands and of personal estate: in the latter case, the words are taken in their vulgar sense; that is, a dying without issue living at the time of the death of the first taker; but in the former, standing unexplained, they mean an indefinite failure of issue. Goodright *v.* Pullen, 2 *Ld. Raym.* 1437, may also be mentioned in this connection. There the devise was to N. for life, and, after his decease, to the heirs male of the body of the said N., lawfully to be begotten, and his heirs for ever; but if the said N. shall happen to die without such heir male, then over. It was argued that the use of the word "his," in the singular, brought the devise within Archer's case, and, consequently, the first taker took but an estate for life. But the court answered that, "heirs male of the body" imported an estate-tail, and this was not to be overruled by doubtful expressions; that ever since King *v.* Melling, 3 *Keb.* 100, it was so settled as not to be disputed, that the word "heirs" is, properly, a word of limitation, and not

[George v. Morgan.]

of purchase, and so, in a will, is "issue" unexplained, though it is different in a deed.

Indeed, it may be safely asserted that the words "if he shall leave issue," or "in default of issue," and the like, are uniformly construed to mean an indefinite failure of issue, unless there be something in the context to qualify the general expression, or the reference be expressly to persons then existing. As early as Wilde's case, this doctrine was averred, and it is said that whenever the term "issue" is used in reference to persons not in *esse*, it is synonymous with the terms "heirs of the body." Nor is it enough, to avoid this consequence, that the person named as the source of inheritable blood had issue at the date of the devise, unless it appear such living issue was, particularly, in contemplation of the testator at the moment, as the commencement of an inheritable stock. Of this, Goodright v. White, 2 *Bl. Rep.* 100; Long v. Beaumont, 1 *P. Wms.* 229, and Bagshaw v. Spencer, 1 *Ves. Sen'r* 142, are usually cited as examples. They were devises to the heirs of the body or issue of persons known to the testator to be in full life, having children, and the questions were whether there was a sufficient designation of the persons to take? From the very nature of the case, it was held the parties thus pointed to might take *designatione personæ*, and as though they had been specifically named. It is scarcely necessary to add, this doctrine has no application in the instance before us, though the first Mordecai had a son living at the time of the devise. Had that son died, it cannot admit of doubt any subsequently born issue would have taken under this devise, as heir of the body and competent to carry on the succession by inheritable blood.

To the cases already noticed, I will only add Morris v. Le Gay, cited by Lord KENYON in Denn v. Puckey, 5 *D. & E.* 324, and with approbation, in our own cases of Carter v. McMichael, and Paxson v. Lefferts. I introduce it, because it appears to me to be exactly alike, and decisive of the present. The devise was to A. for life, remainder to the heirs of the body of A. *and their heirs*, and if A. died *without issue of her body*, over. It was decided that A. took an estate-tail.

The adjudications I have referred to, and those upon which they are based, furnish an answer to the objection most prominently urged for the defendants below, that the superadded words, serving to limit a fee in the issue of the first taker, show the testator intended to constitute them the stock of a new descent as purchasers, and they are, therefore, not to be treated as branches of their own progenitors. It has long been settled that superadded words of limitation engrafted on words of procreation will not operate to turn these into words of purchase, unless the super added word denote a different species of heirs from that described by the first words, thus showing an intent to break the ordinary

[George v. Morgan.]

line of descent from the first taker: *Har. Law Tr.*, 504; 1 *Ferne Rem.* 181. Following Ferne, Mr. Justice KENNEDY lays it down, in Paxson *v.* Lefferts, 3 *Rawle* 59, that if the words be "heirs," or "heirs of the body," or "issue of the body," words of inheritance engrafted on them, if not inconsistent with the nature of the descent pointed out by the first words, will not convert them into words of purchase.

But it is urged upon us that as, in England, an intention to change the line of descent is sufficiently manifested wherever the superadded words import eventual distribution of the estate among several, as if it be limited over as a tenancy in common, or to be divided equally among all the heirs of the first taker,—in Pennsylvania, since the abolition of the right of primogeniture, such a devise as we have here, must be taken as changing the descent; the superadded words, "and to their heirs for ever," necessarily importing, not the heir in tail, who is generally the right heir in England, but all the lineal descendants of the *præpositus*, who take as parceners with us, under the general title of heir. I confess, I was much struck with the view when it was first presented, and very much inclined to adopt it as consistent with reason. But further reflection has satisfied us it is inadmissible. In the first place, it frequently happens that, even in England, the right heirs of a devisor may be of persons entirely different from him who would alone take as heir in tail, and yet it has always been there held as essential, that to withdraw the devise from the power of the rule, distribution must be expressly contemplated, and shown to be so by some precise direction. Secondly, though in Findlay *v.* Riddle, 3 *Bin.* 139, Mr. Justice YEATES seemed much inclined to adopt the idea that, with us, a limitation to heirs general always imports distribution, and is therefore repugnant to the rule in Shelly's case, it was not received in our subsequent cases, though expressly urged upon the attention of the court, where full scope was afforded for its operation, had it been thought tenable. In the last case of Heilman *v.* Bouslaugh, the reasoning of the chief justice is in direct repudiation of it. All this is conclusive that, in this State, a testator is to be regarded as speaking in reference to the common-law system of descent.

The exception taken to the admission in evidence of the deed from Joshua Morgan to the plaintiff below was but little urged. Though inoperative to bar the entail, it is, questionless, good to convey the grantor's right of possession. A tenant in tail may convey his life estate, and surely an attempt to convey a larger interest, which fails from a merely technical objection, may carry such an estate as would pass without the omitted ceremony. As his beneficial right of present enjoyment may be sold under an execution, without affecting the future tenant in tail, Armstrong *v.* Dunager, 16 *Ser. & R.* 323; Elliot *v.* Pearsoll, 8 *W. & Ser.* 38,

[George v. Morgan.]

it will certainly pass by private grant; and this may exist under semblance of a grant of his whole estate, just as an agreement to convey a larger estate than the party has, is good for such estate as he may hold; Rohr v. Kindt, 3 *W. & Ser.* 567. The conveyance works, in fact, two distinct effects; one at common law, to pass the present interest; the other under the statute, to bar the entail, a defect in which can only be objected by a tenant in tail.

Judgment affirmed.

COULTER, J., dissented.

CASES

IN

THE SUPREME COURT

OF

PENNSYLVANIA.

MIDDLE DISTRICT—HARRISBURG 1851.

McClellan's Appeal.

1. The discretion given to the register as to granting letters of administration is limited to a selection from those asking the administration, if competent; from each class entitled to administer, in its order.

2. The widow is entitled to administration upon the estate of her deceased husband, and if she renounces, the register may select from the children or next of kin, preferring males to females; but the widow or next of kin or both combined cannot pass by one of the children or next of kin competent and willing to take the administration, and vest it in a stranger.

3. Though the widow released her right to the administration in favor of persons whom she designated, but who were not entitled to the same, and certain of the children afterwards joined with her in a petition in favor of such persons, it was held, that this was not an absolute, but only a qualified release or renunciation, and the designation being beyond her power, the paper was inoperative, and left her rights and those of the children as before.

APPEAL by James D. McClellan from the decree of the Register's Court of the county of *Lancaster*.

Joseph P. McClellan, late of Paradise township, Lancaster county, died intestate, at the residence of his son James, in Chester county, on the 25th of February last.

On the 5th day of March last, a renunciation, dated the 4th of the same month, of the right to administer, was filed by the widow with the register of Lancaster county, in which she desired that letters

[McClellan's Appeal.]

of administration be granted to James L. Jones and Samuel B. Thomas; and on the same day, without notice or citation to James D. McClellan, the appellant, letters of administration on the estate of the intestate were granted to those gentlemen.

The paper was as follows:

To the Register for the probate of wills and granting letters of administration in and for the county of Lancaster and State of Pennsylvania.

Whereas, my late husband, Joseph P. McClellan, late of the township of Paradise, in said county, deceased, died intestate, whereby the right of the administration of the estate of said deceased did devolve upon me, Mary E. McClellan, widow and relict of the said deceased. Now, know that for divers good causes and considerations, me, the said Mary E. McClellan specially moving, I have released and hereby do release all my right and title to the administration of the said estate to James L. Jones and Samuel B. Thomas, both of the borough of West Chester, in the county of Chester and State aforesaid, and desire that the same may be granted to the said James L. Jones and Samuel B. Thomas, my appointees. Witness my hand and seal, the 4th day of March, A. D. 1851. MARY E. McCLELLAN, [*Seal.*]

On the 11th day of April, A. D. 1851, James D. McClellan appealed from the decree of the register granting said letters. A citation was issued to the administrators to show cause why the decree of the register in granting letters of administration should not be set aside.

On the hearing before the Register's Court, the counsel for the appellees presented and read a petition addressed to that court, signed by the widow and her four children, Martha A. Jones, Francis E. McClellan, Joseph F. McClellan, and Robert M. McClellan. It was as follows:

In the matter of the citation to James L. Jones and Samuel B. Thomas, administrators of Joseph P. McClellan, deceased, to show cause why letters of administration should not be revoked. } In the Register's Court of Lancaster county.

To the honorable the judges of the Register's Court of Lancaster county:

The petition of Mary E. McClellan, widow of said Joseph P. McClellan, &c., respectfully represents,

That the said Joseph P. McClellan died on the twenty-sixth day of February last, leaving to survive him the above-named widow and five children, to wit: Martha Ann Jones, Francis E. McClellan, Joseph F. McClellan and Robert M. McClellan, aforesaid, and James D. McClellan, the eldest son aforesaid, by a former marriage; that the said Joseph F. McClellan is a minor above the

[McClellan's Appeal.]

age of twenty years, and the said Robert M. McClellan is a minor above the age of seventeen years.

The petitioners further represent that the said Mary E. McClellan released her right to administration of the estate of said decedent, and, with the approbation and consent of the petitioners, requested the register of wills, &c., of said county, to grant such administration to the aforesaid James L. Jones and Samuel B. Thomas; and that in pursuance thereof the said register did on the 5th day of March last grant letters of administration on said estate to the said James L. Jones and Samuel B. Thomas; that the said administrators duly filed an inventory of the personal estate of said deceased, and have proceeded in the administration of the same to the satisfaction of your petitioners; that your petitioners have full confidence in the integrity and capacity of said administrators, and believe that a change of administrators would subject the estate to increased expense and create unnecessary delay in its settlement; and that they are entitled to thirteen-fifteenths of the personal estate of said deceased. They therefore respectfully request that your honors will not revoke said letters of administration granted to the said James L. Jones and Samuel B. Thomas, as aforesaid. And they will, &c.

(Signed) MARY E. McCLELLAN, and others.

The appeal was heard on the 26th of April 1851, and the claim of James D. McClellan to administer was rejected entirely, and the decree of the register confirmed, the court being equally divided.

The intestate left to survive him a widow, Mary E. McClellan, (his second wife,) and issue five children, to wit, James D. McClellan, (the appellant,) *by his first wife*, Martha Ann *intermarried with James L. Jones, one of the appellees*, Francis E., Joseph F., and Robert M. McClellan, the last two of whom are minors.

Exceptions were filed:

1. That the court erred in rejecting the claim of right of James D. McClellan to exclusive administration, after appellees presented the declination of all the other next of kin.

2. In giving the letters to strangers, while any one of the next of kin remained capable to take and asking for them.

3. Even if any discretion were left in this case with the Register's Court, it erred in the exercise of that discretion.

The case was argued by *Parke*, for appellant.—1. He contended that the letters to Jones and Thomas should be revoked and given to James D. McClellan, the appellant. That the widow, having renounced, had no right to dictate to the register who shall administer. He being a judicial officer, must be governed by the law and his own judgment, particularly when there are next of kin of

[McClellan's Appeal.]

age, capable, and willing to take administration. The appellant is of the first class, has not declined, and is competent and willing to take the administration.

2. The next of kin, who have not renounced, preferring males to females among them, are entitled to the administration in preference to creditors and strangers, unless incompetency, unfitness from peculiar circumstances, or inability be established.

3. That the persons to whom the letters in this case were granted had no interest in the residue of the personal estate after payment of debts, and no action of the widow and a portion of the next of kin could deprive the appellant of his right to administer, or at least take part in the administration, and give it to strangers to the estate; the fact of Mr. Jones being intermarried with one of the next of kin, not destroying his character of a stranger under the former, and particularly the present law of this State.

4. If Jones's wife had not declined by her petition presented to court by her husband, he could not administer for her or in her right. By the former law, administration was committed to a *feme covert* alone, the husband assenting and entering into the bond in her place. If he did take part, it could only be by taking letters jointly with her *during coverture*. By the present law it is presumed that a *feme covert* is independent of her husband as to administration, and may administer and give bond, or decline as Mrs. Jones did, as if a *feme sole*. But if she had not declined, with assent of her husband, her right to administer could not be considered while any male next of kin, asking letters, remained undisposed of. Females next of kin, where there are males, are in a second class.

The act of 1832, *Dunlop* 521, has made very little alteration in the law as before understood, in relation to the right to administer: Ellmaker's Appeal, 4 *Watts* 38, per ROGERS, J. The commissioners, in their first report, p. 33, have endeavored in this section to arrange and condense the material provisions of the statute 21 *Hen*. 8, c. 5, *Rob. Dig.* 250, in relation to the persons entitled to letters of administration.

Section 22 of the law of 1832 prescribes with exactness who first, who second, who third, and who fourth are entitled, in classes. The discretion of the register, and, upon appeal, of the Register's and Supreme Court, is limited to select from those *asking*, if competent, in each class, in their order.

The English statute, *Rob. Dig.* 250, says the ordinary shall grant letters to the widow, or to the next of kin, or to both; and when divers, equal in degree of kin, claim, the ordinary to be at his election and liberty to accept any one or more making request where divers require; where any one person as next of kin asks, he is entitled.

The decisions in England upon this statute were that "the ordi-

[McClellan's Appeal.]

nary is to grant administration of the effects of the husband to the widow or next of kin; but he may grant it to either or both at his discretion. If the widow renounce administration, it shall be granted to the children, or other next of kin, in preference to creditors:" *Toller* 86.

The ordinary may grant administration *quoad* part to the wife and, as to the other part, to the next of kin; for in such case there can be no ground to complain, as the ordinary is not bound to grant it exclusively to either: *Tol.* 87; *Rob. Dig.* 252, note.

"But the administration is so much a *claim of right*, that a *mandamus* will be issued by the Court of King's Bench in favor of the party entitled to enforce it:" *Tol.* 87; 1 *East* 408.

It seems then the widow is not *exclusively* entitled first, but is only in the first class with the next of kin, from which class the ordinary has a discretion to select either or both, or a part of the next of kin, or a part with the widow.

And so it was here, before our statute of 1832; and is since by section 22, as *it* is but a condensation of the English statute, and not substantially altered: 4 *Watts* 38; 1st *Report of Commissioners* 53.

If then the register could not select beyond the first class, if any of them claimed, neither could the widow, nor the widow and all the next of kin but one who claimed, dictate by nomination or otherwise a person of an inferior class or a stranger; or *they* would be a judge, and more powerful than the law, the register, or the court; for neither could exclude or pass by a competent next of kin claimant of the first class.

This was the principle settled on argument, in Williams's Appeal, 7 *Barr* 259. The circumstances material were precisely similar in that case with the present. There, as here, all the persons entitled of the first class declined, except the claimant, (and his sister,) and the court affirmed the decision of the Register's Court, reversing the decree of the register who had given the letters to two strangers put in nomination by the persons entitled to consideration of the first class, who had declined, giving the letters to the male next of kin who claimed.

Here the very reverse has taken place, the Register's Court confirming the letters to two strangers, because nominated by all the first class who declined; and rejecting the claim of one of that class who had not declined but claimed to be appointed.

This decision has never been shaken or questioned, is in accordance with the English decisions, and is conclusive. He cited also *Williams on Executors* 246; 3 *Curtis's Rep.* 429; 1 *id.* 50; 10 *Barr* 454, Hassinger's Appeal; 1 *Jones* 157, Beaver's Appeal.

P. F. Smith, for appellees.—He contended that the register had authority to grant administration to the widow at his discretion, or to

[McClellan's Appeal.]

join with her any of the next of kin, preferring males to females, without notice to the next of kin or creditors.

2. The register was bound to respect the nomination of the widow, especially when there is no other person claiming: and *a fortiori*, the nomination of the widow and all the next of kin but one.

3. The widow having released, if the register was not bound by her nomination, the case was taken out of the statute, the next of kin had no claim *de jure*, and the register was authorized to grant administration to any fit person.

4. Should the grant to the present administrators be invalid, it is still to be referred to the register, to whom to grant administration of the class entitled; and the Supreme Court will not designate any individual of the class entitled as the proper person.

5. Should the present grant be invalid, the register is bound to make the grant to such individual of the class entitled as may be selected by a majority of interests.

The opinion of the court was delivered May 19, by

ROGERS, J.—The argument of the counsel for the appellee is based on the erroneous assumption that the widow is placed in a class by herself, and as such entitled to the administration of the estate; and this would appear to have been the apprehension of the Register's Court. The statute of 21 *Hen.* 8, c. 5, which, in relation to persons entitled to administration, is the same as the act of 1832, places the widow and next of kin on the same platform: 4 *Watts* 38, Ellmaker's Appeal; *Rob. Dig.* 250. Under the construction given to that act, the ordinary or register in this State, grants administration of the effects of the husband to the widow, or next of kin, or he may grant it to either or both, at his discretion. If the widow renounces administration, it shall be granted to the children, or other next of kin, in preference to strangers or even to creditors. The discretion given to the register is limited to a selection from those *asking, if competent*, in each class in their order: *Tol.* 86; *Wms. Ex'rs* 246. When the widow renounces her right to administer, it is the duty of the register to select from the children, or next of kin, a person or persons competent to perform the duties of administration, preferring males to females. In making the choice among this class, doubtless, great respect ought to be paid to the recommendation of those persons who have the most interest in the assets, on the reasonable presumption that those who have the greatest interest to increase the estate, are most fit to advise as to the administration. Thus far the cases go, but no further. It has never been understood, as is contended, that the widow or next of kin, or both combined, having the greatest stake in the estate, can pass by any one of the children, or next of kin, competent and willing to take, and vest the appointment in a stranger.

[McClellan's Appeal.]

On the contrary, directly the reverse is ruled in Williams's Appeal, 7 *Barr* 288. There, two of the sons of testator, who were his executors, having renounced, the register, at their request, granted letters of administration to a stranger, to which a third son and two of the daughters assented. A fourth son and a daughter having petitioned for a revocation, it was held that the register was bound to revoke the letters and grant administration to the person who consented to act. The facts of the case cited are precisely similar, with the immaterial exception that here the widow concurred in the nomination. There, as here, all the persons entitled of the first class declined, except the claimant and his sister, and the court affirmed the decision of the Register's Court, reversing the decision of the register, who had given the administration to two strangers, put in nomination by persons of the first class. Judge COULTER correctly says, that although the executors (also next of kin) may relinquish their own right, they cannot take away the rights of others. In principle, we perceive no difference in the cases. Williams's Appeal rules this point. We cannot affirm this, without reversing that.

But is the paper put in evidence to be viewed as an absolute or conditional, qualified renunciation of the widow and children? We think the latter is the correct interpretation. It is a release of her right to the present administrators, and nothing more. It would not have been executed, as we are warranted in believing, except on the erroneous supposition that it conferred, the register assenting, on the persons in whom they put trust and confidence, an unimpeachable title to administer the assets. The widow released all her right and title to the administration of the estate to James L. Jones and Samuel B. Thomas, and desired that administration be granted to the said James L. Jones and Samuel B. Thomas, her appointees. It is not an absolute, but qualified release or renunciation. It was, as we think, the obvious intention of the parties, to release on condition that their appointees be permitted to settle the estate. Having attempted what they had no power to do, the whole instrument becomes inoperative, leaving the rights of the widow and the heirs, or next of kin, as before. Being then of opinion that letters of administration were improperly granted to the appellees, the same are hereby revoked. The proceedings are remitted to the register, with directions to grant letters of administration according to law, to the widow, or next of kin, to one or more of them, according to his best discretion.

Kirkpatrick *versus* Muirhead.

1. In an action on a negotiable note brought by the payee against the drawer, the defendant may prove that the note in suit was given with another note, in lieu of a former note, which with other notes had been given by the drawer and another who was his partner, to another firm, for the purchase of certain personal property, and the lease of real estate, and that a portion of the personal property to a greater amount than the note in suit, had never been received by the purchasers, through default of the sellers, whereby there was a failure of consideration; and that the *original notes* had been transferred by the payees to the payee of the note in suit, not in the usual course of business, but merely as *collateral security* against certain liabilities incurred by the holder for the payees, no new consideration passing between the holder and payees of the original notes at the time of the transfer.

2. The circumstance that the suit upon the note had been tried several times before, and that the defence made in this suit was not then made, and that the note in suit had been given after a knowledge by the maker of the failure of consideration, will not preclude the defence, if the silence of the maker as to the failure of consideration did not mislead the holder, or unless the latter relinquished some advantages of which otherwise he might have availed himself, evidence being offered that the drawer, at the time of the giving of the new note, supposed that the transfer of the original note to the holder was in due course and for a valuable consideration.

3. Consideration, like every other part of a contract, must be the result of *agreement;* and the circumstance that the new note was not signed by both of the parties to the original note, (one being accidentally absent,) and that it was payable at a longer period than the original note, will not preclude the defence, the old note having been split into two, and further time being given, merely for convenience, and not because of any new consideration contemplated by the parties, the release of the other party not inducing the execution of the new note; but if this hypothesis as to time and party were *unfounded,* it was not for the court to say so; whether there was any new consideration leading to the execution of the new note sued, was a question of fact for the jury.

4. The party whose name was omitted in taking the new note, being released by the defendant, the maker of the note in suit was a competent witness in his favor, to prove a failure of consideration of the original notes, partial or total, after the original notes reached the plaintiff's hands, and that the note in suit was given for one of them.

5. The testimony of one of the payees of the original notes, given on a former trial of this case on the new note, was admissible on the part of the defendant to prove the consideration of the transfer to the plaintiff below of the original notes, the object not being to impeach the original notes; and it was not a valid objection to this testimony, that the jury might infer from other portions of the same testimony that the first notes were accepted as payment of pre-existent debts.

6. The inventory of the property for the purchase of which the former notes were given, was evidence, if the fact of its containing such an enumeration was established.

ERROR to the Common Pleas of *Lancaster county.*

This was an action of debt on a promissory note, brought by William Muirhead against William Kirkpatrick. The note was as follows:—

[Kirkpatrick v. Muirhead.]

11 March 1842, sixty days after date, I promise to pay to William Muirhead or order, at the Lancaster Bank, $186.22, without defalcation, value received.

WILLIAM KIRKPATRICK.

The case had been tried in December 1842, when verdict was rendered for defendant. The judgment was reversed. Tried again in March 1844, and verdict rendered for defendant. The judgment was reversed in May 1846. In 1848, again tried and verdict rendered for defendant; a new trial was granted. The pleas were payment, and payment with leave.

On the part of the plaintiff, the note was given in evidence.

It was alleged on the part of defendant, that the note in suit was given for the balance of a negotiable note, for $500, given by William Kirkpatrick and Ephraim Kirkpatrick to Jonathan Muirhead and John M. Capron, doing business under the firm of J. M. Capron & Co., dated June 17, 1839.

The defence set up by defendant was as follows:—

William Kirkpatrick purchased of Capron & Co. certain machine-shops, threshing-machines and castings, some of them being at the time of purchase at the foundry of Darling & Co., the manufacturers in Reading. After they were transferred to the plaintiff, he exchanged them for negotiable notes, amounting in all to $9047.40. The note of $500 above mentioned was the last of them, the others having all been paid. The following notice of special matter showed the defence:—

Under the pleadings in this case, defendant will give in evidence that the consideration of the note on which this suit is founded, was another note, given by William and Ephraim Kirkpatrick, for the purchase of certain personal property, and the lease of certain real property in the counties of Lehigh, Northampton, and Berks, from John M. Capron & Co. That said notes had been transferred to plaintiff, to secure him for certain liabilities that he had incurred for said Capron & Co., or some of said firm. That the consideration of said notes failed to a much larger amount than this note, which is all that remains unpaid of said notes. That among the articles sold, and which were to have been delivered, were 10 sets of castings, 7720 lbs. at 4½ cts., amounting to $347.40
  Fitting up, 450 cts... 45.00
  Patterns 150 cts... 150.40
————
$542.40

That said articles never were delivered to defendant, but were lost to him. That said Capron & Co. were to have paid the rent of a shop at Reading, to William Darling, Esq., amounting to $36.41, which defendant was compelled to pay. The said defendant was obliged to pay to William Darling, Esq., $87.93 for articles to com-

[Kirkpatrick v. Muirhead.]

plete the goods purchased as aforesaid from said Capron & Co., and which they by their contract were bound to pay or furnish.

On the trial of the cause, defendant called E. Kirkpatrick as a witness. He was objected to on the ground of interest. Defendant produced a release from William Kirkpatrick, defendant, to E. Kirkpatrick, for all cause for contribution and liability on account of any of the notes given for the purchase of the property in question; and especially on account of the note referred to, of the 17th of June 1839, and all liabilities in this suit. Witness rejected and excepted to by the defendant.

Defendant then proved by C. Anthony, that the notes of Kirkpatrick were transferred to plaintiff by Capron & Co., within ten days of their date, *as collateral security* for several notes endorsed by plaintiff for Capron & Co. in various banks. He also proved by George W. Houser, that the note in suit was given for the balance of one of the notes thus pledged.

Defendant then offered the inventory of the goods purchased, (for which the notes were given,) and offered to prove that the articles specified in the notice of special matter were never received by Kirkpatrick, but were retained by the makers (in whose shop they were) because they had not been paid for by Capron & Co. The court rejected the evidence, and defendant excepted.

Defendant offered to read from the notes of Judge HAYES, so much of Jonathan Muirhead's testimony, taken on a former trial of this case, as showed what the notes given by the Messrs. Kirkpatricks to Capron and Muirhead were transferred to defendant for, and when transferred, and that the note in suit was given for one of the above-stated notes, and that the transfer was not made in the regular course of business. This was offer 8.

And defendant offered to prove the same facts by Ephraim Kirkpatrick.

This evidence was offered for the purpose of introducing the defence already offered and specified in the previous bills of exception. This constituted the whole defence to the note.

The testimony of Muirhead was objected to, on part of plaintiff, because he is one of the firm of J. M. Capron & Co., and one of the payees of the original note, and an endorser of the same. Evidence rejected, and exception on part of defendant.

Defendant offered to prove that he did not know that the notes given by him and Ephraim Kirkpatrick were endorsed to William Muirhead for security merely, but supposed they were actually negotiable for value, in the regular course of business, until after he had given the note in suit; and that he had taken counsel to know whether, if the fact were as he supposed, he could set off failure of consideration as a defence, and was advised by the counsel that he could not. This advice was obtained shortly after the notes were

[Kirkpatrick *v.* Muirhead.]

transferred to William Muirhead; and then renewed the offer of the evidence just excluded. This was offer 9.

PER CURIAM.—There is no offer to prove that William Muirhead concealed from defendant the consideration, or that any fraud was practised upon defendant by plaintiff—defendant was bound to make diligent inquiry; he knew of the partial failure of consideration now complained of, when he gave the note in suit, obtaining the release of his joint payor and obtaining further time of payment. The defence as against plaintiff, if made out as offered, is destitute of equity. The testimony now offered is rejected.

Defendant excepted.

June 4, 1850, verdict for plaintiff for $276.28.

It was assigned for error:—1. The court erred in rejecting E. Kirkpatrick as a witness. 2. Also in rejecting inventory and proof in second bill of exceptions. 3. Also in rejecting Jonathan Muirhead to prove under what circumstances the notes were assigned to plaintiff, and to show that it was not in the regular course of business nor for value. 4. Also for rejecting offer 8. 5. Also for rejecting offer 9.

The case was argued by *Stevens*, for plaintiff in error.—The court rejected the principal part of the defendant's evidence, on the ground that if all was proved that was offered, it would form no defence to the note in suit. It seems the court acted on the following reason:

1. The original notes being negotiable and endorsed before due, no defence could have been set up to them.

2. The note in suit being given for one of the original notes after the failure of consideration was known to defendant, no defence could be made to it.

When a negotiable note is transferred as collateral security for liabilities already incurred, and not for value in the regular course of business, it is subject to the same defence in the hands of the endorsee as it would have been in the hands of the payee: 6 *Ser. & R.* 537, Harrisburg Bank *v.* Myer; *Chitty on Bills* 68–9; 5 *Johns. Ch. R.* 56; *Idem* 637, Bay *v.* Coddington; 3 *Kent* 79, 80, 81; 3 *B. & Cres.* 154, Gill *v.* Corbit; 13 *Wend.* 570, Rant *v.* French; *id.* 605.

The same defence lies to the new note as to the old one for which it was given: 15 *Mass.* 92, 96, Bridge et al. *v.* Hubard.

Defendant offered to show that he did not know what was the consideration of the transfer of the notes to plaintiff, and supposed it to have been for value, in the regular course of business. But as soon as he found that the transfer was only as collateral security, he refused to pay. He gave the note in ignorance of the facts.

The suggestion that further time was a part of the consideration

[Kirkpatrick v. Muirhead.]

had no foundation in fact. Nor was the note given to settle a dispute.

As to first bill of exceptions. Ephraim Kirkpatrick was a competent witness. He never was a party to the suit or to the note. The old note was cancelled, and he was released from all liability.

Second bill of exceptions. Jonathan Muirhead was a competent witness to prove what the transfer to plaintiffs was for, and that it was not in the regular course of business, and the time of endorsement.

"A party to a negotiable instrument actually negotiated may prove facts subsequent to its creation, yet he cannot *invalidate* it in its original consideration:" 9 *Ser. & R.* 236, Bank *v.* Walker; 10 *John. R.* 231; 11 *id.* 128; 1 *Phil. Ev.* [35–36], and the notes thereto; 11 *Pick.* 418, Sprig *v.* Louett, to prove the time of endorsement; *Chit. on Bills* 674.

Besides, it had been already proved, by Conrad Anthony, that the notes were transferred to plaintiff only as collaterals; and it has nowhere been proved that he was damnified. It was also proved that the notes originally transferred to plaintiff were not negotiable, and that he afterwards got defendant to give negotiable notes for them.

Frazer, for Muirhead, defendant.—Kirkpatrick was not a competent witness; he was one of the drawers of the old note, and although discharged by the new note, he was liable to defendant in the suit for contribution, and the release at law could not avail: 7 *W. & Ser.* 44, Reed *v.* Patterson; 8 *id.* 272; 5 *id.* 509, Post *v.* Avery; 5 *Barr* 395.

As to third error.—Muirhead was incompetent on the ground of policy. The offer was to show what took place *at the time the note was negotiated*, not after: 4 *W. & Ser.* 287, Parke *v.* Smith; 5 *Barr* 52, 53, Griffen *v.* Howell.

Fourth error.—The defence being an equitable one, defendant must show that he is entitled to equity. Plaintiff was a *bona fide* holder for value of the original note; the note in suit being in consideration of further time and a release of Ephraim Kirkpatrick from the former note, and no allegation of failure of consideration being made for nine years, the note in suit being a new contract, and the old note given up, takes from defendant all equity.

The opinion of the court was delivered May 19, by

BELL, J.—On the trial of this action, brought by the plaintiff below as payee of a promissory note drawn by the defendant below, the latter offered to prove, as a full defence, that the note in question was given in lieu of another note previously drawn by William and Ephraim Kirkpatrick in favor of Capron & Co., and delivered to them, with other notes, in payment of certain personal property,

[Kirkpatrick v. Muirhead.]

and the lease of certain real estate, purchased by the defendant for the drawees; that a portion of the personal chattels so purchased, to an amount greater in value than the sum called for by the note in suit, was never received by the purchasers, through the default of the sellers, whereby there was a total failure of consideration, and that the original notes were transferred by Capron & Co. to the plaintiff, not in the usual course of business, but simply as collateral security against certain liabilities incurred by him for the firm.

By the evidence given, or proposed to be given, it appeared that in the year 1840 William Kirkpatrick, or he with his brother Ephraim Kirkpatrick, purchased from Capron & Co., (of which firm Jonathan Muirhead was a partner,) certain machine-shops, with castings, materials, and patterns, necessary in the construction of machines, in payment of which the Kirkpatricks drew and delivered to the vendors their promissory notes for between seven and eight thousand dollars. Very shortly after this transaction, Capron & Co., who were in failing circumstances, transferred these notes to third persons, one of whom was the plaintiff below, who received two of the securities, as the defendant below alleges, merely as security for a pre-existing debt, or to protect him against certain prospective and contingent liabilities he had assumed in favor of the endorsers. One of the notes thus held being unpaid, it was, in the year 1842, on the proposition of the defendant below, broken into two notes, drawn by William Kirkpatrick alone, in favor of the plaintiff below, payable in thirty and sixty days. The reason given why Ephraim Kirkpatrick did not join in them, was his absence from home at the time; and this appears to have been accepted as sufficient by the plaintiff's agent. No objection was then made by Kirkpatrick to the original note, nor was any thing said about the defence now set up. As an excuse for this omission, evidence was offered to show that the defendant, until very recently, was under the impression the plaintiff had received the original notes in due course, and for a valuable consideration, and having, before the present note was given, consulted counsel, was instructed that if such was the fact, the defence now attempted would be unavailing, from whence he would deduce the reason for his silence in 1842.

One of the notes last given was paid, but the other remaining unsatisfied at maturity, the present suit was brought upon it shortly after it fell due. The action has been four times tried. On the first three investigations the defence was made to rest upon an averred set-off, and it was not until this failed, and upon the last trial in 1849, the objection now relied on was set up.

The Court of Common Pleas rejected the evidence offered to establish the facts I have briefly recapitulated, on several grounds. One of these was that, if made out, they would not constitute an

[Kirkpatrick v. Muirhead.]

available defence against the plaintiff's claim. In this conclusion we cannot concur.

Whatever contrariety of opinion may have existed elsewhere on this subject, it is the undoubted law of Pennsylvania that, though the holder of a negotiable instrument received in *payment* of a pre-existing debt, before maturity, cannot be subjected to equities which might have furnished a defence as between the original parties, and of which he had no notice, yet, if the paper be taken as *collateral security merely*, for the payment of a debt, or for protection against previously assumed liabilities, the defendant may aver any ground of defence which would have been competent between antecedent parties to the bill or note; unless, indeed, there was some new and distinct consideration moving between the parties to the transfer; such as giving up some other available security; releasing another party, drawer or endorser; conceding further time for payment, and the like: Petrie v. Clark, 11 *Ser. & R.* 377; Walker v. Geissee, 4 *Whar.* 258; Depeau v. Waddington, 6 *Whar.* 220. In all these cases, it is laid down that the transfer of mercantile paper as collateral security does not constitute the transferree a holder for a *valuable* consideration. The doctrine here proclaimed is in strict accordance with the decisions of several of our sister States. Thus in the leading case of Bay v. Coddington, 5 *Johns. Ch. R.* 54, it was ruled that the *bona fide* holder of negotiable paper, who has received it for a *valuable* consideration, without notice or reasonable ground to suspect a defect in the title of the person from whom it was taken in the usual course of business or trade, is entitled to full protection. But where he has taken it for an antecedent debt, either as nominal payment or as security for payment, without giving up any security he previously had, paying any money, or affording some new consideration, he is not a holder for *value*, who may recover, in despite of fraud practised by the person putting the note in circulation, or the failure of the consideration from which it originally sprang. "It is," said Chancellor KENT, who decided the cause, "the credit given for the paper, and the consideration *bona fide* paid on receiving it, that entitle the holder, on grounds of commercial policy, to extraordinary protection, even in cases of the most palpable fraud." In the same case, on appeal, 20 *Johns. Ch. R.* 637, WOODWORTH, J., observed, that "the reason of the rule affording protection would seem to be founded in the loss incurred by an innocent holder by giving credit to the paper, and having paid a fair equivalent for it." And he stated the true question to be, has he paid value for the note transferred, or made any new engagements as the consideration of the transfer? So in Kimbro v. Lytle, 10 *Yerger* 428, it was determined that, to prevent a note from being subjected to previous equities, it must be taken in due course of trade, that is, by one who has given his

[Kirkpatrick v. Muirhead.]

money for it, his goods, or his credit, at the time of receiving it, or who, then, on account of it, sustained some loss, or incurred some liability. Nichol v. Bate, in the same court, 10 *Yerger* 429, is to the same effect. There the note sued had been taken in lieu and by way of satisfaction of a previous note with a distinct endorser, which was given up at the time, and the learned judge who delivered the opinion, very clearly pointed out the distinction between such a case and that presented in Bay v. Coddington, where the paper sued on had been given to the holder as collateral security only, for liabilities incurred by him as endorser. This was followed by Wormley v. Lowry, 1 *Humph. (Tenn.) R.* 468, where the broad proposition was laid down, that a bill assigned before it fell due, for a pre-existing debt, is not an assignment within the meaning of the words "due course of trade," and it is, therefore, subject to be defeated in the hands of the assignee, upon proof of failure of consideration. In both these latter instances, it was particularly noticed, that the admissibility of the defence turned upon the question whether, by permitting it, the holder of the transferred securities would be placed in a worse or different situation than he would have occupied had he never received them. Where, said the court, one receives a note for a pre-existing debt, due from him only who assigns the note, he parts with nothing; he is in the same situation after a successful defence by the maker, as before he took the note.

I am not unaware of the apparent conflict of opinion, on this subject, between the Supreme Court of the United States, in Swift v. Tyson, 16 *Peters's R.* 16, and the courts of New York, in Bay v. Coddington, and other adjudications, the last of which is Stalker v. McDonald, where all the prior determinations are collected and reviewed in an elaborate and very able opinion pronounced by Chancellor WALWORTH, 6 *Hill* 93. That conflict does not, however, touch the precise question before us, for though Mr. Justice STORY, who delivered the judgment of the Federal tribunal, does intimate that a note endorsed simply as a collateral, is not open, in the hands of a stranger, to prior equities, the point for decision was, whether a negotiable instrument, received in *payment* of a pre-existing debt, is so open? A query, it was thought, the New York courts had answered affirmatively. Perhaps the seeming discrepancy is satisfactorily explained by Mr. Justice SHEPLEY, in Holmes v. Smyth, 4 *Shep. Maine R.* 177, as originating in the New York rule, which is said to be the English also, that a bill or note, whether of the debtor or a third person, taken for a prior debt, is not considered as payment, unless expressly so agreed; while in Maine and some other of the States the rule is different. Under this difference it is pointed out that, while in Maine and elsewhere the loss of the note taken in exchange would, consequently, occasion the loss of the whole debt, in New York it

[Kirkpatrick v. Muirhead.]

would put the party only where he was before; a difference of result which, as we have seen, works the whole distinction between a *bona fide* transfer for a *valuable* consideration, and such a transfer for a *valid* consideration only. Whether these suggestions are competent to reconcile the seeming jar, I need not stop to inquire, since, for our present purpose, it is enough to know that our decisions have recognised the difference between payment and security only; ruling that the former protects the *bona fide* holder against all defences founded in fraud or latent equities practised upon or existing between the original parties; while the latter leaves the door open to every inquiry which would have been pertinent had there been no transfer of the paper.

Conceding then as proved what the defendant below offered to prove, there can be no hesitancy in saying that were this action founded on the negotiable notes first transferred to the plaintiff, the defence relied on must have been available, since its success would leave the plaintiff in the same plight he was before he accepted the collateral security. The proposition is this:—The plaintiff having incurred certain liabilities as endorser of the paper of Capron & Co., the latter being in failing circumstances and unable to meet their engagements, transferred to the former one or more of the notes just before drawn by the Kirkpatricks in favor of the firm, as a security against any eventual loss that might overtake the plaintiff in consequence of his endorsements. Now, a failure of this security would leave him precisely in the position he occupied before the transfer; and consequently, in reference to the notes first transferred, he is to be regarded as a holder for a *valid*, and not a *valuable* consideration.

Did the subsequent transaction, which resulted in the creation of the note now sued, change this position, and, as a consequence, invest the holder with rights and remedies not before possessed? The court below seems to have so thought, for as one reason for rejecting the proffered proof, it is said the facts averred, if proved, would constitute no defence against the plaintiff, after giving him a new note, *upon a new consideration as to time and parties*, three years after knowledge of the alleged failure of the consideration. If, otherwise, the proposed defence is sustainable, the mere lapse of time before averring it, and even the making of a new note in silence, would not operate to destroy it, unless the *laches* misled the plaintiff into the assumption of fresh liabilities, or induced him to relinquish some advantage he might otherwise have availed himself of. No feature of this kind appears to characterize the case. Were it so, the neglect to inform the holder of the failure of consideration might possibly compromise the defence. But, in the absence of such an element, I cannot concede it was the duty of the drawer to inform himself of the terms of the transfer, or that he was culpably remiss in entertaining, without special inquiry, the

[Kirkpatrick *v.* Muirhead.]

impression that his notes had been passed to the plaintiff for a valuable consideration and in the due course of business. Certainly, up to the time when the two last notes were given, his silence will not operate to stop his averment of failure of consideration; and I do not perceive how the mere fact of his giving new notes should work such an effect, or why this should preclude him from showing the reason of his silence, as explanatory of what might otherwise be a suspicious circumstance. Nor will his neglect to avail himself of his present defence until that first set up failed him detract from its vigor. One having several answers to a legal claim, may choose which he will first aver, and can only be precluded from resorting to others by a final verdict. Here, the prior verdicts were set aside, and consequently, upon the last trial the field of attack and defence was as open and unincumbered to both parties as though no prior jury had passed upon the dispute.

But a more serious reason for the rejection of the evidence is found in the assumption that the last notes were given upon a new consideration as to time and parties. If this were so, it would be decisive. I have already intimated that where the transferred bill or note is taken upon a distinct consideration, it is within the general rule of protection; and certainly the extension of the time of payment, or the release of an endorser or other party before bound might constitute such a consideration. But upon the case as it is now presented, I have failed to perceive any such. Consideration, like every other part of a contract, must be the result of agreement. The parties must understand and be influenced to the particular action by something of value or convenience and inconvenience, recognised by all of them as the moving cause. That which is a mere fortuitous result flowing accidentally from an arrangement, but in no degree prompting the actors to it, is not to be esteemed a legal consideration. Now, in the instance before us, it is true that when Houser, as the agent of the plaintiff, called on William Kirkpatrick, the latter complained he was not ready to pay, and proposed, *if he could have more time,* to divide the note then in Houser's possession into two notes, and it was accordingly so done. But it is nowhere said, or hinted, that the extension of the time of payment, was the consideration which influenced Kirkpatrick to give, or Houser, as representing the plaintiff, to accept the new notes. Indeed, it is difficult, under the circumstances, to entertain any such belief. The plaintiff could derive no advantage from taking new notes, unless he intended to negotiate them; more especially as the name of Ephraim Kirkpatrick was omitted, and time could as well have been given on the old note as upon the new. Looking to the facts developed, I should incline to say the old note was split into two merely for the convenience of payment, and not because of a new consideration contemplated by the parties. As to the omission of Ephraim Kirkpatrick as one of the drawers,

[Kirkpatrick v. Muirhead.]

it certainly did not enter into their imagination that release of his prior liability induced, in the slightest degree, the execution of the new notes. William, from the beginning, appears to have been the principal party, and the one looked to for payment. On the negotiation between him and Houser, not a word was said about releasing his brother Ephraim, nor does it appear to have been considered as of any importance whether he joined in the new notes or not. All said upon the subject was, that if Ephraim was at home, he would put his name to the paper. His absence seems to have been accepted without comment, as a sufficient reason why he did not, and no proposition was submitted for preparing the notes with reference to his joining in them at some other time. In short, Houser was profoundly indifferent as to Ephraim becoming a party, and the transaction was finally concluded as though he never had been. At least it so appears to me. But if the hypothesis I have indulged, as to time and party, be entirely unfounded, it was not for the court below to say so. Whether there was a new consideration leading to the execution of the note sued, was a question of fact for the jury. By altogether excluding the offered evidence, the court precluded the jury assuming of itself to determine the fact. In this, a mistake was committed.

There is yet, however, another objection urged against the admissibility of the proposed evidence. The witnesses called to prove the facts to which reference has been made, were Ephraim Kirkpatrick and Jonathan Muirhead one of the firm of Capron & Co., and, as such, an endorser of the note in question. The former of these was first objected to on the ground of interest, but he was released at the bar. It was insisted that, notwithstanding this, he remained incompetent, either under the doctrine of Post v. Avery, 5 *W. & Ser.* 509; Read v. Patterson, 7 *W. & Ser.* 44, and the subsequent cases of that class; or, as a party to the note, excluded from impeaching it on grounds of policy. But neither of these grounds of objection are tenable. The rule established by the cases just cited is applicable only to assignors of *choses in action*, called to assist in their recovery by their oaths. It was so applied to the very witness adduced on a former trial of this cause to prove an alleged set-off: 2 *Barr* 225; but his present relation to the contest is entirely different. It is unnecessary to say more on this point, after the repeated reviews this rule of evidence has recently been subjected to.

As to the remaining objection, it might be sufficient to say the proposed witness is not a party to the note in suit. He was purposely omitted as such, and it may therefore admit of strong doubt, whether, for any purpose, he can be so treated. If, however, it be conceded the last notes were emanations of the first, and so connected with them that Ephraim's original relation to them must be considered as still subsisting, he will stand in the same category as

[Kirkpatrick *v.* Muirhead.]

Jonathan Muirhead, the other proposed witness, and subject to the same objection. We may, therefore, conveniently consider as one the exceptions taken to the admission of each of them.

Though, in a great measure, departed from in England, the rule of policy broached in Walton *v.* Shelley, has been adhered to in Pennsylvania, where the contest is in reference to mercantile paper. That rule prohibits a party to a negotiable instrument, actually negotiated, from impeaching it as a witness, by showing facts destructive of its validity which had place at its inception. The law says, one who assists to give currency to negotiable security is not afterward receivable to prove that it is not, in truth, what it purports to be on its face, or to show fraud or other defect in its origin. Nor will he be permitted to remove a preliminary difficulty to make way for his evidence in chief; as, for instance, by testifying that one apparently a *bona fide* endorser is, in fact, an original party to the paper, or that he paid no value for it; for, say the cases, if he could thus clear the way for his evidence attacking the note itself, he might as well be admitted to swear in chief at once, since both species of proof are equally within the prohibitory policy. While a primary objection remains to his competency unremoved, he cannot be permitted to open his mouth. Following prior cases, so much was determined in Bank of Montgomery *v.* Walker, 9 *Ser. & R.* 236, and Griffith *v.* Reford, 1 *Rawle* 296. But admitting the validity of the transfer, there is no rule which closes the mouth of a party from stating facts subsequent to the date of the note, tending to discharge it or to destroy the title of the holder. Thus in Woodhull *v.* Holmes, 10 *Johns. Rep.* 231, it was ruled the endorser of a note is a good witness to prove the note was fraudulently put in circulation by an agent to whom it was delivered to be discounted, but who, instead, put it into the hands of a broker; "for," said the court, "though a party cannot be called to invalidate the note in its inception or creation, by showing force or fraud, or that the consideration was corrupt or illegal, he may be called to show that after it was regularly drawn and endorsed and delivered to a third person, for a lawful purpose, and consistent with the validity of the note, that person deceived them, and fraudulently circulated the note." So in White *v.* Robbing, 11 *Johns. Rep.* 128, an endorser was admitted to prove payment of a note before its transfer. In Gilpin *v.* Howell, 5 *Barr* 52, a party to a note was received to show a subsequent failure of consideration, upon the broad ground that he may prove any subsequent facts subversive of the holder's right to recover, which do not touch its original validity. An examination of the numerous cases cited for the defendant in error, will manifest that in every case where the witness's mouth has been closed, the proposition was to impeach the instrument in its concoction, or, by attacking the propriety of the transfer, to open

[Kirkpatrick *v.* Muirhead.]

the way for such an impeachment. But nothing of this kind was offered here. The validity of the original endorsement to the plaintiff was fully conceded, together with the entire effectiveness of the original notes as securities at their inception. Making this concession, the defendant proposed nothing more than to show a subsequent failure of consideration, partial or total, after the notes reached the plaintiff's hands. Any party to the note, having no interest in the issue, was competent for this purpose.

The defendant had a right, too, to introduce so much of Jonathan Muirhead's former testimony as showed the consideration of the transfer to the plaintiff, simply because the object was not to destroy the original notes; and it was no objection to this course that the jury might infer from other portions of the same testimony that the first notes were accepted as payment of pre-existent debts.

The paper-book states the offer of the inventory and the proof connected with it, so obscurely, it is difficult to say whether or not it was properly rejected. If it contained an enumeration of the goods for the purchase of which the first notes were given, certainly it was evidence. But some proof must be given of this. It is said there was some. Probably no difficulty will be experienced on this head upon another trial.

Judgment reversed and a *venire de novo* awarded.

Hamilton alias Thacker *versus* The Commonwealth.

In the case of an indictment for murder in the first degree, it should appear from the record that the prisoner was present in court when he was sentenced to be executed, and it should be demanded of him whether he has any thing to say why sentence of death should not be pronounced upon him.

ERROR from the Oyer and Terminer of *Lancaster county*.

This case came before the court on an application made by George Ford, attorney for the defendant in the court below, for a special *allocatur* for a writ of error, for cause shown, and the presentation of an authenticated copy of the record, &c., as follows, viz:

| Commonwealth
v.
James Hamilton, otherwise James Thacker. | August Session, 1847. |

Indictment, 1st, 2d, and 3d counts, murder; 4th count, manslaughter. True bill. April 21, 1847. Same day, the defendant, James Hamilton, otherwise called James Thacker, being arraigned in open court, pleads *not guilty*, and *de hoc*, &c.; attorney-general similiter, issue, and rule for trial. April 21, 1849, the case continued to August sessions by consent of counsel for the commonwealth and counsel for the defendant. And now, August 20, 1847,

[Hamilton alias Thacker v. The Commonwealth.]

the court in session, and all the judges on the bench, viz. ELLIS LEWIS, Esq., president, and JAC. GROSH and EMANUEL SHAEFFER, Esqs., his associates; same day, James Hamilton, otherwise called James Thacker, indicted for murder, having been brought into court, the clerk was directed to draw from the box containing the names of the jurors regularly and legally drawn, a jury in the case of the Commonwealth v. James Hamilton, otherwise called James Thacker, which having been complied with by the clerk, the following jury came; to wit, David Weiler, affirmed, &c., twelve sober, intelligent, and competent men, who, upon their oaths and affirmations, respectively do say, that the defendant, James Hamilton, otherwise called James Thacker, is "guilty of murder in the first degree, and in manner and form as he stands indicted." The jury (at the request of *George Ford* and *W. L. Campbell*, Esqs., counsel for prisoner) was polled, and each for himself pronounced the defendant, James Hamilton, otherwise called James Thacker, "Guilty of murder in the first degree." The jury rendered their verdict August 22 (Sunday) 1847.

August 23, 1847, the court, after hearing all the testimony and the verdict of the jury, sentenced the prisoner, James Hamilton, otherwise called James Thacker, as follows, to wit: "Whereupon all and singular the premises being seen and understood by the court here, it is considered by the court that the said James Hamilton, otherwise called James Thacker, be taken from hence to the place from whence he came, and from thence to the place of execution, and that he be there hanged by the neck until he be dead."

"The prisoner, James Hamilton, otherwise called James Thacker, was present in court during every stage of the trial, from the time of his arraignment up to the period when the sentence was pronounced by the Honorable ELLIS LEWIS, president judge of the court, upon him. In short, the whole trial, from its commencement to its termination, was conducted according to law."

Ford, for plaintiff in error, in support of the application for *allocatur*, argued,—1. The record was imperfect, because it does not appear that the jurors were sworn to try whether the prisoner was guilty or not of the felony in the indictment specified: 1 *Chit. Crim. Law.* 720; 3 *Saund.* 393, and note 1, Rex v. Perin; 11 *East.* 510; 4 *Bl. Com. Appen.* sec. 1; act of May 31, 1718. sec. 6, 1 *Sm. Laws* 112.

2. It does not appear upon the record that the prisoner was present when the sentence was passed on him, nor does it show that he was asked whether he had any thing to say why sentence of death should not be pronounced against him. This is an important part of the record, and cannot be omitted: *Chit. Crim. Law* 700, 720; 4 *Bl. Com. Appen.* 1; Dunn v. Com'th, 5 *Barr* 384.

[Hamilton alias Thacker v. The Commonwealth.]

3. The record shows that the sentence was passed against the prisoner, not in the second, but the third person, and as a mere direction from the president of the court to the clerk.

4. From the record it appeared that the trial was had in the Court of Quarter Sessions, and not in the Oyer and Terminer: *Const. of Penn.* art. v. sec. 5.

Champneys, contra.—The witnesses for commonwealth on the trial proved that the homicide was committed by the prisoner in the perpetration of a robbery; and as the degree of the offence was therefore expressly designated by the act of Assembly, there was nothing left for the discretion of the jury. That the injury inflicted by the prisoner occasioned the death of Hunter, was ascertained after a careful *post mortem* examination. There was evidence of gross negligence in omitting to procure the proper medical attention to the wound; and, although the death of Hunter was hastened by this inattention, yet it was apparent that the wound, and not the improper treatment, caused the death; and the intelligent jury who tried the cause could not do otherwise than convict the prisoner. Having had doubts as to the propriety of the conviction from testimony subsequently discovered and presented to me by General Ford, the prisoner's counsel, both the late and present executive received the information which induced them to suspend the warrant of execution. The present executive very properly urged upon the legislature the enactment of a law which would invest the court with authority, in convictions of murder in the first degree, where the warrant of execution was suspended, to direct that the prisoner should be committed to solitary confinement at labor, so as to receive the moral discipline and punishment prescribed by our admirable penitentiary system. The legislature did not act upon this recommendation, under the apprehension, it is presumed, that it might lead to a general commutation of punishment in cases of conviction of murder in the first degree; and, notwithstanding the plausibility of the objection, I have been long impressed with the necessity of the provision suggested, as essential to the proper and humane administration of justice.

As to the first error urged by prisoner: The brief statement of the clerk in making up the record of the session of the court; the names of the judges; the direction to the clerk to draw the jury; the actual drawing of the jury, and that they were duly sworn or affirmed, &c., is in entire conformity with all the precedents in our county; and I believe will be ascertained upon examination to be equal in particularity to the records of any other county in the commonwealth. The British precedents require much greater precision and particularity than our practice demands. Brief entries, showing substantially what has been the course of proceeding during the progress of the trial, are all that has been required; and the

[Hamilton alias Thacker v. The Commonwealth.]

policy of our legislature and our judicial decisions have equally tended to sanction this practice: Dyott v. Com'th, 5 *Whar.* 67; Jacobs v. Com'th, 5 *Ser. & R.* 315; *Whar. Am. C. L.* 617; Com'th v. Smith, 2 *Ser. & R.* 300.

As to the second error assigned. It does appear distinctly that the prisoner was present during the trial. Until the decision in Dunn v. Com'th, 6 *Barr* 384, it was not the practice to insert a certificate of the presence of the prisoner during trial upon the record. The arraignment of the prisoner and his plea, the challenges of the prisoner and the statement that he was brought in for sentence, sufficiently indicate the trial in person which the constitution and laws demand.

As to the error alleged in the omission to place upon the record the inquiry made of the prisoner after conviction if he knows or hath any thing to say for himself why the commonwealth ought not to proceed to judgment, &c.

From a careful examination of the records of our county from 1692 to the present date, there are but three instances of the numerous cases of homicide tried, in which this question, the *allocatur*, as it has been termed, was inserted upon the record. These were the Com'th v. Lechler, Com'th v. Shaeffer, and the Com'th v. Hagerty, in all of which I was counsel. In the first case the record was made up, according to my impression, under the direction of Judge FRANKLIN, whose accuracy and ability are well known to the profession.

The British precedents clearly require its insertion upon the record; but it appearing in this case that the prisoner was brought into court for sentence, this would seem to indicate with sufficient clearness that the court had not failed to afford him all the safeguards required by the constitution and the laws. I was not aware, until my learned friend showed me the record a few days since, that the clerk, who was a very competent officer, had added the unnecessary and superfluous appendage that the proceedings were *according to law.* This entry is mere surplusage, without any legal effect, and which cannot add to or detract from the merit of the record: *C. Cir. Com.* 28, Com'th v. Pennock, 3 *Ser. & R.* 199; Com'th v. Immel, 6 *Bin.* 403.

3d and 4th. As to the third and fourth errors, it is sufficient to remark, that the sentence is recorded in the usual form, according to the precedents, and, in reference to the objection urged to the tribunal that tried the case, it is only necessary to say, that it distinctly appears from the bill of indictment and all the proceedings of record, that the trial was before the president and his associate judges, composing a Court of Oyer and Terminer.

The opinion of the court was delivered May 20, by

GIBSON, C. J.—The artistic form in which the sentence stands

[Hamilton alias Thacker v. The Commonwealth.]

recorded, proves that the clerk of the court had consulted a precedent. The verb is in the present tense and third person, and the words of the pronouncing judge are not put down exactly as they dropped from his lips. Even the prayer for mercy is properly omitted, as it is no part of the judgment. So far all is unusually well. But for every thing besides, it is plain from the journalizing of the proceedings in the past tense, that the clerk's knowledge of the principles and forms of criminal law was too limited to serve him in applying his precedent to the proceedings with entire advantage. The details of the trial, embracing as they do, the bringing of the prisoner into court; the direction of the court to draw a jury from the proper box; the clerk's compliance with it; the qualification of the jurors as "sober, intelligent, and judicious men;" the polling of the jury, and much more of the sort, show that the officer was too intent on the small beer of the case to attend to essentials; for the entries seem to have been made with a view to obviate some of the exceptions taken in Dunn v. The Commonwealth. However that may be, we find no entry that the prisoner was demanded whether he had any thing to say why sentence of death should not be pronounced on him, the absence of which was ruled in Rex v. Geary, 2 *Salk.* 630, and the King v. Speke, 3 *Salk.* 358, to be fatal. In fact, there is nothing on the docket to show even that the prisoner was present when he was sentenced, except the supplementary memorandum that " he was present in court during every stage of the trial, from the time of his arraignment up to the time when the sentence was passed by the honorable ELLIS LEWIS, president judge of the court, on him. *Indeed, the whole trial, from its commencement to its termination, was according to law.*"

A record is constituted of proper and legitimate elements set down in their order; for it is certainly not law, that all the gossip a clerk or prothonotary writes down in his docket, *ipso facto*, becomes the very voice of undeniable truth. The judges of a court of error must determine for themselves, and consequently on facts instead of sweeping assertions. The premises to found a sentence of death are set forth in 1 *Chitty's Crim. Law* 720, and the form of the entire record is given in 4 *Black. Com.* Ap. 1, in which there is a demand of the prisoner "if he hath or knoweth any thing to say wherefore the said justices ought not, on the premises and verdict, to proceed to judgment and execution against him," together with his answer, that he "nothing further saith unless as he before had said." With us a full record is seldom, perhaps never, formally made up; but the docket, which stands in its place, must contain the substantial parts of it, from which, together with the other records in the office, such a record might be formed. It is because the proceedings remain in paper that we have been able to dispense with strict form as to tense and person, holding fast

[Hamilton alias Thacker v. The Commonwealth.]

however to matter of substance. But even the forms of records are deeply seated in the foundations of the law; and as they conduce to safety and certainty, they surely ought not to be disregarded when the life of a human being is in question. Our practice of rotation has excluded experience from the county offices, and it would perhaps be profitable were the presiding judge to superintend the entries. It would at least prevent our judicial records from becoming entirely barbarous. The clerk is the immediate officer of the court, which is consequently responsible for his acts. Writ of error allowed.

At a subsequent day, the counsel for the prisoner applied for and obtained a writ of *habeas corpus;* and the prisoner having been brought before the Supreme Court by Jacob Huber, Esq., the high sheriff, in obedience to the writ, *T. E. Franklin*, Esq., Attorney General, appeared and stated that it was not the intention of the officers of the commonwealth to prosecute the case any further.

Judgment was reversed and the prisoner discharged.

Sheidle *versus* Weishlee.

1. A *feme covert* joined with her husband in a mortgage on their separate estates to secure a debt of the husband. Afterwards the husband sold his own property, and the purchaser received a deed from the husband and wife, and paid to the husband a sum supposed to be sufficient to pay the mortgage which bound both estates, but which, in fact, was not sufficient. Out of the proceeds of sale of the real estate *of the wife*, the court directed to be paid the balance due on the mortgage: *Held*, that the wife was entitled to recover from the purchaser of the husband's real estate sold as above, the amount which was paid out of the proceeds of sale of her property in discharge of the balance due on the mortgage.
2. In a suit by the wife alone, her coverture or the non-joinder of her husband can be taken advantage of only by plea in abatement: perhaps, however, since the act of 1848, a *feme covert* can maintain a suit in her own name alone.

ERROR to the Common Pleas of *Lancaster county*.

This was an action on the case, brought by Elizabeth Weishlee v. Jacob Sheidle, to recover arrears of interest on a mortgage, and also the taxes on the mortgaged premises unpaid at the execution of a deed in 1848. The plea was *non assumpsit*. Elizabeth Weishlee joined her husband in pledging her property, together with his, to secure the payment of his debt to Hatz. Afterwards her husband sold *his* property to Sheidle, for a sum more than sufficient to pay the debt, and she joined in the deed; it was alleged under the assurance that the debt would be paid out of the purchase-money. She was, notwithstanding, compelled to pay Hatz a part of the mortgage debt, which it was alleged that Sheidle

[Sheidle v. Weishlee.]

ought to have paid; and she sued him to recover the amount so paid, together with taxes.

February 3, 1851. Jury sworn.

26 Oct. 1842. Rosina Sheller to Elizabeth Sheller, the plaintiff, deed for tenement on the north side of East King street, Lancaster.

Admitted that Elizabeth Sheller afterwards became wife of Jacob Weishlee.

15 Oct. 1846. Jacob Weishlee and wife to Christian Habacker, mortgage on plaintiff's property, above mentioned, for $500. *Eo die* recorded.

19 April 1847. David Hartman, sheriff, to Jacob Weishlee, for a two-story house and lot on south side of East King street.

Deed in partition of land.

26 April 1847. Jacob Weishlee and wife to John Hatz, mortgage on both properties to secure payment of $1400 with interest, from date, to secure bond of Jacob Weishlee. *Eo die* recorded.

1 Dec. 1848. Jacob Weishlee and wife to Jacob Sheidle, deed, consideration $1700, for the lot of Weishlee, (the same that was included in the mortgage to John Hatz,) "free of all encumbrances," except ground-rents.

Nov. 1849. Sci. fa. v. Elizabeth Weishlee, who survived Jacob Weishlee.

No. 31, January 1850. Levari facias. Sale of this property. Sheriff paid plaintiff's mortgage, and paid into court $565.48 on 7 Feb. 1850.

January 29, 1850. Rule to show cause, &c.

March 23, 1850. Court direct $175.38 to be paid to John Hatz on his mortgage of 26 April, 1847, and the residue to be paid to Elizabeth Weishlee.

27 March 1850. Receipt of John Hatz to prothonotary for the above sum of $175.38.

Jacob King, sworn:—I am witness to deed of Weishlee and wife to defendant. That evening there was about $300 paid in gold—after that Weishlee said it was customary for the wife to have something, and defendant gave her a $5 gold-piece. It was said this was the balance of the money besides the mortgage. Weishlee said this is the balance of the money besides the mortgage. There was something mentioned about a mortgage. I signed my name as a witness to the deed; it was in the neighborhood of $300; I don't know the exact amount; it was mentioned this is the balance of the money besides the mortgage. I have not seen Weishlee since he left.

Plaintiff closes.

Evidence on part of Defendant.—Admitted that there was $140 of interest due on the mortgage of 26 April 1847, to John Hatz.

[Sheidle v. Weishlee.]

at the time of the conveyance to the defendant on 1 Dec. 1848; also, that taxes were due to the amount of $35.58, which were liens on the property purchased by defendant.

John Hatz, sworn:—I had a mortgage on the two properties; I was not present when Sheidle bought the property, and knew nothing about it. Afterwards I told him there was a good deal of back interest due. I had no conversation with Sheidle till after he bought it.

Admitted that the tax-collectors had no conversation with Sheidle about the taxes until after he purchased.

Wm. Frick, Esq., sworn:—Witness to deed to Sheidle. I took the acknowledgment; there was a lien on the property; the money that was paid was paid in gold; I can't say the exact amount; it might have been somewhere about $300 or $400; I did know the amount, but have forgotten; the purchaser was to pay the lien on the premises; that was left on the property, and the balance was paid down in gold. Mrs. Weishlee was present; it took place at Weishlee's in the front-room; it appeared to me that there was $300 or upwards paid; I can't be confident of the amount. There was only one claim spoken of that stood against the property, and that appeared to be Hutz's mortgage or judgment. It is a mere guess as to the amount paid; I have no definite recollection of the amount.

Lewis, Pres't, charged as follows:—This is an action to recover money paid to the use of defendant. The plaintiff was the owner of a house and lot in Lancaster, and married Jacob Weishlee, who owned another house and lot in the same city. On the 15th Oct. 1846, she joined her husband in a mortgage on her house to Christian Habacker, to secure a debt of $500 due from her husband. On the 26th April 1847, she joined her husband in another mortgage, to secure another debt of her husband, of $1400, which was due to John Hatz. This mortgage included both houses and lots, as well that of her husband as the one which belonged to her. On the 1st Dec. 1848, Jacob Sheidle, the defendant, purchased of Jacob Weishlee the house and lot which belonged to him, and received a deed from Weishlee and wife, for the consideration stated in the deed, of $1700. At the time of executing this deed a sum, in the neighborhood of $300, was paid by Sheidle to the husband, Weishlee, in the presence of the plaintiff, which was expressed, at the time and in her presence, to be the balance, deducting the mortgage or lien of John Hatz, which Sheidle, the purchaser, was to pay. The mortgage of Habacker not being paid, the plaintiff's property was sold by the sheriff, by virtue of proceedings thereon, and on the 7th Feb. 1850, the sheriff paid into court the sum of $565.48, arising from the sale of the plaintiff's house and lot aforesaid. Out of this sum the court directed the sum of $175.38 to be paid on the mortgage of John Hatz, which was all that was

[Sheidle v. Weishlee.]

claimed. It is alleged that the *principal* of the mortgage debt has been adjusted by the defendant, and this sum was the arrearages of *interest* due on the mortgage.

When Elizabeth Weishlee joined her husband in the mortgage to John Hatz, to secure the debt of her husband, she became entitled to all the rights of a surety as against her husband: she had a right to insist on the sale of his own house and lot, to pay his own debt, before resorting to her property included in the mortgage. And in case she was compelled to pay the debt to Hatz, or any part of it, she was entitled to subrogation *pro tanto*, and had a right to enforce the Hatz mortgage against her husband's house and lot. In equity, her husband was bound to pay the debt, and his property stood pledged for that purpose. She had a right to take his house and lot into consideration when she entered into the mortgage, and it is presumed that its inclusion in the mortgage formed an inducement with her to become bound in the mortgage. This being the nature of her rights, at the time of becoming her husband's surety to Hatz, what circumstances have deprived her of her equitable claim? When Sheidle, the defendant, purchased the house and lot of her husband, the Hatz mortgage was upon record, and it appeared upon the face of it, that it was given to secure a debt of Jacob Weishlee, and that Elizabeth Weishlee was but a surety. Not only was the purchaser affected with *constructive* notice of the mortgage, but it appears from the evidence of the subscribing witnesses to his deed, that he had *actual* notice of it, and that he only paid about $300, retaining the residue of the consideration-money, and agreeing to pay the mortgage to Hatz. The money which was paid (except a $5 gold-piece to the wife for signing the deed) was paid to Jacob Weishlee himself. The plaintiff received no part of it. So that there is nothing in this to postpone her. She must be presumed to have signed the deed upon the inducements made known to her; and when it was mentioned in her presence, by the parties, that the defendant was to pay off the Hatz mortgage, she could have no reason for withholding her signature. On the contrary, this agreement would necessarily operate on her mind as an inducement to execute the conveyance, because by the proceeding she would be relieved from the Hatz mortgage. But it is complained that the defendant mistook the amount of that mortgage—that is, that he did not know that any *interest* was in arrears upon it. This was his own fault, and he cannot throw the loss upon the plaintiff. There is no evidence that she deceived him in regard to it, or even that she had any knowledge herself of the arrears of interest due. On the whole, we see nothing in the case to deprive her of her equity as surety to the extent of the sum of $175.38, which she has been compelled to pay. She is entitled, under the evidence, to recover that sum, with interest from the 23d March 1850, when

[Sheidle v. Weisblee.]

it was paid for the use of this defendant in discharge of the Hatz mortgage upon his property.

We do not know whether Jacob Weishlee is dead or alive; and, since the act of 1848, securing the rights of married women, we are not disposed to embarrass them in prosecuting suits for their property, by requiring the husband to join the action. It has been decided that a woman, in such case, is to be treated as a *feme sole*. It is true that the act of 25th April 1850 provides that a suit in such case *may* be brought in the names of husband and wife, for the use of the wife; but we think it does not enjoin it. At all events, with our present views of the law, we are not disposed to turn this woman out of court on a mere matter of form. If the Supreme Court should feel bound to do so, we are prepared to obey their direction.*

*The action was sustained in the name of the plaintiff on the general ground; but it is conceived that advantage could not be taken of the coverture without pleading it.—Per LEWIS, J.

The defendant excepted to the charge.

February 3, 1851. Verdict for plaintiff, and damages assessed at $184.44.

It was assigned for error:
1. The court erred in that part of the charge as to plaintiff's right to recover the $175, and all the reasoning and inferences which precede it.
2. In deciding that the suit was well brought, in the name of plaintiff alone, she being a married woman.

The case was argued by *Fraser*, for plaintiff in error.—The error of the court consisted in treating the case as if Jacob Weisblee had not sold, *with the plaintiff, his own property to the defendant below*, (*Sheidle*.)

When Weishlee sold his property, in December 1848, "*free of all encumbrances except ground-rent,*" to said Sheidle, his wife (the plaintiff below) was a co-grantor; the consideration was $1700, of which $300 were paid in cash, and the remainder, $1400, was to remain in grantee's hands to meet Hatz's mortgage, which $1400 was the amount of same. A mistake was made in not keeping back the interest on the mortgage.

If this co-grantor can be subrogated in Hatz's mortgage, she stands precisely in the same position that Hatz would, had Hatz been a party in the deed with Weishlee. Could he have claimed more out of the mortgaged premises than the amount left in the grantee's hands? Would he not be estopped by his own deed? Can Elizabeth Weishlee do more than Hatz could have done? Her claim is through Hatz, and shall an innocent purchaser suffer, and

[Sheidle v. Weishlee.]

pay more than the consideration-money for the property on account of the acts, errors, or silence of either of the grantors?

Again, the court below having ordered the payment of these arrears of interest, &c., out of the money in court, arising from the sale of the real estate of Elizabeth Weishlee, she cannot now recover in this suit: that proceeding bars her. Also, there is no privity of contract between her and Sheidle.

Under the act of 1850, the suit cannot be sustained in her name, as the husband is alive.

Franklin, for defendant.—The first objection made to a recovery in this case is, that Mrs. Weishlee being the wife, is not entitled to the ordinary rights of a surety of her husband.

But the contrary is the doctrine of the courts of equity; and the rule seems well established, that a wife, mortgaging her inheritance for the debt of her husband, is entitled to all the rights and remedies of a personal surety : 2 *Story's Eq. Juris.* sec. 1372 –1373, and cases cited; 2 *Vernon* 437, Huntingdon v. Huntingdon; 2 *id.* 604, Pocock v. Lee; 2 *Atkyns* 383, Parteriche v. Powlett; 3 *Paige Ch. Rep.* 614, Neimcewitz v. Gahn.

True, in the early case of Tate v. Austin, 1 *P. Wms.* 264, Lord Cowper seems to limit this principle, so as to postpone the wife to all the other creditors of the husband, but gives no reason for the distinction, which is not recognised in other cases.

And Ashley v. Tankerville, 3 *Brown's Ch. C.* 545, and S. C. *Cox* 82, was decided on the contrary principle.

So Aguilar v. Aguilar, 5 *Mad. Rep.* 414, is opposed to Tate v. Austin.

And Gahn v. Neimcewitz's Executors, 11 *Wend.* 312, affirming the chancellor's decree in 3 *Paige* 614, above cited, discards Lord Cowper's distinction.

2. She could not resist Hatz's claim; he was entitled to receive the money under his mortgage. She was not therefore bound by the decree.

3. There was sufficient privity of contract to sustain *indebitatus assumpsit*: 8 *Term Rep.* 308; 8 *Taunt.* 865; 14 *Mees. & Wels.* 762; 5 *Wend.* 558; 6 *id.* 284; 7 *id.* 119.

4. A recovery is resisted, because Mrs. Weishlee is alleged to be a married woman; that her husband must be presumed to be still living, as no proof was given of his death. The only evidence on that point on either side was the scire facias on Habacker's judgment, which issued against Elizabeth Weishlee, who survived Jacob Weishlee: on which judgment was entered against her, and her property sold.

But coverture of *feme* plaintiff at the time of suit brought must be pleaded in abatement. It cannot be pleaded in bar, much less

[Sheidle v. Weishlee.]

given in evidence under the plea of *non assumpsit:* 3 *Term Rep.* 627, Milner *v.* Milnes; *Bacon's Abr.* tit. *Abatement,* G.

Again, since the act of 1848, the wife may bring suit to recover property belonging to her, in her own name, without joining her husband. He has no longer any right in nor dominion over it: Cummings's Appeal, 1 *Jones* 272; Goodyear *v.* Rumbaugh, 1 *Harris* 480.

May 20.—PER CURIAM.—Let the judgment be affirmed on the opinion of the judge below.

McKissick *versus* Pickle.

1. An individual granted and conveyed for a nominal consideration, a lot of ground to certain persons in trust for those who had subscribed or may thereafter be subscribers towards the erection of a school-house and house of public worship thereon, and towards the support of a school, or the support of the gospel, in the said building, and providing, that if at any time thereafter, the premises should be converted to any other use than as aforesaid, and for a burying-ground, that in such case the lot shall revert to the grantor and his heirs *and assigns*. It was *held*, that the mere permission by one of the trustees to a female in distress, to occupy the premises temporarily, as a tenant at will, without rent, though she and her family remained in it for years, did not work a forfeiture of the estate to the grantor or his assigns.

2. The declaration or admission of one of the trustees of a charitable trust in real estate, that the trust title had been divested, cannot affect the right of the persons interested under the trust. The trustees have no right to relinquish the trust property.

3. Though in the case of a condition *in law,* none but the grantor or his heirs can enter for a condition broken, yet in Pennsylvania, where the doctrine of maintenance does not prevail, there is no policy of law which forbids the reservation of a right of entry *to the assigns* of the grantor. Therefore, in the case of such a reservation, a purchaser of the grantor's conditional interest in the premises, at a sheriff's sale, is within the terms of such a reservation, and if a forfeiture exist, he may take advantage of it, though his purchase was *before* the condition was broken.

ERROR to the Common Pleas of *Lancaster county.*

This was an action of ejectment by Arthur McKissick *vs.* Leonard Pickle, for a lot of ground. Summons issued March 22, 1850.

On the 25th of October 1819, Samuel Ferguson and wife conveyed by deed a lot of ground in Georgetown to Arthur McKissick and Robert Patterson, in trust, and as trustees "for all those person or persons who has or may hereafter be subscribers towards the paying the expense of erecting a school-house and meeting-house (or house of public worship) and keeping the same in repair, (on the following described lot of ground,) and all those persons that has or may hereafter subscribe for the payment of money towards the support of a school, or the support of the gospel, or both of them, in the said school-house or meeting-house, of the second part."

Witnesseth, that the said party of the first part, for and in con-

[McKissick v. Pickle.]

sideration of the sum of $100, "doth grant, bargain, and sell unto the said party of the second part, all that lot of ground situate in Bart township aforesaid, and in the town of Georgetown, known in general draught of said town, filed in register's office of said county on the 13th day of March, 1813, by No. 81, and bounded as follows, viz. beginning," &c.

"Together with all and singular the houses and outbuildings thereto belonging," &c.

"To have and to hold the said lot of ground, hereditaments and premises, with the appurtenances, unto the party of the second part, to the only proper use and behoof of the said party of the second part, and to their heirs and assigns for ever."

"Provided always nevertheless, that if at any time hereafter the above-described property, or any part of it, should be converted into any other use than for the use of a school-house for the education of youths, and a meeting-house for promulgating the gospel, and also a burying-ground, and such other improvements as may be advantageous and of use to the promotion of the aforesaid three objects, that then and in that case, the said lot shall revert to the party of the first part and to his heirs and assigns."

This deed was recorded in book No. 22, p. 232, on the 15th day of April, 1822.

A school-house was built by subscription on said lot immediately after, school kept therein, and preaching on Sunday and other days. School continued there until 1839, and preaching until 1842. It was the main school in the township, and larger than any school-house in the same. In 1841, Susanna McCaffery, with four small children, and her sick husband, who died in a month after, were permitted by Arthur McKissick to occupy said school-house, on account of her poverty and destitution. No part of the house was altered or changed. She used the school-house stove for all purposes, and some bed-clothes were nailed to the ceiling to conceal the bed; some benches were put out. She paid no rent, and remained there seven years (April 1848) when she went out; defendant took possession, and shortly after tore down the school-house and farmed the whole lot.

Jacob Eshleman obtained judgment to August 1823, No. 251, against Samuel Ferguson and John Bachman for $400, real debt. A sci. fa. was issued on this judgment to December 1828, No. 38, and on December 23, 1829, judgment was entered for plaintiff; a fi. fa. on same to August 1830, No. 29, and a levy under same of all the right, title and interest of Samuel Ferguson *in all the lots, streets and alleys in Georgetown*, enlarged, &c., and on *vend. exp.* to April 1831, No. 19, real property sold for $85. June 13, 1831. sheriff's deed to Jacob Eshleman for consideration $85, acknowledged.

1845, August 20, Jacob to B. B. Eshleman, deed for same.

[McKissick v. Pickle.]

1847, April 22, B. B. Eshleman to Leonard Pickle, deed for same.

Robert Patterson, one of the trustees, died before suit brought, and title was admitted to have been in Samuel Ferguson, on 25th of October 1819.

The main question was whether the title vested in the trustees by Ferguson's deed in 1819 has been divested; and whether the defendant had title to the premises. On the trial, on the part of the defendant it was offered to prove that the condition in the deed of 1819 was broken since the sheriff's sale, and that Jacob Eshleman, the sheriff's vendee, entered, and that Benjamin B. Eshleman and defendant came into possession under sheriff's vendee.

Plaintiff objected to the evidence:—1. Because the lien of the judgment commenced after plaintiff's right accrued, and was recorded without notice to him. 2. Because the levy is upon all the lots together, without describing this lot or levying upon the reversionary interest, if any, of Ferguson. 3. A stranger cannot enter for condition broken : 55 *Law Library ; Crabb on Real Prop.* 555. If condition in deed be broken, none shall take advantage but feoffer or his heirs, and right of entry given to a stranger is void. Distinction between condition in *deed* and in *law*.

Court overruled the objections and admitted the evidence, and exception on part of defendant.

Amos Pickle testified :—I am defendant's brother; no school has been taught in the house in question since 1839; it was not used for a meeting-house until the Mormons used it in 1839 ; I went to McKissick in 1839 for the key, and he gave it to me. I asked if he had any objections to preaching in the house, and he said not ; the house did not belong to him, it belonged to Jacob Eshleman. He knew it was a Mormon that was going to preach there and had preached there. He said he had nothing to do with it, it belonged to Jacob Eshleman. He never asked me for the key again; I cannot tell that he ever got it. In 1841, a man named Edward McCaffrey moved in, and he died there, and his widow remained there for seven years after 1841. It was never used as a burying-ground; the land has been occupied as farm-land for potatoes, corn, and oats, by my brother, since 1847; the house he pulled down, the last of it in 1849; the other part in the same year or the year before.

Cross-examined :—*Before my brother had purchased, he knew what McKissick had told me about it ; I told him some time after McKissick had told me;* the conversation with McKissick was in 1838 or 1839; John Alt was present. There was no school kept in it at that time ; the last school kept there was in 1839; I don't know who built the school-house ; I unlocked the house with the key, and left it in the lock. The widow was there from the spring of 1841 to the spring of 1848; she was gone when my brother commenced tearing the house down ; no change was made in the

[McKissick v. Pickle.]

building; she just occupied the school-house, and lived there without any change in the building. I know of no preaching before or after the Mormons preached there. After Mrs. McCaffrey moved there, there was preaching there; in spring of 1841, but not after.

On the part of the plaintiff, General James Caldwell testified: This school-house was built immediately after getting the deed; Samuel Ferguson spoke to me to prepare a deed; I prepared one; I heard the deed read. I lived a very short distance of it for twenty years; it was the main school in the township; it was a larger school-house than any in the township; school was kept there until, 1838 when it closed. Heard of worship in it frequently; I heard Mr. Barr, Presbyterian, and Peter Miller, and I heard the Mormons frequently. After the school was quit, no use was made of it till Mrs. McCaffrey went in; in the latter end of March 1841 or 1842, Mrs. McCaffrey came to my house and stated they had been in a distressed way all winter, that her husband came home sick in the fall, and asked me if she could go into the school-house. I sent her to plaintiff; she told me again that she had went to Arthur McKissick and he had given her leave in consequence of her distressed situation; she went in. They hung up some bed-clothes to make a partition around the bed. She went in in April. Her husband died the last of April; she had three or four children, all young; she remained there some years; she went out into a house of Leonard Pickle's brother after she had been there seven years. The next morning I heard that the building, except the walls, was pulled down; all the wood-work taken out; I saw defendant pulling the walls down; he hauled the stone home to build a barn; very little repair would have made it a good school-house. I heard plaintiff three times tell Pickle he would bring suit if that school-house business was not settled; that was after it was pulled down.

Isaac Riley, sworn :—In 1841—latter part of March—Mrs. McCaffrey moved into this house; in about a month after her husband died; she lived there seven years; during the time she lived there, there was preaching several times in 1841 and 1842; I can't tell whether there was any since.

Admitted that plaintiff put Mrs. McCaffrey in possession.

LEWIS, President, after stating the evidence, instructed the jury substantially as follows :—

1. That the evidence of *non user* is not sufficient to work a forfeiture of the estate.

2. That the defendant was not, under the circumstances of this case, bound to make any other demand, previous to taking possession, than that disclosed in the evidence.

3. That if the jury believe the lot in question is included within the description of the "lots, streets, and alleys of Georgetown en-

[McKissick v. Pickle.]

larged" levied on and sold, the sheriff's sale passed the interest of Samuel Ferguson, notwithstanding that there was no specific description of the lot, or of the reversionary interest of the said Ferguson.

4. That the sheriff's sale is sufficient to pass the title of said Ferguson, notwithstanding that the judgment of 1823, and its revival in 1829, were both entered without notice to Arthur McKissick or Patterson, the trustees.

5. That, for the present, and until the question be further considered, the jury are instructed that notwithstanding the sale by the sheriff took place before any forfeiture had accrued, the sheriff's vendee and those claiming under him, had, under the provisions of the deed of 1819, a right to enter for the breach of the condition as fully as the grantor or his heirs might have entered.

6. That the original owner, Ferguson, had a right to give the property for the uses designated in the deed of 1819, and the trustee had no right to divert the property from the uses thus designated. The trustee had no right to devote trust property to such purposes, contrary to the nature of the trust.

That if the jury believe that the plaintiff, in the spring of 1841, consented that Mrs. McCaffrey should remove into the house with her husband and her family, and occupy the premises as a dwelling-house, without any limitation as to time, and that, with the acquiescence of the plaintiff, and all others interested in the trust, she continued thus to occupy the property as a dwelling-house for seven years—and that during that time no school was taught in the house, and no worship except the occasional preaching stated in the evidence, while the family so occupied the premises, and that the property never had been used as a burying-ground, the defendant is entitled to retain his possession against the present plaintiff. If the jury believe the facts here stated, the plaintiff cannot recover.

The plaintiff excepted to the charge of the court before verdict. November 26, 1850, verdict for defendant.

It was assigned for error:
1. In charging the jury on all the points but the first in favor of defendant, and particularly in that part relating to the use of the property by Mrs. McCaffrey working a forfeiture.
2. In ruling that the defendant could enter, if the condition of the grant was broken by the title he acquired under the sheriff's sale.
3. In admitting the evidence referred to in the offer on part of defendant, and contained in bill of exceptions.

Frazer, for plaintiff in error, who was plaintiff below.—As to

[McKissick v. Pickle.]

first exception. The occupancy by a destitute woman, without changing the building in any way, the possession being at will, did not work a forfeiture.

The grant was a charity, and could not be forfeited for *non user* or *misuser ;* and even if it could be, under an express condition or contract, it must be clearly, expressly, and strictly shown *that the condition was broken.*

No act or permission of McKissick could work a forfeiture of the interest of *cestui que trusts*, nor would a mere acquiescence on their part produce that result: 5 *Watts* 493, Martin *v.* McCord ; 9 *Barr* 433, Wright *v.* Linn.

The subscribers to this school-house were not alone beneficially interested: the children around were the beneficiaries. Could such a benevolent purpose and gift be forfeited by the occupation of the building as detailed in the evidence?

The real interest of a minor or beneficiary in land cannot be divested by the act of the guardian or trustee.

The law raises every intendment in favor of a charity against the grantor or those claiming under him.

Public schools are favorites of the law in Pennsylvania.

2. The court erred in ruling that the defendant could enter if the condition of the grant was broken by the title he acquired under the sheriff's sale.

It is well settled that none but the grantor or his heirs can enter for condition broken—no assignee or stranger can do so: See 55 *Law Lib. Crabb on Real Prop.* 531, 550, sec. 2150, 2189, 2190, and the authorities there cited ; also, 5 *Watts* 493, Martin *v.* McCord ; 9 *Barr*, Wright *v.* Linn, 433 ; 1 *Jones* 444, Klinkener *v.* School Directors, &c. ; 3 *Caines* 345, Newkirk *v.* Newkirk ; 5 *Ser. & R.* 385, Hamilton *v.* Elliott, where GIBSON, Chief Justice, says, "*none but the feoffer or his heir can enter; and the reason why a right of entry cannot be assigned is, that a contrary doctrine would favor maintenance and promote litigation:*" 1 *Inst.* 216 ; 1 *Wend.* 395, Jackson *v.* Topping ; 9 *Mass.* 500, Wardens of King's Chapel *v.* Pelham.

No demand or notice of entry was given by Pickle to McKissick.

Stevens, for defendant.—The plaintiff claims the lot in question by virtue of a deed in trust to hold it for a school-house. In the deed there is an express condition that if it should cease to be used as a school-house, or be used for any other purpose, it should revert to the grantor, *his heirs or assigns.* The plaintiff contends that the title cannot be forfeited by *non user* or *misuser*, and relies on the case of Wright *v.* Linn, 9 *Barr* 433 ; and Klinkener *v.* School Directors, 1 *Jones* 444.

There are two kinds of conditions ; one in fact, which is by express words ; and one in law, where the forfeiture is not *expressly*

[McKissick *v.* Pickle.]

provided for, but is implied by law, arising from the nature of the condition.

The condition in the cases relied on by plaintiff are conditions in law, which have no bearing on this case.

The condition in this deed is a condition in fact, expressly stipulating the terms on which the title was to revest in the grantor, his heirs or assigns. The courts in Pennsylvania have never undertaken to declare such condition inoperative. Indeed they could not without violating the contract.

The condition in this case was proved to have been violated; and the plaintiff had surrendered the possession to the sheriff's vendee, as proved by the evidence of Amos Pickle and another.

The only real question here is, had the grantor such an interest in land after the grant to the trustees as could be levied on and sold by the sheriff; and could the purchaser at sheriff's sale take advantage of the condition broken? In Pennsylvania, all possible rights and titles—contingent or otherwise—in lands where there is real interest, may be taken in execution—every *scintilla* of interest may be thus sold: 1 *Yeates* 427; *id.* 27. Even if the land be in the possession of another claiming by a paramount title: 3 *W. & Ser.* 114, Janett *v.* Tomlinson.

In England, while real estate could be conveyed only by feoffment, it was held that a condition was not assignable, and could be taken advantage of only by the feoffor or his heir, as he could not enter until the condition was broken, and consequently could not convey the title to land of which he was not in possession. Nor could the same be devised. But since the mode of conveying real estate by deed of bargain and sale, and the passage of the statutes of *trusts* and of *uses* converting such deeds into perfect titles, a condition is devisable even in England: *Equ. Abr.* 106–107; Marks *v.* Marks, 1 *Strange* 129; 2 *Bac. Abr.* 318–319, tit. *Condition*, (edition of 1843,) in note. The reason why a condition was not assignable in England, was because *no title* could be made to land held by another adversely, as that was against the law which forbid maintenance. No other reason was ever attempted to be given for it. But in Pennsylvania, the law against maintenance never has been adopted: *Kent's Com.* 448. While in England it would have been mischievous to allow great men to uphold their dependants in lawsuits, yet in Pennsylvania there are (in theory) no great men and no dependants; and therefore maintenance is not forbidden. Besides, our titles have always been by deed, and not by livery and seisin. Every reason against the sale of a conditional interest is wanting in Pennsylvania.

In Lampit's case, 10 *Coke* 48, it is said, "that although a possibility or condition cannot be granted to a stranger, because it would tend to multiply contentions to the great oppression of the people, yet all rights and titles, whether in *præsenti* or *futuro*, may

[McKissick v. Pickle.]

be released or assigned—1. To the tenant of the freehold in fact or in law without any privity. 2. To him in remainder. 3. To him in reversion without privity. 4. To him who has right only in respect of privity without any estate. 5. In respect of privity and without right."

In Pennsylvania a sheriff's vendee is not a stranger, but may take, even if the condition be to the grantor alone. But here there are express words, *heirs* and *assigns*.

It was once held that on condition broken, it was necessary to have an actual entry to support ejectment. That has long ceased to be the law: 1 *Salk.* 250; 2 *Ld. Raym.* 750; 3 *Burr.* 1897; 1 *Johns. Cases* 125, Jackson v. Crysler. Here the question can hardly arise, as defendant is in possession: 5 *Ser. & R.* 375; 5 *Mass.* 34.

In 5 *Pick.* 528, Hayden v. Stanton; 10 *Pick.* 306, Brigham v. Shattuck, and 462, Clapp v. Staughton, the question of the devisability of a condition, or interest in real estate depending upon forfeiture for condition broken, is fully considered. The court held that such interest or possibility was transferable by devise, and that the residuary legatee took to the exclusion of the heir at law.

In the first of these cases land had been devised to a town for a school-lot. The town took possession, but for twenty years neglected to build the school-house. The residuary legatee recovered it. The court say, "there was a contingent interest, which the devisor might have disposed of, if he pleased, to take effect on the forfeiture of the estate."

In the last case, it was decided that such interest vested in the residuary legatee *and descended to his heir, although the residuary legatee died before the condition broken.*

In Marks v. Marks, 1 *Strange* 129, it was held that "though a condition, in strictness of law, is not devisable, yet since the statute of uses the devisee may take advantage by an equitable construction."

"The possibility of performing a condition was an interest or right, or *scintilla juris* which vested it in B. and consequently descended, et cetera:" 2 *Bac. Abr.* 320, *Cond.* (P.)

The conclusion of these authorities is, that the right to take an estate in lands on the breach of a subsequent condition is an interest in real estate descendable to the heir, and now even in England, and always in this country, devisable and transferable to a stranger, who could enter even when the right was reserved to the grantor personally.

But this investigation was hardly necessary for the case in hand, because such right or interest is *expressly* granted to the "assigns," and there is no policy of law in Pennsylvania which prohibits such contract. It also appears that defendant is in possession by the consent of plaintiff, who admitted, that "it had fallen to Jacob Eshelman, and that he had nothing more to do with it."

But even if the grantor had consented that he would not sell such contingent right, still the law might have sold it for the benefit of creditors. "A covenant not to assign without license" applies only to voluntary sales; but the creditors may seize and sell: 4 *Kent. Com.* 123, (4th edit.)

The opinion of the court was delivered May 21, by

ROGERS, J.—As this presents the case of a condition in fact, and not a condition in law, it must be conceded that the property conveyed to the trustees, though for a charitable use, may be forfeited by *misuser*. The condition is, that if at any time hereafter the above described property, or any part of it, should be converted unto any other use than for the use of a school-house for the education of youths, and a meeting-house for promulgating the gospel, and also a burying-ground, and such other improvements as may be advantageous and of use to the promotion of the aforesaid three objects, that then, and in that case, the said lot shall revert to the party of the first part, and to his *heirs and assigns*. The proviso in the deed is entitled to a fair, liberal, and benign interpretation, not according to its letter, but its spirit. Viewing it in this aspect, I cannot bring myself to believe that it was in the contemplation of the parties (the grantor and those who contributed the funds to the erection of the building) that an occasional use of the property by a tenant at will, for purposes other than those mentioned in the deed, would work a forfeiture of the estate. To produce that effect, it must be by some permanent use different from those enumerated in the deed, such for example, as converting the building into a factory, or the land attached to it into arable land or pasture. The grant, being for a charity, could not be forfeited for *non user*, nor for *misuser* except under an express condition or contract; and although, in the latter case it may, yet it must be clearly, expressly, and strictly shown that the condition was broken : 5 *Watts* 493, Martin *v.* McCord; 9 *Barr.* 433, Wright *v.* Linn. The law raises every intendment in favor of a charity, against the grantor or those claiming under him. Public schools intended for the children in the neighborhood are favorites in this State, and must receive the protection and support, as far as is reasonable, of the public tribunals. It must be kept in view, that it is a *misuser*, and not a *non user*, which produces the forfeiture. So runs the deed. Throwing therefore, the *non user* out of consideration, what is the evidence of *misuser ?* It consists simply in this, that one of the trustees, from motives of humanity, there being no school kept in the building at the time, nor afterwards, allowed a destitute woman, as a shelter for her sick husband and helpless children, to occupy the building as

[McKissick v. Pickle.]

a tenant at will, without rent, and without charging the building in any way. General Caldwell in substance states, that after they had ceased to keep school in the building, no use was made of it till Mrs. McCaffrey went in. In the latter end of March 1841-42, Mrs. McCaffrey came to his house and stated that they had been in a distressed way all winter, that her husband came home sick in the fall, and asked him if she could go into the school-house. He sent her to plaintiff. That she afterwards told him that she had gone to Arthur McKissick, and that in consideration of her distressed situation, he had given her permission to occupy the premises—she took possession in April—her husband died the last of that month—she had four children, all young, and that she remained there some years. The only alteration that was made was, that some of the benches were put out. The school-house was used by Mrs. McCaffrey, as she testifies; she also proves she paid no rent, and that there was nothing said about the length of time she was to occupy the building.

We think the defendant has failed to prove such a permanent use or occupation of the building, within the meaning of the deed, as to work a forfeiture: and so the court ought to have instructed the jury. The evidence shows, that although they had ceased to use it for a school, yet there was occasional religious worship in the building, one of the objects mentioned in the deed, by permission of the trustees, thereby exercising such control of it as to be inconsistent with the idea that Mrs. McCaffrey had any interest except at their will and pleasure. That the occupation continued for seven years makes no difference; for as it was in the commencement a possession at the will of the trustees, so it continued during the whole period to be held at their pleasure. It was temporary in its nature, and not a *permanent* use of the building, which alone can work a forfeiture. The declaration of one of the trustees, that the property had fallen to Jacob Eshleman, and that he had nothing more to do with it, cannot affect the right of the corporation, who alone are the persons really interested in the property. The trustees have no right to relinquish property belonging to others.

On this point we think the judgment must be reversed. But as the cause goes down for another trial, it becomes necessary to notice another point, and that is, can the sheriff's vendee enter for the condition broken. The deed provides that the property shall revert to the party of the first part, and to his heirs and assigns. The sheriff's vendee is not an heir, yet is he not legal assignee by operation of law, within the true intent and meaning of the deed, which reserves the right of entry, not only to the heirs, but his assigns. That a grantor cannot reserve such a right, will hardly be contended, as in Pennsylvania there is no policy of law which forbids it. The law against maintenance has never been

[McKissick v. Pickle.]

adopted in this State. The reason assigned why a condition in England could not be assigned, is, because no title could be made to land held by another adversely, as that was against the law, which forbid maintenance. And hence the rule, that none but the grantor, or his heirs, can enter for condition broken. This reason does not apply here, where the grantor expressly reserves the right: 55 *Law Library, Crabbe on Real Property* 531, 550, sections 2150, 2189, 2190, and the authorities there cited; 5 *Watts* 493, Martin v. McCord; 9 *Barr* 433, Wright v. Linn; 1 *Jones* 444, Klinkener v. School Directors, &c.; 3 *Caine* 345, Newkirk v. Newkirk; 5 *Ser. & R.* 385, Hamilton v. Elliott. In the last case, Chief Justice GIBSON says, none but the feoffor or his heirs can enter; and the reason why a right of entry cannot be assigned is, that a contrary doctrine would favor maintenance and promote litigation. This is a fair case for the application of the maxim, *cessante ratione cessat ipse lex.*

But a doubt has been suggested whether the grantor had such an interest in the land, the condition not being broken at the time, as would be the subject of levy and sale by the sheriff. This point we think is expressly ruled in Hayden v. Stanton, 5 *Pick.* 528. That was an estate, as here, devised for the use of a school-house, on a condition subsequent. This was held to be a devise of a conditional, and not an absolute fee; that an interest still remained in the devisor, and his heirs. The court say, it is clear the whole interest is not disposed of to the beneficiaries. If then, an interest in the land remain in the grantor, notwithstanding the grant, it may be sold by the sheriff, for in this State all possible contingent titles in land accompanied with a real interest, may be seized in execution and sold by the sheriff: Humphrey's Lessee v. Humphries, 2 *Dal.* 223; 1 *Yates* 427; Rickert v. Madeira, 1 *Rawle* 432. The sheriff in these cases levied on all the right, title, and interest of Samuel Ferguson, the grantor, in all the lots, streets and alleys in Georgetown, &c. The interest of Ferguson therefore, whatever it was, passed to the sheriff's vendee, and as such, his vendee had a right of entry by the express terms of the deed. In a condition at law, it is true that none but the grantor and his heirs can enter for a condition broken. No assignee or stranger can do so. But I know of no rule of policy in this State, where the ancient doctrine of maintenance does not prevail, which prohibits a grantor or devisor from directing otherwise.

Judgment reversed and a *venire de novo* awarded.

Wither's Appeal.

Interest on the balance in the hands of an administrator from the time of its receipt is not of course; circumstances may be shown by the administrator, which would exempt him from the payment of interest.

2. Interest is an incident to a decree of the Orphans' Court, as it is to a judgment in the Common Pleas.

3. Where an auditor to whom the account of the administrator was referred to report upon exceptions to it, made report that a certain amount was in the hands of the accountant on the day of exhibiting his account, which report was simply confirmed in the Orphans' Court: *Held* that it was error in an auditor to whom the account was referred for distribution of the balance, to charge interest on the balance reported from the day of the exhibition of the account, instead of from the day of the decree of the confirmation by the Orphan's Court. The auditor appointed to report distribution is confined to the decree of the Orphans' Court.

APPEAL by John H. Withers, administrator of the estate of Samuel McKinney, deceased, from the decree of the Orphans' Court of Lancaster county, confirming the report of the auditor, distributing the assets in his hands among creditors, &c.

John H. Withers, administrator of Samuel McKinney, deceased, on the 18th day of November 1847, filed his account on said estate in the register's office of Lancaster county.

December 20th, 1847, in the Orphans' Court an auditor was appointed to pass on the exceptions.

March 19, 1849, auditor's report read and confirmed *nisi*, in which he reported the sum of $3857.05 *in the hands of accountant as of the day of exhibition of his account on the 18th of November* 1847.

This report was excepted to, and, on the 20th of August 1849, *was confirmed.*

September 10, 1849, appeal by John H. Withers to Supreme Court. July 1, 1850, *decree affirmed.*

February 5, 1851, report of auditor distributing assets, &c., read and confirmed *nisi* in Orphans' Court.

In the report, the auditor charged the balance of account, viz..	$3857.05
To which he added interest from 18th November 1847, to 1st February 1851....................................	740.55

This charge of interest was excepted to by the accountant, and on the 22d of April 1851, exceptions overruled. From this decision John H. Withers, accountant, took this appeal.

Exception was filed:

That the Orphans' Court erred in confirming the report of the auditor, charging the accountant with $740.55 interest.

[Wither's Appeal.]

Frazer, for appellant.—The report of the auditor on the administrators account was filed *March* 19, 1849, afterwards confirmed *in the Orphans' Court on the 20th of August* 1849. This report finds $3857.05, *in the hands of accountant as of* 18*th of November* 1847, *day of exhibition of the account, but does not find or charge accountant with interest on that sum.* Nor does the Orphans' Court charge interest. *Both court and auditor expressly avoid doing so,* and the report and decree thus *disallow interest*, and report $3857.05 *as in accountant's hands.*

The auditor of distribution was clearly unauthorized to charge interest; he was going beyond the report and decree of the court, and thus in *effect reversing their decree.*

This decree was confirmed by the Supreme Court, and could not in *any way be altered or added to*. It was conclusive on the subject-matter.

Again, even if open, no interest can be charged against an administrator, &c., while his accounts are pending before auditors: 8 *Watts* 73, Hoopes *v.* Brinton; 5 *Barr* 413, Stehman's Appeal.

Stephens, contra.—There was no evidence before the auditor of distribution, that the administrator had *not* used the money in his hands. The confirmation of the report of the auditor that he had a balance of $3857.05 in his hands in November 1847, was a decree for the aggregate amount of principal and interest. He referred to Yundt's Appeal, 1 *Harris.*

The opinion of the court was delivered May 23, by

ROGERS, J.—The auditor appointed to distribute the assets, in ascertaining the amount in the hands of the administrator, to be distributed, is confined to the decree of the Orphans' Court. He cannot go behind the decree for the purpose of increasing or diminishing the sum there ascertained. This is indubitable, and therefore the only question here is as to the construction of the decree; that is, has the court decreed the sum to be paid as $3857.05, or have they decreed that sum with the addition of interest; the auditor to ascertain the amount of the assets having reported that sum in the hands of accountant, as of the day of the exhibition of his account, to wit, the 18th day of November 1847. It is very certain that the auditor might, if he had thought proper, have charged the accountant with interest on the money in his hands, and perhaps ought to have done so, particularly in the absence of proof that it had not been used by accountant, or that it was lying idle, leaving it open to the natural presumption that the money was applied to his own purposes. But although he might, yet it is clear he has not done so. He seems to have left the question of interest to be settled by the court. The charge of interest as against an administrator, is not a matter of right, a ne-

[Wither's Appeal.]

cessary consequence of money being in his hands; but depends on a variety of circumstances, such, for example, as the money being needed for the payment of debts, or other purposes connected with the settlement of the estate. If, therefore, it was the intention of the auditor, that interest should be added, it ought to have formed part of the report. The Orphans' Court, instead of passing upon the question of interest, which they had unquestionable power to do, have confined themselves (purposely, we suppose,) to a simple confirmation of the report. The entry is that the report was excepted to, and, on the 20th August 1849, was confirmed. This decree, we apprehend, cannot relate back to the 18th November 1847, for the purpose of charging the accountant with interest, but must be considered as a decree of the 20th August 1849, when the auditor's report was confirmed by the Orphans' Court. Had the auditor given interest, a simple confirmation of the report would carry interest. But having omitted, or purposely avoided doing so, which is the same thing, we cannot see how it can be viewed as a decree for more than is contained in the report itself. It does not purport to go beyond the report, and must be confined to that. It is highly probable that if the attention of the Orphans' Court had been directed to it, and a special decree in the proper form been made, as ought to be the practice of that court, the accountant would have been charged with interest. But this is not certainly so; the accountant might have shown circumstances which would exempt him from the payment of interest. As no mention is made of interest, either by the auditor or the court, we cannot undertake to charge the administrator on probability or conjecture. There was error therefore in charging accountant with interest from the 18th November 1847.

But is the accountant chargeable with interest at all, and if so, from what time? That an administrator is chargeable with interest from the decree cannot be doubted. In that respect a decree is like a judgment, to which interest, in this State, is a necessary incident. The decree of the Orphans' Court was made the 20th August 1849; and from that time, the accountant is chargeable with interest on the sum of $3857.05, (the amount decreed to be paid,) up to the time of the affirmance of the decree, to wit, the 1st day of July 1850. The interest is thus to be calculated on the aggregate sum of principal and interest, from the said 1st July 1850, until this time. It seems that the administrator appealed on the 10th September 1849; and July 1, 1850, the decree was affirmed by the Supreme Court. It must be remarked that in this court, as well as in the Orphans' Court, a loose practice has prevailed as to decrees on appeals, which ought to be corrected. Instead of ascertaining the amount due, and making a special decree, the decree is usually entered, "decree confirmed." The proceedings are then

154 SUPREME COURT [Harrisburg

[Wither's Appeal.]

remitted to the Orphans' Court to carry the decree into effect, giving interest from the time of the decree in the Orphans' Court.

And now to wit, this 23d day of May 1851, after argument and due consideration, it is ordered and decreed that accountant be charged with the sum of four thousand two hundred and seventy-five dollars and forty-one cents, principal and interest in his hands. Record remitted to the Orphans' Court to carry this decree into effect, by distributing the amount so decreed to the persons entitled to the same according to the decree of the Orphans' Court. Appellee to pay costs.

Thurston *versus* Franklin College.

In the case of an action to recover damages for breach of a parol contract for the purchase of land, the right of action accrues when the vendor conveys to a stranger. It exists *before eviction* by the grantee.

ERROR to the Common Pleas of *Lancaster county*.

This was an action of trespass on the case, by Lyman Thurston and John M. Taylor for the use of Lyman Thurston vs. The Trustees of Franklin College, in the borough and county of Lancaster.

It was an action for damages for a breach of an alleged contract for the purchase of land. Summons issued April 3, 1849. Defendants plead *non assumpsit* and *non assumpsit infra sex annos;* and subsequently, with leave of court, added the plea of *actio non accrevit infra sex annos*. February 3, 1851, verdict for defendants.

On the part of the plaintiff in error, the case was stated partly as follows:—

Samuel W. Morris, Esq., was appointed attorney in fact of the trustees of Franklin College, and authorized to sell the college lands, situated in Bradford county, with directions to give settlers residing upon the land the preference in disposing the same. Morris lived in Tioga county, and was not usually in Bradford, except at the sessions of the courts. He told many of the settlers, and requested them to inform the rest, that if any of them wished to purchase, he might at any time pay fifty dollars into the Towanda Bank, to the credit of the said Morris, and that upon doing so, he (Morris) would give the person thus paying a written contract for the land. In 1840, Lyman Thurston and John M. Taylor were living upon a portion of said lands, and had made some improvements thereupon. The proposition of Judge Morris having been communicated to them, they paid the fifty dollars into the Towanda Bank, to the credit of Judge Morris, by whom the money was

[Thurston v. Franklin College.]

afterwards drawn. Subsequently, in a conversation, in September 1840, between Taylor and Morris, the latter promised to send the written contract by mail, which he omitted to do.

It was alleged that Thurston and Taylor continued in possession for some time, making valuable improvements, and then Taylor sold out his interest in the land to Thurston.

On the 24th day of March, A. D. 1841, the college sold all her lands in Bradford county, including the Taylor and Thurston tract, to John McCord, who brought an action of ejectment against Thurston. The cause was tried at May term 1843; and May 10, jury discharged, and judgment for the plaintiff.

Thurston was in possession when the contract was made. Having been ejected, Thurston brought this action within six years from the time of the verdict against him.

The only defence offered was the statute of limitations, and the question was, whether the action was barred six years from the time when conveyance was made to McCord, or from the time that Thurston was ejected; and further, whether the trustees have not been guilty of fraud, so as to prevent them from availing themselves of the statute of limitations.

On the part of the plaintiff below, J. D. Goodenough testified, *inter alia:*—Samuel W. Morris, of Tioga county, acted as agent and attorney in fact for the trustees of Franklin College. I purchased two lots or tracts of the Franklin College land of said Morris. Purchased one of said lots upwards of twenty years ago, and the other about fifteen years ago. I paid two dollars and fifty cents per acre for both tracts. I am not positive as to the time, but I think some time in the years 1837 or 1838, I made a payment to Judge Morris on my land; he was in Towanda, and requested me to pay it to the Towanda Bank, which I did. At this time he told me when I wished to make payments, I need not go to Tioga county, but to pay into the Towanda Bank. At this time he said that the college wanted to sell their lands, and he wanted to sell it for them, and that if anybody wanted any of the lands, they might deposit fifty dollars in the Towanda Bank, and when he came out he would give them a contract, and they should be sure of the land; said they might rest contented, the land was theirs as soon as they had deposited the fifty dollars in the Towanda Bank; said they might pick out any lot they had a mind for, that was not contracted, and bring him the number of the lot, and the first time he came to Towanda he would give them a contract; and if he did not the first time he came out, he would the second. He told me to tell all the setlers that wanted to purchase or contract for Franklin College lands, that they might have any of the Franklin College lands that was not previously contracted, by paying fifty dollars on a lot into the Towanda Bank, as mentioned above. This fifty dollars was to be the first instalment, which was

[Thurston v. Franklin College.]

to be paid before they could have a contract. I informed these plaintiffs, Taylor and Thurston, as well as other settlers, what Morris requested me to inform them. At the time I informed Thurston and Taylor, I knew the lot that they were on was not contracted for, as I lived close by, and knew what lots were contracted for. Judge Morris had a uniform price for the Franklin College lands, of two dollars and fifty cents per acre. Cannot say whether it was before or after Thurston went on, but it was near that time. I never knew him to ask more than three dollars per acre for any lands in that vicinity, excepting for a very heavy timbered lot that he sold for four dollars per acre, just before John McCord purchased. I was present on the trial of an ejectment, in the Common Pleas of Bradford county, in favor of John McCord, against said plaintiffs, Taylor and Thurston. That suit was, as appears by the certified copy No. 121, February term 1842, Bradford county Common Pleas. The land mentioned in the summons in that case is the same land that Taylor and Thurston were in possession of, as before mentioned. The defendant, Taylor, moved off the land some time before the trial of the cause, and Thurston a few weeks after the trial. I was called and sworn as a witness in said trial. The defendants alleged on that trial that they had a right to hold said land, by virtue of a parol contract. The plaintiffs alleged that as the defendants were in possession of the land at the time the contract was made, they could not hold the land.

Nelson Gilbert testified:—In the season of 1840, I think at September term, I saw M. C. Mercur and Samuel W. Morris meet upon the sidewalk in Towanda. Mr. Mercur was then an officer in the Towanda Bank; either cashier or teller; cannot say which. He has been both. I understood Mr. Mercur to say to Mr. Morris, that there had been fifty dollars paid into the bank to his credit. Mr. Morris asked him who by, and Mercur replied by John M. Taylor and Lyman Thurston. Morris then replied that he was very glad to get money at any time, and that he would call over and get it. I know the land upon which Taylor and Thurston were living in 1840; Thurston and Taylor both occupied the lot in 1840, and had for two years previous. Taylor had longer; I think he commenced there in 1836. In 1838 I understood from both Taylor and Thurston that Taylor had sold an undivided half of the lot to Lyman Thurston. This I understood both before and after Thurston took possession, and at the time I helped Lyman Thurston to raise his house. I think the land was worth ten dollars per acre in May 1843, with the improvements upon it. I think all the improvements had been made by Taylor and Thurston; I know of no one else making any improvements.

Testimony was also given on the part of the defendant. On the trial, the following points were submitted on the part of the plaintiffs:—

[Thurston v. Franklin College.]

1st. The plaintiffs are entitled to recover from the defendants, as the measure of damages, the difference of the price agreed upon for the land, and the enhanced value of the same when the defendants were ejected on the 10th day of May 1843.

2d. The plea of the statute of limitations will not operate against the plaintiffs, as the injury and cause of action accrued only on the 10th of May 1843, a period of less than six years at the time this suit was brought.

3d. The conduct of the defendants was fraudulent, and they cannot therefore take advantage of the statute of limitations.

Charge of LEWIS, J.—This is an action to recover damages for breach of a contract to give the plaintiff a contract in writing for 114 acres and 40 perches of land in Bradford county, at $2.50 per acre, payable in four equal annual payments, in consideration that the defendant would deposit in the Towanda Bank, to the credit of the defendant's agent, the sum of fifty dollars. That sum was deposited in February 1840, and in September 1840, Judge Morris, the defendant's agent, had notice of it, and on demand being made for the contract in writing, promised to send it by mail. On the 24th March 1841, the defendants conveyed the land to John McCord, who, within three or four weeks after, requested Taylor, the plaintiff, then in possession, to leave the premises, and endeavored to make some arrangment with him respecting giving up possession. About this time, Taylor applied to Judge Morris, relative to the contract with him, but could get no satisfaction. On the 19th January 1842, he issued an *estrepment*, and this was followed by an attachment for disobeying the writ of *estrepment*. The attachment was issued on the 25th February 1842. On the 10th May 1843, the plaintiffs in this action (defendants in the ejectment) confessed judgment in the latter action, and were turned out of possession. The question is, When did the present right of action accrue? At the time the contract with Morris was violated by the conveyance to McCord, and notice thereof given by the latter to Taylor and Thurston? or at the time the judgment was confessed in ejectment? It is material in this case that the plaintiffs did not *receive possession under the contract with Morris*, but Taylor, the only one ever in possession, was there long before as a trespasser, cutting timber and exercising ownership, without any title whatever. By the terms of the contract with Morris, the whole consideration-money was to have been paid in four years, so that there is no ground for saying that the parties had a lifetime to fulfil the contract. In these two particulars, the present case differs from the cases cited. In Eames v. Savage, 14 *Mass.* 425, the party seeking to recover back the money paid had been *put into possession under the contract*, and, upon the eviction, it might be well said that the consideration failed, and that a right of action accrued to recover back the money. Besides, that case was de-

[Thurston v. Franklin College.]

cided more on the form of the pleadings than on the effect of the evidence under the statute of limitations. In Walter *v.* Walter, 1 *Whar.* 292, the action was founded upon a partition which was not perfected until within six years from the commencement of the suit, and consequently no right of action for the money payable for *owelty* existed, until the partition was perfected by conveyance. In Leinhart *v.* Forringer, 1 *Watts* 492, it was held that the right of action accrues when the defendant has put it in the power of the plaintiff to rescind the bargain, and it is plainly intimated in that case, that "if the defendant *had conveyed to a stranger, and the plaintiff was apprized of the fact six years before suit was brought,*" the action would have been barred : *Id.* 494. That is plainly the case now before us—the defendant conveyed to a stranger in March 1841, and that stranger not only apprized the plaintiffs of it within three or four weeks afterwards, but, in January 1842, brought ejectment on his title, and in February 1842, pursued his claim, and denied the plaintiff's right to exercise acts of ownership over the property, by an *estrepment* and an attachment for disobedience to the writ. There then was decisive evidence of a violation of the contract in March 1841, and full notice of it in that year, and in the year 1842, but this action was not brought until 30th April 1849. It is our opinion that the action is barred by the statute of limitations, and that the plaintiffs are not entitled to recover. Entertaining these views, we must necessarily decline giving the instructions requested in the points presented by the plaintiff's counsel.

Plaintiff's counsel excepted to the charge.

It was assigned for error:
1. The court erred in charging the jury that plaintiff's cause of action was barred by the statute of limitations.
2. The court should have submitted the question of fraud to the jury.
3. The court erred in refusing to answer specially the plaintiff's points.

Amwake and *Mathiot*, for plaintiffs in error.—It was contended that no complete cause of action had accrued to plaintiff before the 10th day of May 1843, when he was evicted by defendant's vendee, and, therefore, the statute of limitations was not a bar to plaintiff's action.

That there was no evidence of breach of contract on the part of the vendor until upon the trial of the ejectment. The commencement of the action was no notice, for it was not inconsistent with an affirmance of the contract, and therefore the presumption was a reasonable one that the suit was instituted for the recovery of the balance of the purchase-money. But on the case being called for

[Thurston v. Franklin College.]

trial, the defendant first ascertained that the plaintiff wholly repudiated the contract; and the six years commenced running from that time: Jones v. Trimble, 3 *Rawle* 381; McCaskill v. McCaskill, 3 *Rich.* 196; Baricks v. Edwards, 11 *Paige* 289; Leinhart v. Forringer, 1 *Pa. Rep.* 492; Walker v. Bradley, 3 *Pick.* 261; Shearman v. Akin, 4 *Pick.* 296; Eames v. Savage, 14 *Mass. Rep.* 425; Walter v. Walter, 1 *Whar.* 292; Richards v. Allen, 5 *Shep.* 296; Hall v. Vandegrift, 3 *Bin.* 374; Kerns v. Schoonmaker, 4 *Ham.* 331; Mercer v. Watson, 1 *Watts* 330.

It is further contended that in this case the defendant acted fraudulently in suffering the plaintiff to remain in possession of the premises, and make valuable improvements on the same, on the strength and faith of the contract entered into to give a deed of conveyance for the same, and afterwards selling the property with the improvements thereon to John McCord, who evicted the plaintiff. The court ought therefore to have submitted the same to the jury as a matter of fact, for them to decide whether the plaintiff acted fraudulently or not; and, if fraudulently, the statute would not operate, or at least only commence running when the fraud was consummated, to wit, the 10th day of May 1843, the time plaintiff was evicted by defendant's vendee: Pennock v. Freeman, 1 *Watts* 410; Jones v. Conoway, 4 *Yeates* 109.

Thompson, for defendant.—The deed to McCord and notice of it put it into the power of Taylor to rescind the contract, and the right of action for a breach of it occurred: 1 *Pa. Rep.* 494, Leinhart v. Forringer. The conveyance and notice was eight years before suit brought.

The cases of Jones v. Trimble, Walker v. Bradley, and Shearman v. Aken are not analogous cases; and the case of Barick v. Edwards, 11 *Paige* 289, was a bill in chancery to establish the equitable right to certain premises, by one who had been evicted. *This is an action for breach of contract.*

The conduct of the defendants in error was not fraudulent; at most, they merely broke the alleged contract, and it would have been error on the part of the judge to have submitted the question of fraud to the jury, without any evidence whatever tending in any degree to prove fraud: 1 *Whar. Dig.* 576; *Syl.* 200, 210, 215.

May 26.

PER CURIAM.—The right of action clearly accrued when the defendant conveyed to a stranger. Let the judgment be affirmed on the opinion of the judge below.

Stewart and Others *versus* Kelly.

In an action on a contract for the sale of hogs, the declaration of the plaintiff alleged their delivery, which the proof failed to establish: an application was made during the trial for leave to amend the declaration by averring the readiness of plaintiff to deliver and the refusal of the defendant to receive and pay for the hogs, which amendment the court refused to permit: *Held*, that such refusal was error.

ERROR to the Common Pleas of *Lancaster county*.

This was an action in *assumpsit* by Stewart, Stinson, and others, against Patrick Kelly, for not complying with his agreement for the purchase of a quantity of hogs. Plaintiff had agreed to deliver to Kelly, at Baltimore, from 500 to 1200 head of hogs, for which Kelly was to pay at the rate of $6 per 100 net weight when delivered.

In the narr. filed, the delivery of the hogs was alleged. The evidence not establishing the delivery of the hogs, the plaintiffs' counsel on the trial asked leave to withdraw the narr. on file, and substitute a new one, in which it was alleged that the plaintiffs had the hogs in Baltimore ready for delivery, of which the defendant had notice and refused to accept them.

Defendant's counsel objected to the amendment proposed, because it varied the cause of action—did not aver an offer to deliver the number of hogs required by the contract; and because the evidence had been taken in Maryland, under the cause of action set forth in the original declaration. The amendment converts an executed contract into an executory contract.

LEWIS, J., refused to permit the amendment to be filed, on the authority in 2 *Rawle* 337, Diehl *v.* McGlue.

The plaintiffs' counsel excepted.

The plaintiffs having rested their case on the parts of the depositions already given in evidence, the court instructed the jury that the declaration set forth an executed contract; the averment of delivery of the hogs in the city of Baltimore, "according to the terms of the agreement," must be understood to be an averment of delivery to *the defendant*. The breach assigned is the non-payment of the price. The testimony does not sustain this allegation, and does not establish the plaintiffs' case as set forth. The defendant is therefore entitled to a verdict.

It was assigned for error:

That the court erred in instructing the jury that the plaintiffs could not recover, and in refusing the amendment offered.

Stevens, for plaintiffs in error.—The evidence proved that all the hogs were at the place appointed for delivery, viz. Baltimore,

[Stewart and Others v. Kelly.]

and were weighed, and that defendant was at the place and informed on the subject.

The amendment was allowable. The amended offered recited the *same* article of agreement as referred to in the original narr. The cause of action was the same: 8 *Ser. & R.* 444; 2 *id.* 1; 8 *id.* 287; 11 *id.* 101. So long as the plaintiff adheres to the contract on which the declaration is founded, an alteration of the grounds of recovery, or of the modes in which the defendant has violated the contract is admissible: 4 *W. & Ser.* 277; 11 *Ser. & R.* 101, Newlin v. Palmer; 15 *Ser. & R.* 83; 4 *W. & Ser.* 277; 7 *Barr* 433, Schoneman v. Fegley.

Franklin, with whom was *Fordney*, for defendant.—The amendment offered was inadmissible. The narr. filed set forth a contract executed; the amended narr. set forth an executory contract, thus introducing a new state of facts: 2 *Rawle* 337, Diehl v. McGlue.

The plaintiffs filed a declaration presenting the issue on the delivery of the hogs; then took depositions; and the defendant, relying on the plaintiff's inability to prove a delivery, took no steps for cross-examining the witnesses. The case being on trial, these depositions were read in evidence; and after that, the plaintiff offered to amend so as to change entirely the issue presented.

The opinion of the court was delivered May 19, by

CHAMBERS, J.—This action is one of *assumpsit* on special contract, in writing of defendant, to pay the plaintiffs a certain price for a number of hogs to be delivered the defendant at Baltimore by a time appointed. The plaintiffs declared on an executed contract, alleging performance by delivery of the hogs, and claimed damages of the defendant for a refusal to pay. The evidence furnished by the plaintiffs proved that they had, at Baltimore, the hogs contracted for at the time appointed; and that they were then and there ready to deliver the same to Kelly, the defendant, who refused to accept the hogs, or pay for them, but there was no delivery. As the plaintiffs failed to prove a performed contract on their part as laid in the narr., the court below was right in saying that the plaintiffs could not recover.

The second error assigned is that the court refused to allow the plaintiffs to amend the pleadings by filing another narr., reciting the same agreement between the plaintiffs and defendant as was described in the first narr. as the foundation of the plaintiffs' action. In the narr. submitted as an amendment, the cause of action was substantially the same, being on the same contract, assigning the breach of the contract according to the facts, varying the allegation of delivery as contained in the first narr. to the allegation of being ready to deliver the hogs to the defendant, and his refusal to accept and pay for the same. The construction of the contract,

[Stewart and Others *v.* Kelly.]

the injury to the plaintiffs, and the measure of damages were the same under one allegation as under the other.

Such an amendment was within the letter and spirit of the act of 21st March 1806, and it was mandatory to the court to permit it. This act, though susceptible of abuse, to be restrained by judicial discretion, is still a salutary and remedial one, which ought to receive a liberal construction.

There would rarely occur a more appropriate case for its application than the amendment here submitted, and one more within the policy of the law. The amendment proposed was in accordance with the principles well settled by this court in the application of this law of amendment. In the case of Cox *v.* Tilghman, 1 *Whar.* 287, it was said by SERGEANT, J., "that an examination of the decided cases will show that in an action *ex contractu*, so long as the plaintiff adheres to the original instrument or contract on which the declaration is founded, an alteration of the grounds of recovery on that instrument or contract, or of the modes in which the defendant has violated it, is not an alteration of the cause of action." In Cassel *v.* Cook, 8 *Ser. & R.* 268, which was covenant with an averment of performance by plaintiff, after the jury were sworn and made progress, the plaintiff offered an amendment of a new count, excusing the omission of the plaintiff to perform, which was admitted, and was, as Justice DUNCAN said, "the assignment of a breach of the same covenant, on the same instrument, to be covered by the same penalty." In Shannon *v.* The Com'th, 8 *Ser. & R.* 444, it was held by the court, that in an action on a sheriff's bond, the plaintiff might amend his declaration by assigning new breaches of the condition of the bond. In accordance are the cases of Newlin *v.* Palmer, 11 *Ser. & R.* 98; Cunningham *v.* Day, 2 *Ser. & R.* 1; Schoneman *v.* Fegley, 7 *Barr* 434; Caldwell *v.* Remington, 2 *Whar.* 132; Rodrigue *v.* Curcier, 15 *Ser. & R.* 83.

The learned judge who refused the amendment would seem to have been misled in the hurry of a jury trial, by the case of Diehl *v.* McGlue, 2 *Rawle* 337, which was a case very distinguishable. In that case, the plaintiff's declaration was an *indebitatus assumpsit*, with the usual various counts, and on the trial the plaintiff, to introduce evidence inadmissible under any of his many counts, offered an additional count stating a special agreement and promise of defendant, entirely variant from that declared on, and which the court below received. But this court, on error, "held that it was improperly admitted, because it introduced a new cause of action." In this case, the contract declared on, the cause of action alleged, and the redress sought were the same under the amendment proposed as under the narr. last filed. It was not a case in which a plaintiff, with an explicit written contract and a cause of action substantiated by uncontradicted testimony, was to be cast out of court by mere form in the pleadings, and in favour of a defendant

[Stewart and Others v. Kelly.]

who refused to execute his contract, and who offered no excuse or defence for his failure to perform.

In the opinion of the court, there was error in the court below in refusing the amendment. Judgment is reversed, and a *venire facias de novo* awarded.

The Commonwealth *versus* Fraim.

In the appropriation act of 11th April 1848, it was provided that the *common school system* shall be held to be adopted by all the school districts in the commonwealth, and that each school district levying a tax, shall be entitled to a deduction of twenty-five per cent. of all moneys paid into the county treasury by such district, for State purposes, during the *two next ensuing school years;* which school years by a former act, were to end on the first *Monday of June* of each year: It was held that the abatement was to be limited to the taxes assessed for the school years of 1848 and 1849, and was not to extend to taxes which had been assessed for the school year commencing on the first Monday of June 1850, but which had been advanced or paid into the county treasury *before* that day.

Error to the Common Pleas of *Lancaster county*.

This was an application in the name of the Commonwealth *ex rel.* the School Directors of Manheim township, Lancaster county, for a *mandamus* to be issued to Miller Fraim, treasurer of Lancaster county.

The petition was as follows:—

To the honorable the Judges of the Court of Common Pleas of Lancaster county.

The petition of John S. Hostetter, Christian Hostetter, John Miller, David Harnish, John Huber, and John Gerber, school directors of the school district consisting of Manheim township, in the said county, respectfully represents:

That by an act of the General Assembly of this commonwealth, passed the eleventh day of April, A. D. eighteen hundred and forty-eight, entitled "An act to provide for the ordinary expenses of government, the repairs of the canals and railroads belonging to the State, and the payment of other claims upon the commonwealth," it is among other things enacted, "that the common school system, *from and after the passage of this act,* shall be deemed, held, and taken to be adopted by the several school districts of this commonwealth: and that the school directors of the respective school districts from which the undrawn school appropriations were taken by the act of the twenty-ninth of April, one thousand eight hundred and forty-four, entitled 'An act to reduce the State debt, and to incorporate the Pennsylvania canal and railroad company,' shall, during the month of May of the present year, levy and assess a tax, as required by existing laws, to enable school districts to receive their portion of the State appropriation: and each of said school districts in which a tax shall be so levied and

[The Commonwealth v. Fraim.]

assessed as aforesaid, shall thereupon receive its portion of the aforesaid appropriation of two hundred thousand dollars, and shall be entitled to a deduction of twenty-five per cent. of all moneys paid into the county treasury by such district for State purposes, *during the two next ensuing school years:* which money so deducted shall be paid to the treasurer of the board of school directors of such school district, and shall be exclusively appropriated to the erection of school-houses in such school districts." That by an act of Assembly, passed the thirteenth day of June, A. D. eighteen hundred and thirty-six, entitled "An act to consolidate and amend the several acts relative to a general system of education by common schools," it is provided that the school year shall be taken and understood *to end on the first Monday of June of each year.* That the said township of Manheim was one of the school districts from which the undrawn school appropriations were taken by the act of twenty-ninth April, eighteen hundred and forty-four, referred to, and that the school directors thereof did, during the month of May of the year eighteen hundred and forty-eight, levy and assess a tax as required by existing laws, to enable school districts to receive their portion of the State appropriation; and did in all other respects fully and faithfully comply with the requisitions of the act of assembly hereinbefore in part recited.

And your petitioners further represent that during the two school years next ensuing the passage of the said act of Assembly, that is to say, from the first Monday of June, A. D. eighteen hundred and forty-eight, to the first Monday of June, A. D. eighteen hundred and fifty, the moneys paid into the county treasury by the said school district for State purposes, amounted to the sum of ten thousand five hundred and sixty dollars and seventeen cents: by reason whereof, under the provisions of the said act, the said school district became entitled to a deduction of two thousand six hundred and forty dollars and four and one-fourth cents, being twenty-five per cent. of such moneys, to be paid to the treasurer of the board of school directors of said district, and appropriated in the manner prescribed by the said act.

And your petitioners further represent, that although the late and present county treasurers of Lancaster county have paid to the treasurer of the said board the sum of seventeen hundred and sixty-four dollars and eighty-three cents, part of the said sum, yet Miller Fraim, Esq., present county treasurer of said county, has refused to pay to Henry B. Bowman, treasurer of the board of school directors of said district, eight hundred and seventy-five dollars and twenty-one and one-fourth cents, the balance of said sum so payable as above stated, and still refuses to pay, and illegally withholds the same.

Your petitioners therefore humbly pray the court to award a writ of *mandamus*, to be directed to Miller Fraim, Esq., county

[The Commonwealth v. Fraim.]

treasurer of Lancaster county, commanding him to pay to Henry B. Bowman, treasurer of the board of school directors of Manheim township school district, in the said county, the said sum of eight hundred and seventy-five dollars and twenty-one and one-fourth cents, due and payable as hereinbefore set forth, or show cause to the contrary, and upon the return thereof, to award such other writ or writs and make such further order as may be necessary in the premises, and they will pray, &c.

In the answer of Miller Fraim, it was, *inter alia,* alleged that the whole amount of tax assessed and levied and charged against

Manheim township for the year 1848 was	$3490.32
Tavern and retailers' licenses for 1848,	131.50
Whole amount	$3621.82
Deducting for exonerations and commissions,	179.98
There was paid into the county treasury	$3441.84

The treasurer of the school district received from the county treasurer $872.58, which was $12.12 more than twenty-five per cent. on the net amount.

That the State tax assessed, levied, and charged against said Manheim township for the year 1849 was	$3575.77
Tavern, retailers' and distillers' licenses for 1849 was	178.50
Whole amount	$3754.27
Deducting amount of exonerations and commissions	185.25
	$3569.02

$892.25, being twenty-five per cent. on the net amount, was paid by the county treasurer to the treasurer of the school district.

It was admitted that the following payments for State purposes were made by Manheim township, into the county treasury, on account of the tax assessed and levied for State purposes by the said township for the year 1850, to wit:

1850, May 2, on account of tax of 1850	$ 50.00
" June 1, on account of tax of 1850	3380.35
" " 1, retailers' licenses, 1850	7.00
" " 1, tavern licenses, 1850	31.75
	$3469.10

It is alleged that the said school directors are not entitled to any percentage on the above tax of 1850 paid into the county treasury. But if entitled to any, they have no claim for that portion paid *on the 1st day of June,* A. D. 1850, because, prior to that day, the two next ensuing school years specified in the act of the 11th day of April 1848 had expired.

[The Commonwealth v. Fraim.]

It was asked that the petition be dismissed with costs. The 1st day of June 1850 was *Saturday*.

To the answer the relators demurred, and judgment was entered for the respondent with costs.

To this judgment error was assigned.

Franklin, for the school directors.—He cited the act of 8th April 1833, by the first section of which, undrawn balances were to remain in the State treasury, and accumulate for the use of the districts, for any time not exceeding two years from the 1st November 1843. The act of 1844 withdrew the right to undrawn balances. By the act of 11th April 1848, all school districts were made accepting districts, and it was provided that those districts which complied with the school system should receive a portion of the township taxes paid for *two* years. The 25 per cent. does not equal the amount which had been withdrawn from the township by the act of 1843. The act of 11th April 1848 provided that the two years should commence on the 1st Monday of June 1848, and it was contended by him that *all payments made before the 1st Monday of June* 1850 were liable to the abatement of 25 per cent. When the taxes were paid by Manheim township in May and on 1st day of June 1850, the school year for 1850 had not begun to run. That it was a fallacy to say that the payments made on and previous to the 1st day of June 1850 were not *then due and payable*. The tax had been assessed, the duplicates had been committed to the collectors, and the taxes were payable within thirty days, though the collector could not levy till the thirty days had expired. The 1st day of June 1850 was Saturday, and the school year which terminated on the first *Monday* of June had not then expired.

Mathiot, for the respondent.—He contended that under a proper construction of the act of 11th day of April, A. D. 1848, the relators are entitled to a percentage upon State revenue derived from their school district for *two years* only, to wit, the years 1848 and 1849, and this has been paid to them. If they have thought proper to advance the amount of their State tax for the *third year*, viz. 1850, so that its payment falls into the treasury prior to the first Monday of June 1850, this does not enable them to draw their percentage for *three years*.

The payment of the tax for 1850 was an advancement, by reason of which the township, under the act of 1844, became entitled to an abatement of five per cent.; but it was never contemplated that the school directors would set up a claim for the abatement of twenty-five per cent. upon money which was not due and payable to the commonwealth during the two school years.

The construction placed upon the act by the auditor-general, the superintendent of common schools, as well as the court below,

[The Commonwealth v. Fraim.]

should not be disturbed. He cited act May 31st, 1844, *Pam. Laws* 583; act April 16th, 1845, *id.* 508; act April 29th, 1844, *id.* 485; act April 11th, 1848, *id.* 521; act April 10th, 1849, *id.* 639; act May 10th, 1850, *id.* 732.

He observed that if a township which had *not* been in arrear had advanced, it would not be entitled to 25 per cent.; and that a township which had been in arrear should not be entitled to an abatement to that amount.

Mr. *Franklin* replied, that the taxes in 1850 were payable before the first Monday of June 1850, and being so payable during the school year of 1849–50, were liable to abatement.

The opinion of the court was delivered May 22, by

CHAMBERS, J.—This case depends on the construction of the act of Assembly of 11th of April 1848, in which, amongst other things, it is enacted, "that the common school system, from and after the passage of this act, shall be deemed, held, and taken to be adopted by the several school districts of this commonwealth; and that the school directors of the respective school districts from which the undrawn school appropriations were taken by the act of 29th of April 1844, entitled 'An act to reduce the State debt, and to incorporate the Pennsylvania Canal and Railroad Company,' shall, during the month of May of the present year, levy and assess a tax as required by existing laws, to enable school districts to receive their portion of the State appropriation; and each of said school districts in which a tax shall be so levied and assessed as aforesaid, shall thereupon receive its portion of the aforesaid appropriation of two hundred thousand dollars, and shall be entitled to a deduction of twenty-five per cent. of all moneys paid into the county treasury by such district for State purposes during the two next ensuing school years, which money so deducted shall be paid to the treasurer of the board of directors of such school district, and shall be exclusively appropriated to the erection of schoolhouses in such school districts."

The township of Manheim, in the county of Lancaster, was one of the school districts that had not before adopted the common school system, and from which the undrawn school appropriations were taken by the act of 29th April 1844. Under the act of 1848 recited, the school directors of that township, during the month of May of that year, did assess and levy a tax, as required by existing laws, to enable school districts to receive their portion of the State appropriation.

The whole amount of taxes assessed, levied, and charged against the township of Manheim for State purposes, and paid over to the county treasury, after exonerations and commissions, for the year 1848, was $3441.84, and of this there was paid by the county treasurer of Lancaster county to the treasurer of Manheim school

[The Commonwealth v. Fraim.]

district in 1849 the sum of $872.58, which was an excess of $12.12 beyond the 25 per cent. to which such district was entitled.

The total amount of taxes assessed, levied, and paid by the same township, after exonerations and commissions, to the treasurer of Lancaster county for State purposes, was the sum of $3569.02. This year's State tax was settled up on the 11th February 1850, being for the year 1849, at which time there was paid by the county treasurer of Lancaster county, to the treasurer of the Manheim school district, the sum of $892.25, being 25 per cent. on the amount of the state taxes for that township thus paid in for 1849. Are not the two yearly payments made as stated by the treasurer of Lancaster county to the treasurer of Manheim school district a full compliance with the legislative appropriation under the act of 1848? The school directors say not, for that afterwards there was paid by Manheim township into the Lancaster county treasury, on the 2d May 1850, $50, and 1st June 1850, $3419.10, for State purposes, being nearly the total of the State tax of that township for the year 1850; and on this they claim to be paid 25 per cent. by the county treasurer, as on moneys paid in by Manheim township into the county treasury for State purposes *during* the school year which ended on first Monday of June 1850. This is refused by the county treasurer of Lancaster county; and by the proceeding in this matter it is sought to compel him to pay with the aid of the process of this court. In putting a construction on this act to effectuate the intention of the legislature, reference must be had to the system of taxation within this commonwealth. The taxes assessed in the autumn and winter of one year are collected and paid over during the ensuing year, and are called the tax of the latter year. To induce the counties to pay their quota of State tax as early as fifteen days before the first of August of each year, an abatement of 5 per cent. is allowed; and if the county's quota is not paid into the state treasury before the second Tuesday of January following, the county delinquent is therefore charged 5 per cent. interest.

Whilst the State encourages the payment of the State tax by the middle of July, by allowing the abatement, it does not treat the county as a defaulter until after the second Tuesday of January. The township of Manheim did not settle up its State tax for 1849 till the 11th of February 1850, and within four months thereafter pays into the county treasury $3419, being nearly the total of its tax assessed for State purposes for that year. This unprecedented despatch, in paying over such an amount for State taxation is accounted for by the claim made of 25 per cent. on the amount last paid, which, in effect, if allowed, would be to give 25 per cent. on the State tax for a third year, instead of two. The legislature may be supposed, in estimating the amount of their grant for building school-houses, to have had regard to the amount assessed and

[The Commonwealth v. Fraim.]

paid by such townships for State purposes annually, and did choose to grant as a bounty to the township for building school-houses, one-fourth of the said State tax for two years. It was not, we presume, anticipated that the townships who were to be partakers of this bounty would hasten their yearly payments, so as to crowd three years' assessments for State purposes into payments during the two school years. If payment within the time were alone the measure, then if the township had been delinquent for balances of State taxes for the previous year, and had, after the passage of the act of 1848, elected to have paid up all its arrearages within the next school year, it was, under the construction placed on the law by the claimants, to have 25 per cent. on this indebtedness.

By confining the bounty of the legislature to one-fourth of the tax assessed and paid over for the next two school years, the intention of the legislature, we believe, will be fulfilled, and the execution of the law will be certain and uniform with all the townships to which it may apply.

Statutes are to be construed so as may best effectuate the intention of the makers, which sometimes may be collected from the cause or occasion of passing the statute, and, when discovered, it ought to be followed, with judgment and discretion in the construction, though that construction may seem contrary to the letter of the statute. It is said a thing within the letter of the statute is not within the statute unless it be within the intention of the makers; and such construction ought to be put on it as does not suffer it to be eluded: People v. Utica Ins. Co. 15 *Johns. Rep.* 381; 8 *Bac. Abr.* tit. *Statutes* 247.

Entertaining the opinion that the appropriation by the act of 1848, has been complied with by the payments made by the treasurer of the county of Lancaster to the treasurer of the Manheim school district, being 25 per cent. on the amount of the State taxes assessed and paid by that township for the two years contemplated, this court refuses the mandamus applied for to compel the payment demanded on the tax assessed and paid for a third year. To allow this would be to elude the law and extort from the treasury more than the bounty intended by the legislature. If the court should be mistaken in this construction of the act of Assembly, and are instrumental in curtailing the legislative bounty to the school directors below what was intended by the legislature, it will be competent to the legislature to remedy it by subsequent enactment.

Petition of relators refused.

Summers' Appeal.

1. By the 4th section of the act of 16th April 1849, judgments confessed to evade the act of 17th April 1843, concerning preferences in assignments, followed by an assignment of real estate, are void as against other creditors, and are not entitled to preference out of the proceeds of sale of such real estate, but are entitled only to a *pro rata* payment with the other debts of the debtor.

[Summers' Appeal.]

2. A debtor, after suit against him, voluntarily executed five judgment bonds in favor of other creditors, intending at the time to make an assignment of his *real estate*, and about the same time selling portions of his personal property; after the entry of judgments on the bonds he executed an assignment of his *real estate* only, in trust for creditors. On the day it was recorded, an award, in favor of the plaintiff in the suit, was filed. The remaining *personal estate* of the debtor was sold on a fi. fa. on a judgment on a bond executed subsequent to the recording of the assignment. The real estate was sold by the trustee, for a sum not sufficient to pay the five judgments: *Held*, that the five judgments were not alone entitled to the proceeds of sale of the real estate, but that the same were to be distributed *pro rata*, amongst all the creditors.

3. If the debtor at the time of confessing the judgments knew that he was insolvent, his subsequent execution of the assignment is conclusive evidence that the judgments were given in fraud of the act of 1843.

This was an appeal by Samuel Summers, a creditor, from the decree of the Court of Common Pleas of *Lancaster county*, confirming the report of the auditor appointed to distribute the balance on the account of John Strohm, Esq., assignee of the real estate of Christian Shultz, Sr., and wife.

Christian Shultz, Sr., was the owner of sixty-two acres of land in the county of Lancaster, and of personal property, when, on the 22d of May 1849, Samuel Summers brought an action of debt in the Common Pleas of Lancaster county, to August term 1849, No. 58, against him, to recover the amount due upon a single bill for $2800, with interest, from October 14, 1843. On the same day a narr. was filed, and a rule entered by plaintiff's attorney, to choose arbitrators on the 7th day of June 1849, on which day the parties, by their attorneys, chose arbitrators, to meet on the 25th day of June 1849.

In the mean time, to wit, on the 18th day of June 1849, seven days before the time fixed for the meeting of the arbitrators, Christian Shultz, Sr., executed five several judgment bonds—one to Benjamin Barr, for $267.75; one to Jacob F. Herr, for $700; one to Benjamin Shultz for $500; one to Magdalena Eckman for $2200.02; and one to John Groff for $183; at the same time selling portions of his personal property to divers persons; which said five judgment bonds were, on the 19th day of June 1849, entered in the prothonotary's office. Three days after the entry of these judgment bonds, to wit, on the 22d day of June 1849, Christian Shultz, Sr., and wife, executed a deed of assignment of his *real estate only*, to John Strohm, Esq., in trust for the benefit of the creditors, which, on the 25th day of June 1849, was entered in the recorder's office of the county of Lancaster, *and on the same day* the award of arbitrators in the suit of Samuel Summers (the appellant) *v.* Christian Shultz, Sr., was filed in the prothonotary's office for $3097.83. On the 27th day of June 1849, Christian Shultz, Sr., executed a judgment bond to Joseph Armstrong for $545, which on the same day was entered in the prothonotary's office, and a fi. fa. immediately issued thereon; upon which the remaining portion of his personal property was sold by the sheriff.

The assignee of the real estate, John Strohm, Esq., sold the

[Summers's Appeal.]

same, and on the 11th day of May 1850 filed his account in the prothonotary's office of the Court of Common Pleas, which on the 17th day of June 1850, was confirmed *nisi*, there being a balance in his hands for distribution, being the proceeds of the real estate, deducting the expenses of the trust, of $3424.54¼. This account showed that Christian Shultz, Sr., was insolvent at the time he executed the five judgment bonds, to wit, on the 18th day of June 1849, and the proceeds of the real estate were not sufficient to pay the five judgments in full.

On the 17th day of June 1850, an auditor was appointed to distribute the balance in the hands of the assignee among the persons entitled to receive the same. On the hearing before the auditor, John Strohm, Esq., the assignee, was examined as a witness, who testified as follows:—

To the best of my recollection, I drew the five judgment bonds given by Shultz to Barr, Herr, Groff, Shultz, and Eckman. I also drew the deed of assignment. I conversed with Christian Shultz about the deed of assignment before those judgments were given. I don't recollect of any terms being arranged, except that the real estate only was to be assigned to me; and this conversation was on the Saturday previous to the giving of the judgments. The deed of assignment was made (I suppose) because he was unable to meet his obligations. He told me that he had got into difficulties, and wanted to make an assignment to me for the benefit of his creditors. This was before the judgments were given. I do not think that he alluded to the claim of Summers, except that he said at the outset, that "Sam" had pushed him. By "Sam" I understood him to mean, at the time, Summers; although I did not ask him who he meant by "Sam," I so understood him. I can't tell why the personal property was not included in the assignment, except what I might infer from the subsequent proceedings. I do not think that any thing was stated to me why these judgments were given. I was not consulted as to the propriety of giving those judgments before he came to me about the assignment, nor even then. He had spoken, I presume, to other persons: he said he had informed himself that he could make an assignment of real estate alone: he did not consult me about the form of assignment—I did not act in the drawing of these instruments of writing as his counsel, only as scrivener. At the time the deed of assignment was written and executed, nothing was said about these judgments. He did not state to me his reasons for assigning the real estate alone. A portion of the personal property was levied on by the sheriff on the judgment of Armstrong. Shultz sold a portion of it about the time the judgments were given to Jacob Diffenbaugh and others. Mr. Shultz was engaged in distilling.

The attorneys for Samuel Summers claimed a *pro rata* dividend of the fund for distribution on his judgment against Shultz: the

[Summers's Appeal.]

attorney for the five judgment creditors claimed the whole of the fund in satisfaction of the five judgments. On the 21st day of December 1850, the auditor reported that the five judgments entered on the 19th day of June 1849 were entitled to the balance remaining in the hands of the assignee, and therefore distributed it among those judgments *pro rata*.

This report was filed in the Court of Common Pleas, and was afterwards excepted to by the counsel of Samuel Summers, upon the ground that the auditor erred in not distributing the fund *pro rata* to all the debts of Christian Shultz, Sr., and not in awarding a *pro rata* dividend to Samuel Summers. These exceptions were argued in the Court of Common Pleas, and on the 18th day of March 1851, the court confirmed the report of the auditor. From this decree of the Court of Common Pleas this appeal was taken.

The act of 17th April 1843, to prevent preferences in assignments, provides that all assignments of property in trust, which shall hereafter be made by debtors to trustees, on account of inability at the time of the assignments to pay their debts, to prefer one or more creditors, (except for the payment of wages of labor,) shall be held and construed to inure to the benefit of all the creditors in proportion to their respective demands; and all such assignments shall be subject in all respects to the laws now in force relative to voluntary assignments: *Provided*, that the claims of laborers thus preferred shall not severally exceed the sum of fifty dollars.

The 4th section of the act of 16th April 1849 (*Acts* 664) enacts, that any condition in assignments of property made by debtors to trustees on account of inability at the time of the assignment to pay their debts, within the meaning of the act entitled "An act to prevent preferences in assignments," approved April seventeenth, one thousand eight hundred and forty-three, for the payment of the creditors only who shall execute a release, shall be taken as a preference in favor of such creditors and be void, and the assignment be held and construed to inure to the benefit of all the creditors in proportion to their respective demands: *Provided*, that no *bona fide* judgment or lien acquired against the property of any debtor, or any sale or transfer of the property of such debtor, unless the same shall have been obtained, acquired, or made with intent to evade the provisions *of the said act*, shall be avoided or defeated by the subsequent discovery that such debtor was insolvent at the time such judgment was obtained, lien acquired, or transfer made.

Thompson and *Stevens* were for Summers, the appellant.—By the 4th section of the act of April 16, 1849, the legislature intended to prevent and avoid all preferences by a man in failing circumstances, who, at the time of granting such preference by

[Summers's Appeal.]

judgment or other lien, knew that he was insolvent, and contemplated making an assignment for the benefit of his creditors, and gave such lien for the purpose of preferring such of his creditors to others.

The evidence in the case proves that at the time of giving the judgments in question, Christian Shultz knew that he was insolvent—had determined to make an assignment—had spoken to a scrivener for that purpose, and gave the judgments in order to prefer the plaintiffs therein to his other creditors, and especially to Samuel Summers. *A deed of assignment* with a preference was void, though the *creditor* did not know of the intent to defraud; and the proviso in question contains general language. The proceeds of sale of the land will not pay the five judgments. Shultz was thus insolvent.

Frazer, contra.—The first five judgment creditors of Christian Shultz knew nothing of the situation of his estate when the judgment bonds were executed; nor is there any testimony to show any other intention on their part than to obtain judgments for *bona fide* debts. The proviso to the act of 1849, however, is, to a great extent, without meaning, or merely declaratory of the law as it stood before.

There is no proof that Christian Shultz *knew* he was insolvent when he gave the judgments—and his land afterwards selling at a certain price does not prove such knowledge, nor that he had given these judgments in order to prefer the appellees.

The act of 1849 merely prohibits preferences *to releasing creditors*, and does not prohibit confession of judgments to honest creditors. No time is fixed within which a judgment is to be void. It might run back for years. The proviso did not mean this, but was intended only to meet the decision in Lea's Appeal, 9 *Barr* 504. The judgments and assignment are different and distinct acts: Blakey's Appeal, 7 *Barr* 449. Does the proviso go farther than the act; is it not a mere check to the act itself. If no assignment had been made, the judgments would have been valid. Can the judgments be defeated by the mere act of Shultz alone? The act of 1843 does not prohibit the confession of judgments.

The opinion of the court was delivered May 26, by

COULTER, J.—The hardship of withholding from a debtor the right of securing an honest and *bona fide* creditor, by confessing a judgment to him, although such debtor might afterwards execute an assignment for the benefit of his creditors, and the anomalous character of an interdict upon doing that voluntarily which the creditor could compel him to do by suit, as well as the apparent invasion of private right, by taking from a man dominion over his affairs, exercised for an honest and fair purpose, while he continued

[Summers's Appeal.]

sui juris, were fully pointed out in the case of Blakey's Appeal, 7 *Barr* 449. In that case, it was ruled that a judgment confessed by a man in embarrassed circumstances was neither fraudulent nor void, but good in favor of the judgment creditor, although the debtor ten days afterwards executed an assignment. We held that the act of 17th April 1843, entitled "An act to prevent preferences in assignments," did not avoid such *bona fide* judgments, and was confined to preferences contained in the assignment itself, according to the plain meaning of the act. But in the opinion delivered in that case, it was stated, that if the legislature extended the interdict to confession of judgment by a man in embarrassed circumstances, who afterwards executed an assignment, this court would cheerfully carry out such enactments. The statute of 16th April 1849, entitled " An act supplementary to the act about lunatics and habitual drunkards," 4th section, seems to have been an acceptance of the overture, and was no doubt enacted in consequence of that decision. The act is exceedingly obscure—counsel pronounced it insensible—but there is a glimmering of intent in it. The clause is as follows : " Provided, that no *bona fide* judgment, or lien acquired against the property of any debtor, or any sale or transfer of the property of any debtor, unless the same shall have been acquired or made with intent to evade the provisions of the said act, shall be avoided or defeated by the subsequent discovery that such debtor was insolvent at the time such judgment was obtained, lien acquired, or transfer made."

At first blush, the section would seem intended to save, not destroy; but there is nothing going before to which the section can apply. It must be considered, and is, an independent and positive enactment. There are three affirmations to be extracted from it. 1st, That judgments, &c., made to evade the act of 1843, are void. 2d, That knowledge of insolvency at the time the judgment, &c. were made, shall in itself be evidence that they were made with intent to evade the act. 3d, That if the debtor was actually insolvent at the time, but did not know it until afterwards, that the judgment shall remain good. The whole thing, then, hinges upon the *scienter* of the debtor as to his solvency or insolvency at the time he gave the judgment or made the transfer. The knowledge of the creditor or the alienee seems not to enter into the account any more than it did in judgments or transfers before bankruptcy. The objects of the acts of 1843 and 1849 seem to be to force a debtor who makes an assignment *in invitum* into a sort of bankruptcy, so far as the creditors are concerned, without equivalents of bankruptcy to himself.

Did, then, Shultz know, at the time of giving or making the judgments to the several judgment creditors, that he was insolvent at that time? If he did, as he executed an assignment a few days afterwards, these judgments are void, because, by the act of 1849,

[Summers's Appeal.]

that is made conclusive, that they were given in fraud of the act of 1843, and therefore void. It seems clear enough that he did know that he could not pay his debts, and that his property would not do it. Mr. Strohm testifies that he drew the five judgment bonds, and also the deed of assignment; that the bonds were given a few days before the assignment, but that he talked to him about drawing the assignment before he wrote the bonds. Strohm was the assignee, and he says that Shultz told him he could not pay his debts. But there is pregnant evidence in the deed itself, which recites his inability to pay his debts, and directs his trustee to pay his just debts equally and ratably. It appears that the money produced by the sale of the assigned property will not pay the five judgments, and is applied to them by the auditor *pro rata*, leaving the judgment of Summers, the appellant, for $3009, and the judgment of Armstrong for $545, untouched, and, perhaps, other debts which don't appear on the record. We are of opinion that by the 4th section of the act of 16th April 1849, the five judgments confessed to B. Barr, J. F. Herr, B. Shultz, M. Eckman, and John Groff, are void, as against the other creditors, and have no preference. The decree of the court below is reversed, and this court decrees the fund to all the creditors of Christian Shultz *pro rata ;* and the record is remitted to the court below to carry this decree into effect.

Bear *versus* Bitzer.

The land of a judgment debtor was sold by the sheriff and deed made to the purchaser whilst the grain growing on the same was the property of the debtor. After the execution and acknowledgment of the deed, an execution creditor of the debtor levied on the grain, and sold it, and the purchaser brought suit against the tenant of the purchaser of the land, for cutting and removing the grain: *Held*, that the grain passed by the sheriff's sale of the land, and that the purchaser of the grain could not recover in the suit.

ERROR to the Common Pleas of *Lancaster county*.

This was an action of trover and conversion, brought by George Bear against Isaac Bitzer, for the value of about 390½ bushels of wheat in the straw and unthreshed, and about 25 loads of straw, upon the following facts, viz :

George Heller, being the owner of a tract of land, on the 6th of August 1849 confessed judgment to Peter Heller for $600. On this judgment fi. fa. was issued on the 20th August 1849, and on the 15*th of September* 1849 the sheriff levied on the real estate of the said George Heller, being the above-mentioned tract of land—the same on which the grain and straw in controversy were sown. On the same day inquisition was waived and sale on fi. fa. authorized. On the 12*th of October* 1849, Heller's real estate was sold,

[Bear v. Bitzer.]

and on the 24th of November 1849 the sheriff acknowledged a deed to B. G. Herr for the same, dated 19th November 1849.

The grain was sown *for George Heller*, on the 20*th of September* 1849, and was sold by him to Peter Heller *towards the latter end of October*. This contract was rescinded on the 29th day of November 1849, when Peter Heller gave up his right to the grain.

On the 3d December 1849, a fi. fa. was issued at the suit of George Bear against George Heller, upon a judgment obtained by the said Bear against George Heller, on the 27th of August 1849. Under this fi. fa. the sheriff, on the 8th of *December* 1849, levied on the aforesaid grain in the ground, and subsequently sold the same to George Bear, the plaintiff, who now claims the value thereof from Bitzer, the defendant, who came to the premises as tenant of B. G. Herr, on the 1st of April 1850, and cut the grain and converted it to his own use, or that of his landlord.

Peter Heller, affirmed :—In fall of 1849, I sowed wheat for George Heller on that ground that was sold by the sheriff. I sowed 16 acres, more or less, on the same property defendant came into possession of the following April. George Heller owned the land at the time I sowed it.

Cross-examined :—I had rented this property from George at the time I sowed the grain, and was then in possession. When I came on the land I got a crop—and the bargain between us was that when I went off I was to leave a crop. This was the crop I left in lieu of the one I got.

On part of defendant was given in evidence the judgment of Peter Heller *v.* George Heller, on August 6, 1849. Fi. fa. to November 1849, levied on *real* estate of defendant, viz. the tract of land on which the grain was. October 12th, 1849, real estate sold, and sheriff's deed to Benjamin G. Herr acknowledged 24th November 1849. Defendant entered into possession as tenant of B. G. Herr.

Plaintiff's rebutting evidence.—Peter Heller, affirmed :—This grain was sowed on the 20th September 1849. I bought the grain from George Heller some time towards the latter end of October, and I threw it up on the 29th November 1849. We rescinded the contract. He (my brother) told me I should not have it, and I told him I did not want it—I had given my note for it, and he gave the note up to me.

Lewis, President.—This is an action of trover and conversion for wheat and straw. The property in dispute belonged, at one time, to George Heller, who was also the owner of the land on which the wheat grew. The plaintiff claims the property in dispute by virtue of a levy made by the sheriff on the 8th December 1849, and a sale of the grain in the ground by the sheriff.

The defendant claims under Benjaman G. Herr, who purchased the land on which the grain grew, by virtue of a fi. fa. levied on

[Bear *v.* Bitzer]

the land on the 15*th* September 1849; a condemnation of the same date, with an agreement that the sheriff might sell on the fi. fa.; a sale to the said Herr, on the 12th October 1849, and a sheriff's deed duly acknowledged on the 24th November 1849,—all of which proceedings were perfected before the date of the levy under which the plaintiff claims. The grain was sown about the 20*th* September 1849. It is not necessary to attempt any frivolous distinctions, for the purpose of reconciling conflicting cases. It is sufficient to say that subsequent decisions are in conflict with the case of Stambaugh and Yeates, 2 *Rawle* 161, and that that case is not now the law of Pennsylvania. It is now settled that the crops in the ground, so far as they belong to the execution debtor, go with the land on a sale of the land by the sheriff, and that under the facts in evidence in this case, the defendant is entitled to the verdict.

The plaintiff excepted to the charge.

Verdict for defendant.

Error was assigned to the charge.

Eshleman and *Patterson*, for plaintiff in error.—In Stambaugh *v.* Yeates, 2 *Rawle* 161, where, after a fi. fa. levied on *land* and returned, grain was sown on it; another creditor levied on the grain and sold it; afterwards the *land* was sold on a *venditioni exponas* issued on the first fi. fa.—it was held that the creditor who levied on the grain, had the right to the proceeds. This case was afterwards sustained, and the principle reaffirmed in Myers's Assignees *v.* White, 1 *Rawle* 353.

In the case under consideration, the grain in the ground was *separately disposed of* previous to the delivery of the deed by the sheriff. The defendant in execution sold the grain to his brother, Peter Heller, "towards the end of October." The sheriff's deed was not acknowledged and delivered till the 24th of November. The purchaser at sheriff's sale has no right to the possession or profits of land *until the acknowledgment and delivery of the deed.* By act of 1836, the purchaser shall have all rent accruing after acknowledgment of the deed: Thomas *v.* Connel, 5 *Barr* 13; Jones *v.* Striker, 1 *Johns. Ch. C.* 285. The interest in the grain was at that time a *separate interest.* On the 29th November, Peter Heller gave up the grain to George Heller, and on the 3d of December George Bear's execution issued, under which he claims the grain.

In this view of the case, it was contended that under the case of Stambaugh *v.* Yeates, the plaintiff is entitled to the value of the grain levied upon and sold under his execution of the 3d of December 1849.

Franklin, for defendant in error.—The grain which was the subject of this action was put out by Peter Heller, *as tenant of*

[Bear v. Bitzer.]

George Heller. Peter Heller was in possession of the real property as tenant, and sowed the crop under his agreement. It may therefore be regarded as rent, going to the purchaser of the land under the sheriff's sale: 10 *Watts* 362; 5 *W. & Ser.* 432.

That this case differs from Stambaugh v. Yeates. In the latter case the land was levied on, and after that grain was sown, and the grain was sold on execution *before the land was sold*. He contended that the crop growing on the land when the land was sold at sheriff's sale, and which has not *been severed*, passed by the sale of the land. In the case of Sallade v. James, 6 *Barr* 144, the purchaser disaffirmed the lease, and it was not decided on the principle of rent. In that case it is said that the grain passed by a sale of the land.

The opinion of the court was delivered May 26, by
COULTER, J.—In Stambaugh v. Yeates, 2 *Rawle* 161, the grain growing in the ground had been sold on a judgment and execution against the debtor, before the sale of the land on *vend. exponas*, and the court held that grain growing was so far personal property that it could be sold either privately by the owner, or by judicial process against him; and that such sale was an implied severance, and the grain did not pass by a sale of the land. And in Myers v. White, 1 *Rawle* 353, the mortgagor, while the grain was growing, assigned all his property, real, personal, and mixed, for the benefit of his creditors; it was held, that the grain growing passed to the assignees, and did not pass to the purchaser of the land on a judgment on the mortgage, because the assignment amounted to a severance, and vested the right in the trustees. In Sallade v. James, 6 *Barr* 144, which is alleged to be in conflict with the two preceding cases cited, there was judgment against the owner of the land and a levy in the spring, after which the debtor leased the premises, and the tenant paid the rent in advance. In September the tenant sowed the crop, and in October the sheriff sold the land, and the purchaser gave him notice to quit. The tenant paid the rent in advance when he leased. When the grain was ripe he entered, cut, and carried it away, and on replevin by the purchaser it was held that the tenant could only take the way-going crop when he had a right to sow; that his right was no greater than his landlord's, the debtor. That although the judgment creditor has no present interest in the land, he has a lien which may presently be turned into one; and that if a tenant, under such circumstances, pays the rent in advance, he takes the risk of losing it. If he had withheld the rent till due, he would have been entitled to protection for a disturbance, and to a remedy on his covenants. The question there was on the right to enter for the way-going crop, after a judicial sale of the land. As there had been no severance of the crop from the realty, either by a private sale or

[Bear v. Bitzer.]

judicial sale, it was held to pass as appurtenant to the land. The case is in entire accordance with those cases which establish that by a private sale of land the growing crop passes as appurtenant, unless there has been a reservation of it. By the act of 21st March 1772, grain growing was made subject to distress and sale for rent, and the act provided that the purchaser should have free egress and ingress to cut and carry it away; and in analogy to that act, it was held in Pennsylvania that it might be sold privately or judicially and the purchaser have egress and regress to cut and carry it away, because it was in contemplation of law severed by the sale. But nothing of that kind existed in Sallade v. James, 6 *Barr*, as it did emphatically exist in Stambaugh v. Yeates, and Myers v. White.

In the case on hand, the land was sold on the 12th October 1849, by the sheriff, and on the 24th November of the same year, a deed was made by the sheriff to Herr, while the grain growing was the property of the judgment debtor; and under Sallade v. James, and analogous cases, both in England and Pennsylvania, it passed to the sheriff's vendee as appurtenant to the land. After deed made to Herr by the sheriff, an execution creditor levied on the grain and sold it, and the purchaser of the grain brings this suit against Herr's tenant who cut it. He is not entitled to recover, and such was the judgment of the court below, which is now affirmed

Judgment affirmed.

Groff *versus* Levan.

After the execution and recording of a mortgage, but before the issuing of a scire facias thereon, the mortgagor leased a portion of the mortgaged premises for a year, to a cropper, who paid the rent *in advance*, and sowed grain upon it. Before the grain was cut, the land was sold at sheriff's sale, under proceedings on the mortgage commenced after the making of the lease: *Held*, that the grantee of the purchaser of the land was entitled to recover damages from the cropper for cutting and removing the grain.

ERROR to the Common Pleas of *Lancaster county*.

This was a suit by George Levan v. Levi W. Groff, involving the right to grain. A case was stated, embracing, with others, the following facts:—

March 19, 1844, mortgage, Samuel W. Groff to the Farmers' Bank of Lancaster, on 18 acres of land—same day, mortgage recorded.

To November term 1847, scire facias on the mortgage. November 22, 1847, judgment for plaintiff for $8450.66.

Levari facias to January term 1848. Returned "real estate sold to Farmers' Bank of Lancaster for $4700."

[Groff v. Levan.]

January 22, 1848, sheriff's deed to the Farmers' Bank of Lancaster, for property mortgaged. Same day, acknowledged.

April 1, 1848, deed, Farmers' Bank of Lancaster to George Levan, plaintiff, for same property, and on the same day Levan entered into possession of the premises.

At the time of the sale by the sheriff to the Bank, and of the conveyance by the Bank to Levan as above stated, there was a growing crop of rye on about eight acres, parcel of the premises mortgaged and sold. In July 1848, Levi W. Groff, the defendant, cut and carried away the said rye with the straw thereof, and kept and retained the same with the straw, and refused upon demand to deliver the same or any part thereof to the plaintiff. The quantity of rye was 132 bushels, of the value of 65 cents per bushel; and the straw, 400 bundles, at 6 cents per bundle; making the whole value $109.80. The plaintiff seeks to recover this, allowing defendant a credit of $21.45, the expense of harvesting the grain: making his claim $88.35, with interest from 1st August 1848.

The *defendant* claimed the whole of the said rye and straw, on the following facts:—On the 15th day of *September* A. D. 1847, he rented the eight-acre field on which the grain spoken of grew, from Samuel W. Groff, *for the ensuing year*, rent to be paid in advance, and on that day paid the price agreed on, to wit, $142, as per receipt of Samuel W. Groff of that date. He took possession and sowed the grain; and protected, harvested, and took away the grain.

Defendant claimed all the grain; or that he was entitled at least to *the half part* thereof; which is the usual condition on which land is given out to farm.

If the court, on this statement of facts, should be of opinion that the plaintiff is entitled to recover, then judgment to be entered in his favor for such damages as he is entitled to, with costs: otherwise, judgment for defendant.

The court entered judgment for $88.35, with interest, being the whole of the claim of the plaintiff.

It was assigned for error, that the judgment should have been for the defendant below, and not for the plaintiff.

Stevens, for plaintiff in error.—In Pennsylvania, grain growing on land is personal, and not real estate; and if sold by defendant, or by judicial sale, before the land is sold by the sheriff, will go to the purchaser, and not to the purchaser of the land. This is very clearly decided in Myers's Assignee v. White, 1 *Rawle* 353, and Stambaugh v. Yeates, 2 *id.* 161.

In Myers v. White, the court show, that notwithstanding a mortgage, the mortgagor may lease the mortgaged premises or sell the grain growing on it; and that a sale on the mortgage before the

[Groff v. Levan.]

termination of the lease, or the harvesting of the grain, does not give the grain to the purchaser.

The act of 16th June 1836 seems to provide for two cases,—where the person is in possession of land sold by the sheriff by *title* younger than the encumbrance on which it was sold; and by a *lease* also younger.

The 119th section of the act of 16th June 1836, relating to executions, provides "that if any lands or tenements shall be sold on execution as aforesaid, which at the time of such sale or afterwards shall be held or possessed by a tenant or lessee, or person holding," &c., "the purchaser, on receiving the deed, shall be deemed the landlord of such tenant, lessee, or other person, and shall have the like remedies to recover any rents," &c., "as such defendant might have had if no such sale had been made." It is very evident that the legislature intended to authorize an eviction only when the person in possession held as purchaser by title subsequent to the judgment; and to give the purchaser at sheriff's sale, only the rights of the landlord, when the defendant was out of possession, and the land farmed by a tenant. Certainly, such lease or tenancy must be *bona fide*, and not made to defraud the mortgage in anticipation of a sale. Here no such fraud is found or pretended. It would be ruinous to hold that property, which had been mortgaged for five or ten years, could not be rented, or grain raised by a tenant, because possibly the mortgagees might sue out a scire facias, and, in two months after grain was sowed, sell on a levari facias, and seize the crops of the tenant. By such doctrine the mortgagor would be deprived of the profits of his property, while it was uncertain whether his creditor would sell him out; and the cultivation of the soil would be greatly discouraged.

But even if the purchaser could have terminated this lease on notice, it was not done here. On the 1st April after the sale, the purchaser's vendee took possession of the balance of the property, the tenant still holding the eight acres so far as was necessary to protect the grain and harvest it. *He had in fact never resided on the property, renting only the field in question.* If therefore the sheriff's vendee had any claim, it was only as landlord entitled to the rent agreed on by the mortgagor. If it be averred that the rent was paid in advance, that can make no difference, as it was paid according to the terms of the lease. This point was well considered and decided in the Bank v. Ege, 9 *Watts* 436. That case and Myers v. White are precisely like the present.

The case of Sallade v. James, 6 *Barr* 144, seems hostile to the above reasoning, and to other adjudged cases. That opinion seems to have been but slightly considered, and does not profess to overrule previous cases. At the worst, plaintiff below and in error can claim but the *half* of the grain, being all that the landlord could have claimed if the land had been worked on the shares.

[Groff v. Levan.]

Franklin, for defendant.—This case is precisely similar in the facts to the case of Sallade v. James, 6 *Barr* 144, the syllabus of which is—"A judgment was recovered against the landlord prior to the execution of a lease for years at a rent payable in advance. After payment of the rent, and sowing of the crop by the tenant, the estate of the landlord was sold by the sheriff under the prior judgment. The purchaser, and not the tenant, is entitled to the growing crop."

That case is sustained by other authorities. It is too late to contend that a purchaser at sheriff's sale may not elect to disaffirm a lease made after the mortgage or judgment under which he purchases. This point must be considered as settled by the cases, 4 *Watts* 195, McCormick v. McMurtrie; 9 *Watts* 439, Bank v. Ege; 4 *W. & Ser.* 535, Hempfield v. Tevis; 5 *id.* 432, Menough's Appeal.

The opinion of the court was delivered May 26, by

COULTER, J.—This case is ruled by Sallade v. James, 6 *Barr* 144, and Bear v. Bitzer decided at this term. The circumstance of Levi W. Groff being *a cropper* makes no difference in the application of the law to the case, because it has been ruled by this court that the 119th section of the act of 1836 is not imperative on the purchaser at sheriff's sale, inasmuch as he claims by a title paramount to the tenant's right. In this case, however, the cropper or tenant cut and carried away the whole crop, and claimed it because he had paid the rent in advance; thus disavowing the act of Assembly as for his benefit. But his lease being after the judgment and levy, and there being no severance by a sale, the purchaser's right was absolute.

Judgment affirmed.

Mifflin *versus* Railroad Company.
Heise *versus* Same.—Bethel *versus* Same.

A *turnpike road* was constructed over the ground of individuals, who, in 1825, receipted in full for damages sustained by its construction. In 1849 an act was passed authorizing the turnpike company to sell its corporate rights to a *railroad* company, and the latter to purchase, for the purpose of laying rails thereon, the same to be laid under the act of incorporation of the railroad company, which provided for the valuation of land occupied by the road, and of all damages which the owner or owners shall sustain or may have sustained by reason of its construction: *Held*, that the obligation imposed on the railroad company to pay damages, was a proper exercise of legislative authority, when conferring on that company the additional privilege; and that one of the original owners of the land and her grantees were not estopped by the receipt to the *turnpike* company, from claiming consequential damages from the

[Mifflin v. Railroad Company.]

railroad company, by reason of the construction of the *railroad*, though the railroad occupied no more of their ground than was contained within the limits of the turnpike road.

APPEAL, certiorari, and writ of error to the Court of Common Pleas of *Lancaster county*, by J. H. Mifflin *vs.* The Harrisburg, Portsmouth, Mountjoy, and Lancaster Railroad Company.

Appeal by Samuel B. Heise in a similar proceeding against the same company. And an appeal by Susan Bethel, in a similar proceeding.

The complaint in each case was for alleged injury done by the construction of a railroad by the company, on the bed of a turnpike road.

The material facts were stated in the proceedings at the instance of Mifflin and Heise.

On the 31st day of March 1823, an act, entitled "An act to incorporate the Columbia, Chiques and Marietta Road and Bridge Company," was passed, authorizing the making of a turnpike road, beginning at the east end of the Columbia Bridge, thence upon or near the shore of the Susquehanna over the Chiques Creek, at or near its mouth, to the borough of Marietta, *Pam. Laws* 1822–3, p. 199, &c. Under the provisions of this act of incorporation, the company was authorized to enter upon lands, &c., and invested with the usual powers, privileges, rights, &c., conferred in those days upon turnpike companies, and as expressed in the act incorporating the Lancaster, Elizabethtown, and Middletown Turnpike Road Company, passed March 5, 1804, *Pam. Laws* 1803–4, p. 131, &c.

Under this act of incorporation, the company went into operation, procured letters-patent, and constructed a turnpike road along the eastern shore of the Susquehanna river, from and to the points designated. In the course of the construction of the road, the company entered upon, took, and for their own use appropriated a portion of the land owned by Elizabeth, Mary, and Susanna Bethel, the value of which was afterwards estimated by the parties; and for which they gave the following receipt, viz :—

"Received, July 19th, 1825, of the Columbia, Chiques, and Marietta Road and Bridge Company, one hundred dollars, in full of all damages and injuries sustained in consequence of the said road having been laid out and opened through our real property, and in full of all demands against them.

$100.

ELIZABETH BETHEL,
MARY BETHEL,
SUSANNA BETHEL."

The road, as originally constructed, continued to be used by the company, until, in the course of the construction of the Pennsylvania Canal, a part of the bed of the old turnpike was taken by the commonwealth, and for that purpose; which being done, the

[Mifflin v. Railroad Company.]

State constructed and completed another road to supply the place of such parts of the old road thus appropriated. Thus matters remained until the 26th day of February, 1836, when the legislature passed the following act, entitled "An act to change the location of that part of the Columbia, Chiques, and Marietta road, which passes through the land of Elizabeth, Mary, and Susanna Bethel, in the county of Lancaster," viz:—

"Sec. 1. *Be it enacted, &c.* That Elizabeth Bethel, Mary Bethel, and Susanna Bethel, of the county of Lancaster, their heirs and assigns, have full power and authority, at their own proper charges and expense, to change the location of that part of the Columbia, Chiques, and Marietta road, that passes through the land of said Elizabeth Bethel, Mary Bethel, and Susanna Bethel, from where the same is now located, and to remove the same to any distance on their own land not exceeding seventy-five feet: *Provided,* That the road shall be made in all respects as good as the present road, and that the distance be no greater. *And provided also,* That the said Columbia, Chiques, and Marietta Road and Bridge Company receive no damage or be put to any expenses thereby."

The alteration of the road thus authorized, was afterwards made by the Miss Bethels,—*under whom the appellant claims,*—and the road thus constructed continued to be used as a turnpike until in the year 1849, when, under the provisions of an act of the General Assembly, entitled "An act relative to the Harrisburg, Portsmouth, Mountjoy, and Lancaster Railroad Company," *passed January* 26, 1849, *Pam. Laws* 1849, 19, the said Turnpike Road Company sold their said road to the said Harrisburg, Portsmouth, Mountjoy, and Lancaster Railroad Company, who thereupon, and under their original act of incorporation, passed June 9, 1832, and the several supplements thereto, passed March 7, 1848, *Pam. Laws* 1848, 177; and also of April 7, 1848, *id.* 1848, 373, relative to the ascertainment and payment of damages, &c., proceeded to make excavations, &c., and to lay down rails on said turnpike road, as authorized and empowered by said acts of Assembly. In doing so, the said Railroad Company made excavations upon, and used the road in part, and through the lands of the appellant, whereby he sustained damages as he alleged. Accordingly, on the 23d day of March 1850, he presented his petition as follows:

To the honorable the Judges of the Court of Common Pleas of Lancaster county.

The petition of J. H. Mifflin, respectfully represents: That in pursuance of the provisions of the several acts of Assembly, supplementary to the act of incorporation of the Harrisburg, Portsmouth, Mountjoy, and Lancaster Railroad Company, respectively passed on the 16th day of March A. D. 1848, *Pam. Laws* 177; the 7th day of April, A. D. 1848, *id.* 373; and the 26th day of January, A. D. 1849, *id.* 18; the said company have,

[Mifflin v. Railroad Company.]

by their engineers and agents, surveyed, and located, and are now constructing a branch of their road, commencing at a point on the said railroad, near the junction therewith of the turnpike road from Marietta to Portsmouth, and extending to and connecting with the Pennsylvania Railway at Columbia. That the said location passes through lands of J. H. Mifflin, in the borough of Columbia, in said county. That he cannot agree with the said company for the sale of such occupied land, nor upon the compensation to be made to him for the damages sustained. He therefore respectfully prays the court to nominate and appoint twelve discreet and disinterested persons of the said county, as an inquest, to view the land so occupied, and the value of the same, and to proceed therein according to the provisions of the act of Assembly incorporating the said company, passed June 9th, 1832, *id.* 590, and of the several supplements thereto for that purpose enacted.

And he will ever pray, &c.   J. H. MIFFLIN.

The 79th section of the act of 9th June 1832, incorporating the Railroad Company provides, that in a proceeding for damages sustained, the viewers shall value the land occupied or required for such railroad or other work, and all damages which the owner or owners shall sustain or may have sustained by reason of the construction of the said railroad and other works, &c.

The first section of act of January 26, 1849, *Pam. Laws* 18, provided that the president and directors of the Harrisburg, Portsmouth, Mountjoy, and Lancaster Railroad Company, be, and they are hereby authorized and empowered to purchase from the president and directors of the Columbia, Marietta, and Portsmouth Railroad Company, and from the president and directors of the Columbia, Chiques, and Marietta Turnpike Company, upon such terms as may be agreed upon, all the right, title, claim, and demand in and to the roads of said respective corporations, to wit, the Columbia, Marietta, and Portsmouth Railroad Company, and the Columbia, Chiques, and Marietta Turnpike Company, for the purpose of laying rails thereon, under the supplements to the act incorporating the Harrisburg, Portsmouth, Mountjoy, and Lancaster Railroad Company, passed the seventeenth day of March and the seventh day of April, Anno Domini eighteen hundred and forty-eight; and the said Harrisburg, Portsmouth, Mountjoy, and Lancaster Railroad Company is hereby authorized to lay rails on said roads, under the provisions of said supplements.

Others sections conferred the right to sell.

An appointment was made in conformity with the prayer of the petitioner, by the court aforesaid, and precept issued to April term 1850, to the sheriff of Lancaster county, to summon the viewers and to hold the inquisition. This was done, and the precept returned to the court by the sheriff, by which it appears that

[Mifflin v. Railroad Company.]

they assessed the damages sustained by the appellant at the sum of twelve hundred dollars.

To the confirmation of this inquisition and report, and against the whole of the proceedings, exceptions were taken and filed on behalf of the Harrisburg, Portsmouth, Mountjoy, and Lancaster Railroad Company, April 30, 1850, some of which were—

1. The proceedings are altogether illegal and void; not being authorized by any act of Assembly.

3. The title to the land occupied by the railroad, and for the taking of which damages are claimed by complainant, is not vested in him.

4. If any title or right or interest in the said land is vested in the complainant, it is in right of his wife, who ought to have been joined with the complainant as co-plaintiff in the petition and proceedings thereon.

5. The complainant was not entitled to receive any damages for the only injury complained of in his petition, and which only the defendant was ready or bound to answer, to wit, the occupation of his land by the said railroad, because the same had been dedicated to public use by the Miss Bethels, and used as a public road by the Columbia, Chiques, and Marietta Turnpike Road Company; and all the rights of the public and of the said Turnpike Road Company are vested in the defendant, for the use of the public.

6. The jury improperly received evidence of consequential injury to complainant's land and houses not taken nor occupied by the railroad, for which no damages were asked in his petition, and of his claim in respect to which the defendant had received no notice, and which the jury had not viewed.

7. The complainant was not entitled to receive any compensation in damages for any fancied consequential injury to the value of any of his land not taken nor occupied nor in any way encroached upon by the railroad.

The petition of Samuel B. Heise was of a similar character with that of J. H. Mifflin, and it was referred to the *same* jury. The jury reported in his favor $288 damages.

On the part of the company it was alleged, that Mifflin and Heise held under the Miss Bethels, the land through which this turnpike road passed. That the survivor of the Bethels had executed to Heise and to Mifflin voluntary conveyances for the several pieces of property which they hold. Also, that the only injury alleged to have been sustained by the petitioners consisted in the depreciation in value of the dwelling-houses by narrowing the pavements in front of them.

On the part of the company, depositions were taken under a rule of court. One of them testified that the railroad was on the bed of the old Columbia turnpike road, and took up from 22 to 23 feet of the bed of the turnpike—that he considered the whole property

[Mifflin v. Railroad Company.]

through the Bethel estate enhanced in value by the construction of the railroad. That he did not think any part of the property was injured in value except the dwelling-houses, &c.

On the part of complainants, a witness was examined, who testified:—I am acquainted with this property of Mr. Mifflin and Mr. Heise. I am acquainted with these houses. They were not all built at once—*were all built within six or seven years last past.* I do not know what they rent for. In my opinion the houses are decreased in value by the construction of the railroad. There is not more than from two to five feet left for a walk in front of them. The excavation in front of them is from six to eight feet deep, in my judgment: I have not measured. I am acquainted with Mr. Heise's property. I cannot say whether this property is increased or diminished by the construction of the road. There is a small dwelling-house upon his property, (which I forgot,) which is inconvenienced in consequence of this road. I am acquainted with Miss Bethel's property. I think that is depreciated in value by this road. There is a very deep cut through it. The cut is from three to twelve feet all the way through Miss Bethel's property.

Cross-examined:—I think the railroad is very nearly on the bed of the turnpike all the way through Miss Bethel's property. It may vary a little about the centre of it. To the best of my knowledge, Mr. Heise's and Mr. Mifflin's property run back from the canal across the railroad. It is from sixty to seventy-five feet from the canal to the railroad—it varies a little. Heise has two warehouses on his property between the railroad and canal. They are owned by Heise and Mifflin together.

The exceptions, &c. were argued; and afterwards, on the 24th of June 1850, the court sustained the exceptions and decided that the petitioner was not entitled to damages.

Opinion of LEWIS, J.—This case comes before us on exceptions to the report awarding to the petitioner $1200 damages, occasioned by the construction of a branch of the railroad upon his land. Various exceptions have been filed, but it is only necessary to notice a single one. It is admitted, that the petitioner claims title to the land under Elizabeth, Mary, and Susanna Bethel; and the evidence shows that a turnpike was laid upon the identical ground taken by the Railroad Company,—that at the time of constructing the turnpike, the land taken for the turnpike was owned by the Miss Bethels aforesaid, and that on the 19th July 1825, they received from the Turnpike Company $100 "in full of all damages in consequence of the turnpike having been laid out and opened on their real property," and executed a receipt in writing for the same. By the act of 26th January 1849, the Railroad Company was authorized to purchase the rights of the turnpike, and lay rails, &c. for a railroad on the line of the turnpike.

[Mifflin v. Railroad Company.]

The purchase was made; and no ground has been taken for the railroad except that previously taken for the turnpike. On the authority of the case in 6 *Whar.* 25, and other cases, we are constrained to decide that the petitioner is not entitled to damages for the change in the manner of using the road.

Report set aside.

There was also a precept before the same jury on the application of *Heise* and *Mifflin*.

A petition by Susan Bethel was presented, in which it was stated that the location of the road was through lands owned jointly by Samuel B. Heise and herself in West Hempfield township, in said county, and praying for the appointment of an inquest. The same persons were appointed. They reported as follows:—

"The undersigned having been appointed by the Court of Common Pleas of Lancaster county, do report: That having met at the house of Joseph Black, in the borough of Columbia, and having been sworn and affirmed, *viewed the land of the plaintiff*, and find that she has sustained no damages by reason of the construction of the Harrisburg, Portsmouth, Mountjoy, and Lancaster Railroad."

Plaintiff's Exceptions.—1. The act of Assembly requires that the sheriff and jurors shall meet *on the lands*, &c. In this case, by the writ to the sheriff, he was commanded to summon the jurors to meet "on a tract or piece of land owned by Samuel B. Heise and Susan Bethel." Yet, notwithstanding the command contained in the writ, and the language of the act of Assembly, the report shows that the jury met at the public-house of Joseph Black, in the borough of Columbia, which is not on or near to the land for which damages are claimed. 2. The report does not show that the jurors went upon the land, or were sworn at the time and place appointed and required by the act of Assembly. 3. The report does not show when or what time the sheriff and jurors met, except that they met at the public-house of Joseph Black, &c. 4. It does not show what the jurors were sworn and affirmed to do; and in this there is a non-compliance with the act of Assembly. 5. The report does not show that the jurors took into consideration the advantages and disadvantages of the railroad to the plaintiff's property, and in determining upon their verdict.

Opinion of LEWIS, J.—The facts of the case are similar to those shown to exist in the case of Heise *v.* same defendant, No. 86, April 1850. From these facts it appears that the petitioner is not entitled to any damages—that no land has been taken by the Railroad Company, except that previously taken by the Turnpike Company, and for which the petitioner has already received compensation. This objection to the petitioner's claim controls all the exceptions which she has filed to the proceedings upon her own peti-

[Mifflin v. Railroad Company.]

tion. The purposes of justice do not require that the report against her claim should be set aside.

Report confirmed.

Exceptions were filed to the opinion, and to the overruling of the exceptions.

From this opinion and judgment in the case of Mifflin, he appealed, and also sued out a writ of error and certiorari, and the following were filed as the exceptions:

1. The court erred in deciding that the receipt for $100, given by the Miss Bethels, dated 19th July 1825, "in full of all damages in consequence of the turnpike having been laid out and opened on their real property," was a receipt in full for all damages sustained by reason of the alteration of it to a railroad.

2. The court erred in holding that "inasmuch as by the act of 26th January 1849, the Railroad Company was authorized to purchase the right of the turnpike, and lay rails, &c. for a railroad on the line of the turnpike," and as "the purchase was made, and no ground has been taken except that previously taken for the turnpike," the said J. H. Mifflin is not entitled to damages for the change in the manner of using the road.

The cases were argued by *Ford* and *Stevens*, with whom was *North*, for appellants.—It was *inter alia* contended that the receipt was for damages done by the *turnpike* road constructed—the company obtained a right of passage for that road *alone*, and the title to the soil remained in the Miss Bethels: 1 *Yeates* 167; 1 *Barr* 336; 2 *Barn. & Ald.* 793; 1 *Bald.* 230; 16 *Mass.* 35; *Woolwich on Ways* 38, *Law Lib.* The moment, therefore, the land of the appellant ceased to be used as a turnpike, it would have reverted. But the legislature, in the exercise of its power, conferred upon the Railroad Company the right to purchase and convert it into a railroad, upon the condition that they should pay the damages thereby occasioned in the manner prescribed in the original act of incorporation, not of the turnpike, but of the Railroad Company. If this had not been done, they could have been proceeded against as trespassers for having used the land for purposes not sanctioned by the act: Ridge Turnpike *v.* Stoever, 6 *W. & Ser.* 378. The construction of a *turnpike* may be a benefit to an individual; that of a *railroad*, from liability of the property to fire or for other reasons, may be to him an injury. If the jury allowed *consequential* damages, they had a right to do so: Railroad Co. *v.* Yeiser, 8 *Burr* 367.

Franklin, for the company.—This property has been long taken and applied to public use, with the consent and at the instance of the Miss Bethels, the then owners, and they received full compensation therefor.

[Mifflin v. Railroad Company.]

The right of entry and possession are therefore vested in the public; and the legislature has a perfect right to direct a change in the mode of the public enjoyment of it, without providing any additional compensation to the owner of the soil.

This is expressly decided in the case of the Philadelphia and Trenton Railroad Company: 6 *Whar.* 25, 43–4.

That case governs the present; and the principle contained in it is recognised and supported in 9 *Watts* 382, Green v. Borough of Reading. A lot-holder cannot recover damages against the corporation of a borough for grading the street opposite his lot and injuring its value.

The legislature may authorize a bridge company to use a highway without compensation to the owner: 6 *W. & Ser.* 101, Mon. Bridge Co. v. Coons; same case, 6 *Barr* 379, see opinion of GIBSON, C. J., 382. A company invested with the right of eminent domain, is not answerable for consequential damages further than provided by the grant.

Neither the State, nor a person, artificial or natural, acting by its authority under a law which the legislature is competent to make, is answerable for consequential damages, occasioned by the construction of a highway, further than is specially provided by the law itself: 8 *W. & Ser.* 85, Henry v. Pittsburgh Bridge Co.

The damages here insisted on are altogether consequential; resulting from the inconvenience to which the occupants of the houses are subjected by not having a pavement in front of them.

The injury does not arise from making the railroad, but from taking away the turnpike road.

If the turnpike road had not been removed, the plaintiff would have no right to put a pavement in front of his houses; as the front of the houses is on the line of the turnpike road, and the steps and cellar-doors are encroachments on the rights of the public.

In the case of Mifflin, and of Heise, the opinion of the court was delivered May 27, by

BELL, J.—In the year 1823, the legislature incorporated a company to construct a turnpike road from Columbia to Marietta, under the title of "The Columbia, Chiques, and Marietta Road and Bridge Company," and prescribed the mode of ascertaining the damages thereby sustained by the owners of the land through which the proposed road might run. The road was accordingly made, and afterwards the then owners of the property, now in the seisin of the appellants, agreed with the company as to the value of the damages inflicted, and accepted the sum of one hundred dollars in full compensation for all injuries sustained in consequence of the road having been laid out and opened through their real property, and in full of all demands against them. Twenty-four years after this, viz. in the year 1849, an act was passed authoriz-

[Mifflin v. Railroad Company.]

ing the Harrisburg, Portsmouth, Mountjoy, and Lancaster Railroad Company to purchase from the directors of the Turnpike Company, all their right, title, and claim in the said road, and empowering the latter to sell and dispose of the same to the former, "for the purpose of laying rails thereon, under the act and several supplements thereto, relative to the incorporation of the said Railroad Company." This statute grew out of two prior enactments, dated respectively the 16th of March and the 7th of April 1848, by which the Railroad Company was invested with power to construct a branch of its road from an ascertained point on the original road, and extending to the town of Marietta. These acts were supplementary to the statute by which the latter company was originally incorporated, in the year 1832, to make a railroad from Lancaster to Harrisburg, and contain the provision "that in constructing and locating the said branch, and after the same shall have been completed, the said Harrisburg, Portsmouth, Mountjoy, and Lancaster Railroad Company shall be subject to all the provisions and restrictions imposed upon the said company under existing laws, as if the same were herein re-enacted in full detail." The purchase was accordingly made, and a branch railroad built, principally on and occupying the site of the turnpike. Where the new road passed through the lands of the appellants, it became necessary to make an excavation of some depth, by which one portion of their property was cut off from other portions, and certain houses built on the edge of the turnpike were isolated and rendered inconvenient of occupation. It thus happened that what had been a convenient appendage as a road of general use, and a means of facilitating intercommunication, was rendered a positive obstruction in the enjoyment of the appellants' property as it had been before used. This may be, and it is said, is more than compensated by increased facilities created by the making of the railroad in the occupation of the land for other purposes; but as this was a subject for the consideration of the inquest which assessed the damages, it cannot legitimately be taken into account here in determining the abstract right of the landholders to claim remuneration for consequential injuries flowing from the construction of the last improvement. The court below thought such remuneration could not be awarded, because the surface occupied by the turnpike road having been dedicated to public use by legislative authority for every purpose of passage and trial, the community had acquired an interest therein, and no ground having been taken for the purposes of the railroad, other than was before appropriated by the Turnpike Company under a purchase of the right of way, the owners of the soil cannot with propriety complain of a mere change in the mode of *user*, which encroached no further on their actual possession. If this reasoning be correct, the case presents the anomaly of substantial injury inflicted without corresponding remedy; for all the numerous

[Mifflin v. Railroad Company.]

laws passed upon the subject of public improvement by canals and roads, and among them that incorporating the appellees, recognise the possibility of damages incurred beyond the mere appropriation of soil necessary to the purpose. The basis of compensation is not to be measured solely by the value of the land taken for public use. The advantages likely to accrue, and the disadvantages to be suffered, enter largely into the estimate.

These considerations may, and frequently do, swell the sum awarded as remunerative, far beyond the worth of the surface occupied, or reduce it to nothing. One mode of occupation may be attended with little or no inconvenience to the owner of the soil, while another may visit him with injuries of a serious character, in reference to the nature of his possessions and the manner of their enjoyment. Nay, while one species of improvement may facilitate his business or add materially to the value of his property, another may hinder the one and largely detract from or entirely destroy the other. The very case before us is illustrative of this, if any reliance can be placed in the correctness of those who measured the amount of injury severally occasioned by the turnpike and railroad. While the first was esteemed, by the parties themselves, as fully compensated by the payment of $100, for the whole line of road passing through the farm then owned by the Misses Bethel, the last is fixed by an inquest at fourteen hundred and eighty dollars, in reference to a part only of the same property. A very limited knowledge and brief reflection will satisfy the inquirer that such a disparity may well occur, under the circumstances which have place here, and it demonstrates, at least, the propriety of making provision for the payment of damages, whether the consequential injuries suffered be the result of an original construction, or flow from the supervention of a new and different work upon an old improvement. Had a railroad been originally made over the lands of the appellants, creating the injuries they now complain of, an omission to provide for remuneration to the owners would have encountered universal disapprobation. The suggestion that the damages suffered were merely consequential could not have been accepted as an answer, except, perhaps, in a discussion relative to the constitutional power of the legislature to concede the right of making such a road over private property, without stipulating for the payment of such damages. In the case of the Philadelphia and Trenton Railroad Company, 6 *Whar.* 25, specially referred to by the court below, the distinction is pointed out between what has been called consequential injuries, and direct damage suffered from actual appropriation of the land, considered in reference to the constitutional prohibition. It is there, and in other cases which follow it, said that though the General Assembly is without power to grant to a corporation the right of *taking* private property for a public use without making compensation, it may

[Mifflin v. Railroad Company.]

authorize the site of a street or highway, dedicated to the use of the people, to be occupied by a supervened railway, without providing for the remuneration of private damages consequent upon it; for, said the court, the constitutional inhibition extends not to mere matters of annoyance. The same doctrine was repeated in the Monongahela Navigation Company v. Coons, 6 *W. & Ser.* 101; and though Mr. Justice HOUSTON there took occasion to dissent from the principle laid down, that an act which incidentally injured or entirely destroyed the enjoyment of property, in a particular way, is not always a *taking* or appropriation of it within the meaning of the constitution, it was again proclaimed in the subsequent case of Henry v. The Pittsburg and Allegheny Bridge Company, 8 *W. & Ser.* 85, where the court declared it to be settled that neither the State nor a person, natural or artificial, acting by its authority or command, under a law which the legislature is competent to make, is answerable for consequential damages occasioned by the construction of a highway, *further than happens to be specially provided.* Notwithstanding, then, some prior difference of opinion, it may now be taken as the ascertained rule, that the lawmakers may legally omit a provision for merely consequential damages, when creating a corporation to construct an improvement for the common benefit. But, I think, such was not the popular impression, and it is certain that, governed either by constitutional scruples or actuated by a sense of common justice, our legislature have always directed payment for consequential injuries suffered by the landholder from the making of public highways or other like works. I say always; for the very few instances where this has been omitted among the numerous acts of this character which load the statute-books, scarcely deserve to be esteemed exceptions. These, to be sure, with one or two instances of departure, relate to original constructions; but what difference can it make in principle, and so far as the dictates of right are involved, whether a railway is laid down on an already made turnpike road, or constructed over a surface newly prepared for the purpose. Had the Columbia, Chiques, and Marietta Turnpike Road Company been at first empowered to make a railway over the appellants' land, doubtless it would have been held expressly responsible, not only for the value of the land actually occupied by the way, but for all incidental injury. Why should a difference of practice be tolerated because such injury flows from a railway engrafted upon a previously made turnpike? There is, obviously, no reason for such a distinction, as perhaps there would have been, had a property in the soil passed to the earlier company by virtue of its payment of damages. The case might then have fallen within the principle which recognises the power of a proprietor to put his possessions to a profitable use, though such *user* may involve an incidental injury to a neighbour; a principle which was recog-

[Mifflin v. Railroad Company.]

nised in Green v. The Borough of Reading, 9 *Watts* 382, and other cases, cited for the appellee. But here, the soil over the surface of which the turnpike ran remains in the original owners or their alienees. During its appropriation to the purposes of the turnpike, those owners might have maintained an action of trespass against the directors of the corporation, had they attempted to construct over its site a railroad, without special authority, or turned it to any other use than that authorized by their charter: Ridge Turnpike v. Stoever, 6 *W. & Ser.* 378; for it is undoubted that land taken, under authority of law, for the construction of a turnpike or other road, cannot be used for some other purpose; but the State is bound to protect the highway and preserve its uses according to the terms of the concession: 1 *Bald.* 230; 16 *Mass.* 35. If, then, by the payment of the original damages, the first company purchased under its charter but the right of constructing and using a turnpike over the surface of the soil, it is obvious it could, of itself, unassisted by legislative action, have conveyed no interest beyond this to the second company. As alienees, the latter corporation could not have excavated a shovelful of earth but at the hazard of an action. Their right to do so is something greater and different from any interest derived or privilege purchased from the older company. It is, therefore, to be regarded precisely as though it were an original grant by an exercise of the legislative power, and its enjoyment is subject to all the conditions and restrictions to which the legislature has seen fit to subject it. We are not here presented with a question of constitutional law, such as occurred in the cases I have referred to, and upon which the learned president of the Common Pleas seems to have founded his determination.

The inquiry is not whether the General Assembly might have empowered the Railroad Company to make a branch railway on the site of the turnpike, without making compensation for the incidental damages consequent upon it? Nor is it, whether a municipal corporation in the exercise of its legitimate functions, may alter or cause the grade of streets and highways, without being accountable to the owners of the adjacent property for loss and inconvenience resulting thereupon? as it was in Green v. The Borough of Reading. It seems to be, simply, whether the legislature may annex, as a condition to the exercise of such a privilege as was here conferred, the duty of reimbursing private owners for injuries suffered by them in the promotion of the interests of a private corporation, or, if you please, of the public, and have so directed in this instance? Upon this point, the most extreme verge to which this court has gone in favor of private corporations is to be found in the doctrine, reiterated in the last case of Coons v. The Monongahela Nav. Co., 6 *Barr* 379, that a company invested with the right of eminent domain is not answerable for

[Mifflin v. Railroad Company.]

consequential damages *further than is provided by the grant.* In that case, too, the court gave effect to an act of Assembly directing remuneration for consequential damages, suffered long before the passage of the statute, from acts committed in pursuance of authority conferred by the original charter, which contained no similar provision. In truth, that adjudication recognises the propriety of legislative interference to an extreme much further than is claimed in this instance. But without this authority, not the slightest doubt could be entertained of the justice of providing for remuneration, where new powers and privileges are conferred either on the original company or another substituted for it. We are thus reduced to the single point, whether such a provision is discoverable in any of the statutes which have been enacted in reference to the branch railway particularly under notice? Happily, not the slightest difficulty is found in returning an affirmative response to this *quære*. We have already seen that by the act of March 1848, in constructing and locating the branch road, the appellees are expressly made subject to all the provisions and restrictions imposed by prior laws; and the act of January 1849, which authorizes the sale and transfer of the turnpike road, enacts that the rails to be laid thereon shall be laid under the act and the several supplements thereto relative to the incorporation of the Railroad Company. These references to the prior statutes, as containing the conditions under which the branch road was to be constructed, are too clear and explicit to admit a moment's hesitancy. They empower the company to make a new piece of railroad, as auxiliary to the principal road then completed, upon precisely the same terms imposed by the original statutes in reference to the original work. One of these terms or conditions was the obligation to pay for consequential injuries, assessed in the manner pursued in this instance. When petitioning the court for inquests, the complainants referred themselves to the original act of incorporation, as we have shown they had a right to do. Consequently, in setting aside the inquisition so found, upon the motion that there is no warrant for the inquiry of damages, the court fell into error, and the decrees quashing the inquisitions must be reversed.

But other exceptions were taken to the finding of the inquests, which the court declined to pass upon, and which, indeed, under the opinion entertained, it was unnecessary to consider. As, however, it may be proper to inquire into the truth of these exceptions, or some of them, the record will be remitted to the court below, with a *procedendo*.

And now, to wit, May 26th, 1851, after argument and due consideration, it is ordered that the decree and judgment of the said Court of Common Pleas, quashing the said inquisition, so as aforesaid found upon the petition of the said J. H. Mifflin, be reversed

[Mifflin v. Railroad Company.]

and wholly set aside; and it is further ordered that the said record be remitted to the said Court of Common Pleas, in order that the said complaint and the finding thereon, together with the exceptions filed thereto in the said court, may be duly proceeded in and finally determined.

A similar decree is to be entered in the case of Heise v. The Harrisburg, Portsmouth, Mountjoy, and Lancaster Railroad Company.

In the case of Susan Bethel, the opinion and decree were as follow, by

BELL, J.—For the reasons just expressed in the cases of Mifflin vs. the above defendant, and Heise vs. the same, we are of opinion the court erred in refusing to entertain the exceptions filed by the complainant, on the ground she is not entitled, at law, to claim the assessment of any damages for consequential injury done to her estate by making the said branch railroad. But as we perceive no merit in the said exceptions so filed, we think the court below was right in refusing to set aside the said inquisition.

Wherefore the said decree, confirming the said inquisition, is confirmed May 27, 1851.

Hackman *versus* Flory.

1. On an appeal from the judgment of a justice of the peace, it need not appear in the *declaration* that the claim of the plaintiff was for an amount within the jurisdiction of the justice; it is sufficient if that appear on the trial.
2. In an action for service rendered, the plaintiff may show service rendered by his wife as well as himself, though her services are not mentioned in the declaration.
3. In an action by the husband for service rendered by himself and also by his wife, the declarations of the wife, during service, as to the terms of her employment, are admissible on the part of defendant.
4. In the case of a hiring for a year, at a specified sum per month, it is not competent for the employer, within the period contracted for, to reduce the amount of monthly pay, without the consent of the other party.

ERROR to the Common Pleas of *Lancaster county*.

Benjamin Flory brought suit against Abraham S. Hackman, before a justice of the peace—referees reported, finding for plaintiff $16.98. Defendant appealed.

In one count in the declaration, were claimed $131 for work done by the plaintiff. The narr. contained other counts, in which the service by the wife of plaintiff was not mentioned. It was stated

[Hackman v. Flory.]

on the transcript from the justice's docket—Demand, book-account, $131. Credit, $91.52. Balance, $39.48.

It was proved, on the part of the plaintiff, that he was hired by defendant at $10 per month, that this service commenced in March 1848, and that he continued in defendant's employ till April 1849.

Defendant objected to the jurisdiction, because the declaration is for $131, without any credits endorsed. Court overruled the objection for the present. Defendant excepted. Plaintiff got married on Christmas 1848. Plaintiff offered to prove work done by his wife, since her marriage. Defendant objected; the evidence was admitted, and defendant's counsel excepted. It was proved that plaintiff's wife kept house for defendant, from Christmas after her marriage, till in March following, as she had done before.

On part of defendant, it was testified that plaintiff told witness that defendant would not give him more than $7 per month from 1st January till 1st April 1849. If he chose to stay at that, he might.

Defendant offered to prove that during the service of Mrs. Flory, she stated that she was working for her board. Plaintiff objected. Court rejected the evidence, and exception on part of plaintiff.

The court, with other instructions, told the jury that if the contract was for the whole year, at $10 per month, defendant had no right to change it without the plaintiff's consent. This part of the charge was excepted to on part of defendant.

Verdict for plaintiff for $8.77.

It was assigned for error:
1. The court erred in sustaining the jurisdiction of the magistrate, as plaintiff declared (and gave evidence to sustain it) for $131. The suit originated before a justice of the peace.
2. In allowing plaintiff to prove work done for defendant by plaintiff's wife, having laid all the work as done by himself.
3. In refusing to allow defendant to prove that Mrs. Flory said, *when doing the work for which the plaintiff charged defendant*, that she was doing it for her board, as she worked mostly for herself.
4. In charging the jury that defendant could not, on notice, reduce plaintiff's wages *in future* to $7 after his marriage, unless plaintiff consented, if the original hiring was for a year at $10 per month.

Stevens, for Hackman, plaintiff in error.—Plaintiff gave evidence of a demand equal to the sum demanded in plaintiff's declaration, giving no credits to reduce it below $100. Defendant then raised the question of jurisdiction, as the suit was brought before a justice of the peace. Court sustained the jurisdiction, and defendant excepted. This is assigned as the 1st error.

[Hackman v. Flory.]

That the plaintiff could not charge defendant with work done by any other person but himself, as he lays it to have been thus done. That defendant ought to have been allowed to prove that while in the act of doing the work, the wife stated on what account she was doing it. It was part of the *res gestæ*, and could not be separated from the thing done. She was living in defendant's house, and working for herself; and when she did occasional turns for defendant, it seems to be competent to prove who she said it was for, and on what account.

Frazer, for defendant in error.—1. The transcript of the justice's docket, in this case, shows the justice's jurisdiction—the plaintiff's claim having been reduced to below $100 by direct payments: Cooper v. Coats, 1 *Dal.* 308; Stewart v. Mitchell, 13 *Ser. & R.* 287. The office of the declaration is to state the plaintiff's cause of action, and not the defendant's defence. The damages suffered by a plaintiff may be less than $100 when a suit is instituted, yet after an appeal, when the declaration is filed, may be more than $100. Therefore, the laying of a sum over $100 in the declaration does not show a want of jurisdiction in the justice: Rankin v. Murry, 2 *Pa. Rep.* 74; 5 *Bin.* 522. In this case, defendant gave in evidence the credits in plaintiff's book, amounting to $91.52.

2. The evidence in the 2d bill of exception was properly admitted, the wife being considered the husband's servant, and the promise, in law, is made to him: *B. N. P.* 126; 2 *Stark. Ev.* 688–9, *Husband and Wife*, 1. A husband, suing alone on a note given to his wife during coverture, may describe it as given to him, without noticing the wife: 4 *Term Rep.* 616; 2 *Ch. Pl.* 136, note.

3. The admissions of the wife will bind the husband only where she has authority to make them. Where he sues for her wages, the fact that she earned them does not authorize her to bind him by her admissions: Hall v. Hill, 2 *Str.* 1094; *Green. Ev.* section 185.

4. The law is rightly stated in the charge of the court, "that if the contract was for the whole year at $10 per month, defendant had no right to change it without plaintiff's consent." It bound both, and could be changed only by consent of both. The plaintiff and his wife both worked for defendant before their marriage, and rendered him as much service after as before.

The opinion of the court was delivered June 2, by

CHAMBERS, J.—This is an action of *assumpsit*, for work, labor, and services rendered by defendant to the plaintiff.

On the trial, defendant offered to prove that whilst Mrs. Flory, the wife of the plaintiff, was doing work in the family of defendant, and for which defendant was charged in this action, she stated

[Hackman v. Flory.]

that she was doing it for her board, as she worked most of the time for herself; which evidence being objected to, was refused by the court, and exception taken by defendant.

Whilst the admissions of a wife are not receivable to charge the husband, is a general rule, to be sustained on sound policy, judicial authority, and a regard to the legal relation of husband and wife; yet the exigencies of trade and intercourse, the habits of society, and family convenience and arrangements, necessarily create exceptions to this rule, to be observed and respected. When there is a division of the labors and employment of a husband and wife, at home or abroad, and the husband permits his wife to act and be employed in the business of life with others, he necessarily commits to her the agency and control of her actions and contracts. His consent is to be presumed as giving to her power to contract and make engagements, for which she is to receive the wages and profit; and if she is thus made competent to contract, she may certainly furnish evidence, whilst engaged in the business, of the terms of the contract in which she is employed, as part of the *res gestæ*. The husband who permits his wife to be engaged in the domestic service of other families by hiring, which is, it is believed, a common occurrence, cannot with propriety object to the terms which she made, and on which she was retained, and the services rendered. She was allowed to obtain the situation, and it must be held on the terms which she made, and of which her declarations at the time, and whilst engaged in the work, are evidence. His consent is to be presumed, and the presumption is only rebutted by objection or prohibition on the part of the husband; and until such objection, her engagement would be the measure of his right for her services. In the case of Spencer v. Tisue *Add.* 819, it is said the cares of matrimony, the duties of management are divided; the husband assumes some parts, and submits other parts to the cares of the wife. When he acts or submits, he is bound. There may be a presumed agency in their common concerns, with which every wife is presumed to be vested, &c. In McKinley v. McGregor, in this court, 5 *Whar.* 569, it is ruled, if husband and wife live together, any business in which she may be engaged is presumed to be conducted by her with his knowledge and as his agent.

The declaration of a wife, at the time of effecting a policy on her life, as to the state of her health, was received in evidence against her husband as a part of the *res gestæ*: Oveson v. L. Kennard, 6 *East* 188.

On principle and authority, it is the opinion of the court that the declarations of Mrs. Flory, made at the time and place of her service, as to what her employment was, and the terms of it, were part of the *res gestæ*, and in a transaction in which she was presumed to be acting with the consent of her husband; and as such

[Hackman v. Flory.]

her declarations ought to have been received. In the refusal of the court below there was error. The other errors assigned not being maintained, it is unnecessary to remark on them in detail.

Judgment reversed and a *venire de novo* awarded.

Staines *versus* Shore.

1. In an action on a note given for the price of a horse sold at auction, where fraud is alleged as to the condition of the animal at the time of sale, the presumption is very slight that the horse was unsound when fully grown, and apparently vigorous, because it had been diseased when a colt; the jury are to judge of the soundness or unsoundness, from the evidence exhibited in the case.
2. There can be no deceit in the sale of a chattel without a *scienter*.
3. The employment of a puffer by the seller to bid for him at an auction vitiates the sale, and it is not material whether the property purchased brought no more than its *general value;* a purchaser has a right to purchase at an under value if he can.
4. When the employment of a puffer has been discovered by the purchaser after the sale, it is his duty to offer to return the property purchased, when the fraud is discovered; but if not discovered till too late to do so, the purchaser's defence is good without it.

ERROR to the Common Pleas of *Huntingdon county*.

This was an appeal from the judgment of a justice of the peace in an action of debt, by Shore *v.* Staines & Kough, on a note for $69.50, dated 18th March 1847, given by Staines & Kough to Shore for a horse sold by Shore, and purchased by Staines, at public auction. The horse died about thirty days after the sale. The purchaser did not offer to return him; but it was alleged that he believed, till shortly before the death of the horse, that he could cure him. It was further alleged that the horse was *unsound* when sold; and also that the plaintiff employed a person to bid him up at the sale.

On the part of the defendant, John Henderson was examined, and testified that the animal was cried out as a young, sound horse in every respect. That he examined him and found that he was scabby. That it was quite evident from the appearance of the skin; he considered the horse unsound at the time. He knew this colt, when a man named Martin owned him. He was in a bad condition. The horse was not much moved about at the sale. He appeared stiff.

Jeremiah Brown testified, that at the time the horse was knocked down to Staines, Aaron Shore was present, within hearing distance. One of the Shores said the man was bit. I asked the reason. The boy said the horse was unsound. Staines was present, but perhaps a little further off.

Burket, the *crier*, was examined, and said he thought he cried

[Staines v. Shore.]

him as a fine, sound, young horse, as far as he knew; and he looked so. That he did not know whether Shore, the plaintiff, was present.

On the part of the plaintiff, John B. Logan testified, *inter alia:* —I think on the morning of the vendue I offered Aaron Shore $55; he refused to take it. I bid him at the sale to about $63 or $64; may be a little more. He was sold at outcry in a public yard. He had nothing of farcy while I knew him. The appearance of the horse on that day was good.

Jacob Gehrett was the person who it was said was employed as puffer. He was examined on the trial, on the part of the plaintiff, and testified, *inter alia*, that Shore asked him to bid in the colt for him. That he saw the horse—he looked well. That he bid on the horse. Thought he started him at $40. That he soon went over that, and he let him go. He further said that he was to bid in the horse for Shore, the plaintiff, for $55.

On the trial, defendant's counsel submitted two points:

"1. If the jury believe that the colt, for the price of which the note in controversy in this action was given, was unsound and unhealthy at the time of the sale of the colt by Martin to Shore, the law presumes that unsoundness continued, unless it had been proven that the colt recovered its health before it was sold to defendant."

TAYLOR, J., charged that such presumption would be but slight in the present case, as the animal had grown to be a horse. Much of the evidence here relates to the growth, appearance, and apparent health of the animal during the period between the purchase by Shore and the purchase by Staines. You will take into consideration the whole evidence—that which relates to the health of the colt before, at the time, and after Martin parted with it—what has been testified to in relation to the nature of its disease, &c.; and thus judge whether the *horse* was sound when sold to Staines.

"2. If the jury believe the evidence of Jacob Gehrett, one of the plaintiff's witnesses, and that Jacob Gehrett was employed by Aaron Shore, the owner of the horse sold, as a puffer at the public sale of the colt, to bid for Aaron Shore, and that he did so bid at the sale, the sale was fraudulent and void; and as the note for which this suit is brought was given for the horse purchased at such auction, in which Jacob Gehrett so acted as a puffer for Aaron Shore, the owner of the horse sold, the plaintiff cannot recover in this action."

We refuse to answer this point as requested. The evidence, as we recollect it, is that Shore had requested Gehrett to bid for him, and not let the horse go for less than $60; that he bid to that point, and then ceased bidding; and that afterwards he was bid by Staines and others to $69.50, and at that knocked down to Staines. Taking the facts, however, to be as assumed in this point, then it

[Staines *v.* Shore.]

would follow, we agree, that the sale at the auction was fraudulent and void; and Staines could not have been compelled to take the horse, (he refusing to do so;) that Shore could not have recovered the amount for which he was struck down *upon the bid.* But it would not still follow, *if he afterwards did take the horse, with an after opportunity for inspection, and ratify the sale by giving his single bill with security for the price, and the horse was a sound horse and worth the money, that the single bill would be without consideration.* If a sound horse at a fair price was the consideration of the single bill, then, as we have already remarked, there was, *in point of fact,* no want or failure of consideration; and it is not disputed that the horse was worth the money if sound. Whether the defence set up should, therefore, avail the defendant, must depend upon your decision of the questions of fact already submitted.

Verdict was rendered for plaintiff for $80.65.

The charge was excepted to on part of defendants.

It was assigned for error:

1. That the court instructed the jury in substance, that although the horse was diseased at the time of the sale, and Shore asserted him to be sound, by which assertion Staines was induced to bid for him, it did not vitiate the sale, unless Shore knew the horse to be diseased at the time he made the assertion.

2. To the answers to the points submitted on part of defendant, and particularly to the part of the answer to the second which is in italics.

Fisher, for plaintiff in error.—That it was not material whether Shore knew that the horse was unsound. If one asserts what he does not know, he is guilty of falsehood: *Story's Eq.* 193; 9 *Watts* 55, McFarland *v.* Newman; *Oliphant on the Law of Horses, Racing &c.* 84, and notes.

[BELL, J.—There must be either a warranty or deceit.]

That it was illegal to employ a puffer: Pennock's Appeal, 1 *Harris* 446; *Babington on Auctions* 48, 49, 52.

Cornyn, for defendant.—The purchaser gave his note and took the horse. He kept him till he died, and he did not, at the time, allege unsoundness.

A naked affirmation is not itself an express warranty, nor evidence of it: McFarland *v.* Newman, 9 *Watts* 55. To constitute a warranty, the words must not be dubious or equivocal, but it must appear that the affirmant intended to *warrant,* and did not express a mere matter of opinion or judgment: 7 *Ser. & R.* 482. The maxim *caveat emptor* is so strictly construed that it has given rise to another principle, *simplex commendatio non obligat;* a simple

[Staines v. Shore.]

assertion by the vendor as to the value or quality of the goods, does not amount to a warranty: 2 *Kent* 484; *Chitty on Contracts* 134–5.

The sale of an unsound horse *without fraud or warranty*, though known to be unsound by the seller, is no defence to an action for the purchase-money: Pulhamus *v.* Pursell, 3 *Pa. L. J.* A fair price implies a warranty of *title* in the sale of a chattel, but not a warranty of *quality:* 2 *Kent* 482.

In Bramley *v.* Alt, 3 *Vesey* 620, it was held that a sale was not fraudulent because a puffer had been employed, if there were real bidders who bid after the puffer had ceased: 12 *Vesey* 477, Smith *v.* Black.

Fraud without damage, or damage without fraud, gives no cause of action; but where they concur and meet together, action lieth: CROKE, J., 3 *Bl. Rep.* 95.

Blair, on same side.

Fisher, in reply.—That the legality of the employment of a puffer does not depend on the price the property brought. That the value of the horse was not a proper element in the case: That it matters not whether the defendant got the worth of his money or not.

The opinion of the court was delivered May 26, by

GIBSON, C. J.—The direction on the first point was right: there is no deceit without a *scienter*. On the second, it was inaccurate. We held, in Pennock's Appeal, 2 *Harris* 449, that the employment of even a single puffer vitiates the sale. In the present case, the ruling judge instructed the jury that if the horse was actually worth the sum to be paid for him, the buyer got the value of his money and could not have been defrauded. The fallacy of the principle is in assuming that there is a standard of value independent of the wishes and wants of the bidders, and that every man is willing to buy by it. A man proposes to sell his horse for a fair price to another, who declines because he has no use for him, and does not choose to take the risk of getting less for him than he gave, with a certainty of losing his trouble, and the expense of keeping in the mean time; but the case would be different did the owner make it worth his while to purchase with a view to profit on a resale. What is the worth of any thing? The apophthegm of Hudibras answers truly, "Just so much money as 'twill bring." A man is defrauded whenever he is incited by artful means to bid more than he otherwise would. He has a right to buy at an undervalue, where the necessities of the owner compel him to sell; and whenever the price is ever so little enhanced by a secret contrivance, he is cheated. A sale by auction presupposes a sacrifice, or at least a willingness to sell for what can be had; but should the vendor

[Staines v. Shore.]

stick for the last penny, it would be idle to set the property up, because his price could be as readily obtained at private sale. Should he, however, see fit to make the experiment, his object could be attained by directing the auctioneer not to let the property go for less than his estimate of its market value; or, if he propose to sell without reservation as to price, let him openly reserve a right to bid. For no fair purpose is the employment of a puffer necessary; and it must vitiate every sale in which recourse is had to it. Had the horse lived in this case, it would have been necessary to return or tender him to the vendor as soon as the fraud was discovered; but as there is no evidence that it was discovered till it was too late for that, the vendee's defence was perfect without it.

Judgment reversed and *venire de novo* awarded.

Dottarer *versus* Bushey.

1. If the words charged in a narr. for slander do not imply a criminal charge subject to infamous punishment, neither an innuendo nor verdict will help them; but when they are used in a double sense, the plaintiff may, by an innuendo, aver the meaning with which he thinks they were spoken, and the jury may find whether they were spoken with that meaning or not.

2. Where the words were that the plaintiff "will lie, cheat, steal, and swear," it was not error for the court, in answer to a broad request of defendant's counsel to charge that the evidence did not support the declaration, to say to the jury that these words may import that the plaintiff steals.

3. To say of a person that "I believe he will steal, and I believe he did steal," amounts to the charge of larceny.

4. To say of a person he "took my wood, and is guilty of any and every thing that is dishonest," connected with the innuendo that the defendant meant that plaintiff was guilty of larceny, is sufficient after verdict.

ERROR to the Common Pleas of *Adams county*.

This was an action of slander, brought by Bushey against Dottarer. The narr. contained seven counts; in the first of which the matter complained of is laid in the following words, viz. "Bushey is guilty of every thing that is mean and dirty. He lies, and swears, steals, and cheats. He has taken my wood."

In the 2d count the words laid are, "Bushey has stolen my property."

In the 3d count they are laid, "Bushey is guilty of theft. He has taken my property."

In the 4th count they are charged as follows: "Bushey took my wood, and is guilty of any and every thing that is dishonest."

In the 5th count, the words laid are, "He lies and swears, steals and cheats."

In the 6th count they are laid, "Bushey stole my property."

And in the 7th count, "Bushey has taken my property. He is

[Dottarer v. Bushey.]

guilty of any and every thing that is mean and dirty. He will lie, cheat, steal, and swear, and then attend preaching on Sundays."

The plea was not guilty.

Upon the trial, the plaintiff produced the following testimony, viz. :

Enoch Routzong :—I was working for Bushey last fall a year. Dottarer came there and wanted me to work for him. I told him I was engaged to Mr. Bushey, and could not. He said that Bushey was such a rascal; that he would lie, cheat, and steal.

Cross-examined :—Nobody else present. I didn't tell it before this suit was started.

Jacob Funk :—In Miller's shop, Dottarer said Bushey would swear, lie, cheat, and steal. This was some time before the township election last spring.

Cross-examined :—James Miller and Nicholas Wilson were present.

Jonas Yetts :—The evening before last spring township election, at Stahle's store, Dottarer said, Bushey would lie, swear, and do any thing that was ornary; that he had taken his wood from him; and what else wouldn't he do?

James A. Miller :—On the morning of last spring election, Dottarer came by my shop. He said he was going to use his influence against Bushey at the election. He said, he will lie, swear, cheat, and steal, and do any thing else that is ornary. Had frequently used the same words before in my hearing; had done it at my shop when Mr. Funk was there. Mr. Bushey was a candidate for justice of the peace.

Nicholas Wilson :—The morning of the election, at Miller's shop, Dottarer said that Bushey would lie, cheat, swear, and steal, and do any thing that was ornary.

Cross-examined :—The same conversation Mr. Miller spoke of.

In chief :—I heard him use the same words at other times.

Abraham Slaybaugh :—At the spring election, Dottarer stopped me as I came by his mill. He said that a man who would do what Bushey had done, would steal, if it was not for the law.

Jacob B. Trostle :—I met Dottarer on his farm. He said, now I have left all good friends except this damned rascal across the creek, Bushey. *I believe he will steal, and I believe he did steal.* This was in April last.

Cross-examined :—We are not good friends.

The counsel for the defendant asked the court to instruct the jury that the evidence of the plaintiff did not support his allegation in the declaration that the defendant had charged him with the crime of stealing.

The charge was as follows :—This is an action of slander, in which the plaintiff seeks to recover damages from the defendant

[Dottarer v. Bushey.]

for charging him with the crime of stealing. Among other things in his declaration, the plaintiff alleges that the defendant, in speaking of the plaintiff in the presence and hearing of different persons, falsely and maliciously said of him as follows: "Bushey is guilty of every thing that is mean and dirty. He lies and swears, steals and cheats."

It is contended by the defendant's counsel, that there is no evidence in support of this, and we are asked so to instruct the jury. A number of witnesses have testified that they heard the defendant say that the plaintiff *would* lie, swear, cheat, and steal. The testimony of these witnesses does not go to support the charge referred to. The charge is that he *does* steal, &c., and the testimony is, that he *would* steal, &c. To say of a man he *would* steal, is but to impute to him a want of honesty, or at most, a thievish propensity, to which he might yield under certain circumstances, as where the temptation is strong, or impunity probable or nearly certain, or if it were not for the law. One witness, however, James A. Miller, testifies that the defendant, in speaking of the plaintiff, said he will lie, swear, cheat, and steal, and do any thing else that is ordinary. If this witness testifies correctly, his testimony establishes the truth of the charge that the plaintiff steals, &c. Though the allegation and the proof are not precisely the same in words, they are the same in *substance*, and that is all that the law requires. The words laid in the declaration and those proved would be understood, by the world, as meaning the same thing. To say of a man that he will lie, swear, cheat, and steal, is, in meaning, the same as to say he is addicted to those vices, or that he practises them, or that he lies, swears, cheats, and steals. To say of a dog he will bite people and kill sheep, would as surely fix upon him the character of a vicious, sheep-stealing dog as would the words, he bites people, and kills sheep; or to say of a child, he will neither obey his father nor mother, would no less amount to a charge of disobedience than would the words, he disobeys the commands of his father and his mother.

Whether Miller is right or wrong in his statement of what the defendant said; whether it was *will* or *would*, is a matter for you to determine. Other witnesses, who were present, as they say, and as he says, at his shop, when the defendant spoke of the plaintiff, give a different version of the charge. They say that it was that he *would* steal, &c., and not that he *will* steal, &c. How it is, you will determine.

This charge was excepted to by the counsel for the defendant, and it was filed at their request. The jury found for the plaintiff $300 damages.

A motion was entered for a new trial in the court below, and overruled by them. Whereupon this writ of error was sued out.

[Dottarer v. Bushey.]

It was assigned for error:
1. The court should have given an affirmative answer to the defendant's prayer.
2. In that part of the charge, when they say to the jury, "to say of a man he will lie, swear, cheat, and steal, is in meaning the same as to say he is addicted to those vices; *or that he practises them*, or that he lies, swears, cheats, and steals," &c.
3. There was error in the distinction taken by the court as to the effect to be given by the jury to the expressions "he will" and "he would," &c., and strongly calculated to mislead the jury.
4. The words laid in the 4th count in the declaration are not actionable, and the finding of the jury being general, and the verdict and judgment general, it is erroneous and should be set aside by this court.

The case was argued by *Hepburn* and *McCreary*, for plaintiff in error.—The charges in the different counts, except the 4th, are of larceny. The testimony of every witness is, that Bushey *would* lie, cheat, steal, &c., except one, who uses the word "will" instead of "would." To say of a man that he will do so and so, characterizes a propensity which he may have in a peculiar emergency, and is not a charge of an indictable offence. To say he will steal, is not a charge that he did steal. To make words actionable, they must convey an express imputation of some crime liable to punishmen: 6 *Term Rep.* 691, Holt v. Scholefield; and C. J. GIBSON, in Harvey v. Bois, 1 *Pa. Rep.* 13, says, "If there is any rule established by universal assent, it is that words which impute an offence against morality are not actionable *unless the offence be indictable or induce some legal disability.*" And 2 *W. & Ser.* 409, unless the charge imported by the words be indictable they are not actionable. Here, as we say, the proof does not establish a direct charge of an indictable offence.

The "substantial agreement" between the words laid in the declaration and those proved, which the law requires, must be found in the language employed, and not, as the court below seems to have supposed, in the effect which those words would probably have upon the minds of the hearers. Words must be proved as laid, and it is not sufficient to prove equivalent words of slander: Olmstead v. Miller, 1 *Wend.* 506; Watson v. Music, 2 *Miss.* 29; Fox v. Vanderbeck, 5 *Cowen* 513; Johnson v. Tait, 6 *Bin.* 121; Tipton v. Kahle, 3 *Watts* 93; Walters v. Mace, 2 *B. & A.* 756; 1 *Mod.* 86; 1 *Starkie on Slander* 370–72; 7 *Ser. & R.* 223–7.

No valid judgment can be given upon an assessment of entire damages upon several counts in slander, one of which counts discloses no cause of action: Day v. Robinson, 4 *Nev. & Man. Rep.* 384; 1 *Adol. & Ellis* 554, and Ruth v. Kurtz, 1 *Watts* 489. In the 4th count in the declaration, no cause of action is set forth.

[Dottarer v. Bushey.]

McConaughy and *Smyser*, for defendant.—The words are to be taken in their popular acceptation: 1 *Stew.* 384; 2 *Port.* 212, Hog v. Dorah; 9 *East* 93. The charge need not be made in direct terms: 2 *Watts* 352; 2 *Wend.* 534; 3 *id.* 291; 4 *id.* 320.

The words, "you will steal," are actionable, when it is averred in the declaration that by the speaking of the words defendant meant and intended to have it understood and believed that the plaintiff had been guilty of larceny: Cornelius v. Van Slyck, 21 *Wend.* 71. The words are so laid in the 1st count in the declaration in this suit; and the other counts contain the clause, "the said defendant further contriving and intending as aforesaid, then and there," &c. But the testimony of Jacob B. Trostle fully sustains the narr., for he swears that defendant said of plaintiff, "*I believe he will steal, and I believe he did steal.*" These words are actionable, and are none the less so, because of the expression, "I believe:" Beehler v. Stoever, 2 *Whar.* 313.

The 4th count, taken in connection with the prefatory matter in the 1st count, and with its context, comprehends the charge of larceny; and the jury, by their verdict, having found that such was their meaning, the court ought not to disturb it. Each successive count need not be prefaced with all the inducements and allegations set forth in the first. A reference to them in the subsequent counts is sufficient: Loomis v. Swick, 3 *Wend.* 205; Chambers v. Shultz, 8 *Watts* 300. Even if the words laid in the 4th count were not in themselves necessarily actionable, yet the 1st and 4th counts, taken together, connect the plaintiff with the slanderous imputation, and give them an actionable meaning as applied to the plaintiff: 1 *Chitty's Pl.* 681. After verdict, it shall be taken that the jury intended to find that the defendant spoke the words with reference to the commission of a larceny by plaintiff: 1 *id.* 677, 678.

The opinion of the court was delivered May 26, by

COULTER, J.—If the words charged in a narr. for slander do not imply a criminal charge subject to infamous punishment, neither an *innuendo* nor a verdict will help them. But when the words be used in a double sense, or will bear several meanings, the plaintiff may, by an *innuendo*, aver the meaning with which he thinks they were spoken, and the jury is the proper tribunal to pass on the truth of the *innuendo* and find whether the words were spoken with that meaning or not. In this case, the counsel for the defendant requested the court to "instruct the jury that the evidence of the plaintiff did not support the allegation in the declaration that the defendant had charged him with the crime of stealing." This is a very broad request, and the court did not comply with it. The words in all the counts were laid with an *innuendo*, to wit, thereby meaning that the plaintiff had been guilty of larceny. Now, if the

[Dottarer v. Bushey.]

words spoken or proved, without torturing them, would bear that meaning, the court had no right to say that they did not support the allegation in the narr. The words proved were, the plaintiff will "lie, swear, cheat, and steal, and do every thing else that is ornary." The court say that these words may import that the plaintiff "lies, swears, cheats, and steals." This was not taking from the jury the right to say, if they so thought, that they were not spoken in that sense, but were intended to mean that he will lie, cheat, and steal in future, if he thinks proper. The frequent repetition of these charges in the same or equivalent words, the number of persons to whom they were spoken, evinced a determination on the part of the defendant to fix on the plaintiff a character rotten in corruption, especially as they were spoken with the avowed purpose of preventing his election as a justice of the peace. All that can fairly be implied from the answer of the court is, that these words may implicate a charge of larceny. They could not take from the jury the right to say that they were spoken in that sense. And nobody will say that the circumstances, the manner of speaking them, and their constant repetition, may not give to them the character of a direct charge. The defendant was very indefinite in his point put to the court, if he wished a more particular instruction. I understand the judge to mean that the words proved are substantially as laid, and that if found as laid, that is, with the *innuendo*, they do support the action.

But the testimony of one of the witnesses comes fully up to the mark, who says that he met Dottarer on his farm, and he said, "Now I have left all good friends except this damned rascal across the creek, Bushey. I believe he will steal, and I believe he did steal." If this does not mean that he stole, I don't know what it does mean.

The addition of "I believe," does not soften the charge; it is a charge of larceny: 2 *Whar*. 313.

The words in the 4th count are connected with the *innuendo*, that the defendant thereby meant that the plaintiff was guilty of larceny, and after verdict, are sufficient. They may import the crime of larceny without torturing them, especially when spoken in connection with the other words with which they are coupled. The whole testimony was before the jury, and they were the proper judges with what intent the words were spoken, and in what sense the defendant intended them to be understood. The error assigned, therefore, as to the damages being assessed on all the counts, the fourth being bad, fails.

Judgment affirmed.

Harbold's Executors *versus* Kuntz.

1. To take a case out of the statute of limitations, the acknowledgment must be clear and unequivocal; and it ought to be so distinct in its *extent* and form as to leave no room for doubt or hesitation.
2. In a claim by a son-in-law who had lived on the farm of his father-in-law, for ten years' service, and for rents of a house of plaintiff, received by defendant, testimony that defendant (the father-in-law) said to the witness that "he had never settled with the plaintiff, nor paid him for the ten years' service, and he did not know what he would charge him; that he owed him for his ten years' service; that he had never paid him, and that he could pay him and would pay him; that he had not settled with him for the rent of the house and lot; that he would settle with him and pay him all he owed him, that he was old and wanted to settle up for the ten years' service and the rent; that he had paid debts for him (the plaintiff) and hauled stone for him:" was held to be too vague and uncertain to remove the bar of the statute.

ERROR to the Common Pleas of *Adams county*.

This was an action on the case, brought by John Kuntz against Michael Harbold. The executors of Harbold were substituted, after his death. The suit was brought January 17, 1849. In the declaration, the plaintiff claimed to recover for services of himself, his wife Susanna, and minor children, Michael, Elizabeth, and Sarah, alleged to have been rendered to defendants' testator from 1831 to 1841; and also certain rents, accruing during said period, from a house and lot claimed as plaintiff's, and which he alleged defendants' testator rented out and received the rents, as agent for plaintiff.

Defendants contended that the plaintiff never rendered services to their testator, as hireling, either by himself, his wife, or children; that their testator had taken the plaintiff (his son-in-law) and family into his family, when in poverty, and from considerations of affection and charity, and had supported them in his family and upon his farm, and had paid debts for plaintiff—that no wages were to be paid for any service done by them—and that the decedent had not received rents for the use of plaintiff; and, further, that if there had been any indebtedness by defendant to plaintiff, for services or rents, the same was satisfied and paid—and, further, the defendants interposed the bar of the statute against all claims by plaintiff for alleged services of plaintiff, his wife and family, and for rents.

The declaration contained a number of counts, and the pleas were *non assumpsit*, and *non assumpsit infra sex annos*, and payment.

On the trial, Samuel Blake was examined on the part of the plaintiff. A part of his testimony, which was considered by his Honor DURKEE, J., to be material as to the bar of the statute, was as follows:—Blake said in conclusion, Kuntz was not

[Harbold's Executors v. Kuntz.]

present when the old man said he would pay him; nobody but myself, that I recollect. He told me about paying debts for him, and that he had hauled stone for him. Kuntz worked out at carpentering, in the ten years, for Simpson and Baker. I communicated to Kuntz what the old man said to me about paying him, that same evening.

Testimony was given as to the value of the services rendered.

DURKEE, J., charged, in part, as follows:—On the 17th of January 1849, this suit was instituted by John Kuntz against Michael Harbold, who was his father-in-law. Shortly after the suit was brought, Michael Harbold died, and the present defendants, Jacob George and George Brown, his executors, having been substituted in his place, make defence to the action.

The plaintiff seeks to recover compensation for work and labor done and performed by him for Michael Harbold, in his lifetime. He alleges, that with his family he moved on to the farm of Michael Harbold, at his request, in the spring of 1831, and that he remained there, working and laboring for him, until the spring of 1841—a period of ten years—for which work and labor he had never been paid. And, further, that Michael Harbold for a number of years received the rents of a house and lot belonging to him, (the plaintiff,) and which he ought to have paid over to him, but did not.

The defendants deny that the plaintiff ever worked and labored, as he alleges, for Michael Harbold at his request, or, if he did so work and labor for him, they contend that it was done with an understanding between the parties that he was not to be paid for it; or, if he was to be paid for it, they contend that he has been paid and satisfied for it. And, lastly, that if he has any claim for such work and labor, it is barred by the statute of limitations, the suit not having been brought within six years from the time the services were performed.

They also deny the receipt by Michael Harbold of any rents belonging to the plaintiff. If any were so received, they contend that they were paid over to him or accounted for; and, at all events, that he is barred by the statute of limitations from recovering any thing for them in this suit. * * *

The latest period at which it is pretended that the plaintiff performed any services for Michael Harbold was the spring of 1841. His suit was commenced, as I have already stated, on the 17th of January, 1849, more than six years after all the alleged services had been performed. More than six years having elapsed, then, after the services were rendered, before the suit was brought, the plaintiff's claim for those services is cut off and barred by the statute of limitations, unless there is proof in the case that Michael Harbold said or did something in his lifetime that rescues it from the statute, or takes the case out of the statute. If there is any

[Harbold's Executors *v.* Kuntz.]

such proof, it is to be found alone in the testimony of Samuel Blake, Esq. If you believe his testimony to be true, then the plaintiff's claim is unaffected by the statute—is no more barred by it than though all the services had been rendered within six years before the suit was brought. If you disbelieve it, the plaintiff cannot recover for services, and ought not, for the statute of limitations is a wholesome act, and should not be violated, even though it should, in the opinion of the jury, work the grossest injustice. Esquire Blake testifies in regard to the point under consideration as follows. Speaking of the house in which both parties resided, he says:—" I went to the house the last of March 1843, and remained there as a boarder, until the spring of 1848, boarding part of the time with Kuntz, and part of the time with the old man. The old man detailed to me about bringing Kuntz and his family from York county, to work on his farm, from 1831 to 1841; he said he was $2000 in debt for the farm; that Kuntz was a great worker, and he brought him along to work on the farm; that Kuntz had a house and lot in Washington township, York county, and that he (Kuntz) told him (Harbold) that he should rent it out and pay his (Kuntz's) little debts. He said he had never settled nor paid him for the ten years' service, and he did not know what he would charge him. He told me, in 1847, that he owed Kuntz for his ten years' service; that he had never paid him, and that he could pay him and would pay him. On the same day, he said he had not settled with him for the rent of the house and lot; that he would settle with him and pay him all he owed him; that he was old, and wanted to settle up for the ten years' service and the rent. He told me that after the ten years he gave Kuntz the place on rent for the third bushel; Kuntz to get the third bushel. I had a settlement with the old man in February 1847, and his settlement with Kuntz was repeatedly brought up by him that day."

Verdict was rendered for plaintiff for $1401.91.

Various errors were assigned: one was to the charge, that the testimony of Samuel Blake was sufficient to take the case out of the statute.

D. McConaughy and *M. McClean*, for plaintiffs in error, contended that the testimony of Blake was not sufficient to take the case out of the statute: 6 *Watts* 219; 10 *id.* 172–9; 7 *W. & Ser.* 180; 3 *Barr* 418; 4 *id.* 321–4; 1 *Jones* 365. In this case there is no admission of *a clear balance:* 1 *Peters* 351, Bell *v.* Morrison.

D. M. Smyser and *R. J. Fisher*, in reply.—The claim was a *quantum meruit* for an amount unliquidated, not only at the time

[Harbold's Executors v. Kuntz.]

of the acknowledgment, but from and during all the time of the continuance of the implied contract between the parties. The acknowledgment went to the *entire* claim—the *whole claim* for ten year's services. It acknowledged an indebtedness coextensive with any that ever existed, before the statute began to run. In the very nature of the case, it could name no sum or amount.

But the *acknowledgment* was accompanied by an *express promise to pay*. This *promise*, if the testimony of the witness is true, was as extensive as the acknowledgment, and went, like it, to the full extent of the original demand. There is, it is true, no admission of a clear balance. There could be none, as there never had been any thing between the parties by which the amount of the balance was known to either, but an undertaking to pay whatever the services were worth. If, one day before the statute interposed, the defendant would have been liable to pay the value of the services, to be liquidated by a jury in case of disagreement between the parties, we say that the declaration of Harbold, in 1847, "that he owed Kuntz for his ten years' services; that he had never paid him, and that he could pay him, and would pay him," restored that liability to where the statute found it. Such a declaration, made within six years, with proof of previous service, would have made out a good case for the plaintiff. Why should it not be sufficient to reinstate his case.

The opinion of the court was delivered May 26, by

COULTER, J.—In order to take a case out of the statute, the acknowledgment of the debt must be clear and unequivocal, otherwise it is not equivalent to a promise to pay; and it ought to be so distinct in its extent and form as to leave no room for doubt or hesitation: Farley v. Kustenbader, 3 *Barr* 418; Berghaus v. Calhoun, 6 *Watts* 220; Magee v. Magee, 10 *Watts* 172; Hazlebacker v. Reeves, 9 *Barr* 258; Gilkyson v. Larue, 6 *W. & Ser.* 213. The extent of the promise, whatever may be said on that subject, is as important as any other of the ingredients. And this is strongly manifested in Farley v. Kustenbader.

The old debt is gone. It is the new promise which is efficacious and creates the liability, and which supports the action. But how can that be, if you don't know its extent, either by positive admission, or by reference to something admitted which makes it certain. The law delights not in shadows and uncertainties, but in distinct proof, on which the mind can rest with certainty in establishing a liability. To say that I will settle with you, and pay you what I owe you, and all such forms of admission, are wholly uncertain, because you cannot tell what was in the mind of the person; he perhaps thought nothing was due. The case on hand is strongly evincive of the value of the statute, and the danger of making it of no effect by loose testimony.

[Harbold's Executors v. Kuntz.]

The alleged promisor was dead at the time of trial. The claim is for alleged services by Kuntz, his wife Susan, and his minor children. The services are alleged to have been rendered between 1831 and 1841, during which time it is also averred that Harbold received the rent of a house belonging to Kuntz. The suit was not instituted till 1849. The court say that the testimony of Samuel Blake, if believed, removes the bar of the statute. But Blake's testimony, thus thrown before the jury in a lump, is altogether too vague and ill-defined. We cannot ascertain whether it was one conversation, two, three, or more.

It is uncertain whether he meant that he had not settled and paid for the ten years' service of Kuntz himself, or for himself and family. It is uncertain whether, when he said he would settle and pay all he owed him, he referred to the rent merely, or to the whole claim. He afterwards said that he wanted to settle up for the ten years' service (but of whom he did not say) and the rent, and he would pay all he owed him. He also said he did not know how much Kuntz would charge him. Now there is nothing certain in this. All the while Kuntz was living on the farm of Harbold, and must have been furnished, I should suppose, with much material for clothing and subsistence. But the witness testifies that his services were worth $150 per year. Here is a claim and a recovery to the amount of $1401, for alleged services, the last of which were rendered eight years before suit brought, and all depending upon the misty recollection of one witness, who testifies merely as to admissions, the easiest mode of testimony to lead to error, the kind of evidence most apt to be misapprehended and mistaken, and in relation to which a facile conscience may stretch itself like India rubber. At the close of his testimony, he says that Harbold told him he had paid debts for Kuntz and hauled stone. We may suppose also that he had a claim against Kuntz for occupying his premises. What then was the balance on settlement—how much, what sum was in the mind of Harbold when he said he would settle and pay what he owed? Was it a hundred dollars, or was it two thousand? The evidence gives no data, acknowledged and stated by Harbold, from which it can be fixed with certainty.

The direction of the court is too general in throwing the vague and uncertain testimony of Blake before the jury as removing the bar of the statute.

Judgment reversed and a *venire de novo* awarded.

Alexander *versus* Miller, Reed & Co.

A wife cannot make any contract to bind her husband without his authority express or implied, or dispose of his property, except perhaps in case of necessity for the immediate use of his family. And where the husband is a *lunatic*, she cannot transfer his property to pay a particular creditor to the prejudice of others.

ERROR to the Common Pleas of *Mifflin county*.

This was a *scire facias* on a recognizance, issued in favor of Miller, Reed & Co., against Napoleon B. Alexander, as bail for stay of execution on a judgment before a justice of the peace, in favor of Miller, Reed & Co. *vs.* William A. Alexander. The recognizance of N. B. Alexander, on which the sci. fa. was issued, was dated 30th January 1843, and the stay of execution expired on the 12th October 1843. On the 28th July 1843, before the stay of execution had expired, and when William A. Alexander, the defendant in the above judgment, was in a deranged state of mind, and then confined, for his cure, in the Insane Hospital, in the county of Philadelphia, Edith, (wife of William A. Alexander,) Napoleon B. Alexander, the above named defendant, and David C. Miller, one of the firm of Miller, Reed & Co., entered into the following agreement:

KISHACOQUILLAS, July 28th, 1843.

Agreement for the purchase and sale of a crop of wheat, made the above date, by and between Edith W. Alexander, by and with the advice of Napoleon B. Alexander, of Union township, Mifflin county, of the one part, and David C. Miller, of Brown township, county aforesaid, of the other part, witnesseth, that the said party of the first part agrees to sell to the said David C. Miller, of the second part, all their crop of wheat, now in the barn, and in one stack beside the barn—say one hundred bushels, more or less—whatever will be of it, except what will be bread for the family, and pay what school-tax he owes to James Poe—at one dollar per bushel, or market price. The wheat is considered to be now delivered; and if N. B. Alexander can thresh and haul said wheat for said Edith, he is to do it as soon as he can get it done so as not to stop his other farming or putting out his seed.

Received pay at the rate of one dollar per bushel, for one hundred bushels—the balance to be understood or ascertained when the wheat is threshed. Signed by Edith W. Alexander, Napoleon B. Alexander, and D. C. Miller.

The wheat was not taken away by Miller, Reed & Co., but, on the 3d of October 1843, was levied upon by the sheriff of Mifflin county, as the property of the said William A. Alexander, and, on

[Alexander v. Miller, Reed & Co.]

the 14th of the same month, was by him sold upon a fi. fa. at the suit of J. & J. Milliken v. William A. Alexander. The stay of execution upon the said judgment of Miller, Reed & Co. vs. William A. Alexander, expired on the 12th of October 1843, and on the 19th of that month an execution issued thereupon, and was returned "no goods;" whereupon this action was brought by scire facias upon the recognizance; tried March 17th 1849, and verdict rendered in favor of the plaintiff.

On the trial, WILSON J., charged, *inter alia:*—The defendant alleges that he was released, by the agreement entered into on the 28th of July 1843, between David C. Miller, the wife of William Alexander, and Napoleon Alexander, (William, at that time, being insane, and in the hospital, as testified to.) Miller, Reed, & Co. had taken out an execution on their judgment, on the 14th of August, returnable on the 3d of December 1843, which was before the stay of execution was up, which he directed to be returned; *and while it was in the hands of the constable, this agreement was entered into,* by which David C. Miller was to get the grain, which was afterwards sold by Millikens, on their judgment. Miller, not in the name of Miller, Reed & Co., but in his own name, entered into the agreement, and the parties acknowledged a receipt of $1 per bushel, for 100 bushels of the grain, the balance to be understood or ascertained when the wheat is threshed. How, or under what circumstances, the execution in August was issued before the expiration of the stay, we are not informed. But, to this agreement we find Napoleon B. Alexander, who, there is some proof, was attending to the affairs of William Alexander on the farm, for his wife, a party. It may have been at his instance, to secure this property for his liability on the judgment. James says there was no money paid to Miller, but that the amount receipted was considered to satisfy a judgment of Miller, Reed & Co. against William A. Alexander, in which Napoleon was bail.

We do not think that the agreement for the sale of this property, under the circumstances, could be enforced; and, certainly, the property not having been taken into actual possession by Miller, it was subject to levy and sale on Millikens' judgment; still, if you are satisfied that Miller took the risk of the agreement, and agreed thereby to discharge Napoleon from his liability on his recognizance, the defendant would not be liable in this suit. There is no question that, the grain remaining in the possession of William A. Alexander or those having the custody of his effects, and it being sold by legal process and applied to William's debts, William A. Alexander would remain liable on the judgment; and the question, as we have said, is, if Miller, by his agreeing to treat the property as delivered, and in discharge of Napoleon Alexander from his recognizance, took upon himself the risk under the agreement, whether the plaintiff cannot recover. But if he did

[Alexander v. Miller, Reed & Co.]

not take upon himself the risk of the agreement being carried out, and Napoleon and Mrs. Alexander agreed to deliver this grain in payment of the judgment, which was not done, it would not be a payment, and the plaintiff is entitled to recover the value of the personal property William A. Alexander had on hand when the recognizance was entered into, towards or in satisfaction of his debt.

To this opinion defendant's counsel excepted.

Verdict was rendered for plaintiff, for $116.35.

It was assigned for error:

1. The court erred in instructing the jury that the agreement made between Edith W. Alexander, Napoleon B. Alexander, and D. C. Miller, under the circumstances, could not be enforced.

2. The court erred in submitting to the jury a fact of which there was no evidence, to wit, whether or not N. B. Alexander and Mrs. Alexander agreed to deliver the grain mentioned in the agreement to Miller, Reed & Co.

3. The court erred in saying to the jury that "while" an execution "was in the hands of the constable, this agreement was entered into."

4. That the court erred in instructing the jury that plaintiff could recover, but should have instructed that the defendant was discharged by the agreement from his liability.

J. Alexander, for plaintiff in error, contended that where a wife is left with the care of her husband's farm, goods, and effects, she is, in the absence of her husband, to be considered as the head of the family and the general agent of her husband; and more especially, as in this case, where the husband is prostrated by disease, and wholly unable to make any contracts or to provide for his family; her contracts made for the payment of his debts, and for the support of the family, are binding upon the husband, and all other parties thereto. Felker v. Emerson, 16 *Ver.* 653.

That the court, in their charge, mis-stated the evidence to the jury, by saying to them that "Miller, Reed & Co. had taken out an execution on their judgment, on the 14th of August, returnable on the 3d of December 1843, which was before the stay of execution was up, which he directed to be returned, and while it was in the hands of the constable, this agreement was entered into."

E. L. Benedict, for defendant.—The facts of this case appear to be correctly stated in the charge of the court, except that "while the execution was in the hands of the constable, the agreement was entered into, by which David C. Miller was to get the grain which was afterwards sold by Millikens on their judgment," which was entirely *immaterial*, and was evidently an oversight, as

[Alexander v. Miller, Reed & Co.]

the dates of the executions and the agreement are correctly stated by the court.

The agreement could not be enforced under the circumstances. There was no evidence that Mrs. Alexander was the agent of her husband; and if she were authorized to act for him, the agreement was void as against creditors, and the grain mentioned in it was sold by the sheriff, and the proceeds applied to the payment of Alexander's debts. It was to be threshed and delivered by her, or N. B. Alexander, the quantity ascertained, and an amount deducted sufficient for the family, and to pay the school-tax due to Poe. The property remained where it was at the date of the agreement, when levied on by virtue of Millikens' execution. A transfer of personal property, unaccompanied by a corresponding change of possession, is void as against creditors: Streeper *v.* Eckart, 2 *Whar.* 302; Hoofsmith *v.* Cope, 6 *Whar.* 58; Stark *v.* Ward, 3 *Barr* 329; Jordan *v.* Frink, 3 *Barr* 443; McBride *v.* McClelland, 6 *W. & Ser.* 94; Cadbury *v.* Nolan, 5 *Barr* 326; Clow *v.* Woods, 5 *Ser. & R.* 278; Baab *v.* Clemson, 10 *Ser. & R.* 419; Cunningham *v.* Neville, 10 *Ser. & R.* 202.

David C. Miller acted for himself individually, and not for Miller, Reed & Co.

Alexander, in reply.—It would be unfortunate if nothing could be done for the support of the family of a lunatic until the appointment of a committee.

The opinion of the court was delivered May 27, by

ROGERS, J.—This case may be safely rested on the opinion of the learned judge who tried the cause. The facts are correctly stated by Judge WILSON, with the exception of the immaterial error contained in the remark "that while the execution was in the hands of the constable the agreement was entered into by which David C. Miller was to get the grain which was afterwards sold by Millikens on their judgment."

The court charged the jury that the agreement for the sale of the property, under the circumstances, could not be enforced. On this point the whole case turns. For if the court be correct in this position, it puts an end to the defence, for the defence is confessedly based on the validity of that contract. The agreement referred to is for the sale of a crop of wheat belonging to the husband, William A. Alexander, which Edith W. Alexander, his wife, by and with the advice of Napoleon B. Alexander, the bail on the recognizance now in suit, undertook to make to David C. Miller, one of the firm of the plaintiffs, Miller, Reed & Co. The objection to the sale is, that there is no evidence, either express or implied, that Mrs. Alexander was the agent of her husband, and

[Alexander v. Miller, Reed & Co.]

consequently no title to the property passed to the vendee. The law, with a view to the safety of the husband, disables a wife from making any contract, or incurring any debt binding her, without his concurrence or authority. An express or implied authority is the test by which all cases must be determined in regard to the husband's liability for her engagements while they cohabit; for a married woman cannot make any contract to bind her husband, except by his express or implied authority : 2 *Roper, Husband and Wife*, 110–11. It is, however, said that there are exceptions to this rule, on the principle of necessity, and that this is a case of that description; that the husband was a lunatic, and, at the time of the contract, in the Insane Hospital in the city of Philadelphia; that the contract was advantageous to the husband, being made to save his estate from the executions of creditors. The plaintiff in error assumes that the contract was for the benefit of the estate; but of this I see but little, if any evidence. That it was for the benefit of Napoleon B. Alexander, the bail, may be admitted; but it is not so clear it was for the advantage of the husband; certainly not so much so as to justify them in disposing of the husband's property, the only effect of the sale being to prefer one creditor to another. Nor was there, that I perceive, any necessity for the sale. The law points out a mode of meeting a case of this description, namely, by a commission of lunacy and the appointment of a committee to take care of the person and estate. It would be disastrous to that unhappy and unfortunate class of citizens, to be stripped of their property at the will and pleasure of persons wholly irresponsible, under specious pretexts of necessity. That the wife had express authority cannot be pretended, for the husband was incapable of giving consent, nor can it be implied, for the plain reason that from imbecility of mind he was incapacitated from giving assent. Felker *v.* Emerson, 16 *Ver.* 653, is relied on by plaintiff in error. Not having an opportunity of consulting the case itself, we must take the principle declared from the syllabus, as stated in 2 *U. S. D.* 125. That case rules, that where a wife is left with the care of the husband's farm, goods, and effects, she is, in the absence of her husband, to be considered as the head of the family, and the general agent of her husband; more especially (it is added) when the husband is prostrated by disease, and wholly unable to make any contract, or to provide for his family, her contracts made for the payment of his debts, and for the support of the family, are binding on the husband, and all parties thereto. If that case be as I suppose, I have not the slightest disposition to disturb it. It accords with the acknowledged principle that a husband may be bound by her contracts where room is left for the implication of authority in her to contract. The court thought, with some show of reason, this to be the case where she was permitted to superintend his affairs

[Alexander v. Miller, Reed & Co.]

with his knowledge, and therefore, as might well be presumed, with his consent. Under those circumstances, she might with great propriety be deemed his general agent. Although confined to his bed by sickness, and therefore incapable of attending personally to business, yet he had, as I suppose, mind to assent to her acts as his agent; at least the contrary does not appear. But how can you imply an authority to act for him, when, reason having left its throne, the party is incapable of giving any consent whatever? To imply an assent under such circumstances, with respect be it spoken, would be absurd. And where is the necessity of the implication of agency, when the law has made ample provision for the protection of all parties placed in this unfortunate position? That sudden exigencies may arise which would justify the sale of part of the property for the immediate use of the family, it is not my purpose to deny. It ought, however, to be a clear case of necessity, very different from the one here presented.

Judgment affirmed.

Meals *versus* Brandon.

Though in order to render a conveyance admissible in evidence, but slight evidence of title in the grantor is sufficient, yet *some* interest in him must be shown: therefore, where in a deed by N. to W. and wife, purporting to convey all lands in certain counties and all other lands wheresoever the same may be, but without a particular description of any of them, *it was recited* that they were those which were the same day conveyed to the said N. his heirs and assigns by the said W. and wife, *the deed to N. not, however, being produced* and no evidence of its existence being given, and W. having had title to the premises as heir, *independent of the deed: Held*, that without such deed or evidence of its existence, the deed by N. to W. and wife was not admissible against the plaintiff in an ejectment brought by the executor of the will of a *bona fide* purchaser at sheriff's sale, under a judgment against W. in his lifetime, against one who claimed through a conveyance from the wife of W., who survived her husband: Without such deed or evidence, it did not appear that W. had been a party to it, and the title or interest of *a bona fide purchaser* is not to be affected by vague and uncertain evidence of another title.

ERROR to the Common Pleas of *Adams county*.

This was an action of ejectment to August term 1849, by William Brandon, executor of the will of Templeton Brandon, deceased, against William Meals, Jr., to recover the possession of 13 acres 115 perches of unenclosed woodland in Huntington township, Adams county, in the possession of William Meals, Jr., the defendant below.

Brandon, the plaintiff below, after showing title out of the commonwealth in David Waltemeyer, claimed the land through Ludwig Waltemeyer, son of David, who died intestate, and on his death

[Meals v. Brandon.]

this land descended to his son Ludwig, who it was alleged had had adverse and continued possession thereof for more than twenty-one years before his death, which occurred in March 1838; and through a sheriff's deed of the property to plaintiff's testator, as the estate of said Ludwig, dated 27th August 1840, founded on an execution against Ludwig Waltemeyer's executors, upon a judgment obtained against him in his lifetime, and revived against his executors.

Meals, the defendant below, claimed title through Agnes Waltemeyer, the wife and survivor of Ludwig, alleging that whatever title Ludwig originally had to the land in dispute, the title had been changed as far back as the 4th June 1805, by a conveyance of the land by L. Waltemeyer and Agnes his wife to William Norris, and a reconveyance on the same day by Norris to Waltemeyer and wife, "*their heirs and assigns for ever, and the survivor of them, and the heirs and assigns of such survivor;*" and deduced his title directly from her, by conveyance after her husband's death; and that both husband and wife, on the 4th June 1805, were separately seized in fee of lands within the three counties of Adams, Cumberland, and Mifflin, were childless, and that the conveyance to Norris, recited in his deed to Waltemeyer and wife, and his reconveyance to them, were made with the intention of vesting title to the whole in the survivor.

On the 20th August 1850, the cause was tried before his Honor Judge BLACK.

The plaintiff gave in evidence an application of David Waltemeyer, dated 16th November 1785.

The plaintiff then gave in evidence warrant to David Waltemeyer, 60 acres, adjoining Thomas Brandon and William Moore, on the South Mountain, dated 30th November 1785.

Plaintiff then gave in evidence survey for 13 acres 115 perches, dated 9th May 1786.

Plaintiff then proved, by several witnesses who had known the land for a period of thirty or forty years, that Ludwig Waltemeyer, son of David Waltemeyer, had used and occupied this land as his own for a long series of years, and was in possession of it at the time of his death in 1838.

Ludwig Waltemeyer did not live on it, nor was it enclosed. It was all woodland, and adjoined his lower place.

The assessments for Huntington township, Adams county, (the township in which this land lies,) from 1814 to 1843, were given in evidence by the plaintiff. From these it appeared Ludwig Waltemeyer was charged with taxes on lands in that township, from 1814 to 1840 inclusive; the quantity of land with which he appears to have been assessed varying in different years from 180 to 350 acres. In none of them was this tract separately named or assessed; nor did it appear to have been assessed in the name of any other person.

[Meals v. Brandon.]

Plaintiff then gave in evidence a deed, dated 27th August 1840, from George W. McClellan, sheriff of Adams county, to Templeton Brandon, for lands in dispute, sold on a judgment of George Himes, for use of William Moore, as the property of Ludwig Waltemeyer, deceased—consideration $800.

Plaintiff then gave in evidence, will of Ludwig Waltemeyer, dated 20th January 1838, and proved 17th March 1838, in which he directs that the land in dispute be sold.

Proof of service of writ.

Meals, the defendant, claimed under Agnes Waltemeyer, wife and survivor of Ludwig Waltemeyer.

Defendant offered in evidence the following deed, dated 4th June 1805, from William Norris to Ludwig Waltemeyer and Agnes his wife, and to the survivor of them.

This indenture, made this 4th day of June 1805, between William Norris, of the borough of Carlisle, county of Cumberland, and State of Pennsylvania, of the one part, and Ludwick Waltermen, of Dickensen township, county and State aforesaid, and Agness his wife, on the other part, witnesseth:—That the said William Norris, for and in consideration of five shillings lawful money of Pennsylvania, to him in hand well and truly paid by the said Ludwick and Agness, at and before the ensealing and delivery hereof, the receipt whereof is hereby acknowledged, have granted, bargained, sold, aliened, enfeoffed, released, assigned, and confirmed; and by these presents do grant, bargain, sell, alien, enfeoff, release, assign, and confirm unto the said Ludwick Waltermen and Agness his wife, and their heirs and assigns, all lands, tenements, and hereditaments situate in the counties of Adams, Cumberland, and Mifflin; and all other lands, tenements, and hereditaments, wheresoever the same may be or lay, together with all and singular the buildings, improvements, and appurtenances, and the remainders and reversions, rents, issues, and profits thereof, to have and to hold all the lands, tenements, and hereditaments, with the appurtenances, situate and described as aforesaid, (and which was this day conveyed to the said William Norris, his heirs and assigns, by the said Ludwick Waltermen and Agness his wife,) unto them the said Ludwick Waltermen and Agness his wife, and their heirs and assigns for ever, and the survivor of them, and the heirs and assigns of such survivor; to the only proper use, benefit, and behoof of the said Ludwick Waltermen and Agness his wife, and their heirs and assigns for ever, and the survivor of them, and the heirs and assigns of such survivor for ever.

Receipt as follows:—Received the day of the date of the foregoing indenture, from the within-mentioned Ludwick Waltermen, the full consideration therein stated.

WM. NORRIS.

[Meals v. Brandon.]

The deed was acknowledged on the 5th June 1805, by Wm. Norris, and recorded on June 6th, in *Cumberland* county only.

By the court.—This deed being offered, is objected to on the ground that there is no evidence before the court of title in Norris. The court, on examining the deed and considering the recital, is of opinion that it does not, of itself, import or imply that the land in dispute had been previously conveyed to Norris, or that it was intended to be conveyed by Norris to Waltemeyer and wife. There is nothing in the recital of the conveyance from Waltemeyer and wife that can be said to refer to this land. It is therefore rejected.

To this, defendant's counsel excepted.

It was assigned for error:
That the court erred in rejecting the deed from William Norris to Ludwig Waltemeyer and wife.

Smyser and *Reed*, in the argument submitted on the part of plaintiff in error, contended that the generality of the terms of description used in the deed and recital constituted no sufficient objection to the admission of this evidence; words of general description in a deed or mortgage, are sufficient to pass the grantor's title: 11 *Johns. Rep.* 365; 13 *id.* 537.

The court should have submitted to the jury to say whether the language used included the land or not: 5 *W. & Ser.* 78; 7 *Barr* 198; 6 *Ser. & R.* 185.

To show title in the grantor, any evidence of title, however small, is sufficient: 8 *Watts* 382; 7 *Barr* 237; 3 *id.* 239.

The recital in deed from Norris to Ludwig Waltemeyer and wife, and the survivor, &c., that the same land was conveyed by deed by Ludwig Waltemeyer and wife to Norris, is evidence of the fact, in this case, against the plaintiff, because he claims under Ludwig Waltemeyer, by title derived from him since the date of the deed from Norris. That deed is a part of his title, and he is bound by every recital in it: 4 *Bin.* 235; *id.* 328; 6 *Bin.* 417–18; 1 *Greenleaf's Ev.* sec. 23.

Hepburn, *Stevenson*, and *Biddle* were for defendant.—A deed from Ludwig Waltemeyer and wife to Wm. Norris, supposing it to describe accurately the land in dispute, would, by the act of Assembly of 18th March 1775, be void as against Brandon, a subsequent purchaser for a valuable consideration, unless recorded in *Adams* county within six months from its execution: *Dunlop's Digest*, edition 1849, 116–17.

And the effect of this statute could only be avoided by actual or constructive notice to him, neither of which would arise from recording such deed in another county. *A fortiori*, would the mere recital of a conveyance by Waltemeyer and wife to Norris of lands

[Meals v. Brandon.]

in Adams county, in a deed from the latter to the former, recorded in Cumberland county, be inoperative against Brandon, the subsequent purchaser for a valuable consideration. If, then, in strictness the court should have admitted the testimony, it is an error for which this court would not reverse, as it did no substantial injury to the party complaining: Unangst v. Kreamer, 8 *W & Ser.* 391; Gilpin v. Howell, 5 *Barr* 41.

The deed to Norris was not offered, and until some interest is shown to have existed in a grantor, a deed from him cannot be given in evidence: Faulkner v. Lesser and Eddy, 1 *Bin.* 188; Hoak v. Long, 10 *Ser. & R.* 9; Kennedy v. Skeer, 3 *Watts* 95.

The opinion of the court was delivered May 27, by

BELL, J.—Influenced by the statement of the plaintiff in error's paper-book, that Waltemeyer and wife had conveyed the tract in dispute to Norris, I sat down predisposed to discover, if possible, enough in the rejected deed to cover the subject of this controversy, or, at least, to warrant its reference to a jury, under the rules that generality and even looseness of description of the object of a conveyance form no objection to it as evidence, and that where there is latent ambiguity of description, creative of doubt in its application, the application is properly to be made by that portion of the tribunal to which the common law accords the determination of questions of fact. But I have looked into this deed in vain, for a phrase or sentence in chief or by way of recital, which by the most liberal construction, can be accepted as descriptive of, or as even remotely referring to the land here sought to be recovered. Had the defendant below produced the alleged deed from Waltemeyer and wife to Norris, conveying all the lands of the former, situate in the three counties named, in connection with proof that one tract then lay in one of those counties, the recital in the reconveyance might, and probably would be held as sufficiently descriptive by reference, and binding on Waltemeyer and his assigns as parties or privies to the conveyance. The statement of title would then stand thus: Waltemeyer and wife being seized of lands in the three counties, including the tract in question, conveyed them to Norris, who immediately reconveyed to Waltemeyer and wife all the lands in those counties, just before conveyed by them. But without the prior conveyance, and looking only to the proof given and offered, nothing can be extracted further than that Norris conveyed to Waltemeyer and wife all lands in Adams, Cumberland, and Mifflin which were just before conveyed to Norris by his grantees. Now, there is nothing here evidencing that Waltemeyer had before conveyed to Norris *all* the grantor's lands in those counties, and consequently, though we may conjecture, we cannot safely deduce as fact, that the subject of this controversy was so conveyed. Norris conveys all the land before conveyed to him,

[Meals v. Brandon.]

but it does not follow *this* land was so conveyed; *ergo*, there is nothing to show it passed under the last conveyance. I am aware of the rule that in order to the admissibility of a conveyance in proof, very slight evidence of title in the supposed grantor is sufficient; yet, some interest must be shown: Faulkner v. Eddy, 1 *Bin.* 118; Hoak v. Long, 10 *Ser. & R.* 9; Kennedy v. Skeer, 3 *Watts* 95. But here, there is absolutely no glimmer of title in Norris to the 13 acres and 115 perches. So that were the rejected deed admitted, it would avail the defendant below nothing, since it must instantly encounter, not only the insuperable objection just stated, but the reasonable principle that the title of a *bona fide* purchaser for value is not to be affected by vague and uncertain evidence: Boggs v. Varner, 6 *W. & Ser.* 469.

I have hitherto considered the question as though the recital relied on is binding on Waltemeyer and those claiming under them. The rule is that recitals are evidence against parties and privies to the conveyance or other instrument containing them. They are not binding on strangers. But to make Waltemeyer and, through him, the plaintiff below parties to the rejected deed, the supposed prior conveyance to Norris is absolutely necessary. Without this it is not apparent Waltemeyer had any connection with the latter conveyance, for it is in proof he was the owner of this land, independently of that deed. Surely, a third person could not compromise that ownership by recital in a pretended conveyance, which the true owner may have never seen. Had there been any evidence that he claimed under the Norris deed, as, for instance, causing it to be recorded, (Plumer v. Robinson, 6 *Ser. & R.* 185,) there would be reason for esteeming and treating him as a party to it. But as he neither executed it, nor, so far as appears, claimed under it, it is wholly inadmissible to say he was a party to it. Were such a proposition tenable, nothing would be easier than to defraud an owner of his estate, by a pretended conveyance to him of a different estate, reciting a supposed conveyance from him, and placing it of record. This would, indeed, be a most mischievous application of the rule invoked for the defendant below, and inviting to the grossest fraud.

The latter may in truth be entitled to hold the land in contest, but, if so, he has unfortunately lost an indispensable link in the chain of his title.

Judgment affirmed.

Gordon *versus* Bowers.

1. If the interest of a witness in the event of the cause be *doubtful*, the court should receive his testimony and refer it to the jury to decide whether he has such an interest or not. But whether the question of interest be determined by the court or tried by the jury, and the witness is not examined on his *voir dire*, but evidence is adduced to show his incompetency, the testimony of the witness himself, in support of his own competency, should not be received.
2. *Ex parte* conversations are not admissible against the adverse party.
3. In a suit on a contract to deliver wheat in the interior of the State, evidence as to its price in Philadelphia, at and soon after the time agreed upon for its delivery, is receivable as corroborative of the testimony as to its value at the place at which it was to be delivered.

ERROR to the Common Pleas of *Centre county.*

This was an action on the case, brought by Thomas Bowers against James Gordon, to recover damages for the non-performance of a contract made between the plaintiff and defendant, for the purchase and sale of a quantity of wheat. Upon the trial, the plaintiff gave in evidence a receipt given to him by defendant for $25 in part, for 300 bushels of wheat, to be delivered in the storehouse of Sterrett, Hughes & Packer. The store-house was at Howardsville, Centre county.

The receipt was as follows:

9th April 1847.—" Received of Thomas Bowers, per John Cummings, twenty-five dollars in part for 300 bushels of wheat at $1.10 per bushel, of which there are about 60 bushels of the same red, all to be delivered in the store-house of Sterrett, Hughes & Packer. JAMES GORDON."

The defendant relied upon two grounds of defence:

1st. That a certain John Cummings was a partner with the plaintiff in this purchase, and the action cannot be maintained in the name of the plaintiff alone.

2d. That by agreement of the parties at the time of giving the receipt, the wheat was to be retained by the defendant until a certain time agreed upon, at which time plaintiff was to call upon defendant and the wheat was to be delivered, and that the plaintiff failed to come at the stipulated period.

The alleged errors in this case were confined to exceptions taken upon the trial to the admission and rejection of evidence.

The plaintiff offered John Cummings as a witness, to whom defendant objected on the ground that he was interested in the event of the suit. In support of this objection, defendant produced several witnesses who testified that, at different times, both Cummings and the plaintiff had declared to them that they were partners in the business of buying and selling wheat. The *plaintiff* then

[Gordon v. Bowers.]

called a witness who testified that he had resided in the same place with the plaintiff in the spring of 1847, and that he never knew of such a firm as J. J. Cummings & Bowers. They also read the memorandum-book of plaintiff, and the depositions of Miller, Nesbitt, and Garretson. Upon this state of facts, the court, being of opinion that the weight of evidence submitted to the court on the question of competency was in favor of the witness, overruled the objection, and admitted the witness. Defendant excepted, and the witness was examined.

During the examination of Cummings, the plaintiff proposed to ask him if he had any interest in this contract or in the event of this suit. Objected to by defendant's counsel on the ground that his competency had been tried on evidence to the court, and that it is not competent to prove by the witness himself to the jury that he has no interest. The objection was overruled, and the question admitted: defendant's counsel excepted.

John Cummings:—I am not interested in the event of the suit; nothing to gain and nothing to lose by it. I am not a partner of Mr. Bowers in any of these contracts; was not when they were made. I bought for Mr. Bowers; he furnished every cent of money.—He was cross-examined.

The deposition of John Miller was offered on part of plaintiff, and the parts in italic were objected to. He testified:—In May 1842, I was employed by Mr. Bowers as captain of his boat Princeton. *Mr. Bowers instructed me to go to Centre county, to Curtin's Forge, to load wheat, which Mr. Cummings had bought for Mr. Bowers. I went to the Forge; got there on Friday in the forepart of May. While we lay at Curtin's Forge, Mr. Cummings asked me to go with him to Gordon's (the defendant) to lift the receipts for 300 bushels of wheat, that Mr. Cummings had bought of him for Mr. Bowers, and to pay him the balance of the money.* On our arrival at James Gordon's, Mr. Cummings asked for the receipts for the delivery of the wheat, as above stated, and offered to pay the balance of the money. Gordon told him he was too late, that the wheat was sold, and that he (Cummings) had not come according to contract. We went to Howardsville the next day, but found no wheat there subject to the order of Mr. Bowers. *I asked Hughes, Sterrett & Co. to look over their books; they did so, but found no entry of wheat for Mr. Bowers. The boats were hired at or about this time, for $6 per day. Grain was high, and every one was anxious to get to the market.* When I got to Philadelphia with this boat, wheat was worth $2.20 per bushel. *To fill out the load, there was some wheat bought by Mr. Bowers, at $2 per bushel.*

Defendant's counsel excepted.

John P. Packer testified that the price of wheat at Howard was $2 per bushel.

[Gordon v. Bowers.]

The plaintiff also offered in evidence the depositions of Alexander Nesbitt and Edmund Garretson, to prove the prices of wheat in Philadelphia, in the spring of 1847, and also to show on whose account sales of wheat were made; to which defendant's counsel objected, on the ground that the facts stated in them, if true, were wholly irrelevant. The court overruled the objection, and permitted the deposition to be read. This formed the basis of the third error assigned.

WOODWARD, J., charged *inter alia:*—

Defendant insists that plaintiff and Cummings were partners. If they were, the plaintiff cannot recover in his own name on this contract, and Cummings could not be a witness. The true criterion of partnership is a right to participate in the profits of the enterprise. There may be no profits in point of fact; but if the jury are satisfied from the evidence that Cummings had a right as between him and Bowers to share the profits, if profits resulted, their verdict must be for the defendant. Is such a relation proved? (The court referred to the evidence bearing on this point.)

It was assigned for error:
1. The court erred in admitting John Cummings as a witness.
2. The court erred in allowing the parts of the deposition of John Miller, which were underscored, (*italicized,*) to be read in evidence.
3. The court erred in admitting the depositions of Nesbitt and Garretson.   4. The court erred in permitting Cummings to testify as to his interest in the contract.

The case was argued by *Linn*, for plaintiff in error.—He contended that Cummings was interested, and should not have been admitted: 8 *Mass.* 487, Pierce v. Chase. That the part of Miller's deposition admitted related to *ex parte* conversations. As to the third error, that the measure of damages, if the plaintiff is entitled to any, is the difference between the contract-price and the value of the article at the *time* and *place* of delivery, and that it is not competent for him to give in evidence the value of the article at a *different time* and at a *distant place:* Chitty on Contracts 870 in note; Gilpin v. Consequa, 3 *W. C. C. R.* 184; 5 *Watts* 15, 109; Andrews v. Hoover, 8 *Watts* 239.

As to the fourth error, it was certainly improper to allow Cummings to testify to his interest, when the question had been already tried in another form: 4 *Ser. & R.* 298; Mott v. Hicks, 1 *Cowen* 513; 1 *Greenleaf on Evidence* 496.

Curtin and *Burnside*, for defendant.—As to the admission of Cummings, reference was made to Hart v. Heilner, 3 *Rawle* 411. If the interest be in the least degree doubtful, the court will not decide the question of interest in the witness, but receive his testi-

[Gordon v. Bowers.]

mony, and leave it to the jury to determine whether or not he has an interest in the event of the suit. See also Martin *v.* Jones, 6 *Barr* 82, and Cowen and Hills, *Phillips*, in note on page 1501.

In determining the question of interest, where the evidence is *aliunde*, and it depends upon the decision of intricate questions of fact, the judge, in his discretion, may take the opinion of the jury upon them: Sec. 425, *Greenleaf's Ev.* vol. 1. This was done in the case trying, by the judge submitting the question of partnership to the jury. Reference was made to Bent *v.* Baker, as reported in Smith's Selection of Leading Cases, page 39, and the note thereon.

2d Error. A reference to the depositions of Miller, will show that the court excluded all, if not more than all, that was not evidence.

3d Error. The depositions of Nesbitt and Garretson showed the price of wheat in Philadelphia, which would be the price at Howard, less freight and toll, and were only corroborative of the testimony of Mr. Packer, who fixed the price at Howard.

4th Error. While it is true, we could not examine Cummings as a witness on the question of competency, yet having been adjudged competent by the court, he was as competent to disprove that partnership, as would have been any other witness; his credibility was for the jury, and they have passed on it by their verdict.

The opinion of the court was delivered June 2, by

ROGERS, J.—This is an action on the case, to recover damages for the non-performance of a contract for the purchase and sale of a quantity of wheat.

The plaintiff gave in evidence a receipt by defendant for $25, in part payment for 300 bushels of wheat, to be delivered in the storehouse of Sterrett, Hughes & Packer, at the village of Howard.

The defendant relied on two grounds of defence:

1st. That a certain John Cummings, being a partner with the plaintiff in the purchase, the action cannot be maintained in the name of the plaintiff alone.

2d. That by agreement of parties, at the time of giving the receipt, the wheat was to be retained by the defendant until a certain time agreed upon, at which time plaintiff was to call upon defendant, when the wheat was to be delivered; and that the plaintiff failed to come at the stipulated period.

The plaintiff called John Cummings, the alleged partner, as a witness, to whom defendant objected, on the ground that he was interested in the event of the suit. Whereupon the court overruled the objection, and admitted the witness.

During the examination of Cummings before the jury, plaintiff proposed to ask him if he had any interest in the contract, or in

[Gordon *v.* Bowers.]

the event of the suit: to which question defendant objected, but the objection was overruled. In both cases exception was taken.

As the exceptions are intimately connected, it is most convenient to examine them together. There are two ways of proving a witness to be interested in a cause; first, by examining him on his *voir dire;* or, secondly, by showing his interest by other evidence. But both ways cannot be pursued at the same time: Mifflin *v.* Bingham, 1 *Dal.* 275; 1 *Peters's Rep.* 338, Evans *v.* Eaton.

The defendant elected to show interest in the witness by testimony *aliunde.* It is ruled that on a trial *before the court*, if one party prove by evidence a witness to be interested, the witness cannot purge himself of the interest by his own oath: Vincent *v.* The Lessee of Huff, 4 *Ser. & R.* 298. It is most certain, says C. J. Tilghman, that the witness could not be examined to prove his own competency. The defendant might have examined him on his *voir dire* to prove his interest; and if he had taken that course, he could have resorted to no other. But having adduced evidence of interest *aliunde*, it was not competent to the plaintiff to rebut it by the testimony of the witness himself.

In support of his objection, the defendant produced several witnesses who testified that, at different times, both Cummings and the plaintiff declared to them that they were partners in the business of buying and selling wheat. There was strong affirmative testimony on that point. The plaintiff then called a witness, who testified that he had resided in the same place with the plaintiff in the spring of 1847, and that he never knew of such a firm as Bowers, Cummings & Co.

He also read the memorandum-book of plaintiff, and the depositions of Miller, Nesbitt, and Garretson, proving they had never heard of such a firm, and that contracts were entered into in the name of Bowers alone. The court being of opinion, that the weight of testimony submitted to the court, on the question of competency, was in favor of the witness, overruled defendant's objection.

On the view I have taken of the evidence, I should have great difficulty in coming to the same conclusion, nor should I have admitted the witness to testify, except on the principle and in the manner settled in Hart *v.* Heilner, 3 *Rawle* 411. If the interest, as is there ruled, be in the least degree doubtful, the court will not decide the question of interest, but receive his testimony and leave it to the jury to determine whether or not he has an interest in the event of the suit. See also Martin *v.* Jones, 6 *Barr* 82, to the same effect. In determining the question of interest, when the evidence is *aliunde*, and it depends on intricate questions of fact, the judge, in his discretion, may take the opinion of the jury upon them. Section 425, 1 *Greenleaf's Ev.* This was the course pursued by the judge, as the counsel for the plaintiff admit, referring

[Gordon v. Bowers.]

to the charge in proof of the assertion, and which the counsel for the defendant do not deny. Taking this to be so, there was no error in admitting the witness, and referring the question of interest to be determined by the jury. There was, at least, some doubt as to his interest. Viewing the case in this aspect, we are relieved from the necessity of deciding whether a mistake of the judge (unless it be a very gross mistake) in determining the weight of parol evidence can be corrected on error; and if it can, (as I suppose it may,) whether the court was wrong in the view taken of the conflicting testimony.

Waiving, then, this question, and conceding the witness to be properly admitted, the next question is, was Cummings the witness competent to testify that he had no interest? in other words, was he at liberty to prove his own competency? We have already seen that this will not be permitted where the question is tried by the court: 4 *Ser. & R.* 298, Vincent v. Lessee of Huff. Conceding this, it may be inquired what reason (if any) can be assigned, why he should be at liberty to testify before the jury, when substituted to try the same fact in place of the court. It may be asked, ought not the latter to be bound by the same rules as the former? Why should there be any difference, in this respect, between the court and jury, when performing the same office. That the rules of evidence, which it is important to preserve, should be relaxed before the latter tribunal, seems to be reversing the order of things. No reason has been assigned for making any change, and none occurs to my mind.

We also think the court erred in admitting that part of the deposition of John Miller which is underscored. It relates to *ex parte* conversations between the witness and Bowers, and between Bowers and Cummings, and was consequently clearly inadmissible.

There is no error that we perceive in admitting the depositions of Nesbitt and Garretson. Their evidence is merely corroborative of the testimony of Packer, who proves the price of the wheat at Howard, where it was to be delivered.

Judgment reversed and a *venire de novo* awarded.

Gratz *versus* Hoover.

1. The marks on the ground of an old survey, indicating the lines originally run, are the best evidence of the location of the survey, and if any evidence of such lines exist, it should be referred to the jury.

2. Where a survey returned called for others on three sides, and on the fourth for J. H. *or vacant*, there being no evidence given that the line on that side was run, it was not error for the court to charge the jury that the return was equivocal, or indicated nothing more than that the line on that side was left open or undecided upon by the surveyor.

3. Where a question existed whether the larger part of a tract of land lay in Centre or Clearfield county, which were there bounded by the Mushannon Creek, it being the usage to tax lands in the county in which the greater part of the tract was situate, the official book of the treasurer of Centre county was evidence to show that the tract in question was *not* returned for taxation in Centre county, although other tracts in the same lot of surveys were so returned, the taxes on the tract in question having been paid by the claimant in the county of Clearfield; and especially, when taken in connection with the deposition of the treasurer of Centre county, that the present claimant had furnished to him a list of his lands *in Centre county*, in which the tract in question did *not* appear.

Error to the Common Pleas of *Centre county*.

Ejectment by John T. Hoover, against Jacob Gratz and Joseph Gratz, for a tract of land, situate partly in Snowshoe township, Centre county, and partly in Morris township, Clearfield county, containing 406 acres or thereabouts.

This action was in the nature of an appeal from a decision of the board of property, and was brought in obedience to the directions contained in the 11th section of the act of 30th April 1792: *Dun.* 1st ed. 146. On the 16th day of August 1849, a warrant was granted to John T. Hoover (the plaintiff below) for "four hundred acres of land (unimproved) adjoining land surveyed on warrant in the name of William McPherson on the south, and on the north, east, and west, by lands of Joseph Gratz and brothers, situate partly in the county of Clearfield, and partly in the township of Snowshoe on the Mushannon creek." In pursuance of this warrant, a survey of 406 acres and allowance was made October 4th 1849. On the 12th of October 1849, Jacob Gratz, on his own behalf and as attorney of Joseph Gratz, entered a *caveat* against the acceptance of this survey, alleging that the land applied for was not vacant, but owned by Jacob and Joseph Gratz. A hearing was had before the board, on the first Monday of January 1850, and it was decided that the surveys and patents claimed by the Gratz's covered the land in dispute, and the survey of Hoover was placed upon the rejected files. This decision seems to have been made 7th January 1850. On the 23d of February 1850, this suit was brought. At August term 1850, the plaintiff moved for judgment for want of an appearance, *sec. reg.* The

[Gratz v. Hoover.]

motion was entertained, and ordered to be placed on the argument list for adjourned court, and on the 9th of September the motion was taken up, when Mr. *Hale* appeared for defendants *de bene esse*, and at his instance a rule was granted to show cause why the service of the writ should not be set aside. On the 14th of September, after argument, the court discharged the rule, dismissed the plaintiff's motion for judgment, and the defendants appeared by their counsel and pleaded "not guilty." On the trial, the *plaintiff* relied on the title already stated.

The defendants alleged that the land in dispute was covered by a survey in the name of Clement Stocker, the title to which was in them. There being no dispute about the paper titles of the respective parties, the only question in the cause was the proper location of the Stocker survey; whether it covered the land surveyed upon the Hoover warrant? This was a question for the jury under the evidence; but the plaintiffs in error complained that the court erred in their instructions to the jury, in not giving to the calls for adjoiners, in the returns of the Stocker survey, a sufficient degree of conclusiveness.

The Stocker tract is one of a block of fifty surveys which were made in pursuance of an application entered by Aaron Levy on the 3d of August 1792, for 20,000 acres of land. The surveying of this block of surveys, known as "the Levy lands," seems to have been commenced on the 21st of June 1793, and to have been continued until the 26th, when the work was completed. These surveys are all laid so as to adjoin each other, and bounded by parallel lines crossed by other parallel lines, so as to throw each tract into a rectangular form, and make the contents equal. Clement Stocker, according to the official draft, is an exterior tract, and occupies the north-east corner of the block. On the north-east side of and adjoining this body of Levy surveys, another block of surveys was located in 1792, known as the Wallis lands, three of the exterior tracts of which, and which were alleged by the *defendants* to adjoin the Levy lands, were surveyed on warrants in the name of John Harris, Henry Harris, and Benjamin Harris. But the *plaintiff* contended that these tracts do not adjoin the Levy lands, but that, on the contrary, a vacancy was left between them, which he had a right to apply to his warrant of 1849, and this state of facts he undertook to establish by proof of the actual condition of the *marks upon the ground.* The defendant claimed that the Stocker survey adjoins the surveys in the name of John Harris and Henry Harris; and if this were so, then the Stocker survey would cover the vacancy claimed for the Hoover warrant.

Joseph F. Quay, an experienced surveyor, testified that at the instance of Mr. Gratz, and under the guidance of a draft furnished by him, he surveyed the Levy lands in 1834—that he found them well marked upon the ground—that the leading warrant (Robert

[Gratz v. Hoover.]

Morris) corresponded with the location as indicated by the return of survey, it being designated by such permanent and distinct marks as could not be mistaken—that in running the line bounding Clement Stocker on the east, and which is an old, well-marked line, and common to several surveys of the block, he ascertained that the Stocker tract did not adjoin Henry Harris by 198 perches, and that he blocked the east line of the Stocker tract, which was parallel to the line of Henry Harris, and at 198 perches distance from it, and found that the line counted to the date of the survey of Stocker. He further testified that if the block were so moved as to make Stocker adjoin Henry Harris, it would throw the intersection of the Mushannon with the Indian Path entirely off the leading warrant, and thus deprive it of marks which clearly identify and distinguish the Robert Morris survey. He further swears that if Stocker were made to adjoin John Vaughan, Paul Cox, Henry Harris, and John Harris, which would be placing it in its official connection, it would then contain more than 1000 acres, whereas by the return of survey it contains but 433 acres and 153 perches. Mr. Green corroborated Mr. Quay, and further stated that he examined whether there were any marks on the ground which would throw Stocker out of its official connection with Cox and Vaughan, and found none. Wm. Harris was examined, who, on behalf of the defendants testified that he never examined this block of Levy lands with a view to the proper location of the Stocker tract. He said the Clement Stocker must be located according to the official draft and the stream, so as to join the John Harris and Henry Harris, and having regard to the marks on the ground, he would say the same, because he found the line of Henry Harris and John Harris just where Mr. Quay says he found them; that there was no dispute about them; and there he found a line from the maple to the Mushannon Creek, counting to date of survey, the line between Cox and Stocker.

That the John Vaughan was so far west as not to be reached by Clement Stocker. There would be vacant lands according to lines of official survey.

Cross-examined :—Never located Robert Morris or any of this body; did not examine the W. O. corner of Mr. McPherson, and my location of Clement Stocker would be 200 rods east of that corner. If Stocker were to be fixed by the adjoiners, it must go to Paul Cox and John Vaughan; but the natural marks decide its location beyond a doubt.

The warrant to Clement Stocker was dated 3d August 1792, for 400 acres, adjoining John Vaughan, 26th June 1793; survey calls for Paul Cox on south, Henry Harris on east, north *John Harris or vacant*, and John Vaughan on west.

8th May, 1837, patent to Joseph Gratz, Jacob Gratz, and Benjamin Gratz.

[Gratz v. Hoover.]

The court, *inter alia*, instructed the jury that if they believed the east line found and blocked by Green and Quay, to be the line of the Stocker tract, then the actual marks as found on the ground, must control the calls for adjoiners as indicated in the return of survey.

The charge of WOODWARD, J., was as follows:—The plaintiff took his warrant on 16th Aug. 1849, for land as vacant, which defendants then claimed, and had long claimed, and still claim as their property, under and by force of a warrant and survey of 1793, in the name of Clement Stocker. The burthen of proof is on the plaintiff. A body of surveys are found in the land-office, calling for each other as adjoiners, and the whole claiming to adjoin an older body; the plaintiff has undertaken to satisfy a jury that between these bodies of surveys, professing to adjoin, there is a considerable strip of vacant land, open to his warrant of 1849. The presumptions are all against him, and are to be overcome only by full and adequate proof. It is a question of location. What is the proper location of Clement Stocker? If it be located where the plaintiff places it, there would seem to have been vacant land where he laid his warrant. If it be located where the defendant insists it lies, there was no vacant land for the plaintiffs' warrant, and the verdict of the jury would be for the defendant.

This is a question of fact, and belongs exclusively to the jury to decide. I may, however, state a few general principles which affect questions of location, and which never should be lost sight of by a jury, when they have to deal with such a subject.

1st. The artificial marks on the ground constitute the survey, and where they are found and verified, they are the highest proofs of location.

2d. Subordinate, but very important evidence of location, are natural objects, especially streams of water; and adjoining surveys called for, and where location is not questioned.

3d. Returns of surveys into the land-office as adjoining, permitted to remain there for 21 years and upwards, raise a conclusive presumption of an actual survey somewhere, and afford evidence of location which, in the absence of other proof, may determine the question.

4th. The location of a tract of land, which is one of a body of surveys calling for each other, may be determined by fixing any one of the body, whether the leading survey or another, and then laying the rest as returned into the land-office.

The plaintiff alleges that the actual lines, as marked on the ground and found remaining, show that the calls of Clement Stocker for John and Henry Harris are inaccurate and should be disregarded. If the jury are satisfied of this, the cause is with the plaintiff, for the defendant must be stopped by the actual lines on the ground. Here is the main point of the case, and the tes-

[Gratz v. Hoover.]

timony of Quay, and Green, and Harris is to be carefully weighed as bearing on this point.

But the defendant insists, that though the lines of Robert Morris, and of the other tracts of this body, may be found as claimed, yet if marked lines or corners be not found on Clement Stocker, to control its peculiar position, it must be permitted to go to the adjoiners called for. This proposition is correct with only one qualification, and that is, that in pushing Clement Stocker to its adjoiners you do not *dislocate* any other tract of the body of which it is part. Clement Stocker is one of a body of surveys, and while its calls must, if possible, be all answered, yet we must not forget that it maintains on the ground certain relations to other tracts, and the rights of property in them are not to be disturbed, and a scene of universal litigation introduced, merely to satisfy one of the calls of Clement Stocker. But if, unrestrained by marks found on itself, Clement Stocker can be made to adjoin Henry and John Harris without affecting the fixed location of the other tracts with which it is associated, let it go to them. With this necessary qualification, the defendant's point is affirmed.

Is the line which Quay and Greene found marked on Clement Stocker, its eastern boundary? Was that line run and marked as part of the survey of the tract? Their testimony founded, in examinations of the whole body of fifty surveys, inclines the mind powerfully to an affirmative conclusion, and if the jury are brought to it, their verdict will be for the plaintiff.

But Mr. Harris's testimony and highly respectable opinion, the maple corner common to Henry Harris and Clement Stocker, the Tompkins surveys, the returns into the land-office, and the lapse of time, together with the waters as described by him, tend strongly to the locating of Christian Stocker where the defendant has always claimed it to be. It is to be regretted that Mr. Harris did not make a more general examination of this body of surveys. This would have enabled him to speak more confidently as to the line which Quay and Green found on the ground, and which the plaintiff insists is the eastern boundary of Clement Stocker.

The jury will take the drafts of the surveyors and their testimony, and if they believe the marks on the ground to locate Clement Stocker so as to leave vacant land between it and the Harris surveys, they will find for the plaintiff. If they do not, they will consider all the other matters that have been pressed on their attention as tending to fix this tract. Henry Harris being an older warrant, *and whose location is conceded on all hands*, Clement Stocker, if not restrained by marks of an actual survey on the ground, must go to it and adjoin it as called for. I cannot say the same as to John Harris, for the call of Clement Stocker on that side is for John Harris or vacant land, an equivocal call, which under the circumstances of the case and in respect to the

[Gratz v. Hoover.]

question before the jury, is indecisive. It indicates nothing more *than that the line on that side of Clement Stocker was left open;* and there is no other evidence before the jury that tends to prove that it was run.

To which the counsel of both parties excepted.

Verdict was rendered for the plaintiff.

As to treasurer's book and the deposition of treasurer, see the opinion of ROGERS, J.

A. G. Curtin, for plaintiff in error.—The location of the Clement Stocker tract is, as the court below properly said, the important question in the cause. He contended that the court erred in not instructing the jury that, as there was no evidence whatever of any marks on the ground to restrain the Clement Stocker tract from going to its call on the north, viz. John Harris, a well-known tract, that there was therefore no vacant land between these tracts upon which to locate the plaintiff's warrant in 1849, and consequently, as to so much of the plaintiff's survey, as lay between the Clement Stocker and the John Harris surveys, there must be a verdict for defendants.

We think there was no sufficient evidence of marks upon the ground to restrain the Clement Stocker from going to its call on the east, viz. Henry Harris, also a well-known survey. The only evidence upon their point is, the testimony of Mr. Quay, of a line running from a white oak, supposed by him to be a corner of the Paul Cox, Sharp, and Delaney tracts.

He says he found this line running past the end of the Clement Stocker, but he found no corner whatever below the white oak, nearly a mile from Clement Stocker. Now we do not think this is such evidence of marks upon the ground as should separate the surveys that call for each other, and have been so returned for upwards of fifty years in the land-office. The court ought to have told the jury, that in order to contradict this return of survey, acquiesced in for more than fifty years, and presumed to have been made as returned, evidence of the most *undoubted character* of marks on the ground, made at the time, and made for this survey, must be adduced to justify a separation of the tracts; and that the evidence in this case on the Henry Harris's side, was not of that character to justify such a conclusion.

The court endeavor to overcome the defendant's position, that the Clement Stocker must adjoin the John Harris survey, by saying that the call upon that side is equivocal, being for John Harris or vacant land. There would seem to be no force in this, when the John Harris survey is actually found and located upon that side of the Stocker survey. The call being for John Harris or vacant land on that side, the true meaning is, that if the John Harris survey is really located on that side, it becomes then a certain call,

[Gratz v. Hoover.]

and they must adjoin, and so all the drafts returned to the landoffice show it to be.

The surveys of Clement Stocker and John Harris, it appears, were made at different times and by different persons, and it is probable the surveyor who located the Stocker survey was not certain of the location of the John Harris survey; but that he intended to adjoin that survey on that side, is manifest, and so returns it to the land office.

Norris v. Hamilton, 7 *Watts* 93; Neiman v. Ward, 1 *W. & Ser*. 69; Hall v. Turner, 4 *Barr* 245; Schnable v. Doughty, 3 *Barr* 393.

McAllister, Burnside, and *Linn*, for defendant in error.—The treasurer's book was evidence, and the purpose for which it was offered was proper. The defendants claimed that the Stocker tracts were located principally on the east side of the Mushannon Creek, which formed the boundary between Centre and Clearfield counties, and while other surveys belonging to the Levy lands, were taxed in Centre county, the Stocker tract was not taxed there. It was evidence bearing upon the point in dispute, being a state of things somewhat under the control of the defendants, and was therefore properly admitted for what it was worth.

The court were right in saying that the call for the John Harris tract being *equivocal*, was not conclusive of the location of Clement Stocker, even where marks are not found restraining it short of John Harris. The return of the surveyor is only conclusive of what it contains, and not of what it does not pretend to assert: Hall v. Powell, 4 *Ser. & R*. 162; Phillips v. Sheaffer, 5 *Ser. & R*. 215; Walker v. Smith, 2 *Barr*. 43; Hall v. Tanner, 4 *Barr* 244; Henry v. Henry, 5 *Barr* 447; Schnable v. Doughty, 3 *Barr* 393.

The opinion of the court was delivered June 2, by

BELL, J.—Of the thirteen supposed errors assigned in this record, but four have been pressed upon our attention with any show of confidence. Of these, three present but a single point, and may therefore be considered together.

The leading question in the cause was as to the proper location of what is called the "Clement Stocker" tract, in the block of surveys made under the warrant issued on the application of Aaron Levy, in 1792. The survey of that tract calls for, as conterminous, the tracts returned in the names of Henry and John Harris, and the court instructed the jury that if unrestrained by actual marks of survey found upon the ground, the "Clement Stocker" must be permitted to extend to the surveys called for as adjoining, unless by so doing the relative position of the other tracts of the block would be disturbed and deranged; that the "Henry Harris" survey being under an older warrant, and having a conceded location, the tract in dispute must be taken as adjoining it, if this presumption was not contradicted by ascertained existing marks of the original survey; but that, on the other side, the call being for "John Harris" *or vacant land*, it was equivocal and indecisive, and indicated nothing more than that the line of the survey on that side was left open. The plaintiff in error complains of this portion of the charge as not being sufficiently favorable to him. He thinks there was no adequate evidence of marks on the ground to be left to the jury as restraining the survey on the "Henry Harris" side, and as on the north the "John Harris" was found and indisputably fixed, the call ceased to be equivocal; wherefore the instruction should have been that in the absence of restraining marks found on that side, the jury was bound to accept the southern line of the last-mentioned tract as the true boundary of the one in controversy. But in this we cannot concur. Notwithstanding the long acquiescence in the drafts of surveys returned to and filed in the surveyor-general's office, it is undoubted that actual indications of the lines originally run on the ground are the best evidence of the true location sought for; and as there was, to say the least of it, some proof of such indications in the surveyor's marks testified to by Quay and Green, the court had no choice other than to submit to the jury what was properly matter of fact for its determination. To the other branch of the objection, the answer is found in the obvious meaning of the surveyor's return, that although he was aware a tract had been located in the immediate neighborhood in the name of John Harris, he had not taken upon himself to ascertain exactly where that tract lay. It might join the "Clement Stocker" on that side, or the land there might be vacant. This was the interpretation given below, and we think the correct one.

The other exception principally urged was that taken to the admission of what is known as the book of the treasurer of Centre county, containing lists of unseated lands situate in that county liable to taxation. The defendant below claimed that the Stocker tract was situate principally on the east side of the Mushannon Creek, which there divides Centre and Clearfield counties; while the location assigned to it by the plaintiff below threw the greater portion of it to the west side of the stream. It seems the custom in that district of country is to levy the tax of unseated tracts of land in that county in which the larger part of it may be found to lie. In this discussion as to locality, it became of importance to show in which of the counties the larger portion of the disputed tract actually is. As one means of making this manifest, the plaintiff below offered the deposition of the treasurer of Clearfield county; but it was objected, the best evidence of the unseated lands returned in Clearfield for taxation was the treasurer's book. The court was of this opinion, and accordingly rejected the deposition. After this, the book of the treasurer of Centre, being duly proved,

[Gratz v. Hoover.]

was received, to show the Stocker tract was not returned for taxation in Centre, although most of the other tracts of that survey were so returned; the former, with three others, having in fact been transferred from Centre to Clearfield. It is objected that, at best, this was the work of the treasurer himself, without reference to the owner, whose interests were therefore not liable to be affected by it. But we cannot admit this transfer of his lands for the purposes of taxation was a subject with which the owner was wholly unconnected. By the act of March 1806, it is made the duty of the owners of unseated lands to return a statement of them to the commissioners of the proper county; a duty to which it is not to be doubted the Messrs. Gratz had given their attention. It is not to be supposed that of their own mere motion the commissioners or treasurer of Centre would have assigned these tracts to Clearfield, and as the owners had regularly paid the taxes assessed upon them, it cannot be questioned they were cognizant of the fact. Indeed, I find in the paper-book of the plaintiff in error, the deposition of John G. Lowry, taken after notice, in proceedings relative to the tracts, before the board of property, and read on the trial of this cause. Mr. Lowry was treasurer of Centre county from 1829 to 1843, and also in the years of 1846 and 1847. He testified he presumed the transfer of the four tracts from Centre to Clearfield was made in pursuance of directions from Jacob Gratz; that no taxes for these four tracts had been paid in Centre since 1835; and that Mr. Gratz had furnished to the witness, as treasurer, a corrected list of their lands in Centre for the years 1848 and 1849, in which the Stocker tract did not appear. With this deposition, it will not be questioned the treasurer's book was properly received, and without it, I think it was good evidence, under the circumstances, of the fact sought to be proved.

The remaining errors, but faintly pressed on the argument, are sufficiently answered by the printed remarks submitted for the defendant in error, except the tenth, which is not there noticed. It avers the court erred in refusing to set aside the service of the writ of summons issued in this case. Were this now assigned as error, the record presents no ground upon which the court could with propriety have interfered with that service. The sheriff's return is regularly made of a regular service, and there is absolutely nothing to contradict it or to call it into question. As for the bill of exceptions signed on the hearing of the rule to show cause, because of the rejection of Sheriff Musser's testimony, by which it was intended to contradict the return, it is enough to say it is a mere nullity. . The notion of an exception to evidence on a preliminary inquiry is indeed novel.

Judgment affirmed.

Baxley *versus* Linah.

A judgment in a sister State is to be deemed to have the effect of a *domestic* judgment, in relation to the cause of action; and where the defendant had notice it is conclusive of the subject-matter, and the original cause of action is merged in it: therefore, a suit pending in the State of Maryland, and a judgment subsequently obtained therein, is a bar to a proceeding between the same parties and for the same cause of action, by foreign attachment, instituted in Pennsylvania, after the bringing of the suit and before judgment therein.

ERROR to the Common Pleas of *Adams county.*

This was a proceeding by foreign attachment, in the name of James Baxley, for the use of David H. Thomson and J. Hamilton Goll, partners in trade, under the firm of D. H. Thomson & Co., vs. Samuel L. Linah.

A writ of foreign attachment in debt, on promissory note, not exceeding $800, issued out of the Court of Common Pleas of Adams county, in this case, on *the 2d day of January* 1847. Real debt, $473.64. Interest, from 16th Nov. 1846.

On the 6th of Jan. 1847, sheriff returned that he had attached certain real estate and book-accounts, &c. of defendant, (prout return,) and on the 26th of March 1847, further returned that he had advertised the writ, in pursuance of the order made thereon.

On the 9th of Aug. 1847, defendant filed a plea in abatement to the writ, setting forth that the plaintiffs had, *prior to the issuing of this foreign attachment*, instituted a suit in Baltimore county court, in the State of Maryland, for the same cause of action, on the 30th Dec. 1846, and that the same *was still pending* in said court.

On the 12th Aug. 1847, plaintiffs filed narr. On the 16th Nov. 1848, plaintiffs filed a demurrer to defendant's plea in abatement. On the 16th April 1849, defendant joined in demurrer.

On the 18th Oct. 1849, argued—Hon. F. WATTS presided; and on the 30th Oct. 1849, the court directed that judgment of *respondeat ouster* be entered.

On the 5th of Dec. 1849, defendant plead *in bar* that the plaintiff's had, on the 31st of Jan. 1848, *obtained a judgment* for the same cause of action against the defendant in Baltimore county court, Maryland, and that the judgment still remained unsatisfied, and is a bar to this action.

On the 8th Dec. 1849, plaintiffs filed demurrer to defendant's plea in bar; and on 20th Dec. 1849, defendant joined in demurrer.

On the 21st Jan. 1850, argument before Hon. ELLIS LEWIS.

On the 9th March 1850, the court decided that the judgment recovered in Maryland was a bar to the action, and ordered that judgment be entered on the demurrer in favor of the defendant. Judgment was accordingly entered.

[Baxley v. Linah.]

The opinion of LEWIS, J., was in part as follows:—Under this article of the constitution (1st sec. of 4th art.) and the act of Congress made in pursuance of it, the courts of the United States have repeatedly determined that a judgment recovered in any State of the Union, before a court of competent jurisdiction, upon due notice to the defendant therein, is not to be regarded in any other State as a *foreign* judgment, but is to be treated as a *domestic* judgment throughout the United States, so far as to give it the same effect in every other State as it would have in the State from whence it may have been taken: 7 *Cranch* 481; *id.* 408; 3 *Wheat.* 234; 6 *id.* 129; 1 *Peters' C. C. R.* 155; 1 *Bald.* 617; 6 *Peters* 317; 4 *Dal.* 412; 9 *Cranch* 122; 11 *Wheat.* 392.

The State courts appear, at last, to have fully adopted the same doctrine. In Vermont, 2 *Ver. Rep.* 263; 14 *id.* 92; in Maine, 1 *Fairf.* 278; 2 *id.* 89; 4 *Greenl.* 124; in New Hampshire, 1 *N. H. Rep.* 242; in Connecticut, *Kirby's Rep.* 124; 1 *Day* 168; in Massachusetts, 14 *M.* 515; 12 *id.* 25; 6 *Pick.* 232; 10 *id.* 470; 13 *id.* 53; in New York, 3 *Johns.* 517; 15 *id.* 121; 19 *id.* 162; 3 *Wend.* 263; 5 *id.* 148; 7 *id.* 435; 5 *id.* 161; 6 *id.* 447; 13 *id.* 417; 8 *Cow.* 311; in New Jersey, 1 *Hals.* 236–275; 1 *Green's Rep.* 68; 1 *Penn.* 399; in Maryland, 5 *Gill & Johns.* 500; in Virginia, 4 *Munf.* 241; 2 *Leigh's Rep.* 172; in North Carolina, *Cane & Nor.* 486; 3 *Hawk's Rep.* 393; in South Carolina, 1 *Baily* 242; 2 *Bay* 485; 1 *Hill* 439; in Louisiana, 5 *Martin's N. S.* 661; 2 *id.* 599; 10 *Louis. Rep.* (*Curry*) 189; in Ohio, 1 *Ham.* 264; *id.* 259; 5 *id.* 545; 1 *Wright* 348; 1 *id.* 430; *id.* 127; in Indiana, 2 *Blackf.* 108; in Kentucky, *Hard.* 413; 5 *Lit.* 349; 3 *Mon.* 62; and in Tennessee, 2 *Yerg.* 484; *id.* 379; 6 *id.* 412, and *id.* 142, we have decisions of the State courts in conformity to the principles recognised by the federal tribunals. And in Pennsylvania we have full authority to the same point: 10 *Ser. & R.* 240; 9 *id.* 259; 12 *id.* 203; 1 *Dal.* 302.

With the principles of international law, the constitution of the United States, the act of Congress, the decisions of the United States courts, and the adjudications of the State courts, including that of Pennsylvania, before us, we see no ground for raising or attempting to raise a doubt upon the question whether the judgment obtained in Maryland, and pleaded in bar, is to have the same effect in barring the action in this State that it would have if the present action had been brought in the State of Maryland. The question is fully decided in the affirmative.

The inquiry then is, what effect would the judgment have in the State of Maryland, where it was recovered? No question was raised in the argument touching the omission in the plea of an averment setting forth the local law of that State, and the effect which the judgment would have under that law. Nor was any question raised respecting the proper method of *ascertaining* the

[Baxley v. Linah.]

local law, and the effect of the judgment under that law. The practice of treating the judgments recovered in other States as foreign judgments has become so inveterate, that some judges have entertained the opinion that the local law of the State in which the judgment was recovered must be established by evidence, as a matter of fact, in order that the judgment may have the effect it would have in the State where it was recovered: 3 *Wend.* 267; 7 *id.* 435; 2 *Blackf.* 31; *id.* 82. But it must be remembered, that this question arises under the constitution and laws of the United States, that the decisions of the State courts thereon, denying the right claimed under the federal enactments, are subject to review in the Supreme Court of the United States, and that in that high tribunal the several States of this Union are not regarded as foreign States, nor are their laws and judgments held to be foreign laws and judgments. In that court the States, their laws, and their judicial proceedings, are essentially domestic, and are taken notice of as such. It would be a very imperfect administration of justice for the court of original jurisdiction to adopt one rule of decision, while the court of final resort was governed by a different one. It follows necessarily, that the State courts, in determining questions of federal cognizance, ought to adopt the rules of decision known to prevail in the tribunal entitled to give the controlling decision. By the act of Congress of 1790, the judgment recovered in Maryland is to have the same effect in Pennsylvania that it has in the former State. In that State the courts take judicial notice of the existence of the common law, and of those principles of that law which render the judgment conclusive upon the parties and privies. A fair execution of the act of Congress, requires that the judge in Pennsylvania should also take notice of the system of jurisprudence which prevails in a sister State, united under a common government, and should give effect to the judgment as fully as would be given to it in the State in which it was pronounced. In cases not arising under the constitution and laws of the general government, the laws of the several States may properly be regarded by each other as foreign laws. But we apprehend that an entirely different rule prevails in all cases where a right is claimed under the constitution or laws of the Union.

In the case of Mills *v.* Duryee, 7 *Cranch* 481, the court of the District of Columbia, and the Supreme Court of the United States took notice, without proof, of the local law of New York and of the effect of a judgment recovered in that State. The question was decided on demurrer to the plea of *nil debet*, without hearing evidence, and without averment of the local law. In Hovie *v.* Wright, 2 *Ver.* 263, PRENTIS, J., referred to the Massachusetts statute for the effect which a judgment had in that State. In Clark *v.* Day, 2 *Leigh's Rep.* 172, the court held that the act of

[Baxley v. Linah.]

Congress had made the judgments of other States domestic judgments, and took notice of the local law, without proof, sustaining the position taken in this respect by an argument not readily answered. In Evans v. Tatem, 9 *Ser. & R.* 260, the plea was *nil debet* and on demurrer, and without any proof of the local law as a fact, the court took judicial cognizance of it, and gave judgment for the plaintiff, on the ground that the judgment recovered in another State was, under the constitution and act of Congress, conclusive.

It is therefore the opinion of this court, that the judgment recovered in Maryland is a bar to the action; and it is ordered that judgment be entered on the demurrer in favor of the defendant.

It was assigned for error:

1. The court erred in their opinion that the judgment of a foreign State is final and conclusive in our courts, or the courts of any other foreign State, so as to be a good plea in bar to a suit for the same cause of action: 1 *Bacon's Abr.* 29; 1 *Har. Dig.* 26; 3 *Rawle* 320-4.

2. The court erred in the opinion that the States of the Union, with regard to their municipal regulations and judicial tribunals, are as to each other domestic and not foreign—and that a judgment recovered in one State is to be treated as a domestic judgment throughout the United States, so as to give it the same effect in every other State as it would have in the State where it was recovered: 2 *Peters's U. S. S. C. Rep.* 586-90, Buckner v. Finley & Van Lear; 3 *Kent's Com.* 94, note; 2 *W. & Ser.* 129-33, Lowry v. Hall.

3. The court erred in its opinion that the plea in bar was sufficient, notwithstanding the omission in the plea of an averment of the local law of the State of Maryland and the effect of the judgment under it: 3 *Wend.* 267.

4. The court erred in the opinion that the local law and the effect of the judgment under it must not be established by evidence as a matter of fact, in order that the judgment may have the effect it would have in the State where it was recovered, but could be ascertained otherwise, even where no allegation of it is contained in the plea in bar: 7 *Wend.* 435; 3 *id.* 267; 2 *Blackf.* 31, 82.

5. The court erred in the opinion that by the act of Congress the judgment recovered in Maryland and pleaded in bar, is to have the same effect in barring the action in this State that it would have if the present action had been brought in the State of Maryland: *Act of Cong.* May 26, 1790.

6 The court erred in the opinion that a judgment obtained in another State of the Union is a bar to a suit brought in Pennsylvania for the same cause of action, and in directing judgment to be entered on the demurrer in favor of the defendant instead of for

[Baxley v. Linah.]

the plaintiff: 2 *W. & Ser.* 210–13, Lowry *v.* Lumberman's Bank; *id.* 129–33, Lowry *v.* Hall; *id.* 190, Irwine *v.* Lumberman's Bank; 1 *U. S. Dig.* 6, (plac. 131, 132,); 3 *Barb. & Harr.* 146; 3 *Rawle* 320, Toland *v.* Tichenor.

McClean and *McConaughy* were for plaintiff in error.—In McElmoyle *v.* Cohen, 13 *Peters's U. S. S. C. Rep.* 326, the Supreme Court of the United States in a very elaborate decision upon the construction of the act of Congress of 26th May 1790, held that a judgment of a State court is only distinguishable from a foreign judgment in this, that where suit is brought upon it it is conclusive of the merits. It does not carry with it, into another State, *the efficacy* of a judgment. It merely has the dignity of record evidence, for the purposes of evidence. In the case of the Merchants' Bank of Baltimore *v.* Bank of United States, it was held by the County Court of Baltimore, that the decision of the Supreme Court of the United States in McElmoyle *v.* Cohen necessarily involved the conclusion that, as the judgments of one State, although conclusive upon the matter in controversy, did not operate as judgments in any other State, they would not take effect by way of merger or extinguishment of the original cause of action, and consequently that a judgment obtained in Pennsylvania could not be pleaded in bar to a suit commenced by attachment between the same parties and for the same subject-matter in Maryland: 2 *Amer. Lead. Cases* 574 (note); *Pa. Law Jour.* (*N. S.*) vol. i. No. 3, 142. This case ruled in Maryland is in all points the same as the present.

In Lowry *v.* Lumberman's Bank, 2 *W. & Ser.* 210, it is held that a judgment on a foreign attachment in New York is not the subject of a plea in bar in this State in an action by the original creditor against the debtor. There must have been *satisfaction* either by actual payment or levy.

There is a material difference between a personal action pending and a foreign attachment pending, where a judgment in another State for the same cause of action is pleaded in bar to it. The proceeding here to which the plea in bar is attempted to be interposed is a foreign attachment—it is a proceeding *in rem*—no suit upon a judgment obtained in it could be brought in another State—it ends here—it is simply *a remedy*: 4 *Cow.* 523, 524 (note); 7 *W. & Ser.* 447, Steel *v.* Smith; 2 *Kent* 124 and note; 2 *Amer. Leading Cases* 574 (note).

In England it has been held that "if A. is indebted to B., and C. is indebted to A. and B. brings suit in B. R. against A., *pending this action*, B. may affirm a plaint in London against A. for the same debt, &c., and attach the debt in the hands of C:" *Cro. Eliz.* 593, 3 *Bac. Abr.* 53. There the distinction between a personal action and an attachment or proceeding *in rem*, is broadly

[Baxley v. Linah.]

taken. Because the last proceeding is an attachment, a former action pending or judgment obtained is not a good subject of a plea in abatement or in bar. There the jurisdictions were not foreign to each other.

Why may not the garnishee in a foreign attachment in another State, plead the judgment therein as a bar to a suit for the same cause of action in this State? Because there has been *no satisfaction* or payment. It is that alone which constitutes the bar.

Why then shall the defendant here be permitted to plead a judgment obtained in another State, in a suit on the note or cause of action, in bar to the foreign attachment laid upon his real or personal estate, for the recovery of the claim in this State? Not because of satisfaction or payment—there has been none—that is not pretended. Does it put the defendant in a worse position? It opens up the merits and lets him in to a full defence. Is this an injury? Then why defeat him? Even in England, we have shown that the proceedings are consistent. Much more so where the jurisdictions are distinct and foreign to each other: 1 *Mass. Rep.* 430, Bartlett v. Knight; 9 *Johns. Rep.* 221, Brown v. Joy, 4 *Cow.* 521, 523 (note).

Stevenson, for defendant in error.—As to 1st error. The plea of a former recovery for the same cause of action, and between the same parties, constitutes an *absolute bar*, &c.: 7 *Bac. Abr.* 633; 2 *Kent. Com.* 120 and note; 3 *East Rep.* 357, Outram v. Morewood; *Story, Conflict of Laws* 500; 13 *Ser. & R.* 246, Garvin v. Dawson; 1 *Phil. on Ev.* 333 and note; 5 *Watts* 120, Duffy & Mehaffy v. Lytle; *Chitty on Con.* 786; 3 *Cow.* 259, Gardner v. Buckbee; 4 *Cow.* 559, Burt v. Sternburgh.

As to 2d error. A judgment obtained in a sister State takes the same dignity, has the same effect, and is as binding and conclusive on the parties, as a judgment rendered in this State. It is put on the footing of a *domestic* judgment, and is not *foreign*: 2 *Amer. Leading Cases* 546 and note; 5 *Gill & Johns.* 500; 13 *Pet.* 326, McElmoyle v. Cohen; *Pet. C. C.* 74, Green v. Sarmiento; 3 *Wheat.* 234 Hampton v. McConnel; 7 *Cranch* 481, Mills v. Duryee; 3 *Story's Com.* 183; 9 *Ser. & R.* 259-60-2, Evans, Adminstratrix v. Tatem; *Chitty on Con.* 790 and note; 7 *Watts* 315, Ellsworth v. Barstow; 10 *Ser. & R.* 242; 16 *id.* 286.

As to 3d and 4th error. They are not now assignable under plaintiff's general demurrer. Were they so, the local law need not be proved. The proceedings, judicial acts, and jurisdiction of a court of another State are *prima facie* deemed correct—issue not being taken upon these questions: 2 *Caine's Cas.* 110; 3 *Bin.* 239 and note; 9 *Ser. & R.* 260; 4 *Bin.* 371; 12 *Ser. & R.* 209; *Story's Conf. of Laws* 500.

[Baxley v. Linah.]

The opinion of the court was delivered June 2, by

CHAMBERS, J.—The case presents the question of the character and effect of a judgment had in the State of Maryland, between the same parties, on the same cause of action, in a suit instituted before the issuing of the foreign attachment in this case, and in which the judgment so obtained in the State of Maryland is pleaded in bar. To this there was a demurrer and a joinder in demurrer.

In considering this case, it is not deemed necessary to go beyond the constitution of the United States, the acts of Congress made in pursuance of it, and the adjudication of the courts of the United States and of this State on the subject.

By that constitution it is declared that "full faith and credit shall be given in each State to the public acts, records, and judicial proceedings of every other State; and the Congress may, by general laws, prescribe the manner in which such acts, records, and proceedings shall be proved, and the effect thereof." And by act of 26th May 1790, Congress provided for the mode of authenticating the records and judicial proceedings of the State courts, and then further declared, that the "records and judicial proceedings, authenticated as aforesaid, shall have such faith and credit given to them, in every court within the United States, as they have by law or usage in the courts of the State from whence the said records are or shall be taken."

The courts of some of the States were, in the early history of the federal government, jealous of the alleged control under the constitutional provision and act of Congress recited, and inclined to controvert the effect which it was the purpose of both to grant. Nothing would have been obtained to remedy the inconvenience that had been experienced in the intercourse, commerce, and trade of citizens before the adoption of the constitution, if the records and judicial proceedings of the States courts were to be received and regarded in the courts of other States of this Union as of no greater weight or dignity than what was attached by the comity of nations to those of foreign countries.

From the facilities enjoyed by the citizens of these States for transportation and conveyance in their infinitely varied internal trade, they regard, but little, State boundaries and jurisdiction, but seek and change their marts of trade, dealing, and residence, where their inclination, convenience, or interest may seem to require, within the Union. The national government, established by the American States and the American people "to form a more perfect union," would have been left by its wise and patriotic founders deficient, had it allowed the States and citizens to stand in no higher relation to each other than foreigners. In all commercial relations we are one people, and in many other respects, the American people are one, and the government which rules their interests in these respects is the government of the Union.

[Baxley v. Linah.]

The constitutional provision adopted came recommended by every consideration of wisdom, convenience, of public peace and private security; and subsequent experience has attested its necessity and incalculable utility, in the more diversified and extended relations of the States and citizens of this republic.

A sound view of this constitutional law was taken at an early period, in the Circuit Court of the United States for the District of Pennsylvania, by WILSON, J., who decided that no defence was admissible to an action on a judgment of another State, which would not have been available had the suit been brought in the State where the judgment was rendered: Armstrong v. Carson's Executors, 2 *Dal.* 302; and in Bissel v. Briggs, 9 *Mass. Rep.* 462, the opinion of the court, delivered by PARSONS, C. J., gave that sanction and effect to the judicial proceedings of other States, which the public exigencies required, and which it was the object of the framers of the constitution to confer.

This question came before the Supreme Court of the United States in the case of Mills v. Duryee, 7 *Cranch* 481, and received the consideration which its importance required; and after solemn argument, it was ruled that the enactment of Congress does declare the effect of the records as evidence when duly authenticated. It gives them the same faith and credit as they have in the State court from which they are taken. If in such court they have the faith and credit of the highest nature, that is to say, of *record evidence*, they must have the same faith and credit in every other court.

This decision was subsequently confirmed by the same court in Hampton v. McConnel, 3 *Wheaton* 204; McElmoyle v. Cohen, 13 *Peters's Rep.* 544, and Reed v. Ross, 1 *Baldwin's Rep. Circuit Court United States.*

In Pennsylvania, the rule and exposition thus established in the courts of the United States have been adopted as authority, having their entire approbation and controlling their action. In the case of Benton v. Burgot, 10 *Ser. & R.* 240, it was decided that in a suit on a judgment in the court of another State, the pleas of fraud in obtaining it, imposition, mistake, and want of consideration, are bad on demurrer, and that *nul tiel record* is the only plea of which the defendant can avail himself,—that there can be no inquiry into the mistakes of the court which gave the judgment, provided the defendant was notified and the court had jurisdiction.

In Evans v. Taylor, 9 *Ser. & R.* 252, where the action was brought on the decree of a court of equity of Tennessee for the payment of money, it was held that although *nul tiel record* was not a good plea, as proceedings in equity do not possess the character of records, yet that *nil debet* was also bad, as leading to an inquiry into the cause of action, which was not open to examina-

[Baxley *v.* Linah.]

tion. The same principle was further recognised and affirmed in Kean *v.* Rice, 12 *Ser. & R.* 203.

An objection presented as to the effect claimed for the judgment of a court of another State was, that the courts to which it is removed are not enabled to issue execution upon it. It was well said, "This objection, if it had force, would apply to every other court of the same State where the judgment was rendered. The right of a court to issue execution depends upon its own powers and organization:" 7 *Cranch* 485. All which pertains to the means of execution, or the remedy of the party to obtain satisfaction, is left open to the law of the forum in which it is sought to be carried into effect.

Whilst for a time there was a reluctance in some of the State courts to give that faith and credit to the public acts, records, and judicial proceedings of the courts of other States, as provided by the constitution and acts of Congress, yet experience, more mature consideration, and a regard to constitutional law, to judicial uniformity and State harmony, have brought the courts of the States, with scarcely an exception, to concur in considering the judgments of the courts of each State as conclusive in every other, in all instances in which they had jurisdiction of the cause and the parties. So numerous and consistent are the authorities of the State courts on this important principle as to render a detailed reference to them unnecessary in this opinion.

In Pennsylvania we consider the question settled so decidedly by repeated adjudications, as to be no longer open to discussion.

The judgment of another State is put by the constitution on the same footing as a domestic judgment, with this qualification, that this does not prevent an inquiry into the *jurisdiction* of the court in which the original judgment was given to pronounce it, or the right of the State itself to exercise authority over the persons or subject-matter: *Story's Com.* sec. 183.

As the judgment in the courts of one State are judicial obligations of record there, so they are, under the provisions of the constitution, in every other, and are consequently conclusive in pleading and evidence; and they are a merger and extinguishment of the original cause of action, where the defendant had been summoned or appeared.

The judgment here exhibited from the State of Maryland is to be deemed to have the effect of a domestic judgment, and be so regarded in relation to the cause of action. It is presumed that the court in which it was rendered had jurisdiction of the subject-matter and of the parties, and which has not been controverted. The inquiry then is, what effect this judgment would have had in the State of Maryland, if presented under like circumstances. It is a judicial obligation of record there, conclusive of the subject-matter and a merger of the cause of action on which it is founded.

[Baxley v. Linah.]

Such is the opinion of the Supreme Court of the United States; and it necessarily follows that the State courts, in determining questions of federal cognizance, ought to adopt and be governed by the rules of decision adjudicated in that tribunal of controlling authority. If the constitution and courts of the United States should not be competent to give efficacy and uniformity to the law on this subject, as they are, what would be the contradiction and confusion if open to the decisions of the State courts of thirty independent States! We know that the courts of the State of Maryland have a system of jurisprudence under the common law and the principles of that law, little distinguishable from that which prevails in Pennsylvania, under a common government: under that law the effect of a judgment in a court of common law jurisdiction, and with notice to the parties, is, that such judgment is a merger of the original cause of action, which by it has become one of record. As such, does not public policy and authority make it a bar to the prosecution of any other action on the original cause of action? The law discourages a multiplicity of unnecessary actions, as vexatious to the parties and an abuse of the administration of the laws. It is settled that where a judgment has been already obtained in a prior action by the plaintiff against the defendant, for the *identical* demand, contract, or obligation, it is merged by the superiority of the record security, acquired by the judgment; *transit in rem judicatam*, and the creditor can no longer prosecute suit upon the original demand, though it were a specialty. If he do so, the defendant may plead, in bar, the judgment recovered against him by the plaintiff for the same cause of action: *Chitty's Con.* 7th ed. 787–8; 3 *Chitty's Pl.* 6th ed. 793.

It is therefore the opinion of this court that the judgment recovered in Maryland, between the parties in this case, and for the same identical cause of action, is a bar to the further prosecution of this action.

Judgment of the court below is affirmed.

Lange *versus* Stouffer.

In a sci. fa. to revive a judgment, the pleas were *nul tiel record*, payment, and payment with leave. Replication *non sol* and that there is such a record. Arbitrators appointed under a rule entered under the act of 1836, found for plaintiff a gross sum: *Held*, that the plea of *nul tiel record* did not exempt the case from arbitration, but that the arbitrators had jurisdiction of the whole cause.

ERROR to the Common Pleas of *York county*.

This was a scire facias on a judgment issued in the name of Sarah Caroline Stouffer, by her next friend, George W. Stouffer, *in re* judgment of Elizabeth Caroline Lange vs. Daniel Philip Lange. Scire facias on judgment, No. 339, April term 1845, to revive it and continue the lien thereof in the name of Sarah Caroline Stouffer, &c., one of the residuary legatees under the will of Elizabeth Caroline Lange, deceased, and all other persons who may be interested in said judgment.

April 23d, 1850, defendant pleads *nul tiel record*, payment, and payment with leave, &c. July 8th, 1850, plaintiff replies *non solvit* and that there is such a record. September 3d, 1850, plaintiff enters a rule to refer on 20th September 1850; on which day arbitrators were chosen. October 4th, 1850, report of arbitrators filed, finding for the plaintiff twelve hundred eighty-seven dollars and one cent, with costs of suit. Judgment *nisi*. November 5th, 1850, rule to show cause why the award of arbitrators, and the judgment entered thereon, should not be stricken off, because at the time of entering the rule of reference, appointing the arbitrators, and entering the award, the plea of *nul tiel record* was pending and undisposed of, and is still pending and undisposed of. February 26, 1851, rule discharged by the court, (LEWIS, J., holding a special court at York,) and judgment absolute.

It was assigned for error:
1. The arbitrators had not jurisdiction of the case, and the judgment entered on their award is therefore erroneous.
2. The court erred in discharging the rule of 5th of November 1850, and in entering judgment thereon, and in not setting aside the award of arbitrators.

Campbell, for plaintiff in error, contended that the plea of *nul tiel record* could not be tried by compulsory arbitration: Roop v. Meek, 6 *Ser. & R.* 545; Hill v. Crawford, 8 *id.* 478; 3 *Watts* 176. These decisions *were under the act of* 1810; but if the legislature had intended that demurrers, certioraris, and pleas of *nul tiel record* might be tried by arbitration, it is probable that they would have said so decidedly in the act of 1836. That it

[Lange v. Stouffer.]

was not so intended is evident from the oath prescribed, which is, *justly and equitably* to try all matters in variance submitted to them. See also 9 *Watts* 192. That a writ of error is the remedy of the plaintiff in error. The rule on this point seems to be that the Supreme Court will not hear the errors when they are to be established by *affidavits*, and go to the merits; but that when the errors are on *the face of the record*, they will hear them, and sometimes even act on *affidavits* to determine the regularity of the proceedings: Drenkle *v.* Garber, 7 *Watts* 122; Biggs *v.* Funk, 5 *id.* 481. Especially will this be done when the court below refuses to grant relief. In the present case, the errors are on the face of the record, and the court below refused to strike off the award and the judgment entered thereon. In Hill *v.* Crawford and Stevenson *v.* Docherty, writs of error were taken: 2 *Barr* 435.

Mayer, with whom was *Evans* and *Naille*, for defendant in error.—The "matters in variance" are submitted, not the issues on the pleas. Arbitrators are constituted judges of the law and the facts: *Section* 40 *of act of* 1836. Though they may not know the meaning of the plea of *nul tiel record*, they can tell whether there is a judgment and whether the defendant has a defence: 5 *Whar.* 309, Waage *v.* Weiser.

The cases specially excepted in the act of 1836 leave all others subject to its operation. A matter may be submitted to arbitration without narr., plea, or issue; the right of submission is not to be taken away because the plea of *nul tiel record* is pleaded. As to *certioraris* they are prerogative writs, authorized by the constitution, issued in the name of the commonwealth to an inferior tribunal to send up the record. It might as well be said that writs of habeas corpus were embraced within the terms "civil suits or actions," and that an exception was necessary to exempt them from the jurisdiction of arbitrators.

The opinion of the court was delivered June 4, by

GIBSON, C. J.—Arbitrators, though less skilled in technicalities than a court, may be made legally competent by the legislature to determine an issue of law; and the question is whether such an issue is a subject of reference within the intent and meaning of the compulsory arbitration act. The words, "all matters in variance in the suit between the parties," are too comprehensive to exclude any part of the controversy. Nor is there a reason why they should. The reference of even a naked issue of fact draws the decision of incidental questions of law to the arbitrators. They are substituted for the primary tribunal in all respects, and are both court and jury. The framers of the act doubtless looked no further than to a speedy decision of the merits; and it may be that a cause depending exclusively on an issue of law is not within

[Lange *v.* Stouffer.]

the purview of it—though even that construction would delay a creditor in obtaining a lien—but it is more reasonable that an issue of fact should draw other issues to it than be drawn by them, else a principal object of the act might be frustrated by sticking in a plea to the court. Suppose that the court, to avoid this, should bring on the argument of such a plea and decide it for the defendant, what would become of the rest of the cause before the arbitrators? On the other hand, to reserve it for subsequent decision by the court, and arbitrate a plea to the country, would raise doubts and difficulties not easily resolvable. An award under the act is declared to have the force and effect of a judgment " until reversed upon *appeal* or satisfied according to law." It would not be reversed by any decision of a plea of *nul tiel record*. It would continue to stand as a judgment against the defendant, who could get rid of it only by appealing; and when he had brought the cause back, it would be immaterial whether his plea to the court had been referred and determined against him, as the whole would be rejudged. Besides, to refer half a cause, if it could be done, would present an entangled question of costs. But the plea of *nul tiel record* sometimes leads to an issue of fact. In Esplin *v.* Smallet, *Sayer's Rep.* 208, it was held that a plea embracing matter of fact and matter of law, might conclude to the country. To a scire facias on a recognizance of special bail, the defendant pleaded that a fieri facias was sued out against the principal, and that the money was levied of his goods: the plaintiff replied that the writ was not sued out, and that *the money was not levied*, and concluded to the country: the defendant demurred, and the replication was held good. The same principle in Peter *v.* Stafford, *Hob.* 244. Proper averments may raise a question of fact, whether a former recovery was for the same cause of action; and though that could not have been done in this case, nothing would be gained by excepting it from the general rule. But, for paramount reasons, already given, it seems the arbitrators had jurisdiction of the whole cause.

Judgment affirmed.

W

Welsh *versus* Anthony.

Under the 3d section of the act of 29th March 1824, either trespass or trover may be maintained for entering upon plaintiff's land, without his consent, and cutting and removing timber trees. If there be a *trespass merely, double* damages may be given; if, in addition, the trees felled have been converted to the use of the wrong-doer, *treble* damages may be recovered in trespass, and also in *trover*. By the words "as the case may be," is meant that if the trespass to the close *be waived*, and trover brought, *treble* damages for the injury done may be recovered in that form of action.

2. Either the jury or the court may assess the double or treble damages.

3. Double or treble *costs* mean, in Pennsylvania, double or treble the single costs: and so with respect to *damages*. The English rule as to costs in such cases does not prevail in this State. Per ROGERS, J.

ERROR to the Common Pleas of *Clinton county*.

This was an action of trespass *quare clausum fregit*, brought by Joseph B. Anthony and others *vs.* James Welsh, for entering upon land and cutting timber trees, and removing and disposing of the same to his own use.

The plea was not guilty and *liberum tenementum.*

The 3d section of the act of 29th March 1824, under which the plaintiffs below brought suit, is as follows:—

" SEC. 3. In all cases where any person, after the said first day of September, shall cut down or fell, or employ any person or persons to cut down or fell any timber, tree or trees, growing upon the lands of another, without the consent of the owner thereof, he, she or they, so offending, shall be liable to pay to such owner *double* the value of such tree or trees, so *cut down or felled ;* or in case of the *conversion* thereof to the use of such offender or offenders, *treble* the value thereof, *to be recovered* with costs of suit, by *action* of *trespass* or *trover*, as *the case may be ;* and no prosecution by indictment shall be any bar to such action."

On the trial, WOODWARD, J., instructed the jury that the action of trespass was well brought. That under the 3d section of the act of 29th March 1824, *either trespass or trover* would lie where there had been not only a cutting down and felling of timber trees, but *a conversion* of them by the offender to his own use, and that if the jury believe there had been such trespass and conversion by the defendant, they were bound to render to the plaintiffs a verdict for *treble* the value of the trees cut on their land and taken away. To which opinion, so far as the court held that trespass would lie, and that trover was not the exclusive remedy, the counsel for defendant excepted and prayed that the charge be filed.

Verdict for plaintiffs for $202.59.

It was assigned for error:

1. The court erred in their instruction to the jury, that in *this*

[Welsh v. Anthony.]

form of action, the plaintiffs were entitled to recover *treble* the value of the trees cut on their land and carried away.

2. The court erred in saying that *trespass* would lie, and *trover* was not the *exclusive* remedy to recover *treble* the value, for the felling and conversion of timber trees, under the 3d section of the act of 29th March 1824.

The case was argued by *J. W. Quiggle*, for the plaintiff in error.—The 3d section of the act of 29th March 1824 creates two offences, prescribes a penalty, and gives a remedy *in each*.

At *common* law the plaintiffs could simply recover the value of the timber cut or converted. But by this statute two separate and distinct offences are made. The one, the *cutting down or felling* of any timber, tree, or trees; the other, the *conversion* to the offender's own use. For the former offence, *double* the value of the tree or trees may be recovered; for the latter *treble* the value, to be recovered "by *action* of trespass *or* trover, as *the case may be*." As the *fact* may be; or as the *suit* or *action* may be? Surely not the latter. For if it be construed to mean the latter, then *trover* would lie for a mere cutting *down or felling*, which would be absurd. It must then mean as the *fact* may be. If a cutting or felling, then *double* the value to be recovered by action of *trespass*. If a conversion to the use of the offender, then *treble* the value to be recovered by *action* of trover. The remedy in each case being given by *statute*, must be *pursued*.

That *trover* is *the remedy* to recover *treble* damages under this act, for the cutting and conversion of timber trees, is settled in the case of Tammany *v*. Whitaker, 4 *Watts* 221.

Armstrong, for defendant.

The opinion of the court was delivered June 12, by

ROGERS, J.—The action of trespass is well brought. The plaintiff having alleged in his narr. that the defendants took and carried away the property severed from the freehold, and converted the same to his own use, the jury were at liberty to assess treble damages under the statute. The suit is brought on the 3d section of the act of the 29th of March 1824, which reads thus: "In all cases where any person shall cut down or fell any timber, tree or trees, growing upon the lands of another, without the consent of the owner, he, she, or they, so offending, shall be liable to pay to such owner double the value of such tree or trees so cut down or felled; and in case of the *conversion* thereof to the use of such offender or offenders, *treble* the value to be recovered, with costs of suit, by action of trespass or trover, as the case may be," &c. The design of the act cannot be doubted. Where there is a trespass merely, double damages only are to be given, but where in addi-

[Welsh v. Anthony.]

tion the trees felled are converted to the use of the wrong-doer, treble damages are to be awarded. The remedy given for the injury to the owner, is trespass or trover, *as the case may be*. By the latter words, *as the case may be*, nothing more is to be understood than that when the owner chooses to waive the trespass to the close and elect trover, (as he may,) he may recover treble damages; but it certainly could not be intended that when he proceeds as well for the trespass as the conversion, he shall be restrained to double damages merely. It seems clear that where there is a conversion, treble damages may be recovered as well in trespass as trover. The owner may elect trover if he pleases, but surely he ought not to be compelled to do so, and thereby lose the damages sustained by the illegal and tortious entry.

A doubt was suggested at the bar whether the jury or the court should assess double or treble damages when given by the statute. In England the rule is that the jury who try the issue may assess the double or treble damages, but if they neglect to do so, the court may award the damages, on a writ of inquiry for assessing them. I perceive no reason why a different rule should prevail in this State: *Rob. Dig.* 116, *Bro. Damages*, pl. 76; *Sayer on Damages* 244.

According to the *English* practice, double or treble costs are not understood to mean twice or thrice the amount of single costs; but double costs consist of the single costs and half the single costs; and treble costs of the single costs, half the single costs, and half of that half: 2 *Arch. P.* 233; *Brightly on the Law of Costs*, 298. But this rule is not in practice in Pennsylvania, as is ruled in Shoemaker *v.* Nesbit, 2 *Rawle* 201. I am not aware that even in England the same artificial rule applies when double or treble *damages* are given by statute, but if it be, it is certain it has never been adopted in this State.

Judgment affirmed.

Ervine's Appeal.

1. A testator in his will directed that after the decease of his wife, his executors should rent out his lands, and out of the proceeds his son Daniel to be supported, and willed and desired that none of his real estate should be sold during the life of his said son, but that he be supported out of the same; and provided further, that it was his will and desire that, after the death of his son Daniel, then his real estate should be sold, and all his children to receive share and share alike. After the death of the widow, an act was passed, at the instance of Daniel, providing that on his application, the Orphans' Court shall make an order appointing a trustee to make sale of the said real estate, and to invest the proceeds under the direction of the said court, so that the interest thereof shall secure to him that support during his natural life which

[Ervine's Appeal.]

the will intended him to receive out of the produce of the said real estate, provided that such sale shall be approved by the said court—and providing further, that the annual interest only of the proceeds of sale be paid to the said Daniel or his trustee, and the principal sum be invested, subject to all the provisions of the will: *Held*, that the other parties in interest being of full age, under no disability, and objecting to the sale, the court below was right in refusing to direct it; that the legislature does not possess the constitutional power, in such a case, to direct a sale against the consent of the other parties in interest who were of full age and under no disability, *within the time during which the sale was forbidden by the testator;* and that the act in this case was *unconstitutional*.

2. The provision in the 5th article of the amendments to the Constitution of the United States that no person shall "be deprived of life, liberty, or property without due process of law," and the equivalent provision in the Constitution of Pennsylvania, that no one shall be "deprived of his life, liberty, or property, unless by the judgment of his peers or *the law of the land*," imply the right to notice to appear and answer, and to a remedy in court. Per COULTER, J.

APPEAL from the decree of the Orphans' Court of *York county*.

This was an appeal from the decree of the Orphans' Court of York county on the petition of Daniel Ervine, a legatee under the will of Patrick Ervine, deceased, praying for an order to sell certain real estate. The petition was as follows:—

To the Honorable the Judges of the Orphans' Court of York county:

The petition of Daniel Ervine, son and legatee under the last will and testament of Patrick Ervine, late of York township, York county, deceased, respectfully represents:

That by the said last will and testament, the said Patrick, after providing for his widow, Julia Ann, directed as follows:—"After the decease of my said wife, it is my will that my executors should rent out my lands to the best advantage, and out of the proceeds of the same my son Daniel to be supported; and it is further my will and desire that none of my real estate should be sold during the life of my said son Daniel, but that he is to be supported out of the same as above mentioned; and it is further my will and desire that after the death of my said son Daniel, that then my real estate shall be sold to the highest bidder, and all my children to receive share and share alike."

Your petitioner further states that the said Julia Ann, widow of the said testator, is dead, and that the proceeds of the said real estate are insufficient to support him, as was contemplated by the testator in his last will, a copy of which will is hereunto annexed and made part of this petition.

Your petitioner further states that by an act of Assembly, passed at the present session of the legislature, it was enacted "that on the application of Daniel Ervine, or any other person interested in the estate of Patrick Ervine, late of York county, deceased, the Orphans' Court of said county shall make an order appointing a

[Ervine's Appeal.]

trustee to make sale of the real estate of said decedent, and to invest the proceeds thereof under the direction of said court," &c., *prout* said act of Assembly, a certificate copy of which is hereunto annexed and made part of this petition.

Your petitioner further states that the real estate now unsold, belonging to the said Patrick Ervine at the time of his death, consisted of twelve acres of woodland, more or less, situate in York township, and bounded by lands of Leonard Weisenbaugh, David Kettle, Jacob Young, and perhaps others: also the mansion tract now situate in Spring Garden township, York county, bounded by lands of Samuel Weaver, John Horn, York Water Company, Thomas Baumgardner, Jacob Spangler, Michael Shellenberger, Samuel Frey, Henry Spangler, and Samuel and Jacob Rudy, containing about one hundred and thirty acres.

Your petitioner therefore prays your honorable court to appoint Samuel Weiser, (farmer,) of the borough of York, trustee, to make sale of the said real estate and to carry into effect the provisions of the said act of Assembly relative to the proceeds of said sale of said real estate, and the maintenance and support of your petitioner thereout, &c. And he will pray, &c.

his
DANIEL × ERVINE.
mark.

An act was passed on the 29th March 1849, which, in its 17th section, provided that the Orphans' Court in and for the county of York are hereby authorized, *if the said court shall deem it expedient*, to cause an order to be made for the sale of the real estate in question: See *Acts of* 1849, 273.

The Orphans' Court refused to decree a sale of the said estate, on the ground that the provision above referred to was unconstitutional. An appeal was taken to the Supreme Court, and the decree was affirmed on the ground that the matter was submitted by the act to the discretion of the court below. It was, however, added in the *per curiam* opinion that the constitutionality of the act was established by the case of Norris *v.* Clymer, 2 *Barr* 277.

On the 2d April 1850, the act was passed which is referred to in the petition. The preamble and 3d section of the act (see *Acts of* 1850, p. 337,) were as follow:—

Whereas Patrick Ervine, of York township, in the county of York, died during the minority of his son Daniel, who was incapable of managing the property left for his benefit, and it appearing that the property, the income of which was designed for his support and maintenance, has not been controlled or managed in such manner as to secure the true intention of the testator; and as the said Daniel, who is blind, does not receive the means which the said property is abundantly able to produce for his support, and

[Ervine's Appeal.]

inasmuch as the will does not authorize the sale or disposition of said property to fulfil the clear design of the said Patrick Ervine, to wit, the proper support and comfort of his son Daniel, who is now forty-two years of age, and is in a suffering condition and totally helpless; the said property being worth seven thousand dollars, would, if sold, furnish ample means to comply with the object of the testator: Therefore,

SECTION 3. Be it enacted by the authority aforesaid, that on the application of Daniel Ervine, or any other person or persons interested in the estate of Patrick Ervine, late of York county, deceased, the Orphans' Court of said county shall make an order appointing a trustee to make sale of the real estate of said decedent, and to invest the proceeds thereof, under the direction of said court, so that the interest thereof shall secure to the said Daniel Ervine that support for and during his natural life, which the will of said decedent intended him to have and receive out of the produce of the said real estate; provided that such sale when made shall be approved of by the said court, after which a deed shall be made, conveying to the purchaser or purchasers such estate as the said Patrick Ervine had and held in the premises at and immediately before the time of his decease; provided also that before receiving any of the proceeds of sale, said trustees shall give such security as the said Orphans' Court may require, conditioned for the faithful execution of said trust; and provided further that any person or persons interested may appeal to the Supreme Court from any order or orders, decree or decrees that the said Orphans' Court may make, said appeal to be taken within thirty days from the making of such order or decree; and provided further that the annual interest only of said principal sum arising from the sale of the real estate aforesaid shall be paid to the said Daniel Ervine or his trustee, and that the principal sum aforesaid shall be and remain permanently invested, subject to all the provisions of the will of the said Patrick Ervine, deceased.

The Orphans' Court of York county dismissed the petition. The opinion of his Honor DURKEE, President, was as follows:—

In regard to his real estate, Patrick Ervine directed by his last will and testament, as follows:—"After the decease of my said wife, it is my will that my executors should rent out my lands to the best advantage, and out of the proceeds of the same my son Daniel to be supported—and it is further my will and desire that none of my real estate should be sold during the life of my said son Daniel, but that he is to be supported out of the same as above mentioned—and it is further my will and desire that after the death of my said son Daniel, that then my real estate should be sold to the highest bidder, and all my children to receive share and share alike." By the express direction of the testator in this clause of his will, then, his real estate is not to be sold until *after*

[Ervine's Appeal.]

his son Daniel's death. It is *then* to be sold, and what it shall *then* bring is to be equally divided amongst his other children. He doubtless supposed his real estate, which is situated near the borough of York, would increase in value for many years, and that the longer the sale should be deferred the more there would be to divide amongst his children—and we are far from believing he was mistaken. If it would bring three times as much now as it would have sold for twenty years ago, we can see no reason for supposing that it would not bring more twenty years hence than it would sell for now, nor can we see on what principle his children, who are entitled, by the express terms of the will, to all that it can be sold for, after the death of Daniel, can be justly deprived of the benefit of its increasing value, by a premature sale, made against their consent. Such a sale, made under such circumstances, it strikes us, would not be a mere conversion or alteration of their property, without injury to their rights, but a measure (could it be effected) that would *deprive* them of their property—a thing which cannot rightly be done, "unless by their peers or the law of the land." Between depriving them of a part of what they are entitled to, according to the provisions of the will, and depriving them of all to which they are so entitled, there seems to us no difference in principle. At all events, we can see no occasion for legislative interposition in the matter, as it is not pretended that any of the parties interested are minors, or that they labor under any legal disability, or that the will has, from any supervening cause, become impracticable, or that any power is wanting to carry it out according to the expressed intentions of the testator—nor is any public benefit sought to be effected by legislative interference with the will, in some of which particulars, at least, this case differs from all others, as we believe, in which legislative interference has received judicial sanction. These being our views, and the prayer of the petitioner being opposed in behalf of Peter Ervine and six others, children of the testator, without whose consent or knowledge, it is alleged, the act of Assembly on which this proceeding is based was passed at the instance of Daniel Ervine, the petition is dismissed by the court.

An appeal was taken to this court, and the exceptions filed were:
1. The court erred in dismissing the petition.
2. The court erred in not granting the prayer of the petitioner.

Fisher, for the appellant, contended that the act of Assembly directing the court to make an order appointing a trustee to make sale of the real estate of Patrick Ervine, deceased, is constitutional: Braddee *v.* Brownfield, 2 *W. & Ser.* 275; Menges *v.* Wertman,

[Ervine's Appeal.]

1 *Barr* 218; Norris *v.* Clymer, 2 *Barr* 277; Sergeant *v.* Kuhn, 2 *Barr* 293.

In the matter of Ervine's Appeal, (not reported,) the Supreme Court say that the case of Norris *v.* Clymer settles that the 17th section of the act of 1829 is constitutional, authorizing a sale of the property mentioned in the will of said Patrick Ervine.

The act of Assembly does not *divest* any fee; no fee descends to the heirs; the will, by directing a sale after the death of Daniel Ervine, converts the estate into personal property, and the act of 1850 only hastens the time of sale: Miller *v.* Meetch, 8 *Barr* 425; Allison *v.* Kurtz, 2 *Watts* 185; Allison *v.*Wilson, 13 *Ser. & R.* 330; Morrow *v.* Brenizer, 2 *Rawle* 188; Craig *v.* Leslie, 3 *Wheat.* 563; 16 *Mass.* 329; 2 *Peters* 629.

Mayer, with whom was *Evans*, in reply.—I. 1. The act is mandatory on the Orphans' Court of York county to appoint a trustee to make a sale, with the *proviso*, however, that "*such sale when made shall be approved by the said court.*" The opinion of the court shows that they refused to execute this mandate, because such a sale would be a plain violation of the will of the testator, and no power to make it could be conferred on the court or would be sanctioned by them. Had they yielded so far as to appoint the trustee, they could not have *approved* the sale when made; and it was therefore idle to take the initiatory step in the proceeding.

2. We do not see therefore what this court can do in the matter on this appeal. The appeal given in the act presupposes the action of the court in the furtherance of the object, when the matter to be decided would be some question arising in the course of the proceeding; not a refusal to act at all. On an appeal, the court above generally delivers a final decree; but in this case no power is conferred on this court to *appoint a trustee* and *approve the sale*, if the court below refuses to do it, and consequently no such decree can be made here. If this court did not agree with the court below in its opinion of the matter, no power exists to compel the court below to think otherwise, or to *approve the sale*, without which approval the appointment of the trustee would be nugatory.

3. The exercise of a judicial function may be enforced by mandamus, but not the manner of its exercise: Com'th *v.* Hultz, 6 *Barr* 469; Griffith *v.* Cochran, 5 *Bin.* 87, 103; Com'th *v.* Judges, &c. 3 *Bin.* 275. And clearly, if a discretion is vested in the inferior tribunal *to approve* or *disapprove* an act, no power can circumscribe its discretion: Com'th *v.* County Commissioners, 5 *Bin.* 536. This case cannot be reached on an appeal.

II. But the court below was right. Far as courts have gone in sanctioning the conversion of property by sale with the consent of all parties, it has not yet sustained a project of sale like this. The interest and wishes of the parties, and sometimes of the public,

[Ervine's Appeal.]

seemed to require a dispensation with legal disabilities, in order to substitute a mere *modal* change in the enjoyment of the property. There was no "case of controversy between party and party," "nor any decree or judgment affecting the title to the property. The only object of the authority granted by the legislature was to transmute real into personal estate, *for purposes beneficial to all who were interested therein.*" Per PARKER, C. J., Rice *v.* Parkman, 16 *Mass. Rep.* 329; see Blagge *v.* Miles, 4 *Law Rep.* 256; Wilkinson *v.* Leland; 2 *Peters* 627. Such was the fact in Clymer *v.* Norris, 2 *Barr* 277; Sergeant *v.* Kuhn, *id.* 393. Sometimes, indeed, in those cases where a conversion is authorized by a will, but the time only is postponed, the anticipation of it might have seemed to be demanded by the testator's *intention*, in which case the parties, all consenting or being benefited, might have proceeded to anticipate the time without a special law authorizing it: Gast *v.* Porter, 1 *Harris* 533.

But, "Here the *time* is not matter of form, but substance:" Loomis *v.* McClintock, 10 *Watts* 279; Seweigart *v.* Frey, 8 *Ser. & R.* 299. Above all, *here stands upon the face of this will the formal prohibition by the testator of any sale before the time he has fixed for it.* This feature distinguishes the case from all others. "If the legislature, by *ex parte* enactment, can alter the will of a private individual, whose will shall escape? Brown *v.* Hummel, 6 *Barr* 94; Greenough *v.* Greenough, 1 *Jones* 495.

The sale is not yet made. The prohibition is in full force. The parties in remainder are *sui juris*, and may be considered as vested with the fee notwithstanding the ultimate power of conversion, having the right to treat their interest as land: Smith *v.* Starr, 3 *Whart.* 62; Boshart *v.* Evans, 5 *id.* 562. The *cestui que trust* of the usufruct alone demands a conversion. The others resist it. *They were not represented when the act was passed*, and their rights cannot be disregarded: Bumberger *v.* Clippinger, 5 *W. & Ser.* 311; Rogers *v.* Smith, 4 *Barr* 93. The trial by jury is inviolate under the constitution. The parties interested *are resisting, not consenting to the act.* The court below, knowing all the facts, and specially appointed to approve the execution of the statute, refused to sanction it.

In the report of Norris *v.* Clymer, 2 *Barr* 277, it does not appear that the persons interested opposed the passage of the act.

Special acts "are passed by the legislature without hearing the parties to be affected, but with the express understanding of every honest member, of leaving the question of their constitutionality to the judiciary." Per BURNSIDE, J., Dale *v.* Medcalf, 9 *Barr* 111.

The chief objects of the testator in his will were to provide for his son Daniel—to provide for his other children—and to provide for the security and prospective increase of the fund. It is directed that the land shall be rented by the executors, and Daniel be sup-

[Ervine's Appeal.]

ported out of the income; that the land *shall not be sold during Daniel's lifetime;* and that at his death it shall be sold, and the proceeds be divided among the other children. Here is a clear trust—and the duties of the trustee and the rights of the parties are well defined. The act procured by Daniel proposes to take the property out of the hands of the trustees, and to place it in the hands of others, to sell it, contrary to the express letter of the instrument creating the trust and the will of the donor, and to appropriate not, merely his support, but the whole annual product of the fund to his use. We may well ask as this court has done in a similar case, speaking by one of its members, "where this power was or is derived, I am at a loss to perceive." Per COULTER, J., Brown v. Hummel, 6 *Barr* 94. No difficulty has occurred in the execution of this trust showing its defects or impractability. On the contrary the testator's foresight has been verified by the event in every particular, unless it be in the amount of Daniel's expenditure. The property has greatly increased in value, and will probably continue to do so, while the fund is safe, as he intended it should be, against all dangers either from the improvident habits of any whom he meant to favor, or the unfortunate investments of those to whom the care of the fund was intrusted.

Notice was not given of the contemplated enactment, and the proceeding was not "according to the law of the land."

Fisher, in reply.—In Brown v. Hummel, 6 *Barr* 94, the act divested an estate.

The opinion of the court was delivered June 12, by
COULTER, J.—The Constitution of the United States ordains "that no person shall be deprived of life, liberty, *or property,* without due process of law," and the constitution of this State contains an equivalent provision in words nearly alike.

It is an affirmation of a great doctrine contained in Magna Charta: "neither will we pass upon any one but by the lawful judgment of his peers or by the law of the land." And Lord COKE says that the words *"per legem terræ,"* mean, by due process of law, and being brought into court to answer according to law. The whole clauses in our constitutions on the subject were established for the protection of personal safety and private property. These clauses address themselves to the common sense of the people, and ought not to be filed away by legal subtleties. They have their foundations in natural justice, and, without their pervading efficacy, other rights would be useless. If the legislature possessed an irresponsible power over every man's private estate, whether acquired by will, by deed, or by inheritance, all inducement to acquisition, to industry and economy would be removed. The principal object of government is the administration

[Ervine's Appeal.]

of justice and the promotion of morals. But if property is subject to the caprice of an annual assemblage of legislators acting, tumultuously, and without rule or precedent, and without hearing the party, stability in property will cease, and justice be at an end. If the government is interdicted from taking private property even for public use without just compensation, how can the legislature take it from one man and dispose of it as they think fit. The great principle is, that a man's property is his own, and that he shall enjoy it according to his pleasure (injuring no other man) until it is proved in a due process of law that it is not his, but belongs to another. Many acts of Assembly have been passed, it is true, authorizing guardians, trustees, and executors to convey lands. This power has been sustained by this court where the persons in interest were minors and lunatics, and could not act for themselves, and where the guardians, &c. requested the passage of the laws. Among the first of the private acts in such cases was that in Estep v. Hutchman, 14 *Ser. & R.* 435. That was sustained on the ground that the *cestui que trusts* were minors. The court say that of necessity, in such cases, the power must reside in the government somewhere; and where it has not been granted to the courts, it must reside in the legislature. This proceeds on the ground that the conveyance itself was lawful, for the maintenance of minors or lunatics, as the necessities of the minor or lunatic might absolutely require it. In such cases a court of chancery would order the sale. It was considered that the ordering of the sale was merely modal, as it is termed in Norris and Clymer; that is, doing in one way that which might be done in another. And that principle is quite suitable, when the *cestui que trust* is legally disabled from acting and the *parens patriæ* acts for his benefit. But to say that because a man who is under no disability may convey his property, that therefore the legislature may, as a mere mode, order and direct another to convey it against his will, is a perfect *non sequitur* from those cases. In Norris and Clymer the legislative decree of sale was for the benefit of *cestui que trusts* who consented, and who alone were interested, except issue was born who had cross remainders, and the trustees appointed in place of those named in the will requesting the sale, as well as all persons concerned in interest and *in esse*, so far as appears from the reported case. And the opinion there seems to be that a chancellor might have ordered the sale; and a distinguishing feature of that case was that the estate, after conversion, remained in the hands of the trustee.

But there is no adjudicated case where the legislature ordered the sale of one man's land when he was *sui juris*, under no legal disability to act for the benefit of another person, also *sui juris*, and where such legislative decree was sustained. The case of Brown v. Hummell, 6 *Barr* 94, is, in all its principles, directly the

[Ervine's Appeal.]

other way; which case has received, I believe, the sanction of the profession and the approving judgment of the community. The case on hand presents an act of Assembly, requiring the Orphans' Court of York county, on the petition of Daniel Ervine, or any other person interested in the estate of Patrick Ervine, in said county, to make an order appointing a trustee to make sale of the real estate of said testator, and invest the proceeds for the benefit of Daniel during his life, &c. The devisees of said estate were all of full age, and under no legal disability, at the time of passing the law, and who had power themselves to convey, if they thought fit, all residing in York county, and all, save Daniel, objecting to the law. It is alleged that, as Daniel was to receive from the executors during the life of said Daniel, the rents, issues, and profits of the estate, and as the executors were directed to sell after his death, and divide the product among his surviving brothers, it was not real, but personal estate. But it is of no consequence whether it was real or personal estate, because the constitution protects a man in the enjoyment and dominion of his personal as potentially as his real estate. There could be no reason for the distinction; and the language of the constitution is, that no man shall be deprived of his "*property*," &c. The legislature contemplated no such distinction, for the act denominates it real estate of the decedent. But if it was personal estate so far as regarded the children who survived Daniel, under the authority of Morrow v. Brenizer, 2 *Rawle* 188, and Craigo v. Leslie, 3 *Wheaton* 563, yet it was real estate as it regarded the executor, who was to receive the rents, issues, and profits, during the life of Daniel, and the fee was vested in him, he had an interest coupled with a power to sell. Two things were evidently in the mind of the testator: 1st, that the realty would be more secure for Daniel, who was probably improvident, than money at interest. And, 2d, that the rents, issues, and profits, as well as the land itself, would increase in value, as it lay near the borough of York; and this increase would benefit the children who survived Daniel. This probable increase was a substantial interest secured by the will. It is this probability of increase in value which induces men to buy lands which they do not intend to cultivate. Beside, the children who survived Daniel could elect to take the land itself, instead of requiring the executor to sell it. These interests, first in the executor himself, and second, in the children who might survive Daniel, being secured by the positive terms of the will, they ought to be as inviolable as interests secured by deed. A just government ought as emphatically to protect wills as deeds and contracts. Because, by so doing, not only the rights of the living are secured, but also the rights of the dead—rights which all civilized nations regard. Those who are now the living will shortly be the dead. And we labor not only for the present, but for the future, and for

[Ervine's Appeal.]

those who shall be in that future. The will provides that the land shall not be sold until Daniel's death. The children of testator, except Daniel, insist on the will being observed and their rights under it preserved. Daniel applies to the legislature, who pass an act that the court shall appoint a trustee, who shall sell immediately. Here is an act deciding between two parties, and nullifying the provisions of the will, and requiring the court to disregard it. A power to sell, either in a will or deed, to be exercised upon the happening of a particular event, cannot by law be exercised until the happening of that event; in fact, the power does not exist until then. This has been so often ruled, and is so consonant to common sense and natural right, that no authority need be cited. But the legislature say the court shall appoint a trustee, to execute the power immediately; that is, makes a law for a particular case between two contesting parties, which rule is contrary to existing law, and orders the court to enforce it. Suppose the right of entry was barred by twenty-one years' adverse possession, and the legislature, choosing to pass a law for a particular case, should enact that A might bring his action of ejectment against B for a messuage or tenement, and order the court to give judgment in favor of A, notwithstanding twenty-one years' actual adverse possession, alleging some reason not sufficient in law to prevent the statute from running. Here would be legislation for a particular case, contrary to the general law. Such legislation would, I apprehend, find few approvers, because it would be taking that which the general law made the property of one man and giving it to another. But after all, the excuse would be that they were only giving the estate to him who had the title, merely removing the impediment of the statute. In the case on hand, the legislature not only removes the legal impediment contained in the will, which prevents the executors from selling before the death of Daniel, but also annihilates the provision of the will that the executors shall rent out the land and pay the rents and profits to Daniel during his life, and takes from the sons of the testator the probable increase of the land during Daniel's life, and the privilege of taking it as land at his death. By what warrant may they do all this? Not by the power of a judicial decree, because the legislature have no judicial power. And that is not legislation which adjudicates in a particular case, prescribes the rule contrary to the general law, and orders it to be enforced. Such power assimilates itself more closely to despotic rule than to any other attribute of government.

It is sought to cover the act under the case of Braddee *v.* Brownsfield, 2 *W. & Ser.* 275, which rules that the legislature possess a mixed jurisdiction, being partly legislative and partly judicial; under which many hybrid acts were passed. But that case received a fatal blow in Greenough *v.* Greenough, 1 *Jones,* in which

[Ervine's Appeal.]

it is said the legislature possess no such power. It was utterly overthrown in De Chastellux *v.* Fairchild, 3 *Harris* 18, in which it was emphatically ruled that the legislature possess no judicial power, and Braddee *v.* Brownfield was declared not to be law.

But these parties were before the court on a former occasion. A previous act of Assembly authorized the Orphans' Court of York county, if they deemed it expedient, to appoint a trustee to make sale, &c. On the petition of Daniel, the court declined to make the order, in which case the court below said, " It is admitted on part of the petitioner that the act referred to in the petition was in no wise procured by the other heirs or legatees, but against their consent ;" and the prayer of the petitioner being opposed by them, the court refused the prayer, on the ground that it had not the constitutional power to grant it. On appeal to this court, that decree was affirmed, on the ground that the matter was submitted by the act to the discretion of the court below. It was added, however, in the *per curiam* opinion, that the case of Norris *v.* Clymer established the constitutionality of the act. That, however, was an *obitur dictum*, probably hastily thrown out, not being an element of the decision, and not sustained, in the opinion of a majority of the court, by the case of Norris *v.* Clymer.

The subsequent act, being the one now under consideration, was then passed, enjoining and ordering the court to appoint a trustee, &c. The court declined to make the order, and Daniel appeals to this court, and relies upon the *obitur dictum* in the former case. But in Norris *v.* Clymer, the case on which the *dictum* rests, all parties concerned in interest and *in esse*, so far as appears from the case reported, consented to the enactment, as well as the trustee appointed by law in place of the assigning executors, and, by themselves or their legal representatives, requested its passage. The act positively required that a majority who had vested estates should consent to the sale ; and it is to be inferred from the case that they all consented. And there was no other mode, perhaps, (although it seems to me that the powers of a court of chancery would have been adequate,) to convert the real estate into money, or change the nature of the estate in the manner mentioned in that act. The measure was eminently to the advantage of the parties ; and that case rested on the same ground as that of Estep *v.* Hutchman. In the case on hand, all the parties were of full age, labored under no disability, and could themselves sell. The object, then, of the present act, is to force a sale against the executors' consent, and against the consent of the remainder men ; and to take the property out of the hands of the executors, contrary to the will. This circumstance, alone, separates this case by an impassable gulf from Norris *v.* Clymer, which case we design not to impugn or touch. Here are individuals, all without legal

[Ervine's Appeal.]

disability, to transact their own business and take care of their own property; and the interest of some of them, and the rights of the executors under the will, attempted to be wrested from them by a summary process, unknown in any court of justice, by an *ex parte* statute. But these parties stand here under that irremovable decree of the constitution, that for any injury done an individual in his lands or goods, he shall have remedy by due course of law, in the commonwealth's courts, where right and justice shall be administered.

This court have so determined in Brown *v.* Hummel, 6 *Barr*. In closing this opinion, I may say that when, in the exercise of proper legislative powers, general laws are enacted, which bear or may bear on the whole community, if they are unjust and against the spirit of the constitution, the whole community will be interested to procure their repeal by a voice potential. And that is the great security for just and fair legislation.

But when individuals are selected from the mass, and laws are enacted affecting their property, without summons or notice, at the instigation of an interested party, who is to stand up for them, thus isolated from the mass, in injury and injustice, or where are they to seek relief from such acts of despotic power? They have no refuge but in the courts, the only secure place for determining conflicting rights by due course of law. But if the judiciary give way, and, in the language of the chief justice in Greenough *v.* Greenough, 1 *Jones*, confesses itself "too weak to stand against the antagonism of the legislature and the bar," one independent co-ordinate branch of the government will become the subservient handmaid of another, and a quiet, insidious revolution effected in the administration of the government, whilst its form on paper remains the same.

Decree of the court below affirmed.

BELL, J., dissented from the judgment pronounced, as being in direct hostility to Norris *v.* Clymer and other cases, and filed his reasons in writing; the law prohibiting the publication of dissenting opinions.

With this dissent and reasons therefor, GIBSON, C. J., concurred.

Oyster *versus* Longnecker.

1. The judge trying a cause should not withdraw the facts from the consideration of the jury, or induce the jury to infer that they are not at liberty to pass upon disputed facts; but he may express an opinion as to the tendency of the facts in evidence; and an erroneous opinion concerning facts not withdrawn from the jury, is no ground for reversal.

2. Usury is not committed by payment of a premium *less* in amount than the legal interest. The offence consists in taking more than six per cent. on the loan, and till more has been taken the penalty is not incurred.

3. A return to the lender of part of the sum on which interest is reserved, reduces the contract essentially to a loan of *the residue*. The money returned is not a premium, but a discount. Therefore, if $700 were paid to the borrower, and he immediately handed back to the lender $35, and eventually received interest on $700, the offence of usury became complete *on the actual receipt of the interest;* and every fresh taking of interest on the $700 was a fresh consummation of the same offence.

ERROR to the Common Pleas of *Cumberland county*.

This was a *qui tam* action of debt, by *Jacob* Longnecker, who sued as well for himself as for the Commonwealth of Pennsylvania, against Oyster, brought to April term 1850, under the act of 2d March 1723. The act is as follows:—

SEC. 1. No person shall directly or indirectly, for any bonds or contracts to be made after the publication of this act, take for the loan or use of money or any other commodities, above the value of six pounds for the forbearance of one hundred pounds or the value thereof, for one year, and so proportionably for a greater or lesser sum.

SEC. 2.. If any person or persons whatsoever do or shall receive or take more than six pounds per cent. per annum on any such bond or contract as aforesaid, upon conviction thereof the person or persons so offending shall forfeit the money and other things lent, one-half thereof to the governor, for the support of government, and the other half to the person who shall sue for the same, by action of debt, bill, plaint, or information, in any court of record within this province, wherein no essoin, protection, or wager of law, or any more than one imparlance shall be allowed.

The 6th section of the act of 26th March 1785 provides that all actions, &c. which shall be brought for any forfeiture upon any penal act of Assembly made or to be made, the benefit and suit whereof is or shall be by the said act limited to the commonwealth, and to any person or persons that shall prosecute in that behalf, shall be brought by any person or persons that may lawfully sue for the same, within one year next after the offence was committed; and in default of such pursuit, then the same shall be brought for the commonwealth any time within one year after that year ended, &c.

[Oyster v. Longnecker.]

It was alleged, on part of the plaintiff below, that Longnecker borrowed from Oyster, on the 27th April 1847, $665, and that he gave to Oyster an obligation dated *twelfth* day of April 1847, for $700, which was on 20th March 1850 satisfied in full.

On the part of the plaintiff, was given in evidence No. 314, January term 1847, a judgt. in favor of Oyster *v.* Isaac Longnecker. Real debt $700, by amicable action, dated 12th April 1847, with interest.

20th March 1850, acknowledgment of satisfaction in full.

Isaac Longnecker affirmed on *voir dire:*—I have no interest in this suit. I never asked my son for a cent. I did not employ counsel. I did not instruct counsel to bring the suit.

Sworn in chief:—(Paper of the 12th April 1847 shown the witness.) I told Oyster I was on the hunt of money, and heard he had some to put out; he told me he had; he asked me how much I wanted, and I told him $644. I did not get the money that day—when I came down again, he told me he could do better with his money than take simple interest, and that I must give him a premium of five per cent. I told him that was a hard case. He said if I did not choose to give it, I could not have it. I did not get the money that day. I went down again to give him a bond for the money; he then told me he had a little business at Carlisle; he would ride up with me. Then he came up, and in the office he gave me $665, and I gave him a judgment for $700. That judgment remained not quite three years, and we settled it on the 20th March 1850. I paid the whole, principal and interest, 20th March 1850; on that day I paid him, I think it was $824.

Cross-examined:—Oyster paid me $665, and not a cent more—he never did pay me $700. Nothing said about a settlement between him and me for straw. I do not know that I applied to anybody but him for the money. I was not at Squire Wills's that spring for the money, nor at Bretz's. There never was any agreement that I should pay Oyster for coming to Carlisle. The plaintiff, Jacob Longnecker, is my son. He lives with me on my farm. The stock is mine—he is in my debt for bail-money paid by me for him.

Jacob Bretz, affirmed.—I was in the prothonotary's office when the judgment was paid. Mr. Longnecker wanted Oyster to drop $35, which he had taken off him; Oyster was not agreed to it. Oyster said that he had told Longnecker the conditions on which he would give him the money, and that he had agreed to take it on those terms. Mr. Longnecker said that he was pushed for the money, and had been ill used and could not do without it. Oyster was not agreed to forgive him the $35.

Cross-examined:—Mr. Oyster did not deny at the time that he had taken the bonus. I heard nothing about Mr. Oyster saying that he had given him the money to compensate him for coming up to Carlisle.

[Oyster v. Longnecker.]

The following testimony was given on part of the defendant:—
Wm. M. Beetem, Esq., sworn:—This amicable action is in my hand-writing. The parties came into the office, and Mr. Oyster said he was about loaning to Longnecker $700, to pay a debt he owed for about that amount. Mr. Oyster requested me to draw the amicable action; I did so, and Mr. Oyster paid him down the $700. I counted the money—it was first counted by Oyster and handed to me; I counted it and handed it to Mr. Longnecker, saying it was right. After the amicable action was signed, and I had passed the money to Mr. Longnecker, they both moved to the end of the desk and had some conversation, which I think I did not hear. I saw money passing between them then at the end of the desk, and I think it was the opposite end of the desk. The notes were all large bills. Mr. Oyster did come up, I think twice, to ask me if there were any liens against Longnecker; I examined the docket, and referred him to a judgment in favor of Bretz.

Cross-examined:—A great deal of business done in the office in the spring of 1847.

On the part of defendant, points were submitted as follow:—

1. If the jury believe that the agreement between Mr. Oyster and Mr. Longnecker was that he (Oyster) was to loan to Longnecker $665, for which he was to give him an obligation for $700, and that in fact Mr. Oyster did, upon the execution of the obligation by Longneker, 12th April 1847, actually gave him $700 in money, and that Longnecker then handed him (Oyster) back the bonus of $35 of the money, the offence of usury, if any was committed, was then consummated, and the statute which limits the action to two years then began to run, and the action now trying, which was brought 30th March 1850, is barred by that statute.

2. If the jury believe that Oyster paid to Longnecker $700, and that Longnecker executed an amicable judgment for that amount and received the money, and subsequently paid to Oyster any amount as a bonus for the accommodation, then, if any offence was committed, the offence was complete on 12th April 1847, and the plea of defendant is a bar to the recovery in this case.

WATTS, President, charged as follows:—The facts of this case are so clearly proved as to be beyond any reasonable doubt. Indeed, it does not seem to be seriously argued that Mr. Longnecker did receive more than $665 from Mr. Oyster; but the counsel for the defendant has requested the court to charge the jury that "if you believe that the agreement between Mr. Oyster and Mr. Longnecker was that he (Oyster) was to loan Longnecker $665, for which he was to give him an obligation for $700, and that in fact Mr. Oyster did, upon the execution of the obligation by Longnecker, 12th April 1847, actually give him $700 in money, and that Longnecker then handed him (Oyster) back the bonus of $35 of the money, the offence of usury, if any was committed, was

[Oyster *v.* Longnecker.]

then consummated, and the statute which limits the action to two years then began to run, and the action now trying, which was brought 30th March 1850, is barred by the statute." In answer to which, we instruct you that the plaintiff's cause of action is not barred. In his declaration, he sets out that on the 20th of March 1850, the defendant received $158.43 for the forbearance of $665 for the time Mr. Longnecker had the use of the money—which, by a calculation, you will find to be the interest upon the entire principal of $700, and the bonus of $35 added, *and we instruct you that the device made use of, paying over the* $35 and immediately paying it back, is a mere fraud upon the statute, and affords the person practising it no shield from the effect of its penalty. If you believe the facts as proved, the case is as plain as facts and law can make it. The plaintiff's claim is $665. *Your verdict can make it no more, nor can you make it less.* If the plaintiff is entitled to recover, that is the amount.

The charge was excepted to by defendant's counsel.

The second point submitted, we think does not in any thing but phraseology differ from the one put and answered—but we answer it as we answered the first.

Excepted to.

Verdict was rendered for the plaintiff.

It was assigned for error:
1. The court erred in withdrawing from the consideration of the jury, the question of fact, whether or not any offence had been committed.
2. The court erred in charging the jury that the facts testified to by William M. Beetem were a fraud perpetrated on the statute, without there being any testimony in the cause showing fraud.
3. In charging the jury in the negative on defendant's second point.

Todd, for plaintiff in error.—The court assumed that $35 was paid back. There was no evidence of it: the judge should not have charged peremptorily as to it. Nothing should appear in the charge from which the jury might infer that they were precluded from considering the facts: 4 *Ser. & R.* 329; 4 *Rawle* 356; 3 *Pa. Rep.* 370; 2 *Ser. & R.* 415; 1 *W. & Ser.* 68.

As to 2d point:—The court instructed the jury that the payment of the $700 was a device and a fraud, when there was no evidence of fraud, or that there was any money handed back as a bonus. Longnecker explicitly denied any such state of facts as testified to by Beetem, who swore as to the payment of the $700, and said nothing nor knew any thing about money being paid back as a bonus. The court should have left the conflict in the testimony to the jury, to determine for themselves which of these wit-

[Oyster v. Longnecker.]

nesses told the truth, and whether or not any offence was committed.

As to 3d point:—There can be but one penalty. There must be a usurious contract at the time of the loan, and a usurious taking in pursuance of it: 4 *W. & Ser.* 453.

Hence the court should have instructed the jury that if they believed the testimony of Beetem, rather than that of Isaac Longnecker, there was no evidence of a usurious contract, and, without the finding of such a contract, the plaintiff was not entitled to recover.

Under the testimony, the court should have submitted to the jury the question whether any money had been paid on a usurious contract, or voluntarily after the contract of loan was consummated; and if in the latter mode, then the plaintiff could not recover.

Biddle, for defendant in error.—The opinion of a judge concerning facts is not the subject of a writ of error: 3 *Bin.* 80; 3 *Ser. & R.* 500. Nor the expression of the opinion of a judge as to the weight and credibility of the evidence: 10 *Barr* 296; unless it distinctly appear that the jury were led to suppose that they were precluded from judging of the facts.

It is contended that the court erred in charging the jury that the facts testified to by William M. Beetem were a fraud perpetrated on the statute without there being any testimony in the cause showing fraud. It will be perceived by a reference to the charge of the court that this is a mistake: what the judge said is in substance, that assuming the facts in the points to be true, the statute limits would not be a bar, and he added, "that the device made use of, paying over the $35 and immediately paying it back, is a mere fraud upon the statute, and affords the person practising it no protection." The rule as to this is well stated in *Comyn on Usury* 117: "It signifies not in what shape the profit on the money lent is to accrue: it is sufficient that such profit should exceed the legal rate, in order to bring the transaction within the statute." And as to the statute of limitations, the very case cited on the other side, Lamb v. Lindsey, 4 *W. & Ser.* 449, decides the point. It was there held by the court that "under the act of 2d of March 1723, the offence of taking usurious interest is committed by every successive receipt of such interest, and under the 6th section of the act of 26th of March 1785, a suit to recover the penalty may be brought within a year after the last successive receipt of such interest."

GIBSON, C. J.—It is settled that usury is not committed by payment of a premium less in amount than the legal interest. The offence consists by the statute, in taking more than six per cent. on the loan; and till more has been taken, the penalty is not incurred. Lamb v.

[Oyster v. Longnecker.]

Lindsey, 4 *W. & Ser.* 449; Fisher *v.* Beasly, 1 *Doug.* 235; Wade *v.* Wilson, 1 *East* 195, and Scurry *v.* Freeman, 2 *Bos. & Pul.* 381, are sufficient for the principle. The only cases that might seem to collide with them, are Musgrove *v.* Gibbs, 1 *Dal.* 216, and Kirkpatrick *v.* Houston, 4 *W. & Ser.* 115, which ruled that any taking of interest, however small, on a usurious contract, is a completion of the offence. A distinction between interest and a bonus may seem to be a flimsy one; but it is not. A return of part of the sum on which interest is reserved, reduces the contract essentially to a loan of the residue. The formal delivery of the whole with one hand, and the retrenchment of a part of it with the other, like the formal delivery of a chattel returned at the execution of a bill of sale of it, is, in either case, simply a transparent artifice to elude the statute. The money returned, unlike the silk gown sometimes exacted by a wife for joining in a conveyance, is not a premium, but a discount; and the detention of part of a bank loan, as payment of interest in advance, is legalized only by inveterate custom. If there was such a detention in this case, the contract for the nominal sum was usurious, but the offence was not committed till something had been received on it. In this view of the subject, it would seem to be indifferent whether the sum detained were greater than the amount of the interest or not: payment of interest on the usurious loan would still be necessary. But the point is immaterial, as the whole interest was taken within the period of limitation; for it was ruled in Lamb *v.* Lindsey, and Scurry *v.* Freeman, the latter of which is precisely like the case we have to deal with, that every fresh taking is a fresh consummation of the same offence.

Judgment affirmed.

COULTER, J., objected to the manner in which the evidence as to the receipt of usury had been submitted to the jury.

Walls *versus* Stewart.

1. A testator devised to his son Eli, his heirs and assigns for ever, two tracts of land, *subject nevertheless to, and charged and chargeable with* the payment of six hundred dollars, to certain of the children of his son Joseph, to be paid to them or the survivors, share and share alike, viz: "one-half of the said sum to be paid one year after his decease, and the other half two years after his decease, which sum of six hundred I do hereby bequeath to my said grandchildren, to be paid them as above stated and directed, and I do hereby charge the payment of the same on the tracts or parcels of land herein and hereby devised to my said son Eli, his heirs and assigns."
After the execution of his will, the testator sold the devised lands to his son James for part cash and the major part of the purchase-money in payments, which did not become due till after the testator's death. He devised to others of his children and grand-children pecuniary legacies; and he further directed that after the legacies and debts were paid, the balance of his estate should be equally divided amongst all his children, and the children of any that are deceased, share and share alike: *Held*, that as the legacy charged on the land devised to Eli, was to be paid by him as devisee in respect of the devise, and as a means of distribution among the testator's children, the land being the sole source of payment, the sale of the land by the testator effected an ademption of the legacy.

2. If a legacy be given with reference to a particular fund, only as pointing out a convenient mode of payment, it is to be considered *demonstrative*, and the legatee will not be disappointed, though the fund wholly fail. But where the gift is of the fund itself, in whole or in part, or so charged upon the object made subject to it, as to show an intent to burden that object alone with the payment, it is esteemed *specific*, and consequently liable to be ademed by the alienation or destruction of the object. In such matters, the *intention* of the testator is principally to be ascertained; and it is necessary, in order to render a legacy specific, that the intention so to make it, clearly appear. Per BELL, J. See this opinion as to specific and demonstrative legacies.

ERROR to the Common Pleas of *Huntingdon county.*
John Walls, being the owner of three farms, made his will on the 13th day of July 1844, wherein and whereby he devised one of these farms to his son *Eli*, his heirs and assigns for ever; subject nevertheless to, and charged and chargeable with a legacy of $600 to the children of *Joseph* Walls, the defendants in error. On the 27th of May 1847, the said John Walls, being still in full life, agreed to sell to his son *James* Walls, for the sum of $3000, the farm he had previously devised to Eli Walls, and upon which the legacy of $600 to defendants in error was charged by the will of the said John Walls as aforesaid; and on the 16th day of August, 1847, the said John Walls and wife, executed their deed for the land aforesaid to James Walls in fee simple. John Walls died the 17th day of July 1848, and his will, made as aforesaid on the 13th of July 1844, was duly proven on the 30th of July 1848, and same day letters testamentary were granted to the defendants below.

This amicable action, which was in the form of a case stated, was by the children of *Joseph* Walls, the defendants in error, to

[Walls v. Stewart.]

recover from the executors of the testator, John Walls, deceased, plaintiffs in error, the $600 legacy, charged on the devise to Eli Walls by the will of their grandfather, John Walls, as aforesaid; who, after making his will containing said devise to Eli and this legacy of $600 charged thereupon, sold and conveyed to James Walls the lands so as aforesaid devised to Eli, and upon which the legacy in controversy in this case was charged by his will.

The case stated was as follows:—

J. Sewall Stewart, Guardian of Isaac Walls, Margaret Walls, Susannah Walls, and George Walls, *vs.* James Walls and Rebecca Walls, executors of John Walls, deceased. In the Court of Common Pleas of Huntingdon county, No. 70, August term 1850. Amicable action of debt for a legacy under the will of John Walls, deceased, late of West township; and case stated therein for the opinion of the court.

On the thirteenth day of July, A. D. eighteen hundred and forty-four, John Walls made and executed his last will and testament, and died on the seventeenth day of July, A. D. eighteen hundred and forty-eight, leaving as executors thereof his son James Walls, and his daughter Rebecca Walls, which said will was duly proven in the register's office of Huntingdon county, on the thirtieth day of July, A. D. eighteen hundred and forty-eight, and letters testamentary granted to said executors. The said testator, in his said will, among other things, bequeathed to his grand-children, Isaac, Margaret, Susannah, and George Walls, children of his son Joseph Walls, the sum of six hundred dollars, the one-half thereof to be paid in one year after his decease, and the remaining half in two years thereafter, by virtue of the following clause, *pro ut* said will:—

"Thirdly.—To my son Eli Walls I do give and devise all that farm, plantation, or tract of land, on which he now lives, as surveyed and divided off and its boundaries designated by William Reed, Esq., the 10th June 1831, containing seventy-eight acres and eighty-five perches and allowance, &c., and also thirty-three acres and thirty-nine perches of woodland, part of a larger tract surveyed on a warrant in the name of George Wilson, the said part being surveyed off at the same time, and designed by me to belong to the above-mentioned tract or parcel of farm land; which two tracts or parcels of land I do give and devise to my said son Eli, his heirs and assigns for ever; *subject nevertheless to, and charged and chargeable with* the payment of six hundred dollars to Isaac, Margaret, Susannah, and George Walls, children of my son *Joseph* Walls, to be paid to them or the survivor or survivors of them, (if any of them should die without issue before the six hundred dollars be paid,) share and share alike, as follows, that is to say, one-half of the said sum to be paid one year after my decease, and the other half two years after my decease; which sum of six hundred dollars *I do hereby*

[Walls v. Stewart.]

bequeath to my said grand-children, *to be paid them as above stated and directed*, and I do hereby charge the payment of the same on the tracts or parcels of land herein and hereby devised to my said son Eli, his heirs and assigns."

The whole of which said will is made part of this case stated.

The said testator, by articles of agreement, dated the twenty-ninth day of May, A. D. eighteen hundred and forty-seven, (*pro ut* the said articles,) agreed to sell and convey all the lands mentioned and described in the above devise to his son Eli, to his son James Walls, for the sum of three thousand dollars, payable as follows, to wit:

$1000.00	on the first of April	1848.
333.33½	"	1849.
333.33½	"	1850.
333.33½	"	1851.
333.33½	"	1852.
333.33½	"	1853.
333.33½	"	1854.

To be secured by bond and mortgage; the deed to be made on or before the first day of April, eighteen hundred and forty-eight. In pursuance of the said agreement, the said testator and Susan his wife, on the sixteenth day of August, eighteen hundred and forty-seven, made and executed their deed of conveyance for the lands mentioned in the said article of agreement, (*pro ut* the said deed, being the same lands devised to Eli Walls, by the said testator in his will,) to their son James Walls, his heirs and assigns for ever, the said James Walls having paid and secured to be paid the purchase-money therefor. The whole of which said articles of agreement and deed are made part of this case.

The inventory returned by the said executors into the register's office of Huntingdon county, shows a personal estate amounting to $6981.25, which includes the unpaid purchase-money then owing on said sale, (*pro ut* the said inventory.) The whole of which said inventory is made part of this case.

The said J. Sewall Stewart was appointed guardian of the said Isaac, Margaret, Susannah, and George Walls, by the Orphans' Court of said county, on the 20th August 1849, who gave security on the 18th of September, 1849, agreeably to the order of the court.

If, on the above and foregoing state of facts, the court shall be of the opinion that the case is with the plaintiff, the judgment to be entered for the plaintiff for $600, with interest on $300 thereof from the 17th day of June, 1849, and interest on the remaining $300 from the 17th day of June, 1850; and if the court shall be of opinion that the case is with the defendants, then judgment to be entered for the defendants.

[Walls v. Stewart.]

Each party reserves the right to take a writ of error.

Defendants' attorney objecting to the item of interest on the legacy as set forth and claimed in the above statement of the case, it is hereby agreed that the interest, if any, and what amount and when payable, shall be for the determination of the court upon the facts stated in this case, and made part of their opinion, if the said court shall be of opinion that the plaintiff is entitled to recover the legacy aforesaid, each party reserving a right to writ of error as aforesaid.

It was signed by counsel.

After preliminary matter, the first, sixth, seventh, and ninth items of the will of John Walls, the testator, were as follow:—

1st. I do order and direct that all my personal property (except what may hereinafter be otherwise disposed of) be sold by my executors at public sale, as soon after my decease as practicable, and also that all moneys due and owing to me be by them collected as soon as possible.

6thly. To each of my four daughters, Mary, Rebecca, Sarah, (intermarried with Jacob Walls,) and Elizabeth, (intermarried with John Jacobs,) I give and bequeath the sum of $600; the sums heretofore given by me to three of my said daughters to be reckoned as so much paid on the legacies now herein and hereby bequeated to them respectively and to be deducted therefrom, that is to say, $170 paid by me to my daughter Rebecca, to be retained and deducted out of the $600 dollars now bequeathed to her; $387 paid by me to my daughter Elizabeth Jacobs, to be retained and deducted out of the $600 now bequeathed to her; and $360 heretofore paid by me to my daughter Sarah Walls, to be retained and deducted out of the $600 now bequeathed to her; the said legacies to be paid by my executors to my said daughters in three equal annual payments without interest, the first payment to be made in one year after my decease.

7thly. To Isabella Paxton and Juliann Paxton, children of my daughter Susannah Paxton, now deceased, I give and bequeath each $50, and to Aaron, Isaac, Azariah, and John Paxton, children of my said daughter Susannah, each the sum of $5; the said legacies to these my grand-children to be paid by my executors within one year after my decease.

9thly. It is my will, and I do order and direct that after the death of my beloved wife Susannah, all my household and other personal property, heretofore directed to be retained for the use of my said wife, shall be sold by my said executors; and after all the legacies hereinbefore bequeathed, and all debts and expenses, including the expense of supporting with necessaries my said wife, shall be paid, I do order and direct that the balance and residue of my estate, if any, shall be equally divided amongst all my children, and the children of any that are or may be deceased, share

[Walls v. Stewart]

and share alike; the children of any that may be deceased to have divided amongst them the share that would fall to the parent, if living.

Lastly. I do hereby nominate, constitute and appoint my son, James Walls, and my daughter, Rebecca Walls, to be the executors of this my last will and testament.

April 19, 1851, judgment was rendered for plaintiff for $647.60.

It was assigned for error:

The court erred in giving judgment for defendants in error for the legacy of $600 with full interest, when, from the facts stated, and the law of the case, judgment should have been given for the plaintiffs in error.

The case was argued by *D. Blair*, for the executors, plaintiffs in error.—He contended that the legacy in question was charged on the land devised, and the land having been sold by the testator, the legacy *was adeemed*. The following authorities were cited: *Dunlop's Dig.* 1st ed. 521, sec. 59, act of 1834; 1 *Rop. on Legacies* 152, sec. 2; Downer v. Downer, 9 *Watts* 60–3; Cuthbert v. Cuthbert, 3 *Yeates* 486; Blackstone v. Blackstone, 3 *Watts* 335; Alsop's Appeal and Riley's Appeal, 9 *Barr* 374; Richardson v. Brown, 4 *Vesey* 377; *Ward on Legacies* 27, 21; 2 *Jarmin on Wills* (marginal page) 594; *Ram on Assets* 124; *Law Lib.* No. 22, April No. 1835, 84; Gettins v. Steele, 1 *Swans.* 24; Arnold v. Arnold, 1 *Brown's Ch. C.* 401; Bridges v. Phillips, 6 *Vesey* 571; Ashbruner v. Maguire, 2 *Brown's Ch. Rep.* 109; 1 *Rop. on Legacies* 151–2; *id.* 149; Walton v. Walton, 7 *Johns. Rep.* 258; Tole v. Hardy, 6 *Cow.* 333; Cryder's Appeal, 1 *Jones*, 72; Page v. Leapingwell, 18 *Vesey* 463; 2 *Freeman's Rep.* 21 and 24.

J. S. Stewart, with whom was *S. S. Wharton*, for defendants in error, contended that the legacy was not adeemed; that it should be declared to be demonstrative, that is, a legacy of so much money, and payable out of a particular fund.

The question in this case is, whether the legacy of $600 given by John Walls to the children of Joseph Walls is specific or demonstrative. If specific, it is adeemed by the sale made by the testator in his lifetime of the land or fund upon which it was charged. If demonstrative, it is payable out of his general estate; 1 *Rop.* 150.

A specific legacy is the bequest of *a particular thing*, so described by the testator in his will as to distinguish it from all other things in his possession. In this case there is no specific money or thing given to Joseph's children; but simply a general legacy of six hundred dollars, with the property devised to Eli charged with its payment. If specific at all, it must be so in con-

[Walls v. Stewart.]

sequence of a specified property being appropriated to bear that burden, and that in such way as to manifest an intention to give the very property, or part of the very property itself, or the proceeds, under a direction to sell. Here no specified part of the farm devised to Eli was given as these children's legacy, or in lieu of it; neither were the proceeds of a sale of it, nor a rent issuing out of it, nor a term of which it was the subject,—which have been held to be specific. It is merely a bequest of $600, *charged upon the land as a security for its payment*, without any intention manifested *to give the security itself*, or any part of it. There is no adjudged case in which a legacy, considered one of quantity, with a fund, either real or personal, upon which its payment is merely charged, has been held to be specific; but such cases have been universally held to be *in the nature of specific or demonstrative:* 1 *Roper* 192–3. The land was to be merely subject to the payment, and it is not directed in the will that Eli shall pay it.

A demonstrative legacy is one of *mere quantity*, with a specific fund appropriated for its payment; the mention of the fund being considered rather by way of demonstration than of condition; rather showing how or by what means the legacy may be paid, than whether it shall be paid at all: *Ward on Legacies* 21, (margin;) 1 *Roper* 150.

A gross sum given out of a term or estate, considered demonstrative: 1 *Roper* 153–4; *Ram on Assets* 121, (marginal page.) A legacy charged upon land is demonstrative: Saville v. Blacket, 1 *Peere Williams* 778–9; Hoover v. Hoover, 5 *Barr* 351–56; Fowler v. Willoughby, cited in 1 *Roper* 154. Courts are desirous of constructing the bequests to be general: Walton v. Walton, 7 *Johns. C. Rep.* 263; Blackstone v. Blackstone, 3 *Watts* 339.

In the ninth item of the will, the testator directs, after the death of his wife, all his personal property to be sold, and after *all* the legacies thereinbefore bequeathed, &c. shall be paid, then disposes of the residue, which is an indication that the legacy in question is a general one.

A legacy to be paid by the devisee of a farm was held *not* specific: *Ward on Legacies* 29, (margin;) Cotterell v. Chamberlain, *Bunbury's Rep.* 32.

The opinion of the court was delivered June 12, by

BELL, J.—As is truly said in Walton v. Walton, 7 *Johns. Ch. Rep.* 258, and elsewhere, in applying the doctrine of ademption, it is sometimes extremely difficult to perceive the distinction attempted to be kept up between specific, demonstrative, and general pecuniary legacies. Many of the English cases rest upon points of difference so refined as often to baffle the most microscopic examination; a subtlety referable to an anxious desire to treat bequests as general or demonstrative, wherever the slightest pretext can be

[Walls v. Stewart.]

found for such a construction. This is particularly observable where a bequest is charged on or refers to a personal fund as the source of payment; of which the English books offer a large variety of perplexing instances, owing to the very general practice which there obtains of investing in stocks and other public securities. The courts are disinclined to recognise specific legacies, because of their liability to sink with the destruction of the thing bequeathed or the fund charged. But as it was obviously impossible to esteem as purely pecuniary many of the testamentary gifts which judges inclined to withdraw from the class of specific legacies, they were driven to borrow from the civilians a term thought to be descriptive of a species of donation holding a middle place between specific and pecuniary, the only kinds distinctly recognised when Swinburne wrote. They are called *demonstrative*, and, like general legacies, are gifts of mere quantity, but differ from these by being referred to a particular fund for payment. They are so far general, that if the particular fund be called in or fail, the legatees will be permitted to receive their legacies out of the general assets; yet so far specific as not to be subject to abatement, with general legacies, on a deficiency of assets. They are thus specific in one sense, and pecuniary in another; specific, as given out of a particular fund, and not out of the estate at large; pecuniary, as consisting only of definite sums of money, and not amounting to a gift of the fund itself, or any aliquot part of it, the mention of the fund being considered rather by way of demonstration than of condition—rather as showing how or by what means the legacy may be paid, than whether it shall be paid at all: Smith v. Fitzgerald, 3 *Vesey & B.* 2; *Ward on Legacies* 21. A familiar instance, given in the last book cited, is of a bequest of £10, *which J. S. owes to the testator:* when in truth J. S. does not owe any such money, the gift fails; but if he gives £10, and wills that the same be paid out of the money he has in a certain place, or out of a particular debt due to him, the devise is good, notwithstanding there should appear to be no money in the place or no such debt owing. The distinction seems to be this:—If a legacy be given with reference to a particular fund, only as pointing out a convenient mode of payment, it is considered demonstrative, and the legatee will not be disappointed though the fund totally fail. But where the gift is of the fund itself, in whole or in part, or so charged upon the object made subject to it as to show an intent to burden that object alone with the payment, it is esteemed specific, and consequently liable to be adeemed by the alienation or destruction of the object. In this, as in other questions springing from the construction of wills, the intention of the testator is principally to be ascertained, and it is said to be necessary that the intention be either expressed in reference to the thing bequeathed, or otherwise clearly appear from the will, to constitute

[Walls v. Stewart.]

a legacy specific. If it be manifest there was a fixed and independent intent to give the legacy, separate and distinct from the property designated as the source of payment, the legacy will be deemed general or demonstrative, though accompanied by a direction to pay it out of a particular estate or fund specially named. Of the application of this principle, Mann v. Copland, 2 *Mad.* 223, is a pregnant example. There a testator bequeathed to his servant an annuity of £10 during life, to be paid out of the rents of a certain freehold, if the testator's brother would cancel a conveyance theretofore made of the freehold; if not, he directed £200 to be secured out of £2000, 5 *per cent.* Navy, in trust for the servant during life. The question was, whether the bequest was general or specific, for, if the latter, it could not take effect. Sir THOMAS PLUMER, V. C., determined, on the construction of the will, the legacy was not specific, for he thought the intention was clearly marked to give the legacy in every event: that it was not so connected with the fund as to fail if there was no such fund, it appearing there was *a fixed, independent, separate, and distinct* intent to give the legacy, the particular property out of which it was to be paid being a secondary thought. The determination was evidently influenced by the direction consequent upon the anticipated refusal of the testator's brother to cancel the prior conveyance of the freehold. In Long v. Short, 1 *P. Wms.* 403, where, excepting the feature just noticed, the disposition was similar, the determination was different. It was a bequest of £40 a year to B for life, *out of* the testator's chattel estate at R. and £10 a year to C for life, *out* of the same estate which he devised to D. And Lord Chancellor COWPER decreed these bequests to be specific, remarking that the devise of a rent-charge out of a term is as much a specific devise as if it had been of the term itself. The subsequent case of Creed v. Creed, 1 *Drury & Warren* 416, was decided by the House of Lords upon somewhat broader grounds. The testator gave an annuity or yearly rent-charge of so much for "life, charged upon and payable out of all my real and freehold estate and property, (except Ballynanty,) and I do hereby charge and encumber the same therewith, and also empower the annuitant to take all and every remedy for recovery thereof, as in cases of rent-service, as usual." He then gave several general legacies, irrespective of any particular fund for payment, and in a subsequent clause directed them to be paid out of his personal estate remaining after payment of debts; and such part of such legacies as should remain unpaid out of the personal estate, was to be raised and paid by *his executors,* out of his real and freehold properties, (except Ballynanty,) " and I do hereby charge and encumber the same therewith." The judgment was delivered by Lord COTTENHAM, who said that the rule laid down by Lord HARDWICKE, in Lewin v. Lewin, 2 *Vesey. Sen.* 416, that all simple gifts of annuities are held to be pecuniary

[Walls v. Stewart.]

legacies, had no application to the gift of a rent-charge or annuity arising out of land, "for that is an *interest in the land itself*, and necessarily specific," and he accordingly decreed the annuities in question to be so. But of the after given legacies he remarked that, though charged on the land on a deficiency of the personalty, it would not alter their character or make them specific; and he added, "general legacies do not, necessarily become specific, because they are payable out of the proceeds of real estate, but the gift of the proceeds of real estate may be specific, as in Page v. Leapingwell," 18 *Vesey* 463.

The principle of construction will be found the same where a gross sum is charged upon or directed to be paid out of the proceeds of realty. If an intention is apparent to give the legacy at all events, though with reference to a fund for its payment, the legatees' remedy is not as of course confined to the fund adverted to. This, indeed, is often considered as merely auxiliary in aid of the personal assets. Of this class is Savile v. Blacket, 1 *P. Wms.* 778, where A, having a power of charging lands, (which power he afterwards destroyed) bequeathed to his child £1000 out of the lands, and also £1000 charged on the personal estate. The power to charge having failed, the question was whether the first bequest was not specific, and, therefore, a failure. But Lord MACCLESFIELD, on the ground that the testator intended to give two sums of £1000 each, though one was directed to be paid out of the land, decreed that the failure of the *modus* appointed for payment should not defeat it. This case can only be reconciled with prior and subsequent determinations, on the foot that the reference to the land chargeable under the power was for convenience, and secondary to the main intent. In remarking upon it, Mr. *Roper*, in his treatise upon legacies, says the principle of the decision was the intention of the testator not to make the legacy dependent on the due execution of his power, but to bequeath a sum equivalent to what he was entitled to charge on the estate, with reference to that estate as the primary fund for the payment of it; and that such appeared to the court to be the testator's design, upon the construction of the whole will. It is also said that Fowler v. Willoughby, 2 *Sim. & Stu.* 354 was ruled on the same principle. It was a bequest of £1400, to be raised, for the benefit of the testator's two children, by the sale of an estate for which he had, just before, contracted. After his death, it was found the contract could not be enforced against his assets; and the question arose, whether the legacy could take effect, though it could not be raised in the manner directed by the will? Sir JOHN LEACH, declaring it was neither *legatum nominis* nor *legatum debiti*, but a pecuniary legacy with a particular security, directed that it should be paid out of the testator's general estate, as a demonstrative legacy.

Wilcox v. Rhodes, 2 *Russ.* 452, is another instance of the same

[Walls v. Stewart.]

kind. The testator had given, with other legacies, £500 to the plaintiff for life, with remainder to her children, and added, "*I guaranty* my leasehold in, &c. for the payment of the above legacies." The leaseholds failed, and it was insisted, that being exclusively charged upon them, the legacies were specific. But the vice chancellor, and afterwards Lord ELDON, on appeal, held the legacies were general, and, consequently, charges on the general personal estate, the property particularly specified being merely an auxiliary fund in case the personalty should be found deficient. In the still more recent case of Newbold v. Roadknight, 1 *Russ. & M.* 677, Fowler v. Willoughby was cited by the eminent counsel who argued for the plaintiff, as ruling the question agitated in the principal case. It presented a devise of lands to trustees to sell, and, out of the proceeds thereof, to pay to A £1000, and to divide the residue among certain persons named. This was followed by a gift of other lands and of personal property, in trust to sell the same and divide the avails among the same persons. Afterwards, the testator sold and conveyed the land first devised. In answer to the argument I have noticed, Sir THOMAS PLUMER, in pronouncing the judgment, said, "The gift to one of a sum of money, part of the produce of real estate directed to be sold, followed by a gift of the residue of the purchase-money to others, is *substantially a gift of the estate, and not a gift of legacies with a collateral charge on the estate.* This distinguishes the present case from Fowler v. Willoughby, and the legacy to A is therefore adeemed."

This reasoning, it will be perceived, is in accordance with that which governed the determination in Creed v. Creed, and will, also, be found to harmonize with many other cases in the books, some of which I shall have occasion more particularly to notice. Indeed, I think an examination of the authorities, English and American, will show that wherever an intent is exhibited to make distribution of the value of lands, either by means of a sale and division of proceeds, or by the charge of a sum *in numero*, payable by the devisee of the land as a *quasi* partial purchase of the estate devised, the bequests are always treated as specific, and, consequently, liable to be adeemed by an alienation of the land in the lifetime of the testator. I may add, this is also true where the only gift of a legacy is found in the direction to pay it out of the land devised: 2 *Jarman on Wills* 593, and the cases there cited; or, as it is elsewhere expressed, where a testator charges his real estate with a sum of money, and then bequeaths the sum so charged: Dickin v. Edwards, 4 *Har.* 273; though it is commonly otherwise where there is a distinct bequest, afterwards generally charged on the lands of the donor.

Among the earlier illustrations of these rules of construction is an anonymous case, reported in 2 *Freem. Ch. Ca.* 21. It was there ruled, that if a man gives a legacy and charges it on Black

[Walls v. Stewart.]

acre, although this be not sufficient to answer the full value of the legacy, yet it shall not be charged on the personal estate. So, if one devises £100, *out* of a lease for years, and the lease be determined, yet the legatee shall never resort to the personal estate for this legacy. The same book (*Ca.* 124) furnishes us with the report of Colchester *v.* Lord Stamford, in which TREVOR held, that "if a man hath two daughters, and deviseth to one £1000 out of his real estate, and to another £1000 out of his personal estate, then if the real estate be evicted, that legacy is lost, and shall never come into average with the other on the personal estate." So far as I am informed, these determinations have never been called into question. On the contrary, they are frequently cited in other precedents, as furnishing authoritative ground upon which the inquirer may safely stand, and a basis for future decision. They have been followed by a multitude of others to the same effect. Of some of these I may be pardoned a particular notice, as affording reliable guides through the somewhat intricate mazes of this branch of our law. Among the first which present themselves, in point of time, is Whaley *v.* Cox, 2 *Eq. Ca. Abr.* 549. It was a devise of land charged with the payment of a legacy of £500, followed by this clause: "I have devised the said estate to my nephew Cox, on condition he pay the said £500." It was ruled by Sir JOSEPH JEKYLL that, though both the condition and devise were void, the devisee being the heir at law, yet, as these showed the intention of the testator, the land was liable in the first instance.

In Gittins *v.* Steele, 1 *Swan.* 24, a legacy of £7000 was charged upon certain freehold and leasehold estates, devised in trust to sell the same and pay the legacy out of the purchase-money. The testator afterwards sold some of the devised estates, and the sum produced by a sale of the remaining portion, after his death, was insufficient to pay the legacy. On a question made, whether the legatee was entitled to come in on the personal assets for the balance, Lord ELDON decided the personal estate was not subject to pay any part of it. "Legatees," said he, "as volunteers, are not entitled to resort to any other than the particular fund the testator or the law has assigned." "Entertaining no doubt that the intention of the testator has been frustrated by a subsequent sale of a part of his estates, I am not authorized to advert to that fact as affecting the construction of the will. I am bound, as a judge, to assume that the testator supposed he should leave, at his decease, freehold and leasehold estates sufficient for the payment of the legacy of £7000; and I protest as being understood to give my judgment on the ground of the subsequent sale. My duty is to apply the funds which, at his death, are applicable, by the operation of the will, to the payment of this legacy. If they are insufficient, the court, whatever may be the hardship of the case, cannot supply other funds." I have cited

[Walls v. Stewart.]

these remarks somewhat at length, as furnishing an answer to the considerations of supposed hardship which, on the part of the defendant in error, were urged on us in argument.

Amesbury v. Brown, 1 *Vesey, Sen.* 481, is a striking instance of the same class. The testator devised his estate generally, after payment of his debts, but, in this part of the will, said nothing about legacies. Then followed bequests to his four sisters, and, in the same clause, he added, " all which legacies I mean shall be paid out of my freehold estate at N." It was insisted, for the devisee, that a legacy generally given is payable out of the personal estate, and though afterwards made a charge on the real, yet, as the heir is not likely to be disinherited, the court looks to it that unless the personalty is expressly exempted, the legacies shall be payable out of the latter assets. But Lord HARDWICKE answered, " This is not within the common rule, not being a common charge on the real, in aid of the personal, but an express encumbrance upon that estate; an express gift of the legacy out of the real estate, which, wherever done, the real must bear the burden.

Then followed Reade v. Litchfield, 3 *Vesey* 475. The will directed a term to be raised out of the testator's real estate, upon which he charged several sums in favor of his children *nominatim*. It was held, that as he intended these as a provision for his children, and a charge upon his real property *by way of distributing it among his family*, the personal estate was not applicable to their payment.

Spurway v. Glynn, 9 *Vesey, Jr.* 483, is to the same effect. There was a devise of estates in certain counties, (except the estate called Portledge,) subject to debts, funeral and testamentary expenses, and pecuniary legacies thereafter given. Then followed a devise of the Portledge estate, in trust to demise, sell, or mortgage the same, or out of the rents and profits, to make up the sum of £400, and pay the same to the plaintiff; and after payment thereof, and *subject thereto*, upon trust for J. P. for life, with remainder over. The testator then made specific bequests of chattels, and gave some pecuniary legacies, and directed the residue of his personal effects to be turned into money and applied in payment of his debts and legacies, in exoneration of his real estate; and if any thing remained of these proceeds, he gave it to the devisees of the first-named estate. Upon the intention of the testator, it was decreed by Sir WILLIAM GRANT that the £400 was a charge exclusively upon the Portledge estate, with the observation, " There is no direct bequest to the plaintiff of £400, but that sum is directed to be raised out of the particular estate and paid to him; and the general words at the close of the will clearly refer to the first devise, and were intended to exonerate the estates there charged."

These determinations but follow the earlier case of Ward v.

[Walls v. Stewart.]

Dudley, 2 *Bro. C. R.* 316. After a gift of certain real estate to the defendant, the testator proceeded, "I charge the last-mentioned estate with the payment, as well of the said sum of £5000, (a sum stipulated in a prior marriage settlement) as of the further sum of £5000," &c. The devisee insisted these sums were first payable out of the personal estate. But Lord THURLOW said "there was no ground for argument. This is, clearly, a *real devise;* it is purely a gift out of the real estate, and cannot fall upon the personalty."

I shall notice but three other English cases, which, though occurring under wills containing directions to sell, proceed upon the same principles. They are, indeed, in that respect, like Gittins v. Steele. The first of them is Brydges v. Phillips, 6 *Vesey* 567. The devise was of all the testator's lands, in trust to sell so much thereof as might be deemed expedient, and with the proceeds, in the first place to pay debts, and in the next place to raise and pay to his half-sister £1000; and, in the last place, to pay to his wife £4000; with a devise over of all the residue of his unsettled real estate. Sir WILLIAM GRANT decreed these legacies a charge exclusively on the land devised, saying, "Legacies given, payable out of the real estate, must be paid out of the real estate, for there is no other fund. They have no existence but by the will, and must come out of the fund the testator points out."

The next case, Hancock v. Abbey, 11 *Vesey* 179, is very decisive of the grounds of distinction I have ventured to deduce from the authorities. It was a devise of all the testator's lands, upon trust to sell so much of the same as should be sufficient for after-mentioned purposes, and to apply the proceeds to discharge a mortgage of £3000, and to raise the sum of £2000, which he bequeathed to his two daughters, to be invested for their benefit; his wife to have the usufruct of the residue of his real estate during life, and afterwards to go to his said daughters in fee. The residue of his personal estate, after payment of his debts, legacies, and funeral expenses, was given to his wife. Upon a question made whether the personal estate ought not to be called on for payment of the two sums of £3000 and £2000, in relief of the realty, it was insisted for the daughters, that a general charge on real estate, followed by a residuary bequest of personalty, does not exonerate the latter estate; and besides, by this will, the personal assets were expressly subjected to debts and legacies. But the master of the rolls answered, he could not consider this as a general legacy; for the sum is given only *as a part of the produce of the real estate.* The daughters, therefore, could claim it only in that shape.

The remaining case, drawn from the English Chancery, is Page v. Leapingwell, 18 *Vesey* 463, noticed in Creed v. Creed. Without

[Walls v. Stewart.]

here particularly stating its general features, it may suffice to say it asserts the same doctrine which governed in the two last cases.

To these overruling authorities it is scarely necessary to add any thing further than our own recent cases of Cryder's Appeal, 1 *Jones Rep.* 72, and Balliot's Appeal, 2 *Harris* 451. The first of these arose under a direction to sell and apply the proceeds of realty in discharge of certain legacies bequeathed; and the last was a devise of land, *subject* in the hands of the devisees to the payment of a certain aggregate sum, given by the same will to named legatees. In both it was ruled the legacies were specific, and in the latter that they were adeemed by sale of the land charged, by the testator in his lifetime. Although, in delivering the judgment in the last case, some stress is laid upon features peculiar to the will, it is obvious both determinations are based on the doctrine I have brought to view, that although a legacy is not necessarily *specific*, because referred to a particular fund as a means of payment, yet, if it be not only charged on real estate, but deducted from its value in the hands of the devisee, the legatee is confined to that fund alone.

Downer v. Downer, 9 *Watts* 63; S. C. 9 *Barr* 302; Lobach's case, 6 *Watts* 167; Shickler v. Shaeffer, 5 *Barr* 440; Read v. Read, (in note to last case;) Hoover v. Hoover, 5 *id.* 351; Miltenberger v. Schlegel, 7 *id.* 241; Mohler's Appeal, 8 *id.* 27, and Schaeffer's Appeal, *id.* 38, all point in the same direction. They all proceed upon the ground that a legacy directly charged upon land devised is payable out of the land alone, or personally by the devisee, who by accepting the thing devised makes himself responsible; and that the remedy is in the Orphans' Court, against the devisee, or other holder of the estate, without reference to the executor named in the will, who, as such, has no interest in the subject of controversy.

By the will before us, the legacy here sought to be recovered is directly charged upon the land devised to Eli Walls, to be paid by him as devisee, in respect of the devise, and as a means of distribution among the testator's children. It was regarded by the devisor as the sole source of payment, and therefore, according to the cases I have passed in review, the sale of the principal thing by the testator destroyed its accessory, the legacy. The sale may have frustrated the intention entertained in favor of the plaintiff below, but however we may regret this, we can but repeat the declaration of Lord ELDON, in Gittins v. Steele, that it is not in the power of the court to supply other means of payment than those pointed to by the creator of the intended gift.

Something was said, in the argument, of a supposed efficacy found in the ninth clause of the will, to save the legacy in question. But it is perfectly obvious that the words there used, "after

[Walls v. Stewart.]

all the legacies hereinbefore bequeathed," have reference only to the pecuniary legacies just before given in the sixth and seventh clauses of the will. A similar direction occurred in Brydges v. Phillips, (*supra*,) and was construed in the same way.

As our conclusions are adverse to the plaintiff below, the judgment rendered on the case stated, by the Court of Common Pleas, must be reversed, and judgment entered here for the defendants below.

Judgment accordingly.

McCulloch *versus* McKee.

1. Parol evidence is receivable in Pennsylvania to prove that a bond was fraudulently obtained, or that the consideration has failed.
2. An agent having authority only *to collect a debt*, has no right to take a note for the amount of it, from the debtor to himself, and thus substitute himself as creditor; but if such an arrangement be afterwards *ratified* by the principal, the latter is bound by it, and the debtor is released from liability to the principal on the original claim.

ERROR to the Common Pleas of *Cumberland county*.

This was an action of debt, commenced before a justice of the peace, and brought by the defendant, David J. McKee, into the Common Pleas by appeal. The action was commenced by David W. McCulloch, for use of James H. Spriggs, against David J. McKee, to recover the amount of a sealed note, bearing date the 27th day of March 1844, signed and sealed by David J. McKee, the defendant, for the sum of $53.28, payable ten days after date, with interest, to David W. McCulloch or order.

The plaintiff filed his statement in the Common Pleas, setting forth his claim, and the defendant entered the plea of "payment with leave," &c. The cause came on for trial before the Honorable FREDERICK WATTS, at April term 1851.

The plaintiff read the note and rested. The defendant opened, and then called John Auld, Esq., the justice before whom the suit had originally been commenced.

He offered to prove by this witness that the note in suit was given in consideration of an indebtedness of the defendant, David J. McKee, to a certain Lewis Carpenter; and that when this note was given, it was under an arrangement between the plaintiff and defendant that he, the plaintiff, would pay the money for the defendant to the said Lewis Carpenter, and that he did not then, nor has ever since paid the said money, by which the consideration of the said note has entirely failed.

Objected to by the plaintiff, that the note is sealed, and im-

[McCulloch v. McKee.]

ports a consideration which *this* parol testimony cannot affect so as to defeat a recovery.

Objection overruled, and exception by plaintiff's counsel.

Witness:—This suit was brought before me; McKee objected to paying the note because McCulloch had not paid over the money. McCulloch answered that he had endeavored to pay it through General Miller. When he got the note from McKee, it appeared by the conversation between them that McKee was scarce of money, and that McCulloch agreed to satisfy the debt to Lewis Carpenter; that he, McCulloch, had money standing with General Miller, who was going to Gettysburg, (where Carpenter then lived,) and that he would get him (General Miller) to pay the money over to Lewis Carpenter. McCulloch said that General Miller had seen Lewis Carpenter, and had offered him the money, and that he refused to take it, but sent it back. At the same time, McCulloch stated that he had sent the money a second time with General Miller, and that time Miller could not find him. McCulloch also said that he had procured an order from Lewis Carpenter to lift this money from McKee, and he asked McKee if he had not the order, and McKee said that it was either mislaid or lost. It was admitted by McCulloch that the money had not been paid over. There was no other consideration for the note mentioned at the time of this conversation than McCulloch's agreement to pay Carpenter the money.

Cross-examined:—McCulloch said in the office, at the time of the conversation, that Lewis Carpenter had told General Miller, when the money was offered him, that he did not need the money, and that this was the reason he sent it back.

Isaac Marquart, sworn:—I was in Esquire Auld's office when the parties were there about the suit. It was said that the note had been given instead of the one which McKee had given to Lewis Carpenter. McCulloch said he had told General Miller to pay it to Lewis Carpenter when he was in Gettysburg, but that he could not find him. I understood that McCulloch was to pay Lewis Carpenter the money for the debt which McKee owed to Lewis Carpenter. I remember a letter from Carpenter to McCulloch being read in the office at the time; don't remember what it contained.

28th March 1849, the note in suit transferred to James H. Spriggs by D. W. McCulloch.

For plaintiff, Linn McCulloch affirmed:—I remember Lewis Carpenter. He lived with my father about a year. I think he went away in 1837. I remember he gave father a note on Mr. McKee, and told father to collect it and keep it until he called for it.

Cross-examined:—I saw the note, but could not identify it now. arpenter went to Gettysburg.

[McCulloch v. McKee.]

Hugh McCulloch sworn:—I know my brother David paid me a debt which Lewis Carpenter owed me when he went away. My debt may have been fifty cents, or it may have been $1.50.

31st October 1837, due-bill to Lewis Carpenter by D. J. McKee, for $39.

27th July 1840, receipt of David McCulloch, the agent, on the back of it, for having received it in full.

Order, without date, of Lewis Carpenter to D. J. McKee to pay the note to D. W. McCulloch.

WATTS, President, charged as stated in the opinion delivered by CHAMBERS, J.

It was assigned for error:
1. The court erred in admitting the parol evidence to explain or to attach conditions to the note; no fraud or mistake being pretended.
2. The court erred in the whole of their instructions contained in the first paragraph of their charge.
3. After telling the jury that the original indebtedness of the sealed note of defendant to McCulloch was to Lewis Carpenter, who authorized McCulloch to collect the money—that McCulloch agreed with McKee to give him time for its payment, and took a note in his own name for it, giving up to McKee the original note with a receipt upon the back of it, in consideration whereof McCulloch then agreed with McKee that he would pay the money—that he never did pay it—the court erred in instructing the jury that "if these are the facts, though made out by parol proof, the plaintiff would not be entitled to recover."
4. The court erred in instructing the jury that it is to be observed in this view of the case, (as stated in the 3d error assigned,) that the authority of D. W. McCulloch was to collect the money, but, *without authority* and *without the payment of the money*, he undertook to release the debt, and take a note to himself for it; to change Carpenter's debt from McKee to himself without Carpenter's consent; and that his having changed the relationship, as stated in the evidence, would not change the relationship of debtor and creditor between McKee and Carpenter, and the liability of the former to the latter to pay the money was not changed thereby.

The case was argued by *Miller*, for plaintiff in error.—He contended that the parol evidence admitted to impeach the sealed note was not admissible: 1 *Green. Ev.* 398, &c.; 4 *Barr* 493; 10 *Shep.* 517; 8 *Miss.* 161; 14 *id.* 154; 8 *Ser. & R.* 473. As to 2d assignment. McCullough had authority to take whatever means he thought best to accomplish the object: *Smith's Mer. Law* 61; *Law Lib.* 17; 4 *Camp.* 43; 5 *Bin.* 442; 5 *Esp.* 75;

[McCulloch v. McKee.]

15 *East* 408; 8 *T. Rep.* 531; 24 *Wend.* 240; 5 *Barr* 335. When the agent has a beneficial interest in the performance of the contract he makes, he can sue in his own name: 4 *Iredell* 275; *Smith's Mer. Law* 76.

McKee could not disaffirm the note when no evidence was given that Carpenter disapproved of it, and when he could have plead the statute of limitations in a suit on the original note: 5 *Johns.* 43; 6 *Barr* 277.

Biddle, for defendant.

The opinion of the court was delivered June 12, by
CHAMBERS, J.—On the trial of this cause, the defendant offered to prove that the single bill of defendant given in evidence was in consideration of the indebtedness of the defendant to Lewis Carpenter, and that it was given under an arrangement between McCulloch and the defendant, that McCulloch would pay the money for the defendant to Carpenter; but that he never paid said money, by which the consideration of the note failed. This was objected to, and the objection overruled—evidence admitted, and exception taken, which is now assigned for error.

It is well settled in Pennsylvania that fraud or failure of consideration may be given in evidence, under the plea of payment with leave, &c., in an action on a note or bond: Baring v. Shippen, 2 *Bin.* 166; Stubbs v. King, 14 *Ser. & R.* 206.

Evidence is received to prove that a bond was fraudulently obtained or *that the consideration has failed:* Carpenter v. Groff, 5 *Ser. & R.* 162; Geiger v. Cook, 3 *W. & Ser.* 266; Houk v. Foley, 2 *Pa. Rep.* 245.

This jurisprudence is too well established in Pennsylvania as a part of our system of laws, to be departed from or influenced by the decisions on the subject in other States—and in the admission of the parol evidence offered there was no error.

The other errors assigned to the charge of the court may be considered together.

It appears from the evidence, which consisted of the admissions of McCulloch before the justice, that he was authorized by Carpenter to receive from McKee the amount of a note, or due-bill, held on him by Carpenter, which was given in 1837, for $39—that McKee was scarce of money, and McCulloch agreed to satisfy the debt to Carpenter—that he, McCulloch, had money standing with General Miller, who was going to Gettysburg, where Carpenter then lived, and that he would get him, Miller, to pay the money to Carpenter. McCulloch said that Miller had seen Carpenter and had offered him the money, and that he refused to take it, but sent it back, and that he had sent the money a second time with General Miller, and that Miller could not find Carpenter. There was

[McCulloch v. McKee.]

no other consideration for the note, and no part of the money was paid by McCulloch to Carpenter, whose residence, at the trial, was unknown, and who had not been heard of for many years. It was also in evidence that Carpenter had lived with McCulloch and went away in 1837, leaving with McCulloch the note of McKee, with directions to collect it and keep it until he called for it. In 1844 McKee executed to McCulloch a single bill, given in evidence, for the amount of his due-bill to Carpenter, payable ten days after date, and had delivered up to him the due bill, and the order of Lewis Carpenter without date, to D. J. McKee to *pay* the note to D. W. McCulloch. McCulloch, as was admitted, was to pay Carpenter for McKee, which was not done.

The court below, after stating the evidence and remarking on the consideration of the single bill being a proper subject of inquiry, through the medium of parol proof, further observe, " that the authority of McCulloch was to collect the money; but without authority and without the payment of the money, he undertook to release the debt and take a note to himself for it, to change Carpenter's debtor from McKee to himself, without his consent. His having done so would not change the relation of debtor and creditor between McKee and Carpenter, and the liability of the former to the latter to pay the money was not changed thereby." The court also say, " We have only considered the case in this aspect, to enable us to answer the plaintiff's points, which he desired us to consider abstractly, for these facts do not constitute the whole case as exhibited by the testimony," and added, " It will be observed that the evidence which makes up the facts, consisted of the acknowledgments of the plaintiff as to what the consideration of the note was; and it was a part of those acknowledgments, that after he had taken the note of defendant, he sent the money to Carpenter, who declined taking it, saying that he wanted Mr. McCulloch to keep it, as he then had no need of it. If this be the truth of the case, of which the jury must judge, and there is as much evidence of it as of the other facts embraced in the conversations of McCulloch alluded to, then, by Carpenter's consent, his debtor was changed, the arrangement of Mr. McColloch, by which he took the note, was *ratified*—he thereby became the debtor of Carpenter, and McKee was released. In this view of the case, the plaintiff is entitled to recover." Taking the entire charge into consideration, we think it presented the case to the jury as favorably for plaintiff as he could require.

The court, in the first part of their charge, instructed the jury that "the authority of McCulloch was to collect the money, but, *without authority and without the payment of money*, he undertook to release the debt and take a note to himself for it, to change Carpenter's debtor from McKee to himself, *without his consent.*"

[McCulloch v. McKee.]

Carpenter's authority by the order to McKee was to pay the money to McCulloch. McCulloch was a special agent to receive the money from McKee, and as such he had not authority to substitute any thing else for the money so as to discharge McKee. An agent specially employed to receive payment in money cannot vary from his authority in receiving a bill: 2 *Lord Ray.* 930; 2 *Salk.* 442; Hays & Wick *v.* Lynn, 7 *Watts* 524; *Story on Agency* 115, 451. It is true that if the article substituted is delivered over to the principal, and he agrees to it, or, when informed of it, he approves of or assents to it, it is a ratification of the act of the agent that will bind the principal.

The court did submit to the jury the evidence, with the instruction that if the facts were as stated, of Carpenter sending back the money to McCulloch, with directions to him to keep it for him, that he had no need of it—the arrangement of Mr. McCulloch with McKee was *ratified*, and Mr. McCulloch became the debtor of Carpenter, and McKee was released. In this view of the case the plaintiff is entitled to recover, as McCulloch had commuted for the money without authority, and had not paid McKee according to his engagement, when he took to himself McKee's note. The material inquiry was whether Carpenter had assented to the arrangement made by his agent, and dispensed with the payment over to him by McCulloch. This was matter of fact for the jury. The acknowledgments of McCulloch were to be taken entire as evidence. As an admission, it would not have been competent for the court to have received part and rejected part: the whole must be submitted to the jury. What credit is to be given to the whole or part, is a question for the consideration and discretion of a jury: 2 *Stark. Ev.* pl. 4, p. 49. The question arising on this admission, as to assent and ratification and the legal effect of it, was submitted fairly to the jury, and favorably to the plaintiff, and it was for their decision. The jury, as within their province, found for the defendant. As the plaintiff has failed to sustain the errors assigned,

Judgment affirmed.

Lex *versus* Potters.

The second section of the act of 29th March 1819, authorizing stock held in corporations by individuals, in their own names, and which is not claimed by any other person, to be taken in execution and sold in the same manner as goods and chattels, is not repealed by the act of 16th June 1836, relating to executions.

ERROR to the Common Pleas of *Centre county*.

This was a proceeding by foreign attachment by Jacob Lex against James Potter and John Potter, with clause of summons to the Centre and Kishacoquillas Turnpike Road Company.

The firm of J. & J. Potter failed on or about the 7th December 1847. On that and the following day amicable judgments, to a large amount, were entered against them in the Common Pleas of Centre county. All of these judgments, with the exception of two or three, stipulated for a stay of execution for one year. On the 7th of December 1847, executions were issued upon the judgments of Simon Cameron *vs.* J. & J. Potter, and William Allison *vs.* Same, by virtue of which the personal property of the defendants, including 165 shares of stock in the Centre and Kishacoquillas Turnpike, was levied on and sold by the sheriff. The stock was purchased by James Burnside, Esq., who afterwards, as was admitted on the trial, received one or more dividends on the same, but no transfer was ever made to him upon the books of the corporation.

On the 9th of December, a judgment was confessed by J. & J. Potter to Jacob Lex for $4000, and entered at No. 167, November term 1847, upon which there was a stay of execution for one year. To No. 5, April term 1849, an attachment execution was issued upon this judgment against J. & J. Potter, with clause of scire facias to the Centre and Kishacoquillas Turnpike Road Company, by virtue of which the 165 shares of stock above mentioned were attached in the hands of the corporation. On the trial of the case, at November term 1850, James Burnside, Esq., asked leave of the court to suggest his interest in the stock in controversy, and be made a party defendant upon the record, *pro interesse suo*, which was granted. The plaintiff contended that notwithstanding the sale to Mr. Burnside by the sheriff, under the executions of Cameron and Allison, the stock remained liable to the attachment of the plaintiff or any other judgment creditors of J. & J. Potter; that a sale under fieri facias conferred no title upon the purchaser as against a subsequent attaching creditor. Mr. Burnside contended that by his purchase at sheriff's sale he took a good title, even as against the present plaintiff. This was the only point in the cause.

The second section of the act of 29th March 1819 provides, "That the stock of any body corporate owned by any individual

[Lex v. Potters.]

or individuals, body or bodies politic or corporate in his, her, its, or their own name or names, shall be liable to be taken in execution and sold in the same manner that goods and chattels are liable in law to be so taken and sold, subject nevertheless to any debt due by any holder or holders of such stock to the company or body corporate. And whereas it sometimes happens that the stock of such bodies corporate is held in another name or names than that of those of the real owner or owners thereof, and it is just that such stock so held should be made liable for the real owner or owners, therefore be it further enacted," &c. See acts of 1819, 226–7.

Opinion of WOODWARD, J.—The court, after stating the positions and relations of the respective parties, proceeded to observe, that the plaintiff's counsel insist that the act of 16th June 1836, relating to executions, supplies and repeals the act of 29th March 1819, for taking stock in execution like goods and chattels, and that there is no law to justify the levy and sale under which Mr. Burnside claims to hold the stock in question.

This position is said to be supported, 1st, by the fact that the compilers of all the digests now in use omit the act of 1819, and that Mr. *Sergeant* speaks of it in his work on attachments as repealed by the law of 1836. And 2d, by the fact that the law of 1836 prescribes a mode of taking stock in execution which the legislature has said "*shall*" be pursued, and which mode is inconsistent with the provisions of the law of 1819. As to the first of these objections, it is to be considered that the acts of Assembly in Pennsylvania are so numerous, and touch one another at so many points, that no compiler or commentator, however learned or diligent, can, in the absence of cases, undertake to declare with any confidence what sections or parts of sections of a particular law have been supplied by subsequent legislation. It is only when cases arise, and you come to apply the subsequent law, that it can be clearly seen whether the old law be superseded or not; and therefore it is no uncommon thing to find in our modern digests acts of Assembly and parts of acts, as still in force, which in reality have been supplied and repealed. And the compiler is quite as likely to omit a law as repealed which is really in force, as he is to insert a law as being in force which is really repealed. While the greatest deference is felt, therefore, for the learning and industry of the compilers of our digests and the commentators on our acts of Assembly, their opinions as to what laws are in force are far from being conclusive. It remains for the courts, after all, to determine this point, as cases occur from time to time for their consideration.

2d. In the next place, is the law of 1819 superseded by the act of 1836, so far as a case circumstanced like the present is concerned?

The second section of the act of 29th March 1819 is evidently

[Lex v. Potters.]

confined to the case of stock *held in the name of the real owner.* Such stock "shall be liable to be taken in execution and sold in the same manner that goods and chattels are liable in law to be so taken and sold." The third section provides a peculiar and different proceeding to reach stock that is held in "another name or names than that of those of the real owner or owners thereof." See the preamble to 3d section.

Now the 22d section of the act of 16th June 1836 seems to re-enact and extend the provisions of the 1st section of the act of 1819, and in the most express terms subjects "the stock owned by any defendant in any body corporate" to execution "like other goods or chattels." If this section be limited to stock held in the name of the owner, it may be admitted to have superseded the 1st section of the act of 1819; but if it be construed to embrace all stock, without regard to the mode of holding it, then, undoubtedly, it is to be taken in connection with the 32d, 33d, and 34th sections of the same act. And what is the proper construction of these sections? The latter clause of the 32d section, and the whole of the 33d section, prescribe a mode of seizing stock, "if it shall be held in another name than that of the real owner thereof." That is one class of cases. Stock is often held in the name of a trustee, the beneficial interest in which belongs to a person whose name does not appear on the books of the corporation. When that person is the debtor, the creditor has the remedy prescribed in these sections on complying with the conditions proposed. And here, let it be observed, is a system of measures provided for the very class of cases contemplated by the 3d section of the act of 1819; but which measures are inconsistent with the provisions of that section, and yet, in our later editions of Purdon's Digest, which contains this execution law of 1836, this very 3d section of the act of 1819 is retained as being in force, while the 2d section of the act of 1819 is said to be repealed. See *Purdon*, edition of 1847—title "Corporation."

Now to this class of cases, where the stock is held in another *than the real owner's name*, I apply the provisions of the 32d and 33d sections of the act of 1836, and the imperative "*shall*," which occurs in the first clause of 32d section. In *such* cases, the proceedings "*shall*" be by affidavit and recognizance and process in the nature of an attachment and summons to the trustee, &c.

But there is another class of cases. A defendant in a judgment may hold stock in his own name *which another party claims to belong to him.* To this class I apply the 34th section, and say that in respect to stock that is so situated, the like proceedings, without affidavit or recognizance, "*may*" be had, and the claimant may come in by affidavit and recognizance, and contest with the judgment creditor the right to the debtor's stock. The "shall" of the 32d section cannot be applied to the cases contemplated in the 34th section because the word "may" is used in the latter, and excludes it. Nor can these words both be construed "shall," for that would impute to the legislature ignorance of grammar, and who is bold enough for that?

The creditor "*may*" proceed under this section, for the purpose of settling titles to the stock, with the outstanding claimant to it. He may consider it the most expeditious and convenient mode of testing such claimant's right to the stock, and he is sure of getting security from the claimant before he can be admitted to defend for the interest he claims. Therefore it is that the legislature opened this mode of procedure to a creditor who wished to seize his debtor's stock, that stands in his own name, but is claimed by another, but they did not shut him up to this procedure, even in this case. And when the debtor holds his stock in his own name, and it is *not* claimed by another, how can it be said that he is confined to the proceedings prescribed in this section.

Is it not apparent that here is a *third* class of cases not contemplated or provided for at all in the act of 1836? The case of a debtor, owning and holding stock in his own name, *which no man claims* in whole or in part? Not provided for, I say, unless it be in the 22d section of this act. If provided for in that section, it may be sold on fi. fa. like goods and chattels—if not provided for in that section, then the 1st section of the act of 1819 is not supplied and repealed by the law of 1836, and it may be sold on a fi. fa. under that.

The case before us falls into this third class. The Messrs. Potters held the stock in their own names, and nobody claimed it. Allison and Cameron, their creditors, had no occasion to avail themselves of the provisions of the 34th section for the purpose of extinguishing an outstanding claim, and they were not subject to the imperative provision of the 32d section, because their debtors held their stock in their own name.

The creditors seized and sold the stock by virtue of the appropriate writ, and we cannot say that that sale was void for want of legal authority. Especially ought not this to be affirmed in behalf of a creditor whose first lien upon the stock attached, and whose interest in it accrued for the first, more than a year after that levy and sale.

As to the rest, there is no evidence that Colonel Burnside bid it in for the Potters. He was their counsel in their failure, and was the attorney of Allison and Cameron, their creditors; but these facts furnish no presumption that the sale, which was by the sheriff and was open and fair, and which was recognised by the Turnpike Company, and acquiesced in by the Potters and their creditors, was covinous, designed to cloak the stock for the benefit of the Potters, and, in a word, fraudulent. Nor does the fact, that the Potters preferred these particular creditors, by giving them judg-

[Lex v. Potters.]

ments without that stay of execution which they imposed on their other creditors, make the sale fraudulent.

They had a right to make a distinction among their creditors, and to prefer whom they would, and the exercise of a legal right is not fraudulent. The facts before us, therefore, afford no just ground for impeaching the sale to Burnside, and as I have shown that it had the authority of law, the verdict must be for the defendants.

To which the plaintiff's counsel excepted before verdict, and prayed the court to file the same of record, which is done.

Error was assigned to the charge.

Linn, and *Curtin*, for plaintiff's in error.—1st. The act of 1819 is supplied and virtually repealed by the act of 1836, relating to executions. Act of 1836, sections 22, 32, 33, 34, 36, 37, and 38; *Dunlop's Digest*, 812, 814, and 815; *Ser. on Attachment*, 190, Com'th *v.* Cromley; 1 *Ashmead* 179; Goodenow *v.* Buttrick, 7 *Mass.* 140; Bartlett *v.* King, 12 *Mass.* 537; Ashley Appellant, 4 *Pick.* 21; Com'th *v.* Cooley, 10 *Pick.* 37; Mason *v.* White, 1 *Pick.* 452; Ellis *v.* Page, 1 *Pick.* 43; Rutland *v.* Mendon, 1 *Pick.* 154; Blackburn *v.* Walpole, 9 *Pick.* 97. These cases establish the principle that if a revising statute embrace all the provisions of antecedent laws on the same subject, and reduce them to one system, such revising statute virtually repeals the statutes revised, without any express provision to that effect.

2d. If the first proposition is correct, then the sale of the stock on the fi. fa. was void, and conferred no title upon Mr. Burnside as against a subsequent attaching creditor. Snavely *v.* Wagner, 8 *Barr* 275; 14 *Ser. & R.* 429; 22 *Eng. Com. Law Rep.* 190.

McAllister, for defendant in error.—This proposition is based on the assumption that the second section of the act of 29th March 1819—(which it is admitted fully authorized the sale)—was repealed by the act of 16th June 1836, and that the act of 1836 did not supply the remedy. It is not pretended that the act of 1819 is repealed by express enactment. There is no repealing clause in the act of 1836. It is argued, however, that the second section is repealed by implication. "The doctrine of repeal by implication is not favored in law, and will not be resorted to except when the repugnance or opposition is too clear and plain to be reconciled:" Bruce *v.* Schuyler, 4 *Gilm.* 221. "If there be two *affirmative statutes* or *two affirmative sections* in the same statute upon the same subject, the one does not repeal the other if both may consist together: Bruce *v.* Schuyler, 4 *Gilm.* 221.

An act of Assembly will not be construed to *repeal by implication* an express enactment, unless there be clear and strong incon-

[Lex v. Potter.]

sistency between them: Street *v.* The Commonwealth, 6 *W. & Ser.* 209; State *v.* Taylor, 2 *McCord* 483; Brown *v.* Miller, 4 *J. S. Marsh* 474; Loker *v.* Brookline, 13 *Pick.* 342, 348; Moore *v.* Miller, 1 *Litt*; 6 *Howard* 644.

There is no inconsistency or repugnance between the 2d section of the act of 1819 and the act of 1836.

The 2d section of the act of 1819 provides "that the stock of any body corporate, owned by any individual *in his own name*, shall be liable to be taken in execution and sold in the same manner that goods and chattels are liable in law to be taken and sold." The act of 1836 still further enlarges the property liable to execution, to deposits of money, debts, &c. The 32d and 33d sections provide a remedy which *shall* be pursued by the creditor who desires to reach stock *owned by his debtor*, and which stands in the *name of another*. The 34th section provides a remedy which *may* be pursued by the creditor who desires to reach stock standing in the *name of the debtor, but which is claimed by another*. It provides a remedy by which the parties in interest *may* have the question of the ownership of the stock ascertained and determined *prior* to a sale. The plaintiff, however, we conceive, may proceed at once to sell, under the 2d section of the act of 1819, leaving the question of ownership to be settled between the claimant and the purchaser. And this as to all stock standing in the *name of the debtor*, though it should be claimed at the time by another. The case of stock standing in the name of the debtor, *owned by him and claimed by no one*, as in the case now before the court, does not seem to have been provided for at all in the act of 1836.

PER CURIAM.—Let the judgment be affirmed on the opinion of the president of the Common Pleas.

Miller's Appeal.

The omission of a debtor to give notice before the sale of his real estate, of his claim to property to the value of three hundred dollars, under the act of 9th April 1849, exempting property to that amount from levy and sale on execution and distress for rent, will be a bar to his claim to that amount of money out of the proceeds of the sale. The claim, as it respects real estate, should perhaps be made before inquisition.

APPEAL by Thomas C. Miller, Jr., from the decree of the Court of Common Pleas of *Cumberland county*, appropriating the money arising from the sale of the real estate of George Lee, sold by the sheriff of said county.

Appellant obtained a judgment against George Lee, 22d June

[Miller's Appeal.]

1850, on a breach of contract for sale of land, entered into November 15, 1849, for $207. On this a fi. fa. was issued to August term 1850, on which defendant's real estate, consisting of an improved farm of about 65 acres, was levied, an inquisition held and the property condemned, and a *venditioni exponas* issued to November term 1850, on which said real estate was sold by the sheriff. *After* the sale, defendant served a notice on the sheriff claiming $300 out of the money arising from the sale, under the provisions of the act of 9th April 1849. When the fi. fa. on which the land was levied was issued, or at any subsequent period until after his property had been struck off by the sheriff, Lee did not give notice of his claim, or require the sheriff to have an appraisement made, &c.

The money was brought into court for appropriation. Depositions were taken, which were read on the hearing of the case, and it was proved that prior to the 4th July 1849, defendant's personal estate was sold by the sheriff, and that he then claimed and received at an appraised value the articles of personal property exempt from execution under the acts of Assembly of June 16, 1836, and April 22, 1846. Further, that the attorney of Mr. Miller was present at the sale of defendant's real estate, and bid the same up to a sum sufficient to cover his judgment, and would have bid $300 more for the property, had notice been given that defendant would claim that sum out of the sale. The property sold for $2700—a sum that would have covered Mr. Miller's judgment, and was bought by Holliday Lee, the brother of defendant.

The court, WATTS, President, decreed $300 to be paid to George Lee, the defendant; and no part of Miller's judgment was paid out of the sale.

Error was assigned to the decree directing $300 to be paid to George Lee, the defendant.

The *first* section of the act of 9th April 1849, to exempt property to the value of $300 from levy and sale on execution and distress for rent, provides, that in lieu of the property now exempt from levy and sale on execution issued upon any judgment obtained upon contract and distress for rent, property to the value of three hundred dollars, exclusive of all wearing apparel of the defendant and his family, and all Bibles and school-books in use of the family, (which shall remain exempted as heretofore,) and no more, owned by, or in the possesion of any debtor, shall be exempt from levy and sale on execution or by distress for rent.

Sec. 2. "That the sheriff, constable, or other officer charged with the execution of any warrant issued by competent authority, for the levying upon and selling the property, either real or personal, of any debtor, shall, if requested by the debtor, summon three disinterested persons, who shall be sworn or affirmed, to appraise the

[Miller's Appeal.]

property which the said debtor may elect to retain under the provisions of this act, for which service the said appraisers shall be entitled to receive fifty cents each, to be charged as part of the costs of the proceedings; and property *thus chosen and appraised* to the value of three hundred dollars, shall be exempt from levy and sale on the said execution or warrant, *except warrants for the collection of taxes.*"

Sec. 3. "That in any case where the property levied upon as aforesaid shall consist of real estate of greater value than three hundred dollars, and the defendant in such shall elect to retain real estate amounting in value to the whole sum of three hundred dollars, or any less sum, the appraisers aforesaid shall determine whether, in their opinion, the said real estate can be divided without injury to or spoiling the whole; and if the said appraisers shall determine that the said real estate can be divided as aforesaid, then they shall proceed to set apart so much thereof as in their opinion shall be sufficient to answer the requirement of the defendant in such case, designating the same by proper metes and bounds, all of which proceedings shall be certified in writing by the said appraisers, or a majority of them, under their proper hands and seals, to the sheriff, under-sheriff, or coroner, charged with the execution of the writ in such case, who shall make return of the same to the proper court, from which the writ issued, in connection with said writ."

Sec. 4. "That upon return made of the writ aforesaid, with the proceedings thereon, the plaintiff in the case shall be entitled to have his writ of *venditioni exponas* as in other cases, to sell the residue of the real estate included in the levy aforesaid, if the appraisers aforesaid shall have determined upon a division of said real estate; but if the said appraisers shall determine against a division of said real estate, the plaintiff may have a writ of *venditioni exponas* to sell the whole of the real estate included in such levy; and it shall and may be lawful *in the latter case* for the defendant in the execution to receive from the sheriff or other officer, of the proceeds of said sale, so much as he would have received at the appraised value had the said real estate been divided."

Sec. 6. "That the provisions of this act shall not take effect until the 4th day of July next, and shall apply only to debts contracted on and after that date.

The case was argued by *Miller* and *Graham*, for Miller, the appellant.—Under the first section, the debtor must *request* the sheriff to summon appraisers, and it is only the property *thus chosen and appraised* which shall be exempt from levy and sale.

But where a division of the property may be injurious, or where a division is impracticable, and the appraisers determine against a division, the plaintiff may have a writ of *venditioni exponas* to sell the whole; and in the latter case, the defendant is to receive out

[Miller's Appeal.]

of the proceeds as much as he would have received had the real estate been divided. That the debtor cannot permit all his *personal* property to be sold, and then demand three hundred dollars in money.

2d. That he cannot silently permit all his real estate to be sold, without asking for a division, and then claim money instead of the property. That no provision exists in the act for the payment of *money* in lieu of the *personal* estate, and the only contingency that authorizes the receipt of money in place of *property*, is where there has been an appraisement, and it has been found and so returned to court that the real estate cannot be divided without injury, &c. The language of the act is, "in the *latter case*," that is, where there cannot be a division, the defendant shall receive "so much as he would have received at the appraised value, had the said real estate been divided."

The defendant, by failing to give notice, and to ask for an appraisement and division, has deprived the *plaintiff* of his debt.

Biddle, for appellee.

The opinion of the court was delivered June 12, by

CHAMBERS, J.—The single question presented in this case is whether a debtor, whose farm of about 65 acres was sold at sheriff's sale, has a right to claim out of the proceeds of sale $300 under the provisions of the act of 9th April 1849, on a notice to the sheriff of his claim *after* such sale.

The act referred to is a humane law, and as such is entitled to a liberal construction. But while benevolence is to be indulged, we are not to disregard the rights of creditors, or overlook the provisions of the law in favor of the unfortunate debtor to be complied with on his part to entitle him to this bounty.

The sheriff is to proceed with the executions directed to him, by levying upon and selling the property, personal or real, of the debtor; and shall, if requested by the debtor, summon three disinterested persons, who shall be sworn or affirmed, to appraise the property, which the debtor may *elect* to retain under the provisions of this act. The property thus chosen and appraised, to the value of $300, is to be exempt from levy and sale on execution or warrant, *except for taxes*.

By the 3d section it is provided, that if the property levied on consists of real estate of greater value than $300, and the defendant elects to retain real estate amounting in value to the whole sum of $300, or *any less sum*, the appraisers are to determine whether the real estate can be divided without injury to the whole; and if it can be so divided, they are to set apart so much as will answer the requirement of the defendant, designating the same by

[Miller's Appeal.]

metes and bounds; of all which a return is to be made to the court in connection with the writ.

And by the 4th section it is declared, that if a part of the real estate has been set off, the *vend. exp.* issued is to sell the residue; but if no division is made as provided, the whole is to be sold, and, in the latter case, the defendant is to receive of the proceeds of the sale so much as he would have received at the appraised value, had the said real estate been divided. This act contemplates the debtor getting property at an appraisment as his exemption where practicable; and the right to demand the money out of proceeds of sale, is only in the last resort, when property did not admit of separation.

The debtor, George Lee, made no request to the sheriff, who represented the creditors, to summon appraisers, or gave any notice what property he elected to retain, but is silent, and permits the sheriff to proceed with the sale, at which the brother of the debtor becomes the purchaser. The sum bid for the property by the junior judgment creditor was sufficient to cover the record liens, if the $300 are not withdrawn for the debtor. The omission to give notice would have the tendency of misleading creditors; and in behalf of the junior judgment creditor it is testified that if the claim of the debtor to the exemption had been made even before the sale, he would have bid the property to an amount that would have covered it and the prior judgments. The silence of the debtor during the whole course of the proceedings in execution can scarcely, under the circumstances, be imputed to ignorance of the law, more especially when it appears that as a debtor he had claimed and retained on a former execution the exemptions allowed of personal property under the acts of 1836 and 1846. Ignorance of the law is not an excuse, and it is not for a debtor to plead that ignorance when the provision of law was one of great notoriety, and which conferred on him so substantial a favor. It is the gratuity of the law, which he ought to be satisfied to take under the provisions and guards which the law granting it has imposed, and which are neither expensive, onerous, or unreasonable. The provisions introduced into this act by legislative discretion are not to be dispensed with by the debtor as useless, and are not to be disregarded by the court in the construction and execution of the law.

There is not in this case an analogy to the claim of the landlord to one year's rent on notice to the sheriff before the money is paid over, as decided in Ege *v.* Ege, 5 *Watts* 139. In that case, the claim is for an existing debt which by law is preferred, and by the act of Assembly the sheriff was directed to pay over *after the sale* one year's rent to the landlord.

Under the act of 1849 we do not decide when the request must be made by the debtor to the sheriff to summon appraisers, but we

[Miller's Appeal.]

think it ought to be made at least before the inquisition, and the omission to make it or give notice of the claim before the sale of the realty, is such a failure to comply with the provisions of the law as in the opinion of the court bars the claim of the debtor.

The decree of the court below ordering that the money be paid to George Lee is reversed.

Sample *versus* Robb.

1. On the trial of an ejectment, drafts of land, offered before any title by warrant, location, or improvement is shown, are not admissible.

2. The talk of neighbors as to who has the title to land in dispute, is not evidence.

3. Drafts found in the office of the deputy surveyor, but no authority shown to the deputy surveyor to make them, may be evidence of boundary, on the part of the claimant under an improvement, if it be shown that when the improvement was commenced, the improver claimed to the lines of the draft and adopted them; but the papers of themselves are no evidence of title.

4. Where a justice certified that the witness was sworn and examined at the place specified in *the notice*, on the day and between certain hours, being those specified in the notice which was attached, it is sufficient evidence that the witness was sworn *before* he was examined, there being no evidence to the contrary.

5. A notice being given that a deposition would be taken at the office of Joseph *Stormer*, Esq., in a certain township, a deposition taken at the office of Joseph *Stermer*, Esq., is admissable under the notice, unless it be shown that there were two justices of those names in that township.

6. The declarations of one claiming in his own right by improvement, and living on the land, made at the time of the making of a survey by another under a warrant, are evidence against himself as to the extent of his claim: they are not evidence against another under whom he did not then profess to claim.

7. The declaration or offer of a former improver (since deceased) whilst living on the land, to give his son-in-law, who was living on it, a part of the land if he would improve on it, and his acts of ownership on the land, are evidence that he claimed the same *as his own*, and not under another.

8. It is not error to receive evidence which is pertinent and relevant, because it is not strictly *rebutting;* especially in a complicated case, and where the adverse party is not taken by surprise.

9. The court may intimate to the jury an opinion that there has been an abandonment, and submit the facts to their consideration, with instructions as to what constitutes an abandonment.

10. It is not essential that the court bring to the notice of the jury all the evidence in relation to a subject on which they charge.

11. If one claiming in his own right, by settlement and improvement, did not object to the location of a warrant on land adjoining his improvement, his subsequent deed cannot affect the location of the warrant: if he claimed *under another* when the warrant was located, his agreement to the location of the warrant cannot affect him under whom he claimed, or his alienes.

12. If the description in the writ, of the land for which the ejectment is brought, be defective, the defect may be supplied by another description filed with leave of the court.

[Sample v. Robb.]

ERROR to the Common Pleas of *Mifflin county*.

This was an ejectment brought by James Robb against Samuel Sample, (David W. Hulings afterwards suggested as landlord, and admitted as co-defendant,) to recover "a tract or piece of land in Oliver township, Mifflin county, bounded by other lands of James Robb and others, containing fifty acres or thereabouts."

The plaintiff gave in evidence a warrant of 9th January 1837. Survey, 25th May 1837. Return and acceptance, 6th June 1837.

The defendants relied upon a pre-emption, based upon improvement and settlement, and showed drafts for two adjoining surveys, in the names of William Lewis and William Harris, commenced in 1797, and finished May 22d, 1806. The drafts call for warrant of 18th March 1793; but upon search made at the land-office, no such warrants were found. In 1808 Charles Kemberly made an improvement within the line of the William Lewis survey, which, by deed of 5th April 1810, he sold to William Lewis. Bostian Rhodes made an improvement within the limits of the same survey, about 1820. How he claimed was a subject of dispute. The two surveys of Harris and Lewis were sold at sheriff's sale, as the property of Wm. Lewis, by Foster Milliken, sheriff of Mifflin county, 21st August 1829, to Judge Wilson, who conveyed the same to D. W. Hulings. *No person was living on the Kemberly improvement in* 1837, *when Robb's warrant was laid;* but defendants deny that they had *abandoned* the same. Bostian Rhodes was living on his improvement at the time, but plaintiff alleges that he was holding for *himself*, and not under Hulings in right of Lewis, and that he appeared satisfied; *the surveyor ran round his improvement and left him out of the Robb survey.* This, defendants claimed, could not be done, because Rhodes was holding under Lewis.

The jury returned a verdict in *favor of plaintiff*, upon which a judgment was entered, and defendant sued out a writ of error.

On the trial, on part of *plaintiff* was given in evidence a warrant to James Robb, dated January 9, 1837, for 300 acres of improved land, adjoining lands of Samuel Sunderland on the west, James Robb on the south, Elizabeth McLaughlin and Philip Powell on the east, and Jack's Mountain on the north, situate in Wayne and Oliver townships, Mifflin county. Survey, May 25, 1837, of 300 acres and 73 perches. Returned and accepted, June 6, 1837. The writ was not found in the office, after search made.

On part of *defendants*, John R. Weeks was called. He testified: —I am the county surveyor, and have charge of the official papers of the county surveyor's office; these are papers from the office, one marked A, A. S. W., Oct. 23d, 1846; one marked C, A. S. W., Oct. 23d, 1846; one marked D, A. S. W., Oct. 23d, 1846; one marked E, A. S. W., Jan. 14th, 1851.

Objected to, that they are not official papers; no evidence of

[Sample v. Robb.]

improvement; no warrant shown upon which they are read, nor authority to the office to make them; does not appear for whom made.

David Hough, (to the court):—(Drafts marked A and E.) I have seen the hand; the draft marked A, I think, is the handwriting of William Harris; the one marked E, I would not like to say is. I did not know William Harris. William Harris, as appears from the papers in the office, was once deputy surveyor of Mifflin county, and for a time assistant of James Harris while James Harris was deputy. I only know this from the office papers. I knew these papers to be in the office for about eighteen years. I took charge of the office in 1832. I looked them up this morning for Mr. Weeks. (Paper marked C.) There has been writing by two or three men on this paper; do not know who did the rough draft; part of the writing upon the draft is R. Robinson's handwriting; he was a deputy surveyor. Is also an endorsement by William or John Shaw; I think William; they were both deputy surveyors. I never was called on to run these surveys. I have been on most of the lines and run them. I find these lines as far as I have examined them. I examined the line on Jack's Mountain; have run part of all the boundary lines of the two tracts; the division line, if I ever examined for it, I never found it; I believe surveys were made on the ground, as they purport to be by that draft, except the division line, which I do not recollect to have examined for.

Cross-examined:—I cannot tell when these surveys were made on the ground; I only say I believe they were made, from what I saw on the ground. I do not recollect of blocking any trees; could not tell when they were made. (Paper E.) Mr. Harris does not sign himself as deputy on this paper. (Paper A.) This paper states late deputy; paper E does not show when it was made.

Re-examined:—They were old lines that I saw.

Cross-examined:—Some of the lines I examined must have been lines of these surveys; part of the way on the examination of last survey, I found two lines; running this lower line on the south side of this survey we had to run by this draft; the lines appear, by the trees, to be made about the same time; whether a year or two or three of difference in their ages I cannot say. I run the James Holmes lines once when they sold; when I run that line, about fifteen years ago, I did not know of James Holmes.

Paper now offered to be read again, to show for whom they were made—for Mr. Lewis.

Objected to as above. Objection sustained, and defendant excepts. This was the subject of the defendant's *first* bill, and of the *first* assignment of error.

Robert Rankin sworn:—In the year 1808, I heard a conversation between Charles Kemberly and General Lewis, at my father's vendue; General Lewis told Charles Kemberly that he was not doing

[Sample v. Robb.]

right, putting up buildings there; Kemberly said he would go on; after some conversation, Lewis said he might put up buildings, provided he would not set fire to it and run off by the light. I believe Kemberly did put up the building, and lived in it awhile; cannot tell how long; they had two houses; don't think it was the house Lewis and he were talking of that they lived in. I do not know what year he went on; it was after the conversation; do not know how long after they went. They left there about 1831 or 1832; likely it might be a year or two after 1808 they went on it.

Offer to prove by witness that it was talked of, by all the neighbors, as General Lewis's land. Objected to and objection sustained.

Witness:—I never heard any of the Kemberlies say it was Lewis's land.

The offer above renewed, and that it was always spoken of in the neighborhood as Lewis's land.

Objected to. Objection sustained, and defendant excepts. This was the subject of the *second* bill of exceptions.

After the testimony had been received, George Allen testified:—There was a cabin when Sample lived on the land; from ever I can remember, Charles Kemberly claimed it. I can remember of being there between thirty and forty years ago; was a house and stable, and a few patches of cleared land. They moved from there, I think, in 1832 or 1833. Bostian Rhodes first made his improvement a year or two after 1820, or about that time; he lived there till the fall of 1838 or winter of 1839, when he died. I spoke to the old man once, and asked him if he held the land on his own hook, or under an agreement with any one; he said he had an agreement with Lewis as landlord, and Bratton, who had charge of Lewis's land. I do not know whether Bratton was executor; he had something to do with the land. I think I had more than one conversation with Bostian about it; he worked with me for some time; never acknowledged the title was in any other person than Lewis; I lived near him, &c.

Diagram marked A offered. Objected to.

David Hough:—(Draft marked A and E.) This I do not say is the handwriting of Mr. Harris; it does not look altogether like William Harris's handwriting; I would not like to say it is William Harris's handwriting; it is doubtful whether it is his handwriting. I have examined all these lines, in whole or in part, except the division line. From my knowledge of marks and blazes on trees, I would suppose these would count back to the time they purport to be made on this draft. I have been examining and running lines in this county since 1829; I was deputy surveyor from 1832 to 1836; was appointed to fill out John Shaw's place, and was reappointed; I have been in altogether nine or ten years. William Harris was acting deputy, under his brother James, in 1792; when

[Sample v. Robb.]

he was appointed deputy himself cannot say; the two continued till about 1806.

Cross-examined:—I will not undertake to say the lines I found were lines of adjoining surveys; the east line, running N. 45, W. 88, I think was not made from adjoining surveys; I found that line marked on the ground; south of that line, the line adjoining Elizabeth McLaughlin, may have been the line of an adjoining survey. The line N. 45, W. 88, I have never seen a survey for. I have never seen any Kemberly survey. This draft could not have been made from adjoining surveys all round; it might have been from adjoining surveys; some of the adjoining surveys were as early as this; some were not. The long line run S. 48, W. 502½ perches, was no survey for the line for which it purports to have been made.

A and E objected to, in connection with the proof in the case that Wm. Lewis claimed the lands as early as 1806, and leased them.

Court:—There is no authority from the commonwealth shown to the deputy surveyor to make the drafts; they purport to be made on warrants, and there are no warrants shown. You may show a diagram corresponding with lines found on the ground, and then it will depend on the proof of whether Mr. Lewis or his tenants claimed to these lines. Admitted to show boundary. The rejected show memorandum without authority.

Defendant excepts. This was the subject of the third bill on part of defendant, and the subject of the second assignment of error.

Two diagrams marked F, A. S. W., January 14, 1850, and G, A. S. W., January 14, 1850, admitted under the above exception.

The deed of Bostian Rhodes to D. W. Hulings, dated 3d April 1831, was offered. It purported to have been signed and delivered in presence of Cornwell and James Rhodes.

An affidavit as follows, was read:—

Mifflin county, ss.

Before me, the subscriber, a justice of the peace in and for said county, personally came Wm. C. Cornwell, one of the subscribing witnesses to the within indenture, who being duly sworn, doth depose and say, that he was present and saw the parties, David W. Hulings and Bostian Rhodes, sign, seal, execute, and, as their several act and deed, execute and acknowledge the same, in his presence, and that the names, David W. Hulings, and Bostian Rhodes his mark, are the proper signatures of the said parties, and that he and James Rhodes signed their names as witnesses, at the time, to the execution of the same, ("the representatives of," in the 12th line, being interlined.) WM. C. CORNWELL.

Sworn and subscribed, this 3d day of September 1836, before me.

WM. McCAY.

[Sample v. Robb.]

George Allen was offered on the part of *defendant.*

George Allen, sworn:—Offer to prove by this witness that he has been acquainted with this land upwards of thirty years; that he knows the lines, and that the lines represented by the draft have been known and recognised as the lines of the Lewis lands all that time, or until Mr. Hulings's purchase, and as Mr. Hulings's since that time.

Objected to, that it is too general, as to strangers.

Court:—He may state his own knowledge of the lines, and what was said by the occupants of it and the adjoiners, and that the lines were recognised by them as the boundaries. Objection overruled and plaintiff excepts.

George Allen:—Know this land to be claimed by the Lewises, as long as I can mind, and by the adjoiners; can recollect it upwards of thirty years. I was born on a farm adjoining that land, and have lived there and on another farm adjoining, ever since. I was 45 years of age a few weeks ago. I think I have known the lines 30 years, the southern line particularly. John Allen and James Holmes adjoin on that side. I know the lines all round for some time; I know it as Lewis and Holmes boundary, and knew it from all the neighbourhood. I never knew any difference after the sheriff's sale; always called Lewis's land; heard Hulings was the owner about the time Hope Furnace was started, in 1831.

Cross examined:—We claimed up to that south line, and believed that to be our line. We always called it Lewis's land, Sunderland claimed that line to be the line of his survey. Powell lived on the Jacob Kemberly tract; never heard him say any thing. He bought from Charles Kemberly, son of Jacob. Know that south line as the line of Lewis and Holmes tract; that on the west side was known as the Sunderland and Lewis line.

Defendants close.

On part of the plaintiff, the deposition of Cornwell was afterwards offered. Objected to, *as not taken before the justice named in the notice;* and that it did not appear that the witness had been sworn *before* his testimony was reduced to writing. The objection was overruled and exception on part of *defendant.* This was the subject of the *fourth* bill, and of the *third* assignment of error.

The notice was as follows:—

Take notice that the deposition of William C. Cornwell will be taken in pursuance of the above rule of court, at the office of Joseph Stormer, Esq., in Upper Chanceford township, York county, on the 29th day of December, A. D. 1846, between the hours of one and four o'clock, P. M., of that day, before the said Joseph Stormer, Esq., when and where you may attend, if you think proper.

It appeared that the name of the justice was Joseph *Stermer.* The caption, deposition, and certificate were as follows:—

[Sample v. Robb.]

Deposition of witness, sworn and examined at the office of Joseph Stermer, one of the justices of the peace in and for York county, at Upper Chanceford township, in said county, on the 29th day of December, A. D. 1846, between the hours of 1 and 4 o'clock, P. M., of said day, in obedience to the rule of court, and notice hereto attached, to be read in a cause depending in the county of Mifflin, at Lewistown, in which James Robb is plaintiff, and Samuel Sample and David W. Hulings, defendants.

William C. Cornwell, sworn:—The first acquaintance I had with Mr. Hulings, was in the latter part of the summer of 1838, which was at Matilda Furnace, in Mifflin county, or near the county line of Huntingdon county. The second or third day after I first saw David W. Hulings, I rode in company with him from Matilda Furnace to Hope Furnace, and from Hope Furnace to Lewistown, and stopped all night with him; that was the first time I ever was in Lewistown, which was about two or three weeks after I first came to Mifflin county, which was the first time I ever was in the county of Mifflin. I have no knowledge of witnessing a deed from Rhodes to David W. Hulings, or any other person. I am positive that I never witnessed a deed in 1831, in Mifflin county, and I have no recollection of witnessing one since.

WM. C. CORNWELL.

I certify that the above witness was duly qualified and examined at the time and place stated in the caption, and subscribed his deposition in my presence.

JOSEPH STERMER, Justice of the Peace.

Upper Chanceford, December 29th, 1846.

On part of *plaintiff*, it was offered to prove by John W. Shaw, the declaration of *Bostian Rhodes*, made at the time the survey was made. Objected to.

Court:—This testimony, when before offered, we rejected, because it was *after* his deed to Mr. Hulings. The evidence now raises a question as to the date of that deed; and whether it was made before or after Robb's warrant was located, is a question for the jury; if after that, his declarations at the time may be evidence to show to what extent his claim by his improvement extended; there were two settlers; he may have claimed for himself or Lewis; his declarations, although he may not affect Lewis's claim, and although he then claimed for himself, would be evidence to show to what extent he claimed by his improvement.

Objection overruled, and defendant excepts. This was the subject of defendant's *fifth* bill, and of the *fourth* assignment of error.

John W. Shaw:—He (Bostian Rhodes) stated that he claimed *in his own right, and not under Lewis or Hulings*. I asked if he had marked his boundary to the extent of his claim; he said he

[Sample v. Robb.]

had not. I then told him we would leave him out of the survey, and give him some woodland with his clear land; we did so, and he appeared satisfied. His improvement was very near the mountain line. I did not run the mountain. I could not say positively that the line we run was the mountain line, but it was very near where the mountain line is usually run. I remember what I took down at the time. We next came to the Charles Kemberly improvement; we included that improvement in this survey. There appeared to be three or four acres of land once cleared; no fence round it; house rotted down—no roof on it; no stable. The Rhodes improvement was a house about sixteen feet square. We left out for Sunderland fifty-two perches, running round what is called the Lewis survey. I thought the marks were not all the same age; it might have been run, but I thought they were the marks of the adjoining survey. I searched for the corners of the line shown by the draft dividing Harris and Lewis; could not find any. The adjoining appropriated land was better than this disputed.

Cross examined:—I run all round this land; run by the adjoining surveys; the lines correspond with the adjoining lines and the Lewis survey in evidence. I have a distinct recollection of what Rhodes said, independent of my notes. Never saw Bostian Rhodes's house before; he was a middling old man; do not recollect that I said he could not hold by his improvement; told him we would run round it and leave him his improvement and some wood land; he went with us. I cannot say that he said he was satisfied; he appeared satisfied; he said he had not his boundaries marked; I told him he ought to have had his lines marked. I had all the drafts of the adjoiners, but Allen and Kimberly; I run by the adjoining surveys. I had this Lewis draft with me. I suppose Robb knew of Hulings's claim, but I do not recollect what he said about it. I was concerned in this suit originally. I took all my notes with a pencil and copied it. I have not the original.

Re-examined:—Mr. Robb saw these drafts; I suppose from that that Mr. Robb knew of Hulings's claim, but do not recollect any thing he said. I think I made a draft for Mr. Robb of the adjoining surveys before he got a warrant.

Robert Graham sworn:—I lived on the Kemberly improvement; they had fruit-trees and built a house. It is about eighteen years ago, when I left them and went on to the canal, and never went there since. Kemberly is my father-in-law; he told me he would give me 100 acres if I would build a house. I lived on it seven years under Kemberly.

Objected that the declarations of Kemberly are not evidence.

Objection overruled, and defendant excepts. This was the subject of the defendant's *sixth* bill, and of the *fifth* assignment of error.

[Sample v. Robb.]

Kemberly said he would give 100 acres if I would put a house or cabin on it. I did build one, and lived in it seven years, and left it of my own accord. It was in January, at the deep snow.

Cross-examined:—He never told me how much land he claimed there; he told me he would give me the 100 acres. I am married to his daughter; left of my own accord, never intending to go back; left the old lady and a son there; they remained there two or three years after. Never heard Mr. Kemberly say that he had sold to Mr. Lewis; never heard him say any thing about a deed to Lewis. I heard of Mr. Hulings's claim to the land when I lived there.

Re-examined:—I know Mr. Kemberly had fruit-trees, and exercised acts of ownership over it as his own.

On part of *plaintiff* it was offered to prove by Mr. Graham that there was no improvement on the Sunderland place or the *Lewis* tract, on the land claimed by Lewis; no residence on it. This was objected to: the *objection* was overruled, and exception taken on part of *defendants*. This was the subject of the *seventh* bill, and of the *sixth* assignment of error.

Robert Rankin testified:—There was no house to my knowledge; lived on what was called the Sunderland improvement; was a cabin there, may be fifteen years ago; I saw it; not certain there was a roof on it; no cleared land; may have been burned down when the woods was on fire.

George Allen:—I remember the Sunderland cabin a long time ago; was burned by fire in the woods, upwards of twenty years ago; never knew any person to live in it.

WILSON, President, charged in part, as follows:—

The plaintiff, to maintain this action for the recovery of the land in dispute, shows a perfect title to himself, by a warrant from the commonwealth, dated the 9th day of January 1837, on which he had the land surveyed by the proper officer, on the 25th day of May 1837, and returned to the land-office on the 6th June 1837, where the return was accepted.

The defendant does not show any legal title, emanating from the commonwealth, under which he pretends to hold or defeat the plaintiff, but relies on a right of pre-emption, acquired by improvement and actual settlement. Such right is acquired by an actual personal resident settlement on unappropriated land, with a manifest intention of making it a place of abode and the means of supporting a family, and continued from time to time, unless interrupted by the enemy, or going into the military service during the war; and under such actual occupancy, the occupant and settler, by marking his boundaries could hold against a person attempting to locate a warrant, a quantity not exceeding 400 acres.

To show title by such settlement and occupancy, the defendant, in one branch of his claim, proves a settlement made by Charles

[Sample v. Robb.]

Kemberly, in 1806, or about that time, putting up a cabin-house, clearing parts of the land, cultivating it and improving it, and on which he continued to live, with his family, until 1827, when he died. His widow and part of the family continued to occupy the land until 1831 certainly, and perhaps to 1832 or '33—most probably till 1832. On the 5th of April 1810, Kemberly and wife conveyed their improvement right to William Lewis. Surveys are produced by the defendant, describing this land, but not made by authority of any warrant granted for that purpose, in the name of William Lewis, and were not admitted in evidence for the purpose of showing any title in the defendants, but as matter of description of the extent Lewis claimed, corresponding with lines marked on the ground. A judgment was obtained against the administrator of William Lewis, which was levied, among other lands, on a tract in Wayne township, surveyed in the name of William Lewis, containing 349 acres and 94 perches, which it is said corresponds with the drafts given in evidence, including the Kemberly improvement, which was sold in 1825 to A. S. Wilson, who purchased it for Joseph Milliken and others, who sold it soon after to D. W. Hulings. Mr. Hulings entered into an agreement, on lease, with Susannah Kemberly, to hold the land under him, on the 22d of May 1832. Susannah Kemberly was the widow of Charles Kemberly, and if she left the land in 1831, she never held possession under this agreement. If she was living on the land, as testified to by some of the witnesses, she left possession of it soon after the date of the lease, and never returned to it to occupy it. She went to Bedford county, but returned to this county in 1838 or '39, and, George Allen says, wanted to go on the land, but did not. She did not, however, return to the land. Mr. Allen says that in the spring of 1838, Mr. Hulings got him to put up a cabin house on the Kemberly tract; that he also fenced in an acre or an acre and a half of the land, and sowed some flax-seed and oats, but did not go to reside on the land. The next occupant of the premises that had been occupied by the Kemberlies, was Samuel Sample, who went into possession in 1842. During the time the Kemberlies occupied, no person not having a right under their improvement, could locate a warrant to hold the land they occupied. *Robb's warrant was located, including it, in May* 1837. At this time their improvement was unoccupied. The *defendant* does not pretend to have acquired a title under any warrant for the land from the commonwealth, or to show that any warrant was ever issued to any person for it from the commonwealth. Robb, the plaintiff, took out his warrant in 1837. It remained until then unappropriated, and was vacant land at the time of Robb's survey. "An improvement on vacant land is nothing of itself, and can give the person making it no right whatever to the land, unless it be prosecuted with reasonable diligence, and consummated by an actual personal resident

[Sample v. Robb.]

settlement thereon, with a manifest intention of making it a place of abode and the means of supporting a family, and continued from time to time, unless interrupted by the enemy or going into military service during the war." (He referred to the opinion of Judge KENNEDY, in the case of Atchison v. McCulloch, 5 *Watts* 15.) Although, by the residence of the Kemberlies, they had acquired a right by which they might have held 400 acres, yet that right, where the claimant under such residence does not procure his warrant for it from the commonwealth, may be lost by abandoning the possession of it. The commonwealth is entitled to payment for all her lands; and an appropriator—one who takes out a warrant and pays the commonwealth for her land—is not to be held for ever at bay by an improver who had abandoned the possession and occupancy of land, which he commenced as an inception of title to it. It is a continuance of residence, with occasional exceptions of temporary but indispensable interruption of it as circumstances may require, that will vest the right of pre-emption in the settler of vacant land. A settler leaving his improvement for a temporary purpose, with an intention of returning to it, does not lose his right; but if he leaves the possession and occupation of it without an intention of returning to the premises to occupy it as a place of abode, it becomes open to location by a warrantee who has purchased from the commonwealth; and whether there was such intention of returning, frequently and in most instances, is a question of fact for a jury to determine; but the abandonment may be for such a length of time that the intention to return will not save the improver's claim against a subsequent warrantee from the commonwealth appropriating the land by having his warrant executed. The proof here is that the family of the Kemberlies, under whom the defendant claims, or who may have been his tenants, in actual possession, holding from Mr. Hulings, left the premises in 1831, '2 or '3. When they left, a question is raised, was it with an intention to return to the premises as a place of abode, or was it the intention of Mr. Hulings, the landlord, to put another in possession to hold for him. Mr. Hulings, in 1838, asked Allen to put up a cabin for him. Allen did, and sowed some flax and oats; but this was not the actual resident occupation required by the act of Assembly to enable a settler to hold against the warrantee. Mrs. Kemberly returned to this county in 1838, but did not go upon it, and it was not again occupied until 1842, when *Sample went into the possession of it, under Mr. Hulings.* This intention manifested by Mr. Hulings, of holding claim to the land, and of again occupying, *was after Robb had located his warrant*, and the intention in 1838 to claim will not avail the improver any thing, after proof of non-occupation from 1831 or '32 until 1842. Graham, who occupied a part of the land by Charles Kemberly, left, as he says, with an intention never to return to it. The Kemberlies went

[Sample v. Robb.]

to Bedford in 1831 or '32; the sons never returned to this county, and the mother did not return to the county until 1838. On the improvement commenced by Charles Kemberly there was no occupation, by either residence or cultivation, during that period. George Allen says, Mr. Hulings asked him, when he went to that place in 1835, to look a little after the land for him, and says he built a cabin for Mr. Hulings, where Charles Kemberly lived in 1837 or '38, covered it with boards and fenced up a patch, sowed some oats and flax on it, and kept up the fences for two or three years. On his cross-examination, he says there was no floor in it, and that it was not designed for any person to live in it. *The old Kemberly house* had gone down, and when so suffered to go down for the length of time that elapsed from the time the Kemberlies left until Robb's warrant was located, and from the manner in which the improvement was suffered to dilapidate, was certainly not such a prosecution of a settlement and residence as the law requires to secure title to land by an improver, without a warrant from the commonwealth. Under these circumstances, after an abandonment, an intent merely to resume the settlement is immaterial. To substitute claim for residence, and convenience for prosecution of title, would subvert the whole doctrine of improvement. It is the continuance of residence, with such occasional exceptions of temporary but indispensable interruption of it as circumstances may require, which is the groundwork of the title. The defendant's right does not depend on the intention to return to reside on the land, after abandoning without an intention to return to it, for the length of time that this improvement was unoccupied, and particularly when such intention to return is not manifested until after a warrant granted by the commonwealth is actually located.

The defendant, further, as a defence to the plaintiff's right to recover, interposes an improvement and residence by Bostian Rhodes on a part of the land which the defendant claims under his purchase of the Lewis property. The Kemberlies were occupying their improvements when Bostian Rhodes made his improvement about the year 1822, and continued to reside there until he died, in 1839, which was after Robb's warrant was located. The question under this part of the case is, whether Bostian Rhodes was on the land *as the tenant of Lewis*, or, at the time of the location of Robb's warrant, the *tenant of Mr. Hulings*, holding the improvement for him. If he was so holding, he could not abandon the possession in favor of Robb's warrant.

Kemberly had sold his improvement to William Lewis in 1810, and describes his improvement as bounded on the south by Elizabeth McLaughlin, on the east by Jacob Kemberly, and on the north by Jack's Mountain. Lines are found there by the surveyors, and whether made by Lewis or by the adjoining owners, Kemberly sells by these lines; that is, the two lines mentioned in the deed,

[Sample v. Robb.]

which would be a designation of the boundary to which he claimed on that side of the improvement at that time. It has then to be determined whether Bostian Rhodes, who was in possession of his improvement, was on the land claimed to be held by Lewis under this improvement commenced by Kemberly, or whether he was on the land under Mr. Lewis, as his tenant, or subsequently of Mr. Hulings, when the warrant of Robb was located, and with marked boundaries, including the 50 acres in dispute. George Allen says Bostian Rhodes made an improvement a year or two after 1820, or about that time; he lived there till he died, in 1838, or winter of 1839. I spoke to the old man once, and asked him if he had the land on his own hook, or under an agreement with any one; he said he had an agreement with Lewis, or Sunderland, or Bratton, who had charge of Lewis's land. I do not know whether Bratton was executor; he had something to do with the land. (A record in evidence shows that Bratton was one of the executors of Lewis.) I think I had more than one conversation with Bostian about it; he worked for me sometimes; never alleged the title was in any other person than Lewis. I lived near him. Mr. Shaw, who located the warrant of Robb, says, "He (Bostian Rhodes) stated that he claimed in his own right. I asked him if he had marked his boundary as to the extent of his claim; he said he had not. I then told him we would throw him out of the survey and give him some woodland with his cleared land; we did so, and he appeared satisfied." On cross-examination he says, "I do not recollect that I said he could not hold by his improvement; told him we would run round it and leave him his improvement and some woodland; he went with us. I cannot say that he said he was satisfied; he appeared satisfied; he said he had not his boundaries marked. I told him he ought to have had his lines marked. Robert Graham says: "I lived about half a mile from Bostian Rhodes; was well acquainted with him when he lived there; he told me *he claimed the land for himself;* two or three times during the 7 years, (the 7 years he lived on the Kemberly claim,) and perhaps more, I understood it from him." Cross-examined:—"He did not tell me how much he claimed there. It has passed my recollection when it was; was during the 7 years I lived there. He did not just tell me he was going to hold it as vacant; it was understood. It was understood he had no writings for it."

The defendant has given in evidence a deed to him from Bostian Rhodes, dated the 3d April 1831. There are recitals in this deed acknowledging a holding from Lewis, and would amount to a conveyance by Rhodes of his claim; and if such is the correct date, it was before Robb's warrant was located, and Bostian Rhodes' declarations on the ground, spoken of by Shaw, should have no effect as against Mr. Hulings, his landlord. But if this deed was not executed at the time of the location of the warrant, and Rhodes

[Sample *v.* Robb.]

was satisfied with the location of Robb's warrant, and did not object to the location as made, (being present,) if he was not in under Lewis, this deed could not affect Robb's title. The deed purports to have been executed on the 3d of April 1831. * * * It purports to be executed at that time, in the presence of William C. Cornwell. William C. Cornwell has no recollection of subscribing it as a witness, &c. * * * *If it was not made till* 1838, Mr. Hulings and Rhodes could not then, which was *after* Robb's warrant had been located by actual survey in the presence of Rhodes, execute an instrument between themselves, and to which Robb was no party, to the prejudice of any right previously vested in Robb. You will decide the case on the testimony submitted, and the question for your decision is whether there was an actual resident settlement on the premises, and a claim in pursuance of the improvement made by the settler, that included the land in dispute. If there was, the plaintiff cannot recover. If there was not, the plaintiff will be entitled to your verdict.

Verdict was rendered for plaintiff as before stated.

It was assigned for error:
1. The court erred in rejecting the evidence set forth in defendant's 1st and 2d bills of exception. 2. The court erred in rejecting the evidence set forth in defendant's 3d bill of exceptions. 3. The court erred in receiving the deposition of William C. Cornwell, set forth in defendant's 4th bill of exceptions. 4. The court erred in receiving the evidence of Bostian Rhodes's declarations, as set forth in defendant's 5th bill of exceptions. 5. The court erred in receiving the evidence of the declarations of Kemberly, as set forth in defendant's 6th bill of exceptions. 6. The court erred in receiving the evidence in regard to the Sunderland improvement, as set forth in defendant's 7th bill of exceptions. 7. The court erred in their charge in relation to the Kemberly improvement, commencing with, "The old Kemberly," &c., and ending with "as actually located." 8. The court erred in their charge in relation to the Rhodes improvement, commencing with, "But if the deed," &c., and ending with "title," and in omitting to bring to the notice of the jury, in that connection, Rhodes's declaration of holding under Lewis, as proved by Allen. 9. The description of plaintiff's claim, "A tract or piece of land in Oliver township, Mifflin county, bounded by other land of James Robb and others, containing 50 acres, or thereabouts," is insufficient, and the verdict and judgment thereon are erroneous.

The case was argued by *R. C. Hale* and *J. Fisher*, for plaintiffs in error.

A. Parker and *E. L. Benedict*, for Robb, defendant in error.

[Sample v. Robb.]

The opinion of the court was delivered June 16, by

COULTER, J.—If there had been an actual settlement on the land, and the settler had adopted the lines designated by the old drafts found in the land-office and offered in evidence as the boundaries of his claim, and proved that he did so adopt the lines indicated by them, I can see no objection to their having been received in evidence.

But as the drafts were offered first by the defendant below, without any warrant being given in evidence, improvement, or location, they were properly rejected. The most that would accrue from these papers was evidence of boundary, and not title. But there was no claim in evidence which they could bound. This ends the 1st exception to evidence.

The offer to give "*the talk of* the neighbors" in evidence was rightfully rejected. It is the first time I have heard that such evidence as "It was always spoken of in the neighborhood as Lewis's land," was entitled to any weight whatever on the trial of an ejectment, or was an element of title. The 2d exception is not sustained.

There is nothing in the 3d exception. The paper, if a transcript of lines on the ground, might be evidence if the defendant showed that when his improvement was commenced and prosecuted he claimed up to those lines and adopted them as the boundary of his claim; and that far the court admitted them, and for that purpose, and this was right. The papers in themselves were no evidence whatever of title.

It appears distinctly enough that William C. Cornwell was sworn before he gave his deposition. I do not see how that fact could be doubted after reading the caption. It is sufficiently certain that the deposition was taken at the place appointed. It was taken in York county, Chanceford township, at the office of Joseph Stermer, Esq., a justice of the peace, &c. The rule says it is to be taken at the office of Joseph Stormer, Esq., &c. This is a mere literal error in spelling the name. It would be good under the principle of *idem sonans*, until it was shown that in Chanceford township there were two justices, one Joseph Stermer, and the other Joseph Stormer. Therefore the 4th exception is of no moment.

Rhodes claimed in his own right, as alleged by plaintiff, and not under any one else; he lived on the ground, had built a cabin sixteen feet square, and cleared a little land; his declarations then made on the ground and at the time a survey was to be executed, were good evidence as to the extent of his claim—there could be none better. But these declarations ought not to have affected the right or claim of Lewis. The court, however, distinctly stated that these declarations were good for nothing, except to define the claim or boundary of Rhodes, who was dead at the trial, and to that extent they were admitted in evidence. There is no error in

[Sample v. Robb.]

this exception. Kemberly's declarations were evidence to show how he occupied the land: he was living on it, making improvements, and had built a house; his declarations to Graham that he claimed the land as his own, and his offer to give Graham, who was his son-in-law, a certain portion of the land if he would improve and live on it, were evidence that he did not occupy or claim under Lewis or Hulings.

The argument used against these declarations being received was that Rhodes and Kemberly occupied under Lewis, and that a tenant could not defeat the title of his landlord. That he cannot, is very true; nor can he set up title against him. But the court could not assume that the testimony of Allen in respect to these admissions was in this respect absolutely true, and exclude evidence which went to contradict it.

It was a question for the jury to determine what was the character of the occupancy of Rhodes and Kemberly from the evidence, and particularly of Rhodes, under the circumstances. And the court put the case to the jury on that footing, to wit, that if Rhodes was the tenant of Lewis or Hulings, that those declarations should not affect Hulings, who claims under Lewis. Both Kemberly and Rhodes were dead before the trial, and their declarations made on the land at the time they occupied were admissible in evidence to show how they occupied it.

There is nothing in the 7th bill of exceptions. The testimony of Graham, that there was no improvement on the Sunderland tract, and no residence on the part claimed by Lewis, was not impertinent or irrelevant. It tended to elucidate and explain the matter in controversy; and as to its not being strictly rebutting, that is of little consequence. For, in a case so mixed up with conflicting claims as this, an important fact is sometimes omitted in its proper order, or its necessity and usefulness not perceived until developments on the other side manifest its importance. It could not have taken the other party by surprise, for obvious reasons.

The evidence of abandonment may be so clear as to justify the court in telling the jury, as a matter of law, that there has been an abandonment; but the court does not go so far in this case. They recapitulate the facts and instruct the jury what amounts to an abandonment, and perhaps intimate that in their opinion there was an abandonment. This intimation, however, is to be drawn more from the facts which they recapitulate, and the law which they declare and announce, and in which they do not err, than from any positive declaration. But they submit the whole matter of fact as to the continued actual resident settlement, both as to Rhodes and Kemberly, and also Hulings, to the jury, and instruct them that if such settlement was proved in their judgment, that then the plaintiff was not entitled to recover; and give the jury suitable instructions as to what constituted such settlement.

[Sample v. Robb.]

We see no error in that part of the charge designated in the 8th error assigned. The court distinctly submit the fact whether Rhodes was in under Lewis or not. It is true, they do not mention the evidence of Allen; nor do they mention the testimony of witnesses the other way. But they distinctly say that if Rhodes was *not in under Lewis*, and did not object to the location of Robb's warrant, and was satisfied with the location, that a deed made by him afterwards to Hulings could not affect the location of the warrant, or Robb's title under it: and in this they were right. Taking the sentence in connection with what they had said before on the subject of Rhodes being in under Lewis, the jury could have no doubt but that if Rhodes was in under Lewis, his agreement to the location could not affect Lewis or Hulings, who claimed under him.

There is nothing in the 9th error as to the description of the land in the writ. The defect was supplied by a description filed at the trial.

Judgment affirmed.

Guthrie's Appeal.

Under the act of 13th June 1836, relative to lunatics, when the Court of Common Pleas has decreed an allowance out of the proceeds of sale of the real estate of a lunatic, for his maintenance, the amount is not to be exceeded without the sanction of the court. The estate of a lunatic is subject to the control of that court.

THIS was an appeal by George Guthrie, administrator of the estate of William Guthrie, deceased, from the decree of the Orphans' Court of Centre county, on his administration account.

In 1832, William Guthrie was found to be a lunatic, under proceedings had in the Court of Common Pleas of Centre county, and John Potter and William Iddings were appointed his committee. In pursuance of an order of said court, made 28th January 1837, his real estate was ordered to be sold. George Guthrie, the eldest son, and only one not then in his minority, purchased the land, and on his petition and that of his mother and the other children, the court changed the terms of the sale, and, by a special decree, directed that $2000 should be secured by bond and mortgage on the premises, "conditioned for the payment of all the interest yearly, and so much of the principal as the court may from time to time order and direct, to the maintenance and support of said lunatic, and upon the decease or restoration of said lunatic, then the residue of said money to be paid to such person or persons as by the laws of this commonwealth are legally entitled thereto, under the decree of this court." The hand-money paid and satisfied the debts

[Guthrie's Appeal.]

of the lunatic, and the mortgage was executed in accordance with the decree.

On the 30th November 1837, the committee having settled their account, John Potter was discharged; the purchaser went into possession of the real restate, and his father went to reside with him, and there continued until his death, on the 14th December 1844.

In 1845, George Guthrie, the purchaser of the estate and mortgagor, took out letters of administration, and in his administration account charged the sum of $200 a year for the maintenance of his father. The administrator kept no account against his father; he had no vouchers for any expenses incurred, nor any charges in his books of account. No contract was ever made by the committee with George Guthrie for the maintenance of the lunatic; nor was there ever any application made to the court for any additional allowance for his maintenance.

The account was referred to auditors. The third exception to the administration account was—The annual interest on the mortgage was more than a sufficient allowance for the keeping of William Guthrie, and the administrator should be charged with that excess, and interest thereon.

The auditors reported as to this exception, viz. "The evidence on this subject is somewhat contradictory, but the weight of the testimony goes to prove that the charge is not an unreasonable one, considering all the circumstances, and we therefore feel bound to say that this part of the objection is not sustained. We must not estimate the expense and trouble as we would that of supporting a person in the full exercise of his reason, but we are to take into view the trouble and expense which arise purely from the irregularity of his conduct. Secondly, on this point it was argued that he is entitled to no more annually than the interest accruing on the mortgage, inasmuch as that was all that the committee were allowed to expend for that purpose, until the court so ordered; and as the power of the committee terminated at the death of the lunatic, no further decree can be made in the premises by the Common Pleas. This objection requires us to dispose of another point which was not raised on the argument. Is the accountant required to pursue the committee of the lunatic for satisfaction of his demand, or, were he not the administrator, could he recover the amount from his personal representative? It appears from the evidence that no contract existed between the committee and George Guthrie, relative to maintenance. Mr. Iddings, on the contrary, swears that "he rather considered that he was clear of him when the account was filed." If an express contract were made with the committee, or a contract arose from necessary implication, no doubt the law would drive him to seek his remedy from them. But, on the contrary, it would seem that no dealing

[Guthrie's Appeal.]

was had on that account between the committee and George, and he was left to be taken care of by George, without any understanding on the subject, and Mr. Iddings never took any notice of his trust from the settlement of the account, in 1837, down to the time of the lunatic's death. It is clear, that if the lunatic was not in the hands of a committee, a person furnishing him with necessaries may recover the amount from him after his mind has been restored, or from his administrator after his death; and when the committee, in case there be one, perform their duties and supply his wants, a person furnishing even necessaries to the lunatic could not recover the amount thereof. But the law is otherwise when the committee neglect to provide for their charge; and such appears to be the case. This point is decided in the case of Call v. Ward, 4 *W. & Ser.* 118, where the question arose in reference to another relation, which we look upon as analagous in this respect. The contract being with the lunatic, and not with the committee, the amount to be allowed is not limited by the decree of the Common Pleas, as it might be in case it was necessary to resort to the committee for compensation. If the lunatic had recovered his reason, then, under the decision above referred to, an action of *indebitatus assumpsit* could be maintained against him, and, of course, it would lie against his personal representative after his death. We think, therefore, that the amount of the compensation is in no way affected by the action of the Common Pleas, and must depend upon the evidence in the case.

Exceptions were filed by the heirs of William Guthrie to the report of the auditors, and on the 9th of February, 1849, the Orphans' Court awarded an issue to be certified to the Common Pleas, to settle the amount of compensation to which the accountant would be entitled. Upon the trial of the feigned issue, certain questions of law were raised, which were *reserved* by the court for their determination after the verdict should be rendered. The jury found for the accountant the full amount claimed by him for the maintainance of his father, viz. $1966.49, but the court, after argument, directed the clerk to restate the account, allowing the accountant annually the interest on the mortgage given by him to the committee of the lunatic, being $120 per annum. This was accordingly done. From the decree of the Orphans' Court the accountant appealed.

The opinion of WOODWARD, J., in part, was as follows:—

From the time that a man is decreed a lunatic, according to our act of Assembly, his estate is placed in *custodia legis*. His committee are the agents of the law to manage it and apply the "income." If the income be found inadequate to pay his debts, and to support the lunatic and his family, his personal estate may, under direction of the court, be applied to these purposes; and if this fail, necessary portions of the real estate may be mortgaged or

[Guthrie's Appeal.]

sold, as the court in its discretion, after inquiries and audits, shall decree. * * *

I speak not of imaginable cases, where, after refusal by the committee to provide, and before application could be made to the court, humanity affords temporary relief, nor of circumstances of sudden and extreme emergencies. In these and similar conditions I would be willing to admit that the law would subject the estate to a *quantum meruit* compensation of the benefactor. But when the court has taken orders for his support, sold his real estate, secured the price by mortgage, and devoted the interest to his support, and has not dissolved the commission, nor been asked to discharge the committee, but is maintaining the system that the legislature has provided, I deny that any man, whether a son or a stranger, can, for a period of years, take more of his estate, according to his discretion, or judgment of his neighbor, and apply it to the support and maintenance of the lunatic. That estate, and the owner of it, have been segregated from the community and placed with the court, under a system of rules and regulations, and whoever would touch it, must approach it according to that system.

Although there was no arrangement between the plaintiff and Mr. Iddings, the continuing committee man, that the plaintiff should take his father, and keep down the interest on the mortgage, which he had undertaken to pay, that, nevertheless, would have been a "very convenient and suitable disposition to be made of" the lunatic. And when Mr. Iddings saw the plaintiff taking and keeping him, and withholding the annual interest on the mortgage, it is not strange that he should have let it alone, as the best arrangement for all the parties that could be made. But if Mr. Guthrie found that $120 a year was not compensating him, he was bound to remember, what he very well knew, that the estate of his father was in the keeping of the court, and that until the conscience of the court was further informed, $120 a year was the appointed compensation for keeping him.

He never applied to the court, either to remove the committee or enlarge the allowance, but now, after the father is dead, he asks that the heirs should allow him to take out of the estate $80 a year more than the court had adjudged to be necessary.

That he deserved this extra allowance we are bound to presume, seeing that the auditors and a jury have pronounced in his favor; but he cannot have it, because the law interposes an insuperable obstacle. It is a rule, founded in an express statute, (see act of 1806, not referred to in the argument,) that where a remedy is provided, or a duty enjoined, or a thing directed to be done, by an act of Assembly, "the directions of said act shall be strictly pursued, and no penalty shall be inflicted or any thing done agreeably to the provisions of the common law in such cases, further than shall

[Guthrie's Appeal.]

be necessary for carrying such act or acts into effect." See *Dunlop's Dig.* 243, and 1 *Pa. Rep.* 283.

The fact that the question is raised after the death of the lunatic, cannot change the principle on which it is to be decided. The protection given to the estate extended throughout his life, and although his death dissolved the commission and all proceedings under it, we cannot go back and treat it as an unprotected estate, and order it to purposes *now* which it could not have been made to answer in his lifetime. The rights of the heirs were among the objects of protection contemplated by the act of Assembly. On the whole, I am of opinion that the plaintiff should have credit in his administration account, not for the amount claimed by him, nor for the amount of the verdict, but for the amount of the accruing interest on the mortgage.

Curtin and *Linn*, for appellant.—The plaintiff in error took the lunatic to his house and maintained him comfortably till his death. His *death* discharged his committee, and all his estate passed from the control of the Common Pleas to the Orphans' Court. The charge for his support and maintenance became a debt against his estate, letters of administration were granted to plaintiff, the jurisdiction of the Orphans' Court attached, and the act of 13th June 1836 ceased to control or affect the estate of the lunatic.

The committee could at any time during the life of the lunatic, when the income from his estate became inadequate to his support, have applied to the Common Pleas for power to raise more money. If they had advanced their own money, they could have been reimbursed in the same way. They did not, and the administrator is now in court, asking that to be done which ought to have been done, and in a court which has exclusive jurisdiction of the estate, independent of the act of 13th June 1836.

As to the reasonable character of the claim, reference was made to the administration account passed and allowed by the register, the report of the auditors on exceptions filed to it, and the verdict of the jury allowing to the plaintiff the amount claimed : 11 *Pickering* 304, cited.

Burnside, with whom was *McAllister*, for appellee.—The act of 13th June 1836, relative to lunatics, is a regular system in itself; all the details of the proceedings are minutely set forth ; the manner in which the jurisdiction shall be exercised; the form of the commission ; upon whose application it shall be issued ; the number of jurors; the pay of the commissioner, in short all the provisions of the act constitute the Court of Common Pleas the guardian of lunatics, as fully as is the crown in Great Britain.

It is the duty of the committee (20th section) to apply the income of the real and personal estate to the support of the lunatic.

[Guthrie's Appeal.]

If that is not sufficient, (section 21,) it is lawful for the committee, "*under the directions of the court,* to apply so much of the personal estate as shall be necessary," &c. Should this also prove insufficient, the succeeding sections provide how his maintenance may be supplied from the real estate.

The committee (section 43) are entirely under the order and control of the court.

William Guthrie and his estate were in *custodia legis*. The court had ordered that two thousand dollars should be secured by bond and mortgage on the premises, "conditioned for the payment of all the interest yearly, and so much of the principal as the court may from time to time order and direct, to the maintenance and support of said lunatic;" and no more than that interest could be taken for the support of the lunatic, by the committee, or any one else, without obtaining, in accordance with the act, the sanction of the court. This was never asked during the lifetime of the lunatic.

The opinion of the court was delivered June 16, by

BELL, J.—The conclusion arrived at by the court below is obviously a just deduction from the evidence given and the law applicable to the facts proved. The reasons given by the judge who pronounced the decision are so far satisfactory that I deem it unnecessary to add any thing to his argument, save a reference to Eckstein's case, 2 *Pa. Law Jour.* 138, approved by this court in Wright's Appeal, 8 *Barr* 57, both of which harmonize with and enforce the general view taken below of the extent of protection to which the person and estate of a lunatic are entitled.

Were it necessary to support the decree, I think it might be assumed the law would, from the circumstances proved, imply a tacit agreement on the part of the appellant to keep and maintain his father for the yearly sum assigned by the court for that purpose. Indeed I cannot well see how such a presumption is to be evaded, if any regard be due to probabilities.

Decree affirmed.

Jessup *versus* Smuck.

A testator having devised to his son Samuel, and to his heirs and assigns, the residue of a tract of land, he or they paying thereout and therefor to one of his daughters £50, in *one* and *two* years after his decease, and to his son Joel £50, in *four* years after his decease, and to another daughter £80, *one* year after his decease, or at his option to give them land worth the money devised to them, and to a grandson £10, to be paid *six* years after his decease, "and in case my son Samuel should die before he marries, then all that part of my estate which I have devised to him, in that case I give and devise to my son Joel Willis, his heirs and assigns, to have and to hold to him my said son Joel, his heirs and assigns for ever, in as full and ample a manner as my son Samuel held, or was to have held the same, and subject to the same conditions and payments," and also to the further payment of £460, the money so paid to be divided between all his daughters equally. He further directed that the residue of his estate, real and personal, should be sold by his executors, and the proceeds divided between Joel and the five daughters of the testator; but in case Samuel should die *before he marries*, and the estate devised to him devolve to Joel, then in that case, it was his will that Joel should not have any part of the residual estate, but that it should be divided between his daughters:

Held, that Samuel having died *unmarried*, after the death of the testator, the estate passed by executory devise to the heirs or devisees of *Joel;* that the testator contemplated the death of Samuel, whenever it might happen, *before marriage*, as the event on which the estate devised was limited over in fee to Joel, his heirs and assigns, and as Samuel died *before he married*, the estate by the limitation became the property of the heirs or devisees of Joel; they to take it subject to the payment of the legacies charged on it, if not paid, and to the payment of £460, to the daughters of the testator, or their representatives; and also to the payment to the same of what Joel may have received out of the residuary estate.

ERROR to the Common Pleas of *York county*.

This was an action of ejectment by Jonathan Jessup, administrator with the will annexed of Joel Willis, deceased, against Levi Smuck and Joel Fisher.

A case was stated as if found by a special verdict, and to be subject to a writ of error, without oath, recognizance, &c.

William Willis, of said York county, on the 30th day of the seventh month, A. D. 1800, made his last will and testament in writing of that date. He died in September 1801; and the said will, on the 7th day of October 1801, was duly proved and recorded in the register's office of said county, (*prout* said will hereto annexed and made part of this case.) At the date of said will, and at his decease, the said William Willis was the owner in fee simple of the land for which this suit is brought.

Letters testamentary on the said will were granted to the executors therein named, on the said 7th day of October, A. D. 1801. The said executors administered the said testator's estate, and filed their account of said administration in the register's office, on the 19th of August 1803, which was duly confirmed by the Orphans' Court of said county, December 20th, 1803, by which account there

[Jessup v. Smuck.]

appears a balance in favor of the estate of £608 4s. 8d. ($1622.95½,) (*prout* said account.) The several legacies in the said will mentioned, out of the personal estate, were paid soon after the settlement of the said account, and the residue was distributed and paid according to the first distribution thereof directed by the will; the testator's daughter Susanna receiving one-sixteenth part, and the testator's son Joel receiving his equal share of it, to wit, £136 19s. 9d., ($373.18.) At the date of said will, the testator's son Samuel was twenty-two years of age, unmarried, and resided with his father. Joel, with his wife and two children, resided in North Carolina; and John resided on the property devised to him in the will.

Samuel Willis, at the death of his father, entered into possession of the land devised to him by the will, and held the same to the time of his death. He was never married, and died intestate on the 22d of January, A. D. 1848, leaving also other real estate and personal property undisposed of. The defendants claim to hold the premises as and for the heirs of the said Samuel Willis.

Samuel Willis, after taking possession of the said land, paid in money the several legacies which he was ordered by the will to pay as devisee of the same, and among others, the legacy of £50 to Joel Willis.

Joel Willis died in the State of Ohio, in January 1843. By his last will and testament, which was duly admitted to probate in this State, and letters of administration with the said will annexed, granted by the register of York county to the plaintiff in this suit, he directed as follows:

Item 3. If I should ever fall heir to a certain tract of land, lying in the State of Pennsylvania, willed to me by my father conditionally, my executors shall sell the same, either at public or private sale, and shall make a good and lawful deed to the purchaser thereof, and after the expenses are all paid, divide the purchase-money equally amongst all of my heirs, namely, Lydia Thornburg, Anna Thornburg, Ariah Hyatt, Jonathan Willis, and Jesse Willis, to them, their heirs and assigns for ever. (*Prout* the said will.)

If upon these facts the plaintiff be entitled to recover—then judgment for the plaintiff.

If the plaintiff would be bound to pay to the legatees again, or to refund to the estate of Samuel Willis, the legacies which Samuel Willis was directed to pay and did pay as devisee of said real estate, or to refund the share of the residue of the testator's estate received by Joel Willis, then judgment to be entered for the plaintiff, on condition of his payment of the sums which he would be liable to pay as aforesaid.

If the plaintiff be not entitled to recover—then judgment for defendants.

[Jessup v. Smuck.]

The will of William Willis, deceased, of Manchester township, York county, contained, *inter alia*, the following provisions:—

Imprimis, my will is and I do hereby order that all my just debts and funeral charges be first paid out of my estate as soon as may be conveniently done after my decease, by my executors hereinafter named.

I do give and devise to my son John Willis and to his heirs and assigns all my messuage and tracts of land situate in Newberry township and county aforesaid adjoining lands of James Bane and others and whereon my son now dwells being three several tracts of land lying contiguous and containing in the whole one hundred and twenty acres be the same more or less with all the buildings and improvements hereditaments and appurtenances to the same belonging or in any wise appertaining, to have and to hold to my said son his heirs and assigns for ever he or they paying thereout and therefor to my executors the sum of one hundred pounds lawful gold or silver coin current in Pennsylvania in manner following (viz.) twenty-five pounds thereof one year after my decease and twenty-five pounds yearly till the whole be paid and also one other hundred pounds for which I mortgaged the said land for his use, the money he shall pay to the mortgagee together with all the interest due and to become due thereon.

Item. I give and bequeath to my daughter Susanna (the wife of Samuel Fisher) the best case of drawers now in my house.

Item. I give and bequeath to my daughter Hannah (the wife of Samuel Wilson) the sum of fifty pounds like money aforesaid to be paid to her by my son Samuel Willis as shall be hereafter directed.

Item. I do give and bequeath to my son Joel Willis and to his heirs and assigns an annuity or yearly ground rent of six pounds per annum due from Peter Sandoe for a mill seat situate on a former part of my land in Manchester township aforesaid and which I had leased to a certain Stophel Slagle subject to the said ground rent of six pounds per annum. To have and to hold to him my said son Joel his heirs and assigns for ever. I also give and bequeath to him my said son the sum of fifty pounds like lawful money aforesaid to be paid to him by my son Samuel Willis as shall be hereinafter directed.

Item. I give and devise to my daughter Lydia (the wife of William Farquhar) four acres of meadow ground to be laid off for her from my land in Manchester township aforesaid beginning at a corner of Joseph Updegraff's meadow at Robert Jones's line thence running up said line so far as to make the said quantity of four acres by running a line parallel to said Joseph Updegraff's line through to Jacob Gartner's line of his meadow lot. To have and to hold the said four acres of meadow ground with the appurtenances to her my said daughter Lydia her heirs and assigns for ever.

Item. I do give and devise to my daughter Mary Willis and to her heirs and assigns four acres of meadow ground to be laid off for her from my land in Manchester township aforesaid, beginning at a corner of that devised to my daughter Lydia at Robert Jones's line, thence up said line so far as to make the said quantity of four acres by running a line parallel to the division line of that devised to my daughter Lydia aforesaid through to Jacob Gartner's line. To have and to hold the same with the appurtenances unto her my said daughter Mary her heirs and assigns for ever. I do also give and bequeath to her my said daughter Mary one feather bed and furniture, a bureau, one cow the choice of my stock, and seven pounds like lawful money aforesaid, exclusively of her dividend of my residual estate.

Item. I do give and devise to my son Samuel Willis and to his heirs and assigns all the residue of my dwelling messuage and tract of land situate in Manchester township aforesaid together with all and exclusively the water-right which I reserved in the before mentioned lease to Stophel Slagle and also twenty-five acres of land be the same more or less adjoining lands of Abraham Yost and others situate in York township. To have and to hold the said messuage and several tracts of land hereditaments and appurtenances to the same or either of the same belonging or in any wise appertaining to him my said son Samuel and to his heirs and assigns for ever. He or they paying thereout and therefor to my daughter Hannah Wilson or to her heirs or assigns the sum of fifty pounds like lawful money aforesaid, twenty-five pounds thereof one year after my decease and the remainder two years after, and to my son Joel Willis or to his heirs and assigns the sum of fifty pounds like lawful money aforesaid four years after my decease, and also to my daughter Betty Willis or to her heirs or assigns the sum of eighty pounds like lawful money aforesaid one year after my decease, or he shall lay off and convey to them and each of them respectively so much of my dwelling plantation as shall be worth their respective sums of money, and I do leave it to his option which he shall do, and he my said son Samuel shall also pay to my grandson James Speakman the sum of ten pounds like lawful money aforesaid six years after my decease. I also give and bequeath to my son Samuel two horse creatures the choice of all those I may be possessed of at my decease he paying or allowing to my residual estate the sum of ten pounds for each and he shall have the liberty of taking one other at the appraisement; and I also give and bequeath to him my said son a desk which stands in my dwelling house and is now called his own and one-third part of the grain which may be in the ground at my decease on my said dwelling plantation and one third of that which may have been raised the preceding year or

[Jessup v. Smuck.]

such part thereof as may not have been disposed of before my decease.

Item. I do give and bequeath to my daughter Betty Willis the sum of eighty pounds like lawful money aforesaid to be paid to her by my son Samuel Willis as above directed and also one feather bed and furniture one bureau and a cow the second choice of my stock and seven pounds lawful money aforesaid to be paid to her by my executors exclusively of her dividend of my residual estate.

And it is my will and I do hereby order that if either of my two daughters Mary and Betty should die before they marry such deceased child's part shall be sold and the money arising from such sale shall be divided as my residual estate, and in case my son Samuel should die before he marries, then all that part of my estate which I have devised to him in that case I give and devise to my son Joel Willis his heirs and assigns. To have and to hold to him my said son Joel his heirs and assigns for ever in as full and ample a manner as my son Samuel held or was to have held the same and subject to the same conditions and payments and he or they shall pay the further sum of four hundred and sixty pounds lawful money aforesaid and the money so paid shall be divided between all my daughters equally share and share alike. And I do hereby further order that all the residue of my estate both real and personal shall be sold by my executors and the monies arising from such sale shall be divided between my son Joel and my five daughters Susanna Hannah Lydia Mary and Betty in the following manner (viz.) Susanna shall have one-sixteenth part of the whole and the remainder shall be equally divided between my other five mentioned children. But in case my son Samuel should die before he marries and the estate which I have devised to him devolve to my son Joel, then in that case it is my will that my said son Joel shall not have any part of my residual estate but that it be divided between my aforesaid five daughters in the following manner (to wit) Susanna shall have one-thirteenth part of the whole and the remainder shall be equally divided between my other four daughters.

And lastly I do hereby appoint my son Samuel Willis and my trusty friend John Love executors of this my last will and testament and do hereby authorize and empower them to sell my tract of land situate in Conewago Mountain and all other my estate not herein otherwise disposed of and also such other part as may fall under their care by the decease of any of my children as aforesaid and deeds and conveyances make do and execute to and for the purchaser or purchasers thereof in as full and ample a manner as I myself could or might now do, and I do hereby revoke and disannul all former wills heretofore by me made and confirm this writing for and to be my last will and testament.

In witness whereof, &c.

[Jessup *v.* Smuck.]

October 2, 1850. The opinion of LEWIS, J., was as follows:—
The plaintiff claims under the will of Joel Willis, who was the son of William Willis, deceased. The defendants claim as heirs of Samuel Willis, who was also a son of William Willis, deceased. William Willis, the common ancestor, in his will, made in 1800, devised the land in controversy "to my son Samuel Willis, *and to his heirs and assigns,*" "to have and to hold," "to him my said son Samuel, and *to his heirs and assigns for ever*, he or they paying thereout and therefor" certain legacies specified in the will. The testator then proceeds to make other dispositions respecting his estate, and in a subsequent part of the will there is this provision: " And in case my son Samuel should die before he marries, then all that part of the estate which I have devised to him in that case I give and devise to my son Joel Willis, his heirs and assigns, to have and to hold to him my said son Joel, his heirs and assigns for ever, *in as full and ample a manner as my son Samuel held or was to have held the same, and subject to the same conditions and payments*"—with a further charge of £460 for the daughters.

The authorities seem to concur in establishing the rule of construction, that where the gift is plainly and clearly a fee simple, to take effect immediately in possession, a devise over in case of the death of the first-named object of the testator's bounty is to be treated or intended to provide for his death in the lifetime of the testator. This rule is *professedly* founded upon the necessity of giving such a construction to a will as shall preserve it from repugnancy, and shall allow each clause a full operation. But it may be aided by the public policy, which is averse to the continuance of lands in a condition incapable of transmission by alienation for long periods of time. The rule does not seem to be confined to cases where death alone is mentioned without any qualification, but has been applied to cases where the estate is directed to go over if either of the first named devisees "should happen to die *without child or children lawfully begotten,*" 5 *B. & Ald.* 636, or "should die *leaving child or children,*" 13 *East* 359, or "should die *without issue born alive,*" 1 *Harris* 152. It would seem also from the cases, and from the observation of Mr. Justice BELL, in the case last cited, that this rule is applicable whether the *corpus* of the gift be personalty or realty, where the whole *interest in each is given*, subject to be defeated by the implied contingency, although most of the cases present bequests of movable property: Caldwell *v.* Skilton, *id.* 126. The qualifications which relate to *marriage* or the *birth of children* are insufficient to take the case out of the rule. To have this effect, some qualification must be introduced which refers to the *time of the death*, and not to the *circumstances* of the *devisee* upon its occurrence.

In the case before us, it does not seem to be material whether the testator contemplated the death of Samuel before the *accept-*

[Jessup v. Smuck.]

ance of the devise and *becoming personally bound* for the legacies to be paid "therefor;" or before final distribution of the estate, or before the death of the testator. We incline to think that the testator referred to the period when his will was to take effect, and that Samuel, not having died unmarried before the testator, took a fee simple subject to no other conditions than the payment of the legacies charged. The devise to Joel, we think, was only intended as a substitution in case of the death of Samuel unmarried *before the death of the testator.* Joel was only to take "in *as full and ample* a manner as Samuel held or was to have held, and *subject to the same conditions* and *payments."* The condition of *dying before he marries* could not be annexed to the gift to Joel, who was already married, and yet he was to hold *as Samuel held,* and *subject* to *the same conditions and payments.* From this, and all the other provisions of the will, we are of opinion that the defendants are entitled to judgment on the case stated.

Judgment for defendants.

It was assigned for error:
The judgment should have been for the plaintiff, subject, if the court considered it necessary to make such order, to the payment of the legacies charged on the premises to the estate of Samuel Willis; and of £460 to the daughters of William Willis, or their representatives; and £136 19s. 9d. to the estate of the said William Willis.

Chapin, for plaintiff in error and plaintiff below.—The plaintiff claims that by the will of William Willis, deceased, Samuel Willis took the fee simple of the premises *defeasible* on his death before marriage, and on the happening of this contingency, the fee simple passed by *executory devise* to Joel Willis, the plaintiff's testator.

That a fee simple may by *executory devise* be limited after a fee simple either *vested* or *contingent,* is as well established as any principle recognised in law: *Fearne on Rem.* 395–6–7, and cases there cited; 4 *Wils. Bac. Abr.* 297; 4 *Kent. Com.* 269–70; 2 *Bin.* 532, Hauer's Lessee v. Sheetz.

The defendants in the court below contended, and the court (Judge LEWIS) decided, that Samuel took at once on the testator's death *an indefeasible estate in fee simple*—in other words, that Joel was a mere substitute, to take only in case the devise to Samuel should lapse *by his death in the testator's lifetime.*

To sustain this position, it was claimed as a rule of construction, that a devise over in the event of death, where the first devisee is to take immediately, is construed to mean death *in the lifetime of the testator.*

The cases cited in support of this position were, with three exceptions, cases in which the death was connected with no other

[Jessup v. Smuck.]

circumstance and with no context indicating a longer time. The words used were merely "in case of her death"—"if either should die"—"in the event of her death"—"in case of her demise"—"in case of death happening to her"—"in case of her decease," &c.

Most of these cases were also of bequests of personal property, with respect to which courts have been more reluctant to sustain executory devises. And, even in these cases, the decisions are conflicting. In Cambridge v. Rous, 8 *Vesey* 12, Sir WILLIAM GRANT says, "Words precisely the same were differently construed in Lord Douglass v. Chalmer," 2 *Vesey Jr.* 501; and Hinckly v. Simmons, 4 *Vesey* 160. In the former, the words were "in case of her decease" and the executory legatee took,—in the latter, the words were "in case of her death," and the first taker held. The cases on both sides are exhibited in note A to Billings v. Sandom, 1 *B. C. C.* 394, to all which reference is now made. Upon this rule, Mr. Jarman remarks as follows:—" But although, in case of an immediate *gift*, it is *generally true* that a *bequest* over in the event of the death of the preceding *legatee* refers to that event occurring in the lifetime of the testator, yet *this construction is made only ex necessitate rei*, from the absence of any other period to which the words can be referred, as the testator is not supposed to contemplate the event of himself surviving the objects of his bounty:" 2 *Jarman on Wills* 664–5.

But this rule, artificial at best, and confessedly not universal in its application, even when the event is *death only*, and belonging especially to personal property, is reversed *when other collateral events* are connected with the event of death. Mr. Jarman thus states it:—" It will commonly be found, it is conceived, that *where the context is silent*, the words referring to the death of the prior legatee in connection with some collateral event, apply to the contingency happening as well *after* as before the death of the testator:" 2 *Jarman on Wills*, 687; Allen v. Farthing, same page; and Child v. Giblet, 488.

The cases above alluded to as exceptions, in which other events were connected in the will with the event of death, and yet were brought within this artificial rule, are Clayton v. Lowe, 7 *Eng. Com. Law* 218, in which no reason is given for the decision; in which the words are, "or should die leaving child or children," and of which Mr. Jarman says—"The reasons for the conclusion at which the court arrived do not appear." "Whether the certificate of the Court of King's Bench was confirmed by the vice-chancellor does not appear. Under such circumstances, it would be *unsafe to rely on the case as a deliberate adjudication* in support of so *doubtful a principle:*" 2 *Jarman on Wills* 692. This case is therefore too apocryphal to sustain the defendant's construction.

The next and only other English case of this class cited by defendants, is that of Doe v. Sparrow, 13 *East* 359. Here were

[Jessup *v.* Smuck.]

three contingencies of death, to wit: 1. "In case of the death of either my son or daughter leaving child or children." 2. "In case my said son and daughter shall be both dead at the time of my decease," then to executors and brother. 3. "In case of the death of my said son and daughter at the time before mentioned."

In construing this will, Lord ELLENBOROUGH says, "The limitations to the executors and to his brother are confined in *express terms* to the event of the death of his son and daughter *in his lifetime*, and *from thence it is inferred* that he was contemplating a death in his lifetime in the preceding clause." And further, "the express restriction to death in testator's lifetime in one clause, leads the court to infer that in the other clauses death during the same period was intended."

Of this case Mr. Jarman remarks:—"But this construction was aided by the context, particularly by a gift over of the entire property in case both devisees were dead at the time of the decease of the testator without children, from which the court inferred that in the clause in question he contemplated death at the same period." 2 *Jarman on Wills* 653. How can this case be a guide for one in which *there is no such express limitation?*

In Caldwell *v.* Skilton, 1 *Harris* 153, the only remaining case of this class cited, the decision is distinctly placed, as to the construction of the will, upon the incongruity which must result from any other construction, and the impossibility of harmonizing its provisions, or carrying into effect the obvious general intention of the testator, without fixing the time of the testator's death as the period for the death of the first taker. This case, like the two preceding, and that of Jenour *v.* Jenour, 10 *Vesey* 563, cited in support of it, was a tenancy in common to the first takers with survivorship, (a condition of things on which the court placed some reliance,) and that survivorship, if treated as unlimited in duration, might entirely defeat the obvious general intention of the testator. Hence, in this case there was a necessity of applying, as to time, that which Mr. Jarman says is "so doubtful a principle." In the case before the court there is no tenancy in common, with survivorship, nor in any conceivable contingency would the obvious general intention of the testator be frustrated by giving to the words of the will their common and ordinary interpretation.

None of the cases above cited connect marriage with the event of death.

But the time intended by the testator is in fact fixed by the very sentence which imposes the defeasance and creates the executory estate. "In case my son Samuel should die *before* he marries, *then*" I give, &c. to Joel. Should die! When? Not generally, or at any time, not in testator's lifetime, nor with or without issue, as in the cases of limitation, but "before he marries." Marriage was to render indefeasible, not death to render defeasible, the

[Jessup v. Smuck.]

estate given to Samuel. His non-marriage was the event which made the premises the property of Joel the first moment such non-marriage could be certain, to wit, Samuel's death. Death was never, in the mind of the testator, the contingency on which the estate was to go over, but non-marriage; and death is only named as the farthest boundary of the period for the performance of the condition which should make Samuel's title indefeasible. Time subsequent to the testator's own decease was in his mind throughout his whole will; legacies were to be paid from one to six years after his decease; the last-named time being allowed for the trifling sum of £10. The testator made all the limitations of time he chose to make even in minute matters, and it cannot be supposed that he omitted such limitations as he desired in matters of greater importance.

Non-marriage is a good condition of defeasance: 2 *Strange* 1175: "Devise to A in fee, but if he dies under age or unmarried and without issue, then over; all the events must concur to defeat the estate."

Griffith v. Woodward, 1 *Yeates* 316: "If either of my said sons shall happen to depart this life unmarried and without lawful issue," then survivorship. Marriage prevented executory devisee from taking. Also cited Drinkwater v. Combe, 2 *Sim. & Stuart* 340.

Evans and *Mayer* were for defendants in error.—The defendants do not admit that the will vested in Samuel Willis an estate "defeasible on his death before marriage," *at any time*. It appears to have been the primary object of the testator to provide for Samuel, and to invest him with full dominion over the most valuable part of his property, worth now perhaps $14,000 or $15,000. The case finds that Samuel was twenty-two years of age at the date of the will, was unmarried, and resided with his father. The two unmarried sisters were no doubt also at home.

That the testator contemplated some contingency upon which Joel should take the place of Samuel and become invested with the property devised to Samuel on the same terms and conditions as Samuel "was to have held it," there is no doubt. The devise to Joel is substitutionary to that to Samuel. The contingency which was to determine this substitution was the death of Samuel—*his death in the lifetime of the testator, while yet unmarried.* In that event Joel was to take the place of Samuel. An additional payment of £460 was imposed on Joel, no legacy out of the land was to be received by him, no share of the residual estate was to be paid to him, but the residual estate was to be divided into other and different shares from what was to have been the case in the event of the property vesting in Samuel.

This construction is indeed required by the established rules of law. "All the authorities concur," says Mr. Justice ROGERS, "per-

[Jessup v. Smuck.]

haps without exception, that, when the gift is *immediate*, that is, in possession, it is to be treated as intended to provide for the death of the objects of the testator's bounty in the lifetime of the testator; the devise affording no other point of time to which they could be referred:" Johnson v. Morton, 10 *Barr* 250. It is not only in case of death simply that the time of it is referred to the death of the testator. Death connected with collateral circumstances, as *without leaving children*, has been ruled to refer to the period of the testator's death: Clayton v. Lowe, 6 *Barn. & Ald.* 636, (7 *Eng. Com. Law Rep.* 218.) The authority of this case is faintly impugned by the plaintiff, but is fully sustained by Mr. Justice BELL in the late case of Caldwell v. Skilton, 1 *Harris* 152, which is also direct to the point, and shows that the rule is applied to real as well as personal estate. In the case of Montagu v. Nucella, 1 *Russell's Ch. Rep.* 165, decided since Clayton v. Lowe, there were two bequests to which the rule was applied.

Prior to any of these cases was that of Doe v. Sparrow, 13 *East* 359, in which death *without leaving issue* was referred to death in the lifetime of the testator. It is true that "the construction in that case *was aided* by the context," but that is no objection to it; and we think that such is the fact also in the present case: Child v. Giblet, 3 *Myl. & Keen* 71. Lippincott v. Warden, 14 *Ser. & R.* 115, is disposed of in Caldwell v. Skilton, 1 *Harris*.

We submit, therefore, that the rule is too firmly established to be shaken, that where the devise is *immediate* and *absolute*, a devise to another, in case of the death of the first-named devisee, although connected with some collateral circumstance, is substitutionary only, and refers to the death of the first devisee in the lifetime of the testator. There cannot be any difference whether the collateral circumstance be the *having issue, having children*, or the *marriage* of the first devisee. The conjunction of the circumstance with the event of the devisee's death might be thought to import a contingency in the one case as much as in the other. But the conjunction of such personal circumstances with the event of death does not, under the rule, determine the contingency which the testator contemplated; and to effectuate his intention, and not destroy the estate he has given, it becomes necessary to refer the happening of the event to the period of the testator's death.

The plaintiff, in the course of his argument, dwells on the word "*before*," in the phrase "should die *before* he marries," and seems to think the force of it decisive of the question. The emphasis however is on the word *die*, leaving the office of the word *before*, as a mere preposition, (not an adverb,) having the words *he marries* for its object, to append the collateral circumstance of marriage to the death. It will not do, however, to hinge a cause upon a single word, in opposition to the context and general intent of a will. We

[Jessup v. Smuck.]

may say of this word, as well as of the word *then*, referred to by the plaintiff, what Lord HARDWICKE said of the latter in Beauclerk v. Dormer, 2 *Atkyns* 311: "If the court here were to lay any stress upon the word *then*, it would be going a great deal too far, for it is too ambiguous to be taken as an adverb of time;" "*then*, in a grammatical sense, is an adverb of time, but in the limitation of estates, and framing contingencies, it is a word of reference, and relates to the determination of the first limitation in the estate where the contingency arises."

The opinion of the court was delivered June 16, by

CHAMBERS, J.—William Willis, by his will, made in 1800, devised the lands in controversy to his "son Samuel, and to his heirs and assigns," to have and to hold "to him my said son Samuel Willis, and to his heirs and assigns for ever, he or they paying thereout and therefor certain legacies." And in a subsequent part of the will it is provided, "and *in case my said son Samuel should die before he marries, then* all that part of the estate which I have devised to him, in that case I give and devise to my son Joel Willis, his heirs and assigns, to have and to hold to him my said son Joel, his heirs and assigns for ever, in as full and ample a manner as my son Samuel held, or was to have held the same, and subject to the same conditions and payments," with a further charge of £460 to his daughters. At the date of the will, Samuel was of the age of twenty-two, unmarried, residing on the mansion farm devised, with his father, who lived about thirteen months after the making of his will. Samuel, at the death of his father, entered into the possession of the land devised, and paid the legacies charged in the will, and died in 1848 intestate, and without having been married. The plaintiffs, devisees of Joel Willis, claim the land in controversy under the limitation contained in the will of William Willis in favour of their testator, Joel Willis. This case has been prepared with great industry and research by the counsel on both sides, who have argued it with much learning and ability.

It is ever professed by courts, that the construction to be put on wills is to execute and carry out the intention of the testator, if that intention can be discovered, and does not contravene some established rule or principle of law. Artificial rules of law have been adopted from necessity, and called in to aid in giving effect to a general intent, conflicting with some particular intent in the same will, or to supply some obscurity in the full intent of the testator, and to sustain the policy of the law.

By the will of William Willis, a fee is devised in the mansion farm to his son Samuel, and the question is, when, and on what event was it made defeasible, and limited over to his son Joel, his heirs and assigns?

[Jessup v. Smuck.]

The non-marriage of Samuel was an *event* that received the attention of the testator, as worthy of testamentary provision. It was not on the death alone of Samuel that the estate was limited over to Joel, as it is provided "in case my son Samuel should die before he *marries*, then all that part of my estate which I have devised to him, in that case I give and bequeath to my son Joel Willis, his heirs and assigns."

But it is death, without marriage. The limitation over is not on the contingency of his death in testator's lifetime, as averred by the defendants, nor is it on the event of his death with or without issue, as in cases of limitation—but "before he marries." If he dies before his marriage, *then*, says the testator, I devise the estate to Joel. The estate was to go over on the contingency of the death of Samuel at any time without marriage.

The property was to pass to Joel when such non-marriage could only become certain, to wit, at Samuel's death. The manifest intention of testator was, that of his children, Samuel and Joel were the only ones to have and enjoy his mansion farm as provided in his will.

The testator was providing for the disposition of his estate after his decease, and must be supposed to refer to events, and their occurrence in time subsequent to his death. That time subsequent to his decease was alone in the contemplation of testator is to be inferred from the payment of the legacies charged, which were to extend from one to six years after his decease; and where he imposed limitations of time as to payments and minute matters, we are not to suppose that the occurrence of the marriage of Samuel, which he would seem to have regarded with interest, was not to apply to the devise to Samuel after the death of the testator.

The provisions and terms of this will are strong to show that the testator contemplated and provided for the death of Samuel, without marriage, at any period of his life, as the time and event on which the property in controversy was to pass over to Joel.

It is contended, on the part of the defendants, that Samuel took an indefeasible estate in fee simple on his father's death, subject only to payment of legacies, with no other limitation; that Joel, by the will, was to take only in case the devise to Samuel should lapse by his death *in the lifetime of their father*. To sustain this construction, it was alleged that, by a rule of construction established by authority, a devise over in the event of death, when the first devisee is to take immediately, is construed to mean death *in the lifetime of the testator*, and that the rule is not confined to cases where death alone is mentioned *without any qualification*, but has been applied to cases where the estate is directed to go over if either of the first devisees "*should happen to die without child or children lawfully begotten:*" Clayton v. Lowe, 5 *Barn. &*

[Jessup v. Smuck.]

Ald. 636; or should die without *leaving child or children :* Doe v. Sparrow, 13 *East* 359; or *should die without issue born alive,* Caldwell v. Skilton, 1 *Harris* 152.

Mr. Powell, in the 37th chapter of his treatise on Devises, after reviewing some of the leading cases in relation to the artificial rule, says—" But in cases of *immediate* gifts, it is generally true that a bequest over, in the event of the death of the preceding legatee, refers to that event occurring in the lifetime of the testator; yet this construction is only made *ex necessitate rei*, from the absence of any other period to which the words may be referred, as a testator is not supposed to contemplate the event of himself surviving the objects of his bounty :" 2 *Pow. Dev.* 763–65.

This rule, admitted to be artificial, is not of uniform application where other collateral events are connected with the death. The case of Lippincott v. Warder, 14 *Ser. & R.* 115, is in conflict with the rule of construction insisted on, and is to be respected from the consideration given to it and exhibited by the learned judge who delivered the opinion. Mr. Jarman states, "It will commonly be found, it is conceived, that where the *context is silent*, the words referring to the death of the prior legatee in connection with some collateral event, apply to the contingency happening as well *after* as before the death of the testator :" 2 *Jarman on Wills* 687. The case of Clayton v. Lowe was not a case of such deliberate adjudication as to be relied on; and in the case of Doe v. Sparrow, 13 *East* 359, Lord ELLENBOROUGH, in construing the will, says, "the limitations to the executors and to his brother are confined in *express terms* to the event of the death of his son and daughter in *his lifetime;* and from thence it is inferred that he was contemplating a death in his lifetime in the preceding clause."

In Caldwell v. Skilton, 1 *Harris* 153, the decision is distinctly placed, as to the construction of the will, on the evidence of intent, to be inferred from its context, being in conformity to the rule referred to; and to avoid the incongruity which must result from any other construction, in carrying out the provisions of the will and the general intention of the testator. The case last referred to as made by this court, was a tenancy in common to the first takers with survivorship, a circumstance that had its influence on the opinion of the court. The opinion of the court, as delivered by Justice BELL, in Caldwell v. Skilton, has our entire approbation. In the case of Johnson v. Morton, 10 *Barr* 245, referred to, words giving an estate of inheritance before the act of 1833, were held from the context to pass a fee; and the artificial limitation of the time of death, was recognised, as applying in that case, where there was a devise to several daughters or the survivor of them; and Justice ROGERS, whilst he applied the rule in aid of the intention of the testator to provide for a death in his lifetime, says, "the devise affording no other point of time to which they could be referred."

In this case now under consideration, there is no tenancy in common with survivorship; nor in the contingency contemplated, of the limitation over to Joel on the death of Samuel at any time before marriage, would the obvious general intention of the testator be frustrated by giving to the words of the will their common and ordinary interpretation.

It is to be remarked, that none of the cases referred to and relied on for the defendants, connect marriage with the event of death. Non-marriage is a good condition of defeasance: 2 *Strange* 1175; and in Griffith *v.* Woodward, 1 *Yeates* 316, it was by the will provided, "if either of my said sons shall happen to depart this life unmarried, and without lawful issue, then" the survivor was to enjoy all: it was held that marriage prevented the executory devisee from taking. In the last case, the court say that the testator "probably intended to tempt his sons to marry, and therefore subjected their lands to that condition." If the testator in this case be considered as holding out an inducement to his son Samuel to marry, by making the estate devised to him absolute on marriage, it must be intended as referring to a marriage not during the short time of the testator's nearly spent life, but to a time after his death, when Samuel became acquainted with the devise to him of the mansion farm in fee, but with a limitation over to his brother Joel and his heirs in case Samuel should die before he marries.

In the cases which limit the death to the testator's lifetime, it is admitted that it is adopted from necessity, in aid of what was considered the general intent of the testator, and was not applied where the first taker is referred to or treated as living at a period subsequent to the death of the testator. That the testator did not contemplate the death of his son Samuel to occur before his own, is, as we have observed, to be inferred from the terms used to express the contingency and the limitation; but is also confirmed by other dispositions in the will in relation to Samuel, which have reference to a time subsequent to testator's death. The will devises to Samuel the grain which is growing on the ground *at testator's decease*, allows him to take at low prices, *after testator's decease*, stock which testator shall have left, and other stock at the appraisement; gives him the *option* and the right to give land to his sisters in lieu of pecuniary legacies, payable *one, two*, and *four* years after testator's decease. These and other provisions, to be executed by Samuel after testator's decease, are to be regarded in confirmation of the construction we have adopted to effectuate the intention of the testator in limiting the estate over to Joel on the death of Samuel after the testator's decease, in case Samuel should *die before he marries*. Samuel having died unmarried, the estate passed by executory devise to the heirs or devisees of Joel

[Jessup v. Smuck.]

Willis. There is no rule of law contravened by this limitation. That a fee simple may by *executory devise* be limited after a fee simple vested or contingent, is well established: *Fearne on Rem.* 395–6–7; 2 *Bin.* 532, Hauer's Lessee *v.* Sheetz.

The limitation over is not on an event too remote, but, being to occur within a life in being, is good as an executory devise, as is well settled. However sound public policy may be against locking up estates from alienation or disposition, and protracting the acquisition of the absolute interest in or dominion over property, yet any change of the law on this subject is to be made by legislative provision, and not by the judiciary, who are not to indulge in judicial legislation, but as expounders of the established law are bound to maintain it and the line which divides judicial from legislative functions. Where there exist provisions in the will evidencing a particular intent, and directory in small matters in the distribution of the estate or fund, they must be made to yield and conform to the general intent as manifested and to be executed, and with which they may appear to conflict. The representatives of Joel are to take the estate in fee, and to hold the same in as full and ample a manner as Samuel held or was to have held the same, and subject to the same conditions and payments; and they are to pay the further sum of £460, to be divided amongst testator's daughters or their representatives, as well as refund and pay to the representatives of the estate of William Willis, the testator, what Joel or his representatives may have received out of the residuary estate of the testator. Some of the provisions that were personal in their application to Samuel, and not to Joel, cannot apply to Joel or his heirs or devisees, who from necessity must take the said estate discharged from such conditions as were applicable only to Samuel as dying before he marries, which could not be annexed to the devise to Joel, who was married, and from paying over to legatees legacies already paid by Samuel in his lifetime. Such provisions, being not applicable to Joel or his representatives, are to be rejected as immaterial and inoperative at this time, to effectuate the manifest general intent of the testator in limiting his estate to his sons Samuel and Joel.

It is the opinion of the court on the will of William Willis, that the testator contemplated the death of his son Samuel, *whenever it might happen* before marriage, as the event on which the estate devised was limited over in fee to Joel, his heirs and assigns; and as Samuel did die before he married, the estate, by the limitation, became the property of the heirs or devisees of Joel. Under this opinion, the judgment of the court below on the special verdict is reversed, and judgment entered for the plaintiffs—subject to the payment of the legacies charged on the premises, if not paid, and subject to the payment of four hundred and sixty pounds to the daughters of William Willis or their representatives, and to the

[Jessup *v.* Smuck.]

payment to the same, in the manner provided in the will, of what Joel may have received out of the residuary estate, being, as stated, the sum of one hundred and thirty-six pounds, nineteen shillings and nine pence.

Brandt's Appeal.

The transcript of a judgment in the Common Pleas, entered in another county, in pursuance of the act of 16th April 1840, is not a very judgment of the court of the county in which it is entered, but is a quasi judgment for limited purposes; it is evidence of a judgment in the court in which it was originally obtained. The original judgment having been set aside at the instance of the defendant, for irregularity, and the execution in the second county stayed, the judgment on the transcript fell with it; and the plaintiff having obtained a new judgment in the case, but no transcript of it having been entered, had no lien in the county in which the transcript had been entered.

APPEAL by Samuel Brandt and Charles Beltzhoover, from the decree of the Court of Common Pleas of *Cumberland county*, appropriating the proceeds of sale of the real estate of Michael Mishler.

The appellants claimed the amount of a judgment, Frederick Baugher for their use *vs.* Michael Mishler, obtained to No. 107, April term 1849, in the Common Pleas of *York county*, a transcript of which was filed in the Common Pleas of Cumberland county, on the 16th of April 1849, in pursuance of the act of 16th April 1840.

The facts in relation to the judgment in York are these:—Suit was brought to No. 38, November term 1848, and summons served upon Mishler, 30th September, 1848. On the 11th November, 1848, the plaintiff filed his declaration and signed judgment for default of appearance. A writ of inquiry of damages, dated 30th November 1848, was issued; and on 27th December 1848, damages were assessed at $435.20, which was duly returned by the sheriff and approved by the Court of Common Pleas on the 2d January 1849.

On the 16th April 1849, a transcript of this judgment was regularly filed and entered of record in the Court of Common Pleas of Cumberland county.

Upon this judgment a fi. fa. issued the same day to No. 2, August term 1849.

On the 25th April 1849, upon the petition of *Mishler*, the defendant, the Court of Common Pleas of York county granted a "rule to show cause why the original judgment and proceedings had on the writ of inquiry in this case should not be stricken off, because the original judgment was irregularly entered, the decla-

[Brandt's Appeal.]

ration having been filed on the 11th November 1848, and judgment taken the same day—and also rule to show cause why the said judgment should not be opened and defendant let into a defence—and also why the writ of inquiry should not be set aside and the finding quashed—all proceedings to stay in the mean time —ten days' notice of this rule to be given to the assignees of the judgment."

On the 30th April 1849, on the application of Mishler, the president judge in Cumberland county endorsed on the fi. fa. No. 2, August term 1849, "I do hereby order that the proceedings on this execution in the hands of the sheriff as within mentioned be stayed until the first day of next term."

No further action was had in Cumberland county upon this order of the judge, nor were the court asked to interpose, on the first day of the succeeding term, or at any time thereafter.

On the 22d March 1850, the Court of Common Pleas of York county disposed of the rule entered as stated before, and filed the following opinion:—" In this case, the declaration having been filed after the return day of the writ, the judgment (entered for a default of appearance) and subsequent proceedings thereon were for that reason set aside, there being nothing from which the defendant's acquiescence in the irregularity could be inferred."

On the 6th of April 1850, arbitrators were chosen by the parties in York county, who reported, on the 18th June 1850, after hearing the parties in favor of the plaintiff, $483.70, with costs, being the amount for which judgment had been entered, with accumulated interest. And on the 9th July 1850, judgment absolute was entered on the award.

On the 19th July 1850, a fi. fa. No. 77, August term, was issued on the judgment in Cumberland county which had been entered on the transcript from York.

On this fi. fa. the defendant's lands were levied upon—an inquisition held upon them, of which the defendant had notice, and they were condemned.

A *venditioni exponas* issued upon this same judgment to No. 11, November term 1850, and the lands levied and condemned and sold by the sheriff, as per return *on No. 6, November term* 1850, which was also a *venditioni exponas* vs. *the same defendant*, for sale of same lands, and the only ones then in the hands of the sheriff, on which the premises were sold, producing the money in court for appropriation.

It was admitted on the argument that Michael Mishler, the defendant, was *insolvent*.

Isaac Mishler and Henry Mishler, two sons of Michael Mishler, the defendant, on the 28th November 1849, obtained an amicable judgment against their father for $4500, which was entered to November term 1849, in the Common Pleas of Cumberland county, and

[Brandt's Appeal.]

on the day the argument of the rule for the appropriation of the money made by the sheriff from the sale of Mishler's property was to be heard, Samuel Brandt, one of the plaintiffs in the judgment before recited, made affidavit, which he presented to the court, for the purpose of obtaining a rule to show cause why this judgment of the two Mishlers vs. their father, should not be set aside on the ground of its being fraudulent. This application the court held under advisement until the hearing of the merits on the Baugher judgment for the use of Brandt and Beltzhoover before referred to.

The fund in court was more than sufficient to pay the Baugher judgment, and was claimed by Brandt and Beltzhoover, *the assignees of it*, on the lien of the transcript from York county, filed in Cumberland county 16th April 1849; and also by George Brindle and the two Mishlers on the judgment obtained on the 28th November 1849, Brindle being the assignee of a part of it.

It is provided in the act of 16th April 1840, that "In addition to the remedies now provided by law, hereafter any judgments in any district court or court of common pleas in Pennsylvania, may be transferred from the court in which they are entered, to any other district court or court of common pleas in this commonwealth, by filing of record in said other court, a certified copy of the whole record in the case; and any prothonotary receiving such certified copy of record, in any case in which judgment has been entered by another court, or in another court by transcript from justices of the peace, shall file the same, and forthwith transcribe the docket entry thereof into his own docket, &c. And as to lien, revivals, executions, and so forth, it shall have the same force and effect, and no other, as if the judgment had been entered, or the transcript been originally filed in the same court to which it may thus be transferred." *Purdon's Dig.* 662.

WATTS, J., decided that when the original judgment in York county was set aside by the Court of Common Pleas of that county, it had the effect of setting aside the lien of the transcript: 7 *Watts* 540, Hastings v. Lolough. That if this be the case, it was not necessary to entertain the inquiry attempted to be raised as to the judgment of Isaac and Henry Mishler, "as it can be of no consequence to any one but a lien creditor, whether the judgment is fraudulent or not: it is certainly good as to the parties to it." He decreed *that* judgment to be paid.

It was assigned for error:
1. The court erred in refusing the issue prayed for to test the fairness of the judgment of the Mishlers.
2. The court erred in decreeing the money to the judgment of the Mishlers, instead of to the appellants.

[Brandt's Appeal.]

Hepburn and *Graham*, for appellants.

The court declined to hear *Biddle*, for appellees.

The opinion of the court was delivered June 18, by

GIBSON, C. J.—Is the transcript of a judgment itself a judgment, or a dependent emanation from one? By the act of 1840, a judgment of a county court may be transferred to the court of any other county by filing a certified copy of the whole record—not a transcript of the judgment merely—and it is provided that it shall have, "as to lien, revival, execution, and so forth, the same force and effect *as if* the judgment had been entered in the same court to which it may thus be transferred." It is not then a very judgment of that court, but a *quasi* judgment, and that too only for limited purposes. Of what court, then, is it *evidence* of a judgment? Certainly the court from which it came. It will not be pretended that the record filed to support it is a record of any other. An exemplification of it as evidence elsewhere could be made only by that court. That the original is not removed by the transcript is shown by the provision that the lien of the judgment in the proper county shall not be impaired by transmission of the certified copy. The judgment in this case, therefore, was a judgment exclusively of the Common Pleas of York county, and the regularity or merits of it could not be overhauled elsewhere, further than to stay execution on it, which was done. Had the defendant moved the Common Pleas of Cumberland to set it aside, he would have been told that the power of that court was restricted to the enforcement of it. He properly went to the fountain head, had the irregular judgment set aside in York county, and execution stayed in Cumberland. The judgment was set aside because it had been surreptitiously obtained; and the rule in Drury's case, 8 *Rep.* 142, is that, as to things executory, a judgment annulled is as if it had never been; and nothing is more executory than an unexecuted writ. If there never had been a judgment in York county, the court in Cumberland might have struck the transcript from its record even when the money was brought in for distribution; and it virtually did so by disregarding it. There may be a judgment on a mortgage and a judgment on a bond for the same debt, but a legal mind cannot conceive of two independent judgments of the very same kind, each binding the person, and each for the same thing; to avoid the absurdity of which, the law allows the pendency of a prior action to be pleaded in abatement, or a former recovery to be pleaded in bar. The object of the legislature was not to create a new lien, but to enlarge the field of an old one and enforce it by local authority; to which end the transcript was endued, as a graft, with no greater measure of life than that of the parent stock. If it were independent and self-sustained, it would not be

[Brandt's Appeal.]

discharged by payment of the original, and the plaintiff would be bound to make more than one entry of satisfaction. After this irregular judgment had been succeeded by a regular one, the plaintiff ought to have filed a new transcript, instead of relying on an exploded one. He insists that it is still at least a judgment *de facto*, and that a creditor cannot take advantage of an irregularity in it. But the defendant himself took advantage of it, abated the original in the proper forum, and its accessories followed it. He procured an order from the court in Cumberland to stay an execution which had been sued out in the mean time; and what more could he do to warn the plaintiff that he did not mean to acquiesce. The plaintiff neglected to file a new one, and his lien is gone.

Decree affirmed.

Rheem *versus* Holliday.

An improvement of a machine for which a patent may be obtained may consist of the introduction of a new element into an old machine which produces a new and useful result or greater facility in the application of power; and though it appear from the description or specification of the claimant for a patent for an improvement, that part of the elements included in the description or specification were not new, *but which he claimed to be newly combined with new elements, the patent is not therefore void.*

ERROR to the Common Pleas of *Cumberland county*.

This was a suit by Jacob Rheem *vs.* Samuel Holliday, to recover the amount of a note dated 16th March 1847, given by Samuel Holliday to Michael McMath or bearer, for $200, and endorsed by McMath to Jacob Rheem. Defendant gave evidence that the note was negotiated after its maturity, and that the consideration for said note was the sale of the patent-right of Howd's improved water-wheel, for the county of Mifflin, Pennsylvania. The defence relied upon was, that the aforesaid patent-right was not a new and original invention; that the patent-right was void, and consequently that no consideration had been received for the note.

Evidence was given on the one side for the purpose of showing that Howd's patent was not a new and original improvement. Witnesses were examined, and models exhibited to the jury, for the purpose of sustaining the allegations of the defendant. On the other hand, plaintiff exhibited a model of his patent, and examined witnesses to establish the fact that his patent was a new and original improvement.

The errors complained of were in the answers of the court to points put by defendant's counsel, and in the general charge to the jury.

[Rheem v. Holliday.]

Defendant's counsel, among others, put the following points, to wit:—

3d. If the jury believe that machinery, such as the spouts or schutes for giving the water a direction with the motion of the wheel, the cylindrical gate, or any other part of the machinery of the Howd patent water-wheel, described and set out in the specification of said patent as a substantial and material part thereof, was not new and original with Howd, having been used before the date of his patent by others in this country, or having been described in some printed publication prior to the date of his patent, then the patent is void, and the plaintiff cannot recover.

4th. If the jury believe that machinery for giving the water a direction with the motion of the wheel, similar to that in Howd's wheel, was used before the date of Howd's patent for giving the water a direction with the motion of wheels, differing from Howd's, and that reaction-wheels such as Howd's were in use before the date of his patent, and that Howd's invention consisted only in applying such previous known machinery to such previous known wheels, then Howd, as he has not claimed for such combination, takes nothing by his patent, and the plaintiff cannot recover.

Both of these points were answered by the court in the affirmative.

The court, also, in their general charge to the jury, instructed them as follows, to wit:—"It is a principle of this branch of the law, that if the applicant for a patent claims several elements or parts combined, as being original with him, and forming or producing a certain mechanical result, and if it appears in evidence that one or more of these parts is not original, it avoids the patent issued upon such specification of claim. It is the duty of the applicant so to specify what he does claim, as to avoid the appearance of claiming what does not belong to him or his inventive genius. If then the specification by Samuel B. Howd includes that which is not new, the plaintiff is not entitled to recover in this action."

Howd claimed, as his *invention*, the application of the water upon the outside of the wheel, and operating upon the principle of reaction, by discharging inwardly on a wheel constructed and combined so as to operate as above described, with the spouts or schutes giving the water a direction with the motion of the wheel, applied to a reacting wheel as aforesaid. A specification preceded the claim, which terminated as follows:—My said improvement being above described as applied to a horizontal wheel, I hereby declare that the same is not intended to be limited to that position of the wheel, but is applicable to vertical and inclined wheels.

Letters-patent issued to Howd on 26th July 1838, which set forth that he alleged that he has invented a new and useful improved water-wheel, which he states has not been known or used before his application; and, therefore, there is granted to him, for

[Rheem v. Holliday.]

the term of fourteen years, the full and exclusive right and liberty of making, constructing, using, and vending to others to be used, the said improvement, a description whereof is given in the words of the said Samuel B. Howd, in the schedule hereunto annexed, and is made a part of these presents.

The case was argued by *Todd* and *Graham*, for plaintiff in error.—It is not necessary that *any part of the machinery* should be new or original with the patentee, to constitute a valid patent. Every part of the machinery may have been known and used for ages, if there is a new combination by which a new result is produced. Nor is it necessary, where there are certain elements or parts combined, forming and producing a certain mechanical result, that all parts thus combined should be original, to constitute a valid patent. Again, although the specifications may include that which is not new, if any of the parts are new, or there is a new combination of old parts, the patent is valid.

In the language of Judge KANE, "combination is patentable if it effect a new result, or an old result by a new mode of action. There must be novelty either of product or process." Yet the court, in answer to defendant's third point, instruct the jury that if the cylindrical gate or *any other part of the machinery* of the Howd patent was not new and original with Howd, the patent is void. If this is the law, there will be an end to patenting improvements upon prior patents, and Howd's patent is only for an *improvement* on water-wheels. He does not even claim the cylindrical gate as his invention; but if any juror ever saw or heard of such gate used in connection with a water-wheel, under the charge of the court, he was bound to find a verdict for defendant.

The law applicable to the case will be found clearly stated in the following references, in connection with an abstract of the principles decided.

A machine or improvement may be new and the proper subject of a patent, although the parts of it were before known and in use. Therefore, the combination of old machines to produce a new and useful result is a discovery for which a patent may be granted: Evans *v.* Hetrick, 3 *W. C. C. Rep.* 408.

Although an implement may have been long in use, yet an invention of a mode of making it in a different manner, which produces a new and useful result by a new combination of old materials, entitles the inventor to a patent for the new implement, and not alone for an improvement of an old one: Geiger *v.* Cook, 3 *W. & Ser.* 266.

In that case the court say, "Though Sharp was not the inventor of the forge-hammer arm, but it had been long before in use, yet if his invention is of a mode of making that arm in a different manner from any ever before made, and it thereby produces a new

[Rheem v. Holliday.]

and useful result by a new combination of old materials, then he could not well claim in a better manner than as a new arm. When there is an addition to an old machine or a mere alteration of some of its subordinate parts, the claim may be *for an improvement only*, but where the whole mode of forming a thing and its effects are new, it may be claimed *as new*."

Combination is patentable if it effect a new result, or an old result by a new mode of action. There must be novelty of product or process: Batten *v.* Clayton, December 1848, KANE, J., 2 *Wharton's Dig.* ed. 1850, title *Patent*, pl. 21.

If old materials and old principles be used in a state of combination to produce a new result, the inventor may obtain a valid patent for such result: Pennock *v.* Dialogue, 4 *W. C. C. Rep.* 538; Barrett *v.* Hall, 1 *Mason* 437; Earle *v.* Sawyer, 4 *Mason* 1.

"If the patentee claims more than he has invented, his patent is not void; but so far as his invention goes, he is protected:" Peterson *v.* Wooden, 3 *McLean* 248.

A patent for an entire machine is valid, although the invention consists only of an improvement on such machine, but the patentee is entitled to the exclusive use only of his improvement: Goodyear *v.* Matthews, *Paine* 300.

Where plaintiff, in the specification of his patent, described the invention to be "a new and useful improvement," whereas in fact it consisted of a combination of several improvements, distinctly set forth in the specification, it was held that the patent was good, not only for the combination, but for each distinct improvement, so far as it was his invention, and that the descriptive words were to be construed in connection with the specification: Pitts *v.* Whitman, 2 *Story* 609; 2d vol. *Sup. U. S. Dig.* 503, pl. 8.

Wm. M. Penrose and *Biddle*, for defendant in error.—In this case there was no evidence that any part of Howd's patent improved water-wheel, set out in his specification as a substantial and material part thereof, was new and original with Howd. One witness testified, "that the application of the water to Howd's wheel is the same as that described in the Journal of Science, (a work printed, as shown by the judge's notes, in the year 1818.) There is a difference in letting off the water from the wheel. I can see no difference in the principle. In looking at the wheel described in the Century of Inventions, (published in 1822, see record,) I think the principles are the same by which the water is conducted to the buckets."

Another witness testified, "the wheel described in Journal of Science, is the same as Howd's. In this case the schutes give direction to the water corresponding with the motion of the wheel. The Howd wheel interferes with the Parker patent. I have seen the Parker wheel. The Howd wheel interferes with it in this, that

[Rheem v. Holliday.]

the direction of the water corresponds with the wheel's motion. The cylindrical gate in the Howd wheel does infringe the Parker patent."

Curtis on Patents, (published in 1849,) section 131: "The statute requires the patentee to give a written description of his invention or discovery. This involves the necessity, in all cases where the patentee *makes use of what is old, of distinguishing between what is old and what is new. He is required to point out in what his invention or discovery consists; and if he includes in his description* what has been invented before, without showing that he does not claim to have invented that, his patent will be broader than his invention, and therefore void. Whatever appears to be covered by the claim of the patentee as his own invention must be taken as part of the claim; and therefore, if it turns out that any thing claimed is not new, the patent is void, however small or unimportant such asserted invention may be." These positions are fully sustained by the cases cited in the notes, and to which we refer.

Reference was made to Carpenter v. Smith, *Webster's Patent Cases* 530, 552; Lowell v. Louis, 1 *Mason* 188; 2 *Brockenbrough's Rep.* 298; 2 *Mason* 112, 118; *Davies's Patent Cases* 295; *id.* 329: 1 *Mason* 449; 2 *Kent*, 5th edit. 370-1; 2 *Hindmarsh on Patent Privileges* 115-16.

In the 15th section of the act of Congress of 4th July 1836, on the subject of actions for infringing patent-rights, it is provided that the defendant may give in evidence any special matter tending to prove that the patentee was not the original or first inventor or discoverer of the thing patented, or of a substantial or material part thereof claimed as new, or that it had been described in some public work anterior to the supposed discovery thereof by the patentee, &c.

The cases and authorities cited by the plaintiff in error are to the effect that combination is patentable if it effect a new result or an old result by a new mode of action; that a combination of old machines to produce a new and useful result is a discovery for which a patent may be granted; that if old materials and old principles be used in a state of combination to produce a new result, the inventor may obtain a *valid patent for such result*. Now none of these cases meet the real question in this case, the inquiry here not being what is the proper subject for a patent, but whether Howd could claim, as new and original with him, certain substantial and material parts or elements of an invention, which were not new and original, without invalidating his patent. And that he could not, the authorities to which we have referred clearly show.

The opinion of the court was delivered June 19, by

COULTER, J.—In part answer to the defendant's fifth point, the court were perfectly right in stating that it is the duty of the ap-

[Rheem v. Holliday.]

plicant for a patent so to specify and describe the machine, instrument, or improvement, as to avoid the appearance of claiming what he did not invent. But an improvement often consists in the introduction of a new element into an old machine; and in order to make this new element of power or convenience intelligible and apparent, it is absolutely necessary to specify and describe the whole machine, as well the old part as the new. The court were, therefore, in error in saying, in part answer to the same point, that if it appears that one or more of these parts is not original it avoids the patent.

Because in such improvement or invention the discovery consists of the new application of old principles, or the new distribution of old elements so as to produce new power or greater facility in the application of power. The specification of Samuel B. Howd did undoubtedly include what was not new, as the description of every improvement in machinery of necessity must do; but the patent was not therefore void. In this case, Howd described and specified the whole, and its mode of operation. But he distinctly and clearly stated in it what was new, and what he claimed as his invention, and the reason why it was an improvement. Thus, after very fully describing the whole wheel and all its parts, he says—"I claim as my invention the application of the water on the outside of the wheel, and operating upon the principle of reaction, by discharging inwardly on a wheel constructed and combined so as to operate as above described, with the spouts or schutes giving the water a direction with the motion of the wheel, applied to a reacting wheel as aforesaid." Now, the reaction-wheel, as used in Parker's patent, in many parts is the same as this of Howd's. But in Howd's, the direction of the water corresponds with the wheel's motion, and is thrown on the wheel at the periphery, and not at the centre. It is new and different from Parker's and other reaction-wheels in that particular. Whether it is a valuable improvement or not is not the question, but whether it is new; and this was for the jury to decide upon the evidence. But Mr. Holliday's letter, in which he so much extols Howd's wheel, is certainly of value to show that this change of Howd's was a substantial improvement.

But the point to which this case converges is, that Howd did particularly specify and describe what he claimed as new, and as his invention. The patent was not void, therefore, because, in the description or specification of the whole wheel including the element that he said was his invention, he included in that general specification or description elements which were old, but which he claimed to be newly combined with new elements.

Judgment reversed and *venire de novo* awarded.

Quigley *versus* The Commonwealth.

The 48th section of the act of 29th March 1832, relating to Orphans' Courts, which enables the *Orphans'* Court to require security from a husband before money payable to his wife under proceedings in partition is paid to him, does not apply to the case of a female *unmarried* at the time of the partition; and the payment to a *future* husband, without security, will discharge the recognizance, so far as the wife is interested.

ERROR to the Common Pleas of *Clinton county.*

This was an action of debt to September term 1849, in the name of the Commonwealth for the use of George Geise and Maria his wife, formerly Maria Quigley, in right of said Maria, against Jacob K. Quigley. The suit was on a recognizance acknowledged by defendant in the Orphans' Court of Lycoming county on the 6th September 1838, for the sum of $4284, the valuation of a tract of land belonging to the estate of William Quigley, deceased, which had been appraised in pursuance of proceedings in the Orphans' Court, and which was taken at the valuation, by defendant, on the 6th September 1838. There was claimed for plaintiffs in interest, the husband and wife, the one-fourth part of the valuation, viz. $1071, with interest.

On the part of *plaintiffs*, was given in evidence the record of proceedings in the Orphans' Court of Lycoming county, in the matter of the partition of the real estate of William Quigley, deceased, from which it appeared that, on 27th February 1827, William Quigley died intestate, leaving a widow and four children, to wit, Jacob K., Samuel M., Amanda, and Maria—and seized of real estate described in the plaintiffs' declaration.

30th April 1838, Asher Davidson appointed guardian for Maria.

30th April 1838, petition of widow, Jacob K., Samuel M., Amanda, and Maria by her guardian Asher Davidson, for partition and valuation of real estate.

30th April 1838, inquest awarded.

9th June 1838, inquisition held, and real estate appraised at $4284.

6th September 1838, inquisition confirmed.

6th September 1838, Jacob K. (eldest son and heir) accepts real estate at the valuation and appraisement.

6th September 1838, recognizance of Jacob K. Quigley to Commonwealth in the sum of $4284—conditioned as set out in plaintiffs' narr.

It was admitted that Maria Geise (formerly Maria Quigley) was one of the four heirs of William Quigley, deceased; that the said Maria was married to George Geise on the 25th August 1842; that the widow Quigley died on the 25th December 1847.

[Quigley v. The Commonwealth.]

The *defendant*, to maintain the issue on his part, called Dr. Asher Davidson, who testified as follows :—I was the guardian of Maria Quigley, and there was a settlement at one time between these parties. I went up and had some conversation with the heirs, and we made an estimate of the money that was coming on the landed property. We took the widow's dower out first, and then divided the balance into four parts, and made an estimate of what they agreed was paid. I then took notes from S. M. Quigley and Jacob K. Quigley, for the balance that appeared to be due to Maria on the recognizance. I handed over the notes to George Geise and wife, and took their receipts. * * * Mr. and Mrs. Geise were there ; can't say whether we had the recognizance. But I was present at the appraisement, and knew exactly what it was. The settlement of the amount due on the recognizance was made *on the 27th May* 1843.

The defendant then offered the note of George Geise to J. K. Quigley, dated January 18, 1845, for $125, payable one day after date, in connection with proof that it was advanced in payment of his wife's interest in the fund set apart for the widow, her mother. Admitted by the court to apply *to the interest* of the present claim only.

WOODWARD, J., instructed the jury in the above cause that the settlement of defendant with the plaintiffs and Dr. Davidson as guardian of Maria Geise, made on the 29th May 1843, was evidence of the indebtedness then due to Maria ; but that the payment of the amount ascertained to be due to her was improperly made to her husband, without her acknowledgment agreeably to the provisions of the 48th section of the act of 29th March 1832, entitled " An act relating to Orphans' Courts ;" and having been made by the defendant in disregard of the act, he must pay the money over again.

But as her husband was entitled to have the interest on the money, she could not in this suit compel the defendant to pay more than the principal ascertained on the 27th May 1843 to be due.

From the time of the death of her mother, however, she would be entitled to recover interest on her share of the widow's third, as well as her share, one-fourth of that fund.

The two sums ascertained to be due to her on the 27th May 1843, were $345.24 and $309.39, together amounting to $654.63. Amount agreed to be due by counsel on account of widow's
fund 357.00
$1011.63

For the above sum, $1011.63, the jury were directed to find for plaintiffs. Defendant's counsel excepted.

It was assigned for error :

[Quigley v. The Commonwealth]

1. The court erred in their charge to the jury that the payment of the amount found due on the recognizance, on the settlement of the parties and Dr. Davidson of the 27th May 1843, was improperly made, and must be paid over again.

2. The court erred in their charge to the jury that the plaintiffs were entitled to recover in this action.

The 48th section of the act of 29th March 1838, relating to orphans' courts, provides, "when, upon any proceedings in the orphans' court, a sum of money shall be awarded by the court for the share or portion to which a *married* woman may be entitled, such money shall not be paid to her husband until he shall have given security to the satisfaction of the court that the amount thereof, or so much thereof as the court shall deem proper, be paid after his death to his wife, or if she shall not survive him, to her heirs, as if the same were real estate; or if the husband shall be unable or refuse to give security as aforesaid, the same may be vested in trustees, to be approved by the court, for the same purposes, but reserving to the husband the *interest* thereof during his life, unless the husband shall desire the same to be settled for the separate use of the wife," &c. The act further provides that if the wife declare before a judge that she does not require the money to be so secured, the declaration being made voluntarily and certified by the judge and filed of record in the said orphans' court, the husband shall not be required to secure the money as aforesaid.

The case was argued by *J. W. Quiggle* and *Linn*, for plaintiff in error.

It was contended that at the time of the acceptance of the real estate by defendants below, Maria Quigley, one of the plaintiffs, was *unmarried*, and that the 48th section of the act of 1832 applies to the shares of married women.

That the share of Maria was converted into *personalty* by the proceedings in the Orphans' Court: 11 *Barr* 374. That Maria was then a minor, and her guardian would have been entitled to receive her share. A payment to her husband, or, as in this case, a payment to her and her husband, on a settlement with them and her guardian, was good.

William Quigley, the intestate, died in 1827; the act of 1832 does not apply to estates then vested. That if the act of 1832 apply, the husband could not sue without giving security, or the declaration of the wife being given, as provided in that act.

C. W. Scates, for defendant in error.—The husband had no right to the money without the declaration of his wife as provided for in the act of 1832. Reference made to the remarks of the Codifiers: 2 *Parke & Johnson's Dig.* 843; 2 *Whar.* 246, Walton's Estate.

[Quigley v. The Commonwealth.]

The guardianship of a female is terminated by marriage: *Cummings's Appeal*, 11 *Barr* 272.

The wife's joining with the husband in giving the receipts of the 27th May 1843 is a mere nullity. They are the receipts of the husband alone: Dorrance v. Scott, 8 *Whar.* 309.

It is not material for whose use a suit of this kind is brought. On a recovery by the commonwealth, the legal party, the court will determine who is entitled to the money: Commonwealth v. Lightner, 9 *W. & Ser.* 117.

The opinion of the court was delivered June 23, by

GIBSON, C. J.—The legislature evidently contemplated the case of a female married at the time of the partition. "When upon any proceeding in the Orphans' Court," it is said, "a sum of money shall be awarded by the court for the share or portion to which a married woman may be entitled, such money shall not be paid to the husband until he shall have given security to the satisfaction of the court that the amount thereof, or so much thereof as the court may deem proper, be paid after his death to his wife." Married at what time? Evidently at the time of the partition; for a feme sole might never marry, and it cannot be supposed the legislature looked so far ahead as to provide for a contingency which might not happen. There was to be a married woman in the case at the time of the partition. And by what court was her portion to be secured? Certainly by the Orphans' Court; for the Common Pleas had not been mentioned. The security was to be a part of the proceedings, and consequently to have regard to the time of the partition. The proceeding was to be, in effect, a chancery one; and a chancellor would finish it, the wife's provision included, at a single operation. Had the intent of the legislature been to provide for the contingency of a future marriage, it is reasonable to suppose the statute would have contained some expression indicative of it; but, according to the text, the Orphans' Court was to deal with married women, and consequently with women married at the final settlement of the estate. A different construction might send a second or any subsequent husband to the Orphans' Court, at the end of twenty years, for leave to receive his wife's chose in action, or recover it by process in a court which the Orphans' Court could not control. It would have been impossible, and perhaps unfortunate, if it were not, for the legislature to provide for the contingency of marriage. As may be seen in Hammersley v. Smith, 4 *Whar.* 126, decided on the authority of Massey v. Parker, 2 *Mylne & Keen* 174, and other cases cited in the argument, a separate use, even when created by a father, lasts no longer than the existing or an impending coverture; and there is no reason to suppose the legislature intended to go further. A wife, having no individuality at the common law, could not resist

[Quigley *v.* The Commonwealth.]

an attempt by her husband to convert her real estate into personalty and make it his own by partition in the Orphans' Court; but a feme sole, having the capacity of a man to take care of her property, needed no protection. Should she think proper to marry without a settlement, when her land has been turned into money or securities, so be it: the legislature can no more protect an unmarried woman from the consequences of an imprudent match, than it can protect a weak man from the consequences of an imprudent bargain. In the present case, the plaintiff was sole at the time of the partition; and when she married, her portion of her father's land had long been converted. To her it was the same as if it had been converted in his lifetime; and had it been, no one would assume that her husband would not have been entitled to receive it in money without having settled any part of it on her. The payment of it to him, therefore, discharged the recognizance.

Judgment reversed.

Knouff *versus* Thompson.

A plaintiff whose deed for real estate has been duly recorded is not bound to give actual notice of his title to another, who claiming under another title, and being in possession, is about to make some improvement on the property, the latter claiming under a deed to one which contained a reference to the deed to the plaintiff. Therefore, S. T., whose name was the same as that of his father, but who claimed under a deed from another, was not debarred from asserting his title, by omitting to give notice of it to one, who, being in possession, was making some improvement on the premises, the latter claiming by virtue of a sheriff's sale of the interest of one who claimed under a deed from the father executed after the conveyance to S. T. the son was executed and recorded, and which deed referred to or recited the deed to S. T. as of record, without however distinguishing between the father and the son, but the grantee in which conveyance from the father had *actual notice* at the time of that conveyance that the title was in the son and not in the father.

This was an action of ejectment, brought by Samuel Thompson, Jr., against Joseph B. Knouff, to recover a lot of ground in New Buffalo, Perry county.

On the trial, both parties admitted that the title to the lot in dispute had been in Jacob Baughman, and they both claimed through him.

Plaintiff gave in evidence a deed for the above lot from Jacob Baughman and wife to Christian Baughman, dated 19th June 1820, and recorded 3d May 1824. Consideration, $60.

Also, deed from Christian Baughman, to *Samuel Thompson, Jr.* dated April 14, 1824, and recorded May 3, 1824. Consideration $85.

The defendant then gave in evidence a deed from Samuel

[Knouff v. Thompson.]

Thompson and wife (the parents of Samuel Thompson, Jr.) to the above named Christian Baughman, for a fishery on the Susquehanna, dated April 14th, 1824, and recorded May 3d, 1824. Consideration, $85.

This deed was of same date, for same consideration, acknowledged before same justice, and recorded at same time as the deed from Christian Baughman to Samuel Thompson, Jr. Baughman was the brother-in-law of Samuel Thompson, and uncle of Samuel Thompson, Jr., to whom he conveyed, who was then a lad about eight years of age.

Defendant then gave in evidence a deed from Samuel Thompson and wife (the parents of Samuel, Jr.) to William Parson, for the lot in dispute, dated March 2d, 1829, and recorded July 6th, 1833. Consideration, $30. This deed referred to the deed to Samuel Thompson (omitting *junior*) as being of record.

Sheriff's deed for same lot sold as property of William Parson to Christian Livingston, dated April 5th, 1836. This deed embraced other property as well as the lot in dispute.

Deed of Christian Livingston to Henry Thatcher for lot in dispute, and other property adjoining, dated August 1, 1843, and recorded November 7, 1843.

Deed of Henry Thatcher to Joseph Knouff, the defendant below, for lot in dispute and adjoining lot, dated September 11, 1845, and recorded August 5, 1846.

Defendant then proved that in 1824, the time of the execution of the deed from Baughman to Samuel Thompson, Jr., Samuel Thompson, the father, was insolvent—that judgments were entered against him to more than all his property sold for afterwards—that his son Samuel was twenty-one about 1836—that William Parson, after he bought, fenced and used the lot as a garden to the adjoining house, which he built after he purchased this lot. Christian Livingston bought in 1836, and occupied the lot till 1843. During all this time the plaintiff lived within two hundred yards of the property, was of full age, and never made any claim. Henry Thatcher bought in 1843, and sold in 1845. He lived on the adjoining lot for seven years before he purchased, as tenant, and occupied the lot in dispute as a garden to the house he lived in. Thatcher fenced the lot while he owned it, and it was alleged on part of defendant below, that neither he nor Livingston ever heard or knew of the present claim while they occupied or owned the lot now in dispute.

Thatcher sold to Knouff, the defendant, in 1845, who has occupied it since that time, put a good fence of palings round it, built a smoke-house, and there was no evidence that he ever heard or knew of the present claim *until this suit was brought,* the 16th of January 1850, but one month and sixteen days before the claim would have been barred by the statute of limitations, (Parsons hav-

[Knouff v. Thompson.]

ing occupied from March 2, 1829,) and fourteen years after plaintiff attained the age of twenty-one.

During all this time plaintiff lived within two hundred yards of the lot, from 1829; knew of the purchase by Thatcher and his sale to Knouff, and knew that the deed by Baughman in 1824, was made in his name.

Samuel Thompson, Sr., was called on part of plaintiff:—I cannot say what was the amount paid me by Christian Baughman for the fishery. I owed Boas & Kepner an account and Christian Baughman assumed to pay it. That was the consideration for the fishery. I did not pay any part of the consideration of the deed from Christian Baughman to Samuel Thompson, Jr. The squire, when writing the deed, asked what consideration he should put in; I told him it was immaterial, he might put in what he chose. He said it would not look well without some consideration. When I sold to *Parson* he was then the owner of the corner lot, which he had purchased about the same time. I cannot remember certainly. But when he was going on to build, he found he could not go on with his building without that lot which is now in dispute. He got at me to sell him the lot adjoining. I told him I had not the title; it was in *Samuel Thompson, Jr.* He said he knew that, but if we would make a deed and give him possession, when *Sam came of age, if he claimed it, he would make it right with him.* He was at me several times before I did it.

Cross-examined:—The limekiln property at the mountain was sold once and bought by Mr. Ramsey. There were executions against Baughman and me both at the same time. I was never out of possession of it. The title of the limestone place was in Noland. I had an interest of $300 in it for my services. I got goods for the $30, the consideration of the deed from me to Parson. Mr. Christian Baughman said that he was giving the lot to the boy, which he conveyed that day when Squire Davis was present. I could live along and pay my debts in 1824—sometimes I was harassed, but I was able to pay all demands against me.

He afterwards said that the fishery was of little value.

The defendant's counsel submitted the following points:—

1. If the jury believe that in April 1824, when the deed was executed by Christian Baughman to Samuel Thompson, Jr., who was then a boy about eight years of age, the consideration for the purchase was paid by his father, Samuel Thompson, Sr., by the conveyance of the interest of the father in a fishery to said Baughman as per deed of same date, and that at the time of said conveyance the father was embarrassed and unable to pay his debts, such conveyance would vest no title in the son, and he could not recover in the present action.

2. If the consideration was paid by the father when the property was conveyed by Baughman to his son, the equitable and beneficial

[Knouff v. Thompson.]

estate would be in the father, and pass by his deed to Parson, and is now by the chain of title in evidence vested in the defendant, and plaintiff cannot recover.

3. If the jury believe that Samuel Thompson, Jr., attained the age of twenty-one in 1836, the same year the lot now in dispute was purchased at sheriff's sale by Christian Livingston, and that said Thompson lived in the same town and within two hundred yards of the property, and saw and knew and permitted the said Livingston and Henry Thatcher his vendee, and the present defendant, the vendee of Thatcher, to fence and improve and occupy said lot by planting trees thereon, converting the same into a garden and building a smoke-house thereon, and this for a period of fourteen years, without giving any notice of his claim or title, he is now estopped from recovering the lot in controversy in this suit.

WATTS, President. This is an action of ejectment for a lot of ground in which both parties claim under the same original title, which was in Christian Baughman; who, on the 14th April 1824, conveyed the same to Samuel Thompson, Jr., the plaintiff. At that date the plaintiff was only six years of age; but a conveyance to him at that age, if otherwise honest and right, is just as valid as if he were of lawful age. But the defendant's title rests upon the allegation that the conveyance was made for the fraudulent purpose of concealing the property by Samuel Thompson, Sr., his father, from his creditors—and in corroboration of this view he has given in evidence a conveyance by Samuel Thompson, Sr., of the property to William Parson, dated the 2d March 1829, and this title has been regularly deduced to the present defendant—and to show the motive which influenced this fraud, evidence has been given of the embarrassed condition of the circumstances of Samuel Thompson, Sr., at the time. Now, this is the point in the cause, a matter of fact, which peculiarly belongs to the determination of the jury. We, therefore, answer the defendant's first point by saying that it is a true exposition of the law, and if the jury believe the facts therein stated, the verdict should be for the defendant.

The defendant's second point we cannot answer affirmatively, for it is competent and lawful for a father at any time to make or procure a conveyance to be made to his child for the purpose of advancing his interests; and if the transaction is honest and with no view of affecting the interests of creditors or any one else injuriously, no exception can be taken to it.

In answer to the defendant's third point the court say:—An estoppel, if the facts which are alleged to constitute it are found by the jury, is a legal bar to an inquiry into the merits of any other question in the cause, and would necessarily in this case produce a verdict for the defendant, independent of the truth of the case, as respects the validity of the deed of Christian Baughman to Samuel Thompson, Jr., as vesting the title in him. We are of

[Knouff v. Thompson.]

opinion that the facts of this case forbid that we should give the instruction asked.

The notice which the law requires that a man should give of his title, is that he record it; and this deed to Samuel Thompson, Jr., was duly recorded and was therefore legal notice to all the world that the title was in him, and this deed was actually recited in the deed to William Parson. The facts, therefore, stated in this point do not estop the plaintiff from a recovery in this case if he be otherwise entitled. Then let us come back to the point from which we started, and determine the cause upon it, for there is nothing else in it.

Was the transaction by which the deed was made by Christian Baughman to Samuel Thompson, Jr., an honest one? Or was the consideration for it paid by his father, and the deed made to the son to conceal that title from his creditors? As you determine this point, so determine the cause for the plaintiff or for the defendant.

To this charge the defendant excepted.

Verdict was rendered for plaintiff.

Graham, for plaintiff in error, contended that the court erred in considering that there could be no estoppel when the adverse title was upon record.

Silence, accompanied by a knowledge of title, will bar a recovery, where the purchase or improvements are made in good faith, without *actual knowledge* of the adverse title. Recording a deed is legal notice, but not actual notice or *knowledge*.

It would be a great hardship, if not fraud, were the law to permit a property that had passed through the hands of three different owners for a period of sixteen years, to be taken from the hands of an honest purchaser, without any *knowledge* of an adverse title, and who had expended his money and time and labor in the purchase and improvement of it for a period of five years—and this by a neighbor, who, with a full knowledge of his title, had silently permitted the purchase and improvement of the property, until only forty-six days were wanting to perfect the title of the occupant under the statute of limitations.

In the case of Carr v. Wallace, 7 *Watts* 394 and 400, the title of plaintiff was on record, and this was relied on by his counsel. But in that case the court say—

"If one knowingly, though passively by looking on, permits another to purchase and spend money on land under an erroneous opinion of title, without making known his claim, he shall not be permitted afterwards to exercise his legal rights against such person."

Hamilton v. Hamilton, 4 *Barr* 193–4, was the case of a sheriff's sale on an award of arbitrators on which no judgment was entered. It was a matter of record, of which all had *legal notice*. The sale could have conferred no title, but the plaintiff permitting valuable

[Knouff v. Thompson.]

improvements to be made while he was quietly standing by and giving no warning of his title, cured all imperfections.

Also cited Pittsburg v. Scott, 1 *Barr* 310; 4 *W. & Ser.* 423; 2 *Pa. Rep.* 22; 2 *Johnson* 589.

Biddle, contra.—The deed from Christian Baughman to Samuel Thompson, Jr., was recorded, and it was recited in the deed to Parsons, under whom Knouff, the defendant in the action, claims. After registry of a deed, the owner need not give notice of his title to one making improvements on the property: 7 *Barr* 233. The law imputes to a purchaser a knowledge of every fact of which the exercise of ordinary diligence would have put him in possession: 2 *Rawle* 90; 4 *Barr* 149, Correy v. Cayton; 11 *Ser. & R.* 389; 10 *Watts* 26–7.

Encouragement to improve may bar a recovery by him who has given it: 7 *Barr* 233; 4 *Barr* 193; 1 *id.* 317; 4 *Watts* 823.

The opinion of the court was delivered June 23, by

CHAMBERS, J.—The title to the lot in controversy in this action is considered as being vested in Samuel Thompson, Jr., the defendant below, under the deed to him from Christian Baughman, dated April 14, 1824, and recorded May 3, 1824, the jury having, by their finding under the charge of the court, negatived the presumption of fraud in the execution of that deed.

The question now raised by the error assigned to the charge of the court is, whether Samuel Thompson, Jr. has been divested of his title, or barred of recovery by his acts, or by operation of law. At the time of the execution of this deed to him, Samuel was of the age of eight years, but, notwithstanding his minority, was capable of taking an estate in the lot as conveyed.

The defendant derives title under a deed from Samuel Thompson, Sr., and wife, to William Parson, for the lot in dispute, dated March 2, 1829, consideration $30, recorded 6th July 1833, which deed recites the deed from Christian Baughman to Samuel Thompson, Jr., referred to as a deed to Samuel Thompson. Parson's right was sold with other property at sheriff's sale to Christian Livingston, in 1836. Livingston conveyed to Henry Thatcher by deed dated August 1, 1843, recorded November 1843, and Thatcher by deed conveyed to Joseph Knouff, the defendant below, dated September 11, 1845, recorded August 5, 1846.

It is testified by Samuel Thompson, Sr., that when Parson applied to him to purchase the lot in dispute, which was adjoining one on which he was about to build, he told Parson that he had not the title, it was in Samuel Thompson, Jr. Parson said *he knew that*, but if he would make a deed and give him possession, when Samuel came of age, if he claimed it, he would make it right with him. That Parson was at him several times before he did it.

[Knouff v. Thompson.]

It was also proved that Thatcher, when told that young Thompson would claim the lot, said he would lose nothing by it, as Livingston was good enough to him for it. Knouff, defendant below, is the son-in-law of Christian Livingston.

A fence was put around the lot by Parson, and cultivated as a garden; it continued fenced and cultivated until defendant occupied it and put up a pale fence, and erected a smoke-house on it. The plaintiff was of age in 1836, and lived within 200 yards of the property. The plaintiff in error assigns for error the answer of the court in their charge to the jury on the third point, as follows:—In answer to the defendant's third point the court says, "An estoppel, if the facts which are alleged to constitute it are found by the jury, is a legal bar to an inquiry into the merits of any other question in the cause, and would necessarily in this case produce a verdict for the defendant, independent of the truth of the case as respects the validity of the deed of Christian Baughman to Samuel Thompson, Jr., as vesting the title in him. We are of opinion that the facts of this case forbid that we should give the instruction asked. The notice which the law requires that a man should give of his title is that he record it, and this deed to Samuel Thompson, Jr., was duly recorded, and was therefore legal notice to all the world that the title was in him; and this deed was actually recited in the deed to William Parson. The facts stated in this point, (say the court,) do not estop the plaintiff from a recovery in this case, if he be otherwise entitled." Was there or not error in this answer of the court?

The title of Samuel Thompson, Jr., was on record, and every person was bound to take notice of it. The lot was not purchased by those under whom defendant claims in ignorance of that title. Parson purchased, not only with the knowledge of the title being in the minor, declaring that when he came of age, if he claimed it, he would make it right with him; but in the deed which Parson receives for the lot the recorded deed to Samuel Thompson, Jr. is recited. In what is the alleged equity of the defendant and those under whom he claims? It is that Samuel Thompson, Jr. remained silent, as the owner of this title, living within a short distance of it. The defendants were cognizant of his title; and why did they maintain silence with him during the many years after Samuel attained the age of 21, which was in 1836? Would not ordinary precaution have induced an inquiry by the purchasers, of the legal owner, living in the same village, about the sale or prosecution of his title? They had the most interest in breaking his silence; they were improving and purchasing at their peril, which they were bound to know, and yet there is neither inquiry nor complaint at the proper source. The improvements made on the property were, it seems, of little value, and the defendants had all the advantage of cultivation and the profits thereof.

[Knouff v. Thompson.]

The defendant, and those under whom he claims, cannot have any defence arising from want of notice. It is decided by this court that whatever puts a party on inquiry amounts to notice, provided the inquiry would lead to the knowledge of the requisite fact, by the exercise of ordinary diligence and understanding: Squire v. Weeks, 7 *Watts* 267; Hood v. Fahnestock, 1 *Barr* 470; Epley v. Watson, 7 *Watts* 167. The very deed under which they derived their title informed them that the title was in the plaintiff, and that the evidence of it was on record in the proper office.

Would silence bar and estop the plaintiff from asserting his title within the time allowed by the law to prosecute his right? We think not.

Equity will not, on the mere ground of silence, relieve one who is perfectly acquainted with his right, or has the means of becoming so, and yet wilfully undertakes to proceed in expending money on the lands of another without obtaining or asking his consent. His ignorance of it is wilful, and he acts at his peril: Carr v. Wallace, 7 *Watts* 401; Crest v. Jack, 3 *Watts* 240.

In Alexander v. Kerr, 2 *Rawle* 90, Chief Justice GIBSON says—"While courts of justice have on the one hand endeavored to repress dishonesty, they have on the other exacted the utmost vigilance and caution. It is difficult to imagine how the concealment of a fact which an individual of common prudence and sagacity can discover, can constitute a fraud."

In Goundie v. Northampton Water Company, 7 *Barr* 233, it is decided that after registry of a deed, the owner need not give notice of his title at sheriff's sale of another title, nor to one making improvements.

The party who has placed his written title on record has given the notice which every person is bound to know and respect. The law does not require him to go further. But if he speaks or acts, it must be consistent with his recorded title. The law distinguishes between silence and encouragement. Whilst silence may be innocent and lawful, to encourage and mislead another into expenditures on a bad or doubtful title would be a positive fraud, that should bar and estop the party, the author of that encouragement and deception, from disturbing the title of the person whom he misled, by any claim of title in himself.

The distinction between the omission to give notice and encouragement by positive acts, is recognised and assumed by Justice COULTER in the case last referred to in 7 *Barr* 233, and by C. J. GIBSON in Alexander v. Kerr, 2 *Rawle* 89. It is this principle that distinguishes the cases herein referred to and applicable to this case, from those of Hamilton v. Hamilton, 4 *Barr* 193; Pittsburg v. Scott, 1 *Barr* 317; McHelvy v. Truly, 4 *Watts* 323.

The title Knouff was receiving, informed him of the title on record of Samuel Thompson, Jr., and in the exercise of *ordinary*

[Knouff v. Thompson.]

caution, he might, on inquiry, have learned from him every other fact which he was desirous of knowing for his protection; and the law imputes to him the knowledge of such facts. Such an imputation rebuts the inference of constructive fraud, to be implied merely from silence. If Knouff remained in ignorance, it was wilful on his part, and he is without equity in his defence.

The charge of the court excepted to, is in conformity to the adjudications of this court and the established elementary principles of law and equity. It is free from error, and the judgment of the court below is affirmed.

McConnell *versus* Wenrich.

Where a husband assigned a bond given to him for his wife's interest in real estate, without receiving value therefor, but by an instrument under seal expressing the transfer to be *for value;* and the assignee during the coverture assigned the same to another *for value;* the second assignee, not having knowledge or the means of knowledge that the former assignment was without consideration, is entitled to the bond or its proceeds against the claim of the wife who brought suit after obtaining a divorce.

ERROR to the Common Pleas of *Berks county*.

This was an action of assumpsit, by Elizabeth McConnell, formerly Elizabeth Shaffer, daughter of John Shaffer, deceased, against John Wenrich, David Wenrich, and Daniel Wenrich.

The material facts in the case were stated in the charge of his Honor D. F. GORDON, President Judge, as follows:—

This is an action of assumpsit, brought to recover money which the plaintiff alleges to have been received by the defendants for her use, under the following circumstances:—The facts will be detailed to you by the court, as they appear to be substantiated by the evidence; but whether they are so or not, and of all matters of fact in the case, the jury are the exclusive judges. John Shaffer died in 1815, leaving a widow and four children, of whom the plaintiff in this action is one. In the same year, proceedings were had in the Orphans' Court of Berks county for the partition of the real estate of the decedent, under which proceedings 114 acres of land were adjudged to John Shaffer, son of the deceased, who entered into a recognizance in the Orphans' Court to secure the purparts of the other heirs. Elizabeth McConnell was at that time the wife of Frederick A. McConnell, and a bond was executed to *F. A. McConnell and his wife* to secure the payment of the wife's share. It would seem that this bond was for the sum payable to Elizabeth McConnell in one year, and also for the sum payable to her after the death of the widow of the decedent Catharine Shaffer. *For the latter sum* a new bond was given by John Shaffer *to F. A.*

[McConnell *v.* Wenrich.]

McConnell alone, dated December 14, 1818. The bond was for the sum of $1190.67, payable after the death of Catharine Shaffer, the widow of John Shaffer, deceased, that being the sum payable to Elizabeth McConnell as one of the heirs of the deceased.

On the 15th January 1819, Frederick A. McConnell, the husband of the plaintiff, assigned this bond to *Robert* McConnell and Daniel Vonneida. The assignment was under hand and seal, and made in the presence of two subscribing witnesses, and is expressed to be *for a valuable consideration.*

Daniel Vonneida, the assignee, who has been examined as a witness in the case, states that the assignment was not made for any stipulated sum, nor in payment and discharge of any debt due to him from the assignor, but he took it, as he says, as security for money due to him from F. A. McConnell, and also for his liabilities as surety of said McConnell, and that afterwards, within a year, as he thinks, from the time of the assignment, he paid for McConnell on account of those liabilities more money than the sum called for by the bond. Daniel Vonneida became the assignee of the whole sum mentioned in the bond; Robert McConnell having assigned to him legally on the 20th February 1819.

On the 15th February 1820, Daniel Vonneida assigned the bond legally to John Wenrich, the father of the defendants, *for a valuable consideration;* that is to·say, in payment of his own debt to Wenrich as to a portion of the bond, and for money paid him by Wenrich for the excess beyond the debt.

In 1827, John Wenrich died, and letters testamentary were granted to the defendants in this suit. Catharine Shaffer died in 1831. To August term 1831, No. 58, an action of debt was instituted on the recognizance of John Shaffer, in the name of the commonwealth for the use of John Shaffer's heirs *vs.* John Shaffer, and judgment was entered for the plaintiff on the 19th January 1832, for the sum of $28,000. To April term 1835, No. 124, a sci. fa. was issued on this judgment for the use of John Wenrich's executors, the defendants in this suit. In 1841, a verdict was rendered in favor of the plaintiffs in that suit for $1881.23, and judgment taken *de terris.* Fi. fa. to August term 1841, No. 20, on which the 114 acres taken at appraisement by John Shaffer were levied on in the hands of Hannah Miller. After this levy was made, the amount of their judgment and interest was paid to William Strong, Esq., the counsel of the plaintiffs in that action, by Christian Seltzer, on an agreement that the judgment should be assigned to him; the sum thus received by the Wenrichs as executors of John Wenrich, deceased, forms the subject of controversy here. It is to recover that sum and the interest due on it that the present action has been instituted. Elizabeth McConnell, the plaintiff in this action, was divorced from her husband, Frederick A. McConnell, by the decree of this court in 1825. She claims to be the owner of this

[McConnell v. Wenrich.]

bond now, and to be entitled to recover the amount of it from the defendants, with interest from the time the money was received by them.

She alleges that the assignments made by her husband, Frederick A. McConnell in 1819, to Robert McConnell and Daniel Vonneida, and by Robert McConnell to Daniel Vonneida, *not being made for a valuable consideration*, did not divest her right to this bond, which was her property when it was executed, subject only to the power of her husband to bar her claim to it in certain formal modes recognised by the law, none of which, as she alleges, have been adopted in the transfers given in evidence here. She contends that the assignments of F. A. McConnell and Robert McConnell were insufficient to bar her claim, and also that the assignment to John Wenrich in 1820 did not bar her, although it would seem, from the evidence, that the latter assignment was made *for a valuable consideration*, to wit, the value of the bond as agreed upon by the parties at the time of assignment: of this fact the jury are the judges.

The defendants allege that the plaintiff took part in the action brought by them to recover the money from Shaffer and Hannah Miller, who was terre tenant of the land taken by Shaffer in the Orphans' Court; that she knew they were claiming the money as their testator's property, and that she suffered them to pay it out to legatees without notice, and is therefore estopped to claim it from them in this action. This is believed to be a full, though brief statement of the matters in controversy here, and will, with the court's explanation of the law and their answers to the legal points propounded to them by the counsel of the respective parties, enable the jury to determine as to the party for whom they shall render their verdict.

He further charged, *inter alia :—*

We have stated that the husband's assignee without value succeeded to all the husband's rights, and among these was the right to assign for value or otherwise; if he assigned the chose without value, it will not be doubted, we presume, that the second or any subsequent assignee without value could reduce it into possession *during coverture*, and the only reason he could not do so afterwards would be his want of equity founded on value paid; this, if correct, would show that every successive assignee without value would succeed to all the husband's rights by virtue of the assignment, and when value has been paid by any assignee during coverture, the thing sought to be recovered by him has been sold, and not given away, and the assignee has the equity of a purchaser to invoke the aid of the law to enable him to recover. In this case, then, the defendant's testator had a right to recover the money due on the bond in question and retain it, unless the jury shall be of opinion that the assignment to him was *without* valuable consideration. If the assignment to John Wenrich was made during the subsistence

[McConnell v. Wenrich.]

of the marriage, and was for the value of the bond as estimated by the parties at the time, then Wenrich's executors were entitled to recover this money and retain it, and the plaintiff cannot recover in this suit.

The *seventh* point submitted on part of *defendants* was as follows:—

That even if the jury believe that the assignment to Robert McConnell and Daniel Vonneida was not for a valuable consideration, yet inasmuch as that to John Wenrich was for value, it amounted to a reduction into possession of the debt, and divested all right of the wife, and she cannot recover.

Ans. If the assignment to John Wenrich was as herein stated, the law is with the defendants, and the assignment made for value during coverture would bar the wife's right to recover.

Error was assigned to the admission of evidence, and that the court erred in charging:

1. In their answer to the plaintiff's *fourth* point. That a subsequent assignee of a wife's chose in action who pays value, during coverture, can recover the amount due after death, or divorce of her husband, and defeat her survivorship, although the assignment by the husband to his assignor was made without value.

2. In their answer to that part of the plaintiff's *fifth* point which relates to subsequent assignees.

3. In their answer to the plaintiff's *ninth* point, that the wife's right of survivorship to her chose in action is barred in the hands of a subsequent assignee, who paid value for it, although the husband assigned it to the first assignee merely as a collateral security and without value.

4. The court erred in their charge to the jury generally.

The case was argued by *J. Glancy Jones*, for the plaintiff in error.—The main point is, whether a wife's choses in action, if assigned by the husband during coverture, without value or as a collateral security, will survive to her on his death or her discoverture; and whether her right of survivorship can be barred by any subsequent assignment made by a stranger, *even for value*.

The first part of this point is not denied, as I understand, and the point stands good as a general proposition; but the court charged, that the latter part formed an exception to the rule, and as this case fell within the exception, they took the case from the jury, and informed them, if they were wrong the Supreme Court would set them right.

And to prove that the court erred in this point, the following authorities were cited:—

Bates *v.* Dandy, 2 *Atkyns* 207; Hornsby *v.* Lee, 2 *Mad.* 16; Purden *v.* Jackson, 1 *Russell* 1; Honner *v.* Morton, 3 *Russell* 298;

[McConnell v. Wenrich.]

Glancy on Married Women, 110, 121–124, and from 140 to 146; *Siter's Accounts*, 4 *Rawle* 472–83; 5 *Johns. Ch. Rep.* 207; Krumbaur v. Bart, 2 *W. C. C. Rep.* 406–9; 5 *Cow.* 597; Petrie v. Clarke, 11 *Ser. & R.* 388; Hartman v. Dowdel, 1 *Rawle* 281; Woelper's Appeal, 2 *Barr* 73; Lodge v. Hamilton, 2 *Ser. & R.* 493; Ferree v. Com'th, 8 *Ser. & R.* 315.

N. and *W. Strong* were for defendants.—The errors assigned in the charge of the court raise the question whether a voluntary assignee of the husband may assign for value and the second assignee hold against the wife after her discoverture.

The court charged that the assignment by the husband of the wife's chose as a collateral security, (being an assignment not for value,) does not defeat the wife's survivorship. It may however be doubted whether even a voluntary assignment, *if it be a legal one*, does not destroy the wife's claim by survivorship. In England no chose in action is assignable at law, but an equitable assignment for value prevails against the wife's title. The reason why a voluntary assignment does not, is that the assignee is destitute of equity, and therefore the chancellor refuses his aid to the assignee: Hartman v. Dowdel, 1 *Rawle* 281. But in Pennsylvania, in some cases, this reason fails. The act of May 28, 1715, makes certain assignments of bonds *legal*. In those cases the assignee needs no aid from the chancellor. In this instance the assignment of the bond was a *legal* transfer, and there is therefore the same reason for the wife's survivorship being barred as exists in the case of a release by the husband. Yet a release by the husband bars, though he does not receive the money. See cases collected in *Glancy on Married Women*, 111; Hartman v. Dowdel, 1 *Rawle* 281.

But the defendant in error need not contest this question. In this case there was an assignment by the assignee of the husband, for value paid. (Vide Vonneida's testimony.)

It matters not that the money was not payable until after discoverture happened: *Shepherd's Touchstone* 333; *Glancy* 111; 4 *Rawle* 475, Siter's case.

By the marriage, the husband succeeded to the wife's power over the wife's choses in action: Siter's case, 4 *Rawle*. He only could exercise it. He may do what she could do if sole, and as she could sell, or constitute an attorney to sell her chose in action, he, having succeeded to her power, may do the same. The assignment by the husband, though voluntary, authorized his assignee to exercise, during the coverture, all the rights of ownership, and among them was the right to sell. The voluntary assignee stood in the place of the husband, and during coverture could reduce the chose into possession, and bar the wife's right by survivorship. This is admitted in Burnet v. Kinaston, 2 *Vern.* 401, which is the leading case. But reduction into possession is reduction of the *title*, not

[McConnell *v.* Wenrich.]

of the money secured by the chose, "*the exercise of some act of ownership over it:* Siter's case, 4 *Rawle* 374; Woelper's Appeal, 2 *Barr* 71; 7 *W. & Ser.* 168, Shuman *v.* Reigart.

A sale by the first assignee was therefore a sale by the husband, and was a reduction of the title to possession, and barred the wife's survivorship.

That the husband may destroy the wife's right by survivorship by the acts of his attorney is undoubted: *Comyn's Dig. Baron and Feme*, E. 3; *Moore* 452, Huntley *v.* Griffith; 5 *Johns. Ch.* 250. BLACKSTONE calls the assignee the attorney of the assignor.

Again, Frederick A. McConnell assigned, it is said, as collateral security, and therefore without value, to Vonneida. But the holder of a collateral may use it to pay the debt due him, either by collecting the sum secured by it, or by sale, and if he sell, the right of the original holder is gone.

John Wenrich bought the bond, seeing upon the bond his assignment purporting to be for value. On the faith of that assignment he released his claim and paid his money. Had the first assignment been fraudulent and therefore void, a subsequent assignee for value *without notice* would be protected. *A fortiori* would John Wenrich in this case: 4 *Watts* 85, Price *v.* Junkin; 4 *id.* 424, Fetterman *v.* Murphy; 3 *W. & Ser.* 479, Thompson *v.* Lee; 1 *Amer. Leading Cases* 67, and cases there cited.

The opinion of the court was delivered June 27, by

ROGERS, J.—This is an action of assumpsit, for money had and received to the use of the plaintiff. The plaintiff seeks to recover on the plea that the bond assigned to the defendant being a chose in action belonging to her, not reduced into possession, nor assigned for a valuable consideration, during coverture, survived to her, after the dissolution of the marriage. That consequently, as survivor, she is entitled to recover the proceeds of the bond, as money received for her use. The plaintiff contends that the assignment of F. A. McConnell, her former husband, to Robert McConnell and Daniel Vonneida, and by Robert McConnell to Daniel Vonneida, not being made for a valuable consideration, does not divest her right to the money, nor does the subsequent assignment to John Wenrich, the defendant, though for a valuable consideration, bar her claim. Numerous errors, as usual, are assigned, most of which touch not the merits of the case. The argument has been narrowed down to two points; to one of which only will the attention of the court be directed, as that disposes of the whole case. The point to which I refer is, granting that as to the original assignees the wife is not bound on the principle of survivorship; yet inasmuch as the transfer by Vonneida to Wenrich is a legal assignment for a valuable consideration, this suit can be sustained. In other words, as in Mott *v.* Clark, 9 *Barr* 405, the question is

[McConnell v. Wenrich.]

whether Wenrich stands in the same or a better situation than his assignor Vonneida. It must be taken as part of the case, and such was the undisputed fact, that Wenrich was entirely ignorant that no value passed between the husband, the original assignor, and his immediate assignees. He therefore stands in the favorable position of an innocent purchaser for value, without notice, either actual or constructive, and, as will be hereafter shown, without any knowledge, or the means of knowledge, to protect himself against combination or fraud. The point arises on the answer to the defendant's *seventh* proposition. The court instructed the jury that if they believed the assignment to Robert McConnell and Daniel Vonneida was *not* for a valuable consideration, yet inasmuch as that to John Wenrich was for value, it amounted to a reduction into possession of the debt, and divested all the right of the wife. We think that the court was right in instructing the jury that on that state of facts the plaintiff could not sustain her suit. It must be borne in mind that the question is not, whether Wenrich knew that the bond assigned was the product of the wife's share of her father's estate, for that may be admitted without affecting the case, but whether he knew, or had the means of knowing, that the bond was assigned to McConnell and Vonneida without consideration. On that point the whole case turns. That he had actual notice of that essential fact is not alleged. Had he then the means of knowledge, is the next inquiry? The assignment, be it remembered, purports on its face to be for a valuable consideration. It must also be confessed the husband had the undoubted right to pass the title of his wife's chose in action for value. If this be so, was there any laches on the part of the defendant, when he purchased and paid his money, in acting on the reasonable supposition that he received a valid title to the bond and its subsequent proceeds. This would appear to me to be equitable and just, for without this he has no means of protecting himself against a fraudulent transfer. As is ruled in Mott *v.* Clark, 9 *Barr* 405, a case very like this, no man can be affected with a latent equity of which he has no knowledge, or possibility of knowledge, and against which it would be impossible for him, with the most careful diligence, to guard himself. In cases of the transfer of the choses of the wife, there can be no safety, for it would be utterly impossible for a subsequent assignee to guard against fraudulent combinations between the husband and his assignee. To whom, it may be asked, could the second purchaser or assignee apply for information? It would be ridiculous to answer, to the apparent owner of the chose, or to the husband of the assignee. They have already asserted, on the face of the assignment, that it was transfered for value. On the supposition that it was an intended fraud, the inquiry would be fruitless, and moreover, the question would imply a doubt as to their honesty and truth. The law is too reasonable to require any thing either vain

[McConnell *v.* Wenrich.]

or frivolous. It has been faintly urged that information could be obtained from the wife. But what information could be drawn from her? That the bond was her chose, even if that was asserted, which it was not, would be beside the question; for be it remembered, the only thing that is material is whether any consideration passed between the husband and the assignee. And on that point, what knowledge could the wife be supposed to have, which would render an inquiry of her either necessary or proper? It would be justly regarded by both, if not an insult, as an impertinent interference with business pertaining to the husband alone, intermeddling with his unquestioned right of absolute disposition and transfer. Our own cases, Mott *v.* Clark, 9 *Barr* 405, and Taylor *v.* Gitt, 10 *Barr* 428, are full to the point. As this disposes of the whole case, we deem it unnecessary to express any opinion on the other points, one of which only has been much pressed.

Judgment affirmed.

Eyster's Appeal.

1. The record of the Orphans' Court is evidence of the appointment of a guardian; the issuing of a certificate of the appointment is not material; an act as guardian, by the person appointed, is an assumption of the trust.

2. Guardians are liable for wilful default or gross negligence; but they are allowed the exercise of reasonable discretion and prudential care in managing the property of their wards. Therefore, where a guardian permitted the rents of a small property to be received by the widow, and the share of the ward in the rents to be applied by her to the maintenance and education of the ward, who was her son and was residing with her, the guardian is not accountable to the ward for the rents, the said rents not being an unreasonable provision for the purpose.

3. The balance due the administrator of the estate in which the ward is interested, upon the settlement of the administration account, and which is a charge upon the estate, if paid out of the rents is a proper credit as against the ward, in a settlement for the rents.

APPEAL by George S. Eyster, alleged guardian of William Adams, from the decree of the Orphans' Court of *Franklin county*.

The petition of William Adams was presented at the Orphans' Court held in Franklin county, in which it was alleged that at an Orphans' Court held in October 1835, George S. Eyster was appointed guardian of the person and estate of the petitioner, then a minor under the age of 14 years; that no account of his guardianship had been filed, and asking for a citation to file an account.

A citation was awarded 29th January 1850.

George S. Eyster replied that he was appointed guardian of William Adams by the Orphans' Court of said county, on the 6th day of October A. D. 1835, as appears by the record of said court; that the account of James Wright, Esq., administrator of Johnston

[Eyster's Appeal.]

Adams, father of said William Adams, was confirmed by said court on the 7th day of October A. D. 1835, and that there was a balance due said accountant of $31.46, as appears by the record of said court; that your deponent never gave bond, nor assumed the duties of said trust, neither has he to his knowledge received any money in the capacity of guardian as aforesaid; that your deponent knows not where moneys to any amount could be due said William Adams, as the only property left by said Johnston Adams has been occupied by said William and his mother since the death of said Johnston, and the greater part of the rents which have accrued have, as your deponent believes, been applied to the liquidation of the debts of said decedent, and the maintenance and education of said William.

An auditor was appointed, who reported that it appeared from the Orphans' Court docket, that George S. Eyster was appointed guardian of William Adams on the 6th October 1835. Also that Henry Ruby was examined, and testified that William Adams, the petitioner, was indentured to him as an apprentice to the printing business, as near as he could recollect, in 1840. His impression was that Mr. G. S. Eyster signed the indenture as guardian of William Adams. The property of the decedent is, he supposed, worth fifty dollars rent a year.

Mrs. Adams, the mother of petitioner, lives in the property of her late husband. He boarded with me while in the printing-office.

Another witness testified that he lived in the property in 1838; that he rented the property from Eyster, and paid thirty dollars rent for half of the house and lot. That he called on Eyster to pay him the rent, who told the witness to pay it to Mrs. Adams, as she was in the habit of receiving the rent; he, Eyster, did not receive any rent from me. I remained in the house three years, the last two rented from Mrs. Adams—she received all the rent. I cannot say whether Mr. Eyster rented the house to me as guardian or agent. Mrs. Adams occupied part of the house—the petitioner boarded part of the time with his mother.

In chief:—Can't say how much of the time he was at home since I left. The old lady often complained to me of trouble in collecting rents of the house and lot.

Another witness testified that the difficulty about the indenture was settled, and that the *mother* paid the witness $50 in consideration of the release of Adams from the indenture.

Another witness testified that he was the administrator of the estate of Johnston Adams, the father of the petitioner; that he filed his account in October 1835, at which time there was a balance due on said account of thirty-one dollars and forty-six cents. I think the widow paid me said sum. The petitioner was a small boy at the death of his father. Mrs. Adams frequently complained

[Eyster's Appeal.]

to me, after 1835, of the difficulty she had in collecting rents from her tenants. The petitioner lived some time after 1835 with his mother.

The auditor alleged, that being of opinion that the current of decisions in Pennsylvania was in favor of petitioner, he reported an account charging the guardian with two-thirds of the rents from 1st April 1835, with interest for most of the time; viz. rents and interest $627.56½; and he allowed credit for $31.46, the balance of the account paid by the widow to the administrator; also for the maintenance of the ward during the time he was living with his mother; also for the payment by the widow for the release from the apprenticeship; and for allowance and fees. From the balance reported against the guardian, the court directed interest to be deducted, and the result was a balance of $194.76 against the guardian.

Exceptions were filed on the part of *petitioner*, to the whole amount of the credits allowed; and others were filed on the part of the *guardian*.

The court ordered that the guardian be credited in the account with interest on the payments, from the time they appear by the report to have been made. The clerk was ordered to make a calculation accordingly, and the report, being so reformed, was confirmed.

It was certified by the clerk that no certificate was issued to Eyster of his appointment as guardian.

McClellan and *Smith* were for appellant.—It was contended that no part of the money charged came to the hands of Eyster as guardian.

That there was not sufficient evidence that he ever assumed the duties of guardian; and if he did, that the allowance to him was not sufficient; and that no interest should be charged against the guardian.

McLanahan, *Reilly*, and *Carlisle*, were for Adams, the petitioner.

The opinion of the court was delivered, June 27, by

CHAMBERS, J.—The first question raised in this case is, was Mr. Eyster the legal guardian of William Adams?

Mr. Eyster was appointed by the Orphans' Court of Franklin county, on petition, the guardian, of which the record is evidence; and whether a certificate of his appointment was issued by the clerk of the court is not material. The act of 1832 makes it discretionary with the Orphans' Court to require bond with security from the guardian of a minor; and the omission to require or to give such bond does not vitiate the appointment. Did Mr. Eyster accept the appointment? It was rightly said by Justice KEN-

[Eyster's Appeal.]

NEDY, in Neutz v. Rutter, 1 *Watts* 235, that any act as guardian was an acceptance of the appointment generally, and he thereby became responsible as such. After his appointment, Mr. Eyster assumed to act in leasing the property of which the ward was part owner, and gave his assent to the binding of him as an apprentice. His authority to act in these matters could only be derived from his appointment as guardian, and is considered as evidence of an acceptance of the guardianship with its responsibility. That responsibility was to attend to and manage the interests of the ward with reasonable attention, and account for them with fidelity.

William Adams, the ward, was of seven or eight years of age, the only child of his mother, a widow, at the time of the appointment of Mr. Eyster. The only property of the mother and son consisted of a small house and lot, the rents and profits of which were estimated at fifty dollars per year. At the time of the appointment of guardian, it appears there was a balance due the administrator of the estate of Johnston Adams, the father of the ward, of $31.46, and which there were not personal assets to pay. The whole property of the ward consisted of his share, being two-thirds, of the house and lot referred to, to be applied to his maintenance and education, and which was subject to the charge stated in favor of the administrator. The comfort of the mother and child would require her to retain, for their shelter and home, a part of the dwelling-house. This she did, and the property, so far as could be rented out, was rented for thirty dollars. The income from this property for the support of the mother and child would be only so much as was left of the thirty dollars, after any charges of repairs, taxes, &c. The ward's share of this small patrimony would not have afforded the guardian the means of supporting him anywhere else than with his mother, whose affection would secure her attention and means of support not to be had from a stranger. We can well suppose that Mr. Eyster, as the guardian, to promote the best interests of his ward, and for her accommodation and the convenience of all parties, would allow the mother to maintain and school her youthful son, receive as she could the small rents receivable, and apply her son's share to that maintenance and education. The mother has continued to reside in the house from the decease of her husband, and with her the son has had his residence and home, whilst he resided in Chambersburg, which was for many years. So far as Mr. Eyster may have allowed the mother thus to act for her child, it was to the benefit of his ward. Her industry would have to supply the means of support, to which we cannot but suppose his share of the rents was inadequate. The widow, with propriety, paid the balance to the administrator, which was a charge on the realty, and, if not paid, might have been increased with costs, and for which she was fairly entitled to a credit out of the rents receivable.

[Eyster's Appeal.]

If the rents receivable were faithfully applied by the widow to the maintenance and education of her son as long as he was a charge to her, and it is not pretended that she acted with imprudence or without frugality, this ward has had the advantage of them, and it would be unconscionable and unjust that he should now make Mr. Eyster, his guardian, pay them over to him, though he never received any part of them. We cannot see that it was to the disadvantage of the ward that his small income was applied to his support, by permission, through the hands of a faithful mother, rather than through the hands of his guardian. The fifty dollars she advanced to relieve him of his apprenticeship, with which we suppose he was dissatisfied, could not have been saved from rents, but must have been the earnings of her own employment. If Mr. Eyster is chargeable with the rents to his ward, the mother, who received all that were received, would be chargeable for the same to the guardian.

It has been said in this court, to be the harshest demand that can be made in equity, to make a trustee answerable for what never was in his hands, or to make up a deficiency not owing to his wilful default. More ought not to be expected of guardians than common prudential care: they should not be made liable, unless under unfavourable circumstances: their acts expose them to the animadversions of the law for supine negligence, showing carelessness of duty and of the ward's interests: Johnson's Appeal, 12 *Ser. & R.* 317; Konigmacher *v.* Kimmel, 1 *Pa. Rep.* 213. If guardians are to be held responsible for all negligence, and are not to be allowed the exercise of reasonable discretion and prudential care in managing the property of their wards, it will deter prudent men from assuming the office, which in itself is sufficiently onerous, and already undertaken by such men with reluctance.

The intelligent auditor who reported the account in this case charging the guardian with all the rents, expresses "his opinion of the extreme hardship of it," under all the facts of the same, and to which he felt himself compelled by the decisions on the subject. We are not aware of any decisions in this court that would subject a guardian to such "extreme hardship," unless he was a wilful defaulter, or guilty of gross negligence, and which do not appear in this case from the facts on the record.

The facts necessary to the proper consideration and decision of this case were not presented as fully to the auditor by the parties as they ought to have been, and are wanting to enable the court to decide on or reform the account; and for want of testimony, the case will stand over, and it is committed to an auditor to ascertain the facts of the time of residence of William Adams with his mother, during his minority and after—his maintenance and education, and by whom, during his minority—the amount of rents received or receivable by the guardian, or by whom, during the same time—and

[Eyster's Appeal.]

payments and disbursements for and in behalf of said William by his mother, or for and on account of the property; and report the same together with an account of the indebtedness of George S. Eyster, as guardian, if there be such indebtedness under the facts and circumstances. *Thomas B. Kennedy, Esq.*, of Franklin county, is appointed auditor for the purpose, who will make report to this court.

Maurer *versus* Marshall.

A testator devised as follows:—"I give to my wife Maria the use and income of my plantation, the whole lying and being situate in Alsace township, for her support and maintenance during her life. Item, I give and bequeath to my youngest son Daniel Maurer, the whole of the aforesaid plantation; also, my woodland, containing about fourteen acres, lying on Penn's Mount, after the decease of my said wife Maria; and if my son Daniel should be a minor at the decease of my said wife Maria, then my will is that my executor, hereinafter named, shall rent or lease the said plantation until my said son Daniel shall arrive at the age of twenty-one years. Item, if my aforesaid son Daniel should die, under the age of twenty-one years, and without lawful heirs, then my will is that my said plantation shall be sold by my executor, providing it be after the decease of my wife Maria, and the whole of the proceeds to be equally divided among the lawful heirs of my son George, the lawful heirs of my daughter Maria, and the lawful heirs of my daughter Sarah, provided, always, that if my son Daniel survives and *begets lawful heirs*, then after his decease, the proceeds of the said plantation to be equally divided, share and share alike, to the heirs of my son Daniel:" A conveyance was made by Daniel to bar the entail, and he tendered a deed *in fee simple* to the purchaser of the estate with whom he had contracted to convey such an estate: *Held*, that Daniel had such an estate in the premises as the purchaser was compellable to take. The estate which he derived under the will was considered by this court to be an estate-tail.

ERROR to the Common Pleas of *Berks county*.

This was an action by Daniel D. Maurer against Jacob Marshall, to recover an instalment of $3000, on an agreement for the sale of a tract of land which was to be conveyed in fee simple to Marshall. The question in dispute was whether Daniel D. Maurer had an estate for life in the land, or a fee-tail, or a conditional fee. The following facts were agreed upon by the parties to the suit, in a case stated.

On the 4th day of December 1819, Maria De Turk, the mother of the plaintiff, became seized and possessed of the said land, in her own right, in fee simple absolute, for the consideration of $12,000, by deed of that date from John Rothermel and Deborah his wife to the said Maria, which deed is duly recorded in the proper office, at Reading, in said county, in book A, vol. 36, p. 324.

Sometime in 1820, the said Maria De Turk, mother of the said plaintiff, intermarried with Jacob Maurer, the father of the said plaintiff.

Subsequent to said marriage, to wit, on the 12th day of Decem

[Maurer v. Marshall.]

ber 1820, the said Jacob Maurer and Maria his wife, for the consideration of £4000, therein expressed, conveyed the said land to Daniel Guldin in fee simple, which said Daniel Guldin and Margaret his wife, on the 16th of the same month, for the same consideration of £4000, conveyed the said described land, in like form, to the said Jacob Maurer. The said Jacob Maurer continued seised and possessed of the said land until in the year 1839, when he died, leaving the said Maria his widow, since deceased, and the plaintiff, who was the only child of the said marriage—and also leaving children of a former marriage, to wit, George Maurer, Susan intermarried with Daniel Weidner, Maria intermarried with Jacob Long, and Sarah intermarried with John Weidner. The plaintiff is above the age of twenty-one years, married, and has an heir, a son.

Jacob Maurer left a will, which contained, *inter alia*, provisions as follows:—Item, I give to my wife Maria the use and income of my plantation, occupying the whole lying and being situate in Alsace township, for her support and maintenance during her life. Item, I give and bequeath to my youngest son Daniel Maurer, the whole of the aforesaid plantation; also my woodland, containing about fourteen acres, lying on Penn's Mount, after the decease of my said wife Maria, and if my son Daniel should be a minor at the decease of my said wife Maria, then my will is that my executor, hereinafter named, shall rent or lease the said plantation until my said son Daniel shall arrive at the age of twenty-one years. Item, if my aforesaid son Daniel should die, under the age of twenty-one years, and without lawful heirs, then my will is that my said plantation shall be sold by my executor, providing it be after the decease of my wife Maria, and the whole of the proceeds to be equally divided among the lawful heirs of my son George, the lawful heirs of my daughter Maria and the lawful heirs of my daughter Sarah, provided, always, that if my son Daniel survives and begets lawful heirs, then, after his decease, the proceeds of the said plantation to be equally divided, share and share alike, to the heirs of my son Daniel.

On the 1st day of April A. D. 1851, according to the terms of the agreement, (a copy of which was exhibited,) the said plaintiff tendered to the said Jacob Marshall a deed *in fee simple* for the said land, according to all the requisitions of the act of Assembly, passed the 16th of January A. D. 1799, entitled an act to facilitate the barring of entails. This deed the defendant refused to accept, and to pay the said sum of $3000, alleging that the said plaintiff had only *a life-estate* in the said land, and had no power to convey an estate in fee simple as specified in the said agreement.

It was agreed, that if upon the facts stated the said Daniel D. Maurer had an estate in the said tract or tracts of land, which might be barred under the said act of Assembly, so as to enable the said plaintiff to convey an estate in fee simple, then judgment shall be entered for the plaintiff for the sum of $3000, the amount of the said first instalment, with interest from the 1st of April 1851. But if otherwise, then judgment shall be entered for defendant, with costs of suit.

May 26, 1851, the court entered judgment in favor of the plaintiff, Daniel D. Maurer, on the case stated.

It was assigned for error:

That the court erred in entering judgment in favor of the plaintiff below.

Filbert, for plaintiff in error, contended that Daniel D. Maurer took an estate *for life only* in the land : 10 *Ser. & R.* 296, Abbot *v.* Jenkins ; 3 *Bin.* 139.

Banks and *N. D. Strong*, for defendant.—It was contended that the devise in this case gives to Daniel Maurer an estate for life in the first instance; and by force of the devise to *the heirs of his body*, he is made the stock from which alone *they* can inherit, and the source alone from which their inheritable blood can spring, and he has an estate-tail : 1 *Harris* 344, Hileman *v.* Bouslaugh. It is to the lawful heirs begotten by his son. This is clearly an estate-tail—not only substantially so, but technically so. He is tenant-tail general. Tenant in tail general is "*where lands or tenements are given to a man, and to the heirs of his body begotten:*" *Coke's Institutes*, book 1, chap. 3, sec. 14 ; 2 *Blackstone Com.* top page 80, margin 114; also cited 3 *Bin.* 374–81 ; 1 *Dallas* 48 ; 1 *Yeates* 338 ; 2 *id.* 400 ; 3 *Ser. & R.* 470 ; 10 *id.* 429 ; 3 *Rawle* 59 ; 1 *Whar.* 139 ; 9 *Watts* 450 ; 7 *W. & Ser.* 98 ; 5 *Barr* 463 ; *Jarman on Wills* 488 ; 8 *Ser. & R.* 268, Cook *v.* Cassel.

A conveyance of real estate to a married woman during her natural life, and after her decease to the heirs of her body, and to them and their heirs and assigns for ever, creates an estate-tail : Hileman *v* Bouslaugh, 1 *Harris* 344.

A devise to one for life, with remainder to the heirs of his body, gives him an estate-tail : *id.*

The opinion of the court was delivered June 28, by

ROGERS, J.—It will hardly bear even the semblance of an argument, that the testator intended to give the plaintiff, Daniel Maurer, his son, merely an estate for life. The only doubt is whether the devisee under the will of Jacob Maurer takes a fee tail or a conditional fee. But whether it is one or the other, on the case stated the plaintiff is entitled to judgment. The parts of the will which bear on the title are contained in the following items. The testa-

[Maurer v. Marshall.]

tor, after devising the use and income of the plantation in question to his wife Maria during her life, proceeds as follows:—"Item, I give and bequeath to my youngest son, Daniel Maurer, the whole of the aforesaid plantation, &c., after the decease of my said wife Maria, and if my son Daniel should be a minor at the decease of my said wife, then my will is that my executor, &c. shall rent or lease the said plantation until my said son Daniel, shall arrive at the age of twenty-one years. Item, if my aforesaid son Daniel should die under the age of twenty-one years, and without *lawful heirs*, then my will is that my said plantation shall be sold by my executor, provided it be after the decease of my wife Maria, and the whole of the proceeds to be equally divided among certain children, naming them, and their lawful heirs, provided always, that if my said son Daniel *begets lawful heirs*, then, after his decease, the proceeds to be equally divided, share and share alike, to the heirs of my son Daniel." The plaintiff survived his mother, is married, and has heirs, one son, and moreover the estate-tail is barred. On this state of facts, the plaintiff has a marketable title which may be assigned to a purchaser, and consequently one which the vendee may be compelled to take. For, as was before remarked, it is of no consequence, for the purposes of this case, whether Daniel's title be a fee tail or a conditional fee. It may however be satisfactory to the parties to say, that on the authority of the cases cited, we are of opinion that the estate in Daniel *is a fee tail*.

Judgment affirmed.

Finney *versus* Finney.

A transfer of certain bonds and real estate was made by a principal debtor to the son of his surety, to indemnify the estate of the latter for being bound in a bond to M. Before M. expressed her assent to the transfer, the principal debtor assigned the fund to another, for whose use suit was brought in the name of the principal against the first transferee, but there was a failure to recover. The bond to M. was never paid: *Held*, that the administrator of the estate of M. could not maintain assumpsit against the first transferee for the amount of money received by him from the property assigned to him, on account of the want of privity of contract between M. and the said transferee.

ERROR to the Common Pleas of *Dauphin county*.

This was an action of *assumpsit*, brought to November term 1846, by Thomas Finney, administrator *de bonis non* of Mary Milligan, deceased, against Thomas Finney. David Ferguson, with *Samuel* Finney as his surety, gave a bond, dated April 7, 1818, to Mary Milligan, for the payment of $800 in one year, with interest. On this bond an action was brought by Mary Milligan against David Ferguson and Samuel Finney, to November term 1823. In October 1823, *Samuel Finney died*, and Thomas Finney, the de-

[Finney *v.* Finney.]

fendant, with others, were appointed his administrators. On the 5th May 1824, David Ferguson gave to Thomas Finney, the defendant, two bonds on Frantz and Brown, for $400 each, and conveyed to him the half of four hundred acres of mountain land, and took from him a receipt in the following words:—

Received, May 5, 1824, of David Ferguson, two bonds payable by Jacob Frantz and Philip Brown, to Adam Brightbill, each bond for $400. The first bond becomes due on 1st May, 1830, the second on 1st May, 1831, and on assignment of the one-half of four hundred acres of land on the Blue Mountain, held by warrant from the commonwealth by Samuel Finney, deceased, and the said David Ferguson, which bonds and land I leave in the hands of the said Thomas Finney, to indemnify him for his father, the said Samuel Finney, being bound as bail in a bond to Mary Milligan, and now in suit, and one note payable by the said David Ferguson to the aforesaid Samuel Finney, amounting now with interest to ———. (Signed) THOMAS FINNEY.

The defendant, Thomas Finney, after these bonds became due, collected and received the amount thereof, and also sold a portion of the land conveyed to him for $244, which he also received—all which moneys, it was alleged, remained in his hands, and were claimed in this suit. The defendant pleaded *non assumpsit* and the statute of limitations. The jury found a special verdict, by which the question reserved for the court was whether the plaintiff as administrator of Mary Milligan, deceased, could sustain this action against the defendant. The court below decided that there was not such a privity of contract or assumption as to enable the plaintiff to recover in this action, and rendered a judgment for the defendant.

Special verdict rendered October 28, 1849, according to the suggestion of the court:—

Thomas Finney, administrator *de bonis non* of Mary Milligan, deceased, *vs.* Thomas Finney. The jury in this case find as follows:—That on the 7th day of April 1818, David Ferguson and Samuel Finney gave their joint and several bond to Mary Milligan, in the sum of $800; Ferguson principal, Finney the surety, *pro ut* said bond. That a suit was brought thereon, No. 57, November term 1823, in the Common Pleas of Dauphin county, and prosecuted, conducted, and discontinued, *pro ut* record. That Samuel Finney died on the 23d October 1823, and letters of administration were granted on his estate to Thomas Finney, Ann Finney, and William Finney, *pro ut* letters. That on the 5th day of May 1824, David Ferguson gave over to Thomas Finney the bonds and lands mentioned in his receipt of that date, *pro ut* receipt, for the purposes therein mentioned. That a deed was made of the land in said receipt mentioned, on the 5th day of May 1824,

[Finney v. Finney.]

pro ut recital in Finney's deed to Casper Heckert, dated July 4, 1825. That Thomas Finney received the money on said bonds, as per endorsements thereon, *pro ut* same, and received on sale of part of the land, $244, *pro ut* receipt in the deed. That Thomas Finney, as acting administrator of Samuel Finney, deceased, settled a final administration account on the 11th February 1836, showing a large balance in his favor, and that no part of the money collected and received on the bonds and land referred to, and named in the receipt of Thomas Finney to David Ferguson, was brought into that account, *pro ut* administration account filed and in evidence, and the estate of the said Samuel Finney was then and yet is entirely insolvent. That David Ferguson, for the use of John Cochran, brought suit against Thomas Finney, for the recovery of the money now in dispute, in the Common Pleas of Dauphin county, No. 98, of April term 1840; said suit also embracing four other bonds; and said suit was terminated by a reversal in the Supreme Court, *pro ut* record. That Thomas Finney, administrator, &c., of Mary Milligan, brought suit against *the administrators of Samuel Finney, deceased*, in the Common Pleas of Dauphin county, No. 200, August term 1843, on the bond given by David Ferguson and Samuel Finney to Mary Milligan, before referred to, and prosecuted the same to judgment, on the 3d day of September 1846, and recovered judgment therein for $1520, *pro ut* the record, which said sum the estate of Samuel Finney is wholly unable to pay. And we find further, that there was no other promise, either express or implied, on the part of Thomas Finney, to pay over the money received on the securities given him by David Ferguson, as aforesaid, except as contained in the aforesaid proceedings, or arising by implication of law, if the law, from the facts aforesaid, raises such promise. If on the aforesaid facts, the plaintiff is the proper party to bring this action and can support the same, then we find a verdict in favor of the plaintiff, for the sum of thirteen hundred and forty-six dollars seven cents, damages, and costs of suit, if in the opinion of the court this action can be sustained; and if the same cannot be sustained, we find for the defendant.

See 1 *W. & Ser.* 112, for a report of the case of Finney v. Cochran, and 3 *id.* 413, for the report of the case of Finney v. Ferguson.

Opinion of PEARSON, President.—The only question presented by the special verdict in this case is, can the plaintiff sustain the action? Is there privity of contract or any assumption in her favor express or implied? Was the money received for her use? Although the action of assumpsit is held in England to be one of the most liberal character, giving a right to recover wherever one man has money which *ex equo et bono* belongs to another, yet it cannot be pretended that this action could be sustained there at law. The promise must be made *to* the plaintiff, or at least to another for his

[Finney v. Finney.]

use: 1 *Stra.* 592; 2 *Keble* 528; 14 *East* 582; 3 *Bos. & Pul.* 147; or the money must be received for his use, 3 *Price* 58. In this country the same rule is established: 5 *Peters* 580; 6 *Watts* 182; id. 349; *Story's Equity Jurisprudence*, sec. 1041, and in note.

Could the plaintiff reach this fund by a bill in chancery, and if she could, can an action be sustained in Pennsylvania?

But for one circumstance to be noticed hereafter, she probably could proceed with success in chancery. Suppose that established, what are her rights of action under our mixed system in Pennsylvania? It by no means follows in all cases that because a bill in chancery can be sustained in England, that the party can enforce his rights by assumpsit for money had and received in this State: Blymire v. Boistle, 6 *Watts* 182, was assumpsit; there Boistle had a judgment against Gladstone, who sold property to Blymire, who, in consideration thereof, and in part payment of his purchase-money, promised to pay Boistle, but that promise was made to Gladstone, and it was held that Boistle could not recover for want of privity. Yet in precisely such a case chancery would have decreed otherwise: *Story's Equity Jurisprudence*, sec. 1041. There can be no doubt but that a chancellor would have decreed the money to be paid in Morrison v. Berkey, 6 *Watts* 349; yet the plaintiff could not support the action for want of privity.

It is very true that our Supreme Court is daily introducing into our system more of the practice and principles of courts of equity; yet in the action of assumpsit they have gone little beyond the rules of the common law.

In Aycinena v. Peries, 6 *W. & Ser.* 243, an action was sustained on very broad equitable principles, in order to reach a particular fund; but there the money was awarded by the Florida commissioners to Mr. Yard "*for himself and others*," and it was known at the time that *others* were interested in it. Of course the money was received for their use as well as his own, and comes within the ordinary principle of money intrusted to one man to be paid over to another, who can unquestionably support assumpsit against the holder on his failure to make payment.

In Matthews v. Stephenson, 6 *Barr* 496, this action was also used as a substitute for a bill in chancery, in order to reach a particular fund which by the terms of a deed of trust stood for the use of creditors.

But liberal as our courts are becoming, we cannot on any legal or equitable principle sustain this case, if a court of chancery, on a bill filed, would not make a decree in favor of the plaintiff. The transaction between David Ferguson and the defendant does not amount to an equitable transfer of the claim to Mary Milligan. If it had, so soon as the money came to Finney's hands it would have been received for her use, and she could have sustained assumpsit. But it was not *her* interest they were desirous to subserve; the as-

[Finney *v.* Finney.]

signment was to indemnify the estate of Samuel Finney; and when the money was received it was held in trust for David Ferguson, provided Finney's estate was not damnified, and if it was, then for its relief. At no period was it held for Mary Milligan. So soon as Ferguson could have indemnified the estate of Finney, he would have been entitled to receive back the fund, although the debt of Mary Milligan remained unpaid. Had the judgment confessed by Ferguson in 1840 been valid, he could have recovered and held the money. Mary Milligan could not have prevented it.

But suppose the receipt or agreement between Ferguson and the defendant had contained express declarations that the money should be for the use of the plaintiff, or be paid over to her when collected, it could have been revoked by Ferguson at any time before Mary Milligan expressed her acquiescence in the arrangement.

Express direction to collect for, or receive and pay over a sum of money to certain creditors, may be revoked before those creditors have expressed their acquiescence: Gilson *v.* Morrit and others, 21 *Eng. C. L.* 381; 5 *Peters* 580; 5 *Whar.* 277; *Story's Equity Jurisprudence*, sec. 1042–43–45–46; and express assignments may be revoked in equity, as well as at law, any time before the creditors have acquiesced therein. See the sections above, also sec. 1036, *id.*; 1196 in note I.; 972 and note 3 to that section; 2 *Mylne & Keen* 482; 3 *Meriv.* 707. The assent express or implied, if any had been given in this case, was revoked by the owner of the fund in 1840, when he assigned the same to Cochran, as appears by the records made part of this special verdict, and suit was brought for Cochran's use the same year.

That was long prior to any assent, express or implied, by Mary Milligan, and, from aught that appears, before she or her representatives knew of the existence of the fund. After this act of revocation no proceeding could be sustained by Mary Milligan, even if the assignment had been originally intended for her benefit. Although the defendant resisted the collection of the money in that suit, yet it was not on account of the interest of the plaintiff, but because the estate of Samuel Finney was not indemnified.

The manifest unfairness of the defendant's conduct in withholding this fund from all parties, in refusing to give it to Ferguson's assignee, or apply it to the payment of plaintiff's debt, rendered us extremely anxious to sustain this action, if it could be done consistent with legal principles, but we are satisfied it cannot be supported, and therefore are constrained to enter judgment on the special verdict in favor of the defendant. But if this fund does not now belong to Cochran—if David Ferguson has got back the right thereto—the plaintiff is not without remedy. Suit can be brought in the name of *Ferguson* for the use of *plaintiff*, which will unite all the interests, and give the action proper legal form;

[Finney v. Finney.]

and the money, when collected, must go in ease of the estate of Samuel Finney, which will be indemnified *pro tanto*.

Or if D. Ferguson will not assent, judgment can be obtained against him on the bond, and an execution attachment issued, and this debt seized, in which proceeding the validity of Cochran's assignment can be tested, and the whole business properly closed, consistent with legal principles as established in Pennsylvania.

We therefore render judgment on the special verdict for the defendant.

It was assigned for error:

That the court should have rendered judgment for the plaintiff, and that there was error in rendering judgment for the defendant.

The case was argued by *McCormick*, for plaintiff in error.—It was contended that the true construction of the defendant's engagement was, that he was to pay over the money when received to Mary Milligan; that in no other way could the estate of Samuel Finney be perfectly indemnified; and that an action of assumpsit for money had and received was the proper remedy: Fleming v. Alter, 7 *Ser. & R.* 295; Com. Bank v. Wood, 7 *W. & Ser.* 89; 9 *Barr* 229; 17 *Mass. Rep.* 400; 19 *Mass.* 287; 1 *Johns. Rep.* 138, Shermerhorn v. Vanderheisen; 12 *Johns.* 276; 2 *Bibb* 62; 3 *Cranch* 492; 2 *Watts* 104, Hind v. Holdship; 1 *W. & Ser.* 112; 3 *id.* 413.

(See Esling v. Zantzinger, 1 *Harris* 50.)

If the plaintiff cannot sustain this action, there is no remedy for him; because the attempt to recover in the name of Ferguson, as the legal plaintiff, has failed; and whether the money, when recovered in a suit in the name of Ferguson, would belong to Cochran or to Mary Milligan, would be immaterial as to his right to recover from Thomas Finney. The legal title to sue is sufficient to support an action, without proving for whose use or at whose instigation it is brought: Armstrong v. Lancaster, 5 *Watts* 68; Commonwealth v. Lightner, 9 *W. & Ser.* 118; Montgomery v. Cook, 6 *Watts* 238. And it is error to allow the defendant in such case to go into evidence that the transfer to the *cestui que use* was obtained by fraud: Blanchard v. Com'th, 6 *Watts* 309.

Fisher and *Fleming*, for defendant in error.—The positions assumed by the counsel for defendant in error are—That this suit cannot be sustained: 1st. Because there is no privity of contract existing between Mary Milligan and the defendant; neither is there any consideration moving from her, nor promise made to her, nor to defendant for her benefit; nor was she prejudiced or her rights in any way affected by the placing of the fund in controversy in defendant's hands. And, 2dly, because even if Mary Milligan might at one time have availed herself of

[Finney v. Finney.]

this fund, she clearly has no right to do so, since it was revoked by Ferguson, its voluntary creator, in 1840.

This action cannot be supported, unless there has been an express contract, or unless the law will imply a contract: 1 *Chitty's Pl.* 98; *Chitty on Con.* 602.

"The plaintiff must unite in himself both the promise and the consideration of it; and if the action in such a case cannot be supported on the foundation of the consideration by drawing the promise to it, it cannot be supported at all:" Edmondson v. Penny, 1 *Barr* 335, per GIBSON.

"In order to support an action for money had and received at common law, a privity of contract must exist between the plaintiff and the defendant, and a consideration either express or implied:" Per ROGERS, J. Aycinena v. Peries, 6 *W. & Ser.* 256, 257.

"To maintain this action, it is necessary for the plaintiff to prove that he does now, or at one time had owned the money sought to be recovered." Per ROGERS, J., *id.* 244.

In assumpsit, we admit that no privity is required where it is or can be shown that the defendant has money in his hands that belongs to the plaintiff, and which the defendant has no right to retain.

The authorities cited by the counsel of plaintiff in error only go to sustain the position, that if this fund was placed in defendant's hands for the use of the plaintiff or for her benefit, then she could recover. That this was a trust for David Ferguson, and not for Mary Milligan, is clear, not only from the words of the receipt, but from the opinion of the Supreme Court in the case of Ferguson for Cochran v. Finney: 1 *W. & Ser.* 118, 119; 3 *id.* 415, 416.

They were placed in the hands of Thomas Finney to indemnify him for his father being Ferguson's bail; and to pay out of the proceeds the amount of a certain note held by his father.

If the estate of Samuel Finney was not damnified by the suit; if it was compelled to pay no money, then a trust resulted for Ferguson as to all of the money beyond what would pay the note and its interest. The writing itself, and the subsequent act of Ferguson in assigning his claim upon this fund to John Cochran, on the 2d of March 1840, shows that this was his understanding of it.

Nothing is here said of Mary Milligan being entitled to any part of this money, or that it was assigned for her benefit, but to indemnify the estate of Samuel Finney.

Samuel Finney's estate was never damnified by reason of this claim of Mary Milligan, for his estate was exhausted in payment of debts, many years before her administrator brought suit on the bond, and recovered a judgment against Finney's administrators on 1st September 1846.

David Ferguson's representatives might have supported this suit, after the verdict and judgment on this bond, on 1st Septem-

[Finney v. Finney.]

ber 1846. Mary Milligan or her representatives cannot, as no promise was ever made, either express or implied, to her, or for her benefit, by Thomas Finney.

There was no implied promise to pay to Mary Milligan. Unless the transactions between Ferguson and defendant in this case amount to an equitable assignment of the fund to Mary Milligan, she cannot maintain this suit; and that it does not amount to that, appears from the following authorities: 1 *Stra.* 592; 2 *Keble* 528; 3 *Bos. & Pul.* 147; 3 *Price* 58; *Story's Eq.* sec. 1041, and note; 5 *Peters* 580; 6 *Watts* 182, Blymire v. Boistle; 5 *W. & Ser.* 511; 3 *Barr* 330, Ramsdale v. Horton; 6 *Watts* 349. Ferguson had the right to revoke the assignment, and having done so, by assigning the fund to Cochran, the administrator of the estate of Mary Milligan cannot recover: 1 *Story's Eq.* sec. 1046; *id.* 972, note; *Chitty on Contracts* 615–16; 14 *East* 582–97; 7 *Taunton* 339.

The opinion of the court was delivered June 28, by ROGERS, J.—Judgment affirmed for reasons given by Judge PEARSON.

Stoner *versus* The Commonwealth.

1. If a husband leave outstanding the share due to his wife in a recognizance in the Orphans' Court, it is not liable to attachment by his creditors.
2. J. S. took land at an appraisement in the Orphans' Court and entered into recoguizance for payment to the other heirs, of whom the wife of S. L. was one. Afterwards the recognizor became the bail of the husband in a note. Subsequent to this, the husband and wife transferred the interest of the wife under the recognizance, which was alleged to have been done to defraud creditors. Separate judgments were afterwards obtained on the note against the husband and his bail, the recognizor; and on the judgment against the husband the interest of his wife under the recognizance was attached, and J. S., the recognizor, made garnishee. Before judgment in the attachment proceeding the recognizor voluntarily paid the amount of the claim: *Held*, that such voluntary payment could not be used by him as a set-off against the claim of the assignee of the husband and wife under the recognizance, nor could it be pleaded in bar as payment of the recognizance; as garnishee he was bound to contest the claim of the attachment creditor, and payment before judgment against him was no defence to a suit on the recognizance for the share attached.
3. Where there is no order for a settlement of the wife's share under proceedings in partition at the time of the partition, the subsequent declaration of the wife made before a judge of the Orphans' Court, that her share of the money payable under the partition should be paid to her husband, is not equivalent to a reduction into possession by him.
4. None but the creditors of the husband can resist an assignment by him of a claim under a recognizance, made for the purpose of defrauding them. The debtor of the claim thus transferred can safely pay it on the foot of a judgment on the recognizance.
5. In the case of an assignment of a claim by one, who it was alleged was incapable from imbecility of mind to make it, the personal representatives of

[Stoner v. The Commonwealth.]

the assignor after her death, and they alone, can contest the *bona fides* of the transaction, and only by an application to the court after the money has been recovered.

ERROR to the Common Pleas of *Dauphin county*.

This was a suit in the name of N. B. Eldred, President Judge of the Orphans' Court of Dauphin county, for the use of Simon Lingle and Susanna his wife, now for the use of Thomas S. Lingle, *vs.* John Stoner, a co-recognizor with John Crall. It was a scire facias on a recognizance entered into in the Orphans' Court of Dauphin county, by John Stoner, with John Crall as his bail, to Amos Ellmaker, President Judge, &c., *on the 31st October* 1815, in the sum of $4500; conditioned to pay to the several heirs of John Stoner, deceased, one of whom was Susanna, then the wife of Simon Lingle, their several and respective shares of and in the real estate of John Stoner, deceased, taken by the defendant at the appraisement under proceedings in partition; and also for the payment to Anna Stoner, widow, &c., the interest annually during her natural life, of $763.05, and the principal at her death to the heirs, &c., one being Susanna, then wife of Simon Lingle.

Anna Stoner (widow) died on the 21st July 1844, and this suit was instituted to recover the one-third of the sum assigned to the widow, to wit, $190.76½, with interest from the time of her death.

Prior to the death of the widow, *Simon Lingle*, husband of the said Susanna, one of the daughters of John Stoner, deceased, became involved in debt; among others, he became indebted, on the 17th November 1830, to Thomas Montgomery, in the sum of $130; and for the payment of which he gave his single bill, with *John Stoner, the defendant*, as his bail. The defendant also became his bail to other persons, whose debts he was compelled to pay.

On the 6th of August 1832, *Simon Lingle and Susanna his wife, for the purpose of defrauding his creditors, as was alleged on the part of defendant*, assigned, without any consideration therefor, to *Anna Stoner*, (widow,) the mother of Susanna, all their share, purpart, and interest in the recognizance, &c.; which assignment having been acknowledged, was on the same day recorded in the recorder's office of Dauphin county.

On the 27th of November 1839, *Thomas S. Lingle*, the plaintiff in this suit, procured from Anna Stoner an assignment *to himself* of the share in this recognizance which had been previously assigned by the said Simon Lingle and Susanna his wife (the father and mother of the said Thomas S. Lingle) to his grandmother, Anna Stoner. This assignment having been acknowledged, was also recorded in Dauphin county on the 29th November 1839.

After the execution of those assignments, to wit, *on the 29th of January* 1845, nearly six months after the death of Anna Stoner, widow, the said *Susanna Lingle* appeared before one of the judges of the Orphans' Court of Dauphin county, and there, in pursuance

[Stoner v. The Commonwealth.]

of the provisions of the 48th section of the act of the 26th of March 1832, declared that she consented and agreed that the money she was entitled to, proceeding from the partition of the real estate of her father, John Stoner, deceased, (all of which was secured by the recognizance on which this suit is founded,) should be paid "to her husband, the said Simon Lingle, without any security or condition whatever;" which declaration was immediately filed and recorded in the Orphans' Court of Dauphin county.

On the same day, at the same time, as part of the same transaction, the said Simon Lingle, by an instrument of writing under his hand and seal, referring to and in part reciting the previous assignments of himself and wife to Anna Stoner, and that of the latter to Thomas S. Lingle, and the declaration of his wife, ratified, confirmed, established, and made good, &c., *the said previous assignments.*

Afterwards, viz. on the 28th of March 1845, the executors of Thomas Montgomery instituted in the Common Pleas of Dauphin county separate suits on the aforesaid single bill of Simon Lingle and John Stoner, *his bail, against Simon Lingle and John Stoner,* to April term 1845, Nos. 54 and 55; in which suits judgments were obtained on the 28th of April 1845, for $242.68.

On the 4th of June 1845, the executors of Montgomery issued an attachment execution against Simon Lingle, (founded on the above judgment against him,) with clause of sci. fa. to John Stoner as garnishee, for $242.68, with interest from the 28th of April 1845, and costs; which attachment was served upon the said John Stoner on the 6th of August 1845, who had then none other of the effects and moneys of the said Simon Lingle in his hands, except the money due upon the recognizance for which this suit was brought, to wit, the sum of $190.76½. And, as alleged by his counsel, having nothing to say why the said judgment should not be levied of the moneys then in his hands, and being unwilling to pay or encounter the risk of paying more money in costs on said attachment execution, the said Lingle being insolvent, he, John Stoner, paid to the plaintiffs in said attachment execution, the sum of $242.68, with interest from date of judgment, and the costs thereon, to an amount, it was alleged, equal to all that was then due and owing by him on the said recognizance.

On the 15th of September 1846, more *than fifteen months after issuing the said execution attachment,* and nearly *a year after John Stoner had paid* $150 *on the said execution attachment,* this suit was instituted by Thomas S. Lingle upon the aforesaid recognizance, to recover for himself and for *his sole use,* the sum of $190.76½, with interest from the 24th of July 1844, the time of the death of the widow, Anna Stoner.

To this suit the defendant, by his counsel, appeared, and, on the 14th of January 1847, pleaded, among other pleas, "payment and

[Stoner v. The Commonwealth.]

set-off, with leave to add, alter, and amend;" and on the 25th of October following, with leave of court, special pleas.

On the trial of the cause in the court below, the counsel of the defendant interposed as reasons why the plaintiff should not recover—

1. That the attachment execution, with clause of sci. fa., issued in the Court of Common Pleas of Dauphin county, to August term, A. D. 1845, No. 57, was a bar to the recovery of Thomas S. Lingle, the plaintiff in interest in this suit.

2. That the assignments by Simon Lingle and wife, given in evidence in this case, and the papers referred to therein, vested the interest in the cause of action in this suit in *Simon Lingle*, the husband.

3. That the assignment by Simon Lingle and wife to *Anna Stoner*, of the 6th of August, 1842, (having been made in fraud of creditors,) though good as between the parties to it, passed to Anna Stoner their interest in this recognizance to such an extent, that Lingle and wife can never controvert the validity of it; but such assignment was not good as to the creditors of Simon Lingle, who may call the same in question; and as to them, it is void.

4. That if the assignment by Simon Lingle and wife was good, and not a fraud upon creditors, then the interest in the recognizance, upon which this suit is founded, was and is vested in Anna Stoner; that her assignment to Thomas S. Lingle was not good, for want of consideration, as well as incapacity from her extreme old age, and from physical and mental debility, to make a contract that would be good, valid, or binding upon her; and particularly in the circumstances under which it was obtained from her.

5. That the payment by John Stoner to Montgomery's executors, of the judgment obtained against Simon Lingle, on the 28th day of April 1845, for $242.68, was a payment made in ease of Simon Lingle, and is a good and valid set-off, or equitable defence to the claim on which the present suit is founded.

6. That issue having been taken by the plaintiff upon the special pleas filed in this case, the question of whether the assignments as therein set forth were fraudulent, must go to the jury; and if they find the facts to be as stated in the special pleas, plaintiff cannot recover.

The court below charged the jury *that the plaintiff was entitled to recover*. That although there was every reason to believe the assignment was made by Lingle and wife to Mrs. Stoner with the intent and for the purpose of delaying, hindering, and defrauding the creditors of Lingle, yet the same was valid against all the world except the creditors who were intended to be defrauded, who must proceed according to law to avoid such assignment. That there can be but little doubt but the assignment made by Anna Stoner to Thomas S. Lingle could readily be avoided by her heirs

[Stoner v. The Commonwealth.]

or legal representatives, on account of the imbecility of the assignor at the time of the assignment, and the apparent overreaching and fraud practised in obtaining it; yet the present defendant cannot avail himself of that as a defence. No one can take advantage of such fraud or overreaching but those injured thereby—the legal representatives of Anna Stoner, deceased.

The court charged against the defendant on all the points propounded by him, and at his request sealed a bill of exceptions.

It was assigned for error that the court erred in charging the jury that the plaintiff was entitled to recover; also in charging against the defendant on the several points propounded by him for the instruction of the court thereon to the jury trying the case; and in their charge in other respects as specified.

The case was argued by *Fisher*, for Stoner the plaintiff in error.

The attachment execution was here plead specially in bar of the plaintiff's recovery, according to the decision in 9 *Barr* 81, Maynard v. Nekervis; cited also 1 *Jones* 361.

As to the payment by John Stoner:—John Stoner knew that Lingle was insolvent, and that to contest the proceedings on the attachment would not only subject him to the payment of the amount of the money he was indebted on the recognizance, but also to costs. Because he knew that the judgment was in full force, not paid nor disputed by Simon Lingle, and that the money due by him on the recognizance was fraudulently assigned by the father to the son, for the express purpose of defeating the recovery of this very debt from Simon Lingle, which debt had been attached in his hands *more than fifteen months before this suit was brought;* and therefore believed he was justified in paying over what he regarded as all that was justly due from him in this recognizance, to wit, $150; and subsequently in paying the amount of the judgment in full.

It was not contended on the trial that the whole amount of that judgment was not due by Simon Lingle to Montgomery's executors, when it was paid by John Stoner, nor that Lingle had ever paid any part of that judgment, nor that the attachment execution had issued for too much, nor that the judgment was an illegal, improper, or surreptitious one. In the case of Ege v. Koons, 3 *Barr* 109, the debtor paid the money to the assignee of his creditor, *after* the attachment was served, and while it was pending.

The garnishee can insist on irregularities in the proceedings on the attachment: 4 *Barr* 296, 301. Though a legal title is sufficient to maintain an action, yet, "where the commonwealth stands as a trustee in an official bond, it may be necessary to show

[Stoner v. The Commonwealth.]

a particular injury as a title to her interference, in order to secure the obligor from an officious intermeddling:" Armstrong v. Lancaster, 5 *Watts* 68.

Rawn, contra.—" A husband has but a naked power over a bequest to his wife, and one which he is not obliged to exercise in favor of his creditors, nor is such bequest the subject of attachment for the husband's debt." " But if these be not taken into his possession or otherwise disposed of by him, they remain to the wife; and if he destines them so to remain, who shall object? Not his creditors, for they have no right to call on him to obtain ownership of his wife's property for their benefit, *especially as their debts were not contracted on the credit of it*," &c. : Dennison v. Nigh, 2 *Watts* 90; 2 *Vesey* 676; 9 *id.* 174; 4 *Rawle* 182, 486; 2 *Watts* 90; 9 *New H. Rep.* 321; 4 *Pa. Law Journ.* 406.

6 *Watts* 238, Montgomery v. Cook, decides that " a person for whose use a suit is brought need show no right in himself; all that is necessary is to show the plaintiff's legal right to recover." See also to the same effect, 5 *Watts* 68, Armstrong v. The City of Lancaster. A wife's choses are not liable to attachment for the debts of her husband: 2 *Watts* 90; 1 *Whar.* 179; 9 *W. & Ser.* 117.

The opinion of the court was delivered June 30, by

GIBSON, C. J.—The key of the case is that Simon Lingle, the husband of the recognizee, never was the owner of the money secured by the recognizance. The defendant's payment of his debt to Montgomery's executors could not be set off as money paid to his use in the character of a surety in the single bill, or pleaded in bar as payment of the recognizance in the character of a garnishee—as the latter certainly not, for he was bound to contest every inch of the ground, and payment before judgment against him could be no defence to a suit on the attached security. Then as to the allegation of fraud in the subsequent assignments, Lingle entertained a groundless fear that his creditors might reach the money secured by this recognizance, and, to prevent them, assigned it. He certainly intended to defraud them, but failed, not for want of will, but for want of capacity. He parted with nothing that was accessible to them; for so long as he saw fit to leave the money secured by the recognizance outstanding, they could not touch it. Nor was his wife's consent before a judge of the Orphans' Court, that he should have it without settling any part of it on her, equivalent to a reduction of the money to possession. At most, it could be the removal of an impediment. But there was no order for a settlement at the time of the partition, and the subsequent assent to dispense with it was superfluous and a nullity. The effect of the assignment to Mrs. Stoner, then, was

[Stoner v. The Commonwealth.]

not to delay, hinder, or defraud Lingle's creditors; and if it were, none but they could resist it. The same thing, in effect, may be said of Mrs. Stoner's assignment to Thomas S. Lingle, the beneficial plaintiff. The fraud supposed to infect it cannot jeopard the defendant, who may safely pay on the foot of a judgment on the recognizance. The executors of Mrs. Stoner alone could contest the *bona fides* of the transaction, and only by an application to the court after the money had been recovered. The judge therefore properly charged against the defendant on all his points.

Judgment affirmed.

Forster *versus* Juniata Bridge Company.

1. Property carried adrift continues to be the property of him who owned it at the time of the flood. When stranded, the owner has the right to enter on the land and remove it, but he is not bound to do so, and may abandon it without incurring responsibility for injury done by it: And it would seem that unless there has been *negligence* in the management of property carried adrift, the owner is not liable for damage done by it, even though he does not remove it after notice to do so. Per GIBSON, C. J.

2. The owner of the land on which property is stranded, after notice to its owner to remove it, and neglect or refusal to do so, may disencumber his property of it by casting it back into the stream; but he has no right *to appropriate it to his own use*. He may remove it at his own expense; but the refusal of the owner of the property to remove it will not divest the right of the latter in it, or bar his entry to reclaim it. He may resume the ownership after abandonment.

3. The owner of the land has no lien on property cast on it by drift. And where the owner of the latter proves his property in it and the actual conversion of it by the owner of the land, the latter is liable in trover and conversion for damages.

ERROR to the Common Pleas of *Dauphin county*.

This was an action of trover and conversion, brought on the 9th of August 1847, by the Juniata Bridge Company against John Forster, who resided in Harrisburg, for the recovery of a portion of the timber and other materials of one span of a bridge that was swept off by the great flood in March 1846, and lodged on the upper end of the island of the defendant opposite to Harrisburg. That portion of the bridge for which suit was brought, lodged on the island of General Forster in the night of the 14th or morning of the 15th March 1846, and, by its lodging there, turned the current of the stream and with it a body of ice over the island, causing damage to the defendant by injuring a peach-orchard and other fruit-trees, stripping off the soil, washing holes in the island, and carrying off interior fences. Two or three weeks after it had lodged there, Forster met Mr. Hollman, the president of the Bridge Company, in Harrisburg, and told him that one span of that bridge had lodged on his island, and asked him if the com-

[Forster v. Juniata Bridge Company.]

pany would take it away, and required of him that the company should remove it from his island. The president of the company replied to him, *that he would not trouble himself about it.* To which Forster answered, If you or the company don't take it away, I will. It was further in proof that previous to this time one of the directors had also been spoken to to the same effect, by General Forster, and a desire expressed that the Bridge Company should remove it. The request was not complied with, nor was any attention paid by the president or the company to the notice and demand made by General Forster upon the president; and it remained where it had lodged, without the company paying any attention to it or taking any steps towards the removal of it, until the first week in July 1846.

Previous to that time, Forster had been urged by the tenant of the island to take the bridge away, because it was an obstruction to his farming the land, and an inconvenience to him. He proved that by reason of its being there, he was obliged to stable his cattle and hogs, as he could not pasture them or turn them out, because it lay in such a position on the island that he could not make his fences and keep the cattle off his cultivated fields. The tenant testified that he repeatedly urged Forster to take the bridge away before he did so. After being thus urged, Forster employed hands to take it apart. They commenced doing so in the first week of July, and in a week or ten days they finished taking it apart carefully, and hauled it (about 600 yards) to an unenclosed yard, near the barn, on the island, and there piled it up; the spikes, bolts, and other iron being hauled to the granary at the barn on the island, and there deposited, and there remained up to and at the time of the trial. Part of the materials were used by the plaintiff in the erection of other buildings.

Woodward, a witness on the part of the plaintiff, proved that he had called upon General Forster, at the request of three of the directors, to see what arrangement could be made about the bridge. That this was while they were working at the bridge, taking it apart—*perhaps had taken it all apart.* That Forster told him he had it, intended to keep it, and the company might help themselves. He further testified that he again called upon General Forster on the 26th July 1846, with a resolution of the board of managers of the company, adopted on the previous day, and told him he came "authorized to demand the bridge, and pay him for taking it apart, *provided he had taken it apart carefully, and had not damaged it much or to a great extent in taking it apart;* that he demanded it then, and had the money along to pay him. He said he had it, intended to keep it, and the Bridge Company might make the most of it." This was after the bridge had been taken apart and hauled to the yard of the barn. This witness further proved that he knew on the 16th of March 1846 that this span had lodged on

[Forster v. Juniata Bridge Company.]

this island, and within two weeks of that time he informed the company where it was. He further proved that he did not go to the island where this span of the bridge had lodged and had been piled up, to demand it of General Forster, or the tenant in possession of the island, or any other person. And that he never was on the island before or after it was taken apart.

The resolution of the company authorized Woodward to call on John Forster and demand that portion of the bridge that landed on said Forster's island, or remuneration for the same if he had destroyed or molested it in any manner; and in case of his refusal, that counsel be requested to bring suit.

PEARSON, J., charged:—This is an action of trover and conversion, brought for the recovery of a portion of the timber of a bridge owned by the plaintiff, and which was swept off by a flood and lodged on the property of the defendant. Many points of law have been raised on the trial, on which we are requested to instruct you.

The defendant contends that he is not responsible for the plaintiff's property, that it came on to the island of which he is owner at a time when it was leased out to a tenant, who is alone responsible, and of whom the demand should have been made. That the remedy of the plaintiff was by peaceably entering on the premises and removing the property. That defendant, as owner of the property, had a right to retain the lumber, materials, &c., until compensated for the damage done his island by its lodging and remaining there. That he has a right to retain it till remunerated for his expenses in removing it, and that no action will lie till tender made of such expense. That the proposed payment by Woodward was no tender, and the demand made by him was insufficient, not being made at the proper place or of the proper person. And that the notice to Hollman, president of the company, to remove the bridge, and his reply, show an abandonment of the property by the plaintiff, and fully justified the defendant in converting it to his own use. And after that he was guilty of no tortious conversion in his appropriation of the property.

This bridge having floated upon the defendant's property without any default of either plaintiff or defendant, the plaintiff would have been justified in entering on the land of the defendant without asking his permission and removing it. He was not bound so to enter, and it would be but proper in every case to ask permission of the owner. After permission asked, if the plaintiff was forbidden to enter, he could resort to his action; he is not bound to enter when so forbidden. No demand of the tenant was necessary. It seems that the defendant exercised all the authority over it that was done by any one; the tenant neither claimed nor touched it; the defendant alone employed hands to take the bridge to pieces, and remove it to his house upon the island, where this tenant re

[Forster v. Juniata Bridge Company.]

sided, and afterwards to use it as his own, made a portion into fences, and built a house or houses of another portion; part still remains in his possession.

The demand, if made as testified to by Woodward, was sufficient, and need not be made *on the island or of the tenant;* and even if no demand had been made, so far as he used the property and converted it to his own use, it would support the action without demand. The defendant had no lien on the materials for the labor bestowed on them; the action can be sustained without a tender, and it would be impossible for the plaintiff to know how much to tender. If the defendant claimed a lien, he should have so stated at the time, and furnished a bill of the amount of his damage and expenses; and then, if the plaintiff refuse to pay, the question would fairly arise. The action can be sustained without a tender, and the only question of any moment is, whether the defendant, under the circumstances, is entitled to have deducted from the value of the property, the expenses incurred in taking it to pieces and removing it to a place of safety or where it would be valued. And we are of opinion and instruct you, that the defendant has a right to be compensated what it was reasonably worth to take the bridge to pieces and remove it, especially after having notified the president of the company to remove it or that he would remove it himself. The damages, if any, should be the value of the materials after deducting all the expense of taking them to pieces and removing them to a place of safety, or to a place of sale, or where they would be of value. The mere declarations of Hollman, president of the company, would not be an abandonment of the property, or bar the plaintiff from removing, and would not justify the defendant in converting it to his own use. If the defendant sustained damages by the bridge being left there an unreasonable time after plaintiff knew it was there, and the president of the company was requested to remove it, that should be paid for or deducted from the amount of damages; but not the injury arising from the accident of the bridge coming upon the defendant's island and causing it to be washed by the flood; but if not removed in a reasonable time, and washing took place in consequence afterwards, it would be a fair subject of deduction.

To this charge defendant's counsel excepted.

Verdict was rendered for plaintiff for $300 damages.

It was assigned for error:

1. The court erred in charging the jury "that the demand, if made as testified to by Woodward, was sufficient, and need not be made on the island or of the tenant; and even if no demand had been made, so far as he used the property and converted it to his own use, it would support the action without demand."

2 The court erred in charging the jury that "the defendant

had no lien on the materials for the labor bestowed on them; that the action can be sustained without a tender, and that it would be impossible for the plaintiff to know how much to tender. If the defendant claimed a lien, he should have stated it at the time, and furnished a bill of the amount of his damages and expenses, and then, if the plaintiff refused to pay, the question would fairly arise. The action can be sustained without a tender."

3. The court erred in charging the jury that "the mere declaration of Hollman, the president of the company, would not amount to an abandonment of the property, or bar the plaintiff from recovering; and would not justify the defendant in converting it to his own use."

The case was argued by *Fisher*, with whom was *Forster*, for plaintiff in error.

It was contended, *inter alia*, that the plaintiff was bound to remove the bridge in a *reasonable* time, especially after request to do so; and not having done so, the company were trespassers, and cannot sustain this action. The demand should have been made at the place where the timber was found or kept: *Story on Bailments*, sec. 117.

If defendant was entitled to compensation, a sufficient tender should have been made before suit brought.

McCormick, for defendant.—1. The plaintiff proved that a resolution was adopted by the board of managers of the company on the 25th July 1846, authorizing their agent, Woodward, to demand from General Forster the part of the bridge lodged upon his island; and on the next day he called on General Forster with a copy of the resolution, and informed him of it, and made the demand; that the defendant replied, "He had it, intended to keep it, and the Juniata Bridge Company might make the most of it." It was also proved that General Forster took the bridge to pieces, and appropriated the materials to his own use, by making fences of the weather-boards, and using other parts in the erection of a frame for a rolling-mill, and afterwards in the building of four frame houses. The timber was used by him *before this suit was brought*, and the iron was put away in his granary: there was, therefore, an actual conversion of the property, and hence no demand was necessary on the part of the Bridge Company to enable them to recover in this action. The defendant did not live on the island, and of course no demand could be made on him there; and the tenant, Van Horn, who was examined as a witness, disclaims having any thing to do with the bridge: he says that after the flood he leased the farm on the shares; that Mr. Forster had to put up the fences.

[Forster v. Juniata Bridge Company.]

and that it was his business to remove the bridge, and that he, the witness, contributed nothing towards the removal of it.

2. No tender of expenses or compensation was required. This question was decided in Etter v. Edwards, 4 *Watts* 65, which was an action of replevin for a raft of boards that went adrift on the Susquehanna River, and it was determined that a person who voluntarily took possession of the boards, and removed them to a place of safety, had no lien on them for expenses thus incurred, and that no tender of such expenses was necessary to sustain the action. The same case decides that the act of 20th March 1812, 5 *Sm. Laws* 335, providing for the compensation of persons taking up timber that may have gone adrift, does not apply to the case of that which has lodged on an island. Treating the defendant as the finder of lost property, it is well settled that he had no lien for expenses gratuitously incurred in taking care of it: Binstead v. Buck, 2 *W. Black.* 1117; Nicholson v. Chapman, 2 *H. Black* 258; *Story on Bailments* 61.

3. The declaration of the president is no better than that of any other member of the corporation; and to lay a ground for it, the defendant ought to have given evidence of the power and duty of the president as derived from the charter or regulations of the company, to show that the matter referred to was within his authority. In the Farmers' Bank of Bucks County v. McGee, 2 *Barr* 318, it is held that to make the agreement of the president of a private corporation evidence, it should be shown to be within the scope of his authority.

The opinion of the court was delivered June 30, by

GIBSON, C. J.—It is not pretended the company had lost its title to this fragment of its bridge by the lodgment of it on the defendant's island. A boat, or a raft, or an ox, driven on it by the current, would continue to be the property of him who owned it at the time of the flood; and why not any other sort of property? Even driftwood, if it could be identified, might be reclaimed. Rails frequently are. The common as well as the civil law allows the owner of stranded property to enter and take it away. Mr. Justice STORY says truly, that if timber be drifted on another's land, not by unavoidable casualty, but by the owner's negligent management of it, he is answerable for damage from it; but he adds that the same rule would probably be applied if the owner were to disregard a notice to remove it, though it had been drifted on the land purely by inevitable casualty. The latter is not so clear. In the Lehigh Bridge Company v. The Lehigh Coal and Navigation Company, 4 *Rawle* 24, it was ruled on good authority, that where a loss happens from an act of Providence, it is not to be borne by him whose superstructure happened to be made the immediate instrument of it; and that to charge him, negligence

[Forster v. Juniata Bridge Company.]

must be mingled with the cause of it. If that be so, there must be negligence in the first instance, and the sufferer must get rid of the instrument and the injury as he may. The company were not bound to follow the wreck of their bridge. They might abandon it without incurring responsibility for it, and the defendant, after notice given, might have disencumbered his land of it by casting it back into the river; but he could not appropriate it to his own use. He certainly might have removed it at his own expense; but the refusal of the company to remove it did not divest their property in it or bar their entry to reclaim it. It was held, in Etter v. Edwards, 4 *Watts* 65, that a riparian owner has neither lien nor claim for preserving a raft cast on his land; and this, on the authority of *Doctor and Student*, c. 51, in which it is said that a man who has abandoned his property may at any time resume the ownership of it. Even a lien would not serve the defendant. It would rebut *evidence* of conversion arising from demand and refusal; but the company proved property and actual conversion, which made their case complete.

Judgment affirmed.

McKinney & Heller *versus* Brights.

One partner without the consent of his co-partner, has no right to give to his own separate creditor an order on a debtor of *the firm;* and the fact that the other partner knew of the order before it was executed and did not express his dissent to the defendants in whose favor it was drawn, and who received the same and its produce, was held not to be a defence to a recovery from the latter, by the firm, of the amount of the order. Notice was unnecessary, as the persons receiving the order had no right to presume the consent of the other partner to a misapplication of the partnership property; and the defendants knew that the firm was not liable for their claim against the individual partner.

ERROR to the Common Pleas of *Berks county:*
This was an appeal from the judgment of a justice of the peace, in a suit by McKinney & Heller, partners, against A. & F. Bright. The plea was *non assumpsit.* A verdict was rendered for the defendants.

The plaintiffs were partners in a clothing store. John Darrah owed them upwards of $100—in payment of which debt they were to take brick. *McKinney* drew an order in the name of the firm, on account of his own separate debt, in favor of the defendants, on Darrah, for brick, to the amount of about $90. Darrah delivered to defendants the brick in payment of the debt *he owed McKinney & Heller*, which debt the defendants agreed to settle with them. To recover from the defendants the amount of the brick thus delivered on the order of the plaintiffs, this action was brought.

The defendants took defence that they were not bound to pay

[McKinney & Heller v. Brights.]

the amount claimed, but that they had a right to retain the same in payment of the separate debt that McKinney owed them.

The following evidence was given on the part of the plaintiffs on the trial :—

John Darrah, sworn :—I know that McKinney & Heller, the plaintiffs, were partners in the clothing business; I got clothes from them, and they got bricks from me. Our agreement was that I was to get clothing from them, and they were to take bricks in payment, whenever they could sell them. I was indebted to them about $130 or $140. A. & F. Bright, the defendants, presented an order of McKinney & Heller on me for bricks; I gave them bricks on that order; I don't recollect the amount; I think they got bricks for $160; they got bricks to an amount exceeding their order; the excess above the order they paid me for; and the balance they agreed to settle for with McKinney & Heller; this balance was about $89.

On the part of defendants was given in evidence, record of a suit, McKinney & Heller v. John Darrah; in the Court of Common Pleas of Berks county :—

John Darrah, again :—I was sued by McKinney & Heller for their bill; the clothing was included, for which their order was given on me in favor of the Brights for the bricks. I got credit in that suit for the bricks I had given to the Brights on the order. I furnished these bricks to the Brights on the order of McKinney & Heller. *Heller* heard of the order which was drawn *by McKinney* in the name of the firm, a day or two after I got it. He said to me that it was not right, or that he did not know of it; the amount of what he said was, that he did not think the order was right.

Cross-examined :—The award against me was for the balance I owed McKinney & Heller, after paying their order to the Brights. I never heard the two Brights say they would pay McKinney & Heller. The objection of Heller was, that the Brights had no right to take a partnership order and get the bricks on it as payment of McKinney's individual debt to them. He said they should not keep the price of the bricks for that purpose. I was a witness in this suit before arbitrators. I did not hear McKinney say, in Heller's presence, that he would give Brights an order, but he told me so before he gave it to me. I was indebted to McKinney & Heller about $130 or $140. The $89, I suppose, was paid them by the bricks I gave on their order to the Brights. The award was for $20, and the excess was paid by some other bricks McKinney & Heller had got from me.

George G. Barclay, sworn :—I was an arbitrator in the case of McKinney & Heller v. John Darrah. The plaintiff's claim was over $100. It was suggested to the counsel of the plaintiffs, that he might proceed against the Brights for the amount of

[McKinney & Heller v. Brights.]

the order produced in their favor on Darrah, and drawn in the name of the plaintiffs. The counsel acted on the suggestion, and allowed the amount of the order to be deducted from the plaintiff's claim, and we rendered an award for the balance in favor of the plaintiffs.

GORDON, President J., charged:—This is an action brought to recover the price of a quantity of brick, furnished to the defendants by John Darrah, on the order of the plaintiffs. The order is not produced, but it is agreed here that it was for about ninety dollars, and that it was drawn by McKinney, one of the firm, on John Darrah, a debtor of the firm, in the name of both the partners. From the evidence it appears that John Darrah was indebted to McKinney & Heller, and that McKinney was indebted to the defendants. The order was drawn by *McKinney* and delivered to the Brights *in part payment of the debt due from him to the Brights*. The plaintiffs in this suit allege that McKinney had no right to apply the debt due from John Darrah, which was the property of the firm, to the payment of his own individual debt, and that such misapplication being known to the defendants, they are liable to the firm in this action for the amount received by them on the order. The law is, that one partner cannot apply the partnership property to the discharge of his own debts; and the creditor who receives such funds, with knowledge of the facts, is liable to repay them to the partners, in an action instituted in the partnership name. In the case before us, however, the defendants allege that Heller, the partner, had knowledge of the order drawn by McKinney on Darrah, in the name of the firm, and that although he made some objections to it in conversation with Darrah, he gave no peremptory instructions to Darrah on the subject; that he did not forbid Darrah to furnish bricks to the defendants on the order, nor give notice to the defendants of his dissent to this application of the partnership fund. These facts seem to be established by the evidence of Darrah, who has been examined here as a witness; but whether it be or not, is for you to decide, as are all the facts of the case. If Heller knew of the order on Darrah before it was executed by Darrah, and did not give notice to the defendants of his dissent from such application of the partnership funds, he is bound by the order, and the plaintiff cannot recover. The defendants might not have been willing to take bricks on any other terms than those upon which these were understood by them to be received, and if they had been apprized of his partner's dissent, they might have resorted to McKinney for payment of, or security for their debt.

To this opinion of the court the plaintiffs by their counsel excepted.

It was assigned for error:

The court erred in charging the jury that, if Heller knew of

[McKinney & Heller v. Brights.]

the order on Darrah before it was executed by Darrah, and did not give notice to the defendants of his dissent from such application of the partnership funds in payment of the private debt of McKinney, he is bound by the order, and the plaintiffs cannot recover.

Banks and *Smith*, for plaintiff in error.—When a note is taken by any one in the partnership name from one of the firm, for what he knows to be his particular debt, without consulting or apprising the other members of his intention, or obtaining their consent, the firm is not bound: Livingston *v.* Haste & Patrick, 2 *Caines's Rep.* 249.

When a note is given in the name of a firm by one of the partners, for the private debt of such partner, and known to be so by the person taking the note, the other partners are not bound by such note unless they have been previously consulted and consent to the transaction: 3 *Pick.* 10.

The knowledge of the creditor that the partnership name is given for the individual debt of the partner renders the transaction fraudulent and void in respect to the co-partnership: Livingston *v.* Roosevelt, 4 *Johns. Rep.* 272; 7 *Wend. Rep.* 326.

One partner cannot apply partnership funds or securities to the discharge of his own private debt, without the consent of the other members of the firm. Without their consent their title to the property is not divested in favor of such separate creditor; the right of such separate creditor depends upon the fact that the other partners had assented to such transaction: Rogers *v.* Batchelor, 12 *Peters's Rep.* 232.

In the case of a partner paying his own private debt out of partnership funds, it is manifest that it is a violation of his duty and of the right of his partners, unless they have assented to it. The act is an illegal conversion of the funds, and the separate creditor can have no better title to the funds than the partner himself had. If the separate creditor knew of the misappropriation, he would undoubtedly be guilty of a gross fraud, not only in morals, but in law: Rogers *v.* Batchelor, 12 *Peters's Rep.* 230.

The separate creditor must show the assent of the whole firm, or they are not bound when he has obtained partnership property for the private debt of one of the firm: Dob *v.* Halsey, 16 *Johns. Rep.* 84; Rogers *v.* Batchelor, 12 *Peters* 231.

The burden of proving that the partner who did not sign the note consented to be bound, is thrown on the creditor: *Story on Partnership*, sec. 127, note i. sec. 132 and 133, (note 2, at page 218.)

If the separate creditor of a partner take a partnership security towards the discharge of his separate debt, that fact alone, unless explained by particular circumstances, is conclusive evidence to

[McKinney & Heller v. Brights.]

charge the creditor with fraud or with gross negligence amounting to fraud: *Collyer on Part.*, Perkins's edition, sec. 496 and 501, note 1.

A creditor who receives partnership property to pay a private debt of one of the partners, becomes a debtor to the firm for the property; and the burden of proving the assent of the other partner is thrown on the creditor who thus receives the property: *Collyer on Part.*, Perkins's edition, sec. 501, notes 1 and 2, note 1 at page 462; Davenport v. Runlet, 3 *New Hamp.* 386; Weed v. Richardson, 2 *Dev. & Bat.* 535; Pierce v. Pass, 1 *Porter* 232; *Story on Part.* sec. 133; Dobbs v. Halsey, 16 *Johns. Rep.* 34, 38; Gansevort v. Williams, 14 *Wend.* 133–5; Wilson v. Williams, id. 146; Darling v. March, 22 *Maine* 189.

A partner has no power to bind the firm for his own private debt, without the assent of his co-partners: Noll v. McClintock, 2 *W. & Ser.* 152. It is not doubted that a partner cannot pay his separate debt with the joint funds, though the creditor may not suspect a misapplication: 1 *Barr* 417, Tanner v. Hall & Easton; 6 *Barr* 494, Purdy v. Powers.

The case of Foster v. Andrews, 2 *Pa. Rep.* 160, is relied on by the defendants in error. In that case it is said, "If the other partner were present and permitted it to be done, it would bind both. So, if it has met his subsequent assent." There the transaction took place in the store of the firm, and it was done by the clerk of the firm, who was the agent of the firm. It was entered on the books of the firm. There the whole transaction appeared. On this same page, immediately under these entries, William Foster, the objecting partner, had made entries. He must have seen the entries made by his clerk and agent. He made no objections to the clerk or any one. Was not this evidence of his subsequent assent? Surely it was. This was the ruling of the judge, and is the law of the case. It does not decide that the absent partner must give notice of his dissent, or he is bound. In that case, assent might be inferred—here it cannot be inferred. Heller objected at once. His entire conduct shows continued dissent. Was he bound to give notice of his dissent? It is submitted to the court that he was not.

Filbert, for defendant, presented the following positions:—
1. That the objecting partner had notice of the order drawn by McKinney, it being entered on the firm's books on the day or shortly after it was drawn and delivered to the defendants.
2. That on principles of fairness, the objecting partner in possession of such knowledge was bound to countermand the said order, as well with Darrah on whom the order had been drawn, as with the defendants in whose favor it was drawn, and which Heller neglected to do: 2 *Pa. Rep.* 160, Foster v. Andrews.

[McKinney & Heller *v.* Brights.]

3. If from all the circumstances, the objecting partner has the necessary knowledge of such an order, and does nothing to countermand and defeat it, the jury may presume that he intends to acquiesce in it, and an attempt after the order has been filled and received, cannot meet with favor from a court and jury: Noble *v.* McClintock, 2 *W. & Ser.* 152.

4. The *onus* of proving assent and acquiescence by the other partner is not always thrown on the separate creditor; but if it appears from the circumstances that such acquiescence was fairly presumable, and the jury so find it, as they have done in this case, the losing party cannot complain: *id.*

5. A separate creditor receiving the firm's property in payment of his debts, does not thereby commit a fraud *per se*, on the partnership: and if he can show knowledge, acquiescence, and a culpable want of vigilance in the objecting partner, he will not become a debtor to the firm so as to be compelled to refund.

6. A partner may take the funds and property of the partnership, to pay his private debts, provided he keeps within the bounds of honesty and justice towards his co-partner and the creditors of the firm; and the law will correct and interfere only in cases of gross and palpable dishonesty, amounting to fraud.

7. If it is insisted, as it appears to be, that the defendants are liable to the plaintiffs on the ground of *mala fides* or fraud, then the suit, being in contract, brought originally before a justice of the peace, will not lie, and the plaintiffs, on a reversal here, could not recover below.

5 *Watts* 159, Fichthorn *v.* Boyer, as to assent to a sealed instrument.

The opinion of the court was delivered June 30, by

GIBSON, C. J.—McKinney was separately indebted to the defendant, and Darrah was indebted to the firm of McKinney & Heller. *McKinney* drew an order in the name of the firm, in favor of the defendants, on Darrah for bricks, which were delivered. After an unsuccessful action against Darrah on his original indebtedness, the firm brought this suit, to follow the property into the defendant's hands, on the ground that it was received *mala fide.* The defence is that *Heller* was apprized of the order before the bricks were delivered, and did not give notice to the defendants that he would not be bound by it. Want of notice not to deliver might have been ground of defence by Darrah; but why should Heller have given notice to the defendants of what they already knew? In Northouse *v.* Parker, 1 *Camp.* 82, it was held that notice would be superfluous where the fact is known. The defendants knew that Heller was not liable for McKinney's debt, and they had no reason to presume that McKinney would consent to have it paid out of the partnership effects, to the prejudice of himself and the joint cre-

[McKinney & Heller v. Brights.]

ditors. They acted at their peril and with their eyes open. With full knowledge of the circumstances they dealt with one of the partners to get their debt paid at the expense of Heller, and they now complain of want of notice that he would not consent to it. Was it necessary to give them notice that they were attempting to do him an injury? Notice that a man will not submit to a wrong, would be absurd. The defendants had no ground to presume that Heller had authorized McKinney to draw in their favor, for there is no circumstance in the case to found a presumption, and it was their business to inquire. If they took McKinney's word for it they must take the consequences. When told of the order before the bricks were delivered, Heller told Darrah that it was wrong. But if the defendants gave a receipt for the separate debt, or delivered up the security for it when the order was drawn, notice would have been too late to save them; and if they did not, a recovery in this suit would leave their right of recourse to McKinney intact, and the parties would be remitted to the position which justice requires them to occupy. In any aspect whatever, the defendants have no case.

Judgment reversed.

Moyer's Appeal.

By the 5th section of the intestate act of 1797, the husband who survived his wife became entitled to her choses in action; and such was the case although he did not administer on her estate, or do any act to make them his own, and died leaving issue.

This was an appeal by Samuel Moyer from the decree of the Orphans' Court of Dauphin county, decreeing that the executor of Ann Margaret Harrison, deceased, should have paid to him out of the land devised to Williamson Harrison by Alexander McKenzie, charged with a legacy to Sarah McKenzie during her lifetime, the sum of, &c.

Alexander McKenzie died testate in 1818, leaving a widow named Sarah, and two daughters, viz. Jane intermarried with Williamson Harrison, and Polly with John Duncan. He devised to his son-in-law, Williamson Harrison, a tract of land, which testator valued at $1600, and charged the said land with the payment of the interest on the one-third of said sum to his widow during her life, and the said third, at the widow's decease, was to be equally divided between his *two daughters*. Williamson and Jane Harrison had issue, four children, one of whom died intestate, unmarried and without issue. Jane Harrison died in the year 1823. Williamson Harrison made his last will and testament on the 24th February 1824, in which he directed his executors to sell said tract of land. On the 29th March 1826, after Williamson Harrison's

[Moyer's Appeal.]

death, his executors accordingly, by their deed duly executed, granted, bargained, and sold said tract of land to John Duncan, who was married to Polly, the surviving daughter of said Alexander McKenzie. The said John Duncan afterwards sold the said tract of land to John Moyer, who transferred his equitable title to Samuel Moyer—whereupon the said John Duncan, on the 23d February 1844, by his deed duly executed, granted, bargained, and sold the said tract of land to Samuel Moyer, the respondent; and in the deed to Samuel Moyer, said land is charged only with the payment of $32 to Sarah McKenzie annually during her natural life. On 12th February 1846, Sarah McKenzie died. These proceedings were instituted to charge said land, now owned by Samuel Moyer, with *Jane* Harrison's alleged interest in the legacy of one-half of the third made payable at the death of the widow McKenzie.

The petition was by Anna M. Harrison, the only surviving child of the said Jane Harrison, who was a daughter of *Sarah McKenzie*, and who claimed to be entitled, with her brother, John C. Harrison, to the one-half of the third devised to the said Sarah McKenzie during her natural life.

The material points in controversy were alleged to be—1. W. Harrison having acquired title to the land, under the will of Alexander McKenzie, charged with the payment of the interest of one-third of the purchase-money to the widow during her life, and of said *third* at the widow's decease, in equal moieties to *his* (Williamson Harrison's) *wife*, and to the wife of John Duncan; and the said Williamson Harrison having survived his wife, what interest had he in said tract of land, as well by purchase as by his marital rights and survivorship?

2. As Jane, the wife of said Williamson Harrison, was entitled, as legatee under the will of Alexander McKenzie, to the one-half of said third payable by her husband at the widow's decease, was not her legacy merged in the fee simple which was in her husband, and did not the conveyance under Williamson Harrison transfer to the purchaser his absolute estate, future, reversionary, contingent, and certain, and operate as an extinguishment of the legacy by way of release or assignment?

There is no pretence that creditors existed. Jane Harrison has been dead twenty-seven years, and Williamson Harrison twenty-six.

The court below decreed that Henry Peffer, executor of Anna Margaret Harrison, deceased, shall have paid to him, out of the land devised to Williamson Harrison by Alexander McKenzie, charged with the legacy to Sarah McKenzie during her lifetime, the sum of eighty-eight dollars and eighty-nine cents, with interest thereon from the 12th day of February 1846, the time of Sarah McKenzie's death—with the costs of this proceeding, and that he have all legal remedies for the collection of the same against said land, being now in possession of the respondent, Samuel Moyer.

[Moyer's Appeal.]

Exception was filed, that the Orphans' Court should have denied the prayer of the petitioner, the claimant not having any legacy unpaid charged on the land of Samuel Moyer, and the proceedings being without proper parties, and unlawful.

The case was argued by *H. Alricks*, for Moyer, the appellant. He cited, *inter alia*, the intestate act of 1797, 3 *Smith's Laws* 298.

Fisher, for appellee.

PER CURIAM.—By the fifth section of the supplemental intestate act of 1797, of which the first and third sections of the act of 1833 are as to this provision a transcript, it was enacted that "where she (a wife) leaves a husband, he shall take the whole personal estate." He is consequently entitled to her *choses* in action without administering, or doing any act to make them his own. At the death of Jane Harrison, therefore, her legacy charged by her father's will on the land devised by him to her husband Williamson Harrison, became the husband's property, and merged, if it had not done so before, in his person as that of both debtor and creditor. The land was consequently discharged of it, and passed disencumbered to the purchaser. It is proper to say that the act of 1797 was not presented to the view of the court below.

Decree reversed.

Schneider's Appeal.

A testator devised to his wife during her life or widowhood, the use and possession of all his real and personal estate, with an exception in favor of his unmarried daughters, with respect to whom he provided—"As each of my married daughters have already received one hundred pounds, Pennsylvania currency, on account of their future inheritance (or heritage) without being obliged to pay interest for the same, so it is my will that the rest of my daughters shall also receive one hundred pounds, Pennsylvania currency, on the same account, whenever they marry and should require the money to purchase real estate, without being obliged to pay interest therefor; and besides each of my daughters shall receive at their eventual marriage the same outfit as the others have received before them."

"And as touching the land or real estate, the same shall remain as above said in the possession and enjoyment of my dear wife till her death or remarriage. The right of possession of the whole of my real estate I herewith devise to my two sons, Daniel and Joseph, however they shall not have the immediate possession and use of the same till after the death or remarriage of my wife, to enter upon and divide the real estate as they may deem it suitable, and they are to pay for my aforesaid land or real estate the sum of two thousand pounds, Pennsylvania currency, which two thousand

[Schneider's Appeal.]

pounds are to be divided in nine equal shares, and each of my beloved children, namely, Daniel, Joseph, Sarah, Susanna, Esther, Catharine, Hannah, Lydia, and Elizabeth, share and share alike.

"All the remaining goods, namely, the money that arises out of the sale of the house and kitchen furniture, the outstanding money and bank stock, shall after the death or remarriage of my wife be divided in equal shares amongst my nine children: *Held*, that the sons were each entitled to receive £100, so as to make them equal with the daughters, and that the balance of the estate be equally distributed among the sons and daughters.

THIS was an appeal by Daniel Schneider and Joseph Schneider, from the decree of the Orphans' Court of *Berks county*, distributing the balance of money in the hands of Daniel Schneider, surviving executor of Daniel Schneider, deceased.

The will of Daniel Schneider, deceased, dated 29th October 1816, was proved on the 22d day of March 1817. It is in German.

It provides, *inter alia*—My dear wife Sarah, from the time of my decease until her death, or as long as she remains my widow, shall have the full and undivided possession, usufruct, use, and enjoyment of all my real and personal estate, (although with the following exceptions in consideration of my unmarried daughters) however in the following manner: all the real estate she shall have in possession for the above-named time, and reap the profit thereof in such a way or manner as she herself may think best and most convenient, and of all the movable things which may be found in my dwelling-house and kitchen, she shall have the possession (*in natur*) for life, after a just inventory and appraisement is made of the same. The bank-stock shall remain as it is at my decease, (except the bank should be wound up,) and my said wife at the appointed time shall receive the dividends thereof. The money on hand shall be loaned out on sufficient security, and the interest arising therefrom my said wife shall receive, keep, and enjoy, for the aforementioned time; the other personal property which does not belong to the house and kitchen furniture shall be sold, and the money arising therefrom shall also be loaned out on sufficient security, and the interest thereof for the aforesaid time shall be received and enjoyed by my said wife. However, as each of my married daughters have already received one hundred pounds, Pennsylvania currency, on account of their future inheritance, (or heritage,) without being obliged to pay interest for the same, so it is my will that the rest of my daughters shall also receive one hundred pounds Pennsylvania currency, on the same account, whenever they marry and should require the money to purchase real estate, without being obliged to pay interest therefor; and besides each of my daughters shall receive at their eventual marriage the same outfit as the others have received before them.

And as touching the land or real estate, the same shall remain as above said in the possession and enjoyment of my dear wife till her death or remarriage. The right of possession of the whole of

[Schneider's Appeal.]

my real estate I herewith devise to my two sons, Daniel and Joseph; however they shall not have the immediate possession and use of the same till after the death or remarriage of my wife, to enter upon and divide the real estate as they may deem it suitable, and they are to pay for the whole of my aforesaid land or real estate the sum of two thousand pounds, Pennsylvania currency, which two thousand pounds are to be divided in nine equal shares, and each of my beloved children, namely, Daniel, Joseph, Sarah, Susanna, Esther, Catharine, Hannah, Lydia, and Elizabeth, share and share alike; however that within one year after the decease or remarriage of my wife, my daughter Sarah's share shall be paid by my sons Daniel and Joseph, within the following year my daughter Susanna's share, and so on, every year one share according to the age next following of my daughters, till the whole is paid; and in this respect my two aforesaid sons, when they take possession of the aforesaid real estate shall enter into an obligation to secure to each of my daughters their share at the time fixed.

All the remaining goods (the German word is *gueter*) namely, the money that arises out of the sale of the house and kitchen furniture, the outstanding money and bank-stock, shall, after the death or remarriage of my wife, be divided in equal shares amongst my nine children.

In case it should happen after my decease, that my wife should marry again, then she shall receive what she is entitled to by law out of the real estate, and shall be secured to her by my sons.

Sarah, the wife of John De Turk, and Susanna Kissling, widow, severally received their £100 and outfit, in the lifetime of the testator, and Hannah, wife of Peter Hill, Catharine, wife of Benjamin Leinbach, also severally received their outfit. The inventory of the personal estate of the deceased amounted to $5697.11.

After the death of Sarah Schneider, the widow, Daniel Schneider, as surviving executor of Daniel Schneider, deceased, filed his administration account, in which he was charged with the inventory, &c., which account was audited. The auditor, after crediting the accountant with the £100 paid to Benjamin Leinbach and Catharine his wife, £100 paid Peter Hill and Hannah his wife, £100 paid to Joseph Esterly and Lydia his wife, and $208.52 paid for the outfit of Lydia Esterly, and $198.89 paid for the outfit of Elizabeth Young, found a balance due the estate of $2079.75½, out of which the auditor allowed to Elizabeth Young, $266.66¼; to *Daniel Schneider* $266.66¼; to *Joseph Schneider* $266.66¼, &c.; and to Daniel and Joseph Schneider and others $159.97 each.

The legatees other than the two sons Daniel and Joseph filed the following exceptions:—

1. The auditor erred in allotting to Daniel Schneider and Joseph Schneider, one hundred pounds each, under the will of the testator, no direction of the kind being in the will.

[Schneider's Appeal.]

2. The auditor erred in not distributing the said two hundred pounds ($533.34) which he allotted in the distribution to Daniel and Joseph Schneider, to all the remaining heirs, distributees, and legatees, in equal proportion, according to the directions of the will.

The court sustained the exceptions, and disallowed the £200 distributed to the sons Daniel and Joseph, and distributed the balance of $2079.75½.

Exception was filed that the court erred in not confirming the distribution made by the auditor, and in not allowing to Daniel Schneider and Joseph each £100 ($266.66½) before distributing the balance in accountant's hands to and among the eight surviving children and legatees.

The case was argued by *Smith*, for appellants.—The sons agree that each of the daughters has a right to an outfit of $200 more than themselves are entitled to, because the testator says they are so to receive, beside or in addition to the £100 directed to be paid them by way of advancement on account of their shares, inheritance, or legacies.

But they also claim to receive each the sum of £100 in like manner as the daughters, before the residue of the assets is equally distributed, because the testator in his lifetime had given several of his daughters £100 by way of advancement, and in order to put all his daughters on an equal footing, directed his other daughters to receive the same sum, *expressly stating, however, that it was to be paid on account of their shares or legacies*, and not as so much over and above what each son was to have.

If the testator had intended to give the daughters £100 more than the sons, he would have said so in plain and appropriate terms. The will in this respect, is plain as regards the outfit.

Filbert, contra.—The daughters were to be kept equal by the advancements among themselves. The married ones having already received one hundred pounds as part of their inheritance, the unmarried daughters were to receive the same sum when they came to take husbands, and on the same principle, as part of their inheritance. This was to go towards buying them a house. The sons needed no house; they had this on the farms devised to them.

The daughters for whom these one hundred pounds are claimed are all married.

When the will speaks of an equal distribution among all the nine children, it does so in specified words, enumerating the sources from which the aggregate to make this equal distribution should come. The *sons* are named in this clause, and if the testator had intended them to receive the one hundred pounds along with the

[Schneider's Appeal.]

daughters, it would have been so stated. The naming of some in this clause, necessarily excludes others not named.

The opinion of the court was delivered June 2, by

COULTER, J.—The primary intent of the testator, to wit, that his whole estate, real and personal, shall be equally divided among his nine children, is quite apparent from the whole will. In the clause before the last, he directs that his real estate shall vest in his two sons, Daniel and Joseph, but that they shall not take immediate possession after his death if his wife survives him. But, that after his death, and upon the death of his widow, or her marriage, they shall enter on the real estate and divide it between themselves as they deem suitable. He further provides in the same clause, that his two sons shall pay two thousand pounds, to be divided into nine equal shares, and that each of them, enumerating them by name, including the two sons to whom the real estate is divided, shall have share and share alike. In the next clause he directs that all his goods, money, and outstanding money and bank-stock, after the death or marriage of his wife, shall be equally divided among his nine children; and then directs that if his wife marries, she shall, in that event, receive what she is entitled to by law out of the real estate, which shall be paid to her by his two sons.

Testator had nine children, two of them sons, to whom the real estate is divided, and seven daughters. The clause of the will on which the claim of the daughters is built, occurs in a previous part of the instrument, and is as follows, to wit:—"As each of my married daughters have already received one hundred pounds *on account of their future inheritance*, without being obliged to pay interest for the same, so it is my will that the rest of my daughters shall also receive one hundred pounds on the same account whenever they marry, and should require the money to purchase real estate, without being obliged to pay interest therefor."

This clause is perfectly consistent with the subsequent ones which dispose of his estate in equal shares among his nine children by name. It was a mere advancement to the daughters at the time of their marriages respectively. Although there is no *technical* advancement in cases of testacy, yet, a testator may provide the same equality and equity in his will which is accomplished by the technical advancement in cases of intestacy. Here the testator intended that his daughters should each receive one hundred pounds as they married, in addition to some outfit always given on such occasions, because this one hundred pounds would be useful in providing a present home. But then, as distinctly as language could express it, he provides that this sum was on account, or to be on account of their future inheritance. That is, on account of their equal share of his estate, which he provided in the same will they

[Schneider's Appeal.]

were to receive out of his real and personal estate. But the rivet is clenched by the provision that they shall not be obliged to pay interest for the one hundred pounds; clearly evincing his intent that the principal should be paid in the mode he pointed out, that is, by being accounted for in their future inheritance. And this corresponds and tallies with the two last clauses, directing that his estate shall be divided in equal shares among his nine children.

There is no evidence to justify the averment that the sons were largely preferred. The two thousand pounds may have been, for aught we know, the value of the estate. But if the widow married, they were bound to pay her dower; and in that event would have been so much worse, to that extent, than the girls. But this is no consequence. We heed not these things, because the intent of the testator, if it be not against law, must be carried out, whether it accords with usage or general or particular feeling. The question before the Orphans' Court was, whether the sons were entitled each to one hundred pounds, so as to be made equal with the daughters who had received that sum before distribution equally among all of them. The court below decreed that they were not, and in that we think they erred. The decree is therefore reversed, and it is ordered and decreed that the sons each receive one hundred pounds, so as to make them equal with the daughters, and that the balance be equally distributed among the sons and daughters. And the record is remitted to the Orphans' Court for the purpose of carrying out this decree.

Porter *versus* Lee.

1. The ordering a cause for trial, or its continuance, is a matter within the discretion of the court below, and is not examinable on error.

2. In a suit upon a note, *defendant* offered to prove by the deposition of a witness (who had a supervision of the store and store-accounts of defendant and his partner, but who did not state that he made the entries, or sell or witness the sale of the goods, or the nature of the charges in the books,) the *balance* of a store-account on said books *which were not produced;* and also that *a pass-book* belonging to the plaintiff and containing entries of goods got by plaintiff from the said store, corresponded with the books, and which pass-book the plaintiff's counsel was notified to produce on the trial, but the notice was too late to admit of its production, and the pleas did not give notice to that effect: It was *held,* that the books of defendant, being the proper evidence, should have been produced, and that it was not error to reject the evidence offered.

ERROR to the Common Pleas of *Dauphin county.*

This was an action of *assumpsit,* brought by Washington Lee, against David R. Porter and Samuel Holland, in which the writ was returned served upon David R. Porter, and *nihil* as to Samuel Holland; to which David R. Porter pleaded payment and set-off. The plaintiff claimed upon a promissory note dated 29th February 1848,

[Porter v. Lee.]

drawn by David R. Porter and Samuel Holland, payable to him at three months, for $1218, at the Wyoming Bank. Upon the trial, had on the 30th of January 1851, a verdict and judgment were rendered for the plaintiff for $1393.37. The only question for review by the Supreme Court arose on the rejection of the deposition of William Stewart, and the court's refusal to continue the cause.

The plaintiff gave in evidence the note before described, and rested.

The counsel of defendant then read a notice to plaintiff's counsel to produce on the trial of the cause in court, *the pass-book* of the plaintiff, referred to by William Stewart in his deposition in this case, taken September 5, 1849; and then offered in evidence that part of the deposition of William Stewart, taken September 5, 1849, relating to the account of the plaintiff, which is in the following words, to wit:—After stating upon his examination in chief, that he was a clerk for the defendants, witness says:—In attending to the mines, I also had a supervision over the store and store-accounts. Colonel Lee had a running account in the store from March 1847 until about the time they stopped. He also kept a pass-book, which was kept to correspond with his store-account. *The account against Lee on the store-book, or rather the balance due on his account, amounts to $1869 and some cents, up to 2d October* 1848. The rent of the store-room had been credited to him at the end of each quarter, or when he settled his account in the store. The rent was credited up to the 1st October 1848. I think the rent for the store and two adjoining buildings was $150 per year. I have seen Mr. Lee's pass-book frequently, and know the custom was to make it correspond with the store-account in which the credits of rent are entered. I don't suppose the quarter's rent due October 1, 1848, was entered in his pass-book. I presume all the others were. *And upon cross examination*, he said:—A considerable part of Colonel Lee's account in the store was for goods furnished to men working under the direction of Andrew Lee, at Colonel Lee's mines, at the village of Nanticoke. Colonel Lee's account was settled at certain times by the clerk in the store. I cannot say how often the balance was struck.

Hamilton Alricks, attorney for plaintiff, being affirmed says—I have not the pass-book in my possession. I received a notice on Tuesday morning last, to produce it, (the 28th instant.) I inquired of Mr. Lee, of Wilkesbarre, if he had brought it. He said he had not; did not know it would be necessary. I have all the papers connected with Lee's case that I know of, but not the pass-book, and do not know of it being in the county.

Washington Lee, Jr., sworn:—Mr. Alricks asked me last Tuesday if I had brought the pass-book. I replied I had not brought it; did not know it would be important. It is in the possession of my uncle, the plaintiff, in Luzerne county, about one hundred and

[Porter v. Lee.]

twenty miles distant. I am here as his agent, attending to the suit.

The defendant then applied to continue the cause to enable him to get in his set-off, and to supply the defect in the deposition, if it be defective. This motion is overruled. The defendant has had the deposition in his possession, or it has been on file since it was taken, and should have known that the evidence was defective, and been prepared with the books referred to. If there is a just account, it can readily be collected, as the plaintiff is admitted to be perfectly solvent.

That part of the deposition relating to the amount of the account for goods, being $1869, *is rejected*, as it appears that the witness refers to defendant's books, which should be produced, and at defendant's request exception sealed. JNO. J. PEARSON. [L. S.]

David R. Porter, sworn to make true answers to the court:—I do not know where the books of Holland & Porter are; I know not where to find them; never had them in my possession, except that they were in the store at Nanticoke. Lee has possession of the office and store-house where the books were kept as I believe. I have inquired for and endeavoured to procure them. Mr. Stewart was agent for Holland and myself.

William Lee, Jr., sworn:—The books of Holland & Porter were in the store-house when I last saw them, in possession of William Stewart; he was clerk of Holland & Porter; this was after the store was sold out, which was in the fall of 1848, in October; that store-room is still unoccupied; I also saw them there as late as April 1849.

It was assigned for error, that the court erred in refusing to continue the cause, and in rejecting the deposition of William Stewart.

Boas and *McCormick*, for Porter, plaintiff in error.—The court ought to have allowed the parts of the deposition of William Stewart, which were offered by the defendant, to be read to the jury. The witness had a personal knowledge of the sale of the goods to the plaintiff, and of the amount or balance due to the defendant. Although he speaks of the books of the defendant, it does not appear that he derived his knowledge of the plaintiff's indebtedness from the books, for he says that he had a general supervision of the defendant's business. No objection was made by the plaintiff at the time of the taking of the deposition to the non-production of the books, and this waiver was further confirmed by the plaintiff's cross-examination in reference to the account contained in the books. The *pass-book* referred to never was in the defendant's possession, and the failure of the plaintiff to produce it at trial opened the way for the defendant to prove its contents. There

[Porter v. Lee.]

are many cases where a witness may speak of books or papers without their being produced.

"A witness who has inspected the accounts of the party, though he may not give evidence of their particular contents, may be allowed to speak to the general balance, without producing the accounts:" 1 *Greenleaf on Evidence*, sec. 93. "Where a witness in his deposition refers to a judgment bond having been given and subsequently paid within his own knowledge; and has been cross-examined as to the same matter by the other side, no objection can be taken to the non-production of the bond:" Bank v. Donaldson, 6 *Barr* 179. "In an action on a note for goods sold, the consideration of the note may be proved by a witness without his producing the book of original entries of the sale of the goods:" Fitler v. Beckley, 2 *W. & Ser.* 458; 9 *Watts* 441.

The defendant asked a juror to be withdrawn and to have the case continued; and if the plaintiff regarded the production of the pass-book as material for him, he should have assented to the offer to continue. His insisting on proceeding in the trial put him in the position of every party who has a paper in his possession, and, after notice, refuses to produce it. He thus put it in the power of the other party to prove its contents.

Hamilton Alricks, for defendant.—The store-books not produced were in the control of defendant. There was no evidence that they were books of original entry, or that articles charged there were the subject of a book-charge. The book itself, supported by the evidence of Stewart only, who did not prove that he made the entries or sell or witness the sale of the goods, would not have been admissible. The evidence was objected to when the deposition was taken.

As to the assignment as to the continuance of the cause, it is not the subject of review.

The opinion of the court was delivered June 30, by

COULTER, J.—The ordering on the trial, and the refusal to continue the cause, was a matter within the discretion of the court below, and is not examinable for error here. But for aught that appears, the court exercised its discretion on that subject with due regard to the rights of all parties, and not with a particular regard to the convenience and laches of one of them.

The pass-book, as it is called, which Colonel Lee kept and sent to the store of Porter & Holland, and in which was entered every thing got from the store by his hands or by his order, was, as his nephew, who attended at the trial, deposed, at his uncle's residence in Luzerne county. The notice to produce it was given two days before the trial, to Mr. Alricks, his attorney, in Harrisburg. No facility of travel nor mode of communication could have brought it

[Porter v. Lee.]

in that time. The plaintiff came to try on the plea of payment; he could have had no notice or legal warning that it was necessary for him to carry this book to the trial. But, as alleged, it was a mere transcript, or equivalent in its entries to the partnership books of Porter & Holland. Why then did they not bring on their own books; they were the proper evidence of the account, or the alleged balance was admissible under the pleadings. The part of the deposition therefore of William Stewart, which relates to the contents of the pass-book, and its alleged equivalent, the store-books of Porter & Holland, was properly rejected. He says that "in superintending the mines, he also had a supervision over the store and store-accounts. Colonel Lee had a running account in the store. He kept a pass-book, which was kept to correspond with his store-account. The balance due on his account amounts to $1869 and some cents, up to October 1848." He does not say who made the entries, what the nature of the charges was nor that he knew the handwriting, or made the entries himself.

It is true that Mr. Greenleaf in sec. 93, vol. 1, of his *Evidence*, says "that a witness who has inspected the accounts of the party, though he may not be permitted to give evidence of their particular contents, may be allowed to speak of the general balance without producing the accounts." But he must be understood to mean when that general balance is incidentally involved in the investigation, and not to extend or embrace cases where that general balance is spoken of or testified to as a distinct charge against the opposite party, and the ground of claim and recovery. Because it is clear that a witness may not speak of particular facts appearing on the books or deducible from the entries without producing the books. For where the writing or entries were not made by the witness himself, his testimony, so far as founded on it, is no more than hearsay. And why should a witness be allowed to give evidence of his inference rather from what a third person has written, than from what a third person has said. These entries in the pass-book and store-book may, besides, have covered things or money which are not the subject of evidence by book-entry, and such evidence, if admitted, would destroy and overturn all the safeguards which the law has thrown around this kind of testimony.

Judgment affirmed.

Ermold *versus* Newkirk.

The real estate of an intestate who left *seven* children, was divided and appraised, and a house and lot, a part of the same, were taken by the eldest son, who gave recognizance, and afterwards died intestate, without issue, and without payment of the recognizance. It was afterwards agreed by others of the heirs and the husband of another heir, that the house and lot be conveyed to the husband, he to allow the consideration-money out of the share of his wife, and if more than that share, he to pay the difference. *The other lands* were sold, and the purchase-money of the house and lot was charged against the share of the wife in the distribution of the father's estate: *Held*, that the object of the proceeding not being *partition*, but the estate of the wife having been *converted*, the proceeds became the property of the husband, by his application of them, and that the title to the premises, to the extent thus paid for by the husband, vested in him; besides, the premises descended as the estate of the *son*, and not of the father, and the money due the wife was in the estate of the father. Whether *a conveyance* was made to the husband was held not to be material. The wife, who brought ejectment after the death of her husband, was held to be entitled to recover only one *sixth* part of the house and lot.

ERROR to the Common Pleas of *Berks county*.

This was an action of ejectment in the Court of Common Pleas of Berks county, by Sarah Ermold *vs.* Jacob Newkirk and John Newkirk, for a house and lot in the city of Reading.

Verdict and judgment for the plaintiff for one undivided sixth part of said lot. The plaintiff sued out this writ of error.

John Spohn, who was the owner of said lot, died intestate about the year 1820, leaving a widow and seven children, possessed of said lot and other real estate, and leaving also a small personal estate. The plaintiff, who was married to Daniel Ermold, who died before this suit was brought, was one of said children.

Proceedings were held in the Orphans' Court of said county for partition and valuation of said real estate, which was divided into three purparts. The lot in dispute was one of said purparts, and valued at $850.

On the 10th of November 1820, said purpart was accepted by Adam, the eldest son, at said valuation and was adjudged to him, and he entered into the usual recognizance.

Adam died soon after, intestate, unmarried, and without issue, not having paid said valuation-money, leaving six brothers and sisters living.

The other lands were not accepted by the heirs. An agreement, as stated hereafter, was subsequently made.

Afterwards various attempts having been made by orders of the Orphans' Court to sell the residue of the lands of John Spohn, the heirs made sale of said lands, partly to some of themselves, and partly *to a stranger*. The proceeds were brought into the administration account for distribution. The whole estate was $8040.54½; of this sum $1313.40 was of the personal estate.

[Ermold v. Newkirk.]

Sarah Ermold was charged in the distribution of the estate with $900, the price of said house and lot, and it was thus paid by *her.*

The plaintiff contended that her husband being dead, she has a right to recover one sixth part of said lot, in her own right, *and also the two sixths of Solomon and John, her brothers.*

The defendants contended that the fee simple was in Daniel Ermold, and claimed under a sheriff's sale of the same as his property.

The article of agreement was as follows:—Memorandum of an agreement made and concluded upon the twenty-fifth of September, A. D. 1822, between Solomon Spohn, John Spohn, John Ingham, Jacob Kerlin, Philip Rush, and Daniel Ermold, heirs and representatives of John Spohn, late of the borough of Reading, Berks county, deceased. Whereas the said heirs do hold and enjoy a certain house and lot of ground in the borough of Reading aforesaid, late in the tenure of Adam Spohn, deceased, which said property they hold in common and undivided, and whereas a contract has been entered into and agreed upon by and between them in the manner following, that is to say, that they, the said Solomon Spohn, John Spohn, John Ingham, Jacob Kerlin, and Philip Rush, do hereby covenant and agree, to and with the said Daniel Ermold, his heirs and assigns, to convey in fee simple all their share, purpart, interest, or their undivided respective shares or interest, of and in the house and lot of ground aforesaid, and the said Daniel Ermold hereby covenants and agrees, by these presents, to allow a consideration of nine hundred dollars therefor, in the distribution of the estate of John Spohn, deceased; and in case it should be more than the share accruing to him in right of his wife, then he hereby covenants and agrees to pay unto the other heirs of the said John Spohn, deceased, such share or shares as shall appear to be payable to them.

It is also understood by and between the parties hereto, that a deed be executed on or before the first of April next ensuing, when possession of the property is to be given; and it is understood that whatever belongs to the property is hereby sold with the same unto the said Daniel Ermold, and in case any difficulties arise as to the validity of the title, each of the heirs and parties hereto are to bear equally in the expense, (if any there be.) In witness whereof the said parties have set their hands and seals.

Signed and sealed by Solomon Spohn, John Spohn, John Ingham, Jacob Kerlin, Philip Rush, Daniel Ermold.

GORDON, President, J., charged, *inter alia:*—This is an action of ejectment, brought by Sarah Ermold to recover possession of a house and lot in the city of Reading.

The plaintiff is the widow of Daniel Ermold, deceased, as whose property the premises were sold by the sheriff in 1843. She contends that she is the owner of the lot in fee simple, and that er husband, who died before the commencement of this action, had

[Ermold v. Newkirk.]

only a life estate in it. The facts, as they appear in evidence, seem to be as follows:—John Spohn died in Berks county, in 1820, intestate, leaving a widow and seven children, and seized of considerable real estate, including the lot in dispute here. On the 17th of May 1820, letters of administration were granted to his widow, Maria Spohn, and Adam Spohn, his eldest son. On the 4th of October 1820, an inquisition in the Orphans' Court, dividing the real estate into three parts, of which No. 1, consisting of the lot in question, valued at $850, was on the 10th of November adjudged to Adam Spohn, who entered into recognizance to secure the shares of the widow and other heirs.

On the 5th of January 1821, all the heirs refused to accept the remaining purparts at the valuation. Several orders of sale were taken out subsequently, and a small portion of the property sold to Solomon Spohn, leaving the principal part unsold.

On the 10th of August 1821, the administration account of Maria Spohn and Adam Spohn was confirmed in the Orphans' Court, showing a balance due the estate of $1313.46½, consisting of personal estate only.

Adam Spohn and Maria Spohn both died before April 1822, and letters of administration *de bonis non* were granted to Solomon Spohn on the 4th of April 1822.

Adam Spohn died intestate and without issue.

On the 25th of September 1822, Solomon Spohn and John Spohn, sons, John Ingham, Jacob Kerlin, and Philip Rush, sons-in-law of John Spohn, deceased, contracted with Daniel Ermold, to sell and convey to him their shares or purparts in the lots of ground in question, for which Ermold was to allow nine hundred dollars in the distribution of the estate of John Spohn, deceased, and in case it should be more than the share accruing to him in right of his wife, he was to pay the difference to the other heirs. By the agreement a deed was to be executed on or before the 1st of April 1823.

On the 1st of April 1823, all the other heirs of John Spohn, deceased, conveyed to Solomon Spohn, for the consideration of $1649.19, a tract of 95 acres of land, in Exeter township, part of the estate of John Spohn, deceased, and on the same day all the heirs conveyed 132 acres in same township to Jos. Romig, for $3966—other part of the land of said deceased. Daniel Ermold with others receipted for the consideration-money in both of these deeds.

On the 8th of August 1823, the accounts of Solomon Spohn, administrator *de bonis non* of John Spohn, deceased, were confirmed in the Orphans' Court, showing a balance due the estate of $8049.54½, including the balance in the account of Maria and Adam Spohn, making the distributive share of each heir amount to $1341.59.

[Ermold v. Newkirk.]

It seems that after the death of Adam Spohn, Daniel Ermold went into possession of the property in dispute, and held it until it was sold as his property by the sheriff in 1843.

The defendants have examined witnesses to prove that a deed for the property mentioned in the article of agreement was executed by the other heirs of John Spohn, deceased, to Daniel Ermold, in pursuance of the agreement.

Solomon and John Spohn, Jacob Kerlin, and Philip Rush, who would have been grantors in such a deed, have been examined by the plaintiff, and testified that none of them recollect the execution of such a deed, and some of them do not believe that one was ever made; and Rush denies that he ever executed it. The existence or non-existence of such a deed is a question of fact for you.

On the facts to which the court have called your attention depends the question whether the title to the lot was in Ermold or his wife. If in the latter, she is entitled to recover in this action, notwithstanding the sale of the property by the sheriff in 1843, as the property of Daniel Ermold. The premises were bought at the sale by Charles Feather, under whom the defendants claim. It does not appear that notice of the claim of Sarah Ermold was given at the sale. Evidence has been given of Ermold's declarations before and after 1840, that the property was not his, but his wife's. You will judge whether this referred to the mode and proceedings by which the property came into his hands, and is to be regarded as an expression of opinion as to the title, or to what else it referred. If the property was not the wife's at the time of the declarations, they would not make it so. It is not alleged that Ermold at any time conveyed to her, or in trust for her.

On the death of John Spohn, his property vested in his children as his heirs, subject to the widow's rights. When Adam died, and shortly afterwards his mother, Adam's property went to his surviving brothers and sisters. Sarah Ermold was one of the sisters, and entitled to one sixth part of it. When the others contracted to sell the lot to Daniel Ermold by the article dated in September 1822, for $900, he was to pay for it by allowing so much out of his wife's share in her deceased father's estate, if so much should be coming to her; if not, he was to pay the difference. As to so much of John Spohn's estate as had been taken at the appraisement, or sold, Sarah Ermold's share was money, which could be paid to no other person than to Daniel Ermold, during his life. He could receive it and make valid acquittances for it. He could assign it for money or lands, or any valuable consideration. The land that remained was to be sold either by order of court, or by the parties in interest. In either case it would become MONEY, which Daniel Ermold would be entitled to receive, if living when the land should be sold. The land was actually sold by the parties, and Daniel Ermold receipted for the money with the other

[Ermold v. Newkirk.]

grantors. It was in contemplation of the sale of the land, which had been refused by all the heirs, that Ermold contracted for the purchase of the lot. It was a disposal of the money coming to his wife in anticipation of its receipt from the sale of the lands, and the money was actually in hand at the time he was to get his deed.

If Ermold had taken this lot at the appraisement, and entered into recognizance to secure the other shares, and had paid the shares by applying his wife's interest in the recognizance of other heirs, or in the purchase-money of other lands sold, the law would give him five-sixths of the lot in his own right, and he would hold the remainder in the right of his wife. Did he vary his rights by purchasing the shares of the other parties in interest, and agreeing to pay for them with the moneys coming to his wife out of her father's estate? We think not. Sarah Ermold's interest in this lot *was as heir to her brother, Adam Spohn.* Her husband did not pay for it with any interest of hers in *Adam Spohn's* property. One sixth part of the lot was hers, as heir to her brother, and that was unaltered by the transaction between Ermold and the other heirs. It was not her interest in the lands of her father with which the lot was paid for. It was with the moneys arising from the sale of those lands, which moneys were the husband's, if he chose to make them so, either by receiving them, or assigning them, or buying land with them and taking the title in his own name. Where lands are devised to be sold, and the proceeds divided among legatees by the executors, and some of the legatees are married women, and all the legatees elect to take their legacies in land instead of money, it is held that the husbands, by taking deeds in their own names, indicate their intention to reduce the money into possession, in the form of land, and the land becomes their own. This is because the husband in such cases, as in the case before us, had the right to control the money and dispose of it at his pleasure. Daniel Ermold, we think, in his written contract with the other parties in interest, indicated his intention to appropriate his wife's share of the moneys arising from the sale of her father's estate to himself, in providing for a conveyance of the land bought with those moneys to himself.

Where partition is had among tenants in common, and lands assigned to each, and mutual releases are executed, and some of the tenants are femes covert, the property assigned for the shares of the wives belongs to them, and not to their husbands, whether the releases be to the wives or the husbands. In the latter case, the husbands will be regarded as trustees for their wives. This doctrine, however, is confined to cases of partition, in which the consideration for the releases is the land of the wife assigned to the releasor, and not to cases where the consideration is money of the wife, which the husband could control and dispose of at

2 L

[Ermold v. Newkirk.]

pleasure. No land was assigned to the parties here agreeing to convey to Ermold. The conveyance to Solomon Spohn was simply a sale for money, and the buyer of the larger tract was a stranger. Under this agreement, Daniel Ermold became a purchaser in his own right of the shares of the other heirs of Adam Spohn in this lot, although he may have paid for them with the moneys to which his wife was entitled out of her father's estate. In her own share, which was one sixth part, he acquired no greater interest than a life estate. After his death the title remained in her. Even in cases of partition, it has been held that a deed of release to the husband with a money consideration expressed in it, and containing no notice of the nature of the transaction, would be sufficient to vest in a purchaser of the land at sheriff's sale, as the land of the husband, without notice, the title and beneficial interest. It is conceded by the defendant's counsel that the title to one sixth part of this lot is in the plaintiff, and the court think she is entitled to recover that proportion of it in this action.

Several points of law have been propounded to us by the counsel of the plaintiff, which it is our duty to answer.

1. That the plaintiff, as one of the heirs of Adam Spohn, deceased, is entitled to one undivided sixth part in the lot in controversy, and that she has a right to recover it in this action.

2. That if the jury believe that the lot in question was paid for by Daniel Ermold out of the plaintiff's portion of the proceeds of the lands to which she had a right as one of the heirs of her deceased father, that then the said Daniel Ermold would have but a life estate in the same, and at his death it would belong in fee simple to the plaintiff.

3. That the article of agreement which was given in evidence was notice to all who claim under Daniel Ermold, that this lot had been paid for with the money of the plaintiff.

4. That there is no legal proof of the execution of a deed by Solomon Spohn and wife, John Spohn and wife, John Ingham and wife, Philip Rush and wife, and Jacob Kerlin and wife, to Daniel Ermold.

5. That under the article of agreement which has been given in evidence, the plaintiff is entitled to the two undivided sixth parts in said lot, to which John Spohn and Solomon Spohn had the right, as heirs of Adam Spohn, deceased, if the jury believe that Daniel Ermold paid for the same with the lands of plaintiff.

1. To the plaintiff's first point, we answer as requested. The plaintiff is entitled to recover one undivided sixth part of the lot in controversy.

2. We answer this point in the negative. We are of opinion that such payment as is herein suggested would vest the title of the property in Daniel Ermold, except as to the one sixth part to which the plaintiff was entitled as heir to Adam Spohn.

[Ermold v. Newkirk.]

3. This point is answered in the affirmative. The law is as herein stated.

4. In the opinion of the court, there is legal proof of the execution of the deed mentioned in this point in the testimony of the witnesses who have been sworn to the fact: whether the execution of such a deed be sufficiently established is a question of fact for the jury.

5. If the jury believe that the shares mentioned in this point were paid for by Daniel Ermold with the lands of the plaintiff, she would be entitled to these shares, unless the jury should be of opinion that a deed was executed to Daniel Ermold by the other heirs, expressing the conveyance to be for a money consideration, and affording no notice that the consideration of the conveyance was the land of the plaintiff; but if the jury believe that these shares were paid for with the proceeds of lands sold under order of the Orphans' Court, or by the heirs, to which she was entitled, then she is not entitled to the shares. The facts of the whole case are for the jury, and the court do not wish to be understood as giving any binding directions with regard to them. To this opinion of the court, the plaintiff by her counsel excepts, and requests that the same may be filed of record, which is accordingly done.

It was assigned for error, that the court erred in charging the jury:

1. That "under the agreement, Daniel Ermold became a purchaser in his own right of the shares of the other heirs of Adam Spohn in this lot, although he may have paid for them out of the money to which his wife was entitled out of her father's estate, and in the answers to the plaintiff's second point."

2. That "it was not her interest in the lands of her father with which the lot was paid for. It was with the moneys arising from the sale of those lands, which moneys were the husband's, if he chose to make them so, either by receiving them, or buying lands with them and taking the title in his own name."

3. In answer to the plaintiff's fourth point, that in the opinion of the court there is legal proof of the execution of the deed mentioned in this point, in the testimony of the witnesses who have sworn to the fact.

4. In the answer to the plaintiff's fifth point, that "if the jury believe that the shares mentioned in this point were paid for by Daniel Ermold with the lands of the plaintiff, she would be entitled to those shares, unless the jury should be of opinion that a deed was executed to Daniel Ermold by the other heirs, expressing the conveyance to be for a money consideration, and affording no notice that the consideration of the conveyance was the land of the plaintiff, but, if the jury believe that these shares were paid for

[Ermold *v.* Newkirk.]

with the proceeds of lands sold under order of the Orphans' Court, or by the heirs, to which she was entitled, then she is not entitled to the shares."

Banks and *Hoffman*, for plaintiff in error.—The wife relinquished by the agreement her right to the one sixth part of her patrimony, so far as it was necessary to pay for this lot, and thus furnished the consideration for it and the means of paying its price.

She was the meritorious person and the party to be benefited. The object was partition of the lands among the heirs as far as possible. Her husband, by being the party to the agreement, took the title to the lot in dispute as her trustee. Her land, which was the fund for payment, was her separate estate, as much so as money settled to her separate use, which, of itself, secures to her a trust estate by implication of law. Her land was conveyed in payment. Her object was not to part with its value, but to secure to herself a portion of its equivalent in the land.

When a husband takes his wife's purpart in land, and it is of less value than her share of the estate, the husband, having nothing to pay out of his own funds, acquires but a life estate: Snavely *v.* Wagner, 3 *Barr* 275; 8 *id.* 397; 5 *id.* 216–19; 7 *Watts* 217, Duncan *v.* Clark; 3 *W. & Ser.* 520, Weeks *v.* Haas; 9 *id.* 131, Kaufman *v.* Crawford.

In the case of Weeks *v.* Haas, Chief Justice GIBSON says that the law raises a resulting trust in favor of the person whose money pays for the land.

In that case, the chief justice says—"By relinquishing her right in the two-thirds of her patrimony, she furnished the consideration for it; and as she was the party to be benefited, the object being *partition, and not conversion*, the law raises a presumption that the husband took the legal title of her share as her trustee, for the same reason that it raises a resulting trust of land paid for with the money of another. With what did he pay? Certainly with his wife's land for all but an inconsiderable part of the value, and this land was as much her separate estate as money settled to her separate use, which, had it been the consideration, would have given her an indisputable trust estate by implication of law. Why then shall not the law imply such a trust estate when her land has been conveyed in payment, and the object is not to part with the value of it, but to reserve or take back an equivalent."

In the case of Kaufman *v.* Crawford, it was ruled that where husbands had procured deeds for the lands of their wives by virtue of a sale by executors where the money was to be divided among testator's daughters, and divided the lands, and executed deeds to

[Ermold v. Newkirk.]

each other, the husbands acquired nothing but the naked legal title, and upon their deaths the fee remained in their wives.

Smith, contra.—In the court below, the plaintiff in error claimed to recover, first, one-sixth; secondly, three-sixths, and the whole. The defendants admitted that she was entitled to recover her own share in the estate of her brother Adam Spohn, deceased, being one-sixth.

The case under consideration was *a sale* by the heirs of Adam Spohn, deceased, to Daniel Ermold, *and not a partition*. At the sheriff's sale, no notice was given of Sarah Ermold's title. The purchaser at sheriff's sale took the title, after seeing the deed made and executed in the usual form.

When Adam Spohn accepted of the lot in dispute, and entered into a recognizance for the payment of his brothers and sisters, the title became vested in him, and he became indebted to each of them for a seventh part of the valuation money, for which they had a lien on the house and lot. But as soon as he died, the same descended to them as his heirs, and the indebtedness and lien were extinguished by operation of law. Where the same hand is to receive and pay, the debt is paid by operation of law.

Land charged with the payment of an annuity, descending to the annuitant, the annuity is discharged: Hefferman v. Adams, 9 *Watts* 529; 2 *Pierre Williams* 604.

If the plaintiff in a judgment becomes the owner of the land upon which the judgment is a lien, the lien is extinct by operation of law: Koons v. Hartman, 7 *Watts* 20.

If partition be made between tenants in common, who are *femes covert*, and mutual releases be executed to the husbands, the husbands hold in trust for their wives: Weeks v. Haas, 3 *Watts & Ser.* 520. But if the release do not recite the partition, but a moneyed consideration, a purchaser from the husband, without notice, would hold the property: *Id.* Where the object is partition, *and not conversion*, the husband would be trustee for his wife. Opinion of GIBSON, C. J., 3 *W. & Ser.* 522.

In Kintzer v. Mitchell, 5 *Barr* 216, 219, and 8 *Barr* 81–82, notice of the wife's title was brought home to the purchaser.

Where, in partition in the Orphans' Court, the real estate cannot be divided into as many parts as there are heirs, and a husband of one of the heirs accepts in right of his wife, and enters into a recognizance to pay the valuation money, and pays the heirs their share of the valuation money with his wife's share of the valuation money of other purparts, he acquires a fee simple to all but his wife's share: Snavely v. Wagner, 8 *Barr* 396.

In Kaufman v. Crawford, 9 *W. & Ser.* 131, the title-papers disclosed the wife's interest.

[Ermold v. Newkirk.]

The opinion of the court was delivered June 30, by

BELL, J.—The view taken by the President of the Common Pleas, of the interest acquired by Daniel Ermold, under the undisputed facts of the case, is entirely correct.

The distinction is between partition and conversion. When the former is the object, the husband takes but a life estate in the land not actually paid for with his own proper funds; but where the estate of the wife is actually converted, the proceeds become the property of the husband by an application of them to his own purposes. Here, it is in uncontradicted proof that the lands which descended from the wife's father *were actually sold and conveyed*, and the money arising from them applied in purchase of the house and lot conveyed or to be conveyed to the husband. This fact brings the case within the distinction pointed out in Weeks *v.* Haas, 3 *W. & Ser.* 520. Besides, the property in dispute came to the plaintiff immediately from Adam her brother, and not from her father. It is therefore not within the purview of the cases cited for the plaintiff.

Under this aspect of the case, it is immaterial whether a deed was actually executed to the husband, or not, and consequently indifferent whether what the court said upon that point be well founded.

Judgment affirmed.

Kidd *versus* The Commonwealth.

1. In a suit on a recognizance in the Orphans' Court given by an heir who took one of three purparts at the appraisement, executed in favor of the Commonwealth for the payment to the other heirs their proportional shares in the purpart, it was admissible for the recognizor, the defendant, under the plea of payment with leave to show that one of the other purparts, not taken at the appraisement, was sold by a trustee under order of the Orphans' Court, and that all of the balance of the proceeds, after payment of debts of the intestate, was paid to the plaintiff, and that the defendant in the suit never made any objection. The fact whether or not it was received as part payment, should have been submitted to the jury.

2. Such a recognizance should be sued in the name of the Commonwealth as the legal party, though it is proper that the name of the persons suing, should be stated on the record. A mistake however, in this respect, will not furnish a defence against the Commonwealth, as the court should look to the distribution of the amount recovered. The judgment should not be for the *penalty*, but for the amount of the interest of those suing.

3. It is not necessary that all the *cestuis que use* should be marked of record. Less than the whole number may sue, and they may recover as much of the fund as they show themselves entitled to, leaving the balance for those entitled who may afterwards sue. But where they represent *one heir*, their joinder in the suit would seem to be peculiarly proper.

ERROR to the Common Pleas of *Berks county*.

This was a scire facias on a recognizance in the Orphans' Court,

[Kidd v. The Commonwealth.]

in the penal sum of $7200, brought in the name of the Commonwealth of Pennsylvania to the use of Samuel Moore and Robert Alexander Moore, who sue by their guardian, John M. Keim, and of James and William Moore, heirs of John Kidd, deceased, *vs.* Mary Kidd.

The plaintiff claimed to recover the one third part of the valuation, amounting to $1200, with interest from 10th January 1841.

The defendant plead payment, with leave to give the special matters in evidence, &c.

John Kidd died in 1829, intestate and without issue, (leaving two sisters, viz. Mary Kidd, the defendant, Anna, the widow of James Shoemaker, and the children of Lydia, wife of Charles Moore, another sister,) seized of two lots in Reading, one situate in Penn street, containing 60 feet, and the other on Hamilton street, containing 30 feet.

Lydia Moore died in the lifetime of the said John Kidd, leaving issue, four children—the plaintiffs in this suit.

In 1839, *John M. Keim, guardian of the children of Mrs. Moore*, presented his petition for an inquest, &c.

The inquest divided the 60 feet lot into two equal parts—appraised purpart No. 1 at $3600, and purpart No. 2 at $1800, and purpart No. 3, on Hamilton street, at $700.

Mary Kidd accepted purpart No. 1, and entered into recognizance; Ann Shoemaker accepted purpart No. 3, and entered into recognizance; John M. Keim, guardian, &c., refused to accept purpart No. 2, and prayed a sale, &c.

The court, at the request of the heirs, appointed A. F. Miller, Esq., trustee to sell purpart No. 2, and granted an order of sale, and he sold the same to Henry Shearer, for $1575.

This sum of $1575 was paid to the creditors of John Kidd, *except a balance of* $468, as appears by the account of A. F. Miller, &c.

This balance of $468 was paid to *John M. Keim, guardian*, on the 6th day of November 1840: one third, viz. $156, *belonged to Mary Kidd, the defendant in this suit;* but as she was debtor to Keim in $1200 for his ward's share in the recognizance, he received the whole sum, including the share of Ann Shoemaker, who was also debtor in $233.33, for the one-third of her recognizance.

Keim died in 1846, but, prior to his death, placed the amount received in the hands of Joseph L. Stichter, with instructions to pay it to his wards, with interest, whenever they should demand it.

The plaintiff had gone to reside in the State of Indiana about the time of the inquest.

To August term 1841, No. 376, Keim brought suit on the recognizance, but nothing was done until April 1850, when William Moore, one of the plaintiffs, employed counsel to proceed with the suit. The case was put at issue and entered for trial.

A petition of William Moore was presented to the Orphans'

[Kidd v. The Commonwealth.]

Court, at the April term 1850, setting forth the receipt of the $468 by Keim, as above stated, and that one of his brothers, to wit, Robert Alexander, died in the West, in July 1846, intestate and without issue, and that the two other brothers had left their former residence, one upwards of twelve, and the other upwards of seven years, and had not been heard of since; and prayed the court to decree the payment of the same to him, as surviving heir.

The court, upon the report of a commissioner of the facts contained in the petition, decreed the money to the said William Moore, upon giving his own bond to refund to his brothers in case they should appear and claim the same. William Moore received the same April 16, 1850, and gave bond as per decree. Upon the trial of the case, the defendant gave notice of these facts, and claimed credit for $156 and interest, which the court refused to allow, and directed the jury to find a verdict for the whole amount of one-third of the valuation of purpart No. 1, with interest.

The notice of special matter, on the part of defendant, was as follows:—

The defendant will offer to prove on the trial of the above cause, that the plaintiffs, by their guardian, some time in the year 1840 or 1841, received from Anthony F. Miller, trustee to sell part of the real estate of John Kidd, deceased, the sum of $468, of which sum one-third belonged to the defendant, and that she is entitled to a credit on the recognizance, upon which the above suit is brought, for so much as she was entitled to receive.

To show that she was entitled to that sum, viz. one-third of the said sum of $468, the defendant will give in evidence the account and report of the auditors thereon, of the said Mary Kidd, administratrix of John Kidd, deceased, and the receipt of John M. Keim, guardian as aforesaid, to the said A. F. Miller, for the said sum of $468, and the proceedings in the Orphans' Court of Berks county, authorizing the sale of the real estate of the said John Kidd, deceased, by said A. F. Miller, to Henry B. Sherer, and the account, &c. of said Miller, filed in the said court, and the decree of the Orphans' Court, directing the payment of the money raised by said sale, to the Farmers' Bank of Reading, and to the said Mary Kidd, and all the records and papers relating to or bearing upon that point.

On the trial, the defendant's counsel moved to have the jury sworn between the Commonwealth of Pennsylvania, for the use of William Moore, and the defendant, Mary Kidd—the said William Moore being the real and only plaintiff in the case; which motion the court overruled, and directed the jury to be sworn as the record stood. To which decision by the court, the defendant's counsel excepted. This was the *first* bill.

The plaintiff having opened his case, offered in evidence the proceedings in the Orphans' Court on the estate of John Kidd, de-

[Kidd v. The Commonwealth.]

ceased, viz. the petition of John M. Keim, guardian, &c., for an inquest on the real estate of the said deceased—inquest awarded 11th December 1839—and offered to read the recognizance of Mary Kidd, on which the said scire facias was brought. To the admission of which the defendant's counsel objected, because the recognizance is joint, and sued by several of the heirs, *but not by all;* which objection the court overruled. This was the second bill.

The recognizance, dated January 10, 1840, was as follows :—

Purpart No. 1, being accepted by and adjudged to Polly Kidd, upon her paying or securing to be paid to the other heirs and legal representatives of the said deceased, their equal and proportionable shares respectively of the net two-thirds within one year, with interest from the first day of April next. " Therefore I the said Polly Kidd acknowledge to owe to the Commonwealth of Pennsylvania the sum of $7200 of the real estate so accepted and adjudged to be made and levied, if default be made in the following condition, that is to say, if the said Polly Kidd shall and do well and truly pay or cause to be paid to the other heirs and legal representatives of the said deceased respectively, their equal and proportionable shares respectively, of and in the said valuation money, agreeably to the adjudication, then this recognizance to be void, otherwise to be in full force and virtue."

The plaintiff closed—and defendant offered, under the plea and notice of special matter, the following evidence, to wit:—An order of court to Anthony F. Miller, trustee, to sell purpart No. 2, and a sale for $1575. The accounts of Anthony F. Miller, trustee to sell, &c., and of Mary Kidd, administratrix of John Kidd, together wiith the decrees of said court, and payments pursuant, &c., and the payment by said Anthony F. Miller to John M. Keim, guardian of the plaintiffs, of $468, (*pro ut* said papers, &c.;) to which the counsel for the plaintiff objecting, the court sustained the objection, and sealed a bill of exceptions. This was the third bill.

The defendant's counsel further offered in evidence the record in the Orphans' Court, to April term 1850, consisting of a petition by William Moore, the plaintiff, setting forth the receipt by John M. Keim, of the said $468, as guardian, &c., and claiming the same in his own right, and as the survivor of the said plaintiffs above named—the decree by the court in his favor and the receipt of it, (*pro ut* the record and proceedings, &c.;) to which the said plaintiff objected, and the court rejected it, and sealed a bill of exceptions. Fourth bill.

The defendant further called Anthony F. Miller, to prove the decease of John M. Keim in 1846, and that Ann Shoemaker, named in the recognizance, on which the suit is brought, is alive and residing in Reading. To which defendant's counsel objected, and the court sustained the objection, and sealed a bill of exceptions. This was the fifth bill.

[Kidd v. The Commonwealth.]

The defendant further called J. B. Gordon, Esq., to prove that William Moore is the only claimant, and that he claims the whole amount of the recognizance in right of said William, as surviving him, &c. Rejected and bill of exceptions sealed. This was the sixth bill.

GORDON, J., charged:—This is a scire facias in the name of the Commonwealth of Pennsylvania against Mary Kidd, on a recognizance in the Orphans' Court of Berks county, entered into by the defendant to secure the payment of purparts or shares of the other heirs of John Kidd, deceased, in land taken at the appraisement in said court by the defendant, Mary Kidd, who was a sister of the deceased. The Commonwealth is the plaintiff in the action, which is brought for the use of the children of Lydia Moore, who was a sister of the decedent John Kidd. The defence made here has reference to the manner in which the suit is brought. It is purely a legal or technical defence, and will sufficiently appear in the points of law submitted to the court by the defendant's counsel. Your verdict will be regulated by the answers given to these points by the court.

Points submitted on part of the defendant were as follow:—

1. That the action cannot be sustained by joining four of the five claiming under the recognizance, and claiming a joint verdict for four. If a specific sum is claimed, each heir should sue for him or herself.

2. If the action can be sustained in the name of the Commonwealth of Pennsylvania, as a trustee for the recognizors, without their appearing on the record, then the verdict and judgment should be for the penalty of the recognizance according to the præcipe and scire facias.

3. The recognizance being given, and made payable to the heirs of John Kidd respectively and severally, the cause of action upon it is several, and the verdict and judgment should be for the specific amount due to each, and must be specifically assigned in the breach of the scire facias.

The first point the court answer in the negative. The Commonwealth is the plaintiff, and as such entitled to recover the shares of those who sue in her name. The respective shares of those for whom she sues in the sum recovered can be adjusted after recovery. There is no question here of joinder or non-joinder of parties. The Commonwealth is the only legal party, and the number of persons for whose use the action is marked is quite immaterial, except that in this action it furnishes information to the court and jury as to the sum for which the verdict should be rendered.

2. The verdict should not be for the penalty of the recognizance, but for the aggregate of the sums due to those who have brought this action in the name of the Commonwealth for their use. Who they are appears in the scire facias and the papers given in evi-

[Kidd v. The Commonwealth.]

dence. If there be other claimants under this recognizance not suing here, the verdict and judgment in this action will be no bar to their recovery of whatever may appear to be due to them in actions to be instituted for their use.

3. The recognizance is not given and made payable to the heirs of John Kidd respectively and severally, as supposed in this point, but to the Commonwealth of Pennsylvania; and it is competent for any one or more of those for whose use it was taken to sue in the name of the Commonwealth for their shares, severally for the shares of each, or aggregately for the shares of those suing. The verdict in this case ought not to be for the specific amount due *to each heir, but for the amount due to all the heirs for whose use the action is brought.*

With this view of the law, the court are of opinion that *the plaintiff* is entitled to recover.

To this opinion of the court, the defendant by her counsel excepted.

November 13, 1850, a verdict was rendered for $1980.

It was assigned for error:
1. The court erred in refusing to swear the jury as requested by defendant's counsel.
2. There was error in the admission of the evidence mentioned in the second bill of exception.
3. There was error in the rejection of evidence mentioned in the third bill of exceptions.
4. There was error in the rejection of the evidence in the fourth bill of exceptions.
5. There was error in the rejection of the evidence proposed in the fifth and sixth bills of exceptions.
6. The court erred in their answers to the defendant's points. They should have answered in the affirmative.
7. The charge is generally erroneous—and especially in directing the jury to render a verdict for one-third of the valuation of the purpart No. 1, instead of for the penalty, or for the claim of *one* heir only.

The case was argued by *Hoffman* and *Banks*, for plaintiff in error.—The evidence was admissible. It proved payment to the plaintiff. *Debt* on recognizance is the *proper* form of action. *Sci. fa.* sustained upon the *practice:* Blanchard v. Com'th, 6 *Watts* 311–12; Good v. Good, 7 *Watts* 159. The recognizance changed the property from real to personal: 1 *Jones* 374. It passed, upon the death of Robert Alexander, to his administrator, and not to William Moore as surviving heir: Lee v. Wright, 1 *Rawle* 149. The action is brought for the penalty, but for four of the five recognizees, and the verdict is for a specific sum; whereas the verdict should have been for the penalty in the first instance, and for the

[Kidd *v.* The Commonwealth.]

specific amount due to each plaintiff for whose use the suit was brought. An obligation given to several co-obligees jointly cannot be sued by some of the obligees and omitting others. It must be sued jointly or severally: Sweigart *v.* Berk, 8 *Ser. & R.* 308; 10 *Wheat.* 406. See also 1 *Chitty* 1, 5, 6, 7, 9, 31; 1 *Saunders* 154, note; act of 29th March 1832, sec. 37, *Purdon* 913, &c. The act of 14th January 1836 authorizes one suit, and all may be made parties by suggestion, &c. *Distributees must bring *several* suits for the balance of an administrator's account.

See further 2 *Penn. Practice* 327 and 335; Taggart *v.* Cooper, 1 *Ser. & R.* 500.

J. B. Gordon and *W. Strong*, for defendant in error.—1. The suit is properly brought in the name of the legal plaintiff for the use of the parties interested.

Where the parties having a beneficial interest in a suit appear on the record, the court will recognise them as such, and treat them accordingly. But it is not necessary to the validity of a judgment that such parties should appear upon the record. If there be *legal* parties, it is sufficient: Reigart et al. *v.* Ellmaker, 6 *Ser. & R.* 45.

The parties interested have a right to the name of the commonwealth in a scire facias on the recognizance given by a sheriff: Brownfield *v.* Com'th for use, &c., 13 *Ser. & R.* 268.

A legal title is certainly sufficient for the maintenance of an action, except, perhaps, where the commonwealth stands as a trustee in an official bond, and then it may be necessary to show a particular injury as a title to her interference, in order to secure the obligor from an officious intermeddling. The equitable owner of a right of action can recover on the legal title only, and any one attempting to use it a second time would be repulsed at once by a plea of former recovery: Armstrong *v.* City of Lancaster, 5 *Watts* 69.

In an action upon a recognizance taken by the Orphans' Court, in the name of the commonwealth, to secure the payment of money, brought for the use of another, proof by the defendant that the person to whose use the suit is brought is not entitled to the money furnishes no defence to the recovery by the legal plaintiff. The right to the money will be determined when it is recovered from the defendant: The Com'th for use *v.* Lightner, 9 *W. & Ser.* 117.

2. The judgment was properly entered for the share of the plaintiffs, and not for the penalty.

Upon a scire facias on a recognizance in the Orphans' Court, to secure the interest of a widow in land, under the intestate law, a finding for the "plaintiff the sum of $1165, and that there is now

[Kidd v. The Commonwealth.]

due to the said plaintiff the sum of $963," with costs of suit and judgment thereon, is erroneous: Stewart v. Martin, 2 *Watts* 200.

A recovery in an action of debt upon a recognizance to secure the payment to several heirs under the intestate laws, by one of them, is no bar to a subsequent suit by another: Good v. Good, 7 *Watts* 200.

The opinion of the court was delivered June 30, by

BELL, J.—The offer by the defendant below, to prove the receipt of the balance of the avails of purpart No. 2 by the guardian of Mrs. Moore's children, was, we think, improperly rejected. Its exclusion, we are told, was put upon the ground that as it did not appear the payment by Miller to Keim was made with the assent of Mary Kidd, the former was subject to her action for her proportion of the funds, and consequently there was no such privity in respect of this transaction established between her and the wards as would entitle her to regard them as debtors; or, secondly, if they may be regarded as standing in that relation, the proffered defence must be treated as set-off, which was not available for want of the proper plea and notice, and because the claim is barred by the statute of limitations. But we are persuaded this view of the ground occupied by the defendant is incorrect. At the time when Miller handed over to Keim, as guardian, the balance remaining in his hands, after payment of the intestate's debts, both Mrs. Kidd and Mrs. Shoemaker were indebted to the children of their deceased sister for their shares of the valuation of purparts Nos. 1 and 3, adjudged by the Orphans' Court to the surviving sisters. All the parties for whose use the action is brought, being minors, were then represented by Keim, as their guardian, who in that capacity received the money in question. He subsequently accounted for the sum so received, to his wards, for a part of the offered proof was that becoming embarrassed, he placed the money paid him by Miller in the hands of one Stichter for the use of the minors, and it was, long after the commencement of this suit, paid to William Moore, as the survivor of his brothers and sisters, by virtue of an order of the Orphans' Court, made upon his application. At the moment of the payment to Keim, he, Miller, and the surviving sisters lived in the same town, and it is obvious, from the accounts settled by Miller as trustee, and by Mary Kidd, the defendant, as administrator of the intestate's estate, as well as from the general circumstances attending the transaction, that the parties interested were aware of the disposition made by the trustee of the money which had come to his hands. Yet, though still living, it is not asserted that either Mrs. Kidd or her sister, Mrs. Shoemaker, ever called upon Miller to pay to them their proportions of the sale made by him, or in any manner indicated they esteemed him their debtor. More than ten years have run since the money was handed to Keim, and at the end of that period we find one of Mrs. Moore's children, who, as representing the others, is the active prosecutor of this suit, claiming and actually enforcing payment of the sum received by his guardian, as money belonging to the wards. Surely, the facts I have imperfectly detailed afford sufficient ground for the inference that payment was made by Miller to Keim, and received by the latter with the knowledge and assent of the surviving sisters, as a payment on account of their indebtedness to the wards. Indeed, under the circumstances, it is difficult, if not impossible, to escape this conclusion, more especially as the defendant below now so avers, and the party beneficially interested as plaintiff claims the fund as belonging to him. As showing or tending to show payments, the offered proof was strictly admissible under the plea of payment, and, we think, ought at least so to have been submitted to the jury. The refusal to permit that branch of the trying tribunal to say whether the actors in the transaction did not so intend it, was consequently erroneous. I may add, it would be a subject of regret were a defence *pro tanto*, apparently so meritorious, defeated by the unnecessary application of a mere technical reason.

In every other particular, the action of the Court of Common Pleas is correct. A recognizance taken in the Orphans' Court, after proceedings in partition, is unlike a sheriff's recognizance or an official bond, where the remedy is regulated by statute. It is simply a common-law obligation of record, taken in the name of the commonwealth, for the security of the several parties in interest. But the commonwealth is, properly, the conusee, and therefore the legal title to sue resides in her. In every instance the action is properly brought in her name, and may be sustained without the suggestion of any other. But as each individual having an interest in the recognizance may use the name of the commonwealth to enforce that interest, convenience requires the name of the *cestui que use* who sues to be suggested of record; and this is constantly done where the proceeding is instituted by any less than the whole number of claimants: Good v. Good, 7 *Watts* 199. Perhaps in every instance, the name of the party suing ought to be noted, since it seems the judgment should not be for the penalty, but for the precise sum found to be due to the individual or individuals: Stewart v. Martin, 2 *Watts* 200. But even a mistake in this particular furnishes no defence against the legal plaintiff. To the defendant it is of no consequence who claims the money, since the court will look to its proper distribution after recovery: Commonwealth v. Lightner, 9 *W. & Ser.* 117; though doubtless the interference of a mere intruder without pretence of equitable title, would be forbidden.

It is objected here, that more than one, and less than the whole number of persons interested, are marked of record as *cestuis*

[Kidd v. The Commonwealth.]

que use. And what of that? The cases show that one of several may proceed under the recognizance, and why not any number less than all? There could be no question of mis-joinder or non-joinder, for the Commonwealth is always the legal party; and as the recognizance is taken for the security of each and all there is no technical difficulty, nor any objection in principle against suggesting the names of as many equitable claimants as choose to join. By the settled rule, they will recover just so much of the whole fund as they may show themselves entitled to, leaving the balance for those of the remaining parties who may afterwards sue. It was ruled in one of the cases already cited, that judgment, in such an instance, ought not to be given for the penal sum, as a cautionary judgment is unnecessary. It would follow from this that the verdict rendered below for an aggregate sum, specifically due to the named *cestuis que use*, is in accordance with established practice. I may remark, in conclusion, that there would seem to be great propriety in the joinder of parties complained of here, since they represented one share of the estate. That the court was right in refusing to discriminate between them on the application of the defendant, or swear the jury in a particular way, is too plain for remark. Even had a mistake been committed in this point, I do not see how it could have affected the defendant injuriously.

Judgment reversed.

Hennershotz's Estate.

A testator devised to his wife "the sum of one thousand pounds, during her lifetime, and after her decease to be equally divided amongst my children, that is to say as follows: the one thousand pounds above mentioned to remain on my plantation in Alsace, as a dower during her lifetime."

"Third, I will and bequeath unto my beloved wife all my household furniture and kitchen utensils, as much as she may choose to keep for her own use. I will that my beloved wife shall maintain and educate my minor children during their minority, out of her yearly dower."

"Fourth, I will and bequeath unto my son William all my plantation in Alsace, together with the woodland at the hill, *he to pay sixty-five dollars ($65) per acre for the same, in the following manner:* First, one year after my death, he shall pay all my just debts, and after deducting my just debts and the above dower of my beloved wife, then the balance shall be equally divided amongst my children, *that is,* my son William shall buy a house and furniture for my daughter Rebecca by the first day of April next, to the amount of $350—and buy a house and furniture for my daughter Lavina, for $350 three months after the day of her marriage—and after having paid all the above items, then I will that the balance remaining, together with all my other property, shall be equally divided, such as bonds, notes, and the different bequests heretofore mentioned, *amongst my children as follows, to wit,* my son William shall pay the one-half of the part that shall fall to one of my children to my youngest son *Augustus* when he shall come to the age of 21 years—and the next or following year he shall pay the one-half of the part falling to my

[Hennershotz's Estate.]

daughter *Catharine*, wife of David Engle—and the following year he shall pay the one-half falling to my daughter *Rebecca*, wife of John Clouser—and the following year he shall pay one-half of the part falling to my daughter *Lavina*, and following year he shall pay the last part to my son *Augustus*—and so on year after year *agreeable to the names above mentioned*, until all the different parts or sums are paid."

Held, that William, the devisee of the land, was entitled to a share of its proceeds in common with the other children, and that the direction to him to *pay* was not inconsistent with the idea of *retention* by him of a portion of the fund.

APPEALS of A. Lucius Hennershotz, for the use of Elizabeth Hennershotz, James H. Adams, and John Clouser, from the decree of the Common Pleas of *Berks county*, distributing the proceeds *of sheriff's sale of real estate* of William Hennershotz in the following suit:—

The property sold for $17,140. Deducting costs, the balance of money for distribution was $16,943.21.

The property sold is part of 212 acres, more or less, of the land devised by Conrad Hennershotz to said William Hennershotz, by will dated August 13, 1838, and proved October 11, 1838. September 16, 1841, William Hennershotz recovered from the Philadelphia and Reading Railroad Company, by finding of sheriff's inquest, $3000, for occupying 11 acres of said land from November 1, 1838. On appeal, he recovered $3100, January 12, 1844.

March 31, 1845, he conveyed to The Philadelphia and Reading Railroad Company about 1 acre of said land for	$200.00
February 17, 1847, he conveyed to Jonas Shalter 7 acres and 128 perches, more or less, of said land for	1,300.00
October 1, 1848, he conveyed to Solomon Horning 8 acres of said land for	1,100.00
February 17, 1849, he conveyed to trustees of church ¾ acre of said land for	1.00
March 17, 1849, he conveyed to Solomon Horning 9 acres, more or less, of said land for	1,237.59
	6,938.50
Amount of sheriff's sale brought forward	17,140.00
Total	$24,078.50

On the part of the appellees, it was alleged that some material facts are omitted in the appellant's statement. That the whole amount of liens chargeable upon the fund in court is $17,799.53, including the judgments of the appellants. That there is *not* sufficient to pay the liens, if the *judgments of the appellants* are chargeable upon the fund.

[Hennershotz's Estate.]

William Hennershotz made a general assignment in trust for his creditors to Charles Fichthorn, dated March 25th, A. D. 1850.

That the statement of the appellant respecting the amount realized by William out of the property devised to him is calculated to produce erroneous impressions. After the death of the testator the railroad was constructed through the plantation, and its effect has been greatly to increase its value; there is a railroad stopping-place and sideling upon it. William Hennershotz, the devisee, opened quarries, built limekilns, a store-house, a large barn as well as made other improvements since the property came to him. The statement of appellants that he had advantages over his brother and sisters is therefore erroneous.

A judgment in favor of James H. Adams against William Hennershotz was entered April 5, 1849, for $286.71; one in favor of A. L. Hennershotz vs. same, was entered on same day for $430; one in favor of John Clouser vs. same, entered on same day for $304.

On motion a rule was entered in each of those cases to show cause why the amount of each judgment should not then be taken out of court. These rules were subsequently discharged, and the plaintiffs severally appealed.

Each of the foregoing three judgments is founded on defendant's note under seal, with the following endorsement, to wit, "Whereas there is a misunderstanding between the parties as to the construction of the will of Conrad Hennershotz, deceased, and the parties have determined to have it settled by the court, this note therefore is not to be paid in case the question shall be determined in favor of William Hennershotz; but if against him, the plaintiff is to have the amount of the note paid to him."

The question presented to the court was whether or not the said William Hennershotz is entitled to a share of the money which by the will of said Conrad Hennershotz he was to pay for the land devised to him by said will.

There was money enough in court to pay the judgments, but the Common Pleas decided that under the will, *William* Hennershotz is entitled to a share, to wit, one-fifth of the said money which by said will he was to pay for said land so devised to him—and this was the only question presented to the Supreme Court for their adjudication—the appellants contended that he was not entitled to any part of the said money payable by him for said land, but that he had his inheritance in the land.

The will of Conrad Hennershotz contained the following provisions, the mispelling being corrected:—

First, It is my will, and do order that all my just debts and funeral expenses be duly paid and satisfied as soon as conveniently can be after my death.

Second, I will and bequeath unto my dear wife Elizabeth, the

[Hennershotz's Estate.]

sum of one thousand pounds, during her lifetime, and after her decease to be equally divided amongst my children, that is to say as follows: the one thousand pounds above mentioned to remain on my plantation in Alsace, as a dower during her lifetime. And further, I will that my beloved wife shall have all that part of the house, that is to say, the back kitchen, and room in the cellar and spring-house, the back room on the first floor, and the back room on the second floor; my son William, or the proprietor of the place, to keep two cows and one horse in pasture, and feed the same during winter; and to provide her with as much firewood as she may need, and cut the same fit for use.

Third, I will and bequeath unto my beloved wife all my household furniture and kitchen utensils, as much as she may choose to keep for her own use.

I will that my beloved wife shall maintain and educate my minor children during their minority, out of her yearly dower.

Fourth, I will and bequeath unto my son William all my plantation in Alsace, together with the woodland at the hill, *he to pay sixty-five dollars ($65) per acre for the same, in the following manner:* first, one year after my death, he shall pay all my just debts, and after deducting my just debts and the above dower of my beloved wife, then the balance shall be equally divided amongst my children, *that is*, my son William shall buy a house and furniture for my daughter Rebecca, by the first of April next, to the amount of $350—and buy a house and furniture for my daughter Lavina, for $350, three months after the day of her marriage—and after having paid all the above items, then I will that the balance remaining, together with all my other property, shall be equally divided, such as bonds, notes, and the different bequeaths heretofore mentioned, *amongst my children, as follows, to wit,* my son William shall pay the one-half of the part that shall fall to one of my children, to my youngest son *Augustus*, when he shall come to the age of 21 years—and the next or following year he shall pay the one-half of the part falling to my daughter *Catharine*, wife of David Engle—and the following year he shall pay one-half falling to my daughter *Rebecca*, wife of John Clouser—and the following year he shall pay one-half of the part falling to my daughter *Lavina*—and following year he shall pay the last part to my son *Augustus*—and so on year after year, *agreeable to the names above mentioned*, until all the different parts or sums are paid.

The will empowers the executors to sell all the testator's other property for the payment of his debts.

Further, I will that my beloved wife shall have one-third of the garden, wherever she may choose it; and further, I will that after the first payment mentioned to my son Augustus, that then, in place of paying the second payment to my daughter Catharine, [it] shall be made to my daughter Rebecca, and the third payment shall be made to my daughter Lavina, and then the fourth payment to my daughter Catharine, and so on.

William and David Engle are the executors named in the will—and they filed their account on the 17th day of October 1839, showing a balance in their favor of $1693.70 for debts paid beyond proceeds of sale of other property and personal assets, to wit, bonds, notes, &c., to which balance is added the sum of $292, a debt subsequently recovered against the estate; amounting together to $1985.70.

Exceptions were filed that the court should have allowed to Adams, Hennershotz, and Clouser, severally, the amount of their judgments.

The case was argued by *Davis* and *Banks*, for appellants.—It was alleged that William Hennershotz got $4289.98 more in the land than either of the other children in the money to be paid for the land.

That it followed from this view of the matter that the intention of the testator was that William was not to have any share of the money. And that this construction is agreeable to the words of the will. In the distribution of the money William is nowhere mentioned as one of the distributees.

That on the part of the appellees it was contended that the terms *equally divided among my children* included William, and that he was entitled to a share of the money as one of the children of the testator.

The appellants contended that those words, wherever they occur in the will, are followed first by the words, "*that is,*" and then the names of Rebecca and Lavina, only two of the other children, are mentioned; secondly, "*amongst my children, as follows, to wit,*" and then the names of only Augustus, Catharine, Rebecca, and Lavina are mentioned. The will, after having directed the time and order in which the several parts payable to Augustus, Catharine, Rebecca, and Lavina shall be paid, proceeds—" and following year he shall pay the last part to my son Augustus, and so on year after year *agreeable to the names above mentioned, until all the different parts or sums are paid.*"

An argument is attempted to be drawn, favorable to appellee, from the second *item* in the will bequeathing one thousand pounds to the wife during her life, and after her decease *to be* equally divided among my *children*—but there also the restriction appears, in the words, "*that is to say as follows;*" and the distribution of the £1000 after the widow's death is provided for and limited by the words, "*and the different bequeaths hereinbefore mentioned, among my children, as follows, to wit;*" showing clearly that the testator intended the dower, as it is called, to go to the same objects of his bounty as the balance of the money.

[Hennershotz's Estate.]

The construction contended for by the appellants excluding William from a share of the money, produces no inequality, except in William's favor, who has his share, and more than his share in the land. He is the *devisee* of the land *nominatim*, the other children are legatees of the money *nominatim*. Besides, the name of *William* is nowhere mentioned in connection with the money, but the names of all the other children are mentioned. If we adhere to the letter, therefore, William is excluded. The terms "*equally divided among my children,*" are satisfied by applying them to *Augustus*, *Catharine*, *Rebecca*, and *Lavina*, who *are the children of the testator*, and named as such. If there had been but two children, e. g. William and Augustus, then those words could not have been satisfied without including William. Not so here. Again, if testator had intended an equal distribution of the balance among *all his* children, he could have said so; but the word *all* nowhere occurs in the direction of distribution among the children. Again, the words "he to pay $65 per acre, in the following manner," &c., and "my son William shall pay," &c., occurring five times in the distribution, closing with "*until all the different parts or sums are paid,*" is inconsistent with the idea that William was to have a share of the money. The testator, had he so intended, would undoubtedly have so expressed himself. It is *petitio principii*, to say that *retainer* means *payment*. A man may *retain* what is his *due:* the question here is, what is the *due* of William, if any *thing* out of the money. We say he gets land, and the will says he shall pay so much for it. If asked to whom, the will names Augustus, Rebecca, Catharine, and Lavina, and not William. Cited Stahl's Appeal, 2 *Barr* 301; Marshall's Appeal, 2 *Barr* 388.

Sallade and *M. Strong*, for appellee.—William Hennershotz, Augustus L. Hennershotz, Catharine, married to David Engle, Rebecca, married to John Clouser, and Lavina, married to James H. Adams, were all children of the testator, five in number.

David Engle and wife claimed and received one fifth part of the sum ordered to be divided, and released on the   day of May, A. D., 1851.

The other children have also received each one fifth part, but they each claim a fourth part, and their judgments are for the difference between one fourth and one fifth; being designed to be operative only in case the will excludes William from participation in the appraised value of the land.

The testator four times declares that the division shall be made equally among his children. This necessarily includes *all*, unless this conclusion be negatived by other parts of the will.

The argument of the appellants is, that because in the last case in which he directs an equal division among his children, he adds

[Hennershotz's Estate.]

"as follows, to wit," and then names but four, the other is excluded.

But for what purpose were they named? Not to designate them as legatees, but to direct the time when the legacies should become payable. He does not say "the following named children," but *shall be divided* as follows, and then directs, not the share of each, but the time of payment.

No direction was made as to the time of payment to William, for his share was in his own hands.

That the words "as follows, to wit," are used to introduce a direction as to the *time* of payment, and not a designation of the legatee, is also apparent from the use which is made in other parts of the will of similar words.

Even if the part of the will which succeeds the words "as follows, to wit," was intended to designate the legatees, and not the time of payment, still William is not excluded.

A gift to children, describing them as consisting of a specified number, which is less than the actual number, is construed to be a gift to all, and includes the actual number. 2 *Jarman on Wills* 108–9–10.

The rule is the same though some are designated *nominatim*. 2 *Cox* 184; 1 *B. C. C.* 30; 18 *Pick.* 162.

It is not asserted however that this rule prevails where there is a distinct legacy to the child omitted, or where the testator has indicated that he considered the child provided for. There is no such legacy or indication in this case.

Where it appears to have been the intention of a testator to make a class of persons the object of his bounty, and in naming them he omits one of the class, the omitted one will still take: Tucker *v.* Boston, 18 *Pick.* 162.

No importance is due to the word "pay," in the clause in which the testator directs that his son William should pay sixty-five dollars an acre. He regarded the devise as a sale to his son, and he was to pay into the fund for distribution. The design of the testator being simply to raise a fund. The expression is common when the devisee is by the will empowered to receive the sum he is ordered to pay: Leiss *v.* Stubb, 6 *Watts* 48; Zeigler *v.* Grim, 6 *Watts* 106; Lobach's case, 6 *Watts* 167. In all these cases the devisee was directed to *pay*, and yet was authorized to *receive* a part of the sum which he was ordered to pay. Such cases are very numerous in our books.

Again: The repeated directions that the fund "shall be equally divided among his children," and that the half of the part that shall fall to one of them shall be paid to Augustus, Catharine, Rebecca, and Lavina, at certain times, are consistent with each other only on the basis that William is entitled to a share. Thus only can effect be given to all parts of the will.

[Hennershotz's Estate.]

The opinion of the court was delivered June 30, by

BELL, J.—The will in question is evidently the work of an illiterate man; of one measurably unaware of the value of the language he employed. The whole instrument is awkwardly constructed, and particularly in those portions of it which give rise to this controversy. It is not, therefore, at all surprising that some hesitancy should be experienced in pronouncing upon the meaning of its author. Still, by treating it with candor, and assigning to prominent sentences, several times used, their natural and ordinary meaning, we may arrive at a conclusion without much hazard of violating the intention of the testator.

Beyond question, his leading object was to provide for the distribution of his property among all his children. For this purpose, his first care is to create a fund capable of division, by assigning to his son William the plantation and woodland mentioned in the fourth item of the will, at an ascertained price. This is, first, subjected to the burden of his debts, making provision for his widow, and purchasing for his daughters, Rebecca and Lavina, certain amounts of household furniture; and then "the balance remaining, together with all my other property, *shall be equally divided*, such as bonds, notes, and the different bequeaths heretofore mentioned, shall be summed together, and *equally divided amongst my children*." Once before, in the same clause, is found a direction for an equal distribution *among all the children*, of the estate remaining after discharging debts, and setting aside a certain sum for the benefit of the widow; and in a prior clause this sum is also directed to be similarly divided. Looking alone to these leading features of the testamentary arrangement, one is prepared to say that, in contemplation of the testator, the fund to be raised from the land assigned to William, united with what should remain of his personal assets, after payment of debts, was regarded as representing his whole disposable estate, which, with trifling exceptions, was to be equally distributed among all the children of the donor. Had the word "all" been introduced before "my children," in the several disposing clauses, there would absolutely be no room for cavil. And yet the language actually employed is as potent to express the intention of general distribution, as though that particular word had been used. "To be divided among my children," standing alone, is as clearly indicative of a design to give to every member of the class designated, as though every child were named *seriatim*. It requires no formal chain of reasoning to establish that the same conclusion must be necessarily arrived at under either form of gift, and, consequently, a distribution among all must be decreed here, unless, indeed, there be found something in the general context, or in particular expressions, to countervail the natural import of the sentences referred to. In the absence of such counteracting influence, there

[Hennershotz's Estate.]

would be no better reason for the exclusion of the devisee of the land as a distributee, than of any other of the children. That he is the recipient of the realty, at a certain value, cannot, of itself, afford a ground for denying him an interest in the fund raised; for, regarded simply as a devisee, he must be accepted as a purchaser for value, and so standing in the same relative position to the subject of the devise as though he were a mere stranger. For the more easy disposition of his property among the natural objects of his bounty, the testator resolves to dispose of his lands, and turns to his eldest son as the individual he proposes to be his successor as tenant of the fee. Admit that by this arrangement he had in view an incidental benefit to be derived by the son from the low price named as representing the land, the latter is not the less to be esteemed as taking for value, and, in the construction of the will, entitled to every advantage flowing from his position of purchaser at the sum fixed by one to whom alone belonged the power of naming the price. I admit, that when interpreting an obscure testamentary instrument, the inquirer may look to the circumstances which surrounded the testator at the moment, to the number and condition of his family, the position in which particular members of it stood towards him, the condition of his estate, and, sometimes, may consider its general value, or of particular portions of it. The latter inquiry is legitimate where there is a declared intent to equalize all the beneficiaries, as in Marshall's Appeal, 2 *Barr* 388; but even then, too much reliance should not be placed on estimated values, and mere conjecture is always dangerous. In the instance before us, we are asked to deduce an argument against the inclusion of William as a participator of the fund, from the asserted fact, that the land devised to him was, at the date of the will, of much greater value per acre than the sum named by the testator, and that, even at this reduced price, he was permitted to enjoy it subject only to the burden of the balance of the debts and the provision for the widow, until Augustus, the youngest son, arrived at full age, a period of eight years and six months, when the yearly payments were to commence, without, however, carrying interest. Of the value of the land, we have no other proof than from sales made long after the date of the will, and when the worth of the farm had been much enhanced by the construction of the Reading Railroad, and by other large improvements the work of the devisee; *data* much too uncertain to furnish ground for such deduction. The other asserted advantages derived from postponed payments, might, possibly, be worthy of more regard, had the testator declared an intention to make all his children equal recipients of his bounty. But there is no such avowal to be found in this will. It is not the estate, as it should stand at the death of the testator, but the fund springing from the land, united with the personal assets remaining after payment of debts, that is to be

[Hennershotz's Estate.]

equally divided. Such a distribution is not at all inconsistent with a design to confer on William large advantages as devisee, irrespective of his claims as one of the designated class of legatees. Were there then nothing else in the way, it might be safely asserted the mere inequality of benefit complained of furnishes no sufficient reason for refusing to the oft-repeated sentence, "to be equally divided among my children," its obvious meaning. But an additional objection is interposed. It is insisted that the words "as follows, to wit," which immediately succeed the last employment of the sentence just cited, followed by an enumeration of the persons who are to take, in which William's name does not occur, demonstrates an intent to exclude him from any participation in the fund. There would seem to be something of soundness in this position were the words relied on used to designate all the persons who are to take under the bequest. But I think it sufficiently plain they were employed, not for that purpose, but as introductory to a direction as to the time and mode of payment to the several legatees particularly named. The testator did not say, "to be divided among the following named children," or "among my four children, namely," as he naturally would, had he so intended. But after giving the whole fund equally among his children, he proceeded to direct when and how that portion of it to be paid by the devisee should be disbursed. In order to this, it became necessary to name all the children entitled to receive from William, so as to fix the period and manner of the several payments; but as William was himself to be the payer, it was unnecessary to include him in the enumeration. That the phrase on which the appellants base their argument was introduced for the purpose I have intimated, and not to designate the legatees, is also apparent from the use made of similar words in other parts of the will. Thus, "that is to say as follows," in the first clause, point to the manner in which the thousand pounds is to be secured, and not the mode of its subsequent distribution; and, in the fourth clause, "that is," immediately following a direction for equal distribution among the children, introduce, not the names of even all the admitted legatees, but simply an order for a partial investment in favor of two of them. These diverse uses of synonymous terms would imply the testator was not fully aware of the value of the language he employed; it, at least, proves he did not always assign to it the meaning insisted on for the appellants; and as, in the present collocation, it admits a different interpretation, it would be, indeed, hazardous to invest it with a signification destructive of the preceding plainly expressed directions for an equal division among the children as a class.

In this connection, it may also be remarked, the direction is, the devisee shall pay to each of the enumerated children "one-half of the part that shall fall to one of my children," and this is repeated

[Hennershotz's Estate.]

four times, necessarily referring to the preceding words of gift as the only means of ascertaining what proportion of the whole that part is.

But were it even conceded the testator intended to enumerate the beneficiaries, when naming his children at the close of the fourth item, it is by no means certain the omission to name William would necessarily exclude him. It is an undoubted rule, that where a testator refers to a class of persons, as the objects of his bounty, but, in an attempted enumeration, omits to name one or more of them, the parties omitted may still take, unless there be something to show the omission was of purpose: Tucker v. Boston, 18 *Pick.* 162. But in this instance, there was a peculiar reason why William should not be specifically named with the other children, in the fourth item. It is, that that enumeration was but of payees, of whom William was not one.

In conclusion, it may be added that the direction to William to pay is not inconsistent with the idea of retention by him of a portion of the fund. In wills, this expression is not uncommon where, beyond all question, the devisee is, himself, to retain.

Judgment affirmed.

McGinnis's Appeal.

The principle of substitution or subrogation rests in equity only, and is not to be carried out when it would work injustice to the rights of others; therefore, G. M., a judgment creditor, whose judgment was entered in *Cumberland* county, was not entitled to be subrogated to the judgments in *Franklin* county of M., whose judgments originally entered in that county had been subsequently entered by transcript in *Cumberland county*, and there paid out of the sale of the defendant's real estate in the latter county, when the substitution would have been to the prejudice of J., whose judgment in Franklin county was entered *after* the judgment of M. was obtained there, but *before* the judgment of G. M. was obtained in Cumberland county.

APPEAL of George McGinnis, in the matter of the distribution of the proceeds of the sale of the real estate of Lawrence Herchelroth, by the Court of Common Pleas of *Franklin county*.

James X. MacLanahan obtained judgment against Lawrence Herchelroth, in Franklin county, on 23d December 1847, for $204, interest, &c. On the 13th April 1848, a transcript of this judgment was filed in Cumberland county. MacLanahan obtained another judgment against the said Lawrence Herchelroth, in Franklin county, on the 26th of March 1849, for $69.66, with interest from the date, which was also filed in Cumberland county, *on the 27th of March* 1849.

Joseph Johnston obtained judgment against Lawrence Herchelroth, in Franklin county, on the 9th of April 1849, for $1100, with interest from the date.

[McGinnis's Appeal.]

John Herchelroth obtained judgment against Lawrence Herchelroth, on the 9th of April 1849, in Franklin county, for $437.73, with interest from the date.

Adam Cressler obtained a judgment against Lawrence Herchelroth, *in Franklin county*, on the *second* day of April 1849, for $800. This judgment was prior in time to Johnston's and Herchelroth's judgments. It was obtained *in Franklin county*, three days before McGinnis's judgment was entered in *Cumberland county*, and was paid out of the proceeds of the sale of the real estate of Lawrence Herchelroth in Franklin county.

On the *fifth* of April 1849, George McGinnis obtained judgment in *Cumberland county*, against Charles Wharton and Lawrence Herchelroth, for $1515, No. 247, January term 1849.

On the 23d of March 1850, the sheriff of Cumberland county sold all the real estate of Lawrence Herchelroth situate in that county, for $6550. Both the judgments of Mr. MacLanahan were reached and paid out of the proceeds of this sale, and also $1289.53 of McGinnis's judgment was reached and paid out of the said proceeds, leaving a balance due on it of $317.21.

The real estate of Lawrence Herchelroth situate in *Franklin county* was sold by the sheriff of Franklin county, on the 9th of August 1850, for $1340, and the money brought into court for distribution. This sale of real estate in Franklin county was sufficient, and more than sufficient to have paid both the said judgments of MacLanahan, according to the liens of the same entered in Franklin county. On the 12th of August, George McGinnis presented his petition to the Court of Common Pleas of *Franklin* county, praying to be substituted in place of James X. MacLanahan in his said two judgments, in Franklin county, and obtained a rule to show cause why he should not be so substituted, and why the said balance of his judgment should not be paid out of the said proceeds of sale in Franklin county. Notice of this rule was given to all the parties interested. If the said two judgments of MacLanahan had not been transferred to Cumberland county, the judgment of McGinnis would have been paid in full out of the proceeds of the sale in the latter county.

On the 24th of April 1851, the court discharged the said rule, and decreed the payment of the money in court to the judgments of Joseph Johnston and John Herchelroth, according to the appropriation of the sheriff of Franklin county, from which decree George McGinnis appealed.

On the application of George McGinnis, the Court of Common Pleas of Cumberland county, at April term 1850, granted a rule on James X. MacLanahan and the parties interested, to show cause why he should not be substituted in the said two judgments of MacLanahan in the Common Pleas of Cumberland county. Nothing further was done on this rule.

[McGinnis's Appeal.]

Exception was filed to the decree of the Court of Common Pleas of Franklin county.

The case was argued by *Smith* and *Caldwell*, with whom was *McClure*, for McGinnis.—If any rule is well established it is that the creditor who has two funds shall not use his legal advantages in a way to exclude the demand of a fellow-creditor, who has but one: 1 *Story's Equity*, sec. 567, 634–5–6.

The right to substitution is founded upon a mere principle of equity and benevolence, and not necessarily upon either privity or contract between the parties: Kyner v. Kyner, 6 *Watts* 221.

If a party has two funds, he shall not by his election disappoint another, who has one fund only; but the latter shall stand in the place of the former, so as to resort to that fund which can be affected by him alone: 6 *Watts* 221; 2 *Watts* 228, Ramsey's Appeal.

Act of Assembly of 16th April 1840, *Dunlop's Dig.* 911, provides that judgments transferred from the court in which they are entered to any other court, by certified copy of the record, &c., shall have the same force and effect as if the judgment had been entered originally in the court to which it is transferred.

Under this act, the real estate of Lawrence Herchelroth, in the two counties, is to be considered as two tracts of land *in the same county*, as two funds in the same county; and MacLanahan having a lien *on both*, and McGinnis only *on one*.

The lien of McGinnis against one of these funds *is prior* to that of John Herchelroth and Joseph Johnston against the other; but MacLanahan has deprived him of the benefit of that lien, by taking the fund that would have discharged it; hence the application of McGinnis to be substituted against the other fund.

Nill, for John Herchelroth; and *MacLanahan* and *Reilly*, for Johnston.

The opinion of the court was delivered June 30, by

CHAMBERS, J.—George McGinnis, the appellant, a judgment creditor of Lawrence Herchelroth, in the county of Cumberland, asks the Court of Common Pleas of Franklin county, to substitute him in two judgments of James X. MacLanahan, Esq., against the same debtor, on the records of Franklin county, on the ground that Mr. MacLanahan had filed transcripts of his judgments in Cumberland, prior to the lien of the judgment of McGinnis there, and had been paid his two judgments out of the proceeds of the real estate sold in Cumberland.

The law of substitution is the exercise of the equitable powers of the court to afford a summary remedy to a meritorious creditor, who may otherwise be subjected to loss by the operation of proceedings at law, against the estate or funds of a common debtor. The exercise of this equitable power is to be approved and en

[McGinnis's Appeal.]

forced, when it does not conflict with the legal or equitable rights of other creditors of the debtor. Mr. McGinnis is not a surety, but a judgment creditor, with the rights and advantages that the priority of his lien may give him over others. Mr. MacLanahan had, by his vigilance, liens on the real estate of Herchelroth, in the two counties. Mr. McGinnis confined his lien to the county of Cumberland, when he might have transferred it to Franklin, having notice on the record of the prior liens of Mr. MacLanahan in Cumberland. He appears to have been satisfied with the security obtained by his judgment, by which, out of Herchelroth's property sold in Cumberland, he received $1289, leaving a balance of $317, for which he asks to be substituted in Franklin county, on the judgments of Mr. MacLanahan. This is not the case of a creditor having a lien on two funds, and another creditor having a lien on one only, within the same jurisdiction. Mr. McGinnis elected to look to the fund in Cumberland as being sufficient for him, and trust to the proceedings in execution in the courts of that county for the recovery of his judgment. Johnston and John Herchelroth, three days after McGinnis entered his judgment in Cumberland, entered their judgments in Franklin county on the security of the fund in that county. To substitute Mr. McGinnis to the judgments of Mr. MacLanahan in Franklin, would be to raise up to life and lien these judgments which were paid in Cumberland, for the purpose of satisfying the balance of McGinnis's judgment in Cumberland, and, in doing so, disturb and postpone the judgments of Johnston and John Herchelroth in Franklin, who would be deprived of every advantage from their security in that county.

The principle which governs in all cases of substitution, is one of equity merely, and is to be carried out in the exercise of a proper equitable discretion, with a due regard to the legal and equitable rights of others. The claimant who asks this equity must be governed by the common sound maxim, "*sic utere suo ut alienum non lœdas.*" The courts in Franklin or Cumberland would not have restrained Mr. McLanahan from proceeding by execution according to his convenience and choice in either county. He was not bound to make room for the admission of one creditor by displacing another who had equal claims. In Miller v. Jacobs, 3 *Watts* 437; C. J. GIBSON, in delivering the opinion of the court, says, "Between subsequent lien creditors, on distinct parts of the general fund, when equities are balanced, the legal course of execution is not to be disturbed." In Erb's Appeal, 2 *Pa. Rep.* 296, Justice ROGERS, in the opinion given by him, says, "When an application is made for substitution, the court will take care that the subrogation of the surety shall work no injustice to the rights of others." And in Ziegler v. Long, 2 *Watts* 206; Judge SERGEANT observes, "This principle must be employed, like all other rules of equity, to the attainment of justice—it is not to be used to overthrow the equity

[McGinnis's Appeal.]

of another person, and thus work injustice." What superior equity had McGinnis from his unsatisfied judgment in Cumberland county, that is to deprive Johnston and other subsequent creditors in Franklin of an appropriation of the funds there in the unsatisfied judgments, according to the priority of their liens, when the sale and appropriation were made? But it is said that McGinnis had a lien in Cumberland, three days before Johnston and J. Herchelroth acquired theirs in Franklin, and that the maxim "*prior in tempore, potior in jure*," gives him a preference. But what has his lien in Cumberland county to do with an estate in Franklin county, bound to the extent of its value by liens there? Had McGinnis entered a transcript of his judgment in Franklin on the same or next day after the entry in Cumberland, by such diligence he would have secured all the advantages, as if both estates had been in the same county. Having declined to do this, he is without equity that would prefer him to the judgment creditors in Franklin, who elected to look to the estate there for their security. To allow McGinnis to be substituted to the judgments of Mr. McLanahan, as if existing, would have given him a preference over a judgment creditor, A. Cressler, whose lien in Franklin, though subsequent to Mr. McLanahan's lien, was prior to the lien of Mr. McGinnis in Cumberland, and it would have been the small amount of Mr. McGinnis's balance that, under such a substitution, would have left any thing for Cressler's judgment, which was prior in time to Mr. McGinnis's judgment. Such a disturbance and subversion of liens on the records of one county to make way for a judgment creditor of another county, in the appropriation of the proceeds of a sheriff's sale, is unknown in the history of judicial sales in this commonwealth. When Mr. McGinnis elected to place his lien in Cumberland county, on an estate encumbered there, he manifested to the other creditors of L. Herchelroth that he was content to rely on it as sufficient for his purpose. They, perceiving that choice, speculated on their chances by placing their liens on the real estate in Franklin. To postpone and displace such creditors, under the pretence of equity by substitution, would be an abuse of this equitable discretion, as exercised by the courts, and by making the liens on real estate in one county dependent on the liens on other real estate in another county, by different creditors, so as to shift and displace them, would render uncertain the priority and security of liens on such real estate, and embarrass beyond measure the courts in the distribution of the proceeds of sheriff's sales.

It is the opinion of the court that there was no error by the court below in refusing the substitution asked by Mr. McGinnis, and decree of appropriation is affirmed.

Stone *versus* Miller.

1. A debtor by book-account assigned to his creditor a promissory note and also a book-account, with an agreement under seal that in case the same could not be recovered of the persons indebted, then the assignor to pay the amount with charges thereupon, the assignor agreeing to notify the counsel of the creditor when the debtors came to the neighborhood where they were to be proceeded against, which information he never gave; the attorney of the creditor agreeing that if any thing remained after discharging the claim of the creditor, it should be returned to the debtor: *Held*, that there being no agreement to receive the note and book-account *in satisfaction* of the original indebtedness, the assignment was but a *collateral* security; that under the 5th section of the bankrupt act, the claim of the creditor on the said contract of guaranty was provable against the estate of the debtor, who was subsequently discharged as a bankrupt, and that the debtor was consequently discharged from liability to the creditor. See remarks on cases of McMullin *v.* Bank of Penn Township, 2 *Barr* 343, and Cake *v.* Lewis, 8 *Barr* 493.

2. Whether a note or bond is accepted *in satisfaction* of the original claim is for the jury to decide, and not for the court as a matter of law.

3. Where claims transferred to a creditor consist of the indebtedness of others, and there is no agreement to receive the same *in satisfaction*, they are to be considered as *collateral* security for the original debt.

ERROR to the Common Pleas of *Clinton county*.

These were two actions of debt by Miller, Bowman & Co. *vs.* Lewis Stone, on contracts of guaranty under seal. The bankruptcy of Stone was pleaded.

The facts were stated in a special verdict as follows:—

Miller, Bowman & Co. *vs.* Lewis Stone. } Two cases—No. 34, September term 1848; No. 28, December term 1848. Action of debt.—Pleas, bankruptcy.

The jurors empannelled and sworn in the above-stated cases, having heard the proofs of the parties, do say they find the following facts:—

On the 16th of November 1841, H. T. Beardsley, Esq., of Lock Haven, Clinton county, had in his hands for collection, as the attorney of the plaintiffs, a book-account against the defendant amounting, on the 27th day of October 1840, to the sum of $564.67, interest to be added after six months. On the said 16th November 1841, the said Lewis Stone assigned and transferred to the plaintiffs, or their attorney, Mr. Beardsley, *a promissory note* of one Emanuel Rubens, to him the said Lewis Stone, dated January 1st, 1841, and drawn at four months, for $581.28, on which $281.28 had been paid and endorsed—and also *a book-account*, which he the said Lewis Stone held against one Levi Bumbgardner, amounting to $289.55; and received from Mr. Beardsley a written agreement "that if any thing remains over and above after discharging our account of $564.67, of October 27th, 1840, interest after six months, credits against said Stone, and costs of collecting the same, it shall be returned to said Stone. Miller, Bowman &

[Stone v. Miller.]

Co., per H. T. Beardsley, their attorney." The assignment by said Stone of the aforesaid *note* of Emanuel Rubens is endorsed on the back of said note, is under seal, and contains the following covenant : " And in case the same cannot be recovered of the within-named Emanuel Rubens, then I do promise and agree to pay the amount thereof, together with all charges thereupon accruing, unto the said Miller, Bowman & Co., their executors, administrators, or assigns." And the assignment by said Stone of the *book-account* aforesaid contained a covenant that the aforesaid sum of $289.55 was due and owing by the said Levi Bumbgardner to him the said Lewis Stone—" and in case the same cannot be recovered of the above Levi Bumbgardner, then I do promise and agree to pay the amount thereof, together with all charges thereon accruing, to the said Miller, Bowman & Co., their executors, administrators, or assigns." And the jurors aforesaid do further find that at the time of making the assignments aforesaid, the said Lewis Stone represented to Mr. Beardsley that the said Rubens and Bumbgardner were pedlars, and were in the West, but that they would return to Clinton county in the next spring, (to wit, of 1842,) and pay the note and account, and that he would let Mr. Beardsley know when they came in—that Mr. Beardsley proposed to send the claims to Pittsburg, where they sometimes came to buy goods, but that Mr. Stone assured him it would do no good, as they were moving from place to place in the Western States, and that he would inform Mr. Beardsley when they returned to Clinton county—that Mr. Beardsley relied on these representations; frequently called on Mr. Stone in spring and summer after the assignment, but never learned that they had come or were within reach of process, and never collected any money on the said claims, or had the opportunity to collect any. And the jurors aforesaid do further find that *on the 9th day of May* 1842, the said Lewis Stone filed his petition in the District Court of the U. S. for the Western district of Pennsylvania, for the benefit of the bankrupt law of the United States. That on the 6*th day of June* 1842, he was decreed a bankrupt by the said court, and on the 22d of November 1842, was discharged as a bankrupt of and from all his debts, contracts, and other engagements due and made by him at the time of the presentation of his petition for the benefit of the bankrupt law. In the schedule of the said Lewis Stone, containing a description of his creditors, filed in the said court, and made part of the record of proceedings in bankruptcy, " Miller, Bowman & Co., Philadelphia, book-account and note $564.67," are found, which schedule was prepared by Mr. Beardsley, as the attorney of the said Lewis Stone.

And the jurors aforesaid do further say, that these present actions commenced in 1848, *are founded on the contract of guaranty contained in the aforesaid assignments of* the said Lewis Stone, and that the only defence set up is the decree and discharge of the

[Stone v. Miller.]

said Lewis Stone as a bankrupt as aforesaid, but whether under the facts aforesaid, the said decree and discharge be a valid defence in law against the plaintiffs' actions, the jurors confess themselves to be ignorant, and referring that question to the court, they do find for the plaintiffs in No. 30, December term 1848, the sum of $432.68; and in No. 34, December term 1848, for plaintiffs $434.91; if the court shall be of opinion that the proceedings in bankruptcy aforesaid are not a valid defence in law to the plaintiffs' actions; but if the court shall be of opinion that said proceedings are such a defence, then they find for the defendant.

In a statement filed, " it was alleged, that the plaintiffs' demand in the above-named suit is founded upon a writing obligatory, under the hand and seal of the defendant, Lewis Stone, in words and figures following, to wit:—

" For a valuable consideration to me in hand paid by Peter Miller, Jonas Bowman, and Philip Erringer, of the firm of Miller, Bowman & Co., of the city of Philadelphia, I do assign and set over the within obligation, and all money due and to become due thereon, unto the said Miller, Bowman & Co., their executors, administrators, and assigns. *And in case the same cannot be recovered of the within-named Emanuel Rubens, then I do promise and agree* to pay the amount thereof, together with all charges thereupon accruing, unto the said Miller, Bowman & Co., their executors, administrators or assigns. Witness my hand and seal this 16th day of November, 1841."

LEWIS STONE. [SEAL.]

Teste, H. T. BEARDSLEY.

Said writing obligatory is endorsed and written upon a promissory note, in words and figures following, to wit:

PINE CREEK, January 1st, 1841.

Four months after date, I promise to pay to the order of Lewis Stone, five hundred and eighty-one $\frac{25}{100}$ dollars, without defalcation, for value received.

$581.25.   EMANUEL RUBENS.

On which said promissory note, the following payments are endorsed, viz. February 14th, 1841, a payment of $181.25—and October 14th, 1841, a payment of $100. And the balance of said promissory note remains due and unpaid. And the said plaintiffs aver that the amount of said promissory note remaining due and unpaid could not be recovered from the said Emanuel Rubens, by means whereof the said defendant became liable to pay to the said plaintiffs the amount of the same—which he refuses and neglects to do.

The opinion of WOODWARD, President J., was as follows:—

Notwithstanding the terms used in the 5th section of the bank-

[Stone v. Miller.]

rupt law of August 19th, 1841, in favor of persons having uncertain or contingent demands against the bankrupt, it seems to be settled in Pennsylvania, that when a man undertakes to pay a sum of money for another, his undertaking alone will not create a debt provable under a commission; and if an act of bankruptcy intervenes between the undertaking and the actual payment, it can never be proved, and the creditor can only resort to the bankrupt personally: Cake *v.* Lewis, 8 *Barr* 493; McMullin *v.* Bank of Penn Township, 2 *Barr* 343.

This principle, judicially established as an exception to the proviso of the bankrupt law, is relied on for defeating the defendant's plea of his certificate of bankruptcy in these cases. The plaintiffs' suits are founded on the most express undertakings of the defendant to pay, not his original debt to Miller, Bowman & Co., but the amount of the assigned claims with all charges thereon, if the same could not be recovered of Rubens and Bumgardner. Now, if these claims thus assigned or guarantied to Miller, Bowman & Co., are to be regarded as a payment of, or a substitute for the original indebtedness of Lewis Stone to them, I see no difficulty in applying the principle of the cases referred to, and holding that, as Stone, at the time of his bankruptcy, was liable to the plaintiffs only as guarantor, which might or might not result finally in an absolute liability, they could not prove their claim and come in under the proceedings in bankruptcy for a dividend of his estate, and consequently that he would be liable to them on the contract of guaranty, notwithstanding his discharge. But if we are to regard the assigned claims and the guaranty of 16th November 1841, merely as a collateral security for the original debt, so that it still subsisted, it is quite apparent that the certificate of discharge is a defence to these actions, for the principal debt being extinguished and sponged out, the collaterals must fall with it.

What then was the nature of the transaction of the 16th November, 1841? Mr. Beardsley himself doubtless regarded the debt of Miller, Bowman & Co. as still subsisting, for he put it into Stone's schedule of creditors prepared by himself. This circumstance, however, cannot affect the rights of the parties in the present question; for though Mr. Beardsley was the attorney of the plaintiffs in the securing and collecting of their claim against Stone, he was Stone's agent and attorney, and not theirs, in the preparation of the schedules of the bankrupt. It is impossible therefore to say with justice to the plaintiffs that they proved their claim, or did any act to entitle them to a dividend of the bankrupt's estate. But even if they had proved their claim, or received part of it under the bankruptcy, it would not, I apprehend, have affected their right to sue upon this present contract for the balance, *provided this contract survived the discharge.* See Kingston *v.*

[Stone v. Miller.]

Wharton, 2 *Ser. & R.* 208. There is nothing therefore in Mr. Beardsley's act, in preparing Stone's papers, that can properly affect this question.

What then was the nature of the transaction of 16th November, 1841? It would seem to have been a *substitution* of the note of Rubens and the account of Bumgardner with the sealed guaranty of Stone, for the book-account held by the plaintiffs against Stone. That book-account was a simple contract debt. *They gave it up*, and obtained similar debts against two men represented to be solvent, and the sealed promise of their debtor Stone to pay if these men did not. It was other and higher security for their money. And with the testimony of Mr. Beardsley before us, we must regard this contract as contemplating a further extension of credit to Stone, until the next spring, when Rubens and Bumgardner were expected to pay; and the covenant of guaranty, or perhaps more strictly of warranty, was, that Stone would pay in the spring of 1842, if they did not. In the spring of 1842 he applies for the bankrupt law. At that time had the plaintiffs a debt against Stone that was provable? Their debt by book-account had been superseded by a higher security. Their *debt*, properly speaking, was against Rubens and Bumgardner. They had only a contingent obligation against Stone, and this, though apparently within the terms of the bankrupt law, was not within its true spirit and meaning as construed *by the Supreme Court in the cases already cited*. It is true that the cases of McMullin v. The Bank of Penn Township and of Cake v. Lewis involved a state of facts and of parties somewhat different from this case,—and I know of no case exhibiting a similar state of facts to the present,—but yet the discrepancy is not such as to render inapplicable the rule stated by Justice BELL, in Cake v. Lewis, 8 *Barr* 494.

Here we have a man undertaking to pay a sum of money for others, "in case the same cannot be recovered of them." Now this undertaking alone did "not create a debt provable under a commission." An act of bankruptcy and a final discharge have intervened since the undertaking; the creditors therefore can only resort to the bankrupt personally. Thus the rule in Cake v. Lewis fits the facts of this case, provided we assume, as I feel at liberty and constrained to do, that the indebtedness by book-account of Stone to the plaintiffs *was superseded* by the debts assigned to them, and that their only claim on Stone now is by virtue of the covenant and undertaking introduced into the assignment. The action was brought on that covenant, and the point decided is that the discharge of Stone as a bankrupt, under the circumstances stated in the special verdict, is not a defence to the plaintiffs' right to recover.

Judgment is therefore entered on the special verdict in favor of the plaintiffs in No. 30, December term 1838, for $432.68; and in No. 34, December term 1838, for plaintiffs for $434.91.

[Stone v. Miller.]

It was assigned for error:

That the court erred in entering judgment on the special verdicts for plaintiffs—and in not entering judgment for defendant.

The case was argued by *Quiggle* and *Armstrong*, for Stone, plaintiff in error.

Linn, for defendants.

The opinion of the court was delivered June 30, by

CHAMBERS, J.—Lewis Stone, on the 16th November 1841, assigned to Miller, Bowman & Co., to whom he was indebted by book-account the sum of $564.67, a promissory note of Emanuel Rubens, dated January 1, 1841, at four months, for $581.28, on which $281.28 had been paid and credited, and also a book-account which Stone held against Levi Bumgardner for $289.55. The assignment of Stone on the back of the note is under seal, and contains the following covenant: " And in case the same cannot be recovered of the within-named Emanuel Rubens, then I do promise and agree to pay the amount thereof, together with all charges thereon accruing unto said Miller, Bowman & Co.," with a like covenant in the assignment of the book-account against Bumgardner. At the time of the assignment, Mr. Beardsley, attorney of Miller, Bowman & Co., gave to Stone a written agreement "that if any thing remains over and above, after discharging our account of $564.67, of October 27, 1840, interest after six months credit against Stone, and costs of collecting the same, it shall be returned to said Stone." At the time of making the said assignment, Stone represented to Mr. Beardsley that Rubens and Bumgardner were pedlars, and were in the West, but that they would return to Clinton county in the next spring and pay the note and account; and that he would let Mr. Beardsley know when they came in. Mr. Beardsley proposed to send the claims to Pittsburg, where they sometimes came to buy goods, but Stone assured him it would do no good, as they were moving from place to place in the Western States; and that he would inform Mr. Beardsley when they should return to Clinton county. Mr. Beardsley, relying on these representations, frequently called on Stone in the spring and summer after the assignments, but never learned that Rubens or Bumgardner had come, or were within the reach of process, and there was no opportunity to collect any thing from them. On the 9th May 1842, Stone petitioned for the benefit of the bankrupt laws of the United States. On the 6th June 1842, he was decreed a bankrupt, and on the 22d November 1842 was discharged as a bankrupt of and from all debts, &c. This action is on the guaranty, to which Stone has put in the plea of bankruptcy, setting forth his discharge. The question arising on the facts stated is the effect of this discharge. The assignments by Stone to Miller, Bowman

[Stone v. Miller.]

& Co. of the note of Rubens and account of Bumgardner, with the guaranty of Stone under seal, were not *per se* an extinguishment or satisfaction of the original indebtedness of Stone. Whether a note or bond was accepted in satisfaction of the original claim is matter for the jury, and it is error in the court to decide it as matter of law: Jones v. Johnston, 3 *W. & Ser.* 276; Leas *v.* James, 10 *Ser. & R.* 307; 4 *Watts* 379, Wallace v. Foreman; Hart *v.* Bollar, 15 *Ser. & R.* 162. As the claims transferred were the indebtedness of others, accompanied with the guaranty of Stone under seal, and no agreement to receive the same in satisfaction of the original indebtedness of Stone, they are to be considered as collateral security for the original debt, and which they exceeded; and in the agreement of the attorney of Miller, Bowman & Co., made at the time, which provided that if from those assignments any thing should remain over and above after discharging Miller & Stone's account of $564.67 and costs, it was to be returned to Stone, there is evidence that such assignments were intended as a concurrent or additional security; and where that appears, they are to be treated according to that intention: Wallace v. Foreman, 4 *Watts* 380.

What was the liability of Stone on his guaranty when he became bankrupt? The assignment and guaranty had been given by him on 16th November 1841, and he assumed and was allowed to direct the measures to be taken by Miller, Bowman & Co., or their attorney, for the collection of the assigned claims. Stone induced forbearance by the assurance that Rubens and Bumgardner, who were pedlars in the West, would return to Clinton county in the next spring and pay the note and account; that to send the claims to Pittsburg for collection would do no good; that they were moving from place to place, and that when Rubens and Bumgardner returned, he would inform Mr. Beardsley, the attorney of Miller, Bowman & Co. Mr. Beardsley called on Stone frequently in the spring and summer, but never learned that these debtors had come within the reach of process. No money was collected from them.

Miller, Bowman & Co. were under obligation to use reasonable diligence to collect these claims; and it was for their advantage to do so, as creditors of Stone. Stone could not complain that they acted in conformity to his advice and suggestions. Clinton county was by him approved of as the place for collection, to which he gave assurance that these itinerant pedlars would return the next spring and pay the note and account. On such assurances and representations he restrained measures for pursuing these debtors elsewhere. After the delay and disappointment occasioned by the representations of Stone, and at his instance, as stated, he became liable to Miller, Bowman & Co. on his guaranty. He had obtained forbearance, and induced expectations by his assurances that were not realized; and by them he waived any right he may have had

[Stone v. Miller.]

to insist on measures of collection by Miller, Bowman & Co. against Rubens and Bumgardner elsewhere. At the time he was an applicant for the benefit of the bankrupt laws, Stone treated this his liability as an existing debt, for in the schedule of his debts as stated, and which was prepared by Mr. Beardsley as his attorney, Miller, Bowman & Co. are returned as creditors on the book-account and note for $564.67. Stone having received his discharge and certificate as a bankrupt under the act, on the 22d November 1842, the question is as to the effect of this discharge under the law and the facts of this case. Was the claim of Miller, Bowman & Co. provable under the bankrupt act against Stone? In the view which we have taken of the existing original indebtedness of Stone, as well as the liability arising on his guaranty of the assigned note and account, there can be no question but that his indebtedness to Miller, Bowman & Co. was provable. By the fourth section of the bankrupt law, it is provided "that a discharge and certificate, when duly granted, shall in all courts of justice be deemed a full and complete discharge of all debts, contracts, or other engagements of such bankrupt which are provable under the act." But if the liability of Stone at the time of the proceedings in bankruptcy had been conditional under his covenant of guaranty, and not fixed and determined by the vigilance of the creditor, or by the waiver of Stone the debtor, yet under the provisions of the bankrupt law and the authority of the adjudications giving it construction and effect, the claim on such covenant of guaranty would have been provable. By the fifth section of the act it is provided that "all creditors whose debts are not due and payable until a future day, all annuitants, holders of bottomry and respondentia bonds, holders of policies of insurance, sureties, endorsers, bail, or other persons having uncertain or contingent demands against such bankrupt, shall be permitted to come in and prove such debts or claims under this act, and shall have a right, when their debts and claims become absolute, to have the same allowed them." Free as this section of the law is from obscurity, yet as to its construction and effect, there has been some contrariety of decision in the State judicial tribunals. In some, too much regard would seem to have been given to the decisions of the English courts under their bankrupt act, distinguishable as it was from the bankrupt act of the United States, which was more general and comprehensive. Our statute not only provided for "debts due at a future day, sureties, endorsers and bail," but includes "all uncertain and contingent demands" as being provable. In this court, too narrow a construction was given to this act in the case of McMullin v. The Bank of Penn Township, 2 *Barr* 343, which was followed by that of Cake v. Lewis, 8 *Barr* 493. In the construction and application of this act to the facts of this case, the learned judge in the court below was governed by the cases named as of conclusive authority and

[Stone v. Miller.]

direction to him on the subject. But as the construction and effect of this bankrupt act is one of cognizance in the judicial tribunals of the United States, the question of the effect of a discharge under this act of a bankrupt against the claim of his surety who had paid after such discharge, came before the Supreme Court of the United States in the case of Mace v. Wells, 7 *Howard* 272, where it was decided that the bankrupt was discharged from his claim, which was provable under the act. As the State tribunals, in determining questions of federal cognizance, ought to adopt and be governed by the rule of construction and decision adjudicated in that tribunal of controlling authority, this court, in the cases of Fulwood v. Bushfield, and McKinney's Administrators v. Same, 2 *Harris* 90, felt bound to depart from the construction of the act before adopted in the cases referred to in 2 and 8 *Barr*, and conformed to that of the Supreme Court of the United States in Mace v. Wells, as one that bound by its conclusion and adjudication this court on the question. In the case of Fulwood v. Bushfield, Justice BELL, who delivered the opinion of the court, remarks, "Whether our adjudication can be sustained upon the difference between guarantors and sureties, strictly so called, it is unnecessary now to inquire, though for myself I may be permitted to say, I see no reason for establishing a diversity in this particular between the two species of undertaking." In this opinion we entirely concur, and that the fifth section of the bankrupt act is comprehensive enough to embrace the liability of the undertaking of the guarantor, which, though "uncertain and contingent," was provable, and consequently that the bankrupt was discharged by his certificate from all future liability under the provisions of the law and the adjudications referred to.

It is the opinion of the court that the plaintiff in these actions was barred by the certificate of bankruptcy of the defendant. Judgment reversed, and judgment entered for defendant.

County *versus* Bridenhart.

1. Though county commissioners are not bound by law to provide a residence for the sheriff whilst the jail is rebuilding, yet, if they lease a house for him, the lessor is not bound to inquire under what arrangement it was made; and if without knowledge of the illegal character of the act of the commissioners, may recover the rent from the county.

2. A lease for a year by the commissioners under their own seals and not the county seal, is binding on the county as an express contract; and if the possession be not delivered up at the end of the term, but the occupancy continued, an implied contract arises against the county. A suit *for use and occupation* however, might not lie against the county, as the occupation was not by the county, nor for its benefit.

ERROR to the Common Pleas of *Dauphin county*.
Elizabeth Bridenhart, the plaintiff below, instituted an action of

[County v. Bridenhart.]

debt against the county of Dauphin for the recovery of one year's rent, with interest, for a certain house and lot belonging to the said Elizabeth, and alleged to have been occupied and enjoyed, with her consent, by the said county of Dauphin.

The declaration in the case contained three counts: one upon an alleged lease of the premises for a year *from* April 1, 1842; another for use and occupation for same time; and another for interest accruing upon the rent claimed.

On June 1, 1841, Elizabeth Bridenhart, by her attorney, John Roberts, leased by agreement *under seal*, to David Hummel, William Orth, and Isaac Rutter, commissioners of the county of Dauphin, a house and lot of ground in Harrisburg for one year from April 1, 1841, to hold until April 1, 1842. At this time, June 1, 1841, John Fox, sheriff of said county, was in possession of said premises under a verbal agreement between the said attorney and Henry Peffer, *clerk to said county commissioners*. The object in leasing the property was to provide a dwelling-house for the sheriff and his family. The rent for the year 1841–2 was paid; the clerk to the commissioners notified the said attorney, prior to the expiration of said lease, that the commissioners did not want the house after April 1, 1842. Fox continued in possession, and this suit was brought to recover from the county rent for said premises *for the year ending April* 1, 1843.

John Roberts, Esq., affirmed:—I rented this property as agent for Mrs. Bridenhart; Mr. Peffer called on me on part of the commissioners; Mr. Fox went in after a verbal and before a written agreement; I did the writing; Peffer afterwards handed it to me signed by them; agreed from the 1st April, with the commissioners; possession was not surrendered on the 1st of April 1842; Mr. Peffer called on me in February or March 1842, said the commissioners would not want the house this year; I said, You are too late, notice should have been sent before 1st January. The commissioners of the county paid the first year's rent in the spring of 1842.

Cross-examined:—Mr. Peffer was clerk for county commissioners in spring of 1841; had the verbal arrangement with him in spring of 1841; I think I had also a talk with the commissioners; Fox went into the possession under the verbal arrangement; he said the commissioners would not rent the house; did not say the commissioners had told him to say so; they neither delivered nor offered to deliver the property to me on the 1st of April; I gave Fox no notice to quit; I had nothing to do with him; nothing passed between us on his going in or going out; I looked to the county alone as my tenant; I demanded the rent of the county, on being informed they would not pay; I demanded it as the quarterly payments fell due; I did not demand,

[County v. Bridenhart.]

that I recollect of, after they refused to pay; may have, before suit brought.

Henry Peffer testified, *inter alia*, that the commissioners agreed to pay the rent till 1st April 1842. It was understood that this payment should not affect the question of liability for the next quarter's rent.

Charge of PEARSON, President J.—The present suit is founded on a lease made by the plaintiff to the commissioners of the county of Dauphin of a house situated in this borough.

The evidence shows that when the old jail was about to be removed and a new one built, the commissioners, under a mistaken idea that they were bound to furnish a residence for the sheriff and his family, leased a house from the plaintiff for one year, commencing on the 1st of April 1841, at a rent of $125, payable quarterly.

In that lease they covenant to give up possession on the 1st of April 1842. Prior to that time, according to the evidence of Mr. Peffer, they instructed him to notify plaintiff's agent that they would not want the premises that year, and received for answer that the notice was too late, it then being some time in the month of January. The tenant of the commissioners, Mr. Fox, continued in possession till the following fall; and it does not appear that even then any restoration of the premises took place.

Under ordinary circumstances, this would amount to a continuation of the former lease for another year at the same rent: when the tenant holds over after the expiration of his term, the law implies a new lease, at the same rent, and on the same conditions.

But it is objected here that the suit cannot be sustained on the old lease. This is true, but as the narr. is lost, we cannot tell for what the party has declared, but take it for granted the special facts are set forth. He might so declare, and the counsel says that he has set forth the lease and its continuance for another year on the same terms, and also has a count for not delivering up the premises according to contract.

The defendant also says that the implied contract to continue another year on the same terms is repelled by the notice that they would not hold longer than till the 1st of April following. Notice to that effect is of no importance whatever against the act of holding over. Had the possession been delivered up on the 1st of April, the plaintiff would have had no claim, whether notice of the intention was served or not; and not being restored, the plaintiff can recover, notwithstanding the notice.

It is also urged that the commissioners transcended their power in leasing the premises at all; that they were not bound to find the sheriff a residence, and their act was void. It is very certain that they were not bound to find a residence for the sheriff, and the county auditors might have charged them with the money paid

[County v. Bridenhart.]

out; but that can make no kind of difference to the person contracting with them. The plaintiff was not bound to inquire under what arrangement with the sheriff they had agreed to furnish the house, or even for what purpose it was to be furnished; for aught she would know, they were under contract to do so; nor was she bound to inquire for what purpose her premises were rented. If informed that it was for an illegal purpose, she could not enforce the contract; but barely receiving information that it was for a residence for the sheriff, would not be sufficient, as she had a right to presume the commissioners were acting in the line of their duty, and that the contract was made for some purpose beneficial to the county.

It is also argued that the county is not bound by an implied contract, and this lease being made under the private seal of the commissioners, and not under the county seal is not obligatory, especially as the county has not had the benefit of the possession.

The mere form of the contract with a corporation is not now considered of much importance: they may be sued for torts or on verbal promises made by their accredited officers or agents, or upon implied contracts. The bargain made was binding for the first year as an express contract, and the possession not being delivered up on the 1st of April as agreed, it is binding the second year, as an implied one. If this was a suit *for use and occupation*, it would not be sustained, as the occupancy was not by the county nor for its benefit. If it appeared from the evidence that the plaintiff or her agent knew that the property was rented by the commissioners under a mistake of the law, she could not recover; or if she had notice of the purpose and object for which it was rented, she was bound to know the law, and would have no valid claim; but she was not bound to know the facts or to inquire of the commissioners under what arrangement with the sheriff they were about to rent her house, or whether it was for a purpose beneficial to the county or otherwise. On the whole facts proved, and about which there is no dispute, we are of opinion that the plaintiff is entitled to recover the rent for the year 1842, as claimed, with interest from the time it fell due.

To this charge the defendant excepted.

Verdict for plaintiff.

Error was assigned on part of the county to what the court said in reply to a point on part of defendants, as to the commissioners transcending their powers in taking a lease of the premises in question; and also to the charge.

Berryhill, for Commissioners.—The power of a county to take and hold real estate depends upon the 3d section of the act of April 15, 1834, entitled "An act relating to counties and townships."

[County *v.* Bridenhart.]

&c., sec. 3. The several counties and townships in this State shall have capacity as bodies corporate " to take and hold real estate within their respective limits, and also personal property: *Provided*, that such real and personal estate shall be taken and held only for the benefit of the inhabitants of the respective county or township, and for such objects and purposes, and none other, as county or township rates and levies are now or hereafter may be authorized by law to be laid and collected, and for such other objects and purposes as may hereafter be expressly authorized by law."

It is contended by plaintiff in error that the commissioners had no legal authority to bind the county by the contract into which they entered; that their right to hold lands is a special one, given for specified purposes, and that whenever they go beyond these, their act is not binding upon the county. It may be obligatory against them in their individual capacity, but it cannot be enforced against a corporation, when the policy of the law and its strict letter prevent the corporation from becoming a party to the contract: 16 *Ser. & R.* 286; Cooper & Grove *v.* Lampeter, 8 *Watts* 125.

The county was not bound to provide a residence for the sheriff and his family, and not being bound, an agreement for this purpose obtains no validity from the consent of the commissioners.

The contracting parties were bound to know the law, and the extent of their legal power: 16 *Ser. & R.* 286, Vankirk *v.* Clark. Mr. Roberts, the agent of plaintiff, knew the object of the lease, and his principal is affected by his knowledge.

2d. The court erred in charging that "*the bargain made was binding for the first year as an express contract; and the possession not being delivered up on the first of April as agreed, it is binding the second year as an implied one.*"

The renewal of the lease, by holding over, is repelled by the notice and inability of the county to surrender.

4th. The court erred in withdrawing the case from the jury, in charging "*that on the whole facts proved and about which there is no dispute, we are of opinion that the plaintiff is entitled to recover the rent for the year* 1842, *with interest from the time it fell due.*"

Fisher, for defendant in error.

The opinion of the court was delivered by

ROGERS, J.—Judgment affirmed, for reasons given by Judge PRARSON.

Beatty *versus* Gilmore.

1. In an action on the case to recover damages for an injury sustained by plaintiff from his falling into an area-way, or passage dug in the pavement, leading into the cellar of defendant's house, erected on a public street in Harrisburg, and through the culpable neglect of the defendant left exposed, by which the plaintiff's leg was broken, it was *held*, that if by ordinary or reasonable care on the part of the plaintiff, he might have avoided the injury, he was not entitled to recover; otherwise he was entitled to recover.
2. What shall be deemed ordinary care must depend on the circumstances of each case, of which the jury is to judge; and if there be no facts proved from which a deduction can be drawn, the presumption is against the defendant whose misconduct rendered the accident possible.
3. In such a case it is not incumbent on the plaintiff to prove the exercise by him of ordinary care to avoid the injury, but the proof of the want of it on the part of the plaintiff lies on the defendant. He who avers a fact in excuse of his own misfeasance, must prove it.
4. It was competent to prove by a witness who examined the place where the accident occurred, but who was not present *when* it occurred, that in his opinion the place was dangerous.
5. It was not error for the court to term a dangerous opening in a much frequented street, in a large town, a public nuisance.

ERROR to the Common Pleas of *Dauphin county*.

This was an action on the case wherein James A. Gilmore was plaintiff, and George Beatty was defendant, to recover damages for an injury sustained by the plaintiff from his falling into an area-way, or passage into the cellar of a house of the defendant, by which the plaintiff's leg was broken. The house referred to was a three-story brick house on Market street, in the borough of Harrisburg, the building of which was commenced in May 1849, and though the upper part of it was occupied in November 1849, the basement story was not entirely finished on the 3d of January 1850, when the accident complained of occurred. The basement room was intended for an oyster-cellar, and the area-way into which the plaintiff fell, led down into it from the street. It was not denied that the plaintiff's leg was broken by his falling into this opening, and it was contended for him that it was occasioned or arose from the negligence of the defendant, whilst the defendant alleged that the accident arose from the recklessness of the plaintiff, and his want of reasonable and proper caution. The accident happened in the night.

On the trial, after other testimony was given, on the part of the plaintiff Jacob Eby was sworn:—I live close by, on the same side; noticed the hole often; open two or three months; hole 16 feet long; near 4 feet wide; 8 or 9 feet deep; no railing around.

Proposed to ask if dangerous or not; objected to, admitted, and exception sealed.

[Beatty v. Gilmore.]

Not very dangerous, but I thought people might fall in by accident; I examined it.

Cross-examined:—A porch projected; 4 feet high; posts at the corners; goes out beyond the area; a person passing would have to turn to the left.

John H. Briggs sworn:—Noticed this place particularly the same day; we turned and looked at it; an area probably 4 feet wide, and 20 feet long, embracing the steps 7 feet deep; no protection there whatever, neither at the side or steps, to prevent falling from the pavement or stone step into the hole; turn to the right or left in coming in or going out of the door, a person would fall in; I did not particularly notice it before.

It was proposed to ask the witness, if in his opinion, from what he then saw, the place was dangerous or otherwise, and what opinion he then formed on that subject. Objected to, admitted, and exception sealed.

I was then of opinion, and still am, that it was a dangerous place.

Another witness testified that he told the defendant before the accident, that the place was dangerous, and some one might fall into it; and that he replied they must look out for themselves. That it was open from the summer till the time of the accident in January following.

Another witness testified that he told the defendant he thought the place very dangerous; defendant said he thought not, no danger of any body falling in from the pavement. I said he ought to have something over it to keep children from falling in. Defendant said he intended to have it railed; that was during the summer, as the building was going up; latter part of July.

Cross-examined:—I thought it dangerous, or would not have said so.

PEARSON, J., charged the jury, *inter alia:* The plaintiff must prove that he was injured in consequence of an unlawful act of the defendant; and if the latter avers that there was want of care on part of the plaintiff, he must prove it. The *onus probandi* rests on the person who attempts to excuse himself through want of proper care in the other.

There are then two points for consideration:

1. Was the place as made and kept up by the defendant, under all the circumstances, a public nuisance? If you believe the description given by the witnesses of both parties, and undisputed as to the nature and extent of this area, the length of time it was left open, and the publicity of the place, it being a great thoroughfare, we feel bound to declare that in point of law it did amount to a public nuisance, and that the defendant is responsible for every injury received by any man thereby in his person or his pro-

[Beatty v. Gilmore.]

perty, provided the person injured was using reasonable caution and care at the time.

2. Was the plaintiff guilty of any rashness or want of proper care in going where he did? for if he was, he cannot recover. And here you will take into consideration the light from the lamps on the out and inside of the house, and whether the glare from the windows would aid the plaintiff in seeing the danger or tend to dazzle his eyes; also, that there was snow on the ground, and what has been said by the witnesses as to the difficulty or facility of seeing, and consider from the evidence whether the plaintiff was sober or not; and if you determine in his favor, then the remaining question is as to the amount of damages he is entitled to recover, which is a question for your sound judgment and discretion.

To this charge the defendant excepted.

Verdict was rendered for plaintiff, finding $1500 damages.

The following was assigned for error:

1. The court erred in the matter contained in the bills of exception taken to the admission of the testimony of Jacob Eby and John H. Briggs. [This related to the admission in evidence of their opinions that the place was dangerous.]

2. The defendant asked the court to charge the jury that "the *onus probandi* as to proper caution, and the absence of negligence on the part of the plaintiff, rests upon plaintiff," which instruction the court refused to give, but said, "it is not necessary for the plaintiff to prove he was using all possible care; the defendant is responsible for his unlawful conduct, unless *he* can prove negligence or want of care on part of plaintiff, by direct proof or by circumstances;" and again, "if the defendant avers that there was want of care on the part of the plaintiff, he must prove it. The *onus probandi* rests on the person who attempts to excuse himself through want of proper care in the other."

3. There was error in the court instructing the jury, that in point of law, the area-way, or opening complained of, did amount to a public nuisance.

The case was argued by *McCormick*, for Beatty, plaintiff in error.

Fisher and *Kunkle*, for defendant.

The opinion of the court, filed July 3, was delivered by

BELL, J.—In Butterfield *v.* Forrester, 11 *East* 60, it was laid down that to support an action like the present, two things must concur—an obstruction or hindrance in the road or highway by the fault of the defendant, and no want of ordinary care to avoid it

[Beatty v. Gilmore.]

on the part of the plaintiff. In that case, the plaintiff had been guilty of actual misconduct in riding furiously through a street of a populous town, and it has been thought this circumstance is to be considered in every practical application of the rule there ascertained. On hearing the motion for a new trial, Mr. Justice BAILEY, before whom the cause had been tried at *Nisi Prius*, remarked, "The plaintiff was proved to be riding as fast as his horse could go, and this was through the streets of Derby. If he had used ordinary care he must have seen the obstruction, so that the accident appeared to happen *entirely from his own fault.*" By way of illustration, Lord ELLENBOROUGH said, "In cases of persons riding upon what is considered the wrong side of the road, that would not authorize another purposely to ride up against them. One person being in fault will not dispense with another's using ordinary care for himself." Of this illustration it was judiciously observed, that of the propriety of one man's abstaining from riding purposely against several others, little doubt can be entertained. What shall be deemed ordinary care to avoid a danger, the existence of which there is no reason to anticipate, does not appear to be equally clear; and it has been thought that the principle upon which the decision proceeded was, that want of care in respect of the probability of injury to others, from riding fast through a public street, is tantamount to a want of care in avoiding that which might be injurious to the party himself, for had he been riding over his own field, at the rate of twenty miles an hour, it would, probably, not be contended he was chargeable with want of care; and had his horse been killed by falling into a pit wrongfully dug there by a stranger, it could scarcely be doubted the latter would be responsible for the injury: Note to Burgess *v.* Gray, 50 *E. C. L.* 580, note a. In subsequent cases, where Butterfield *v.* Forrester was brought to view, it was held that although there may have been negligence on the part of plaintiff, yet unless he might, by the exercise of ordinary care, have avoided the consequence of the defendant's negligence, he is entitled to recover; if by ordinary care he might have avoided, then *he is the author of his own wrong:* Bridge *v.* The Grand Junction Railroad Co., 3 *Mees. & W.* 246; Davis *v.* Mann, 10 *Mees. & Welsby.* What shall be esteemed ordinary care, must of necessity, depend upon the peculiarity of each case. Hence, it was well observed in Robinson *v.* Cone, *Am. Law Jour.* for January 1851, 313, in the Supreme Court of Vermont, that, though Butterfield *v.* Forrester has been considered as furnishing the rule for charging juries in road cases, and, as a general rule, is unobjectionable, yet, in its application to the almost endless variety of incidents attending injuries of this character, perplexing doubts will spring up which the general formula is wholly insufficient to remove. The instances in which it has been generally applied are of accidents occurring during the continuance

[Beatty v. Gilmore.]

of daylight, where usually the exercise of ordinary prudential care is sufficient to avoid injury, and witnesses are commonly found to testify of the circumstances attending the catastrophe. But where, in the darkness and solitude of the night, one suffers grievous injury from the culpable commission or omission of another, the carelessness which would excuse, ought certainly to be of a very gross character, made apparent by direct or circumstantial proof. This reasonable principle seems to have been present to the mind of Lord ELLENBOROUGH, when determining Weld v. The Gas Light Co., 2 *E. C. L.* 350. Speaking of the trenches opened by the defendants to lay gas-pipes, he said that, though authorized to open the streets for this purpose, they were bound to execute it as innocently as possible, even in the daytime, and, *in the night-time*, to take especial precaution that no one shall receive an injury.

In the case before us, the culpable neglect of the defendant in suffering the continuance of what was correctly denominated a dangerous nuisance, upon one of the most frequented thoroughfares of this town, is proved by the verdict. Indeed, under the proofs, it could not well be denied, even by himself. Under this established fact, the court below, applying the rule I have stated, told the jury that, though the owner of the property had unlawfully permitted the excavation complained of to remain open to the danger of passengers, yet if the plaintiff fell into it from his own want of reasonable care, he could not recover in this action; that to sustain it, there must be the concurrence of negligence, or the commission of an unlawful act on the part of the defendant, and reasonable care exercised by the plaintiff; mutual carelessness being destructive of the title to sue. This instruction is certainly in accordance with the doctrine of the most approved authorities on this subject. Yet the plaintiff in error complains because the jury was informed that the *onus* of showing the exercise of proper care and caution by the plaintiff, was not upon him, but upon the party averring it. It was, perhaps, of little consequence, in this case, whether in this particular the court was right or wrong, since the plaintiff's fall into the area was witnessed by many persons, who testified of all the incidents attending it, and thus enabled the jury to ascertain whether the accident was fairly ascribable to his inexcusable carelessness. But it seems to us, the opinion expressed is well founded. The rule, as I have said, is, that apparent negligence on the part of the injured person puts him so far in the wrong as to bar his action. But with perhaps the exception of a single case, to be presently more particularly noticed, I have nowhere met the assertion that, in the absence of all proof on the subject, carelessness is, *prima facie*, to be presumed. Such a principle would involve intolerable hardship, by protecting the culpable party in those instances where the chance of disaster is multiplied by the obscurity of night. To say that the very fact which

[Beatty v. Gilmore.]

increases the danger shall protect him who was the author of it, by rendering the necessary proof difficult, or cutting it off altogether, seems to us too unreasonable to attract the deliberate sanction of tribunals created to watch over the interests of the community. Generally, the direction is that the jury is to judge from the surrounding circumstances, whether the plaintiff exercised the caution which ought to mark the conduct of a prudent person. Such was the instruction given here, and I may say it is in accordance with what was said in a cause tried before me, in Philadelphia, at *Nisi Prius*, where the plaintiff had fallen into an open cellar, while employed about his ordinary avocations before daylight, no one having immediately witnessed the fact. The able counsel for the defendant spoke of an appeal on other points, but finally became satisfied no error had been committed: Myers v. Snyder, *Brightly's Rep.* 489. Indeed, I know of no other guide that can be followed with a due regard to private safety. The jury is to judge from the whole case as proved. If there be no facts shown from which a deduction can be drawn, the presumption should be reasonably against him whose misconduct rendered the accident possible. The precedent in which it is supposed a different view was taken is Law v. Crombie, 12 *Pick.* 176. It was there said that the burden of proof is on the plaintiff, not only to show misconduct in the defendant, but ordinary care and diligence on his own part. The injury complained of was occasioned by a collision in open day, from injudicious driving a sleigh on the highway. The facts, too, are very meagerly reported. In support of the proposition, three adjudications are cited, neither of which go farther than the rule I have laid down; one of them indeed being Butterfield v. Forrester. Had it, however, the sanction of other authority, we should be disinclined to adopt it, as insisted for the defendant, in a case like the present. In addition to its inconvenience, and the gross injustice it might work in a variety of cases, it may be remarked it is hostile to the principle that he who avers a fact in excuse of his own misfeasance, must prove it.

The reception of Eby's and Briggs's testimony as to the dangerous character of the excavation was entirely proper. It was, in truth, rather the assertion of a fact, dependent, in some measure upon opinion, than of an abstract opinion without more. It is a species of testimony always resorted to in cases like the present. In this very instance, many witnesses so testified for the plaintiff before objection was thought of, and the defendant himself introduced a large number to testify the place was not dangerous. The books furnish many similar examples. In Jones v. Boyce, 2 *E. C. L.* 482, a witness testified, "I should have jumped off of the stage, had I been in the plaintiff's place, as the best means of avoiding the danger." In Jackson v. Follett, 3 *E. C. L.* 233, evidence was given to show that the coachman had *adopted*

[Beatty v. Gilmore.]

the most prudent course, in turning out of the middle of the road to avoid a wagon, in doing which the plaintiff's leg was broken. In Bremer *v.* Williams, 11 *E. C. L.* 437, where a coach proprietor was sued for an injury occasioned by the alleged insufficiency of the coach, a coachmaker who had repaired it was received to swear he had *every reason to believe it safe.* In Drew *v.* The New River Co., 25 *E. C. L.* 634, a case like that before us, the plaintiff proved by ten witnesses that mould and stones, taken out of a trench dug by the defendant's servants, were so laid as *to make it unsafe* for persons walking along. And finally, in Wilkes *v.* Hungerford Market, 29 *E. C. L.* 336, an action for a nuisance in stopping up a street, witnesses were called to prove that the complaint was not of the buildings the defendants were authorized to erect, but by keeping up the obstruction in *an unreasonable and unnecessary manner.* These may suffice to show the action of the court below was right, though many others of like character might be adduced.

It is unnecessary to say any thing of the third error further than that the opening in a much frequented street was properly spoken of as a public nuisance under the circumstances.

Judgment affirmed.

Faunce *versus* Burke & Gonder.

1. In a contract between the original contractors with the York & Cumberland Railroad Company and a sub-contractor with them, it was provided that the work should be subject to the supervision and control of the engineer of the Railroad Company; that he should make monthly estimates, four-fifths of which *value* to be paid to the sub-contractor, and when the work was completed, a final estimate; that the monthly and final estimates *as to the quantity, character, and value* of the work done shall be *conclusive* between the parties. And further, that if the contractor should not truly comply with his part of the agreement, or in case it should appear to the engineer that the work did not progress with sufficient speed, the other party should have power to annul the contract, and the unpaid portion of the road be forfeited by the sub-contractor, and become the property of the other party. It was *held*, that the award or decision of the engineer declaring the work forfeited was conclusive and binding on the sub-contractor. Moreover, the action of the plaintiff was in affirmance of the contract, and he cannot impeach the stipulations in it by which he obtained the contract.

2. The term *value* as used in the contract is to be distinguished from the term *price* as applied to the quantity of any of the different classes of work specified in the contract; and the engineer in making the monthly estimates, had the right to deduct from the quantity of work done, what he considered would equalize the part taken out as to quality and value with the whole work, and was not bound to allow the plaintiff for all work done, the price specified in the contract for that kind of work.

3. If the company had withheld the funds due to the sub-contractor, it would be unfair to take advantage of the forfeiture declared for want of prosecution of the work.

4. The retention of the 20 per cent. in case of forfeiture was intended as the

[Faunce v. Burke & Gonder.]

measure of reparation for the failure of the plaintiff to perform his contract, and was not intended as a mere *penalty.*

5. The payment, after the forfeiture, by one of the original contractors of the hands who had been employed by the sub-contractor, and furnishing money to carry on the work, was not a waiver of the forfeiture, and especially if he was then ignorant that the work had been forfeited.

ERROR to the Common Pleas of *Dauphin county.*
This was an action of covenant brought by Samuel Faunce *vs.* Michael Burke and Joseph Gonder, Jr.

Gonder, Burke & Co. were contractors with the York and Cumberland Railroad Company for the construction of their railroad from York to the west end of the Harrisburg Bridge. The plaintiff became a sub-contractor under them, for the graduation and masonry of section 17, from the west end of the Harrisburg Bridge, to a point a short distance below the Yellow Breeches Creek, about $2\frac{1}{2}$ miles in length, and entered into an article of agreement with them, dated the 31st of August 1849.

The action was brought against Michael Burke and Joseph Gonder, Jr., as they alone executed the agreement. Faunce, the plaintiff, entered upon the work and prosecuted it for some months, when the defendants served upon him a notice declaring his contract forfeited and annulled, for reasons therein contained, the principal of which were that the work had not progressed with sufficient speed, and that plaintiff had allowed the use of ardent spirits upon the work, contrary to his agreement. The plaintiff alleged that this abandonment of his work was fraudulent, and that the reasons given for the same as set forth in the notice were groundless and untrue, and he further alleged that in the monthly estimates of the work done by him, by the procurement of the defendants he had not been allowed a full and fair measurement of his work. He therefore claimed damages for the work unpaid for, for the loss of the profits on the job, and for his losses in the erection of shanties, preparation of tools, &c., necessary for carrying on the work. The jury found for the plaintiff $908.10.

Articles of agreement made and concluded this thirty-first day of August, in the year eighteen hundred and forty-nine, between Samuel Faunce of the first part, and Joseph Gonder, Jr., Michael Burke, and others, of the firm of Gonder, Burke & Co., of the second part. The articles were signed by Gonder, Burke & Co., under seal, and by Samuel Faunce.

In the preliminary part of the articles of agreement it was, *inter alia,* stipulated that the work shall be subject to the supervision and control of the engineer of the York and Cumberland Railroad having charge of the work for the time being, who shall have power to order any part of said work which may, in his judgment, be defectively executed, to be remedied by the party of the first part, in any way that the said engineer may direct. It being understood, nevertheless, that said parties of the first and second part

[Faunce v. Burke & Gonder.]

shall give their personal superintendence to said work, and be subject to the same obligations for the proper execution thereof as if no such power of supervision as is hereby given to said engineer was provided for. The said party of the first part shall commence said work at such points and at such times as may be designated by said engineer, and shall at all times when required apply his force as said engineer may direct.

The articles further witnessed that the said party of the first part does hereby promise and agree with the parties of the second part, that he, the said party of the first part, shall and will complete in the manner above described, on or before the first day of June, in the year eighteen hundred and fifty, (A. D. 1850,) the above described work.

In consideration whereof, the parties of the second part do hereby agree with the party of the first part, that they shall and will, for doing the work aforesaid, well and truly pay or cause to be paid to the said party of the first part, his heirs, executors, or administrators, at the rate of fifteen cents (15 cts.) per cubic yard for earth; twenty-five cents (25 cts.) per cubic yard for loose rock; forty-five cents (45 cts.) per cubic yard for solid rock; two dollars and seventy-five cents ($2.75) per perch for masonry.

The payments thus and thereby stipulated to be made, shall be made in the following manner, that is to say, during the progress of the work, and until it is completed, there shall be a monthly estimate made by said engineer, of the quantity, character, and value of the work done during the month, and since the last monthly estimate, four-fifths of which value shall be paid to the said party of the first part, at the office of the party of the second part, in the town of York; and when the said work is so completed, and accepted by the said engineer, there shall be a final estimate made of the quantity, character, and value of said work, agreeably to the terms of this agreement, when the balance appearing to be due to the said party of the first part shall be paid to him upon his giving a release, under seal, to the said parties of the second part, from all claims or demands whatsoever, growing in any manner out of this agreement; and it is expressly understood that the monthly and final estimates of said engineer, as to the quantity, character, and value of the work done during the month, or since the last monthly estimate, and at the completion of the work, shall be conclusive between the parties to this contract. And the said party of the first part further agrees with the said parties of the second part, that in case the said party of the first part shall not well and truly, from time to time, comply with and perform all the terms herein before stated and stipulated on his part, to be performed and complied with, in manner and form, and within the time before mentioned, or in case it should appear to said engineer for the time being, that the work does not progress or go on with sufficient

[Faunce v. Burke & Gonder.]

speed, or in case of interference with said work by legal proceedings, the said parties of the second part shall have power to annul this contract, if they see fit so to do, of which three days' notice in writing shall be given to said party of the first part, when the foregoing agreements on the part of the parties of the second part, and every clause and part thereof, shall become null and void, and the unpaid portion of the road, (except when the contract is annulled in consequence of legal proceedings,) shall be forfeited by the said party of the first part, and become the right and property of the said parties of the second part, and the parties of the second part shall be at liberty and have right and authority, any thing to the contrary notwithstanding, to employ and set to work, or contract with any person or persons whomsoever, in the place and stead of the said party of the first part, and without interruption or interference from the party of the first part.

The right of annulling this contract is not mutual, but may be exercised by the parties of the second part only.

The notice to Faunce, after reference to stipulations in the agreement, proceeded—This is, therefore, to notify you, that for the reasons set forth by the chief engineer, and by the engineer having charge of section No. 17, in their said notices, as well as because you, the party of the first part, have violated the stipulations made with us, the parties of the second part, as regards the use of ardent spirits, by keeping and suffering to be kept and used ardent spirits, on said works, and in the houses and shanties occupied by you and by the workmen under you, on or near the portion of said road contained within the limits of said section No. 17, and have neglected to discharge from your employment every workman, or laborer, or boarding-house keeper, who has kept and used, or who does keep and use, on said works or near it, ardent spirits. And, also, because it appears to the engineer on said section for the time being, that the work on said section does not progress or go on with sufficient speed, and for the reason that the work on said section is delayed and neglected, and not pushed in a proper and suitable manner, or as contemplated by the said agreement between the parties of the first and second part. We, the parties of the second part to the said agreement, and in pursuance of the provisions of said agreement, do hereby declare that at the expiration of three days from and after the day you shall have received this notice, that the contract and agreement made by the said party of the second part with you, the party of the first part, is hereby annulled, and every clause and part thereof shall become null and void; and the unpaid portion of the road, and the work done on the same, shall be forfeited by you, the party of the first part, and become the right and property of the said parties of the second part; and that they will proceed to employ and set to work, or contract with any person or persons, whomsoever they

[Faunce v. Burke & Gonder.]

may think proper, for the completion of said work, in the place and stead of you, the said party of the first part: And you are hereby notified, that after the expiration of said three days, you are not to interrupt or interfere with any person or persons in or upon the said section No. 17.

Various points were proposed on part of the plaintiff, some of which were as follow:—

1. The estimates made by the engineer, though in accordance with the agreement of the defendants with the York and Cumberland Railroad Company, were incorrect, and contrary to the terms of the agreement of the plaintiff with the defendant, which provided for full monthly estimates of the quantity of work done; and if such want of full estimates delayed or embarrassed the plaintiff in his work, it would be a fraud upon him to allow the defendants to annul his contract on the ground of such delay, which was occasioned by their own violation of the agreement.

2. The covenants being mutual and dependent, the defendants cannot insist on the forfeiture if the jury believe they were the first to violate the agreement.

3. The penalty or forfeiture mentioned in the agreement was intended merely to secure a performance by the plaintiff, and it would therefore be unconscionable and against equity that it should be enforced in this action.

4. The conduct of Mr. Burke in encouraging the plaintiff to proceed with his work after the notice of abandonment, his furnishing money to buy powder on the 12th November, and inducing a portion of the hands to go on and work afterwards, under a promise to see them paid, and subsequently charging the wages and expenses of these hands to plaintiff, and his payment to the plaintiff's hands afterwards, are acts that may be regarded as a waiver of the forfeiture if any such existed.

5. If the jury believe that the estimates made by the engineer of the company were incorrect, they may be entirely disregarded, and the jury shall be at liberty to judge of the quantity of work done from all the evidence in the cause.

6. Forfeitures must be strictly construed, and the words used in the agreement, "the unpaid portions of the road shall be forfeited," will not warrant the defendants in withholding the price of plaintiff's labor.

Other points were proposed on the part of defendants, some of which were:—

1. That by the words of the contract the estimates were to be made by the engineer according to the quantity, character, and value of the work done monthly, four-fifths of which estimates, as the engineer *should value them* according to the quality and character of the work done, were to be paid to the plaintiff by the de

[Faunce v. Burke & Gonder.]

fendants, and not four-fifths of the work actually done according to *the quantity*.

8. That as the contract was correctly and properly abandoned by the defendants, the plaintiff is not and was not entitled to recover the October estimate, or any part of the October estimate, and therefore the jury are not to allow the plaintiff any thing for the work remaining unpaid on said 31st day of October 1849.

PEARSON, J., answered plaintiff's points as follows:—1. By the terms of the contract, it is agreed that monthly estimates shall be made by the engineer of the company, of the quantity, character, and value of the work done during that month, or since the last estimate, four-fifths of which value are to be paid to the plaintiffs, and that monthly estimate thus made by the engineer is conclusive between the parties; and if such estimate fixed the amount to be paid, it would be final, unless the plaintiff would prove fraud, or such gross mistake as would amount to fraud; and if the amount was not fixed by the engineer, but the defendants paid according to the quality and quantity reported, and according to the price fixed in the contract, there would be no violation of the agreement on their part. If the defendants had delayed the plaintiff in his work by withholding his funds, it would be unfair to take advantage of the forfeiture declared for want of prosecuting the work with due diligence; but we are unable to see any facts in this case to justify this point.

3. The penalty of forfeiture is inserted in the present contract, in the form usual and long established and known in this State and recognised in our Supreme Court. It is presumed to be inserted with a view of compelling a rigid performance of the contract and turning the plaintiff off the work, and withholding all compensation stipulated for in the contract, should he fail on his part. Equity will often relieve against a penalty or forfeiture, but could not interfere with the action of a party in such a case as this if the plaintiff has done or omitted any act which would justify the defendant in declaring the work abandoned.

4. We can see nothing in the conduct of Mr. Burke which would relieve from the forfeiture. At the time of doing the acts referred to, there is no evidence to show he knew the work was abandoned, but, on the contrary, it is in proof he had just returned from Boston. He furnished money to carry on his own job, which he was bound to prosecute, and encouraged the hands to continue at their labor. Paying plaintiff's hands afterwards, under the circumstances detailed by Mr. Charles, is no waiver of the forfeiture, but an act of duty and justice to the laborers.

The *sixth* point is answered with defendant's *eighth*.

To the first and eighth of defendant's points he answered as follows:—1. The law is correctly stated in this point. Such is the fair and true construction of the contract.

[Faunce v. Burke & Gonder.]

Plaintiff's *sixth* and defendant's *eighth* point:—As I construe this contract, the percentage could be retained till the work was finished, and such clause is common, if not universal, in all similar contracts. If the work was not finished by plaintiff, (of which there is no pretence,) and was properly declared abandoned and forfeited, then, in the language of the article, it was "the unpaid portion of the road" which was forfeited and became the right and property of the defendants, who had the power to take possession at the expiration of the three days fixed in the contract and carry it on themselves; but there would be no forfeiture of the money then earned, excepting the retained 20 per cent., which the plaintiff would be entitled to only on the completion of the work. The engineers had a right to deduct from the quantity what they considered would equalize the part taken out as to quality and value, with the whole; and having done so, their decision is binding on both parties in the absence of fraud or plain and palpable mistake. If there is money coming to the plaintiff according to such estimates after deducting his payments, that amount he is entitled to receive; and the only difficulty in adjusting it is in distinguishing between the work done after the expiration of the three days' notice and that done prior, but subsequent to the October estimate, as the evidence shows that the plaintiff continued to labor for seven days after he should by the terms of his notice have retired from the job. The jury must judge whether that was done with the acquiescence or against the will of the defendants, and if acquiesced in by them, allow it, as they ultimately had the benefit of it, and that work was taken into the estimate. If done against their will, and in defiance of their notice and efforts to get the plaintiff off, he is not entitled to be paid for it.

Verdict for plaintiff for $908.10.

It was assigned for error, that the court erred in their answers to the first, third, fourth, and sixth points of plaintiff, and to the first and eighth points of defendants.

The case was argued by *Kunkle* and *McCormick*, for Faunce, plaintiff in error.—The court erred in their answer to the first point of the plaintiff. By the terms of the contract, the plaintiff was to receive fifteen cents per cubic yard for earth, twenty-five cents per cubic yard for loose rock, forty-five cents per cubic yard for solid rock, and two dollars and seventy-five cents per perch for masonry. He was to receive these prices for each and every yard and perch, taking the easy with the hard, the light with the heavy, and was to be estimated each month for every yard and perch of work done. It probably entered into the plaintiff's calculation, when he executed the contract, that the first part of the work would be the most profitable,

[Faunce v. Burke & Gonder.]

and that his monthly estimates of that work would furnish him the means and facilities of prosecuting more vigorously the more difficult and expensive work to be done afterwards.

The true interpretation of the words "quantity, quality, and value," in the contract is, that the estimates should include every yard and perch of work done by plaintiff during the current month at the contract price. Quantity means, in the contract, the number of yards or perches; character, the kind of work, as earth or rock; and price, the sum fixed by the contract. It could not have been intended by the parties that in addition to all the other provisions favoring the defendants, they should also have the extraordinary power of under-estimating the defendant to any extent, and then in their discretion declaring the work abandoned, and thus hold the earnings of the plaintiff.

In the first point of plaintiff, the court were also asked to charge "that if such want of full estimates delayed or embarrassed the plaintiff in his work, it would be a fraud upon him to allow the defendants to annul his contract on the ground of such delay, which was occasioned by their own violation of the agreement." To which they answered, "If the defendants had delayed the plaintiff in his work by withholding his funds, it would be unfair to take advantage of the forfeiture declared for want of prosecuting the work with due diligence; but we are unable to see any facts in this case to justify this point."

It was not the withholding of plaintiff's funds, but the short estimates of his work that the court were asked to refer to the jury as a reason for plaintiff's delay, if there was any; not the retention of any part of the amount of the monthly estimates, but that the estimate itself was of only part of the work done. The response of the court was not therefore an answer to plaintiff's point, and was calculated to mislead. The court also took from the jury the question as to whether the plaintiff's alleged delay was not occasioned by a prior violation of the contract by the defendants themselves.

The court erred in their answers to plaintiff's third and sixth points and defendant's eighth point. There is no provision in the contract authorizing defendants to retain the 20 per cent. after they annulled the contract, and it would be unjust to allow them to do so. The policy of the law does not regard penalties or forfeitures with favor: 2 *Greenleaf*, sec. 257.

The general rule in equity now is, that wherever a penalty is inserted merely to secure performance, it is not to be taken as liquidated damages; and the test by which to ascertain whether relief can be had in equity, is to consider whether compensation can be made or not: 2 *Story's Equity* 740, sec. 1314.

In the same book, sec. 1316, it is said, "In all these cases, if the party obtains his damages, he gets all that in justice he is en-

[Faunce v. Burke & Gonder.]

titled to;" and in the same section: "In reason, in conscience, in natural equity, there is no ground to say because a man has stipulated for a penalty in case of his omission to do a particular act, (the real object of the parties being the performance of the act,) that if he omits to do the act he shall suffer enormous loss, wholly disproportionate to the injury to the other party."

In sec. 1318 of same book, it is said, "Courts of equity will not suffer their jurisdiction to be evaded merely by the fact that the parties have called a sum damages, which is in fact and in intent a penalty; or because they have designedly used language and inserted provisions which are in their nature penal, and yet have endeavored to cover up their objects under other disguises:" 2 *Greenleaf* 211; *Newland on Contracts* 307.

By the terms of the contract, the defendants in certain contingencies had the power to annul the contract, but it is nowhere said in the contract that they shall retain the price of the work done as liquidated damages, but it was so considered by the court.

The loss of the defendants, if any, by the non-performance of the plaintiff could be compensated in damages, and this was a proper subject to be left to the jury.

A covenant by B that A would deliver two boat-loads of coal at different days, or in default that the covenantee might recover from B the sum of $240, was held to be a penalty, and not liquidated damages; and in the opinion of the court, "The general leaning is that such agreements shall be considered as penalties, so that a party shall recover such damages only as he shows that in justice and fairness he ought to recover:" Curry v. Larer, 7 *Barr* 470.

Where a contractor covenants with a company to construct a specific improvement at a price fixed, and subsequently, before the completion of the whole, the contract is rescinded, the most the contractor can claim in an action against the company, is compensation for the work done at the time the contract was rescinded, according to the price fixed in the contract: Monongahela Navigation Co. v. Fenlon, 4 *W. & Ser.* 205.

The court erred in their answer to the plaintiff's fourth point, in reference to the encouragement given by Burke, one of the defendants, to the plaintiff, after the notice of the abandonment, to proceed with the work, and in taking from the jury the question as to Burke's knowledge and intention in these acts.

R. J. Fisher and *J. A. Fisher*, for defendants.

The opinion of the court, filed July 3, was delivered by

CHAMBERS, J.—This action is brought by the plaintiff for the recovery of damages on account of the alleged violation of a contract between him and defendants for the construction of a section

[Faunce v. Burke & Gonder.]

of the York and Cumberland Railroad. The plaintiff was a subcontractor under the defendants, who had contracted with the York and Cumberland Railroad Company for the construction of the entire road of this company. The article of agreement between the parties contains many stipulations, specifications, and conditions; and also refers to the specifications in the contract between the defendants and the company, which are adopted as part of the contract between the parties in this suit. The plaintiff, after setting forth the agreement and specifications as the foundation of his action, avers a performance of the covenants on his part, and a willingness to perform the same; and that whilst he was, at great expense to himself, prosecuting the work according to the contract, the defendants fraudulently declared the said work abandoned, and the contract annulled, and dismissed the plaintiff from the execution and performance of his contract, and had failed to pay him for the work done according to the said contract. The defendants deny that they annulled the contract and suspended the work without cause, but for causes provided for in the contract, and which were essential to the progress of the work.

The agreement contained the stipulations and provisions that have generally, if not uniformly, formed a part of the contracts between States, corporations, and their contractors, for the construction of railroads and canals, as to the mode of conducting the work, estimating the progress of the work, and the payments to be made from time to time. A provision in this contract which was new, but no doubt proper and useful for the habits of the laborers engaged in the work, as well as for the due prosecution of it, forbid that ardent spirits be kept or used in any building occupied by the plaintiff or his workmen on or near his section, and plaintiff agreed that he would discharge any workman or laborer from his employment that did keep or use it. It was further provided that monthly estimates were to be made by the engineers of the York and Cumberland Railroad Company of the quantity, character, and value of the work done; four-fifths of which value should be paid over monthly to the plaintiff, and one-fifth retained till the work should be finally completed. It was further provided that the monthly and final estimates of the engineer as to the quantity, character, and value of the work should be final and conclusive between the parties; and that if the plaintiff should not well and faithfully perform every portion of his part of the contract, or if the engineer of the company should be of opinion that the work was not progressing as it should do, the defendants might give the plaintiff three days' notice that they had annulled the contract; and from that time the agreement was to become null and void, and they were at liberty to take possession of the work and carry it on, or give it out to others, as they might deem proper; and the unpaid portion of the road, forfeited by the plaintiff, become the right and

[Faunce v. Burke & Gonder.]

property of the defendants. Some of the provisions in this contract, at first view, seem stringent, arbitrary, and penal upon one of the parties, and without the mutuality of obligation and remedy which usually characterize contracts between individuals.

Stipulations and provisions of a like kind form a part of all contracts for the construction of canals or railroads by the parties engaged in undertakings of such character, magnitude, and public interest. It is for the advantage of the prosecution of such improvements and an accommodation to laborers and men of small capital, that the work should be given out in small sections, so as to admit of a large number of contractors, who both work and manage the labor of others on their job. It is important to the company and the public that the work should be prosecuted in all its divisions without delay; and with reasonable diligence and attention, so as to secure its completion at a time appointed. The failure of one or two contractors with their sections might suspend the use of the nearly completed improvement, with all its advantages, to the detriment of the company to an extent that the contractors could not indemnify or repair. To protect the company against such disappointments and failure of contract, it would be necessary to require from the contractors, who would also have to require from their sub-contractors, heavy and responsible security for the faithful performance of their contracts in the prosecution of the work. As such contractors are generally strangers, and men of small capital, the requirement of such security would be an obstacle that would deprive them of the opportunity of becoming contractors for the construction of parts of the road, and lessen to the company the number of competitors for the work. This is obviated by substituting the stipulations and provisions described, in place of personal security not attainable; and which stipulations might have the influence of inducing the diligent prosecution of the work, the faithful performance of the contract, and save the company from the evils of delay and from expensive and harassing litigation, that would retard the work and be onerous and ruinous to both parties. The engineers who were to make the estimates, judge of the progress of the work, and annul the contract, were not the agents of the defendants, but the officers of the company. They were familiar with such works, and from experience of the necessity of such powers to be delegated, were made the judges of the execution of the contract between the company and their contractors; and also between the principal contractors and their sub-contractors. In the execution of these powers, the engineer, by the contract of the parties, was made the absolute judge. The stipulations and provisions in this contract for its execution and termination, and the selection of the engineer as the arbitrator between the parties to adjudge finally on the contract, were all parts of the contract

[Faunce v. Burke & Gonder.]

assented to and adopted, as evidence of their intention and agreement, and as such were binding on them. Stipulations of a like character were brought before this court for its consideration in the case of the Monongahela Bridge Company v. Fenlon, 4 *Watts & S.* 205, and were sustained as legal and binding on the parties. It was there ruled that if the parties by contract appoint an arbiter to settle their difference, they are bound by his award, although he may be interested in the contract which was the subject of reference. This action by the plaintiff on the contract is in affirmance of it, and it is not for him now to impeach the stipulations to which he assented, and by which he obtained the contract. He was bound to know what he was doing when he entered into such contract; and as the court below rightly said, there was no evidence of any fraud or imposition in its procurement.

A great mass of evidence is brought up in the case by the record, and many points for the opinion of the court below were presented by the counsel on both sides. The counsel for the plaintiff in error, with commendable discretion, have confined their assignments of error in this court to a few of the many points presented to the court below, which relieves this court from a review of much of the record, and which was not material to the parties or the public.

The plaintiff has assigned for error the answer of the court to the first and sixth points presented by his counsel, and the eighth point presented by defendant, and as they are connected by the subject-matter, they will be considered together. The court did instruct the jury "that monthly estimates were to be made by the engineer of the company, of the quantity, character, and value of the work done during the month, or since the last estimate, four-fifths of which value were to be paid the plaintiff, and that monthly estimates thus made were conclusive between the parties; and if such estimate fixed the amount to be paid, it would be final, unless the plaintiff could clearly prove fraud or such gross mistake as would amount to fraud; and if the amount was not fixed by the engineer, but the defendants paid according to quality and quantity reported, and according to price fixed in the contract, there would be no violation of the agreement on their part. If the defendants had delayed the plaintiff in his work by withholding funds, it would be unfair to take advantage of the forfeiture declared for want of prosecuting the work with due diligence, but there were no facts in the cause to support this point." In answer to the sixth point the court said to the jury, "that the percentage might be retained till the work was finished, and that such clause is common, if not universal, in such contracts. If the work was unfinished and the contract annulled, the unpaid portion of the road which was forfeited became the right and property of the defendants, but there would be no forfeiture of the money then earned, excepting the 20 per cent., which the plaintiff would be entitled

[Faunce v. Burke & Gonder.]

to only on the completion of the work. The engineers had a right to deduct from the quantity what they considered would equalize the part taken out as to quality and value with the whole; and having done so, their decision was binding on both parties, in the absence of fraud or plain and palpable mistake. If there is money coming to plaintiff according to such estimates after deducting payments, that amount he is entitled to recover." Was there error or not in the answers of the court recited?

By the contract, the engineer of the company was the agent of both parties to make the monthly estimates of the quantity, character, and value of the work done during the month. This estimate would be evidence to all concerned of the progress of the work and furnish a standard for payment according to contract, four-fifths of which value were to be paid the plaintiff. The import of the term *value*, as used in the estimate as well as in the provision for the payment of four-fifths thereof, is in such a contract significant, distinguishable from the term *price*, as contended for by plaintiff, to be applied to the quantity of any of the different classes of work specified in the contract.

The plaintiff excepts to the answer of the court below in saying "that the engineers had a right to deduct from the quantity what they considered would equalize the part taken out, as to quality and value, with the whole; and having done so, their decision is binding on both parties, in the absence of fraud or plain and palpable mistake." Whereas, as the plaintiff contends, the estimate should have included every yard and perch of work done by the plaintiff, at the contract price, and that there had been a large deduction of rock excavation from plaintiff's work by the engineer to equalize what was done with that remaining to be done. Where the heavy part of such work consists of excavations of rock or clay in deep or side cuts, and which by the contract are to be paid for at a certain price per yard, we can well understand that the first part of that work, at or near the surface, could be excavated with more facility and with much less labor and expense than the lower parts of the work. The expense of taking out the lower part of the rock, more solid and less accessible, might require three times or more of labor and expense than what would be required to excavate and remove the same quantity of rock at or near the surface. As the contract price for the entire excavation of solid rock was 45 cents per cubic yard, embracing all of that description to the lowest depth of the grade as well as to the surface, it would have been an unequal estimate to have estimated the work first done at the surface at the full price for all the work of that description, and left the last half to be estimated at the same price. To have made such an estimate, from which 20 per cent. was to be retained, would have given the plaintiff more than the full value of the work done, and left a sum totally inadequate in the hands of the defendants for their indemnity against the labor of plaintiff to prosecute and complete his contract. It would have been made the interest of the plaintiff, after receiving estimates and payments according to the construction claimed by him, without regard to equalization and value, to have withdrawn from his job and leave his unfinished work, which could not, as he would be aware, be completed at any price near what he would be entitled to recover under his contract on the final estimate, the 20 per cent. retained.

The disadvantage and injustice were too great to be overlooked by those whose attention had been given to the construction of such works; and to provide against it, we suppose, the stipulation was introduced into contracts to estimate according to quantity, quality, and value. This appears to this court as reasonable, and, as a part of the contract, was valid and binding on the parties, unless, as was said by the court below in their charge, there was fraud or plain and palpable mistake. It was open to the plaintiff to prove *either*, to relieve himself from the estimates and decision of the engineer, and which would have been facts for the consideration of the jury.

It is alleged by plaintiff that his first point was not answered by the court as to the effect of short estimates on the ability of the plaintiff to progress with the work: to which the court said, that if the defendants had delayed the plaintiff in his work by withholding his funds, it would be unfair to take advantage of the forfeiture declared for want of prosecuting the work with diligence; but that they were not able to see any facts in the case to justify this point.

The short monthly estimates were only injurious to the plaintiff as they lessened the amount of his monthly payments, to enable him to prosecute his work with diligence. It was the funds alleged to be withheld that he was in need of, and the court did answer this point substantially, and as favorable to the plaintiff as if the language used by the counsel had been adopted by the court.

The answer of the court to the third point presented is also assigned for error, as to the penalty or forfeiture inserted in the contract, which the plaintiff alleges was merely to secure performance, and that it would be unconscionable and against equity that it should be enforced in this action. The court said that "equity will often relieve against a penalty and forfeiture, but would not interfere with the action of a party in such a case as this, if the plaintiff has done or omitted any act which would justify the defendants in declaring the work abandoned."

There is an inclination in courts to consider a specified sum as a penalty in contracts, as when such sum is evidently intended as a mere collateral security for the payment of a different sum which is the real debt; or where it is evidently intended to be in the nature of a mere penalty; or where it is uncertain what the parties

[Faunce v. Burke & Gonder.]

really intended; in which latter case the courts have considered and inquired into the reasonableness of the provision for the payment of liquidated damages.

The reservation of the power to annul the contract was rendered necessary by the nature of the work to be constructed and the relation of the parties, and we may say here, as was said by this court in the case of the Monongahela Navigation Company *v.* Fenlon, before cited, that without such a provision as this, plaintiff would never have obtained the contract. It was his substitute for personal security, which it is probable he could not procure. We cannot suppose that the company or their contractors for the entire work would have agreed that the execution of the several contracts, their construction, and any disagreements between the parties in the progress of the work, should be left open to innumerable suits at law, and to the determination of juries unacquainted with the work and such contracts, with all the vexation, expense, and delay attendant upon such litigation. Such a stipulation of forfeiture, under the adjudication of a competent engineer, who was supervising the work, was, we think, a reasonable provision for securing the progress of the work, and a limited indemnity to the defendants in the retained 20 per cent., to allow the employment of other contractors or laborers to complete according to contract the unfinished section. The plaintiff was allowed, under the charge of the court, to recover the balance that might be supposed to be due him exclusive of the retained 20 per cent. It is, we think, to be intended by the parties to this contract, from the peculiar nature of it and the uncertainty of damages, that the measure of reparation on the failure of plaintiff to perform, and the forfeiture as adjudged by the engineer, were the 20 per cent. retained out of the estimates. There are no words evincing an intention that the sum reserved should be considered only as a penalty. The plaintiff chose to contract with such a stipulation, and it was in his power to be relieved from it by the due prosecution of his work, and entitle himself on its completion to the whole sum payable under the contract. Why shall the law undertake to make a new agreement for the parties which they did not intend to make for themselves. They were the best judges of the amount of the injury to be sustained by the interruption of the work and the failure of plaintiff to perform his agreement—an injury uncertain and incapable of estimation until the whole work was completed, and was a proper subject for a stipulated reparation.

The parties contracted upon the faith of that mode of adjustment through the estimates of the engineer and the retention of one-fifth and the forfeiture of that unpaid portion, and it is not for the court to make a different agreement for them than what they intended and did make for themselves; or allow a jury to disregard the stipulation and reparation provided by their estimate

[Faunce v. Burke & Gonder.]

of the supposed injury, at a time subsequent to the transaction and remote from the place, unless there was fraud or palpable mistake.

The fourth error assigned in relation to the payments by Mr. Burke and the effect thereof is not sustained.

As this court is of opinion that the errors assigned are not sustained, the judgment of the Court of Common Pleas is affirmed.

Trimmer *versus* Heagy.

A deed executed before the act of 11th April 1848, by a married woman, conveying real estate to which she was entitled in fee, without her husband joining in its execution, is void. The act of 24th February 1770 requires both to join in conveyances of real estate, and its directions are imperative. *Parol* evidence that the wife executed the deed with the assent and by the direction of her husband, is not admissible. The only legitimate evidence of consent is the execution of the deed in the manner and form directed by the act of 1770.

ERROR to the Court of Common Pleas of *Adams county*.

John Trimmer, the plaintiff in error, brought this action of ejectment against Lydia Heagy and Westley Heagy, for the undivided fourth part of a tract of land containing one hundred and eight acres, in Hamilton township, Adams county, and which was in the actual possession of the defendants. Lydia Heagy, one of the defendants, was formerly the wife of Daniel Heagy, and held the land in dispute, *in her own right, in fee;* her husband being the owner of the undivided three-fourths of the tract.

Daniel Heagy becoming insolvent, his interest in this tract was sold by the sheriff of Adams county, on an execution issued on a judgment against said Daniel, and was purchased by Westley Heagy, the other defendant.

The plaintiff claimed under a deed made by Lydia Heagy, dated March 15, 1848, and which conveyed to him the land in dispute in fee, in consideration of seven hundred dollars paid in hand, and the further sum of three hundred dollars to be paid to the said Lydia Heagy, or her legal representatives, by the said John Trimmer, out of the proceeds of the sale of the said lands, whenever the same should be sold.

Daniel Heagy, the husband of Lydia Heagy, *was living at the time this deed was executed, but did not join in it.* It was executed by Lydia Heagy, the wife, alone; and her separate examination and acknowledgment were taken before a justice of the peace, in due form, as in case of a deed made by husband and wife.

Daniel Heagy, the husband, died before the institution of this suit.

Upon the trial of the cause in the court below, the plaintiff offered in evidence the deed of Lydia Heagy above mentioned, to

[Trimmer v. Heagy.]

be followed by proof that it was executed by the consent, direction, and authority of Daniel Heagy, the husband of the grantor, and for their benefit and advantage.

This was objected to, and the objection sustained by the court, and exception taken by the plaintiff.

Verdict in favor of defendants.

Error was assigned to the rejection of the testimony.

The case was argued by *Cooper*, with whom was *McCreary*, for plaintiff in error. Notwithstanding the general rule that the husband and wife must join in the conveyance of her estate, they submitted that if a married woman execute a conveyance of her estate in due form of law, it will be good against her and her heirs, after the death of her husband, unless avoided during coverture, though he do not join in the deed; especially where, as in this case, the conveyance was made with the consent and authority of the husband.

A *fine* levied by a married woman as a *feme sole* would be good as against her and her heirs, if not avoided by the husband: 2 *Kent* 151; *Sheppard's Touchstone* 7. And what she can do in England by fine, she can do here by deed: 2 *Kent* 168.

A distinction exists between the *conveyance* of a feme covert and her *agreement* to convey; the former being sustained as an actual appropriation of her estate: 2 *Black. Com.* 293, note 12; 2 *Kent* 168. It was admitted that there was no direct proof that she received the consideration money of the deed. Heacock v. Fly, 2 *Harris* 540, the wife shall not keep both money and land. The deed was executed a few days before the passage of the act of 1848. It was offered to be proved that the deed was executed with the assent of the husband.

McClean, for defendant, with whom was *Evans*.—No money passed at the execution of the deed. It was executed for a debt of the husband; but the case had not progressed that far.

By the common law, a married woman could not convey her estate; neither separately nor in conjunction with her husband. Her deed was void. This disability was an incident to her coverture, and was created for her protection: 2 *Roper on Husb. & W.* 95; 2 *Kent's Com.* 152. And she could not waive this protection of the law: per GIBSON, J., Withers v. Baird, 7 *Watts* 228.

Upon the invention of fines and recoveries, the presence of the husband and his participation in the proceedings were made essential to secure to the wife the protection against imposition which the common law guarantied to her; and she was not competent to levy a fine without the concurrence of her husband; and therefore *if it appeared by the record* of a fine that it was levied by a

[Trimmer v. Heagy.]

married woman *alone*, it was voidable for error in the record, and would not bind her or her heirs: 1 *Roper* 141, 32 *Law Lib.* 93; 1 *Shep. Touch. by Preston* 7; 30 *Law Lib.* 32; *Cruise*, tit. *Fine*, ch. 5, sec. 12.

Yet if she did levy a fine *as a feme sole*, not disclosing the fact of her coverture on the record, and the fine was not avoided by her husband, it bound her and her heirs, as they were estopped from averring *against the record* that she was a *feme covert: Id.* But the court would not admit of such a fine if apprized that the conusor was a married woman: 1 *Roper* 141-2, 562.

In some instances married women were permitted, under peculiar circumstances, to levy fines alone, as if unmarried; the court giving no validity thereto, but leaving to the husband and wife the right of avoiding them: 1 *Roper* 142; 1 *Shep. Touch.* 7; *Cruise*, tit. *Fine*, ch. 5, sec. 14, 15, 16. As for perfecting a sale made by husband and wife: *Id.* By particular custom, 1 *Roper* 140; and (by statute) where the husband's concurrence could not be procured: 2 *Kent's Com.* 151, in note.

In lieu of the conveyance by fine, a more convenient and less expensive mode is now provided in England, and in this State, by statute, but without dispensing with any of the guards which were thrown around the married woman. The husband is required *to join* with his wife in the conveyance of land—his assent must appear on the face of the instrument; and in that way be shown his presence for her protection; and "the weight of authority (says Chancellor KENT) would seem to be in favor of the existence of a general rule of law *that the husband must be a party to the conveyance:*" 2 *Kent's Com.* 152.

Our statute in Pennsylvania, of 24th February 1770, provides that the *husband and wife* may make, seal, deliver, and execute any grant, bargain and sale, &c., and then acknowledge the same before a proper officer. To this provision there is no exception in the statute, and we think none can be found to exist by usage or otherwise. Justice KENT, in his collection of exceptions in the States, seems to have found none in Pennsylvania; and he concludes his review of the American law with the remark, that the general rule is as already stated, namely, that the husband *must show his concurrence* to the wife's conveyance, *by becoming a party to the deed:* 2 *Kent* 154.

Her power to convey being a creature of statute law, the prescribed *forms* and solemnities must be pursued: Elliott *v.* Piersol, 1 *Peters's Rep.* 338; 10 *Ser. & R.* 447, DUNCAN, J., in West *v.* West.

"She can waive nothing and consent to nothing, except in the way pointed out by law:" Per GIBSON, J., Withers *v.* Baird, 7 *Watts* 228.

In Willing *v.* Peters, at *Nisi Prius*, 7 *Barr* 288, Mr. Justice KENNEDY instructed the jury that "the deed of the plaintiff was

[Trimmer v. Heagy.]

a nullity, not operating even by way of estoppel, since she was covert *and her husband did not join in the conveyance.*"

Upon these principles the separate deeds of married women, when not brought under the settled exceptions, have been held to be void: Fowler v. Shearer, 7 *Mass. Rep.* 14; Andrews v. Hoover, 13 *id.* 476; Jackson v. Vanderheyder, 17 *Johns. Rep.* 168; and 2 *Bac. Abr.* tit. *Baron and Feme*, 49, note by Bouvier.

The plaintiff refers to the distinction between the *conveyance* of a *feme covert*, and her *agreement* to *convey*. We do not understand what deduction the plaintiff makes from it in his own favor; but we submit that this distinction and the settled law in this respect upon it, afford a decisive argument for the defendant in this case. On her behalf it is contended that her rights are *strictissimi juris;* and the law settled upon this distinction is, that her *conveyance*, if made according to the requisitions and forms of the statute, would bind her, and that any *agreement* of hers *to convey*, not being embraced by the statute, would be void.

The opinion of the court, filed July 3, was delivered by

ROGERS, J.—At the common law, a conveyance of her real estate by a married woman is void. A substitute however of a deed of conveyance, by fine, prevails in most of the States of the Union, and in this. By these acts, for the most part, the husband is wisely required to join with the wife in the conveyance, in order that his assent may appear on the face of the deed, and to show he was present to protect her from imposition. The weight of authority, as Chancellor KENT remarks, would seem to be in favor of the existence of a general rule of law, that the husband *must* be a party to the conveyance or release: 2 *Kent's Com.* 152. Such a rule is founded on sound principles arising from the relation of husband and wife. It is necessary, to avoid family discord and to protect her interests. There are exceptions, it is true, in some of the States; New Hampshire, for example; but I am happy to say Pennsylvania is not one of them. In the act of 24th February 1770, in order, as is expressed in the act, to establish a mode by which husband and wife may hereafter convey the estate of the wife, it is declared that whenever they are inclined to dispose of her real estate, it may be done by deed or conveyance, executed by husband and wife in a manner particularly described in the act. That the mode pointed out is imperative, is not only apparent from the language used in the enactment, but it is ruled to be so by Mr. Justice KENNEDY, in Willing v. Peters, 7 *Barr* 287. In that case it was ruled at *Nisi Prius*, by that distinguished judge, that a release of dower by a *feme covert*, whose husband does not join in the deed, is void, though the deed was separately acknowledged in due form. The doctrine established in Willing v. Peters was not disputed then, nor has it ever

[Trimmer *v.* Heagy.]

to my knowledge been questioned. Indeed it would be difficult to raise a plausible objection in the face of the act of 1770. The case is sought to be supported on the ground of a peculiar equity in the purchaser; but it is one of those bastard kinds of equities which the bar of this State are too prone to invoke. The only equity to which attention can be paid by a court governed by rules, is one founded on precedent and regulated by well-defined principles. Without paying the least regard to the conflicting statements of counsel, it sufficiently appears that the wife's real estate was taken to pay the debts of the husband, an equity which no court ever has or ever will recognise to deprive a wife of her inheritance.

The parol evidence that the deed was executed with the consent, direction, and authority of the husband, was properly excluded. The only legitimate evidence of consent is the execution of the deed in the manner and form plainly pointed out in the act of the 24th February 1770.

What effect the act of the 11th April 1848, securing the rights of married women, may have on this question, we leave to the wisdom of our successors in office.

Judgment affirmed.

Zerbe *versus* Miller.

1. A conveyance of real estate by a father to his son, intended to delay and hinder creditors, is fraudulent as to creditors, whether the consideration amount to the value of the land sold or not.

2. If the conveyance to the son be fraudulent as to creditors, the son cannot set up an outstanding title to the land in another, against the purchaser at sheriff's sale, of the title of the father, who was in possession at the time of the sheriff's sale.

3. Evidence of the value of the land in dispute, without specification as to time, or of its value at the time of the trial, the conveyance in question having been made years before, is not admissible.

4. When a conveyance is impeached on the ground of fraud, considerable latitude is allowable in the admission of evidence; the question is whether the evidence can throw light on the transaction, or whether it is irrelevant.

5. It is incumbent on a party who attempts to deprive the adverse party of a claim apparently due him, and evidenced by a proper voucher, to support his allegation by proof, however slight it may be; if none such be given, the court are not to reject the evidence of the claim, or to submit the question of its invalidity to the jury.

6. A son working after he is of age for his father does not thereby acquire a right of action against his father, unless there has been a previous contract or agreement to pay on the part of the father.

7. An assignment that the court erred in their charge to the jury generally, (without any specification,) is not a proper assignment.

ERROR to the Common Pleas of *Berks county*.

This was an action of ejectment by Samuel, John, and Henry Miller against Henry Zerbe and John Zerbe, for a tract of

[Zerbe v. Miller.]

land, situate in Tulpehocken township, Berks county. It was sold as the property of John Zerbe, on a judgment in favor of John Miller *vs.* John Zerbe. Miller had suit brought upon a bond of John Zerbe, in which an award was had December 7th, 1844, for $3364.96; and an appeal being entered by defendant, judgment was entered for $3553.78, on March 19th, 1846. *Venditioni exponas* issued, and was returned sold to Samuel Miller, John Miller, and Henry Miller, for $60. Deed executed by sheriff.

On the trial of the ejectment, on the part of the plaintiffs was given in evidence the record of the proceedings on the bond above referred to, and evidence of the value of the land.

On the part of the defendants was offered, 1. Deed from David Moyer to John and Jacob Zerbe for the land in question, dated April 3d, 1816, for eighty-two acres and one hundred and ten perches, exact measure.

2. Will of Jacob Zerbe, dated March 31, 1832, and proved May 21, 1833, with letters testamentary to Catharine Zerbe, John Zerbe, and David Brumbach, with power to sell for the payment of debts.

3. Deed, dated April 27, 1844, from John Zerbe to Augustus Zerbe, with names of the executors, John Zerbe and David Brumbach, in the premises of the deed, but signed only by John Zerbe, for a moiety of the same land, and for a consideration of $413.20, and subject to the purchase-money due the commonwealth, and cost of patenting.

4. November 29, 1844, deed of assignment endorsed, from Augustus Zerbe and wife to John Zerbe, for the same consideration as above.

5. Deed, dated November 30, 1844, for the whole of the said land, and for a consideration expressed of $1157.62½.

It was admitted that the said Catharine Zerbe and David Brumbach are still living.

Notice was given by Henry Zerbe, at the sheriff's sale, that the land was his, and not John Zerbe's.

Daniel Whiskyman, testified:—I knew this land very well thirteen years ago, and see it almost every year. It has a two-story frame house and Sweitzer barn. I have not been on the land lately. It may have been worth thirty or forty dollars per acre in 1844–5. It has a good barn and house.

Cross-examined:—I passed the land this summer, but was not on it. It is twelve years since I was on the land; it has a gravel bottom; is hilly and broken. I am not a farmer, but a miller, and work now at Jonathan Miller's. I do not own any land, but *once owned a piece of eighty acres*, in Tulpehocken, *about one mile from this land*. I sold that land; I expect it was not as good as Henry's; there was an old house and old barn on it. May be the meadows on my place were better than on Zerbe's;

[Zerbe v. Miller.]

some part of the land was as good as Zerbe's. I think, take it altogether, it was not better than Zerbe's; Zerbe's was better than mine; the difference was not much; one was like the other.

The witness was then asked the value of this land; to which question, so proposed, the said plaintiffs objected, because not directed to any time, and the court sustained the objection; to which decision of the court the said defendants then and there excepted. This was the first bill of exceptions.

Michael Kalbach, sworn:—I am a subscribing witness to this bond and deed, and saw them executed in Esquire Vanderslice's office, in Womelsdorff; none of the young Zerbes were there that I saw; I think I witnessed other deeds at the same time, but will not be positive; it was all done the same day; I don't know who took the papers away; there was no money paid that I saw.

Cross-examined:—I did not see the papers delivered; am not positive there were any persons there that day but these two.

The plaintiff then offered in evidence the same bond from John Zerbe to Andrew and Henry Zerbe, dated November 30, 1844, for $2400, conditioned for the payment of $1200 on December 1, 1844, together with record of judgment, execution, and proceedings on said bond. To this offer defendants objected, but the court overruled the objection; and exception on part of defendant. This was the second bill.

John Pottinger, sworn, and cross-examined:—My judgment against John Zerbe was $29.23; this Henry paid me at the adjourned court, March 1846. Defendants then proposed to ask the witness if Henry did not work for his father over age, and how long; which question was objected to and overruled, and bill of exceptions sealed. This was the third bill.

Other evidence being given, there was also given in evidence a deed dated November 30, 1844, from John Zerbe and wife to Peter Laucks, for the mill tract and six acres, for the consideration of $1000, subject to Miller's mortgage debt; acknowledged same day before Vanderslice, and recorded December 2, 1844. Mortgage bond before referred to, and another bond from Mr. Zerbe to John Miller, £1078, given in evidence.

The charge of GORDON, President J., was as follows:—

In the year 1844, John Zerbe, one of the defendants in this suit, was the owner of a mill and six acres of land in Berks county, and also of the tract of land in dispute here. He was largely indebted to different individuals, and among them to John Miller, the father of the plaintiffs, in an amount which, when ascertained by judgment, exceeded nine thousand three hundred dollars. *For the portion of his debt,* John Miller held the bond of John Zerbe for £1222, *secured by mortgage* on the mill and six acres, and for the residue a bond of £1078. On the 30th day of November 1844, John Zerbe conveyed *the tract in dispute* (stated in one of the deeds

[Zerbe v. Miller.]

given in evidence here to be eighty-two acres one hundred and ten perches) to his son Henry Zerbe, the other defendant, for the sum of eleven hundred and fifty-seven dollars and sixty-two and a half cents, subject to the payment of the balance of the purchase-money due to the commonwealth. There is no evidence in the cause showing how much of the purchase-money, if any, remained due to the commonwealth. On the same day, John Zerbe executed to his sons, Andrew Zerbe and Henry Zerbe, a judgment bond for $1200, on which judgment was entered in this county; and on an execution issued upon it, the personal property of John Zerbe was levied upon and sold by the sheriff.

On the same 30th day of November 1844, John Zerbe conveyed the mill and six acres of land to Peter Laucks, for the consideration of one thousand dollars, subject to the payment of the mortgage debt due to John Miller. On the sixth of December 1844, John Miller instituted actions on his bonds against John Zerbe, in this court, and obtained judgments thereon. Executions were issued on these judgments, returnable to August term 1846, on one of which the mill property was sold to the plaintiffs in this action, for $4600, about twelve hundred dollars less than the amount of the execution; and on the other, *the property in dispute* was sold likewise to the plaintiffs for sixty dollars.

The plaintiffs having obtained the sheriff's deed, have brought this action of ejectment to recover possession of the land.

The defendants contend that the plaintiffs have no right to recover, because they say that the title and interest of John Zerbe had passed from him to his son, Henry Zerbe, before the judgment of John Miller, on which the land was sold, was obtained, and that the property was at the time of entering the judgment the property of Henry Zerbe, and not liable to be sold on any judgment against John.

As to one undivided moiety of the land, they defend on another ground, alleging that although claimed by John Zerbe and sold by him to his son, Henry Zerbe, yet it never was his in fact, having been at one time the property of his brother, Jacob Zerbe, after whose death it was so informally and insufficiently conveyed by his executors that no title passed by the conveyance, but that the same remained in the heirs or legal representatives of Jacob Zerbe, and remains so still.

The court will dispose of the latter objection first, in order to leave untrammelled for your consideration the question of fraud, which is the principal question to be determined in this action. The defendants have given in evidence a conveyance of the land to John and Jacob Zerbe, dated in 1816, and the will of Jacob Zerbe, proved May 21st, 1833, giving power to the executors to sell his land in Schuylkill county, and also the land of which he owned the half, for the payment of his debts. The executors

[Zerbe v. Miller.]

were Catharine Zerbe, John Zerbe, and David Brumbach, to all of whom letters testamentary were issued.

They have produced a deed purporting to be the deed of John Zerbe and David Brumbach, executors to Augustus Zerbe, for one moiety of the land for the consideration of $413.24; but it is executed *by John Zerbe alone*. Endorsed upon this deed is an assignment by Augustus Zerbe to John Zerbe, of the same interest for the same consideration. Defendants have also shown the deed for the land from John Zerbe to his son Henry, already adverted to. They contend that when a power is committed to several persons to perform an act of a private nature, all those persons must unite in its exercise; and the law is undoubtedly so. But in this case we find John Zerbe on this land, which had been thus sold in 1834–'5, after the time of conveyance to Augustus Zerbe, and from Augustus to him, and from that time forward in possession of it by himself and his family, and in 1844 asserting ownership and exercising the right to convey it as his own. We have in evidence the administration account of John Zerbe and David Brumbach, showing that the purchase-money of this land had been received and accounted for by them. We have the distribution of the balance of the account, consisting of the purchase-money of this land, by auditors appointed by the Orphans' Court, among the creditors of Jacob Zerbe, who were *cestui que trusts* of the fund, and could by the receipt of it confirm the title to the land defectively conveyed; and we have direct proof of the payment of a portion of it to one of those creditors, and the declaration of John Zerbe, while the owner of the land, that he had paid nearly the whole of them. There is no evidence here that the heirs or creditors of Jacob Zerbe have ever made any claim to this land, and we are of opinion, that in the facts before us, there is evidence enough of title to the whole tract in John Zerbe, to entitle the plaintiffs to recover the whole of his property, if there be no other difficulty in their way.

The plaintiffs allege that the conveyance of John Zerbe to his son Henry Zerbe, dated 30th November 1844, was made to delay, hinder, and defraud the creditors of the grantor, of whom John Miller was one, and that the conveyance as against him was utterly void; and that as purchasers at a sale made by the sheriff on the judgment of John Miller against John Zerbe, they have a right to recover the property from John Zerbe and his fraudulent grantee. By the laws of Pennsylvania, every conveyance made to or for the intent or purpose of delaying, hindering, or defrauding creditors, is deemed as against those creditors to be utterly void. A man cannot lawfully give away his property, or any considerable portion of it, without retaining sufficient, without all doubt or question, to satisfy his just debts. If a person who is indebted sell and convey his property for a grossly inadequate consideration, without retaining sufficient to pay his debts, this would be a badge of fraud from which a fraudulent intent might be inferred, and the conveyance declared to be null and void as against his creditors. And even if the consideration be adequate, yet if the intent were to delay, hinder, and defraud creditors, and prevent them from taking the land for the payment of their debts, and this intent were known to the grantee, such conveyance would be null and void as against the creditors. Where the question turns on fraudulent intent deducible from want of or inadequacy of consideration, the important point is, the consideration at the time of the conveyance, which, if fraudulent when made, cannot be aided by subsequent payments not contracted for in the arrangement between the grantor and grantee. When the conveyance is in fraud of creditors, it is void as to the creditors, and they may take the property in execution and sell it as the property of the grantor, which is the usual course adopted for the purpose of trying the question of fraud—a course which has been resorted to in the case before us. The plaintiffs allege that the fraudulent intent of this conveyance is obvious from the circumstances of the case. They say that it is proved by the evidence, that the grantee, Henry Zerbe, was a man of no property; that the sale was suspicious on account of the relation of father and son between the parties; that the suspicion of fraud is increased by the confession of judgment to the grantor's sons, at or about the same time; that the consideration for the conveyance was grossly inadequate; that by the sale to Peter Laucks, at the same time, John Zerbe retained nothing in his hands by which his creditors could be paid; that the appeals from the awards obtained by John Miller against John Zerbe were intended for delay merely, in order to retain the property and derive from it the means of discharging some debts, and thereby give color to the pretence that the consideration of the conveyance was an engagement by the grantee to pay the grantor's debts; that in point of fact, John Zerbe was not at all indebted to his son, Henry Zerbe, at the time of the conveyance to him; that such of the debts of John Zerbe as were paid, were not in fact paid by Henry Zerbe, but by John Zerbe, or with money furnished by him; that the evidence does not prove any undertaking by Henry to pay the debts of John Zerbe, the grantor; that the declarations of John and Henry Zerbe show a fraudulent design on the part of John to divest himself of his property, so as to protect it from the executions of his creditors, and leave nothing in his hands by means of which the creditors could obtain satisfaction of their claims. You are the judges of the credit to be given to the witnesses whose testimony you have heard. It is for you to say what the testimony proves, and to reconcile it, if you can, where part of it contradicts or is in conflict with other parts.

The defendants' counsel contends that the mere fact of indebted-

[Zerbe v. Miller.]

ness on the part of a grantor at the date of conveyance, is no badge of evidence of fraud; and in this the court are of opinion that they are correct in stating the law. They further say that a voluntary conveyance, though made to the son of the grantor when such grantor is in debt, is not of itself fraudulent, provided sufficient property be retained by the grantor, beyond all doubt or question, to pay his debts and satisfy all just claims against him. The law is so. They contend that the sale of this land, by John Zerbe to his son Henry, was a fair and valid transaction, being made for a valuable and adequate consideration, and that John Zerbe, when he conveyed this land to Henry, retained property in his hands abundantly sufficient to pay all his debts. This is for your decision. You have heard the evidence as to the value of the property and the price agreed to be paid for it by Henry, and the manner in which he was to pay it, and also the evidence as to the value of the mill and six acres which were retained by John Zerbe. It appears that the mill and six acres were conveyed to Peter Laucks, by deed dated the same day with the deed to Henry, for the land in dispute, for the sum of one thousand dollars, subject to the payment of the mortgage debt due to John Miller. The mortgage debt was not the whole claim of John Miller against John Zerbe. He had beside a bond for £1078. It has been said here in argument, that this bond was for interest due on John Miller's mortgage, and might be regarded as included in the mortgage debt, subject to which the sale was made to Laucks. There is no evidence in this cause that the bond in question was for the interest due on the mortgage, which renders it unnecessary to decide whether it was included in the lien of the mortgage or not. It is for you to say, from all the evidence in the cause, whether the sale and conveyance to Henry Zerbe, by his father, John Zerbe, on the 30th day of November 1844, was made with the intent and purpose to delay, hinder, or defraud the creditors of John Zerbe or not. If you shall be of opinion that it was so made, your verdict should be rendered in favor of the plaintiffs; if otherwise, then for the defendants. The plaintiffs having given notice that they intend to claim damages for the mesne profits, you will, in case you find in their favor, find also the amount of damages for mesne profits, since their title to the land accrued by the delivery of the sheriff's deed to them.

To this charge the defendants, by their counsel, excepted.

A verdict was rendered for the plaintiffs, and damages assessed.

It was assigned for error, *inter alia*, that the court below erred in the following particulars:—1. In rejecting the evidence offered as in the first bill of exceptions. 2. In admitting the evidence contained in the second bill of exceptions. 3. In rejecting the evidence offered, as in the third bill of exceptions. 8. In charging that if the consideration of the sale was adequate, yet if the intent

[Zerbe v. Miller.]

was to hinder and delay creditors, and this intent was known to the grantee, the deed would be void as to creditors. 9. In *stating* the argument in favor of the plaintiffs below, the court states arguments and suggestions in support of which there was no evidence. 10. In charging that there was no evidence that the mortgage debt to John Miller included the whole debt to John Miller.

The case was argued by *Hoffman* and *N. Strong*, for plaintiffs in error.

Smith, for defendants.

The opinion of the court, filed July 3, was delivered by

COULTER, J.—There is nothing in the first bill of exceptions. The witness said he had not been on the land for twelve years, although he had once passed by it during that time.

The question as to the value of the land might have been pertinent to the matter in issue, if directed to the point of time when the matters in issue occurred; but as it was not so directed, but was indefinite as to time, a direct answer might have misled the jury instead of giving them exact information proper for their guidance. The value of the land might have been ambulatory, owing to surrounding circumstances, and what it was worth at the time of the trial might not have been a correct criterion of its value at the time of the transaction to be elucidated. The question was therefore properly overruled.

The bond of John Zerbe to Andrew and Henry Zerbe was properly admitted in evidence.

Fraud assumes so many shapes, disguises, and subterfuges, that courts always afford a latitude of evidence, by admitting any thing at all connected with the transaction in which it is alleged to exist, in order that it may be detected and exposed, for the safety of society and the benefit of morals. This latitude can never injure an honest man. Covin and deceit avoid the light; but fair dealing invites investigation. The only true test is whether the evidence can throw light on the transaction, or whether it is altogether irrelevant.

This evidence was relevant. It tended to show that the father, by means of deeds and judgments executed about the same time, was stripping himself, not only of his real, but also of his personal property, without consideration paid, in favor of his sons. Men do not act without motive. And when the father gave this bond to his son, and he entered it on the record, took out execution, and sold all his father's personal property, the natural inquiry is, for what was it done? Sons selling out their father! The old man had made a deed to one of them, to wit, Henry, on the same day, for the land in dispute. What was the object of this transfer of his land, and confession of this judgment, by means of which his per-

[Zerbe *v.* Miller.]

sonal property was swept from him? On the same day he had conveyed the mill property to Laucks, subject to the mortgage to Miller. These things being out of the usual course of dealing, and wearing a sinister aspect, afforded a platform on which the judgment could rest; and conduced to establish, with other facts in the cause, that the design was to defraud Miller, and cover up the estate safe from his debt. The evidence was properly admitted.

It has been often ruled by this court, that a son who works for his father after he is 21 years of age, does not thereby establish a debt against his father, unless there has been a previous contract or assumpsit to pay on the part of the father. The evidence rejected, therefore, did not conduce to prove any matter material to the defendant's case. There was no error, therefore, in overruling it.

The fourth error assigned, to wit, that the court erred in their charge to the jury generally, is no assignment of error at all. If the party cannot put his finger upon some error and specify it, we take it for granted that he cannot find any.

The fifth, sixth, and seventh assignments of error relate to the title of Jacob Zerbe. But the court committed no error on that subject. John Zerbe went on this land under a title which, if it can be disturbed at all, must be done by the heirs of *Jacob* Zerbe. But they object not to it. John Zerbe has been long in possession, claimed the land as his own, publicly, notoriously exercised every act of ownership, and had paid at least a considerable portion, if not all, the purchase-money. If then the deed under which he claimed was defective, about which it is not necessary to say any thing, still that circumstance could avail the defendants nothing, because John Zerbe had a title and possession which could be bound by judgment and sold. It was bound, and was sold by due process of law, and the plaintiffs purchased; and they hold the right of John Zerbe, in defiance of all that the alienee of John Zerbe or he himself can do, if the deed was fraudulent against creditors. It lies not in the mouths of the defendants to say that the title of John Zerbe was defective, for the purpose of defeating creditors, and thus preserving the land for themselves. That would be making the law itself to be subservient to their covinous design. But the law is the common parent of all, which all are bound to reverence and respect, and which deals out justice with an even hand. It never helps one man to cheat another. It is to be observed that the defendants below are John Zerbe himself, who was still in possession, and his son Henry, his alienee. If the deed from John Zerbe to his *son* Henry was fraudulent as against the creditors, they are not in that category which would enable them to set up an outstanding title against the purchaser of John Zerbe's interest in the land. Henry Zerbe claims under John Zerbe, whose title was sold, and John Zerbe himself was in possession at the

[Zerbe v. Miller.]

time of the sale by the sheriff, had claimed title, and sold that title to his son Henry. The real question here is whether that sale to Henry was in fraud of his creditors. If it was, they must yield up possession to the purchaser at sheriff's sale. It is, perhaps, not proper here to pronounce upon the title of the creditors or heirs of Jacob Zerbe, who are not parties. But it seems unavoidable to say that from all the facts that appear in this case, their claim upon the land, if they should ever make one, would be hazardous and doubtful in the extreme. The court below put this part of the case upon correct ground. No principle can be better established than that which forbids courts to submit a fact to a jury without some spark of evidence to sustain it. It will not do to allow them to guess at an alleged fact without any evidence whatever. That would not do in a court of justice; no man would then be safe in his cause. The bond for £1078 on its face contains no evidence whatever that it was for interest due on the mortgage. I have looked over the testimony in the cause in vain for any gleam of evidence that it was given on that account. It is the duty of a party who alleges a fact that would deprive his adversary of a sum apparently due to him, and evidenced by proper vouchers, to give some testimony of that fact, be it ever so slight, before submitting it to the jury. We therefore perceive no error in the manner in which that subject was handled by the court below.

The consideration of a sale may amount to the value of the land sold, and yet the sale be fraudulent as against creditors, because such sale may delay, hinder, and obstruct them in the collection of their debts. And a sale for value may not only delay and hinder them, but may also be made for that very purpose and intent. Thus a man may sell and receive bonds at long payments, and thus delay and hinder creditors. It is the intent that gives character to the transaction; and when the act corresponds with the intent, and both concur in delaying and hindering creditors, the deed is void. Where the purchaser had no knowledge of the intent, and was not a guilty party to the transaction, nor implicated in it by the peculiar circumstances, then if he, *bona fide*, actually paid full value, he would be protected. But he must prove *actual payment*. The receipt on the deed and giving bonds are not evidence of *actual payment:* Roger v. Hall, 4 *Watts* 359; Geiger v. Welsh, 1 *Rawle* 349. It was not error therefore in the court below to say, in the course of their charge, " and even if the consideration was adequate, yet if the intent were to delay, hinder, and defraud creditors, and prevent them from taking the land in payment of their debts, and this intent were known to the grantee, such conveyance would be void as against the creditors.' And the reason that there is no error is because in such case the purchaser would be a participant in the fraud, and could not be in the light of an *innocent* purchaser, which affords the real ground

[Zerbe *v.* Miller.]

of protection in all cases where creditors are attempted to be defrauded. But where the purchaser is conusant of the fraud, he is helping a debtor to cheat his creditors ; and after the deed done they might among them dispose of the money and bonds as they pleased. If that would defeat the statute of Elizabeth, it would in effect and in practice make it of no value : Ashmead *v.* Hean & Moulfair, 1 *Harris* 584 ; 8 *Johnston* 451 ; 7 *Barr* 264 ; Kepner *v.* Buckhart, 5 *Barr* 478.

The great question in the case is whether the deed to Henry Zerbe, by his father John Zerbe, was made with intent to defraud his creditors. The case is one of a class. Many of a like kind have been adjudicated in this court, and this one is perhaps as rank in all its facts and circumstances and elements of error as any of them. Johnston *v.* Harvey, 2 *Pa. Rep.* 92 ; Geiger *v.* Welsh, 1 *Rawle* 349, which is a very strong case, and in which it was ruled that a deed made by a father to his sons in consideration of their supporting him during his life, although the consideration was sufficient between themselves, that nevertheless the deed was void as against creditors. In Johnston *v.* Harvey the consideration was to pay off certain judgments on record, and to support the grantor and wife during life ; yet the deed was held void because there were debts due by him not on record. And in that case a purchaser from the sons was held to have no better title than the sons themselves, because the terms of the deed to the sons gave sufficient forewarning to the purchasers that there were creditors unprovided for in the sale.

In this case the court did not pronounce the deed to be a *legal* fraud as regarded creditors, but left it to the jury as a question of *actual* fraud ; and this was as favorable as the defendants below could ask. The court instructed the jury as follows :—" It is for you to say, from all the evidence in the cause, whether the sale and conveyance from John Zerbe to his son Henry Zerbe, on the 30th November 1844, was made with intent and purpose to delay, hinder, or defraud the creditors of John Zerbe or not. If you shall be of opinion that it was so made, your verdict should be in favor of the plaintiffs ; if otherwise, then for the defendants." The verdict was for the plaintiffs, and the jury found the fraud. It is unnecessary for me to recapitulate the facts or dwell upon them, for, as a question of *actual* fraud, it belonged to the jury, and they have put their seal upon it. I may say that we are bound to administer established principles so as to promote honesty and fair dealing, and not encourage covinous contrivances, intended to defeat honest creditors. Such cases never come into court without the dark frown of justice upon them.

Judgment affirmed.

Beck *versus* Uhrich.

1. Where an administrator purchased real estate with funds a moiety of which belonged to himself, and the other moiety to others, in an action of ejectment by the *cestui que trust* against a purchaser of the land from the administrator, without notice of the trust, the purchaser is entitled to be reimbursed the one-half of the purchase-money paid by him before notice of the trust, unless he has been fully compensated to the extent of that moiety out of the rents or profits. It is not, however, necessary that the amount be tendered before suit brought.

2. The administrator, who was a co-defendant in the ejectment, is entitled to be reimbursed for expenses incurred in the creation of the trust, and advances made for the *benefit of the trust*.

3. The administration account settled after the suit brought, is evidence in favor of the defendants, to show the amount of money advanced by the administrator in the purchase of the land in question; but it is not conclusive.

ERROR to the Common Pleas of *Dauphin county*.

This was an action of ejectment by Solomon Uhrich, John Uhrich, Isaac Uhrich, Samuel Uhrich, Daniel Cassell, Emanuel Cassell and Hannah his wife, Casper Hinkle and Barbara his wife, John Feezer and Susan his wife, heirs of George Uhrich, deceased, against Peter Beck, Samuel Rymart, and Joseph Uhrich, for two adjacent tracts of land. The case was up before, and a report will be found in 1 *Harris* 639–40.

John Uhrich, the grandfather of the plaintiffs, conveyed this land to Christian Hynicka, in April 1814, and took from Hynicka a mortgage on the land to secure the payment of fifteen bonds for $400 each, and one bond for $144, payable annually, beginning 1st April 1815. Three of these bonds were assigned by John Uhrich to F. Boas, and by him to D. Krause. John Uhrich died in 1818 intestate, leaving a widow, named Magdalena, and heirs, Joseph Uhrich, the defendant, and the children of George Uhrich, another son, who are the plaintiffs. George having died before his father, letters of administration on John Uhrich's estate were issued in February 1818 to his son Joseph Uhrich and Peter Crum, who settled an administration account, which was confirmed 4th October 1820, exhibiting a balance due to the administrators of $1161.10. This account was in the name of both the administrators, though sworn to by Peter Crum only, who then lived in Dauphin county. Joseph Uhrich, the other administrator, lived in Lancaster county. In this account a credit is asked for the thirteen bonds against Hynicka as outstanding. A judgment was obtained by D. Krause against C. Hynicka in 1818, for $1118.45, the amount of the three bonds assigned to him, on which proceedings were had, and upon a *venditioni exponas* to January term 1829, H. Chritzman, sheriff, sold the two tracts of land to Joseph Uhrich, the defendant, one tract for $410, and the other for $400,

[Beck v. Uhrich.]

for which he acknowledged deeds to Joseph Uhrich, January 21, 1829. An agreement was made between Joseph Uhrich and the administrator of David Krause, that Joseph Uhrich should hold the land purchased, four-fifths for his own use and one-fifth for the use of D. Krause's estate; the three bonds held by D. Krause being about the one-fifth of the whole mortgage debt against Christian Hynicka. The costs of the sheriff's sale, amounting to $73.54, were paid to the sheriff by Joseph Uhrich and D. Krause's administrator, and the balance of the purchase-money, amounting to $736.46, was applied in the same proportions of one-fifth and four-fifths to the mortgage bonds held by D. Krause's administrator, and Joseph Uhrich, as administrator of his father, John Uhrich. Some years after this a partition was made, and Joseph Uhrich set apart and conveyed to D. Krause's heirs one-fifth their portion, reserving four-fifths of the land now in question for himself. Joseph Uhrich held this land until April 1843, when he sold and conveyed it to Peter Beck for $1750, receiving $200 in cash, and taking two judgments against Peter Beck, one for $675, payable April 1, 1844, and the other for $875, payable April 1, 1845, and both entered April 23, 1843, in pursuance of which Peter Beck took possession, and has held it ever since. This action of ejectment was instituted April 24, 1845, by the plaintiffs, who are the children of George Uhrich, and claim the undivided half of this land, on the ground that it was paid for with the bonds of Hynicka, the one-half of which they allege belonged to them. On the 29th of May 1845, Peter Beck served a notice upon Joseph Uhrich, calling upon him to appear to this action of ejectment, and defend the title under the warranty in his deed to Peter Beck; and accordingly Joseph Uhrich did appear and make defence. In September 1845, Peter Beck obtained a rule on Joseph Uhrich to show cause why the judgments against him above stated should not be opened, on the ground of a defect of title to the land sold to him; and on the 26th of February 1847, these judgments were opened by the court, and the defendant let into a defence, and a trial being had on the 27th of January 1848, a verdict was found for the plaintiff. The case was removed to the Supreme Court, where the judgment was reversed in July 1850, a report of which exists in 1 *Harris's Rep.* 636.

Abraham Shope, a witness called by plaintiff, proved that he knew Peter Crum well; that he moved up the river first, eight or ten years ago, and then went West; never back since. His son and wife were back once since; lived up the river two or three years. He also stated, I know the land; it is a poor place; about $50 to $60 is a fair rent from 1829 to 1843; not any better since Beck purchased it. Upon his cross-examination, says—I think it would pay the taxes, keep up the repairs, and pay $50 to $60 a year.

[Beck v. Uhrich.]

Hard times in 1829 and 1830, but don't know what Uhrich got. It is a mile from Linglestown; a good part is mountain.

On the 11th of September 1830, a citation was issued at the instance of Peter Crum to Joseph Uhrich to settle his administration account on John Uhrich's estate, and an attachment issued, returnable February 7, 1831, and an *alias* attachment, returnable May 8, 1831. On the 4th of May 1831, Joseph Uhrich filed his administration account, showing a balance in his favor of $1224.57, in which he prayed credit for the thirteen bonds before named as outstanding and not collected. To this account exceptions were filed on behalf of Peter Crum on the 12th of September 1831. This account and the exceptions were given in evidence by the plaintiffs, who then closed their testimony.

The defendants then gave in evidence the appointment of John H. Briggs, made 4th February 1845, as an auditor, to whom were referred the exceptions to the administration account of Joseph Uhrich, administrator of John Uhrich, which had been filed 12th September 1831, and still were pending and undisposed of. On the 5th of December 1848, this appointment and reference to Mr. Brigg was continued, and on the 7th of October 1850, the same appointment and reference were continued. On the 4th of February 1851, the auditor presented his report to the Orphans' Court, which was on the 8th of February 1851 confirmed absolutely.

The auditor charged Joseph Uhrich, the administrator, with advance on the land sold to Peter Beck, but reported a balance due to him of $224.84.

The defendants gave in evidence a release from the widow of John Uhrich, deceased, to Joseph Uhrich and Peter Crum, administrators, from all demand by her concerning the estate, real or personal, of John Uhrich, deceased.

The case was tried before PEARSON, J., and a verdict was rendered for plaintiffs.

The questions for review arose on the following assignments of error:

1. The court erred in charging the jury that the plaintiffs might recover without previously tendering the $200 which had been paid by Peter Beck to Joseph Uhrich.

2. In charging that the plaintiffs might recover without having tendered to Joseph Uhrich a sum sufficient to reimburse him for his advances for the estate of John Uhrich, deceased; and that they were not required to find a conditional verdict to secure Joseph Uhrich for his advances so made; and in saying that all these questions had been considered by the Supreme Court, and determined in favor of the plaintiffs.

3. In their instruction that the proceedings on the auditor's

[Beck v. Uhrich.]

report in the Orphans' Court since the former trial, did not affect the rights of the plaintiffs, and could have no binding validity against them.

4. The court erred in their construction of the release of Magdalena Uhrich, and in declaring that it enured to the benefit of the estate of John Uhrich, so as to give the plaintiffs one-half of the land; and that this question was before the Supreme Court, and there determined in favor of the plaintiffs.

5. The court erred in charging the jury that the case presented but a question of law, and that they must find for the plaintiffs.

The case was argued by *Boas* and *McCormick*, for plaintiffs in error.

Rawn and *Carson*, for defendants.

The opinion of the court, filed July 3, was delivered by

COULTER, J.—This cause was here once before, and reversed, because the court below charged the jury that Joseph Uhrich, the plaintiff, purchased the land at public sale, and could hold it against the heirs and creditors of John Uhrich, deceased, who must resort to the fund produced by the sale, and in the hands of the administrators of John Uhrich, one of whom was Joseph Uhrich. This instruction altogether cut up the claim of the plaintiff in this action of ejectment, and left nothing to be considered or passed upon by the jury. But this court considered that instruction altogether wrong; and determined that Joseph Uhrich having paid for the land which he purchased, and which is in dispute, with the funds of the plaintiffs, who are the heirs of George Uhrich, deceased, who was one of the heirs of John Uhrich, deceased, he held in trust for them as to a moiety, and which was embraced in this suit, and that they were entitled to recover. This court also determined that the plaintiffs were not compelled or bound to pursue the fund in the hands of Joseph Uhrich, administrator of John Uhrich, deceased, produced by the sale, but had a right to pursue and recover the land which, by force of his purchase, was held by Joseph Uhrich in trust for them. In the reported opinion of this court it was said, incidentally, that Beck, who had purchased from Joseph Uhrich, and who was entitled to be reimbursed so far as he had paid the purchase-money, without notice, had *probably* been compensated by the rents, issues, and profits. But this court did not take that fact for granted. They sent the cause back, in order that it might be tried by a jury, under the principles of law established by this court, to wit, that Joseph Uhrich held as a trustee of a moiety for the heirs of George Uhrich, deceased. I may as well say, however, that as Beck was a mere volunteer, except so far as he had paid his money, ($200,) yet the heirs of George Uhrich were only bound to tender, or could only be held account-

[Beck *v.* Uhrich.]

able for, one-half that sum, as Joseph Uhrich owned one-half the land, as coheir of John Uhrich, deceased, with the heirs of George Uhrich, his brother, and was entitled to one-half the bonds with which the part of the land he got was paid for. So that it was not necessary that the plaintiffs should show that Beck had received two hundred dollars of their money out of the rent and property, but merely that he was fully compensated for the moiety of the two hundred dollars out of the moiety of the profits. Beck received possession in 1843, and, at the time of the first trial, had probably been compensated; at all events had probably been so when the cause was in this court, and long before. This is not a case to be governed by a tender of the amount due at the time of suit brought; because Joseph Uhrich denied the trust, kept it a secret from the heirs of George Uhrich, who were minors, and whose interests he was bound to look after, as well by his office of administrator, as by the dictates of humanity and equity, and his propinquity of blood. He was their trustee of the land, and could take no profit or advantage out of the conversion of the money.

In this proceeding Joseph Uhrich is entitled to be reimbursed for expenses incurred in the creation of the trust, such as costs, &c., and advances made *for the benefit of the trust ;* but he has no lien for any other debts he may claim, either as administrator of John Uhrich or in his own right. Upon the principles of equity the land belongs to the plaintiffs, the expenses of the trust being paid. Executors or administrators will not be permitted, under any circumstances, to derive a personal benefit from the manner in which they transact the business or manage the assets of the estate: 1 *Johns. Chan. Rep.* 620; 4 *id.* 303; 1 *Fonblanque's Eq.* b. 2, ch. 7; *Story's Eq.* 318. More especially if they proceeded secretly, and have not fully disclosed all the facts and circumstances to their *cestui que trusts:* Drysdale's Appeal, 2 *Harris* 531.

An unfaithful trustee is entitled to no favor. He stands exposed to every equity, and every technical legal advantage which accrues to the *cestui que trust.* The statute of limitations, or legal presumption of payment, is a good bar against him, except so far as he has advanced in the creation or for the benefit of the trust: Drysdale's Appeal, 2 *Harris;* 2 *W. & Ser.* 566; 5 *Barr* 413; 4 *W. & Ser.* 456; 5 *Watts* 303.

The estate of George Uhrich cannot be deprived of the plea of the statute of limitations, or legal presumption of payment, by the unauthorized, illegal acts of the administrator of John Uhrich. The administration account may be received in evidence, but it is by no means conclusive, being settled, that is the final account which opened the whole, after the institution of this suit.

The heirs of George Uhrich being the *cestui que trusts,* as the land in dispute was paid for by their money, are in equity the owners of the land, and are entitled to recover it, when they show

[Beck v. Uhrich.]

that Beck has been reimbursed, and the expenses in the creation of the trust satisfied. I understood Beck's attorney to say he was fully reimbursed, and also that the expenses of the trust have been paid: Drysdale's Appeal, 2 *Harris* 531; 2 *Story* 507–8 *et seq.*

The judgment now before this court is reversed, because the court below misconceived the decision of this court. We reversed the former judgment upon instructions in the court below, that went to the root of the cause, and did not grub out every thing in the case. In fact, there might have been and probably were matters in evidence, which no man could descry from the paper-book furnished.

John Uhrich is entitled to be paid for moneys advanced by him in the creation of the trust; that is, if he advanced more money than his share in the original purchase—if more than the half of the bond, by which the land was paid for, belonged to him at that time, throwing out of view the debt or bond due by George Uhrich to the estate of John Uhrich. And it is in this point of view only that the administration account is evidence, in order to show whose money paid for the land. See Drysdale's Appeal, 2 *Harris* 536. The law was always open to the administrator to settle his account rightly and justly, and he has remedies as administrator, unless he has forfeited them by his acts and delay. But he has no right to mingle up his whole administration with this trust.

Judgment reversed and *venire de novo* awarded.

Weidman *versus* Maish.

A testator directed as follows: "As to such worldly estate wherewith it hath pleased God to bless me in this life, I give and dispose of the same in the following manner. Item, it is my will and I order and direct that all my just debts and funeral expenses shall be first paid and satisfied. Item, it is my will and I give, devise, and bequeath unto my beloved wife Elizabeth eighty-five acres and allowance of land of my dwelling plantation whereon I now live, situate in Spring Garden township, in the county aforesaid, she to have the choice of the same wherever she thinks proper; and further I do give and bequeath unto my said wife all my movable property or personal estate of what kind or nature the same may be, together with all the moneys due me, by bond, note or book-account, to and for her only proper use and behoof whatever. Item, it is further my will that my brother and sisters divide the residue of my said plantation amongst themselves, share and share alike:" *Held*, that the widow took only an estate *for life*: that the words "only proper use and behoof" are not words of limitation in a deed, nor do they import perpetuity in a will; that their meaning is too vague except for conjecture; and as to the *introductory words*, there is nothing to which they can be particularly attached, and they are inoperative by themselves.

ERROR to the Common Pleas of *York county*.

This was a case stated, in which Michael Weidman was plaintiff,

[Weidman v. Maish.]

and Jacob Maish, Michael Shriver, and John Lefever were defendants, in the Court of Common Pleas of York county, No. 14, of August term 1848.

Case stated as if found by special verdict, with right to either party to sue out a writ of error.

On the second day of September 1827, John Meyer, of Spring Garden township, York county, Pennsylvania, made his last will and testament in writing of that date, which afterwards and after his death was duly proved and recorded in the register's office of said county, on the 15th day of June 1829, the original of which will is hereto annexed and made part of this case.

Said John Meyer, at the time of making said will, and at the time of his death, was seized of the plantation mentioned therein, being an improved tract of land, situate in Spring Garden township aforesaid, containing one hundred and seventy-nine acres, one hundred and fifty-six perches and allowance, which he had accepted on the 18th day of February 1806, as No. 2 of the real estate of his father, at the valuation of $5564, of which he retained $1096 as his own share, and paid $4468 to his brothers and sisters, and for the costs of the proceeding. His share in No. 1 (being the residue of the real estate of his father) was $1112.80, and his share of the personal estate was $114.66. His wife inherited from her father's estate between $900 and $1000, which he received. The industry of himself and wife, with the proceeds of the farm, were the means by which he was enabled to pay the residue of the charge upon his land, and acquire something beyond it. He had no other real estate.

The testator was married early in life to Elizabeth, a daughter of Christian Herman, of Lancaster county, Pennsylvania, who was his only wife, and survived him. He never had any children. He was between 65 and 70 years of age when he died. He had one brother, Jacob Meyer, of Spring Garden township aforesaid, and three sisters, Barbara, married to Samuel Grimes, of Venango county, Pennsylvania, Christiana, married to John Wolfort, of Franklin county, and Mary, married to John Weidman, of Lancaster county aforesaid, all of whom had issue at the date of his will, and survived him, and were his only heirs at law, and were in good circumstances, but not on terms of intimacy with him. After the death of the testator, his widow made her selection of the eighty-five acres and allowance of land devised to her, including the buildings, which were surveyed off for her, and of which she took possession. The residue of the tract, including the principal part of the woodland and the most valuable, (the buildings being of little account,) was taken into possession by the brothers and sisters of the testator. The sisters sold their interest therein to their brother, and his share still remains in it undivided.

The testator bequeathed the whole of his personal estate, which

[Weidman v. Maish.]

it is supposed amounted to between $1000 and $4000, to his widow, though, no inventory being filed, the amount is uncertain.

The said Elizabeth, the widow, leased her land to Jacob Maish, one of the defendants, on the shares, and he still continues in possession. She died in Lancaster county, Pennsylvania, *about the 1st day of August* 1847, having first made her last will and testament, which was duly proved and recorded in said last-named county. She nominated Michael Shriver and John Lefever, who are the executors of the will of her husband, to be the executors of her will, and directed them to sell said real estate and divide the proceeds among her relations, who reside principally in Lancaster county. A copy of her will is annexed to and made part of this case. The said executors are also defendants in this suit.

At the time of her death, the widow of John Meyer owned a house and piece of ground in York county, worth about $———, and the inventory of her personal estate amounts to $5828.72.

The brothers and sisters of the testator, as well as the husbands of the sisters, are dead, and have all left issue. The plaintiff, Michael Weidman, of Spring Garden township aforesaid, is a son of Mary, the wife of John Weidman, the said Mary having left eleven children, who are all living.

If Elizabeth Meyer, the widow of John Meyer, took under his will *an estate for life* in the eighty-five acres and allowance of land devised to her, then judgment to be entered in favor of *plaintiff* for the undivided one forty-fourth part of said eighty-five acres and allowance, with costs of suit.

If said Elizabeth Meyer took *a fee simple* in said eighty-five acres and allowance, then judgment to be entered *in favor of defendants* for costs.

The second day of September 1827 was Sunday, but the said John Meyer did not die on Sunday.

If any extrinsic fact stated above would not be evidence on a trial before a jury, it is not to be considered by the court in deciding this case stated, and the facts herein admitted are admitted only for the purposes of this case.

The case was argued before the Hon. ELLIS LEWIS, holding a special court at York. The court entered judgment for the defendants, thus holding that the widow took an estate in fee simple.

It was assigned for error, that the court erred in entering judgment for the defendants.

Extracts from the Will of John Meyer.—As to such worldly estate wherewith it hath pleased God to bless me in this life, I give and dispose of the same in the following manner, to wit: Item it is my will and I order and direct that all my just debts and funeral expenses shall be first paid and satisfied. Item it is my will and I give devise and bequeath unto my beloved wife

[Weidman v. Maish.]

Elizabeth eighty-five acres and allowance of land of my dwelling plantation whereon I now live situate in Spring-garden township in the county aforesaid she to have the choice of the same wherever she thinks proper and further I do give and bequeath unto my said wife all my moveable property or personal estate of what kind or nature the same may be together with all the monies due me, by bond, note or book account to and for her only proper use and behoof whatever. Item it is further my will that my brother and sisters divide the residue of my said plantation amongst themselves share and share alike. And lastly I nominate and appoint my beloved friends Michael Shriver and John Lefever of the township aforesaid to be the executors of this my last will and testament hereby revoking all other wills legacies and bequests by me heretofore made and declaring this and no other for my last will and testament. In witness whereof I hereunto set my hand and seal this second day of September one thousand eight hundred and twenty-seven—Signed, sealed, &c.

   (Signed)   JOHN MEYER. [SEAL.]

Potts and *Campbell*, for plaintiff in error.—Did the widow, according to the law of *Pennsylvania* at the time of the death of the testator, take a life estate, or a fee, in the eighty-five acres? We say *the law of Pennsylvania*, because *that* must determine, and because it differs somewhat from the law of some of the other States on the question. "We seem," says Chief Justice TILGHMAN, "to have been more steady in our notions on this point than some of our neighbors, and have thought it prudent to adhere to the law as we had it from England, at the time of our Revolution:" Steele v. Thompson, 14 *Ser. & R.* 89.

The rule of law may be stated in the language of Lord MANSFIELD, who will not be suspected of being too contracted in his notions. "The distinction which is now clearly established, is this: if the words of the testator denote only a *description* of the *specific estate* or *lands* devised; in that case, if no words of limitation are added, the devisee has only an estate for *life*. But if the words denote the *quantum* of *interest* or property that the testator has in the lands devised, there the *whole* extent of such his *interest* passes by his gift to the devisee:" Hogan v. Jackson, *Cowp.* 306. To the same effect are Busby v. Busby, 1 *Dal.* 226; Clayton v. Clayton, 3 *Bin.* 483; and Steele v. Thompson, 14 *Ser. & R.* 88, where most of the authorities are collected. There are no words in this will which denote the *quantum* of *interest*. The words "eighty-five acres and allowance" denote a description of the *lands* devised; and the word "plantation" was held in Clayton v. Clayton, 3 *Bin.* 476, and in Steele v. Thompson, not to enlarge the estate.

The introductory words of the will do not in this case *convert the estate into a fee*. "There is no case where the introduction of

[Weidman *v.* Maish.]

the will has been held to give a fee:" Frogmorton *v.* Wright, 2 *W. Bl.* 889; Burr *v.* Sims, 1 *Whar.* 264. "That the intent," says Chief Justice TILGHMAN, in Steele *v.* Thompson, "was to give an inheritance, is highly *probable;* but something more was necessary: there were no words which give the inheritance to any other person, and therefore it descended to the heir:" Harden *v.* Hays, 9 *Barr* 165.

But it is said that the devise of the eighty-five acres to the widow occurs in a mixed devise of real and personal estate, and therefore she takes a fee in the real estate. It is not disputed that giving real and personal estate in a mixed devise, or to be taken in the same manner or on the same principle, gives an absolute interest in both: Johnson *v.* Morton, 10 *Barr* 245. But it is denied that the devise in this will to the widow is mixed. In the will of John Meyer the devise of the real estate and the bequest of the personal estate are independent and distinct dispositions of the respective estates. Neither of them is "so imperfect as not to be intelligible without referring to the other," but on the contrary each is perfect in itself. Each begins with appropriate words, the devise with, "I give, *devise,* and bequeath," and the bequest with, "I give and *bequeath.*"

The concluding words cannot be carried back to the devise, or called to its aid in this case. An heir at law can be disinherited only by express devise or necessary implication: 7 *W. & Ser.* 284; 1 *Vesey & B.* 466; 1 *Ball & B.* 251; 3 *P. Wms.* 20; 2 *Bin.* 20; 9 *Barr* 154.

It was therefore submitted that the intention to give the widow *a fee* was not *legally expressed* in the will.

Evans and *Mayer,* for defendants, contended that the widow took an estate *in fee.* At the end of the item or sentence comprising the gift to her, are words of limitation *which apply to the property given to her, and define the quantity of interest in it.* No rule of law is better settled than that in a will the word heirs is not necessary to create a fee, as it is in a deed. The words "*to be by her freely possessed and enjoyed*" pass a fee: Campbell *v.* Carson, 12 *Ser. & R.* 54; Loveacres *v.* Blight, 1 *Cowp.* 352; Fox *v.* Phelps, 17 *Wend.* 398; Dice *v.* Sheffer, 3 *Watts* 419. The words "*to and for her only proper use and behoof whatever,*" are of stronger import. They are words of an *habendum* in a deed. They are placed at the end of the sentence, where the *habendum* is always found. In a deed they would be referred to the whole property, and *a fortiori* should they be so applied in a will, in which the *intention* to give a fee is obvious in every point of view: Thellusson *v.* Woodford, 4 *Vesey Jr.* 311. "Where it appears, from the whole will taken together," says Justice DUNCAN, in Campbell *v.* Carson. "that the testator intended a fee, if there are *any words*

[Weidman v. Maish.]

equivalent to perpetuity, it will be held a fee, and the constant struggle of the courts has been to seize hold of any word or any provision to effectuate the intention." This is a rule of law so firmly established, that innumerable titles rest upon it; and we need only open the books of reports to find a number of cases based upon it: Morrison v. Semple, 6 *Bin.* 94; Cassel v. Cooke, 8 *Ser. & R.* 289; Doughty v. Browne, 4 *Yeates* 179, and numerous other authorities there cited; Harden v. Hays, 9 *Barr* 161; Johnston v. Morton, 10 *Barr* 250.

But it is contended that these words are to be read only in connection with the second clause of the sentence, not with the first; and are to be applied *to the personal estate only*, not the real estate. This would render them utterly useless, contrary to another of the established rules for interpreting wills, that, "every sentence and word in a will must be considered in forming a judicial opinion upon it:" Turbett v. Turbett, 3 *Yeates* 187. Legally speaking, they are applicable to the real estate, and "to no other with any propriety of language:" Thellusson v. Woodford, 4 *Vesey* 227.

The whole argument of the plaintiff rests on the hypothesis that there are two distinct, independent sentences, when it is evident that there is but one sentence, one agent, one object, one matter treated of. The word *item* announces the commencement of a sentence or subject throughout the will. The testator in one sentence gives to his wife real and personal property fully describing it, and finally defining her interest in it. It is imagined that the words, "and further" determine the existence of two distinct independent sentences; and reference is made to the case of Burr v. Sims, 1 *Whar.* 264, in which Mr. Justice ROGERS, it will be seen hereafter, decides any thing else. In that case the word "further" was used at the beginning of a separate sentence in a distinct paragraph relating to a different devise to a different person. Its effect was not to disconnect. It had not the power to connect such disjointed things.

In the case before the court, the second clause relates only to personal estate; and to confine the words of limitation to that alone, would be to render them legally inoperative, to treat them as nugatory, and in effect to expunge them from the will. But no words can be treated as inoperative: Harker v. Blean, 3 *Watts* 437. Every word and phrase are to be considered: Turbett v. Turbett, 3 *Yeates* 190. The rules of construction require us to apply them, as was done in the Thellusson case, to all the members of the sentence which require the qualification.

If the will were capable of a twofold construction, by either applying these words to the personal estate alone, or to both the real and personal estate, such construction shall be received as tends to make it (the devise) good: 4 *Vesey, Jr., supra* 311. Whatever may be the strict grammatical construction of the words,

[Weidman v. Maish.]

that is not to govern if the intention of the testator unavoidably requires a different construction : Per MARSHALL, C. J., Smith v. Bell, 6 *Peters* 83, citing 4 *Vezey Jr.* 311, 329, *supra*. And this court say, in Hunter's Estate, 6 *Barr* 107, "The learned, accurate, and searching Mr. Butler, in his note on *Co. Litt.* 379 a, states that no rule of law has a more ancient origin than that if a testator expresses his intention defectively, either by not using technical and artificial terms, or by using them improperly, yet if his intention can be collected from his will, the law, *however defective the language may be*, will construe his words according to his intention."

The court in this case, will apply the words "to and for her only proper use and behoof," as words of limitation or qualification of the estate to all the parts of the sentence, and thus include and reach the one which would be defective without them, according to the maxim, "words added for the purpose of certainty are to be referred to preceding words in which certainty is wanting:" *Branch's Law Maxims* 152.

We have treated these concluding words, "to and for her only proper use," &c., as words of limitation, or equivalent to them in a devise. An unlimited power of disposal carries the absolute property in fee : Morris v. Phaler, 1 *Watts* 389 ; Jackson v. Babcock, 12 *Johns.* 393. They are not of less force certainly than the words, "freely to be by her possessed and enjoyed," which have sometimes been held consistent with a limited interest ; but which have received a judicial construction in this State not now to be shaken, that in connection with an introductory clause purporting to dispose of the whole estate, they are equivalent to words of perpetuity: Loveacres v. Blight, 1 *Cowp.* 352 ; Campbell v. Carson, 12 *Ser. & R.* 54 ; Fox v. Phelps, 17 *Wend.* 398 ; Dice v. Sheffer, 3 *Watts* 419.

The provision for the widow is a gift of real and personal property, in the same sentence, to the same person. It is therefore what is technically denominated a mixed gift of real and personal property, and from its character as such, the law concludes that the same interest was intended by the testator in both species of property. It was therefore submitted that it sufficiently appears that the testator gave *a fee* to his widow in the land devised to her

The opinion of the court, filed July 3, was delivered by

GIBSON, C. J.—Words may be transposed in accordance with the context of a will, to supply a member in a devise or bequest which would else be imperfect ; but the gifts, in this instance, are separately intelligible and complete. No case resembles the present in circumstances; and we are to construe the clauses of it according to their evident meaning, without regard to precedents

[Weidman v. Maish.]

further than they may have established principles of interpretation. The first is in these words: "I give and devise unto my beloved wife Elizabeth eighty-five acres and allowance of land of my dwelling plantation whereon I now live in Spring Garden township, county aforesaid, she to have her choice of the same wherever she thinks proper." Nothing could be more distinct, finished, complete, definite, and entire. He proceeded: "and further, I do give and bequeath unto my said wife all my movable property or personal estate, of whatever kind or nature the same may be, together with all the money due me by bond, note, or book-account, to her only proper use and behoof whatever." This gift, like the other, is separately perfect in its parts, and measurably perfect in its meaning. The only obscure phrase in it is that by which the personalty is given to the wife's use and behoof; and it is precisely this which is invoked to clarify its infinitely less turbid predecessor. Had the whole been jumbled together in one blended gift of the chattels and the land, the words of the latter would have been applicable to every part of it; or rather the confusion of both sorts of property in the same gift, would, on the principle of Morrison *v.* Semple, 6 *Binney* 94, have passed a fee in the land without them. But the testator has thought proper to make separate gifts of them; and we are not at liberty to break through his arrangement in order to give effect to a conjecture. That the two are comprised in one sentence, is of no account. The punctuation is the work of the scrivener: the distribution of the sense according to the context is the business of the court. No case in the books exhibits a transposition of words, where the sense would have been complete without it. Evans *v.* Knorr, 4 *Rawle* 69, was decided on that principle; and Mr. Justice KENNEDY proved, by an array of cases which it would be idle to pass again in review, that it is universal. The only subsequent case which has come to my notice, is Doe *v.* Turner, 2 *Dow. & Ryl.* 398; and no case is supposed to have carried the doctrine of transposition further. "I give," said the testator, "unto Henry Wickham, a messuage or tenement now in possession of Wakely. Item, I give further unto my nephew, Henry Wickham, half part of my garden, and £100 stock in the four per cent. bank annuities. I give further (here he dropped the name) my yard, stable, cow-house, and all other out-houses in the said yard; my sister Wickham to have the interest and profits during her life." Expressly because the last devise would have been imperfect and unintelligible without a devisee of the reversion, a majority of the judges interpolated the word "him" to sustain it. Mr. Justice BEST dissented, because, if the clause were taken by itself, as a distinct and independent devise, the freehold would not be given to Henry Wickham; and because there was no connection between that estate and those estates which were the subjects of those devises: but the four

[Weidman *v.* Maish.]

judges all agreed that the word could not have been supplied, had not the devise been imperfect, and void for uncertainty, without it. In the present case, the two gifts may not only stand separately and alone, but they could not well stand together. "Only proper use and behoof," though significant of something like a gleam of intention, are not words of limitation in a deed; nor do they import perpetuity in a will. They were probably used with a view to a separate use in case the widow should marry again; or, possibly, to give the personal estate absolutely, in contradistinction to the land; or, what is more likely still, they may have been a mere expletive of the scrivener. But whatever their office, their meaning is too vague to found any thing more solid on them than a conjecture. As to the common introductory words, it is enough to say, there is nothing in particular to which they can be attached; and it has been long held that they are inoperative by themselves. We are of opinion, therefore, that Elizabeth Meyer took only an estate for life.

Judgment of the Common Pleas reversed, and judgment by this court for the plaintiff.

COULTER, J., and CHAMBERS, J. dissented.

Johns *versus* Davidson.

1. Title to islands lying within the river Susquehanna, or its branches, could not be acquired by actual settlement and improvement; but by the act of 6th March 1793, directing the sale of certain islands in the Susquehanna or its branches, an improver had two years to obtain a warrant and have a survey made, and in case of his neglect for that time, the island was subject to application by any other person: and though it was incumbent on the improver to state the nature of his improvement and when and by whom made, this was not necessary in the application of another who applied for the island more than two years after the improver had neglected to make application for it.

2. The boundaries of Mifflin county were fixed by the second section of the act of 19th September 1789; and the fact that an island evidently included by the act within the limits of that county, had been assessed for twenty-eight years in *Huntingdon* county, will not avail to disturb the boundary fixed by the act. If the boundary fixed by the act were *uncertain*, such assessments for a long period might be admissible to show where the line was fixed by the act; but are not admissible where the line fixed by the act, viz. the Juniata river, is known. It is a question of law.

3. Where the counties of Mifflin and Huntingdon join at the Juniata river at their southern point of junction, their respective boundaries do not extend *usque ad filum aquæ;* but the *whole bed* of the Juniata river from that point up to Jack's Narrows is in *Mifflin* county, and the islands in the river belong to the latter county.

4. The fact that the island was appraised as a part of the estate of the first improver, of which the plaintiff in right of his wife was an heir, and was sold to the defendant on the proceeding in partition, there being no evidence

that the plaintiff directed it to be so appraised, is not evidence as to the county in which the island is situate, nor sufficient to bar the plaintiff from making application for it: nor will the occupation and cultivation of it for thirty-five years before the application give title to it.

ERROR to the Common Pleas of *Mifflin county*.

This was an action of ejectment, brought by John M. Davidson vs. William Johns, for an island in the Juniata river, containing about 16 acres.

Davidson showed a patent for the island, dated March 12, 1841.

The defendant Johns resisted the recovery by the said Davidson on the ground that no part of the island lay within the boundaries of Mifflin county, but that the whole island lay within the boundaries of Huntingdon county, and had always, since the formation of the county of Huntingdon, composed part of that county.

The defendant offered to prove that for a long time past, to wit, for forty years, and ever since the creation of Huntingdon county, this island had been treated as a part of the territory of Shirley township, in the county of Huntingdon—that it had always been assessed as a part of the township of Shirley, and that the owners and possessors of it had always paid taxes for it in Huntingdon county, and that no taxes had ever been assessed on it or paid for it in the county of Mifflin, and that it had never been claimed or treated as any part of the territory of Mifflin county.

This evidence the court rejected.

The defendant then proved that this island had been valued or appraised as a part of the estate of David Johns, lying in Huntingdon county, and that John M. Davidson, who had an interest in the estate of David Johns, participated in these proceedings in the Orphans' Court of Huntingdon county, in which the island was treated as lying in Huntingdon county.

The defendant then proved that the main body of the Juniata river flows between the island and the Mifflin shore, and that comparatively little water flows between the island and the Huntingdon shore. The court instructed the jury that the island lay in both counties, and that the ejectment was well brought in the county of Mifflin. To which opinion the defendant excepted.

Verdict was rendered for the plaintiff.

On the trial, on the part of the plaintiff, was offered in evidence, January 14, 1835, application of John M. Davidson for an island in the Juniata river, Wayne township, about 18 acres, about two miles below Drake's Ferry, opposite the lands of Smith and David Johns, deceased.

Objected to, that the application does not state whether the island is improved.

Objection overruled, and defendant excepted. This was the first bill of exceptions.

[Johns v. Davidson.]

14th January 1835, order of governor and board of property, read.

Island appraised 6th February 1835. Recorded 16th February 1835, 15 acres 104 perches.

20th September 1836, warrant to John M. Davidson for 15 acres 104 perches, read.

May 31, 1838, survey, 15 acres 104 perches.

March 12th, 1841, patent to John M. Davidson.

Act erecting Mifflin county referred to.

On the part of defendant, James Reed sworn:—I am the clerk of the commissioners of Huntingdon county. I have the assessment lists of Huntingdon county.

Offer to prove that this island has been assessed as a part of Shirley township, Huntingdon county, for the last forty years.

This to show that the land does not lie in Mifflin county, and is not within the jurisdiction of this court.

Objected to by plaintiff, that the assessments are not competent to prove that fact; the assessing of it in that county does not make it in that county, or the subject of assessment.

Objection sustained, and defendant excepted. This was defendant's second bill.

Offered to prove by Henry Buckley that the island is on the Huntingdon county side of the channel.

Witness:—I have known the island since 1810; have lived on the island—worked on it. I always think the largest body of water is on the Mifflin county side of the island; the boat channel is on that side.

Cross-examined:—The island, in the broadest place, is, I suppose, 40 rods wide; cannot tell how wide between the island and the Mifflin county side. Not 100 yards from the island to the Mifflin county shore; more than 50 yards—perhaps 70 yards. From the western side of the island to the Huntingdon shore, about the same distance. Soil perhaps 5 feet above low-water mark. I think the most water is on the Mifflin side. The middle of the river is not on the Huntingdon county side.

Offered in evidence *the record* from Huntingdon county for a partition of the estate of David Johns, deceased, instituted by John M. Davidson, and claiming this land to be a part of the estate in Huntingdon county, (John M. Davidson was married to a daughter of David Johns, deceased,) and that the island was appraised as a part of the estate of David Johns; and that the island was afterwards sold to the defendant on the proceeding in partition, as a part of the estate of David Johns.

This offered to show that the plaintiff has considered it in Huntgdon county; second, to show that the plaintiff has, as one of the tenants in common of the estate of David Johns, acknowledged

[Johns v. Davidson.]

the title to be in the heirs of David Johns, and that his proceeding operates as an estoppel, and whatever title he acquired to the island by his warrant inured to the heirs of David Johns.

Withdrawn for the present.

Joseph Bowers, sworn :—I think I first knew this island in 1827. I rafted on the Juniata river. The main channel is on the Mifflin side of the island. At low-water mark the island is greatly nearest the Huntingdon side of the river, at any stage of water is nearest the Huntingdon shore—would think, at low water, is not more than 3 rods from the Huntingdon shore; at the lowest stage of water, would be 100 yards or more from the Mifflin shore. * * *

Record of the proceedings of the Orphans' Court of Huntingdon county again offered, to show as before, and for the same purposes.

Objected to as irrelevant, and that the island does not appear to be embraced in the proceedings from the beginning to the end of the record.

Objection sustained, and defendant excepted. This was defendant's third bill.

Offered to prove, by one of the inquest, that the inquest appraised this island as a part of the property described in the writ to part and divide—that the sheriff was there, and the inquest acted under his directions, and appraised the island, and that Davidson, the plaintiff, lived about a mile and a half off. Objected to. Objection sustained, and defendant excepted. This was defendant's fourth bill.

Defendant now offers to prove the occupation by cultivation of the land for 35 years, by David Johns, having cleared and fenced the island for the whole of that period.

This offered for the purpose of showing possession in David Johns, and that, as part of his estate, it was appraised in the inquisition held for the partition of the estate of David Johns in Huntingdon county.

Objected to, that neither the possession in David Johns *nor the record* tend to show that the island is embraced in the partition, and if they did, the whole proof would be irrelevant—that the certificate of the record is insufficient.

Court :—The application of John M. Davidson does not show that he included this island in the partition; the application excludes it, and unless it is shown that Davidson directed the island to be appraised, the possession of David Johns of the island gave no title.

Objection sustained, and defendant excepted. This was defendant's fifth bill.

Joseph Bowers :—The heaviest stream is on the Mifflin county side—would amount to two-thirds, or more, on the Mifflin side.

Cross-examined :—My attention was never called to it particu

[Johns *v.* Davidson.]

larly. It is fordable on one side, but I think not on the Mifflin side.

Joseph Morrison sworn: He said, *inter alia*:—I could not say, taking a point in the middle of the island and running to a point in the middle of the river above the island, which side most of the island would be in; suppose on the Mifflin side.

Defendant now offers to prove that for twenty-eight years past, the island has been assessed as part of Shirley township, in Huntingdon county; offer to show this by the assessments of the commissioners.

This offered for the purpose of showing how jurisdiction has been exercised over this island, and to show it lies in Huntingdon county; to show that Mifflin county conceded the right to Huntingdon county.

Court:—This might be considered on a question of boundary, if, from lapse of time, it was difficult to prove the existence of the original line and its marks; but here is a river as the boundary, not alleged to be changed, but confined, opposite the island, by high banks. The necessity for reputation, or hearsay, does not arise.

Objection sustained, and defendant excepted. This was defendant's sixth bill.

On the part of the defendant, the following points were submitted:

1. If, from the evidence, the jury believe the island in controversy lies in Huntingdon county, then their verdict must be for the defendant.

2. If, from the evidence in the case, the jury believe the island lies nearer to the Huntingdon shore than to the Mifflin shore, the island lies in Huntingdon county.

3. That the edge of common low water in the river, is the legal shore of the river.

4. If, at low water, a greater quantity of water flows on the Mifflin side than on the Huntingdon side of the island, the island lies in Huntingdon county.

5. If the narrowest part of the river on the Mifflin side of the island is wider than the narrowest part of the river on the Huntingdon side, and the most water flows on the Mifflin side, then the island is in Huntingdon county.

6. When two counties lie opposite each other, on the same river, and there is no special reservation of jurisdiction over the river in favor of either of the counties, the territory of each county extends to the middle of the main channel of the river.

WILSON, President J., charged as follows:—This ejectment is brought to recover the possession of an island in the Juniata river. Under the provisional government of Pennsylvania, the islands in the great rivers of the State never were the subjects of appropria-

[Johns v. Davidson.]

tion; the proprietors (the Penns) appropriated them to their own use by special warrants. When, by such special warrant, they had appropriated an island, it was excepted from the general proprietary estate, which was vested in the commonwealth by virtue of the act of the 27th of November 1779. This island was not so specially appropriated, and by that act became vested in the commonwealth. The commonwealth, pursuing the same policy, did not, by any law, subject the island to appropriation, either by office right or settlement; but by an act of Assembly in 1795, directed the islands in several of the rivers to be sold at public sale, or otherwise, for the best prices that could be gotten for the same, and declaring that all occupancy and every survey, claim, or pretence for holding the same islands by any other title, should be utterly void. The act of 1793 still continued the sale of islands, limiting a price under which they could not be had, and provided for the appointment of appraisers, to ascertain their value, on the application of a purchaser, and giving a pre-emption right to improvers for two years from the passage of the act. The right of purchase granted to improvers was confined to improvers cultivating the land when the act passed. The object of the legislature always was to sell islands for the best price; and by the act of 1793, to prefer an improver, if he applied within the two years; but if he did not, then to grant it to the first applicant, subject to the regulations and conditions contained in the act. An occupation by cultivating an island for any number of years, where the commonwealth has not parted with her interest, cannot make title to the occupant. The limitation does not run against the commonwealth, and such occupation does not prevent any citizen from applying and purchasing from the commonwealth an island not previously applied for. The only indulgence given to occupants was for two years from the passage of the act of 1793. In this case, from any thing that appears from the evidence, John M. Davidson had the right to make the application he did, and to purchase from the commonwealth; and the application, appraisement, warrant, survey, and patent, given in evidence, make him a good title to the island, and one upon which he will be entitled to recover in this case, provided you shall find that the island for which he took out his warrant is within the boundaries of this county. The territory composing Huntingdon county was erected into a separate county before the erection of Mifflin county. Mifflin county was erected in 1789, and was to include the lands lying within bounds and limits described in the act, and among them is the following description from where it runs from Franklin county—"thence along the said line to the Huntingdon county line; thence along the said line to the Juniata river; thence up the said river to Jack's Narrows." It is in the river, at this line of boundary, the island in dispute is situated. We do not think that the jurisdiction of Huntingdon

2 T

[Johns v. Davidson.]

county, by this division line, is limited to the edge of the river, but that it will extend to the middle of the river; and we mean by this a line equally distant from either shore; and in determining the question, which is one for you, of whether this island is in Mifflin or Huntingdon county, you will not adopt as the line the middle of the heaviest volume of water flowing past this island, but a line equally distant from the shores; and this you will determine from the testimony you have heard from the witnesses in relation to its location and situation, in reference to the shores, and spread of water between the island and main shores.

The first and second points proposed on part of defendant, he answered in the affirmative.

To the 3d:—This, as a general legal principle, is correct.

To the 4th:—For many purposes, the beach on either shore of a river constituting a county line, will belong to the county in which it is situated; but the main channel of rivers may and do often change, and the line adopted for the division by the act of Assembly fixing the boundary, will not always change with a change of the channel. It may deepen it, so as to throw the greater quantity of water on a side of an island where it did not flow when the division line was adopted; and we refuse to answer this point as requested.

To the 5th:—There may be particular parts of the channel, on one side or other of the island, narrower than the narrowest part of the channel on the opposite side, and the most water flow through the widest channel, without determining the line between the counties; and, as a whole, we refuse to answer this point as requested.

To the 6th:—If, by the main channel in this point, is meant the heaviest volume of water, we refuse to answer the point as requested, but say to you that the jurisdiction of counties so situated will extend to a centre line of the river, equally distant from either shore.

If you find that the island is on the Huntingdon side of a centre line between the shores of the opposite sides of the river, your verdict should be for the defendant; if you find the island, or a considerable portion of it, on the Mifflin side of such line, the plaintiff will be entitled to your verdict.

To this opinion both parties except, as well as to the answers to the points, &c.

It was assigned for error:
1. The court erred in receiving in evidence the *application* in defendant's first bill of exceptions.
2. The court erred in refusing to permit defendant below to prove that the island lay exclusively in Huntingdon county, and that no part of it ever was assessed in Mifflin county, as set forth in defendant's second bill of exceptions.

[Johns v. Davidson.]

3. The court erred in rejecting the copy of the record, as set forth in defendant's third bill of exceptions.

4. The court erred in rejecting the evidence of the witness who was one of the jury of inquest on the estate of David Johns, as set forth in defendant's fourth bill of exceptions.

5. The court erred in rejecting the evidence offered by defendant, as set forth in his fifth bill of exceptions.

6. The court erred in rejecting the evidence as set forth in defendant's sixth bill of exceptions.

7. The court erred in the charge, in saying—"The line of Huntingdon county extends to the middle of the river; and by this we mean a line equally distant from either shore; and in determining the question, which is one for you, whether this island is in Huntingdon or Mifflin county, you will not adopt as the line the middle of the heaviest volume of water flowing past the island, but a line equally distant from the shores; and this you will determine from the testimony."

8. In saying—"If you find that the island is on the Huntingdon side of a centre line between the shores of the opposite sides of the river, your verdict should be for the defendant; if you find the island, or a considerable portion of it, on the Mifflin side of such line, the plaintiff will be entitled to your verdict."

The court erred in answering the 4th, 5th, and 6th points of defendant's counsel.

The case was argued by *A. W. Benedict* and *Fisher*, for the plaintiff in error.—The material matter as to which it was alleged error existed, was, that the court erred in holding that the island in question, or any part of it, lay in the county of *Mifflin*.

As to *county* line, evidence of usage may be given to support title: 3 *W. & Ser.* 379, Beale v. Patterson. As to the law arising under the several assignments, the following authorities were cited: 3 *Revised Statutes of New York*, 3d ed.; 1 *id.* 78–9; 3 *Kent's Com.* note, 427–430. See Wright v. Howard, 1 *Sim. & Stewart*, 190; Deerfield v. Orn, 17 *Pick.* 41; Star v. Child, 20 *Wend.* 149; 5 *id.* 423; 6 *Cow.* 518, note a; 6 *id.* 546; 12 *Johns. Rep.* 252; Clement v. Carlton, 2 *New Hamp. Rep.* 269; 2 *id.* 371–372. See 5 *Wheat.* 381; 4 *id.* 339; 7 *Cranch* 84; 9 *id.* 173.

See *Woolrich on Waters*, 38; *Hale de jure maris*, 6; *Fleta*, lib. 3, cap. 2, 446; 2 *Bl. Com.* 261.

It was contended that an island in a river, belongs to that shore between which and the island the *least* portion of the stream flows: 10 *Wend.* 260; 6 *Cow.* 544; 3 *Kent* 430; 14 *Mass.* 149; 5 *Wheat.* 374–81.

Parker, for defendant.—Islands were never the subject of improvement right till 1793. The act limited the application of an

[Johns v. Davidson.]

improver to two years; after that period he had no preference, and the other party had the right to apply for the island.

The act of 1785 includes islands in the Juniata, as a branch of the Susquehanna. The plain words of the act erecting Mifflin county, clearly indicate the western shore as her true boundary. If this be so, the plaintiff has no cause of complaint: 2 *Smith's Law*, 193–4; sec. 2, act of 19th September 1789.

The opinion of the court was filed, July 23, by

COULTER, J.—The application does not describe the improvements. But this, although it is required in the statute, was designed to answer a particular purpose, to wit, to inform the government whether any one was entitled to the preemption under the act of Assembly permitting the appropriation of islands. In this case, the two years during which the preemption was to run had expired long before the application; and therefore, as regarded the commonwealth, it was of no moment that they should be described, because the island was to be valued by persons appointed, who would of course take into consideration the value of the improvements. The commonwealth, after valuation of the island, and after all the preliminary steps except the one of describing the improvements in the application, had been duly taken, granted a patent to Davidson in March 1841. This closed up the matter, and, as far as the commonwealth was concerned, vested the title in the plaintiff below; and this disposes of the first bill of exceptions. The second bill covers exceptions to evidence of assessments of the island in dispute, by the authorities of Huntingdon county offered for the purpose of showing that the island did lie in Huntingdon county, and that therefore the court in Mifflin county had no jurisdiction of the cause. But the lines and boundaries of counties are fixed by statute, and the power is not given to the commissioners or other officers of a county to restrain or expand those boundaries. Whether the assessments were made for a long or short period is of little importance, because local usage or trespass can never repeal positive statutory law. The third and fourth bills of exceptions are disposed of by the same rule and reason which governs the second. The proceedings of the Orphans' Court of Huntingdon county, even if they were properly certified, would not conduce to establish the line of Huntingdon county, or to restrain or limit the line of Mifflin county or oust the jurisdiction of its courts.

As to the fifth bill of exceptions, it may be sufficient to say, that islands have been, from the earliest settlement of the State subject to different rules as to the acquisition of title, than those which applied to the main land. The improvement therefore on the island, being merely an extension of the improvement of Johns on the mainland in Huntingdon county, vested no title in the said Johns to the island. The law of actual settlement and improvement was never extended

[Johns v. Davidson.]

to islands. The sixth bill of exceptions to evidence is closely allied to those considered already. Testimony of assessments in Huntingdon county for twenty-eight years might perhaps be admitted, if the actual location of the line was uncertain, had been obliterated, or had never been surveyed or marked. In such case the assessments for a long period of time might conduce, in the absence of better evidence, to show where the line originally was. But here the line is well known, neither defaced nor shifted by time or accident. It is the Juniata river. And the real question is whether the statute makes the southern bank or shore or the middle of the river the true boundary between Mifflin and Huntingdon counties, as far as it is the boundary. That is a question of law.

Mifflin county was erected out of Cumberland and Northumberland counties. At that time Mifflin embraced the county of Juniata within its limits, which was since erected into a separate county; but that affects not the question here, as the conflicting jurisdiction is between Mifflin in its present limits and Huntingdon. The line of old Mifflin crossed the Juniata and took in a large portion of territory on the eastern and southern side of it; and then intersecting the line of Huntingdon county on the southern side of the river, the statute proceeds as follows: " Thence along the said Huntingdon county line *to* Juniata river, thence up said river to Jack's Narrows," &c. Between Jack's Narrows and where the line of Mifflin strikes the river, lies the island in dispute. It was contended here, and also in the court below, that the middle of the stream was the true boundary; and the court below seemed to be of that opinion, but left it to the jury to say whether part of the island was not on the side nearest the Mifflin shore; and that if that was the case, the Mifflin county court had jurisdiction, under a statute which prescribes that when land lies partly in one county and partly in another, either county has jurisdiction to try title to the whole. But we are of opinion that the jurisdiction of Mifflin county over the island does not depend upon so uncertain a line. We are of opinion that the whole bed of the river and the islands in it, from where the line strikes the southern shore of the stream up to Jack's Narrows, is in Mifflin county.

By the common law, where a river is used as the boundary in a grant, it is used to the centre or middle of the stream, and to that extent the title or fee attaches, so that the proprietor of each bank is the owner of half the land covered by the water, saving to the public the right of highway. And islands in the middle of the stream or close to the shore of either side follow the same rule and are governed by it. This rule has been adopted in several of the states, New York among the number. In the case of Canal Commissioners *v.* The People, 5 *Wend.* 423, it was held that by the rule of the common law which was adopted in that state, grants of lands, bounded on rivers above tide water, extended *usque ad*

[Johns *v.* Davidson.]

filum aquæ, including beds of rivers and islands, but subject to the right of the public to use the waters as a highway. But this rule was never adopted in Pennsylvania. By the act of 1785, appropriating lands in the new purchase, islands were excepted from its provisions, and they were to be sold by special order of the government; and by the act of 1793 the mode of disposing of islands in the Susquehanna and its branches is provided for. By a late act of Assembly the land officers were authorized to issue warrants for land under the beds of certain western rivers, and many warrants were issued under the act. In Pennsylvania, wherever a stream is navigable, and it is made the boundary of a grant by the State, the title passes to low-water mark, but no farther.

The common-law principle of *usque ad filum aquæ* is not applicable to the large streams of this State which are navigable, although there be no flux or reflux of the tide; the beds of such rivers belong to the commonwealth: Carson *v.* Blayer, 2 *Bin.* 475. It is only to small streams not navigable that the principle of *usque ad filum aquæ* applies in Pennsylvania: 8 *Watts* 477. The line therefore of Mifflin county being designated by the statute as coming to the Juniata river, on the southern side of the Juniata, or the side contiguous to Huntingdon, and thence up the river to Jack's Narrows, took in the whole bed of the river to low-water mark; the line did not recross the river until it reached Jack's Narrows.

Although, then, Huntingdon county, opposite the island in dispute, comes up to the river, it goes no farther than *low-water mark;* and the whole of the island is in Mifflin county, whose court had unquestionable legal jurisdiction of the cause. This island was the property of the State, and remained open to appropriation under the terms of the act of 1793. That act expressly recognises cases where improvements have been made; and provides that in any application for the appropriation of an island, the applicant shall state whether any improvement has been made, and also the nature of the improvement, and when and by whom made. And no warrant shall issue directing any island thus improved to be surveyed, except in favor of the person who has made such improvement, or in favor of his heirs or assigns for the term of two years after passing that act; and providing that after the expiration of that time, warrants shall issue for such improved island in favor of any person or persons who shall first apply for the same.

The warrant in favor of Davidson was not issued until long after the expiration of two years from the date of the act of 1793, to wit, in 1835. If the improver, his heirs or assigns, chose to slumber over the privilege accorded to them till it was too late, the fault is their own. The dominion of the State was not thereby lost, and they had a right to grant it to whom they pleased.

Judgment affirmed.

Shell *versus* Haywood & Snyder.

1. A person contracted with machinists for the construction of a steam-engine and fixtures for a grist-mill. A part of the machinery, viz. the boilers and balance-wheel, were delivered, and the boilers fixed in a building attached to the mill. The purchaser became embarrassed, and in an agreement in writing between him and the attorney of the manufacturers, it was stated that the boilers and the machinery attached or to be attached to them were the property of the manufacturers, and they by their attorney agreed to leave the same where they were for three months, in order to give time to the purchaser to make an arrangement with his creditors; and in the event of his inability to make such arrangement, then the manufacturers were *to be left to their legal remedy for the materials already furnished, or to the removal of the same, at their option:* Held, that the machinists had the right to remove the boilers and wheel as against one who had purchased them at sheriff's sale when sold as the personal property of the owner of the mill who had ordered them, without respect to whether they were attached to the *real* estate or not.

2. The acts and declarations of the owner of the mill who contracted for the engine, made before execution issued against him, that he considered the boilers and wheel as the property of the *manufacturers* of them, were admissible on *their* part as evidence of ownership, possession, and the right to remove the same.

ERROR to the Common Pleas of *Dauphin county.*

This was an action of trespass *vi et armis*, brought by Benjamin Haywood and George W. Snyder, doing business in the name of Haywood & Snyder, against Jacob Shell, the sheriff of Dauphin county, for levying upon and selling certain steam-boilers and a balance-wheel, then being in the mill of Thomas McAllen, below Harrisburg. See the opinion of his Honor, CHAMBERS, J., for a statement of the main facts in the case.

The plea was *non cul.*

On the trial, Thomas McAllen was examined as to the contract between him and Haywood & Snyder for the engine. An agreement, as follows, was entered into:—

This article witnesses *that the iron boilers* now in the small building *connected with the mill of Thomas McAllen*, in Lower Swatara township, Dauphin county, and the machinery attached to said boilers, or to be attached to the same, are the property of Haywood & Snyder; and the said Haywood & Snyder agree to leave the same where they now are for three months from the date of this article, giving this time to the said Thomas McAllen for the purpose of making an arrangement with his creditors; *and in the event of his inability to make such arrangement, then the said Haywood & Snyder are to be left to their legal remedy for so much of the materials as are already furnished, or to the removal of the same, at their option.*

And further, in the event of an arrangement with the creditors aforesaid, the said Haywood & Snyder are to put up the engine complete, to the satisfaction of said Thomas McAllen, he securing

[Shell v. Haywood & Snyder.]

the said Haywood & Snyder for the same, upon such terms and time as may be agreed upon between the parties. January 18, 1848. (Signed)
THOS. MCALLEN.
JNO. H. BERRYHILL, Attorney for Haywood & Snyder.

McAllen testified, *inter alia :*—I made no arrangement with my creditors; failed to do so; two would not agree, all the rest willing; the property was sold by the sheriff, all my property, real and personal; the property was left with me by Haywood & Snyder for the time mentioned; I made no payment to them for the engine; nothing was to be paid till it was delivered and put up; they never demanded payment.

Cross-examined:—The materials all delivered in the fall of 1847, which were delivered at all; they remained on the premises till the sheriff's sale; the fly-wheel and part of the binder-plates never moved; the boilers were put in their place; columns and door-frames were walled up before the sale; all was left just as they were when they stopped; no work done after the failure.

After the foundation was built, and boilers on it, Haywood & Snyder were to put up the iron-work of the machinery, put it in order, finish and start it; they were to pay their hands.

It was proposed to prove by the witness that, before the execution issued to the sheriff, he declared to Mr. Berryhill, the plaintiffs' agent, that he (witness) had no claim to the property, and Berryhill might remove it if he insisted on it. This objected to by defendant.

By the court:—" This can have but little weight in determining the right, but may have some, and, as defendants have not shown a legal right to seize, is evidence against the possessor, the witness." Admitted, and exception sealed.

I was owner of the real property, and this engine was building for me as owner. *Berryhill and I had several talks about this property before the agreement was entered into; we came to the conclusion as therein expressed;* I told Berryhill I could not claim the property in consequence of not having paid any thing on it; I never did claim it; always had the same view of it; the boilers could have been taken out by taking the door-frame out; some of the bricks might have fallen; no part of the engine there; the plaintiffs had no person there to superintend the work during erection; had sent their foreman there at first to show the plan; had also a frame-work of wood that the masons were to work round; holes for plates, rods, &c., through it; they worked by that; when finished, that was to be taken out; all the hands about the building were employed and paid by me.

PEARSON, J., charged the jury, *inter alia :*—The arrangement made with Mr. Berryhill creates the principal *legal* difficulty in this

[Shell v. Haywood & Snyder.]

case. Prior to that contract, I have no doubt of the vendors' right to this property, and that they could have removed it at any time. How far did that contract divest them of the right of recaption and vest the title in McAllen.

The contract admits that this property belongs to the plaintiffs, who agreed to permit it to remain in possession of McAllen for three months, to see if he can make an arrangement with his creditors. This, of itself, would not have the effect of giving McAllen the property; it was merely leaving it on the premises, and making him for that time the bailee of the plaintiffs. The contract goes on to provide for the contingency of McAllen's inability to make an arrangement, and leaves it optional with them to remove the goods or to seek their remedy for the materials already furnished. Their remedy how? Unquestionably by suit for their value. In the event of an arrangement with the creditors, plaintiffs are to put up the engine complete, but to be secured their purchase-money upon such terms and time as shall be agreed upon between the parties, evidently contemplating a new contract in that event.

By the terms of this contract no property vested in McAllen, but he might have a vested interest at the end of three months. It was optional with Haywood & Snyder whether he should or not. They left the articles there for nearly one year afterwards. The fair presumption then is, that they made their election under the contract, and agreed to leave the goods with him, although no arrangement was made. Against that presumption you have the evidence of McAllen, that he never considered these articles his, that they were not to be, until paid for, and the improbability that the plaintiffs would agree to part with their property to an insolvent man. But McAllen's understanding alone is insufficient. The plaintiffs, and not he, had the right of election, and you must have some proof to satisfy you that they made the election in order to counteract the presumption arising from their long silence. Mr. Berryhill, it is contended by the plaintiffs' counsel, testified that he had repeated conversations, as well after as before the article was made, and along through the summer, with McAllen, in which he stated his client's intention to remove the goods, but was prevented by Mr. McAllen stating that Mr. Fisher (who had writs in the sheriff's hands the whole time) threatened to bring suit against him if he did. The defendant's counsel contends that these conversations were all before the article was entered into, and that he did not speak of any after. You will have to decide between them. If no conversation took place after the three months expired, the plaintiffs never made the required election, and cannot recover. If it took place soon after, so as to show they made the election in a reasonable time, the article does not stand in the way of a recovery. This is the most important

[Shell *v.* Haywood & Snyder.]

fact you have to decide: almost every thing else has been argued as questions of law.

Were these boilers fixtures? You have heard the evidence as to the purpose for which they were placed in the building, and the manner in which they were built around; that they were not secured in any way, but that it would be difficult, and might be impracticable to remove them without some injury, though slight, to the building. Where a workman contracts to put up machinery of great value, such as this, to be paid for on completion, and, when finished, the person with whom he has contracted refuses to make payment, I have no doubt of his right at once to remove it, although, in so doing, he should to a limited extent injure the building in which it is placed. Such a right is as much secured to him for the benefit and encouragement of trade as to the tenant, who may remove almost every structure placed by him on demised premises to carry on his business. It cannot be that the machinist shall be deprived of machinery worth several thousand dollars because the building in which it is erected may in its removal be damaged to the amount of five or fifty dollars, more especially when a violation of the contract on the part of the owner leads to the necessity of its removal. But the right of recaption in such cases must be *promptly exercised;* a man cannot sell an article to another, and, because he is not paid, go at a distant day to his premises and remove it. Had these boilers been once used as part of the machinery, and detached for a temporary purpose, I should consider them as still part of the freehold. They had never been used nor prepared for use. The whole machinery was in a course of erection. Whether attached to and part of the freehold, is in part a question of intention, to be determined by you. If placed in the building with the expectation that the other part of the machinery should be attached to it, and the whole remain the property of the plaintiffs until completion and payment, according to the terms of the contract, they should not be considered real property, or fixtures, even if some small portion of the building would have to be displaced in order to remove them. The witnesses generally agree that they could not be removed without taking out the door-frame, and all state they could be by removing it, which would do no essential injury. The parties in interest have all treated these boilers as personal property. The sheriff levied on and sold them as such. McAllen said he always considered that they belonged to the plaintiffs, although he would do no act to affect the rights of his creditors.

We are asked to say that the sheriff, by his levy and sale, is estopped from now saying that these boilers are part of the freehold. We do not say so, but his act is a strong admission against him. According to some cases, the sheriff, by his levy and sale, can as effectually sever such property as the owner of the free-

[Shell v. Haywood & Snyder.]

hold. See 6 *Amer. Law Jour.* 355, and the cases there cited. But we are not prepared to say, under all these circumstances, that this is an absolute severance, or that it amounts to an estoppel. The defendant's counsel have urged us to decide, as a question of law under all the circumstances, that these boilers were *fixtures* at the time of the levy and sale. I am of opinion, under all the circumstances proved, that they were not, as between the present plaintiffs and the sheriff, but consider it a question of fact, to be determined by you, and should not have expressed any opinion on the subject but on account of their calling for and urging it.

A number of points were submitted to the court, on the part of the defendants, but none of the assignments of error were sustained by the court.

May 7, 1851, verdict for plaintiffs for $760.22 damages.

Error was assigned to the admissions of the evidence referred to in the bill of exceptions, viz. the admissions or declarations of McAllen, and to various parts of the charge.

The case was argued by *Fisher*, for the plaintiff in error. *Berryhill* and *McCormick*, for defendants.

The opinion of the court, filed July 3, was delivered by

CHAMBERS, J.—The defendants, who were machinists, contracted, in the autumn of 1847, with Thomas McAllen, at a certain price, to construct and put up for use a steam-engine, appurtenant to the flour-mill of McAllen, propelled by a small water-power, to be paid for in part by him when completed, and the balance after a short credit. Haywood & Snyder proceeded to construct the engine, and, in the progress of the work, brought to the mill of McAllen in Dauphin county, the two boilers, a balance-wheel, and some other parts of the machine. McAllen was to prepare the foundation and the enclosure. The boilers were laid loose on the foundation prepared, and the walls and building to enclose them were partially erected, but not completed, when McAllen became embarrassed by the claims of his creditors. It was intended by McAllen to enclose the boilers in a way that would admit of their removal out of the small building that covered them; but some error in the position of the door would not allow of that removal without displacing a small part of the brick wall and the door-frame. Haywood & Snyder had prepared the other parts of the engine, and which were on their way to the place of erection, when, on account of the pressure of McAllen by his creditors, they were stopped, and the progress of the work to completion suspended, with the approbation of McAllen, who said he could not comply with his part of the agreement. McAllen entertained the expecta-

[Shell v. Haywood & Snyder.]

tion that he would still be able to make some arrangement with his creditors that would allow him to retain his real property. By an agreement between Haywood & Snyder, by Mr. Berryhill their attorney, and McAllen, dated 18th January 1848, it was declared that the iron boilers then in the building attached to the mill, were the property of Haywood & Snyder, who agreed to leave the same where they were for three months from that date, giving this time to McAllen for the purpose of making an arrangement with his creditors; and in the event of his inability to make such arrangement, then Haywood & Snyder were to be left to their legal remedy for so much of the materials as were already furnished, or to the removal of the same at their option: and further, in the event of an arrangement with the creditors aforesaid, the said Haywood & Snyder are to put up the engine complete to the satisfaction of McAllen, he *securing* them for the same, upon such terms and time as may be agreed upon between the parties.

The boilers and wheel remained at the same place and in the same condition, when an execution, issued at the suit of Wright & Nephew, against McAllen, on the 11th December 1848, directed to Jacob Shell, sheriff and defendant below, was levied on the boilers and wheel, which wheel had not been put up. Shell, under his levy, sold the boilers and wheel on the 12th January 1849, having on the 8th of the same month made a levy on the mill and other real property, with a minute description. Notice was given Shell that Haywood & Snyder claimed the boilers and balance-wheel as their property, and Shell afterwards acknowledged that he was indemnified, for his proceedings. The mill and real estate of McAllen were sold at sheriff's sale on the 25th of April 1849, for $7005, and a deed made and acknowledged by the sheriff to S. Cameron on the 26th of April 1849.

This action is one of trespass, by Haywood and Snyder against Shell, the sheriff, for the levy and sale of the steam-boilers and balance-wheel. On the trial, the plaintiff was allowed to prove that McAllen, before the execution issued in this case, had declared that he did not claim these boilers and wheel, and that they might be removed; that he could not claim the property in consequence of not having paid any thing on it, and that he never did claim it. The admission of the evidence was objected to by defendant, and exception taken, which is now assigned for error. This evidence does appear to this court to have been pertinent and competent. The property and possession of the boilers and wheel were in Haywood & Snyder and McAllen. The only person who could gainsay the right and control of the property by Haywood & Snyder was McAllen, the other contractor, the owner of the freehold on which the property was; and as such his acts and declarations in relation to this property were proper evidence to be submitted

[Shell v. Haywood & Snyder.]

to the jury, as evidence of ownership, possession, and the right to remove.

Many points were presented by the defendant to the court below, which elicited from the learned judge who tried the cause an elaborate and able charge and reply, and in which many errors are assigned by the plaintiff in error. It is not our purpose to review each one separately, which would extend this opinion unnecessarily, when they present but a few questions requiring the judicial cognizance of this court.

Were the steam-boilers and wheel the property of the plaintiffs below, and the right to the possession of the same in them, at the levy and taking by the defendant?

The defendant alleges that the right of property in the plaintiffs was divested by the delivery to McAllen—and that by the location of the steam-boilers, they became a part of the realty and were not removable.

Was the delivery, according to the evidence, such as passed these parts of the engine beyond the control of Haywood & Snyder, the manufacturers?

They contracted to make and put up a complete machine to be put in operation, finding the materials, and were to be paid for the same a certain price on completion. This machine would require time in the process of manufacture of its parts, as well as in its construction on the premises where it was to be used. McAllen was only bound to receive and pay for a complete machine: for its parts he was not responsible, and to him they were without value. It was said by this court, in the case of Clemens v. Davis, 7 *Barr* 263, that where the contract was for a finished article, nothing but the delivery of a finished article could satisfy it.

That McAllen might progress with the foundation and enclosure the boilers were placed on that foundation loose; and from which they might be removed with but slight injury to the small building for their enclosure. At this stage of the construction, the manufacturers are informed of the insolvency of McAllen and his inability to pay them for the engine, and they were justifiable in suspending the work—in withholding the other parts of the engine that were manufactured, and were at their factory or *in transitu*, and in reclaiming the portion that had been placed on the premises of McAllen.

Whether the same policy of law, which, for the benefit and encouragement of trade, allows a lessee or manufacturer to remove during his term, the buildings, engines, or machines erected on the realty or annexed to it by him, would embrace a machinist, with the like right to remove his machine or engine before its use, on the failure of the vendee to pay for it according to contract, and without his consent, it is not necessary for the court to decide, as

[Shell v. Haywood & Snyder.]

the facts and circumstances in evidence in this case show a consent to removal by the vendee whilst he was owner of the freehold.

The right of removal of improvements on realty by a lessee, when made for the purposes of trade, does not depend on annexation as the criterion, as many parts of a building erected by a lessee may be removed by him, when it can be done without substantial injury to the freehold.

We deem it unnecessary to extend this opinion by the review of the many cases referred to in the argument, on the subject of fixtures, or by the consideration of such fixtures as were removable or irremovable, or of the objects that were appurtenant to realty and not removable as personalty though not annexed to the realty.

The rule of severance and removal is one subject to the control and modification of the parties to the contract and representing the property, who may vary the same according to their convenience, pleasure, or regard to right. That consent will change property otherwise real into personal estate is ruled in Piper v. Martin, 8 *Barr* 211; Mitchell v. Freedly, 10 *id.* 198, and White's Appeal, 10 *id.* 254. For whether attached to the realty or not, or in whatever manner attached, is immaterial, when the parties agree to consider it personal property: 8 *Barr* 211; 2 *W. & Ser.* 116; 10 *Barr* 253.

In the case under consideration, McAllen acted with fairness and integrity to Haywood & Snyder when he found that he was unable to pay for the engine. He said he could not claim it, and that he did not claim it. In this there was the strongest evidence of disclaimer by the owner of the freehold of any claim by him to it as part of the freehold or as his property. By the agreement of 18th January 1848 recited, it is acknowledged by McAllen that these boilers were the property of Haywood & Snyder, which for the accommodation of McAllen were to be left on his premises, for three months, after the expiration of which time they were at liberty to remove them. This agreement was in confirmation of the previous declarations of McAllen disclaiming any right to the boilers, and did not in any degree impair or abridge the rights of Haywood & Snyder. The time given was for the accommodation of McAllen, to allow him to make an arrangement with his creditors; and whatever extension of time there was in allowing the boilers to remain on McAllen's freehold, contravened then the rights of no one but Haywood & Snyder and McAllen. McAllen was the only person who had any right to object or require removal; and as he acquiesced, he is presumed to hold the possession subject to the will and demand of Haywood & Snyder. McAllen no doubt clung to the hope that he could still make an arrangement to the advantage of his creditors; and if this were to be effected by a sale, that the arrangement might provide for the use of the steam-engine to be completed by Haywood & Snyder—McAllen securing them for the price of

[Shell v. Haywood & Snyder.]

the engine. Such expectation may account for the forbearance of the makers to remove, and the willingness of McAllen to hold the possession as bailee for Haywood & Snyder.

The possession of McAllen under the circumstances could not deceive or mislead any of his creditors. The possession of part of an unfinished engine would lead either creditor or purchaser of ordinary vigilance to inquire into the condition of the contract. No creditor or purchaser was misled. The debts contracted by McAllen were antecedent to the delivery of any part of the engine. There was not in this case either legal or constructive fraud to divest Haywood & Snyder of their right of property in the boilers or wheel.

The defendant, who places his defence in part on the allegation that the boilers were a part of the realty, made, as sheriff, his levy on them as personal property to be severed and removed, and sold them at public sale as personal property. After his levy on the boilers and wheel, he levied on the mill and realty, with a minute description of its improvements and advantages, without embracing the boilers, which he had made the subject of distinct levy and sale. The defendant received notice before the sale by him of the claim of Haywood & Snyder to the boilers and wheel, which he did not regard. For his proceeding he said he was indemnified. The purchaser of the realty at sheriff's sale did not purchase in ignorance of the claim by the manufacturers of the boilers and wheel. They had been treated by the sheriff as personal property, removable, and sold as such on the same execution by which the realty was levied. The unfinished condition of the engine was enough to lead a purchaser to inquire whose property it was.

This case, in the opinion of the court, is governed by the intention and agreement of the parties having the control of the rights of property and possession in the boilers and wheel of the unfinished engine; and under the contracts between them, the plaintiffs, Haywood & Snyder, had both the right of property and the right to possession of the boilers and wheel at the time of the levy and sale made by defendant. The right of removal was in the plaintiffs, and the right to sustain this action.

The other errors assigned by plaintiff in error are not, in the opinion of the court, sustained, and the judgment of the court below is affirmed.

Louden *versus* Blythe.

1. The certificate of a justice of the peace in relation to the acknowledgment of a mortgage by a *feme covert* is not conclusive, but parol evidence is admissible to show that the acknowledgment by the wife was not done of her free will and accord, but that undue means were used for obtaining it; and if the mortgagee has a knowledge of facts calculated to put him on inquiry as to the manner in which the acknowledgment was obtained, he must abide the consequences.

2. If interrogatories are substantially answered in the course of the deposition, it is sufficient.

3. The declarations of the wife objecting to making the acknowledgment, made immediately before and at the time of the acknowledgment, though during a period of several hours, are admissible as part of the *res gestæ*.

ERROR to the Common Pleas of *Adams county*.

This was an action of ejectment by Samuel Louden *vs*. Sarah Amanda Blythe and George W. Heagy.

Ezra Blythe and John McCleary, of the town of Fairfield, in the county of Adams, in the year 1843 were partners in trade, doing business under the name and style of Blythe & McCleary. In February 1843, the firm became somewhat embarrassed, and several suits were instituted against it by creditors. On the 27th day of February 1843, to relieve them in their difficulties, at their request, Samuel Louden, the plaintiff in this case, was induced to contribute of his means for that purpose, and as security to him for engagements then entered into by him, three different mortgages were executed in his favor: one by John McCleary, of his individual property in Fairfield—one by Ezra Blythe and two of his brothers, of their undivided interest in a certain tract of land; and one by Ezra Blythe and Sarah Amanda Blythe his wife, for two lots of ground in Fairfield—the said two lots being held in fee by said Sarah Amanda when she married Ezra Blythe.

Samuel Louden complied, on his part, with all the conditions and stipulations embraced in the mortgages referred to.

Ezra Blythe died in August 1844.

Upon the mortgages executed by John McCleary, and by Ezra Blythe and his brothers, nothing was realized.

Samuel Louden brought this action of ejectment, No. 3, April term 1850, upon the mortgage executed by the said Ezra Blythe and Sarah Amanda his wife, against Sarah Amanda Blythe and George W. Heagy, to recover possession of the mortgaged premises.

Mrs. Blythe, one of the defendants, made defence on the ground that her signature to the mortgage had been obtained against her will, and that upon her separate examination she had not declared to the justice of the peace, before whom the acknowledgment was

[Louden v. Blythe.]

made, that she had sealed and delivered said mortgage voluntarily, and of her own free will and accord.

On the 23d day of April 1851, the cause was tried before Judge DURKEE.

The plaintiff first gave in evidence the mortgage by Ezra Blythe and wife, bearing date the 27th February 1843. Witness, Nath'l Grayson.

A certificate as follows was upon it:—

Adams County, *ss*.

Be it remembered, that on the twenty-seventh day of February, eighteen hundred and forty-three, personally appeared before me, a justice of the peace in and for the county aforesaid, Ezra Blythe and Sarah Amanda his wife, parties to the above indenture, and acknowledged the same to be their act and deed, to the intent that as such it might be recorded according to law. She, the said Sarah Amanda, being of full age, and being by me examined separate and apart from her said husband, and the full contents of said indenture having been by me first made known to her, she did declare that she did voluntarily, of her own free will and accord, without any coercion or compulsion of her said husband, sign, seal, and deliver the above and foregoing indenture as and for her act and deed. In testimony whereof, I have hereunto set my hand and seal the day and year aforesaid.

NATH'L GRAYSON. [SEAL.]

Recorded 8th August 1843.

The plaintiff then proved loans by him, his engagements as surety for Blythe & McCleary, and payments made in pursuance of the conditions of the above mortgage, amounting to about $4400, exclusive of interest.

Admitted that defendant is in possession, and was, at the institution of this suit.

On part of *defendants*, the other two mortgages to plaintiff were given in evidence, viz., the mortgage, John McCleary to Samuel Louden, dated 27th February 1843. Recorded 8th August 1843, before referred to.

Mortgage, Ezra Blythe and brothers to Samuel Louden, date 27th February 1843. Recorded 8th August 1843; also before referred to.

It was admitted that the *property in dispute* was held in fee by Sarah A. Blythe, defendant, when she intermarried with Ezra Blythe, and when the mortgage was executed.

On part of defendants it was offered to prove substantially as stated in the testimony of Mrs. M. Blythe. The offer contained the following:—During the whole time, the defendant was in great distress, much agitated, and frequently shed tears. These circumstances took place in the evening by candle-light. The

[Louden v. Blythe.]

plaintiff, Samuel Louden, was present in the sitting-room, with Ezra Blythe and others, where the papers were prepared, at the time the defendant was first requested to execute the mortgage, and refused to do so; but was not present at the time the justice came into defendant's room to take her acknowledgment.

Objection was made on part of plaintiff, but the testimony was admitted. The conclusion of the decision of Judge DURKEE, as to admitting the testimony, was as follows:—In answer to the argument that the plaintiff, not having participated in the fraud, if one was committed, cannot be affected by it, I would say, that I think it was incumbent on him to see that the proper acknowledgment was in fact made by defendant, as her signature, without such acknowledgment, would amount to nothing. In regard to the evidence of what occurred at the time she signed the mortgage, what she said and did, &c, I am inclined to admit it as a part of the *res gesta*, as tending, in some degree, to show whether the transaction was consummated by a due acknowledgment of the instrument. As to her subsequent declarations made after the justice left the house, they are not evidence.

Mrs. Blythe testified substantially as follows:—I was present at the house of Ezra Blythe in Fairfield, when a mortgage was executed. Don't recollect exactly when it was. It was written in the parlor by a brother of Ezra Blythe. Uncle David, Uncle Ezra, and Mr. Samuel Louden were present. I was living there at the time. I was in my aunt's bed-room, and Uncle Ezra came in, and asked her to sign the mortgage. He had it not with him. She refused; told him he was aware of her unwillingness to do it; that she had told him before that she would not put her name to it, and that she was determined that she would not. Uncle still insisted, and turned away apparently agitated; replied that if she did not, he would not live on the property with her, and went out; and the brother who wrote the mortgage came in and insisted upon her signing it. I can't tell what he said to her. She told him that she had told him when he was writing the mortgage that it was of no use, for she would not put her name to it. He offered her his glasses, and asked her if the light was sufficient. She again replied, that it was of no use, that she never intended to put her name to it. He insisted on it again and again. She was in bed. She got up and stood by the side of the bureau, and put her name to it. She then took the pen, and gave it a dash as if to strike out her name. I was not close enough to look at the mortgage. He then left the room, and came back in a few moments with Esquire Grayson. Esquire Grayson asked her if she had put her name to the mortgage with her own free will and consent. She said, Mr. Grayson, it is of no use to deceive you; I had no will in the business; my will was not consulted. He then asked her a second question, one of the same meaning, referring to her signing

[Louden v. Blythe.]

the deed. She said she had not done it of her own free will. Then he asked her if she was afraid of being misused or beaten by Uncle Ezra, or if she had been misused by him. She replied, that uncle had not done that, neither did she fear it; that she had been pressed into it against her will. Mr. Grayson and uncle then went out into the passage, where I heard them whispering, but could not tell what they said. There was no writing done after the justice came into the room. Esquire Grayson did not write any thing that I saw. Aunt was part of the time in the parlor, and part in the bed-room, when the mortgage was being written. Cousin Adeline Massey was in the parlor after the mortgage was written, while the men were yet there. Don't remember that any thing was said between my uncle and aunt while in the parlor. They said something about signing the mortgage; I don't remember what it was. My aunt was in tears most of the time. She was lying on the bed when Esquire Grayson was there. She was in great sorrow, and had been for some days before. She manifested it by tears. *It was about dusk; a candle was lighted.* They were there all the afternoon in the other room, to do the writings. Her health was not very good.

On cross-examination she said, *inter alia*, that Ezra Blythe died in August 1844.

On part of *the defendant* was offered a deposition of Mrs. Massey, taken on commission.

One of the cross-interrogatories, viz. the 8th, filed on the part of *defendant*, required her to state any thing else she knew that would be evidence for defendant in the suit. One commissioner was named on part of defendant, and two were named on the part of plaintiff, or either of them.

The commission returned was executed by the commissioner named on part of defendant. The commission was directed to the three persons named as commissioners, or either of them.

The deposition taken was objected to on the part of the *plaintiff*:—1st. Because the interrogatories on part of defendant are not all answered, viz., the 8th, and because no notice was given to the commissioner named on the part of the plaintiff, and because the commission was not properly directed. 2d. To the evidence, as being inadmissible. Admitted. Exception by plaintiff.

To the third interrogatory she testified, *inter alia*, that she was present when Ezra Blythe called upon his wife, the defendant Sarah A. Blythe, and requested her to execute a mortgage for her house and lot to the plaintiff, and told her that he would be enabled to lift it in a very short time. She replied that she was willing that all her personal property should be sold to pay all the debts of the firm, but she was not willing to sign a mortgage for the house and lot, even for one day, for she felt certain that he would be disappointed in lifting it at the time expected. The said Ezra

[Louden v. Blythe.]

insisted and urged her to agree to sign the mortgage. She declined peremptorily. He still insisted, and said he would send for Mr. Grayson, the magistrate, to take her acknowledgment. She replied that he need not send for Grayson, that she would not execute the mortgage. But her husband did send for Mr. Grayson, notwithstanding her protestations; and when Mr. Grayson came, the said Sarah appeared greatly distressed, and retired to a private room, and went to bed. The said Ezra, Samuel Louden, a brother of Ezra, and Mr. Grayson, were all in a different room from affiant, and were apparently transacting some business. Witness saw pen, ink, and paper taken in, and after they had been there for some time, Ezra Blythe passed into the room where the said Sarah was in bed, heard him talking to her, appeared to be persuading her, she weeping. He then left the room, and shortly afterwards returned, accompanied by a brother of Ezra and Mr. Grayson, and after some conversation between the parties, all three of the gentlemen left her room, and returned to the room where they had been previously engaged in business. Affiant was in a room immediately adjacent, and within hearing of the bed upon which said Sarah was at the time she executed said mortgage. Mrs. Blythe remained in bed for some time after Mr. Grayson and Mr. Louden had left.

To another interrogatory:

Answer—That she, Sarah A. Blythe, was in delicate health, and appeared greatly excited and distressed at the time referred to.

Fourth interrogatory:

Answer—I have stated all the facts within my knowledge, in the preceding answers, that would be of service to either party.

On the part of the plaintiff, Nathaniel Grayson, Esq., was called. He testified that he was confident of the truth of the facts set forth in the certificate as to the acknowledgment. That he never asked Mrs. Blythe if she had been beaten or abused, or feared she would be. On cross-examination, he testified that Mrs. Blythe was standing when he went into the room; that when he entered she appeared to be distressed; there was nothing said for some time, except an explanation by a brother of Ezra Blythe of the reason of getting up the mortgage; it was addressed to witness; the brother read the mortgage; my recollection of the matter is very imperfect; it is a long time since; I never charge my memory with such matters; I must depend upon my manner of doing business. When the mortgage was read, she said, whether in answer to a question, put by me, or not, I don't recollect, "This is done against my will." She said it was not of her seeking; she said she felt confused and at a loss which way to act, or something to that effect. When I spoke of compulsion or coercion, she appeared surprised that any such thing should be used. I think I put my name to the acknowledgment in the front room or parlor. My first recollection is of meeting Mrs. Blythe and taking her by the hand. This conversation of

[Louden v. Blythe.]

Mrs. Blythe that I have detailed, is all that I have any recollection of. There is nothing ridiculous in asking about compulsion or coercion, because it is in the acknowledgment; but to ask her if she had been abused or beaten by her husband, or feared she would be, if she did not, would be, I think, impertinent and improper.

He further testified that Samuel, Ezra Blythe, and two of his brothers, and, he thought, John McCleary, were in the room when he returned. "I have said to Mrs. Blythe and others, that I would never take another acknowledgment under similar circumstances, from a woman who seemed so much discomposed as Mrs. Blythe was—so painful to my feelings was the distress she manifested at the time. It was during the first part of the time that she was discomposed, and she did not seem to be entirely composed while I was in the room."

I don't recollect that the business was introduced to Mrs. Blythe until she had become more composed and began to converse. She was weeping when I first went in. I think she did not continue to weep all the time I was there.

Cross-examined:—I don't recollect any thing further in regard to her condition than I stated on my cross-examination.

Verdict was rendered for defendant.

Error was assigned, in admitting defendants' offer; and, second, in admitting the deposition taken on commission.

The case was argued by *McLean*, with whom was *Reed*, and *Evans*, for Louden, plaintiff in error.

It was contended that it was not competent to falsify by parol evidence the certificate as to the separate examination of the wife, except in cases of fraud and imposition: Jamison *v.* Jamison, 3 *Whar.* 457; Craig *v.* Shallcross, 10 *Ser. & R.* 468-69; Watson *v.* Bailey, 1 *Bin.* 470; 7 *Watts* 228, Withers *v.* Baird; 9 *Ser. & R.* 274, Jordan *v.* Jordan. That no evidence was given that the plaintiff was in the presence of the wife on the day of the acknowledgment, or knew of the circumstances attending it.

That the declarations of Mrs. Blythe were made when the plaintiff was not present, and were admitted.

That *all* the interrogatories should have been put and answered; 1 *Yeates* 404; 2 *W. C. C. Rep.* 184–87.

Cooper, with whom was *McCreary*, for defendant in error.— Parol evidence is admissible to contradict the certificate of the magistrate, in case of fraud or imposition: Jamison *v.* Jamison, 3 *Whar.* 457; also for the purpose of proving forgery or fraud Barnet *v.* Barnet, 15 *Ser & R.* 72; or to prove collusion between the husband and the justice, in consequence of which it was falsely certified that the wife had appeared and made an acknowledgment

[Louden v. Blythe.]

such as is required by law: TILGHMAN, C. J., in Barnet v. Barnet, *id.* 73; or to show that the acknowledgment was obtained by fraud or duress of the wife: Schrader v. Decker, 7 *Barr* 14.

There is nothing in the objection urged by the plaintiff, that he stood in the relation of an innocent person in the transaction. There was evidence in the offer going to charge him with actual notice; and without this, the objection could not avail him, as the defendant stands in equal equity. A purchaser for valuable consideration, without notice of fraud, shall not be assisted against the party on whom the fraud was committed: 2 *Fonblanque's Eq.* b. 2, ch. 6, sec. 2, note h; 1 *id.* b. 1, ch. 4, sec. 25, note. *In æquali jure melior est conditio possidentis.* *Plow.* 296.

As to the second error assigned, we say, that the interrogatories were *all* answered *substantially*, which is sufficient: Nelson et al. v. United States, 1 *P. C. C. Rep.* 235–37; Winthrop v. Union Insurance Co., 2 *W. C. C. Rep.* 7.

The exception goes only to the 8th interrogatory on the part of defendant, which is, in form, a request:—"State any thing else you know that would be evidence for the defendant, Sarah A. Blythe, in this suit." It might be thought strange that the *plaintiff* should object to the entire absence of any answer to this request, if the fact were so; but we find it distinctly answered in the reply of the witness to the fourth or general interrogatory on part of plaintiff, where she says—"I have stated all the facts within my knowledge in the preceding answers, that would be of service to either party." The *order* and *form* in which the interrogatories are answered are not material: Gilpin v. Consequa, 1 *P. C. C. Rep.* 85, 88.

The declarations given in evidence were made at and immediately before the time of the signing of the mortgage, and while it was in the course of preparation; it was all *one transaction*, and at *one time*, though extending through three or four hours; they were admissible, we say, as part of the *res gestæ*.

They were admissible upon another ground. The defendant alleged that she had signed the mortgage under duress, which, as a species of fraud, opens the door for the admission of evidence of the whole context of circumstances in the transaction sought to be affected by it.

The case of Schrader v. Decker is in point; there, the refusal of the wife to sign the deed, *two hours* before it was executed, was part of the offer which this court say ought to have been admitted; and we submit that the fact of the importunity and resistance being continued for a longer time makes the case by so much stronger: Blair v. Coffman, 2 *Overt.* 176. Duress having been pleaded, evidence of conversation and acts before and after the supposed duress may show the state of mind in which the act was done.

It was not proved that the plaintiff was present when the mort-

[Louden v. Blythe.]

gage was executed, but the evidence shows that he was at the house on the afternoon previous to its execution.

McClean, in reply.—No notice was given to the mortgagee of the compulsion. Mrs. B. says that Louden was in the house when the mortgage was prepared, but it was not proved that he was in the room when Mrs. Blythe was asked to sign. The point of Louden *not* having notice was not raised : it was mentioned by the court in admitting the evidence, but that was not to the jury.

The opinion of the court, filed August 2, was delivered by
CHAMBERS, J.—This case presents one instance out of the many that occur, by which a deed is extorted from a wife, conveying her real estate, under the forms of law and the sanction and certificate of a judicial officer, yet in reality against her free will and consent. By the common law the wife's land could be aliened only with her assent, deliberately expressed, on a fair, full, and careful separate examination in a court of record. The condition of real property under the provincial government, its common transfer, as an article of trade and barter, with but little form, and the want of judicial tribunals, induced a departure in this State from the requirements of the common law for the protection of a wife in the alienation of her lands, and substituted the form of acknowledgment which by legislative enactment was confirmed and provided for in February 1770. Whatever the policy or exigency may have been that induced the relaxation of the law for the protection of the rights of *feme coverts* in their real estate, it is not creditable to our jurisprudence or to the intelligence of the times, that, with all the abuses of the exercise of the power by which a wife is divested of her real estate, and which so notoriously prevail, it should not have led to some legislative amendment of the law, providing for the protection of the wife, by a shield that had in it some substance. So great is marital influence, and the defenceless condition of the wife, that it is a rare case that she has firmness and independence to resist, for any length of time, the importunity of a rapacious husband. Whilst she has a husband for her protection against the world, she has, by the law of Pennsylvania, a most inefficient protection against the influence and control of her husband, who has her confidence and the keeping of her will. It is said by Justice GIBSON, in Watson *v.* Mercer, 6 *Ser. & R.* 50, that "the policy of the law should be as far as possible to narrow rather than widen the field of this controlling influence."

It is, we think, for our judicial tribunals to administer to the wife the protection professed to be given by the forms of the law, as far as justice and public security will allow.

In the present case, the plaintiff, S. Louden, claimed the lots and mansion for which the ejectment was brought by him, under a

[Louden v. Blythe.]

mortgage executed by the defendant, Mrs. Blythe, jointly with her late husband, Ezra Blythe, of the real property of the wife. The acknowledgment of Mrs. Blythe was in the *form* required by the act of Assembly, and certified by Nathaniel Grayson, a justice of the peace of Adams county.

On the part of Mrs. Blythe, evidence was offered in the court below to impeach the acknowledgment as certified, for alleged imposition, falsehood, and fraud, as contained in the offer of defendant. This was objected to by the plaintiff, but the objection was overruled, the evidence admitted, and exception taken, and is assigned for error in this court by the plaintiff.

The justice who takes and certifies the acknowledgment of the wife to a deed is acting judicially. He is the commissioner and organ of the law, intrusted with the duty of seeing that it is her act and deed, and that she did voluntarily and of her own free will and accord, without any coercion or compulsion of her husband, sign, &c. His duty is an important one to the wife and her representatives; and it is a responsible one to the public, who are interested that the law be faithfully administered. We cannot cast into oblivion our knowledge that this duty is often, by justices of the peace, and sometimes by other judicial officers, as has been said, "hurried over almost in the presence of the husband." And when the examination is out of the presence of the husband, the justice seems to think, he has only to read over, in a hurried manner, the prepared form of acknowledgment which he has in his hand, and if open resistance is not made by the dependent wife, the acknowledgment is certified in due form, with all its particulars. There is no free and searching inquiry by the magistrate as to the free will and consent with which she is parting with her estate to satisfy the demands of an improvident and importunate husband. The law intends that he should do what is enjoined, and he certifies, under his hand and seal, as a judicial officer, that all was done in conformity to law.

Can it be that such acknowledgments are of so high and sacred character as to import absolute verity, and cannot be assailed by parol evidence? Had the acknowledgment been in a court of record by fine, it would have been open to impeachment for fraud: 1 *Mad. Ch.* 266; Schrader *v.* Decker, 9 *Barr* 14. But, say the court in the last case, " that we would deprive married women of all substantial protection, did we give to the separate examination of a judge or justice of the peace the conclusive effect of an examination by commissioners to levy a fine, which is more private, careful, and searching." " The necessities of justice therefore demand that the transaction be open to objection, not only for fraud, but concealed duress."

In the case of Jamison *v.* Jamison, 3 *Whar.* 457, it was held that parol evidence of what passed at the time of the acknowledgment,

[Louden v. Blythe.]

is not admissible for the purpose of contradicting the certificate, except in cases of fraud or imposition. Parol evidence may be received for the purpose of proving forgery or fraud, or collusion between the husband and the justice, in consequence of which it was falsely certified: Barnet v. Barnet, 15 *Ser. & R.* 72–3.

A regard to the policy of the law, for the security of titles and the protection of the rights of property which are passed by conveyances and assurances of which these acknowledgments and certificates are a common part, will restrain this court from allowing such acknowledgments to be impeached by parol evidence, contradicting the facts certified, in the absence of fraud and imposition; and where there are fraud and imposition alleged, the knowledge of it ought to be brought home to the grantee, or of such circumstances within his knowledge of the want of free will and consent on the part of the wife, as should lead him to inform himself of the reality of a free execution and acknowledgment by the wife whose property was to be divested. Where the grantee has knowledge of facts to put him on that inquiry, if silent and inactive on the subject, it is at his peril, and he must abide the consequences.

In this case it was proposed to be proved, and it was so proved, that when Mrs. Blythe was in the sitting-room with Ezra Blythe, her husband, and S. Louden, the plaintiff, she was asked to execute this mortgage, which she refused to do, and retired to her chamber, where she lay in bed weeping. She was followed there and importuned by her husband to sign the mortgage, which she still refused to do, stating to him that he was aware of her unwillingness to divest herself of this property, which she desired to retain as a home for herself and him, if he survived her. He continued to press her, and she refused. Having persevered for a long time without success, her husband turned away, apparently agitated, declaring that he would not remain on the property if she refused to execute the mortgage; and he went out of the chamber. She was then pressed by the relative of her husband, with repeated solicitation,—when she got from her bed and wrote her name to the mortgage, and immediately gave the pen a dash, as if to strike out her name. The justice, who was in the other room with S. Louden throughout the afternoon, is brought into the chamber of the weeping wife at candle-light, and asks Mrs. Blythe if she signed the mortgage with her own consent, to which she answered, "It is of no use to deceive you: I had no will in the business; my will was not consulted." The justice again asked her whether he understood her to say that she did not sign the mortgage with her own free will and consent, to which she replied, "I did say so." He repeated the question several times, and to which Mrs. Blythe gave the same answer. Her health was delicate, and she was in tears most of the afternoon. She declared that she was willing that all her personal property should go to pay the debts of the firm of

[Louden v. Blythe.]

which her husband was a partner, but that she was unwilling to sign a mortgage of the house and lot, as she felt certain that her husband would be disappointed in lifting it. N. Grayson, Esq., justice of the peace, who certified the acknowledgment, being called on the part of S. Louden, substantially confirmed most of the material facts testified to by witnesses of unimpeached veracity.

The justice testified that when he entered the room, Mrs. Blythe appeared to be distressed, and was weeping, and that when the mortgage was read, she said, " This is done against my will," and that the witness had since said to Mrs. Blythe and others that he never would take another acknowledgment under similar circumstances, from a woman so much discomposed as Mrs. Blythe was; so painful to his feelings was the distress she manifested at the time.

N. Grayson, Esq., who testified to such want of free will and consent on the part of Mrs. Blythe, was the justice of the peace who gave the certificate of her acknowledgment on the mortgage in all the form required by the law, and which, it is contended, is of such solemnity, and of so high a character in legal estimation, that it was not to be assailed by the evidence offered and received. It appears that the justice, on subsequent reflection, felt not a little compunction of conscience, in allowing himself to have been instrumental, as the organ of the law, to take and certify to such an acknowledgment by this distressed, opposing, and defenceless wife. For we have him declaring " that he never would take another acknowledgment under similar circumstances." Well might he regret that on that occasion, as a public magistrate, he did not take an independent stand on the side of the law and of the oppressed wife.

Was not the certificate of the justice to the acknowledgment of Mrs. Blythe on the mortgage exhibited, in view of the facts disclosed, if believed, an imposition and fraud on her?

Can it be that the law interposes any rule or obstacle to prevent the admission of the evidence offered and received by the court below? Here is a wife decidedly refusing to execute the mortgage in the presence of the justice and S. Louden the mortgagee, and flies from the sitting-room to her chamber and bed, to seek solace in tears, having no friend to protect her. In delicate health she lies on her bed and continues to weep throughout the afternoon, where, in the midst of her tears, she is annoyed by a husband's influence, and with the threat, if she did not sign, he would not remain on the property—thus threatening to desert her. It is said, A broken spirit who can bear? Here were the spirit and feelings of a wife crushed by the unkindness of her husband. There were in the circumstances of this case facts proper for the consideration of the jury, as evidence of imposition, undue influence, and fraud.

From the facts in evidence, we cannot suppose S. Louden,

[Louden v. Blythe.]

the plaintiff, ignorant of the circumvention and cruelty by which this wife was to be deprived of her remaining real estate, which she clung to as the home and shelter of her declining years. He was in the sitting-room, about midday, when she refused to execute the mortgage. Why was an afternoon required for the work, and a succession of visits by the husband and others to her weeping chamber, if all was right and voluntary. He saw and heard enough, if believed by the jury, to put him on the inquiry, and make him ascertain for himself, whether she was executing this mortgage "of her own free will and accord."

We are willing to believe that Mr. Ezra Blythe may, like many embarrassed men, have underrated his indebtedness, and did in sincerity suppose that he would be able to extricate himself and lift the mortgage. His wife, with more sagacity, had no such expectations, in which she was right.

Not to have admitted the evidence offered would have been to place the certificate of a justice of the peace in such a case beyond inquiry, and above the most solemn records; left wives as to their real estate in the power of their husbands and any justice of the peace they might select, and been a reflection on the administration of justice.

It is the opinion of this court that there was no error by the court below in admitting the evidence excepted to and assigned for error.

The errors assigned to the deposition taken on commission are not sustained. The charge of the court to the jury, if delivered, has not been brought up with the record.

Judgment of Court of Common Pleas affirmed.

BELL, J., dissented, for reasons assigned in his opinion filed.

INDEX.

ABANDONMENT.
    The court may intimate to the jury an opinion that there has been an abandonment, and submit the facts to their consideration, with instructions as to what constitutes an abandonment.—*Sample* v. *Robb*, 305.

ACKNOWLEDGMENT.
    As to acknowledgment of a mortgage by a *feme covert*, see *Louden* v. *Blythe*, 532.

ACTION. See CONTRACT, 6-10; PARENT AND CHILD.
1. In the case of an action to recover damages for breach of a parol contract for the purchase of land, the right of action accrues when the vendor conveys to a stranger. It exists *before eviction* by the grantee.—*Thurston* v. *Franklin College*, 154.
2. On an appeal from the judgment of a justice of the peace, it need not appear in the *declaration* that the claim of the plaintiff was for an amount within the jurisdiction of the justice; it is sufficient if that appear on the trial.—*Hackman* v. *Flory*, 196.
3. In an action for service rendered, the plaintiff may show services rendered by his wife as well as himself, though her services are not mentioned in the declaration.—*Id.*
4. In an action by the husband for service rendered by himself and also by his wife, the declarations of the wife, during service, as to the terms of her employment, are admissible on the part of defendant.—*Id.*
5. In the case of a hiring for a year, at a specified sum per month, it is not competent for the employer, within the period contracted for, to reduce the amount of monthly pay, without the consent of the other party.—*Id.*
6. A transfer of certain bonds and real estate was made by a principal debtor to the son of his surety, to indemnify the estate of the latter for being bound in a bond to M. Before M. expressed her assent to the transfer, the principal debtor assigned the fund to another, for whose use suit was brought in the name of the principal against the first transferee, but there was a failure to recover. The bond to M. was never paid: *Held*, that the administrator of the estate of M. could not maintain assumpsit against the first transferee for the amount of money received by him from the property assigned to him, on account of the want of privity of contract between M. and the said transferee.—*Finney* v. *Finney*, 380.
7. In a suit on a recognizance in the Orphans' Court given by an heir who took one of three purparts at the appraisement, executed in favor of the Commonwealth for the payment to the other heirs their proportional shares in the purpart, it was admissible for the recognizor, the defendant, under the plea of payment with leave to show that one of the other purparts, not taken at the appraisement, was sold by a trustee under order of the Orphans' Court, and that all of the balance of the proceeds, after payment of debts of the intestate, was paid to the plaintiff, and that the defendant in the suit never made any objection. The fact whether or not it was received as part payment, should have been submitted to the jury.—*Kidd* v. *The Commonwealth*, 427.

8. Such a recognizance should be sued in the name of the Commonwealth as the legal party, though it is proper that the name of the persons suing should be stated on the record. A mistake, however, in this respect, will not furnish a defence against the Commonwealth, as the court should look to the distribution of the amount recovered. The judgment should not be for the *penalty*, but for the amount of the interest of those suing.—*Id.*

9. It is not necessary that all the *cestuis que use* should be marked of record. Less than the whole number may sue, and they may recover as much of the fund as they show themselves entitled to, leaving the balance for those entitled who may afterwards sue. But where they represent *one heir*, their joinder in the suit would seem to be peculiarly proper.—*Id.*

ACTION ON THE CASE. See SLANDER.

1. In an action on the case to recover damages for an injury sustained by plaintiff from his falling into an area-way, or passage dug in the pavement, leading into the cellar of defendant's house, erected on a public street in Harrisburg, and through the culpable neglect of the defendant left exposed, by which the plaintiff's leg was broken, it was *held*, that if by ordinary or reasonable care on the part of the plaintiff, he might have avoided the injury, he was not entitled to recover; otherwise he was entitled to recover.—*Beatty* v. *Gilmore*, 463.

2. What shall be deemed ordinary care must depend on the circumstances of each case, of which the jury is to judge; and if there be no facts proved from which a deduction can be drawn, the presumption is against the defendant whose misconduct rendered the accident possible.—*Id.*

3. In such a case it is not incumbent on the plaintiff to prove the exercise by him of ordinary care to avoid the injury, but the proof of the want of it on the part of the plaintiff lies on the defendant. He who avers a fact in excuse of his own misfeasance, must prove it.—*Id.*

4. It was competent to prove by a witness who examined the place where the accident occurred, but who was not present *when* it occurred, that in his opinion the place was dangerous.—*Id.*

5. It was not error for the court to term a dangerous opening in a much frequented street, in a large town, a public nuisance.—*Id.*

ACT OF ASSEMBLY. See EXECUTION, 3–5.

ADMINISTRATION.

1. The discretion given to the register as to granting letters of administration is limited to a selection from those asking the administration, if competent; from each class entitled to administer, in its order.—*McClellan's Appeal*, 110.

2. The widow is entitled to administration upon the estate of her deceased husband, and if she renounces, the register may select from the children or next of kin, preferring males to females; but the widow or next of kin or both combined cannot pass by one of the children or next of kin competent and willing to take the administration, and vest it in a stranger.—*Id.*

3. Though the widow released her right to the administration in favor of persons whom she designated, but who were not entitled to the same, and certain of the children afterwards joined with her in a petition in favor of such persons, it was *held*, that this was not an absolute, but only a qualified release or renunciation, and the designation being beyond her power, the paper was inoperative, and left her rights and those of the children as before.—*Id.*

ADMINISTRATOR. See EXECUTORS AND ADMINISTRATORS.

AGENT.

An agent having authority only *to collect a debt*, has no right to take a note for the amount of it, from the debtor to himself, and thus substitute himself as creditor; but if such an arrangement be afterwards *ratified* by the principal, the latter is bound by it, and the debtor is released from liability to the principal on the original claim.—*McCulloch* v. *McKee,* 289.

AMENDMENT.
1. In an action on a contract for the sale of hogs, the declaration of the plaintiff alleged their delivery, which the proof failed to establish; an application was made during the trial for leave to amend the declaration by averring the readiness of plaintiff to deliver and the refusal of the defendant to receive and pay for the hogs, which amendment the court refused to permit: *Held,* that such refusal was error.—*Stewart and others* v. *Kelly,* 160.
2. If the description in the writ, of the land for which the ejectment is brought, be defective, the defect may be supplied by another description, filed with the leave of the court.—*Sample* v. *Robb,* 305.

ARBITRATION.
In a sci. fa. to revive a judgment, the pleas were *nul tiel record*, payment, and payment with leave. Replication *non sol,* and that there is such a record. Arbitrators appointed under a rule entered under the act of 1836, found for plaintiff a gross sum: *Held,* that the plea of *nul tiel record* did not exempt the case from arbitration, but that the arbitrators had jurisdiction of the whole cause.—*Lange* v. *Stouffer,* 251.

ARTICLE OF AGREEMENT.
An article of agreement for the sale of land is merged in the deed made in pursuance of it, which is delivered and accepted.—*Jones* v. *Wood,* 25.

ASSESSMENT. See LANDS; ISLANDS, 2.

ASSIGNMENT. See JUDGMENTS.
1. By the 4th section of the act of 16th April 1849, judgments confessed to evade the act of 17th April 1843, concerning preferences in assignments, followed by an assignment of real estate, are void as against other creditors, and are not entitled to preference out of the proceeds of sale of such real estate, but are entitled only to a *pro rata* payment with the other debts of the debtor.—*Summers' Appeal,* 169.
2. A debtor, after suit against him, voluntarily executed five judgment bonds in favor of other creditors, intending at the time to make an assignment of his *real estate,* and about the same time selling portions of his personal property; after the entry of judgments on the bonds he executed an assignment of his *real estate* only, in trust for creditors. On the day it was recorded, an award, in favor of the plaintiff in the suit, was filed. The remaining *personal estate* of the debtor was sold on a fi. fa. on a judgment on a bond executed subsequent to the recording of the assignment. The real estate was sold by the trustee, for a sum not sufficient to pay the five judgments: *Held,* that the five judgments were not alone entitled to the proceeds of sale of the real estate, but that the same were to be distributed *pro rata,* amongst all the creditors.—*Id.*
3. If the debtor at the time of confessing the judgments knew that he was insolvent, his subsequent execution of the assignment is conclusive evidence that the judgments were given in fraud of the act of 1843.—*Id.*
4. None but the creditors of the husband can resist an assignment by him of a claim under a recognizance, made for the purpose of defrauding them. The debtor of the claim thus transferred can safely pay it on the foot of a judgment on the recognizance.—*Stoner* v. *The Commonwealth,* 387.
5. In the case of an assignment of a claim by one, who it was alleged was incapable from imbecility of mind to make it, the personal representatives of the assignor after her death, and they alone, can contest the *bona fides* of the transaction, and only by an application to the court after the money has been recovered.—*Id.*

6. A debtor by book-account assigned to his creditor a promissory note and also a book-account, with an agreement under seal that in case the same could not be recovered of the persons indebted, then the assignor to pay the amount with charges thereupon, the assignor agreeing to notify the counsel of the creditor when the debtors came to the neighborhood where they were to be proceeded against, which information he never gave ; the attorney of the creditor agreeing that if any thing remained after discharging the claim of the creditor, it should be returned to the debtor : *Held*, that there being no agreement to receive the note and book-account *in satisfaction* of the original indebtedness, the assignment was but a *collateral* security ; that under the 5th section of the bankrupt act, the claim of the creditor on the said contract of guaranty was provable against the estate of the debtor, who was subsequently discharged as a bankrupt, and that the debtor was consequently discharged from liability to the creditor. See remarks on cases of McMullin *v.* Bank of Penn Township, 2 *Barr* 343, and Cake *v.* Lewis, 8 *Barr* 493.—*Stone* v. *Miller*, 450.
7. Whether a note or bond is accepted in satisfaction of the original claim is for the jury to decide, and not for the court as a matter of law.—*Id.*
8. Where claims transferred to a creditor consist of the indebtedness of others, and there is no agreement to receive the same in *satisfaction,* they are to be considered as *collateral* security for the original debt.—*Id.*

ASSUMPSIT.
Where a broker was to receive a definite commission for procuring a purchaser for certain lots of ground, and complied with his part of the contract, but the defendant, without good reason, failed to fulfil his part of the contract,—*Held*, that the broker could recover, in *indebitatus assumpsit*, the amount of compensation agreed upon.—*Edwards* v. *Goldsmith*, 43.

ATTACHMENT.
A judgment in a sister State is to be deemed to have the effect of a *domestic* judgment, in relation to the cause of action ; and where the defendant had notice it is conclusive of the subject-matter, and the original cause of action is merged in it; therefore, a suit pending in the State of Maryland, and a judgment subsequently obtained therein, is a bar to a proceeding between the same parties and for the same cause of action, by foreign attachment, instituted in Pennsylvania, after the bringing the suit and before judgment therein.—*Baxley* v. *Linah*, 241.

ATTORNEY.
One who was counsel for the plaintiff at the time of the admissions of defendant, made before the institution of the suit, but not counsel in the suit, and having no interest in the result of it, was a competent witness for the plaintiff to prove admissions by defendant as to the contract on which the suit was founded, and which were made at an interview had in consequence of a note from the counsel.—*Edwards* v. *Goldsmith*, 43.

BAIL. See RECOGNIZANCE.

BANKRUPTCY AND BANKRUPT ACT.
1. A debtor by book-account assigned to his creditor a promissory note and also a book-account, with an agreement under seal that in case the same could not be recovered of the persons indebted, then the assignor to pay the amount with charges thereupon, the assignor agreeing to notify the counsel of the creditor when the debtors came to the neighborhood where they were to be proceeded against, which information he never gave ; the attorney of the creditor agreeing that if any thing remained after discharging the claim of the creditor, it should be returned to the debtor : *Held*, that there being no agreement to receive the note and book-account *in satisfaction* of the original indebtedness, the assignment was but a *collateral* security; that under the 5th section of

the bankrupt act, the claim of the creditor on the said contract of guaranty was provable against the estate of the debtor, who was subsequently discharged as a bankrupt, and that the debtor was consequently discharged from liability to the creditor. See remarks on cases of McMullin *v.* Bank of Penn Township, 2 *Barr* 343, and Cake *v.* Lewis, 8 *Barr* 493.—*Stone v. Miller*, 450.

2. Whether a note or bond is accepted *in satisfaction* of the original claim is for the jury to decide, and not for the court as a matter of law.—*Id.*
3. Where claims transferred to a creditor consist of the indebtedness of others, and there is no agreement to receive the same *in satisfaction*, they are to be considered as *collateral* security for the original debt.—*Id.*

BOND.
1. Parol evidence is receivable in Pennsylvania to prove that a bond was fraudulently obtained, or that the consideration has failed.—*McCulloch v. McKee*, 289.
2. Where a husband assigned a bond given to him for his wife's interest in real estate, without receiving value therefor, but by an instrument under seal expressing the transfer to be *for value;* and the assignee during the coverture assigned the same to another *for value;* the second assignee, not having knowledge or the means of knowledge that the former assignment was without consideration, is entitled to the bond or its proceeds against the claim of the wife who brought suit after obtaining a divorce.—*McConnell v. Wenrich*, 365.

BROKER.
1. In the action of *indebitatus assumpsit* by a broker, to recover compensation fixed by a special contract to sell certain real estate on groundrent, it was not competent for defendant to prove the usual rates charged by brokers for services of a like character.—*Edwards v. Goldsmith*, 43.
2. Where a broker was to receive a definite commission for procuring a purchaser for certain lots of ground, and complied with his part of the contract, but the defendant, without good reason, failed to fulfil his part of the contract,—*Held*, that the broker could recover, in *indebitatus assumpsit*, the amount of compensation agreed upon.—*Id.*

CARRIERS.
1. Though in Pennsylvania a common carrier may *limit* his responsibility by a general notice, yet the terms of the notice must be clear and explicit, and the person with whom the carrier deals must be fully informed of the terms and effect of the notice: the limitation is to be confined to cases of special contract, expressed or implied; and where the notice is in the English language and the passenger a German, who did not understand the English language, it is incumbent on the carrier to prove the knowledge by the passenger of the limitation in the notice.—*Camden and Amboy Railroad Co. v. Baldauf*, 67.
2. If tickets, without more, are evidence of a special contract, yet they must be printed in a language which the passenger understands, or their terms must be explained to him.—*Id.*
3. Where a trunk was lost, and no proof given as to when or how it was lost, the legal inference is that it was lost or mislaid in consequence of the negligence or fraud of the carrier or his agent.—*Id.*
4. Where a trunk of a passenger contains specie, it is not incumbent on him to inform the carrier of its contents, unless inquired of, notwithstanding the advertisement of the carrier that passengers are "prohibited from taking any thing as baggage but their wearing-apparel, which will be at the risk of the owner;" and where the extra weight of the passenger's baggage, including the trunk, was paid for, and the agents of the carrier took charge of it,—*Held*, that it was immaterial whether the trunk was to be viewed as baggage or freight, and that the carrier was responsible for its loss through the negligence or fraud of its agents.—*Id.*

5. Carriers cannot, even by a special agreement with the owner, discharge themselves from the ordinary care incumbent on a bailee for hire. Per ROGERS, J.—*Id.*

CATTLE.
Where the owner of grain takes up cattle trespassing upon it, in order to sell them he must proceed according to the act of Assembly, or he will be deemed a trespasser *ab initio*, and be responsible in damages to the owner of the cattle.—*Fitzwater* v. *Stout*, 22.

COLLATERAL INHERITANCE.
The third section of the act of 11th March 1850, relating to collateral inheritance taxes, which provides that the words "*being within this commonwealth*," in the first section of the act of 7th April 1826, relating to collateral inheritances, "shall be so construed as to relate to all persons who have been at the time of their decease, or now may be, domiciled within this commonwealth, as well as to estates," is applicable to the estate of a person domiciled in Pennsylvania, who died *before the passage of the act*, viz. in December 1849, and is, as to such a case, constitutional, at least as to assets remaining in this State in the hands of the executors; and therefore stocks in corporations in other States, and bonds of such corporations, and cash in a bank in another State, belonging to such a decedent, are liable to the collateral inheritance tax for the use of this commonwealth, and the executors are chargeable with the amount of the said tax, out of the assets in their hands.—*In re Short's Estate*, 63.

COLLATERAL SECURITY. See ASSIGNMENT, 6, 7, 8.

COMMISSIONERS. See COUNTY.

COMMON CARRIERS. See CARRIERS.

CONDITION.
Though in the case of a condition *in law*, none but the grantor or his heirs can enter for a condition broken, yet in Pennsylvania, where the doctrine of maintenance does not prevail, there is no policy of law which forbids the reservation of a right of entry *to the assigns* of the grantor. Therefore, in the case of such a reservation, a purchaser of the grantor's conditional interest in the premises, at a sheriff's sale, is within the terms of such a reservation, and if a forfeiture exist, he may take advantage of it, though his purchase was *before* the condition was broken.—*McKissick* v. *Pickle*, 140.

CONSIDERATION. See BOND, 1.

CONSTITUTIONAL LAW.
1. The act of 13th June 1836, authorizing the laying out of *private* roads, is constitutional.—*Pocopson Road*, 15.
2. A testator in his will directed that after the decease of his wife, his executors should rent out his lands, and out of the proceeds his son Daniel to be supported, and willed and desired that none of his real estate should be sold during the life of his said son, but that he be supported out of the same; and provided further, that it was his will and desire that, after the death of his son Daniel, then his real estate should be sold, and all his children to receive share and share alike. After the death of the widow, an act was passed, at the instance of Daniel, providing that on his application, the Orphans' Court shall make an order appointing a trustee to make sale of the said real estate, and to invest the proceeds under the direction of the said court, so that the interest thereof shall secure to him that support during his natural life which the will intended him to receive out of the produce of the said real estate, provided that such sale shall be approved by the said court—and providing further, that the annual interest only of the proceeds of sale be paid to the said Daniel or his trustee, and the principal sum be

invested, subject to all the provisions of the will: *Held*, that the other parties in interest being of full age, under no disability, and objecting to the sale, the court below was right in refusing to direct it; that the legislature does not possess the constitutional power, in such a case, to direct a sale against the consent of the other parties in interest, who were of full age and under no disability, *within the time during which the sale was forbidden by the testator;* and that the act in this case was unconstitutional.—*Ervine's Appeal,* 256.

3. The provision in the 5th article of the amendments to the Constitution of the United States that no person shall "be deprived of life, liberty, or property without due process of law," and the equivalent provision in the Constitution of Pennsylvania, that no one shall be " deprived of his life, liberty, or property, unless by the judgment of his peers or *the law of the land*," imply the right to notice to appear and answer, and to a remedy in court. Per COULTER, J.—*Id.*

CONTRACT.

1. The evidence of a contract leaving it obscure, it consisting in part of a memorandum in writing by defendant made subsequent to the contract, the same with certain parol evidence, was submitted to the jury to decide what the contract was: *Held,* to have been properly submitted.—*Edwards* v. *Goldsmith,* 43.

2. An article of agreement for the sale of land is merged in the deed made in pursance of it, which is delivered and accepted.—*Jones* v. *Wood,* 25.

3. Fraud will vitiate any contract. Where land is, by article of agreement, agreed to be sold by A. to W., and W. afterwards sells the same to J., *the deed to be made by A. to J.,* which is afterward made and delivered to J. in the presence of W.: in a suit by W. against J. for the value of a certain piece of land, alleged by W. to form a part of his original purchase, but which, by a subsequent deed, had been conveyed by A. to J. for an additional consideration, in order to affect J. with fraud in the transaction as between A. and J., it must be shown that J. participated in the fraud, or at least had knowledge of it.—*Id.*

4. In a suit on a contract to deliver wheat in the interior of the State, evidence as to its price in Philadelphia, at and soon after the time agreed upon for its delivery, is receivable as corroborative of the testimony as to its value at the place at which it was to be delivered.—*Gordon* v. *Bowers,* 226.

5. A transfer of certain bonds and real estate was made by a principal debtor to the son of his surety, to indemnify the estate of the latter for being bound in a bond to M. Before M. expressed her assent to the transfer, the principal debtor assigned the fund to another, for whose use suit was brought in the name of the principal against the first transferree, but there was a failure to recover. The bond to M. was never paid: *Held,* that the administrator of the estate of M. could not maintain assumpsit against the first transferee for the amount of money received by him from the property assigned to him, on account of the *want of privity of contract* between M. and the said transferee.—*Finney* v. *Finney,* 380.

6 In a contract between the original contractors with the York and Cumberland Railroad Company and a sub-contractor with them, it was provided that the work should be subject to the supervision and control of the engineer of the Railroad Company; that he should make monthly estimates, four-fifths of which *value* to be paid to the sub-contractor, and when the work was completed, a final estimate; that the monthly and final estimates *as to the quantity, character, and value* of the work done shall be *conclusive* between the parties. And further, that if the contractor should not truly comply with his part of the agreement, or in case it should appear to the engineer that the work did not progress with sufficient speed, the other party should have power to annul the contract, and the unpaid portion of the road be forfeited by the sub-

contractor, and become the property of the other party. It was *held*, that the award or decision of the engineer declaring the work forfeited was conclusive and binding on the sub-contractor. Moreover, the action of the plaintiff was in affirmance of the contract, and he cannot impeach the stipulations in it by which he obtained the contract.—*Faunce v. Burke & Gonder*, 469-70.
7. The term *value* as used in the contract is to be distinguished from the term *price* as applied to the quantity of any of the different classes of work specified in the contract; and the engineer in making the monthly estimates had the right to deduct from the quantity of the work done, what he considered would equalize the part taken out as to quality and value with the whole work, and was not bound to allow the plaintiff for all work done, the price specified in the contract for that kind of work.—*Id.*
8. If the company had withheld the funds due to the sub-contractor, it would be unfair to take advantage of the forfeiture declared for want of prosecution of the work.—*Id.*
9. The retention of the 20 per cent. in case of forfeiture was intended as the measure of reparation for the failure of the plaintiff to perform his contract, and was not intended as a mere *penalty*.—*Id.*
10. The payment, after the forfeiture, by one of the original contractors of the hands who had been employed by the sub-contractor, and furnishing money to carry on the work, was not a waiver of the forfeiture, and especially if he was then ignorant that the work had been forfeited.—*Id.*

CORPORATION.
Possession and use will not give an individual or a corporation a title to a franchise which is an encroachment on a public right.—*Penny Pot Landing*, 79.

COSTS.
Double or treble *costs* mean, in Pennsylvania, double or treble the single costs: and so with respect to *damages*. The English rule as to costs in such cases does not prevail in this State. Per ROGERS, J.—*Welsh v. Anthony*, 254.

COUNTY. See LAND, 1; ISLANDS, 2.
1. Though county commissioners are not bound by law to provide a residence for the sheriff whilst the jail is rebuilding, yet, if they lease a house for him, the lessor is not bound to inquire under what arrangement it was made; and if without knowledge of the illegal character of the act of the commissioners, may recover the rent from the county.—*County v. Bridenhart*, 458.
2. A lease for a year by the commissioners under their own seals and not the county seal, is binding on the county as an express contract; and if the possession be not delivered up at the end of the term, but the occupancy continued, an implied contract arises against the county. A suit *for use and occupation* however, might not lie against the county, as the occupation was not by the county, nor for its benefit.—*Id.*

COURT. See ERROR.
1. Where there is a spark of evidence of a fact, it should not be excluded from the jury.—*Fitzwater v. Stout*, 22.
2. It is error for the court to submit to the jury, an alleged fact, of which there is *no* evidence.—*Jones v. Wood*, 25.
3. The judge trying a cause should not withdraw the facts from the consideration of the jury, or induce the jury to infer that they are not at liberty to pass upon disputed facts; but he may express an opinion as to the tendency of the facts in evidence; and an erroneous opinion concerning facts not withdrawn from the jury, is no ground for reversal.—*Oyster v. Longnecker*, 269.
4 It is not essential that the court bring to the notice of the jury all the

evidence in relation to a subject on which they charge.—*Sample* v. *Robb*, 305.
5. The ordering a cause for trial, or its continuance, is a matter within the direction of the court below, and is not examinable on error.—*Porter* v. *Lee*, 412.

DAMAGES. See RAILROAD; also, TIMBER.
1. Under the act of 29th March 1824, relative to cutting timber on the land of another, either the jury or the court may assess the double or treble damages.—*Welsh* v. *Anthony*, 254.
2. Double or treble *costs* mean, in Pennsylvania, double or treble the single costs: and so with respect to *damages*. The English rule as to costs in such cases does not prevail in this State. Per ROGERS, J.—*Id.*

DEBTOR AND CREDITOR. See EXECUTION, 5.

DECEIT.
There can be no deceit in the sale of a chattel without a *scienter*.—*Staines* v. *Shore*, 200.

DECLARATION.
In an action on a contract for the sale of hogs, the declaration of the plaintiff alleged their delivery, which the proof failed to establish: an application was made during the trial for leave to amend the declaration by averring the readiness of plaintiff to deliver and the refusal of the defendant to receive and pay for the hogs, which amendment the court refused to permit: *Held*, that such refusal was error.—*Stewart and Others* v. *Kelly*, 160.

DEED.
1. A deed, whether voluntary and without consideration, or for a valuable consideration, made upon a parol trust, declared at the time of the execution of the deed, that the grantee would hold in trust for the children of the grantor, if intended as a fraud upon creditors of the grantor, is void as against the creditors, but it is valid as against the grantor and the children for whose benefit it was designed, and the grantee will be entitled to hold against the children or their vendee; whether the trust be by parol or in writing the rule is the same; and the circumstance of the grantee *of the children* being in possession will not vary the principle. See 7 *Barr* 420.—*Murphy* v. *Hubert*, 50.
2. A deed from a tenant in tail purporting to bar the entail, but never entered on record and recorded, as required by law, and thus incompetent to bar the entail, was nevertheless held to be good to convey the grantor's right of possession, and was therefore admissible in evidence.—*George* v. *Morgan*, 95.
3. Though in order to render a conveyance admissible in evidence, but slight evidence of title in the grantor is sufficient, yet *some* interest in him must be shown: therefore, where in a deed by N. to W. and wife, purporting to convey all lands in certain counties and all other lands wheresoever the same may be, but without a particular description of any of them, *it was recited* that they were those which were the same day conveyed to the said N. heirs and assigns by the said W. and wife, *the deed to N. not, however, being produced* and no evidence of its existence being given, and W. having had title to the premises as heir, *independent of the deed*: *Held*, that without such deed or evidence of its existence, the deed by N. to W. and wife was not admissible against the plaintiff in an ejectment brought by the executor of the will of a *bona fide* purchaser at sheriff's sale, under a judgment against W. in his lifetime, against one who claimed through a conveyance from the wife of W., who survived her husband: Without such deed or evidence, it did not appear that W. had been a party to it, and the title or interest of *a bona fide purchaser* is not to be affected by vague and uncertain evidence of another title.—*M ils* v. *Brandon*, 220.

VOL. IV.—70   2 W

4. A plaintiff whose deed for real estate has been duly recorded is not bound to give actual notice of his title to another, who claiming under another title, and being in possession, is about to make some improvement on the property, the latter claiming under a deed to one which contained a reference to the deed to the plaintiff. Therefore, S. T., whose name was the same as that of his father, but who claimed under a deed from another, was not debarred from asserting his title, by omitting to give notice of it to one, who, being in possession, was making some improvement on the premises, the latter claiming by virtue of a sheriff's sale of the interest of one who claimed under a deed from the father executed after the conveyance to S. T. the son was executed and recorded, and which deed referred to or recited the deed to S. T. as of record, without however distinguishing between the father and the son, but the grantee in which conveyance from the father had *actual notice* at the time of that conveyance that the title was in the son and not in the father.—*Knouff* v. *Thompson*, 357.

5. A deed executed before the act of 11th April 1848, by a married woman, conveying real estate to which she was entitled in fee, without her husband joining in its execution, is void. The act of 24th February 1770 requires both to join in conveyances of real estate, and its directions are imperative. *Parol* evidence that the wife executed the deed with the assent and by the direction of her husband, is not admissible. The only legitimate evidence of consent is the execution of the deed in the manner and form directed by the act of 1770.—*Trimmer* v. *Heagy*, 484.

6. The certificate of a justice of the peace in relation to the acknowledgment of a mortgage by a *feme covert* is not conclusive, but parol evidence is admissible to show that the acknowledgment by the wife was not done of her free will and accord, but that undue means were used for obtaining it; and if the mortgagee has a knowledge of facts calculated to put him on inquiry as to the manner in which the acknowledgment was obtained, he must abide the consequences.—*Louden* v. *Blythe*, 532.

7. The declarations of the wife objecting to make the acknowledgment, made immediately before and at the time of the acknowledgment, though during a period of several hours, are admissible as part of the *res gestæ*.—*Id*.

DEFALCATION. See RECOGNIZANCE.

DEPOSITIONS.
1. Where a justice certified that the witness was sworn and examined at the place specified in *the notice*, on the day and between certain hours, being those specified in the notice which was attached, it is sufficient evidence that the witness was sworn *before* he was examined, there being no evidence to the contrary.—*Sample* v. *Robb*, 305.
2. A notice being given that a deposition would be taken at the office of Joseph *Stormer*, Esq., in a certain township, a deposition taken at the office of Joseph *Stermer*, Esq., is admissible under the notice, unless it be shown that there were two justices of those names in that township.—*Id*.
3. If interrogatories are substantially answered in the course of the deposition, it is sufficient.—*Louden* v. *Blythe*, 532.

DEVISE. See LEGACY.
1. The rule in Shelly's case is a settled rule of property in Pennsylvania; and in deciding whether a devise is within the rule, no influence is to be conceded to any supposed prohibition of the rule by the testator, or to the defeat of a particular intention. The leading inquiry is what is the great object of the devisor; but where the form of the deposition is constituted of terms of art, to which an ascertained meaning has been fixed by decision, the construction settled is binding on courts:

Where a testator devised as follows: "I give and bequeath unto my son Mordecai all that messuage or tenement situate, &c., with all its rights, members, privileges, and appurtenances, to hold to him for and during his natural life, and, after his decease, to the heirs of his body, lawfully begotten, and to their heirs for ever; and, in default of such issue, then to the heirs of my son Samuel, and their heirs for ever:" *Held*, that by the devise Mordecai took an estate-tail, under the rule in Shelly's case.—*George* v. *Morgan*, 95.

In a devise of lands a limitation of them in default of issue, means *an indefinite failure of issue*, unless there be something in the context to qualify the expressions, or the reference be expressly to persons then existing.—*Id.*

Superadded words, serving to limit a fee in the issue of the first taker, engrafted on words of procreation, will not operate to turn these into words of purchase, unless the superadded words denote a *different species of heirs* from that described in the first words, and showing an intent to break the ordinary line of descent from the first taker.—*Id.*

An intention to change the line of descent is not sufficiently manifested when the superadded words *import* eventual distribution of the estate; to have that effect, distribution must be expressly contemplated.—*Id.*

In Pennsylvania, a testator as to real estate is to be regarded as speaking in reference to the common-law system of descent. Per BELL, J.—*Id.*

A testator having devised to his son Samuel, and to his heirs and assigns, the residue of a tract of land, he or they paying thereout and therefor to one of his daughters £50, in *one* and *two* years after his decease, and to his son Joel £50, in *four* years after his decease, and to another daughter £80, *one* year after his decease, or at his option to give them land worth the money devised to them, and to a grandson £10, to be paid *six* years after his decease, "and in case my son Samuel should die before he marries, then all that part of my estate which I have devised to him, in that case I give and devise to my son Joel Willis, his heirs and assigns, to have and to hold to him my said son Joel, his heirs and assigns for ever, in as full and ample a manner as my son Samuel held, or was to have held the same, and subject to the same conditions and payments," and also to the further payment of £460, the money so paid to be divided between all his daughters equally. He further directed that the residue of his estate, real and personal, should be sold by his executors, and the proceeds divided between Joel and the five daughters of the testator; but in case Samuel should die *before he marries*, and the estate devised to him devolve to Joel, then in that case, it was his will that Joel should not have any part of the residual estate, but that it should be divided between his daughters:

Held, that Samuel having died *unmarried*, after the death of the testator, the estate passed by executory devise to the heirs or devisees of *Joel*; that the testator contemplated the death of Samuel, whenever it might happen, *before marriage*, as the event on which the estate devised was limited over in fee to Joel, his heirs and assigns, and as Samuel died *before he married*, the estate by the limitation became the property of the heirs or devisees of Joel; they to take it subject to the payment of the legacies charged on it, if not paid, and to the payment of £460, to the daughters of the testator, or their representatives; and also to the payment to the same of what Joel may have received out of the residuary estate.—*Jessup* v. *Smuck*, 327.

A testator devised to his wife during her life or widowhood, the use and possession of all his real and personal estate, with an exception in favor of his unmarried daughters, with respect to whom he provided—"As each of my married daughters have already received one hundred pounds, Pennsylvania currency, on account of their future inheritance (or heritage) without being obliged to pay interest for the same, so it is my will that the rest of my daughters shall also receive one hundred pounds, Pennsylvania currency, on the same account, whenever they marry and should require the money to purchase real estate, without being obliged to pay interest therefor; and besides each of my daughters shall receive at their eventual marriage the same outfit as the others have received before them."

"And as touching the land or real estate, the same shall remain as above said in the possession and enjoyment of my dear wife till her death or remarriage. The right of possession of the whole of my real estate I herewith devise to my two sons, Daniel and Joseph, however they shall not have the immediate possession and use of the same till after the death or remarriage of my wife, to enter upon and divide the real estate as they may deem it suitable, and they are to pay for the whole of my aforesaid land or real estate the sum of two thousand pounds, Pennsylvania currency, which two thousand pounds are to be divided in nine equal shares, and each of my beloved children, namely, Daniel, Joseph, Sarah, Susanna, Esther, Catharine, Hannah, Lydia, and Elizabeth, share and share alike.

"All the remaining goods, namely, the money that arises out of the sale of the house and kitchen furniture, the outstanding money and bank stock, shall after the death or remarriage of my wife be divided in equal shares amongst my nine children: *Held*, that the sons were each entitled to receive £100, so as to make them equal with the daughters, and that the balance of the estate be equally distributed among the sons and daughters.—*Schneider's Appeal*, 407.

8. A testator devised to his wife "the sum of one thousand pounds, during her lifetime, and after her decease to be equally divided amongst my children, that is to say as follows: the one thousand pounds above mentioned to remain on my plantation in Alsace, as a dower during her lifetime."

"Third, I will and bequeath unto my beloved wife all my household furniture and kitchen utensils, as much as she may choose to keep for her own use. I will that my beloved wife shall maintain and educate my minor children during their minority, out of her yearly dower."

"Fourth, I will and bequeath unto my son William, all my plantation in Alsace, together with the woodland at the hill, *he to pay sixty-five dollars ($65) per acre for the same, in the following manner:* First, one year after my death, he shall pay all my just debts, and after deducting my just debts and the above dower of my beloved wife, then the balance shall be equally divided amongst my children, *that is*, my son William shall buy a house and furniture for my daughter Rebecca by the first day of April next, to the amount of $350—and buy a house and furniture for my daughter Lavina, for $350, three months after the day of her marriage—and after having paid all the above items, then I will that the balance remaining, together with all my other property, shall be equally divided, such as bonds, notes, and the different bequests heretofore mentioned, *amongst my children as follows, to wit*, my son William, shall pay the one-half of the part that shall fall to one of my children to my youngest son *Augustus* when he shall come to the age of 21 years—and the next or following year he shall pay the one-half of the part falling to my daughter *Catharine*, wife of David Engle—and the following year he shall pay the one-half falling to my daughter *Rebecca*, wife of John Clouser—and the following year he shall pay one-half of the part falling to my daughter *Lavina*, and the following year he shall pay the last part to my son *Augustus*—and so on year after year *agreeable to the names above mentioned*, until all the different parts or sums are paid."

Held, that William, the devisee of the land, was entitled to a share of its proceeds in common with the other children, and that the direction to him to *pay* was not inconsistent with the idea of *retention* by him of a portion of the fund.—*Hennershotz's Estate*, 435.

9. A testator directed as follows: "As to such worldly estate wherewith it hath pleased God to bless me in this life, I give and dispose of the same

in the following manner. Item, it is my will and I order and direct that all my just debts and funeral expenses shall be first paid and satisfied. Item, it is my will and I give, devise, and bequeath unto my beloved wife Elizabeth, eighty-five acres and allowance of land of my dwelling plantation whereon I now live, situate in Spring Garden township, in the county aforesaid, she to have the choice of the same wherever she thinks proper; and further I do give and bequeath unto my said wife all my movable property or personal estate, of what kind or nature the same may be, together with all the moneys due me, by bond, note or book-account, to and for her only proper use and behoof whatever. Item, it is further my will that my brother and sisters divide the residue of my said plantation amongst themselves, share and share alike:" *Held*, that the widow took only an estate *for life:* that the words "only proper use and behoof" are not words of limitation in a deed, nor do they import perpetuity in a will; that their meaning is too vague except for conjecture; and as to the *introductory words*, there is nothing to which they can be particularly attached, and they are inoperative by themselves.— *Weidman* v. *Maish*, 504.

DRIFT.
1. Property carried adrift continues to be the property of him who owned it at the time of the flood. When stranded, the owner has the right to enter on the land and remove it, but he is not bound to do so, and may abandon it without incurring responsibility for injury done by it: And it would seem that unless there has been *negligence* in the management of property carried adrift, the owner is not liable for damage done by it, even though he does not remove it after notice to do so. Per GIBSON, C. J.—*Foster* v. *Juniata Bridge Company*, 393.
2. The owner of the land on which the property is stranded, after notice to its owner to remove it, and neglect or refusal to do so, may disencumber his property of it by casting it back into the stream; but he has no right *to appropriate it to his own use.* He may remove it at his own expense; but the refusal of the owner of the property to remove it will not divest the right of the latter in it, or bar his entry to reclaim it. He may resume the ownership after abandonment.—*Id.*
3. The owner of the land has no lien on property cast on it by drift. And where the owner of the latter proves his property in it and the actual conversion of it by the owner of the land, the latter is liable in trover and conversion for damages.—*Id.*

EDUCATION.
In the appropriation act of 11th April 1848, it was provided that the *common school system* shall be held to be adopted by all the school districts in the commonwealth, and that each school district levying a tax, shall be entitled to a deduction of twenty-five per cent. of all moneys paid into the county treasury by such district, for State purposes, during the *two next ensuing school years;* which school years by a former act, were to end on the first *Monday of June* of each year: It was *held* that the abatement was to be limited to the taxes assessed for the school years of 1848 and 1849, and was not to extend to taxes which had been assessed for the school year commencing on the first Monday of June 1850, but which had been advanced or paid into the county treasury *before* that day.—*The Commonwealth* v. *Fraim*, 163.

EJECTMENT. See EXECUTORS and ADMINISTRATORS, 4–6. As to NOTICE. see DEEDS, 3, 4.
1. Notes of the testimony of deceased witnesses taken on a former trial between the same parties and bearing directly on the same subject of dispute, viz: the boundaries and extent of a certain tract of land, are admissible in evidence in a suit for the value of a piece of land adjoining that the extent of which was in dispute in the first suit —*Jones* v. *Wood*, 25.

2. On the trial of an ejectment, drafts of land, offered before any title by warrant, location, or improvement is shown, are not admissible.—*Sample* v. *Robb*, 305.
3. The talk of neighbors as to who has the title to land in dispute, is not evidence.—*Id.*
4. Drafts found in the office of the deputy surveyor, but no authority shown to the deputy surveyor to make them, may be evidence of boundary, on the part of the claimant under an improvement, if it be shown that when the improvement was commenced, the improver claimed to the lines of the draft and adopted them; but the papers of themselves are no evidence of title.—*Id.*
5. The declarations of one claiming in his own right by improvement, and living on the land, made at the time of the making of a survey by another under a warrant, are evidence against himself as to the extent of his claim: they are not evidence against another under whom he did not then profess to claim.—*Id.*
6. The declaration or offer of a former improver (since deceased) whilst living on the land, to give his son-in-law, who was living on it, a part of the land if he would improve on it, and his acts of ownership on the land, are evidence that he claimed the same *as his own* and not under another.—*Id.*
7. If one claiming in his own right, by settlement and improvement, did not object to the location of the warrant on land adjoining his improvement, his subsequent deed cannot affect the location of the warrant: if he claimed *under another* when the warrant was located, his agreement to the location of the warrant cannot affect him under whom he claimed, or his alienee.—*Id.*
8. If the description in the writ, of the land for which the ejectment is brought, be defective, the defect may be supplied by another description filed with leave of the court.—*Id.*
9. A plaintiff whose deed for real estate has been duly recorded is not bound to give actual notice of his title to another, who claiming under another title, and being in possession, is about to make some improvement on the property, the latter claiming under a deed to one which contained a reference to the deed to the plaintiff. Therefore S. T., whose name was the same as that of his father, but who claimed under a deed from another, was not debarred from asserting his title, by omitting to give notice of it to one, who, being in possession, was making some improvement on the premises, the latter claiming by virtue of a sheriff's sale of the interest of one who claimed under a deed from the father executed after the conveyance to S. T. the son was executed and recorded, and which deed referred to or recited the deed to S. T. as of record, without however distinguishing between the father and the son, but the grantee in which conveyance from the father had *actual notice* at the time of that conveyance that the title was in the son and not in the father.—*Knouff* v. *Thompson*, 357.

ERROR.
1. Where there is a spark of evidence of a fact, it should not be excluded from the jury.—*Fitzwater* v. *Stout*, 22.
2. It is error for the court to submit to the jury for their deliberation an alleged fact of which there was no evidence.—*Jones* v. *Wood*, 25.
3. It is not error to receive evidence which is pertinent and relevant, because it is not strictly *rebutting;* especially in a complicated case, and where the adverse party is not taken by surprise.—*Sample* v. *Robb*, 305.
4. The ordering of a cause for trial, or its continuance, is a matter within the discretion of the court below, and is not examinable on error.—*Porter* v. *Lee*, 412.
5. It is incumbent on a party who attempts to deprive the adverse party of a claim apparently due him and evidenced by a proper voucher, to support his allegation by proof, however slight it may be: if none such be

given, the court are not to reject the evidence of the claim, or to submit the question of its invalidity to the jury.—*Zerbe* v. *Miller*, 488.
6. An assignment that the court erred in their charge to the jury generally, (without any specification,) is not a proper assignment of error.—*Id.*

ESTATE-TAIL.
1. The rule in Shelly's case is a settled rule of property in Pennsylvania; and in deciding whether a devise is within the rule, no influence is to be conceded to any supposed prohibition of the rule by the testator, or to the defeat of a particular intention. The leading inquiry is what is the great object of the devisor; but where the form of the disposition is constituted of terms of art, to which an ascertained meaning has been fixed by decision, the construction settled is binding on courts.

   Where a testator devised as follows:—"I give and bequeath unto my son Mordecai all that messuage or tenement situate, &c., with all its rights, members, privileges, and appurtenances, to hold to him for and during his natural life, and, after his decease, to the heirs of his body, lawfully begotten, and to their heirs for ever; and, in default of such issue, then to the heirs of my son Samuel, and their heirs for ever:" *Held*, that by the devise Mordecai took an estate-tail, under the rule in Shelly's case.—*George* v. *Morgan*, 95.
2. In a devise of lands a limitation of them in default of issue, means *an indefinite failure of issue*, unless there be something in the context to qualify the expressions, or the reference be expressly to persons then existing.—*Id.*
3. Superadded words, serving to limit a fee in the issue of the first taker, engrafted on words of procreation, will not operate to turn these into words of purchase, unless the superadded words denote a *different species of heirs* from that described in the first words, and showing an intent to break the ordinary line of descent from the first taker.—*Id.*
4. An intention to change the line of descent is not sufficiently manifested when the superadded words *import* eventual distribution of the estate; to have that effect, distribution must be expressly contemplated.—*Id.*
5. In Pennsylvania, a testator as to real estate, is to be regarded as speaking in reference to the common-law system of descent. Per BELL, J.—*Id.*
6. A deed from a tenant in tail purporting to bar the entail, but never entered on record and recorded, as required by law, and thus incompetent to bar the entail, was nevertheless held to be good to convey the grantor's right of possession, and was therefore admissible in evidence.—*Id.*
7. A testator devised as follows:—"I give to my wife Maria the use and income of my plantation, the whole lying and being situated in Alsace township, for her support and maintenance during her life. Item, I give and bequeath to my youngest son Daniel Maurer, the whole of the aforesaid plantation; also, my woodland, containing about fourteen acres, lying on Penn's Mount, after the decease of my said wife Maria; and if my son Daniel should be a minor at the decease of my said wife Maria, then my will is that my executor, hereinafter named, shall rent or lease the said plantation until my said son Daniel shall arrive at the age of twenty-one years. Item, if my aforesaid son Daniel should die, under the age of twenty-one years, and without lawful heirs, then my will is that my said plantation shall be sold by my executor, providing it be after the decease of my wife Maria, and the whole of the proceeds to be equally divided among the lawful heirs of my son George, the lawful heirs of my daughter Maria, and the lawful heirs of my daughter Sarah, provided, always, that if my son Daniel survives and *begets lawful heirs*, then after his decease, the proceeds of the said plantation to be equally divided, share and share alike, to the heirs of my son Daniel:" A conveyance was made by Daniel to bar the entail, and he tendered a deed *in fee simple* to the purchaser of the estate with whom he had contracted to convey such an estate: *Held*, that Daniel had such an estate in the premises as the purchaser was compellable to take. The estate

which he derived under the will was considered by this court to be an estate-tail.—*Maurer* v. *Marshall*, 377.

ESTOPPEL. See DEED, 4.

EVIDENCE. See PROMISSORY NOTES, 6–7; also, DEPOSITIONS; ISLANDS; PRESUMPTION; STEAM-ENGINE, 2.

1. Where there is a spark of evidence of a fact, it should not be excluded from the jury.—*Fitzwater* v. *Stout*, 22.
2. It is error for the court to submit to the jury for their deliberation an alleged fact of which there was no evidence.—*Jones* v. *Wood*, 25.
3. Notes of the testimony of deceased witnesses taken on a former trial between the same parties and bearing directly on the same subject of dispute, viz: the boundaries and extent of a certain tract of land, are admissible in evidence in a suit for the value of a piece of land adjoining that the extent of which was in dispute in the first suit.—*Id.* 25.
4. One who was counsel for the plaintiff at the time of the admissions of defendant made before the institution of the suit, but not counsel in the suit, and having no interest in the result of it, was a competent witness for the plaintiff to prove admissions by defendant as to the contract on which the suit was founded, and which were made at an interview had in consequence of a note from the counsel.—*Edwards* v. *Goldsmith*, 43.
5. In an action of *indebitatus assumpsit* by a broker, to recover compensation fixed by a special contract to sell certain real estate on ground-rent, it was not competent for defendant to prove the usual rates charged by brokers for services of a like character.—*Id.*
6. The evidence of a contract leaving it obscure, it consisting in part of a memorandum in writing by defendant made subsequent to the contract, the same with certain parol evidence, was submitted to the jury to decide what the contract was: *Held* to have been properly submitted.—*In.*
7. Maps, ancient surveys, as well as reputation are evidence to *elucidate and ascertain a boundary*, but not to impeach official grants on public record, control having been long exercised in conformity to the grants.—*Penny Pot Landing*, 79.
8. Though in order to render a conveyance admissible in evidence, but slight evidence of title in the grantor is sufficient, yet *some* interest in him must be shown: therefore, where in a deed by N. to W. and wife, purporting to convey all lands in certain counties and all other lands wheresoever the same may be, but without a particular description of any of them, *it was recited* that they were those which were the same day conveyed to the said N. his heirs and assigns by the said W. and wife, *the deed to N. not, however, being produced* and no evidence of its existence being given, and W. having had title to the premises as heir, *independent of the deed: Held*, that without such deed or evidence of its existence, the deed by N. to W. and wife was not admissible against the plaintiff in an ejectment brought by the executor of the will of a *bona fide* purchaser at sheriff's sale, under a judgment against W. in his life-time, against one who claimed through a conveyance from the wife of W., who survived her husband: Without such deed or evidence, it did not appear that W. had been a party to it, and the title or interest of *a bona fide purchaser* is not be affected by vague and uncertain evidence of another title.—*Meals* v. *Brandon*, 220.
9. If the interest of a witness in the event of the cause be *doubtful*, the court should receive his testimony and refer it to the jury to decide whether he has such an interest or not. But whether the question of interest be determined by the court or tried by the jury, and the witness is not examined on his *voir dire*, but evidence is adduced to show his incompetency, the testimony of the witness himself, in support of his own competency, should not be received.—*Gordon* v. *Bowers*, 226.
10. *Ex parte* conversations are not admissible against the adverse party.—*Id.*

11. In a suit on a contract to deliver wheat in the interior of the State, evidence as to its price in Philadelphia, at and soon after the time agreed upon for its delivery, is receivable as corroborative of the testimony as to its value at the place at which it was to be delivered.—*Id.*
12. The marks on the ground of an old survey, indicating the lines originally run, are the best evidence of the location of the survey, and if any evidence of such lines exist, it should be referred to the jury.—*Gratz* v. *Hoover*, 232.
13. Where a survey returned called for others on three sides, and on the fourth for J. H. *or vacant*, there being no evidence given that the line on that side was run, it was not error for the court to charge the jury, that the return was equivocal, or indicated nothing more than that the line on that side was left open or undecided upon by the surveyor.—*Id.*
14. Where a question existed whether the larger part of a tract of land lay in Centre or Clearfield county, which were there bounded by the Mushannon Creek, it being the usage to tax lands in the county in which the greater part of the tract was situate, the official book of the treasurer of Centre county was evidence to show that the tract in question was *not* returned for taxation in Centre county, although other tracts in the same lot of surveys were so returned, the taxes on the tract in question having been paid by the claimant in the county of Clearfield; and especially, when taken in connection with the deposition of the treasurer of Centre county, that the present claimant had furnished to him a list of his lands *in Centre county*, in which the tract in question did *not* appear.—*Id.*
15. Parol evidence is receivable in Pennsylvania to prove that a bond was fraudulently obtained, or that the consideration has failed.—*McCulloch* v. *McKee*, 289.
16. It is not error to receive evidence which is pertinent and relevant, because it is not strictly *rebutting*; especially in a complicated case, and where the adverse party is not taken by surprise.—*Sample* v. *Robb*, 305.
17. In a suit upon a note, *defendant* offered to prove by the deposition of a witness (who had a supervision of the store and store-accounts of defendant and his partner, but who did not state that he made the entries, or sell or witness the sale of the goods, or the nature of the charges in the books,) the *balance* of a store-account on said books *which were not produced;* and also that a *pass-book* belonging to the plaintiff and containing entries of goods got by plaintiff from the said store, corresponded with the books, and which pass-book the plaintiff's counsel was notified to produce on the trial, but the notice was too late to admit of its production, and the pleas did not give notice to that effect: It was *held,* that the books of defendant, being the proper evidence, should have been produced, and that it was not error to reject the evidence offered.—*Porter* v. *Lee*, 412.
18. In an action on the case to recover damages for an injury sustained by plaintiff from his falling into an area-way, or passage dug in the pavement, leading into the cellar of defendant's house, erected on a public street in Harrisburg, and through the culpable neglect of the defendant left exposed, by which the plaintiff's leg was broken, it was *held*, that if by ordinary or reasonable care on the part of the plaintiff, he might have avoided the injury, he was not entitled to recover; and what shall be deemed ordinary care must depend on the circumstances of each case, of which the jury is to judge; and if there be no facts proved from which a deduction can be drawn, the *presumption* is against the defendant whose misconduct rendered the accident possible.—*Beatty* v. *Gilmore*, 463.
19. In such a case it is not incumbent on the plaintiff to prove the exercise by him of ordinary care to avoid the injury, but the proof of the want

of it on the part of the plaintiff lies on the defendant. He who avers a fact *in excuse of his own misfeasance*, must prove it.—*Id.*

20. It was competent to prove by a witness who examined the place where the accident occurred, but who was not present *when* it occurred, that in his opinion the place was dangerous.—*Id.*

21. Parol evidence is not admissible to show that a deed executed by a wife alone, conveying her own real estate, was executed with the assent and by the direction of her husband. The only legitimate evidence of consent is the execution of the deed in the manner and form directed by the act of Assembly.—*Trimmer* v. *Heagy*, 484.

22. It is incumbent on a party who attempts to deprive the adverse party of a claim apparently due him, and evidenced by a proper voucher, to support his allegation by proof, however slight it may be; if none such be given, the court are not to reject the evidence of the claim, or to submit the question of its invalidity to the jury.—*Zerbe* v. *Miller*, 488.

23. Where the boundary of a county is fixed by act of Assembly, the fact that an island evidently included in its limits had been assessed for 28 years in another county, will not avail to disturb the boundary fixed by the act; but if the boundary fixed by the act *be uncertain*, such assessments for a long period may be admissible to show where the line was fixed by the act.—*Johns* v. *Davidson*, 512.

EXECUTION.

1. Creditors can attack a judgment *collaterally* only *for collusion*, not for matter of defence, original or subsequent. A judgment creditor who objects to a prior judgment on the ground of failure of consideration, can do so only on the trial of an issue directed as to the prior judgment, to ascertain the amount due upon it; but while it stands as a debt of record, unabated in whole or in part, and unaffected by any such proceeding in relation to it, neither the sheriff nor a subsequent judgment creditor can resist the enforcement of it as a lien, and the sheriff cannot legally disregard it in the appropriation of the proceeds of sale of the real estate bound by it.—*Lewis* v. *Rogers*, 18.

2. Horses purchased by A, B, and C, in partnership, were levied on under an execution against A for his private debt, and on an execution against B and C for the debt of B on a judgment confessed by B against himself and C; *after* the sale the judgment was on motion of C set aside as to him: *Held*, that the vacating of the judgment did not affect the validity of the previous sale under executions against all the partners, but that the proceeds of it represent the property, and the execution creditors occupy the place of the purchaser; that C can claim out of the proceeds only to the extent of the interest he had in the property; and if on the settlement of the account, under the direction of the court, in the course of the distribution of the proceeds of the sale, he appears to have been entitled *to no interest in the horses*, he is not entitled to any share of the proceeds of their sale.—*Kelly's Appeal*, 59.

3. The distribution of the proceeds of a sheriff's sale is, by the 86th section of the act of 16th June 1836, to be made according *to law and equity;* and in the course of the distribution of the proceeds of the sale of property purchased in partnership, and sold on executions against the partners as individuals, for their separate debts, the court may direct an account to ascertain the respective rights of the partners to the proceeds in dispute.—*Id.*

4. The second section of the act of 29th March 1819, authorizing stock held in corporations by individuals, in their own names, and which is not claimed by any other person, to be taken in execution and sold in the same manner as goods and chattels, is not repealed by the act of 16th June 1836, relating to executions.—*Lex* v. *Potters*, 295.

5. The omission of a debtor to give notice *before the sale of his real estate*, of his claim to property to the value of three hundred dollars, under the

act of 9th April 1849, exempting property to that amount from levy and sale on execution and distress for rent, will be a bar to his claim to that amount of money out of the proceeds of the sale. The claim, as it respects *real estate*, should perhaps be made *before inquisition*.—*Miller's Appeal*, 300.

EXECUTORS AND ADMINISTRATORS. See ADMINISTRATION.
1. Interest on the balance in the hands of an administrator from the time of its receipt is not of course; circumstances may be shown by the administrator, which would exempt him from the payment of interest.—*Wither's Appeal*, 151.
2. Interest is an incident to a decree of the Orphans' Court, as it is to a judgment in the Common Pleas.—*Id*.
3. Where an auditor to whom the account of the administrator was referred to report upon exceptions to it, made report that a certain amount was in the hands of the accountant on the day of exhibiting his account, which report was simply confirmed in the Orphans' Court: *Held*, that it was error in an auditor to whom the account was referred for distribution of the balance, to charge interest on the balance reported from the day of the exhibition of the account, instead of from the day of the decree of the confirmation by the Orphans' Court. The auditor appointed to report distribution is confined to the decree of the Orphans' Court.—*Id*.
4. Where an administrator purchased real estate with funds a moiety of which belonged to himself, and the other moiety to others, in an action of ejectment by the *cestui que trust* against a purchaser of the land from the administrator, without notice of the trust, the purchaser is entitled to be reimbursed the one-half of the purchase-money paid by him before notice of the trust, unless he has been fully compensated to the extent of that moiety out of the rents or profits. It is not, however, necessary that the amount be tendered before suit brought.—*Beck* v. *Uhrich*, 499.
5. The administrator, who was a co-defendant in the ejectment, is entitled to be reimbursed for expenses incurred in the creation of the trust, and advances made for the *benefit of the trust*.—*Id*.
6. The administration account settled after the suit brought, is evidence in favor of the defendants, to show the amount of money advanced by the administrator in the purchase of the land in question; but it is not conclusive.—*Id*.

FLOOD. See DRIFT.

FRAUD.
1. Fraud will vitiate any contract. Where land is, by article of agreement, agreed to be sold by A. to W., and W. afterwards sells the same to J., *the deed to be made by A. to J.*, which is afterward made and delivered to J. in the presence of W.: in a suit by W. against J. for the value of a certain piece of land, alleged by W. to form a part of his original purchase, but which, by a subsequent deed, had been conveyed by A. to J. for an additional consideration, in order to affect J. with fraud in the transaction as between A. and J., it must be shown that J. participated in the fraud, or at least had knowledge of it.—*Jones* v. *Wood*, 25.
2. A conveyance of real estate by a father to his son, intended to delay and hinder creditors, is fraudulent as to creditors, whether the consideration amount to the value of the land sold or not.—*Zerbe* v. *Miller*, 488.
3. If the conveyance to the son be fraudulent as to creditors, the son cannot set up an outstanding title to the land in another, against the purchaser at sheriff's sale, of the title of the father, who was in possession at the time of the sheriff's sale.—*Id*.
4. Evidence of the value of the land in dispute, without specification as to time, or of its value at the time of the trial, the conveyance in question having been made years before, is not admissible.—*Id*.
5. When a conveyance is impeached on the ground of fraud, considerable

latitude is allowable in the admission of evidence; the question is whether the evidence can throw light on the transaction, or whether it is irrelevant.—*Id.*

GRAIN.
1. The land of a judgment debtor was sold by the sheriff and deed made to the purchaser whilst the grain growing on the same was the property of the debtor. After the execution and acknowledgment of the deed, an execution creditor of the debtor levied on the grain, and sold it, and the purchaser brought suit against the tenant of the purchaser of the land, for cutting and removing the grain: *Held*, that the grain passed by the sheriff's sale of the land, and that the purchaser of the grain could not recover in the suit.—*Bear* v. *Bitzer*, 175.
2. After the execution and recording of a mortgage, but before the issuing of a scire facias thereon, the mortgagor leased a portion of the mortgaged premises for a year, to a cropper, who paid the rent *in advance*, and sowed grain upon it. Before the grain was cut, the land was sold at sheriff's sale, under proceedings on the mortgage commenced after the making of the lease: *Held*, that the grantee of the purchaser of the land was entitled to recover damages from the cropper for cutting and removing the grain.—*Groff* v. *Levan*, 179.

GUARANTY. See SURETY.

GUARDIAN AND WARD.
1. The record of the Orphans' Court is evidence of the appointment of a guardian; the issuing of a certificate of the appointment is not material; an act as guardian, by the person appointed, is an assumption of the trust.—*Eyster's Appeal*, 372.
2. Guardians are liable for wilful default or gross negligence; but they are allowed the exercise of reasonable discretion and prudential care in managing the property of their wards. Therefore, where a guardian permitted the rents of a small property to be received by the widow, and the share of the ward in the rents to be applied by her to the maintenance and education of the ward who was her son and was residing with her, the guardian is not accountable to the ward for the rents, the said rents not being an unreasonable provision for the purpose.—*Id.*
3. The balance due the administrator of the estate in which the ward is interested, upon the settlement of the administration account, and which is a charge upon the estate, if paid out of the rents is a proper credit as against the ward, in a settlement for the rents.—*Id.*

HORSE. See PARTNERSHIP, 1.
1. In an action on a note given for the price of a horse sold at auction, where fraud is alleged as to the condition of the animal at the time of sale, the presumption is very slight that the horse was unsound when fully grown, and apparently vigorous, because it had been diseased when a colt; the jury are to judge of the soundness or unsoundness, from the evidence exhibited in the case.—*Staines* v. *Shore*, 200.
2. There can be no deceit in the sale of a chattel without a *scienter*.—*Id.*
3. The employment of a puffer by the seller to bid for him at an auction vitiates the sale, and it is not material whether the property purchased brought no more than its *general value*; a purchaser has a right to purchase at an under value if he can.—*Id.*
4. When the employment of a puffer has been discovered by the purchaser after the sale, it is his duty to offer to return the property purchased, when the fraud is discovered; but if not discovered till too late to do so, the purchaser's defence is good without it.—*Id.*

HUSBAND AND WIFE.
1. Acts by a trustee, a married woman, in relation to the trust property,

made as agent of her husband, and her declarations accompanying such acts, are evidence against her husband.—*Murphy* v. *Hubert*, 50.
2. If a deed be made in consideration of a bond executed by the grantee, and the bond was subsequently cancelled by the grantee, *then a married woman*, this would not revest the estate in the grantor, or defeat the estate of her husband.—*Id.*
3. A *feme covert* joined with her husband in a mortgage on their separate estates to secure a debt of the husband. Afterwards the husband sold his own property, and the purchaser received a deed from the husband and wife, and paid to the husband a sum supposed to be sufficient to pay the mortgage which bound both estates, but which, in fact, was not sufficient. Out of the proceeds of sale of the real estate *of the wife*, the court directed to be paid the balance due on the mortgage: *Held*, that the wife was entitled to recover from the purchaser of the husband's real estate sold as above, the amount which was paid out of the proceeds of sale of her property in discharge of the balance due on the mortgage.—*Sheidle* v. *Weishlee*, 134.
4. In a suit by the wife alone, her coverture or the non-joinder of her husband can be taken advantage of only by plea in abatement: perhaps, however, since the act of 1848, a *feme covert* can maintain a suit in her own name alone.—*Id.*
5. In an action for service rendered, the plaintiff may show service rendered by his wife as well as himself, though her services are not mentioned in the declaration.—*Hackman* v. *Flory*, 196.
6. In an action by the husband for service rendered by himself and also by his wife, the declarations of the wife, during service, as to the terms of her employment, are admissible on the part of the defendant.—*Id.*
7. In the case of a hiring for a year, at a specified sum per month, it is not competent for the employer, within the period contracted for, to reduce the amount of monthly pay, without the consent of the other party.—*Id.*
8. A wife cannot make any contract to bind her husband without his authority express or implied, or dispose of his property, except perhaps in case of necessity for the immediate use of his family. And where the husband is a *lunatic*, she cannot transfer his property to pay a particular creditor to the prejudice of others.—*Alexander* v. *Miller, Reed & Co.* 215.
9. The 48th section of the act of 29th March 1832, relating to Orphans' Courts, which enables the *Orphans'* Court to require security from a husband before money payable to his wife under proceedings in partition is paid to him, does not apply to the case of a female *unmarried* at the time of the partition; and the payment to a *future* husband, without security, will discharge the recognizance, so far as the wife is interested.—*Quigley* v. *The Commonwealth*, 353.
10. Where a husband assigned a bond given to him for his wife's interest in real estate, without receiving value therefor, but by an instrument under seal expressing the transfer to be *for value;* and the assignee during the coverture assigned the same to another *for value;* the second assignee, not having knowledge or the means of knowledge that the former assignment was without consideration, is entitled to the bond or its proceeds against the claim of the wife who brought suit after obtaining a divorce.—*McConnell* v. *Wenrich*, 365.
11. If a husband leave outstanding the share due to his wife in a recognizance in the Orphans' Court, it is not liable to attachment by his creditors.—*Stoner* v. *The Commonwealth*, 387.
12. Where there is no order for a settlement of the wife's share under proceedings in partition, at the time of the partition, the subsequent declaration of the wife made before a judge of the Orphans' Court, that her share of the money payable under the partition should be paid to her husband, is not equivalent to a reduction into possession by him.—*Id*
13. None but the creditors of the husband can resist an assignment by him of a claim under a recognizance, made for the purpose of defrauding

them. The debtor of the claim thus transferred can safely pay it on the foot of a judgment on the recognizance.—*Id.*

14. By the 5th section of the intestate act of 1797, the husband who survived his wife became entitled to her choses in action; and such was the case although he did not administer on her estate, or do any act to make them his own, and died leaving issue.—*Moyer's Appeal*, 405.

15. The real estate of an intestate who left *seven* children, was divided and appraised, and a house and lot, a part of the same, were taken by the eldest son, who gave recognizance, and afterwards died intestate, without issue, and without payment of the recognizance. It was afterwards agreed by others of the heirs and the husband of another heir, that the house and lot be conveyed to the husband, he to allow the consideration-money out of the share of his wife, and if more than that share, he to pay the difference. *The other lands* were sold, and the purchase-money of the house and lot was charged against the share of the wife in the distribution of the father's estate: *Held*, that the object of the proceeding not being *partition*, but the estate of the wife having been *converted*, the proceeds became the property of the husband, by his application of them, and that the title to the premises, to the extent thus paid for by the husband, vested in him; besides, the premises descended as the estate of the *son*, and not of the father, and the money due the wife was in the estate of the father. Whether *a conveyance* was made to the husband was held not to be material. The wife, who brought ejectment after the death of her husband, was held to be entitled to recover only one *sixth* part of the house and lot.—*Ermold* v. *Newkirk*, 417.

16. A deed executed before the act of 11th April 1848, by a married woman, conveying real estate to which she was entitled in fee, without her husband joining in its execution, is void. The act of 24th February 1770 requires *both* to join in conveyances of real estate, and its directions are imperative. *Parol* evidence that the wife executed the deed with the assent and by the direction of her husband, is not admissible. The only legitimate evidence of consent is the execution of the deed in the manner and form directed by the act of 1770.—*Trimmer* v. *Heagy*, 484.

17. The certificate of a justice of the peace in relation to the acknowledgment of a mortgage by a *feme covert* is not conclusive, but parol evidence is admissible to show that the acknowledgment by the wife was not done of her free will and accord, but that undue means were used for obtaining it; and if the mortgagee has a knowledge of facts calculated to put him on inquiry as to the manner in which the acknowledgment was obtained, he must abide the consequences.—*Louden* v. *Blythe*, 532.

18. The declarations of the wife objecting to making the acknowledgment, made immediately before and at the time of the acknowledgment, though during a period of several hours, are admissible as part of the *res gestæ*.—*Id.*

INDICTMENT.
In the case of an indictment for murder in the first degree, it should appear from the record that the prisoner was present in court when he was sentenced to be executed, and it should be demanded of him whether he has anything to say why sentence of death should not be pronounced upon him.—*Hamilton alias Thacker* v. *The Commonwealth*, 129.

INTEREST. See EXECUTORS AND ADMINISTRATORS.
1 Usury is not committed by payment of a premium *less* in amount than the legal interest. The offence consists in taking more than six per cent. on the loan, and till more has been taken the penalty is not incurred.—*Oyster* v. *Longnecker*, 269.

2. A return to the lender of part of the sum on which interest is reserved, reduces the contract essentially to a loan of *the residue*. The money returned is not a premium, but a discount. Therefore, if $700 were

paid to the borrower, and he immediately handed back to the lender $35, and eventually received interest on $700, the offence of usury became complete *on the actual receipt of the interest;* and every fresh taking of interest on the $700 was a fresh consummation of the same offence.—*Id.*

INTESTATE ACT.
By the 5th section of the intestate act of 1797, the husband who survived his wife became entitled to her choses in action; and such was the case although he did not administer on her estate, or do any act to make them his own, and died leaving issue.—*Moyer's Appeal*, 405.

ISLANDS. See DRIFT.
1. Title to islands lying within the river Susquehanna, or its branches, could not be acquired by actual settlement and improvement; but by the act of 6th March 1793, directing the sale of certain islands in the Susquehanna or its branches, an improver had two years to obtain a warrant and have a survey made, and in case of his neglect for that time, the island was subject to application by any other person: and though it was incumbent on the improver to state the nature of his improvement and when and by whom made, this was not necessary in the application of another who applied for the island more than two years after the improver had neglected to make application for it.—*Johns* v. *Davidson*, 512.
2. The boundaries of Mifflin county were fixed by the second section of the act of 19th September 1789; and the fact that an island evidently included by the act within the limits of that county, had been assessed for twenty-eight years in *Huntingdon* county, will not avail to disturb the boundary fixed by the act. If the boundary fixed by the act were *uncertain,* such assessments for a long period might be admissible to show where the line was fixed by the act; but are not admissible where the line fixed by the act, viz. the Juniata river, is known. It is then a question of law.—*Id.*
3. Where the counties of Mifflin and Huntington join at the Juniata river at their southern point of junction, their respective boundaries do not extend *usque ad filum aquæ;* but the *whole bed* of the Juniata river from that point up to Jack's Narrows is in *Mifflin* county, and the islands in the river belong to the latter county.—*Id.*
4. The fact that the island was appraised as a part of the estate of the first improver, of which the plaintiff in right of his wife was an heir, and was sold to the defendant on the proceeding in partition, there being no evidence that the plaintiff directed it to be so appraised. is not evidence as to the county in which the island is situate, nor sufficient to bar the plaintiff from making application for it: nor will the occupation and cultivation of it for thirty-five years before the application give title to it.—*Id.*

JUDGMENTS. See ARBITRATION.
1. Creditors can attack a judgment *collaterally* only *for collusion,* not for matter of defence, original or subsequent. A judgment creditor who objects to a prior judgment on the ground of failure of consideration, can do so only on the trial of an issue directed as to the prior judgment to ascertain the amount due upon it; but while it stands as a debt of record, unabated in whole or in part, and unaffected by any such proceeding in relation to it, neither the sheriff nor a subsequent judgment creditor can resist the enforcement of it as a lien, and the sheriff cannot legally disregard it in the appropriation of the proceeds of sale of the real estate bound by it.—*Lewis* v. *Rogers*, 18.
2. A sheriff who does not incur any risk of mispayment in the appropriation of the proceeds of sale of real estate, has no right to impose conditions or take a promise to refund from a judgment creditor, to whom he pays a part of the money arising from the sale of the real estate bound by the

judgment, and to which the judgment was from the record apparently entitled.—*Id.*

3. By the 4th section of the act of 16th April 1849, judgments confessed to evade the act of 17th April 1843, concerning preferences in assignments, followed by an assignment of real estate, are void as against other creditors, and are not entitled to preference out of the proceeds of sale of such real estate, but are entitled only to a *pro rata* payment with the other debts of the debtor.—*Summers' Appeal*, 169.

4. A debtor, after suit against him, voluntarily executed five judgment bonds in favor of other creditors, intending at the time to make an assignment of his *real estate*, and about the same time selling portions of his personal property; after the entry of judgments on the bonds he executed an assignment of his *real estate* only, in trust for creditors. On the day it was recorded, an award, in favor of the plaintiff in the suit, was filed. The remaining *personal estate* of the debtor was sold on a fi. fa. on a judgment on a bond executed subsequent to the recording of the assignment. The real estate was sold by the trustees, for a sum not sufficient to pay the five judgments: *Held*, that the five judgments were not alone entitled to the proceeds of sale of the real estate, but that the same were to be distributed *pro rata*, amongst all the creditors.—*Id.*

5. If the debtor at the time of confessing the judgments knew that he was insolvent, his subsequent execution of the assignment is conclusive evidence that the judgments were given in fraud of the act of 1843.—*Id.*

6. A judgment in a sister State is to be deemed to have the effect of a *domestic* judgment, in relation to the cause of action; and where the defendant had notice it is conclusive of the subject-matter, and the original cause of action is merged in it: therefore, a suit pending in the State of Maryland, and a judgment subsequently obtained therein, is a bar to a proceeding between the same parties and for the same cause of action, by foreign attachment, instituted in Pennsylvania, after the bringing of the suit and before judgment therein.—*Baxley* v. *Linah*, 241.

7. The transcript of a judgment in the Common Pleas, entered in another county, in pursuance of the act of 16th April 1840, is not a very judgment of the court of the county in which it is entered, but is a *quasi* judgment for limited purposes; it is evidence of a judgment in the court in which it was originally obtained. The original judgment having been set aside at the instance of the defendant, for irregularity, and the execution in the second county stayed, the judgment on the transcript fell with it; and the plaintiff having obtained a new judgment in the case, but no transcript of it having been entered, had no lien in the county in which the transcript had been entered.—*Brandt's Appeal*, 343.

8. The principle of substitution or subrogation rests in equity only, and is not to be carried out when it would work injustice to the rights of others; therefore, G. M., a judgment creditor, whose judgment was entered in *Cumberland* county, was not entitled to be subrogated to the judgments in *Franklin* county of M., whose judgments originally entered in that county had been subsequently entered by transcript in *Cumberland county*, and there paid out of the proceeds of sale of the defendant's real estate in the latter county, when the substitution would have been to the prejudice of J., whose judgment in Franklin county was entered *after* the judgment of M. was obtained there, but *before* the judgment of G. M. was obtained in Cumberland county.—*McGinnis's Appeal*, 445.

JURISDICTION.

On an appeal from the judgment of a justice of the peace, it need not appear in the *declaration* that the claim of the plaintiff was for an amount within the jurisdiction of the justice; it is sufficient if that appear on the trial. *Huckman* v. *Flory*, 196.

JUSTICE OF THE PEACE.

1. The rule of the common law as to the computation of time is to include the first day and exclude the last: therefore, where notice to a justice of the peace of an intended suit, given in pursuance of the first section of the act of 21st March 1772, was served on the 19th of May, and suit brought on the 18th of June, it was *held* that the notice was given thirty days before suit. The decision in Goswiler's Estate, 3 *Pa. Rep.* 200, was not well considered.—*Thomas* v. *Afflick*, 14.
2. The certificate of a justice of the peace in relation to the acknowledgment of a mortgage or deed by a *feme covert* is not conclusive; but parol evidence is admissible to show that the acknowledgment by the wife was not made of her own free will and accord, but that undue means were used for obtaining it.—*Louden* v. *Blythe*, 532.

LAND. See ISLANDS, 2–4.

Where a question existed whether the larger part of a tract of land lay in Centre or Clearfield county, which were there bounded by the Mushannon Creek, it being the usage to tax lands in the county in which the greater part of the tract was situate, the official book of the treasurer of Centre county was evidence to show that the tract in question was *not* returned for taxation in Centre county, although other tracts in the same lot of surveys were so returned, the taxes on the tract in question having been paid by the claimant in the county of Clearfield; and especially, when taken in connection with the deposition of the treasurer of Centre county, that the present claimant had furnished to him a list of his lands *in Centre county*, in which the tract in question did *not* appear.—*Gratz* v. *Hoover*, 232.

LANDLORD AND TENANT. See COUNTY, 2.

LEGACY AND LEGATEE. See DEVISE, 6.

1. A testator devised to his son Eli, his heirs and assigns for ever, two tracts of land, *subject nevertheless to, and charged and chargeable with* the payment of six hundred dollars, to certain of the children of his son Joseph, to be paid to them or the survivors, share and share alike, viz: "one-half of the said sum to be paid one year after his decease, and the other half two years after his decease, which sum of six hundred I do hereby bequeath to my said grand-children, to be paid them as above stated and directed, and I do hereby charge the payment of the same on the tracts or parcels of land herein and hereby devised to my said son Eli, his heirs and assigns."

    After the execution of his will, the testator sold the devised lands to his son James for part cash and the major part of the purchase-money in payments, which did not become due till after the testator's death. He devised to others of his children and grand-children pecuniary legacies; and he further directed that after the legacies and debts were paid, the balance of his estate should be equally divided amongst all his children, and the children of any that are deceased, share and share alike: *Held*, that as the legacy charged on the land devised to Eli, was to be paid by him as devisee in respect of the devise, and as a means of distribution among the testator's children, the land being the sole source of payment, the sale of the land by the testator effected an ademption of the legacy.—*Walls* v. *Stewart*, 275.
2. If a legacy be given with respect to a particular fund, only as pointing out a convenient mode of payment, it is to be considered *demonstrative*, and the legatee will not be disappointed, though the fund wholly fail. But where the gift is of the fund itself, in whole or in part, or so charged upon the object made subject to it, as to show an intent to burden that object alone with the payment, it is esteemed *specific*, and consequently liable to be ademed by the alienation or destruction of the object. In such matters, the *intention* of the testator is principally to be ascertained; and it is necessary, in order to render a legacy spe

cific, that the intention so to make it, clearly appear. Per BELL, J. See this opinion as to specific and demonstrative legacies.—*Id.*

LEGISLATURE. See CONSTITUTIONAL LAW.

LIMITATION AND STATUTE OF LIMITATIONS.
1. In the case of an action to recover damages for breach of a parol contract for the purchase of land, the right of action accrues when the vendor conveys to a stranger. It exists *before eviction* by the grantee.—*Thurston v. Franklin College,* 154.
2. To take a case out of the statute of limitations, the acknowledgment must be clear and unequivocal; and it ought to be so distinct in its *extent* and form as to leave no room for doubt or hesitation.—*Harbold's Ex'rs.* v. *Kuntz,* 210.
3. In a claim by a son-in-law who had lived on the farm of his father-in-law, for ten years' service, and for rents of a house of plaintiff, received by defendant, testimony that defendant (the father-in-law) said to the witness that "he had never settled with the plaintiff, nor paid him for the ten years' service, and he did not know what he would charge him; that he owed him for his ten years' service; that he had never paid him, and that he could pay him and would pay him; that he had not settled with him for the rent of the house and lot; that he would settle with him and pay him all he owed him, that he was old and wanted to settle up for the ten years' service and the rent; that he had paid debts for him (the plaintiff) and hauled stone for him:" was held to be too vague and uncertain to remove the bar of the statute.—*Id.*

LUNATIC.
1. A wife cannot make any contract to bind her husband without his authority express or implied, or dispose of his property, except perhaps in case of necessity for the immediate use of his family. And where the husband is a *lunatic,* she cannot transfer his property to pay a particular creditor to the prejudice of others.—*Alexander* v. *Miller, Reed & Co.* 215.
2. Under the act of 13th June 1836, relative to lunatics, when the Court of Common Pleas has decreed an allowance out of the proceeds of sale of the real estate of a lunatic, for his maintenance, the amount is not to be exceeded without the sanction of the court. The estate of a lunatic is subject to the control of that court.—*Guthrie's Appeal,* 321.

MACHINE.
An improvement of a machine for which a patent may be obtained may consist of the introduction of a new element into an old machine which produces a new and useful result or greater facility in the application of power; and though it appear from the description or specification of the claimant for a patent for an improvement, that part of the elements included in the description or specification were not *new,* but which he claimed to be newly combined with new elements, the patent is not therefore void.—*Rheem* v. *Holliday,* 347.

MIFFLIN COUNTY. See ISLANDS, 2–4.

MORTGAGE.
As to acknowledgment by a *feme covert,* see *Louden* v. *Blythe,* 532.

MURDER.
In the case of an indictment for murder in the first degree, it should appear from the record that the prisoner was present in court when he was sentenced to be executed, and it should be demanded of him whether he has any thing to say why sentence of death should not be pronounced upon him.—*Hamilton alias Thacker* v. *The Commonwealth,* 129.

NOTICE. See BOND, 2.
A plaintiff whose deed for real estate has been duly recorded is not bound to give actual notice of his title to another, who claiming under another title, and being in possession, is about to make some improvement on

the property, the latter claiming under a deed to one which contained a reference to the deed to the plaintiff. Therefore, S. T., whose name was the same as that of his father, but who claimed under a deed from another, was not debarred from asserting his title, by omitting to give notice of it to one, who, being in possession, was making some improvement on the premises, the latter claiming by virtue of a sheriff's sale of the interest of one who claimed under a deed from the father executed after the conveyance to S. T. the son was executed and recorded, and which deed referred to or recited the deed to S. T. as of record, without however distinguishing between the father and the son, but the grantee in which conveyance from the father had *actual notice* at the time of that conveyance that the title was in the son and not in the father.—*Knouff* v. *Thompson*, 357.

NUISANCE.
It was not error for the court to term a dangerous opening in a much frequented street, in a large town, a *public nuisance*.—*Beatty* v. *Gilmore*, 463.

ORPHANS' COURT. See PARTITION; RECOGNIZANCE.
1. Interest on the balance in the hands of an administrator from the time of its receipt is not of course; circumstances may be shown by the administrator, which would exempt him from the payment of interest.—*Wither's Appeal*, 151.
2. Interest is an incident to a decree of the Orphans' Court, as it is to a judgment in the Common Pleas.—*Id.*
3. Where an auditor to whom the account of the administrator was referred to report upon exceptions to it, made report that a certain amount was in the hands of the accountant on the day of exhibiting his account, which report was simply confirmed in the Orphans' Court: *Held*, that it was error in an auditor to whom the account was referred for distribution of the balance, to charge interest on the balance reported from the day of the exhibition of the account, instead of from the day of the decree of the confirmation by the Orphans' Court. The auditor appointed to report distribution is confined to the decree of the Orphans' Court.—*Id.*
4. The record of the Orphans' Court is evidence of the appointment of a guardian; the issuing of a certificate of the appointment is not material; an act as guardian, by the person appointed, is an assumption of the trust.—*Eyster's Appeal*, 372.

PARENT AND CHILD.
A son working after he is of age for his father does not thereby acquire a right of action against his father, unless there has been a previous contract or agreement to pay on the part of the father.—*Zerbe* v. *Miller*, 488.

PARTITION.
1. The 48th section of the act of 29th March 1832, relating to Orphans' Courts, which enables the *Orphans'* Court to require security from a husband before money payable to his wife under proceedings in partition is paid to him, does not apply to the case of a female *unmarried* at the time of the partition; and the payment to a *future* husband, without security, will discharge the recognizance, so far as the wife is interested.—*Quigley* v. *The Commonwealth*, 353.
2. If a husband leave outstanding the share due to his wife in a recognizance in the Orphans' Court, it is not liable to attachment by his creditors.—*Stoner* v. *The Commonwealth*, 387.
3. J. S. took land at an appraisement in the Orphans' Court and entered into recognizance for payment to the other heirs, of whom the wife of S. L. was one. Afterwards the recognizor became the bail of the husband in a note. Subsequent to this, the husband and wife transferred the interest of the wife under the recognizance, which was alleged to have been done to defraud creditors. Separate judgments were after-

wards obtained on the note against the husband and his bail, the recognizor; and on the judgment against the husband the interest of his wife under the recognizance was attached, and J. S., the recognizor, made garnishee. Before judgment in the attachment proceeding the recognizor voluntarily paid the amount of the claim: *Held*, that such voluntary payment could not be used by him as a set-off against the claim of the assignee of the husband and wife under the recognizance, nor could it be pleaded in bar as payment of the recognizance: as garnishee he was bound to contest the claim of the attachment creditor, and payment before judgment against him was no defence to a suit on the recognizance for the share attached.—*Id.*

4. Where there is no order for a settlement of the wife's share under proceedings in partition at the time of the partition, the subsequent declaration of the wife made before a judge of the Orphans' Court, that her share of the money payable under the partition should be paid to her husband, is not equivalent to a reduction into possession by him.—*Id.*

5. None but the creditors of the husband can resist an assignment by him of a claim under a recognizance, made for the purpose of defrauding them. The debtor of the claim thus transferred can safely pay it on the foot of a judgment on the recognizance.—*Id.*

6. The real estate of an intestate who left *seven* children, was divided and appraised, and a house and lot, a part of the same, were taken by the eldest son, who gave recognizance, and afterwards died intestate, without issue, and without payment of the recognizance. It was afterwards agreed by others of the heirs and the husband of another heir, that the house and lot be conveyed to the husband, he to allow the consideration-money out of the share of his wife, and if more than that share, he to pay the difference. *The other lands* were sold, and the purchase-money of the house and lot was charged against the share of the wife in the distribution of the father's estate: *Held*, that the object of the proceeding not being *partition*, but the estate of the wife having been *converted*, the proceeds became the property of the husband, by his application of them, and that the title to the premises, to the extent thus paid for by the husband, vested in him; besides, the premises descended as the estate of the *son*, and not of the father, and the money due to the wife was in the estate of the father. Whether a *conveyance* was made to the husband was held not to be material. The wife, who brought ejectment after the death of her husband, was held to be entitled to recover only one *sixth* part of the house and lot.—*Ermold v. Newkirk,* 417.

PARTNERSHIP.

1. Horses purchased by A, B, and C, in partnership, were levied on under an execution against A for his private debt, and on an execution against B and C for the debt of B on a judgment confessed by B against himself and C; *after* the sale the judgment was on motion of C set aside as to him: *Held*, that the vacating of the judgment did not affect the validity of the previous sale under executions against all the partners, but that the proceeds of it represent the property, and the execution creditors occupy the place of the purchaser; that C can claim out of the proceeds only to the extent of the interest he had in the property; and if on the settlement of the account, under the direction of the court, in the course of the distribution of the proceeds of the sale, he appears to have been entitled to *no* interest *in the horses*, he is not entitled to any share of the proceeds of their sale.—*Kelly's Appeal,* 59.

2. The distribution of the proceeds of a sheriff's sale is, by the 86th section of the act of 16th June 1836, to be made according *to law and equity;* and in the course of the distribution of the proceeds of the sale of property purchased in partnership, and sold on executions against the partners as individuals, for their separate debts, the court may direct

an account to ascertain the respective rights of the partners to the proceeds in dispute.—*Id.*

8. One partner without the consent of his co-partner, has no right to give to his own separate creditor an order on a debtor of *the firm;* and the fact that the other partner knew of the order before it was executed and did not express his dissent to the defendants in whose favour it was drawn, and who received the same and its produce, was held not to be a defence to a recovery from the latter, by the firm, of the amount of the order. Notice was unnecessary, as the persons receiving the order had no right to presume the consent of the other partner to a misapplication of the partnership property; and the defendants knew that the firm was not liable for their claim against the individual partner.—*McKinney & Heller v. Brights,* 399.

PATENT.
An improvement of a machine for which a patent may be obtained may consist of the introduction of a new element into an old machine which produces a new and useful result or greater facility in the application of power; and though it appear from the description or specification of the claimant for a patent for an improvement, that part of the elements included in the description or specification were not *new*, but which he claimed to be newly combined with new elements, the patent is not therefore void.—*Rheem v. Holliday,* 347.

PENALTY. See CONTRACT, 9.

PHILADELPHIA.
1. In 1690, Vine street, from Front street to the river Delaware, in the city of Philadelphia, was dedicated to public use, as a street of the increased width of 100 feet or more, by the act of the commissioners of property.—*Penny Pot Landing,* 79.
2. The proprietary, having granted this addition to Vine street for the public use and accommodation, could not revoke the grant by any subsequent act or deed. The rights of the adjacent lot-holders, as well as the public, to Vine street so enlarged, were vested rights, of which they could not be divested.—*Id.*
3. In addition to the right of the city of Philadelphia to the space annexed to and made part of Vine street in 1690, the same piece of ground was expressly granted to the city corporation by the charter of 1701, as Penny Pot Landing.—*Id.*
4. Maps, ancient surveys, as well as reputation, are evidence to elucidate and ascertain a boundary, but not to impeach official grants on public record, control having been long exercised in conformity to the grants.
5. The dedication of a street or landing will be intended to be for the public, and not for part of the public in exclusion of any other part.—*Id.*
6. Street, in a town or city, signifies a public highway. No particular form or ceremony is necessary in the dedication of land to public uses.—*Id.*
7. Possession and use will not give an individual or a corporation a title to a franchise which is an encroachment on a public right.—*Id.*

POSSESSION.
Possession and use will not give an individual or a corporation a title to a franchise which is an encroachment on a public right.—*Penny Pot Landing,* 79.

POWER.
Where the donee of a power to sell land possesses also an interest in the subject of the power, a conveyance by him made without actual reference to the power will not be deemed an execution of the power, unless there be evidence of an intention to execute it, or at least in the face of evidence, disproving such an intention; but where the donee has *no estate in the premises,* and his conveyance can be made operative *only* by

treating it as an execution of the power to sell, it will be so considered. —*Jones* v. *Wood*, 25.

PRESUMPTION. See EVIDENCE, 15.
1. In an action on a note given for the price of a horse sold at auction, where fraud is alleged as to the condition of the animal at the time of sale, the presumption is very slight that the horse was unsound when fully grown, and apparently vigorous, because it had been diseased when a colt; the jury are to judge of the soundness or unsoundness, from the evidence exhibited in the case.—*Staines* v. *Shore*, 200.
2. What shall be deemed ordinary care to avoid accidental injury will depend on the circumstances of each case, and of which the jury is to judge; but if no facts be proved from which a deduction can be drawn, the *presumption* is against the defendant whose misconduct rendered the accident possible.—*Beatty* v. *Gilmore*, 463.

PRINCIPAL AND AGENT.
An agent having authority only *to collect a debt*, has no right to take a note for the amount of it, from the debtor to himself, and thus substitute himself as creditor; but if such an arrangement be afterwards *ratified* by the principal, the latter is bound by it, and the debtor is released from liability to the principal on the original claim.—*McCulloch* v. *McKee*, 289.

PRINCIPAL AND SURETY. See SURETY; CONTRACT, 5.

PROMISSORY NOTES.
1. An engagement endorsed on a bill or promissory note under seal, for $500, of the same date with the note, as follows:—"I hereby acknowledge to be security for the within amount of five hundred dollars, until satisfactorily paid by W. A.:" *Held*, to import the liability of a surety, and not that of a guaranty; that the surety was not discharged by mere forbearance to sue the principal, no notice having been given by the surety to the payees to proceed against the principal; that the plaintiffs were not bound to give notice to the surety of non-payment at the maturity of the note; and that it was not incumbent on plaintiffs to show that they had used due diligence to recover from the principal before suit against the surety.—*Marberger et al.* v. *Pott*, 9.
2. In an action on a negotiable note brought by the payee against the drawer, the defendant may prove that the note in suit was given with another note, in lieu of a former note, which with other notes had been given by the drawer and another who was his partner, to another firm, for the purchase of certain personal property, and the lease of real estate, and that a portion of the personal property to a greater amount than the note in suit, had never been received by the purchasers, through default of the sellers, whereby there was a failure of consideration; and that the *original notes* had been transferred by the payees to the payee of the note in suit, not in the usual course of business, but merely as *collateral security* against certain liabilities incurred by the holder for the payees, no new consideration passing between the holder and payees of the original notes at the time of the transfer.—*Kirkpatrick* v. *Muirhead*, 117.
3. The circumstance that the suit upon the note had been tried several times before, and that the defence made in this suit was not then made, and that the note in suit had been given after a knowledge by the maker of the failure of consideration, will not preclude the defence, if the silence of the maker as to the failure of consideration did not mislead the holder, or unless the latter relinquished some advantages of which otherwise he might have availed himself, evidence being offered that the drawer, at the time of the giving of the new note, supposed that the transfer of the original note to the holder was in due course and for a valuable consideration.—*Id.*

INDEX. 575

4. Consideration, like every other part of a contract, must be the result of *agreement;* and the circumstance that the new note was not signed by both of the parties to the original note, (one being accidentally absent,) and that it was payable at a longer period than the original note, will not preclude the defence, the old note having been split into two, and further time being given, merely for convenience, and not because of any new consideration contemplated by the parties, the release of the other party not inducing the execution of the new note; but if this hypothesis as to time and party were *unfounded,* it was not for the court to say so; whether there was any new consideration leading to the execution of the new note sued, was a question of fact for the jury.—*Id.*
5. The party whose name was omitted in taking the new note, being released by the defendant, the maker of the note in suit was a competent witness in his favour, to prove a failure of consideration of the original notes, partial or total, after the original notes reached the plaintiff's hands, and that the note in suit was given for one of them.—*Id.*
6. The testimony of one of the payees of the original notes, given on a former trial of this case on the new note, was admissible on the part of the defendant to prove the consideration of the transfer to the plaintiff below of the original notes, the object not being to impeach the original notes; and it was not a valid objection to this testimony, that the jury might infer from other portions of the same testimony that the first notes were accepted as payment of pre-existent debts.—*Id.*
7. The inventory of the property for the purchase of which the former notes were given, was evidence, if the fact of its containing such an enumeration was established.—*Id.*

PUFFER. See SALE.

RAILROAD.

A *turnpike road* was constructed over the ground of individuals, who, in 1825, receipted in full for damages sustained by its construction. In 1849 an act was passed authorizing the turnpike company to sell its corporate rights to a *railroad* company, and the latter to purchase, for the purpose of laying rails thereon, the same to be laid under the act of incorporation of the railroad company, which provided for the valuation of land occupied by the road, and of all damages which the owner or owners shall sustain or may have sustained by reason of its construction: *Held,* that the obligation imposed on the railroad company to pay damages, was a proper exercise of legislative authority, when conferring on that company the additional privilege; and that one of the original owners of the land and her grantees were not estopped by the receipt to the *turnpike* company, from claiming consequential damages from the railroad company, by reason of the construction of the *railroad,* though the railroad occupied no more of their ground than was contained within the limits of the turnpike road.—*Mifflin v. Railroad Company,* 182.

RECOGNIZANCE.
1. J. S. took land at an appraisement in the Orphans' Court and entered into recognizance for payment to the other heirs, of whom the wife of S. L. was one. Afterwards the recognizor became the bail of the husband in a note. Subsequent to this, the husband and wife transferred the interest of the wife under the recognizance, which was alleged to have been done to defraud creditors. Separate judgments were afterwards obtained on the note against the husband and his bail, the recognizor, and on the judgment against the husband the interest of his wife under the recognizance was attached, and J. S., the recognizor, made garnishee. Before judgment in the attachment proceeding the recognizor voluntarily paid the amount of the claim: *Held,* that such voluntary payment could not be used by him as a set-off against the claim of the assignee of the husband and wife under the recognizance, nor could it be pleaded in bar as payment of the recognizance; as garnishee he was bound to

contest the claim of the attachment creditor, and payment before judgment against him was no defence to a suit on the recognizance for the share attached.—*Stoner* v. *The Commonwealth*, 387.
2. In a suit on a recognizance in the Orphans' Court given by an heir who took one of three purparts at the appraisement, executed in favor of the Commonwealth for the payment to the other heirs their proportional shares in the purpart, it was admissible for the recognizor, the defendant, under the plea of payment with leave to show that one of the other purparts, not taken at the appraisement, was sold by a trustee under order of the Orphans' Court, and that all of the balance of the proceeds, after payment of debts of the intestate, was paid to the plaintiff, and that the defendant in the suit never made any objection. The fact whether or not it was received as part payment, should have been submitted to the jury.—*Kidd* v. *The Commonwealth*, 426.
3. Such a recognizance should be sued in the name of the Commonwealth as the legal party, though it is proper that the name of the persons suing, should be stated on the record. A mistake however, in this respect, will not furnish a defence against the Commonwealth, as the court should look to the distribution of the amount recovered. The judgment should not be for the *penalty*, but for the amount of the interest of those suing.—*Id.*
4. It is not necessary that all the *cestuis que use* should be marked of record. Less than the whole number may sue, and they may recover as much of the fund as they show themselves entitled to, leaving the balance for those entitled who may afterwards sue. But where they represent *one heir*, their joinder in the suit would seem to be peculiarly proper.—*Id.*

RECORD AND RECORDING ACTS.
A plaintiff whose deed for real estate has been duly recorded is not bound to give actual notice of his title to another, who claiming under another title, and being in possession, is about to make some improvement on the property, the latter claiming under a deed to one which contained a reference to the deed to the plaintiff.—*Knouff* v. *Thompson*, 357.

REGISTER. See ADMINISTRATION.

RIVER. See ISLANDS, 3.

ROAD.
1. Viewers of a private road being required by act of Assembly of June 13 1836, to report whether the same is *necessary;* a report that there is *occasion for the road* was held to be sufficient.—*Pocopson Road*, 15.
2. The act of June 13 1836, authorizing the laying out of *private* roads, is constitutional.—*Id.*

SALE.
1. The employment of a puffer by the seller to bid for him at an auction vitiates the sale, and it is not material whether the property purchased brought no more than its *general value;* a purchaser has a right to purchase at an under value if he can.—*Staines* v. *Shore*, 200.
2. When the employment of a puffer has been discovered by the purchaser after the sale, it is his duty to offer to return the property purchased, when the fraud is discovered; but if not discovered till too late to do so, the purchaser's defence is good without it.—*Id.*

SATISFACTION.
1. Whether a note or bond is accepted *in satisfaction* of the original claim is for the jury to decide, and not for the court as a matter of law.—*Stone* v. *Miller*, 450.
2. Where claims transferred to a creditor consist of the indebtedness of others, and there is no agreement to receive the same *in satisfaction*, they are to be considered as *collateral* security for the original debt.—*Id.*

SCHOOL.
In the appropriation act of 11th April 1848, it was provided that the *common school system* shall be held to be adopted by all the school districts in the commonwealth, and that each school district levying a tax, shall be entitled to a deduction of twenty-five per cent. of all moneys paid into the county treasury by such district, for State purposes, during the *two next ensuing school years;* which school years by a former act, were to end on the first *Monday of June* of each year: It was held that the abatement was to be limited to the taxes assessed for the school years of 1848 and 1849, and was not to extend to taxes which had been assessed for the school year commencing on the first Monday of June 1850, but which had been advanced or paid into the county treasury *before* that day.—*The Commonwealth* v. *Fraim*, 163.

SCIRE FACIAS.
In a sci. fa. to revive a judgment, the pleas were *nul tiel record*, payment, and payment with leave. Replication *non sol* and that there is such a record. Arbitrators appointed under rule entered under the act of 1836, found for plaintiff a gross sum : *Held*, that the plea of *nul tiel record* did not exempt the case from arbitration, but that the arbitrators had jurisdiction of the whole cause.—*Lange* v. *Stouffer*, 251.

SET-OFF. See RECOGNIZANCE.

SETTLEMENT. See case of *Sample* v. *Robb*, 305, &c.

SHERIFF. See SHERIFF'S SALE; EXECUTION; COUNTY.
1. Creditors can attack a judgment *collaterally* only *for collusion*, not for matter of defence, original or subsequent. A judgment creditor who objects to a prior judgment on the ground of failure of consideration, can do so only on the trial of an issue directed as to the prior judgment, to ascertain the amount due upon it; but while it stands as a debt of record, unabated in whole or in part, and unaffected by any such proceeding in relation to it, neither the sheriff nor a subsequent judgment creditor can resist the enforcement of it as a lien, and the sheriff cannot legally disregard it in the appropriation of the proceeds of sale of the real estate bound by it.—*Lewis* v. *Rogers*, 18.
2. A sheriff who does not incur any risk of mispayment in the appropriation of the proceeds of sale of real estate, has no right to impose conditions or take a promise to refund from a judgment creditor, to whom he pays a part of the money arising from the sale of the real estate bound by the judgment, and to which the judgment was from the record apparently entitled.—*Id.*

SHERIFF'S SALE. See EXECUTION, and SHERIFF.

SLANDER.
1. If the words charged in a narr. in an action for slander do not imply a criminal charge subject to infamous punishment, neither an innuendo nor verdict will help them; but when they are used in a double sense, the plaintiff may, by an innuendo, aver the meaning with which he thinks they were spoken, and the jury may find whether they were spoken with that meaning or not.—*Dottarer* v. *Bushey*, 204.
2. Where the words were that the plaintiff "will lie, cheat, steal, and swear," it was not error for the court, in answer to a broad request of defendant's counsel to charge that the evidence did not support the declaration, to say to the jury that these words may import that the plaintiff steals.—*Id.*
3. To say of a person that "I believe he will steal, and I believe he did steal," amounts to the charge of larceny.—*Id.*
4. To say of a person he "took my wood, and is guilty of any and every thing that is dishonest," connected with the innuendo that the defendant meant that plaintiff was guilty of larceny, is sufficient after verdict.—*Id.*

STEAM-ENGINE.
1. A person contracted with machinists for the construction of a steam-engine and fixtures for a grist-mill. A part of the machinery, viz. the boilers and balance-wheel, were delivered, and the boilers fixed in a building attached to the mill. The purchaser became embarrassed, and in an agreement in writing between him and the attorney of the manufacturers, it was stated that the boilers and the machinery attached or to be attached to them were the property of the manufacturers, and they by their attorney agreed to leave the same where they were for three months, in order to give time to the purchaser to make an arrangement with his creditors; and in the event of his inability to make such arrangement, then the manufacturers were *to be left to their legal remedy for the materials already furnished, or to the removal of the same, at their option:* Held, that the machinists had the right to remove the boilers and wheel as against one who had purchased them at sheriff's sale when sold as the personal property of the owner of the mill who had ordered them, without respect to whether they were attached to the *real* estate or not.—*Shell v. Haywood & Snyder*, 523.
2. The acts and declarations of the owner of the mill who contracted for the engine, made before execution issued against him, that he considered the boilers and wheel as the property of the *manufacturers* of them, were admissible on *their* part as evidence of ownership, possession, and the right to remove the same.—*Id.*

STOCK.
The second section of the act of 29th March 1819, authorizing stock held in corporations by individuals, in their own names, and which is not claimed by any other person, to be taken in execution and sold in the same manner as goods and chattels, is not repealed by the act of 16th June 1836, relating to executions.—*Lex v. Potters*, 295.

STRAYS.
Where the owner of grain takes up cattle trespassing upon it, in order to sell them he must proceed according to the act of Assembly, or he will be deemed a trespasser *ab initio*, and responsible in damages to the owner of the cattle.—*Fitzwater v. Stout*, 22.

STREET.
1. In 1690, Vine street, from Front street to the river Delaware, in the city of Philadelphia, was dedicated to public use, as a street of the increased width of 100 feet or more, by the act of the commissioners of property.—*Penny Pot Landing*, 79.
2. The proprietary, having granted this addition to Vine street for the public use and accommodation, could not revoke the grant by any subsequent act or deed. The rights of the adjacent lot-holders, as well as the public, to Vine street so enlarged, were vested rights, of which they could not be divested.—*Id.*
3. In addition to the right of the city of Philadelphia to the space annexed to and made part of Vine street in 1690, the same piece of ground was expressly granted to the city corporation by the charter of 1701, as Penny Pot Landing.—*Id.*
4. Maps, ancient surveys, as well as reputation, are evidence to elucidate and ascertain a boundary, but not to impeach official grants on public record, control having been long exercised in conformity to the grants.—*Id.*
5. The dedication of a street or landing will be intended to be for the public, and not for part of the public in exclusion of any other part.—*Id.*
6. Street, in a town or city, signifies a public highway. No particular form or ceremony is necessary in the dedication of land to public uses.—*Id.*
7. Possession and use will not give an individual or a corporation a title to a franchise which is an encroachment on a public right.—*Id.*

SUBSTITUTION.
The principle of substitution or subrogation rests in equity only, and is not

to be carried out when it would work injustice to the rights of others; therefore, G. M., a judgment creditor, whose judgment was entered in *Cumberland* county, was not entitled to be subrogated to the judgments in *Franklin* county of M., whose judgments originally entered in that county had been subsequently entered by transcript in *Cumberland county*, and there paid out of the proceeds of sale of the defendant's real estate in the latter county, when the substitution would have been to the prejudice of J., whose judgment in Franklin county was entered *after* the judgment of M. was obtained there, but *before* the judgment of G. M. was obtained in Cumberland county.—*McGinnis's Appeal*, 445.

SURETY. See PRINCIPAL AND SURETY.

An engagement endorsed on a bill or promissory note under seal, for $500, of the same date with the note, as follows: "I hereby acknowledge to be security for the within amount of five hundred dollars, until satisfactorily paid by W. A.:" *Held* to import the liability of a surety, and not that of a guaranty; that the surety was not discharged by mere forbearance to sue the principal, no notice having been given by the surety to the payees to proceed against the principal; that the plaintiffs were not bound to give notice to the surety of non-payment at the maturity of the note; and that it was not incumbent on plaintiffs to show that they had used due diligence to recover from the principal before suit against the surety.—*Marberger et al.* v. *Pott*, 9.

SURVEY. See WARRANT AND SURVEY.

TAXES.

The third section of the act of 11th March 1850, relating to collateral inheritance taxes, which provides that the words "*being within this commonwealth*," in the first section of the act of 7th April 1826, relating to collateral inheritances, "shall be so construed as to relate to all persons who have been at the time of their decease, or now may be, domiciled within this commonwealth, as well as to estates," is applicable to the estate of a person domiciled in Pennsylvania, who died *before the passage of the act*, viz. in December 1849, and is, as to such a case, constitutional, at least as to assets remaining in this State in the hands of the executors; and therefore stocks in corporations in other States, and bonds of such corporations, and cash in a bank in another State, belonging to such a decedent, are liable to the collateral inheritance tax for the use of this commonwealth, and the executors are chargeable with the amount of the said tax, out of the assets in their hands.—*In re Short's Estate*, 63.

TENDER. See TRUST, 7.

TIMBER.
1. Under the 3d section of the act of 29th March 1824, either trespass or trover may be maintained for entering upon plaintiff's land, without his consent, and cutting and removing timber trees. If there be a *trespass merely, double* damages may be given; if, in addition, the trees felled have been converted to the use of the wrong-doer, *treble* damages may be recovered in trespass, and also in *trover*. By the words "as the case may be," is meant that if the trespass to the close *be waived*, and trover brought, *treble* damages for the injury done may be recovered in that form of action.—*Welsh* v. *Anthony*, 254.
2. Either the jury or the court may assess the double or treble damages.
3. Double or treble *costs* mean, in Pennsylvania, double or treble the single costs; and so with respect to *damages*. The English rule as to costs in such cases does not prevail in this State. Per ROGERS, J.—*Id.*

TIME. See DEVISE, 6.

The rule of the common law as to the computation of time is to include the first day and exclude the last; therefore, where notice to a justice of the peace of an intended suit, given in pursuance of the first section of the act of 21st March 1772, was served on the 19th of May, and suit brought on the 18th of June, it was *held* that the notice was given thirty days before suit. The decision in Goswiler's Estate, 3 *Pa. Rep.* 200, was not well considered.—*Thomas* v. *Afflick*, 14.

TRANSCRIPT.
The transcript of a judgment in the Common Pleas, entered in another county, in pursuance of the act of 16th April 1840, is not a very judgment of the court of the county in which it is entered, but is a *quasi* judgment for limited purposes; it is evidence of a judgment in the court in which it was originally obtained. The original judgment having been set aside at the instance of the defendant, for irregularity, and the execution in the second county stayed, the judgment on the transcript fell with it; and the plaintiff having obtained a new judgment in the case, but no transcript of it having been entered, had no lien in the county in which the transcript had been entered.—*Brandt's Appeal*, 343.

TRESPASS. See TIMBER.

TRIAL. See COURT.
1. Where there is a spark of evidence of a fact, it should not be excluded from the jury.—*Fitzwater* v. *Stout*, 22.
2. It is error for the court to submit to the jury an alleged fact of which there is *no* evidence.—*Jones* v. *Wood*, 25.
3. The judge trying a cause should not withdraw the facts from the consideration of the jury, or induce the jury to infer that they are not at liberty to pass upon disputed facts; but he may express an opinion as to the tendency of the facts in evidence; and an erroneous opinion concerning facts not withdrawn from the jury, is no ground for reversal. *Oyster* v. *Longnecker*, 269.
4. It is not essential that the court bring to the notice of the jury all the evidence in relation to a subject on which they charge.—*Id.*
5. It is not error to receive evidence which is pertinent and relevant, because it is not strictly *rebutting;* especially in a complicated case, and where the adverse party is not taken by surprise.—*Id.*
6. The ordering a cause for trial, or its continuance, is a matter within the discretion of the court below, and is not examinable on error.—*Porter* v. *Lee*, 412.

TROVER. See TIMBER.
The owner of the land has no lien on property cast on it by drift. And where the owner of the latter proves his property in it and the actual conversion of it by the owner of the land, the latter is liable in trover and conversion for damages.—*Forster* v. *Juniata Bridge Co.* 393.

TRUST AND TRUSTEE.
1. A deed, whether voluntary and without consideration, or for a valuable consideration, made upon a parol trust, declared at the time of the execution of the deed, that the grantee would hold in trust for the children of the grantor, if intended as a fraud upon creditors of the grantor, is void as against the creditors, but it is valid as against the grantor and the children for whose benefit it was designed, and the grantee will be entitled to hold against the children or their vendee; whether the trust be by parol or in writing the rule is the same; and the circumstance of the grantee *of the children* being in possession will not vary the principle. See 7 *Barr* 420.—*Murphy* v. *Hubert*, 50.
2. Acts by a trustee, a married woman, in relation to the trust property, made as agent of her husband, and her declarations accompanying such acts, are evidence against her husband.—*Id.*
3. If a deed be made in consideration of a bond executed by the grantee, and the bond was subsequently cancelled by the grantee, *then a married*

woman, this would not revest the estate in the grantor, or defeat the estate of her husband.—*Id.*

4. An individual granted and conveyed for a nominal consideration, a lot of ground to certain persons in trust for those who had subscribed or may thereafter be subscribers towards the erection of a school-house and house of public worship thereon, and towards the support of a school, or the support of the gospel, in the said building, and providing, that if at any time thereafter, the premises should be converted to any other use than as aforesaid, and for a burying-ground, that in such case the lot shall revert to the grantor and his heirs *and assigns*. It was *held*, that the mere permission by one of the trustees to a female in distress, to occupy the premises temporarily, as a tenant at will, without rent, though she and her family remained in it for years, did not work a forfeiture of the estate to the grantor or his assigns.—*McKissick* v. *Pickle*, 140.

5. The declaration or admission of one of the trustees of a charitable trust in real estate, that the trust title had been divested, cannot affect the right of the persons interested under the trust. The trustees have no right to relinquish the trust property.—*Id.*

6. Though in the case of a condition *in law*, none but the grantor or his heirs can enter for a condition broken, yet in Pennsylvania, where the doctrine of maintenance does not prevail, there is no policy of law which forbids the reservation of a right of entry *to the assigns* of the grantor. Therefore, in the case of such a reservation, a purchaser of the grantor's conditional interest in the premises, at a sheriff's sale, is within the terms of such a reservation, and if a forfeiture exist, he may take advantage of it, though his purchase was *before* the condition was broken.—*Id.*

7. Where an administrator purchased real estate with funds a moiety of which belonged to himself, and the other moiety to others, in an action of ejectment by the *cestui que trust* against a purchaser of the land from the administrator, without notice of the trust, the purchaser is entitled to be reimbursed the one-half of the purchase-money paid by him before notice of the trust, unless he has been fully compensated to the extent of that moiety out of the rents or profits. It is not, however, necessary that the amount be tendered before suit brought.—*Beck* v. *Uhrich*, 499.

8. The administrator, who was a co-defendant in the ejectment, is entitled to be reimbursed for expenses incurred in the creation of the trust, and advances made for the *benefit of the trust.*—*Id.*

9. The administration account settled after the suit brought, is evidence in favor of the defendants, to show the amount of money advanced by the administrator in the purchase of the land in question; but it is not conclusive.—*Id.*

USURY.

1. Usury is not committed by payment of a premium *less* in amount than the legal interest. The offence consists in taking more than six per cent. on the loan, and till more has been taken the penalty is not incurred.—*Oyster* v. *Longnecker*, 269.

2. A return to the lender of part of the sum on which interest is reserved, reduces the contract essentially to a loan of *the residue*. The money returned is not a premium, but a discount. Therefore, if $700 were paid to the borrower, and he immediately handed back to the lender $35, and eventually received interest on $700, the offence of usury became complete *on the actual receipt of the interest;* and every fresh taking of interest on the $700 was a fresh consummation of the same offence.—*Id.*

WARRANT AND SURVEY. See EJECTMENT.

1. The marks on the ground of an old survey, indicating the lines originally run, are the best evidence of the location of the survey, and if any evi-

dence of such lines exist, it should be referred to the jury.—*Gratz* v. *Hoover*, 232.
2. Where a survey returned called for others on three sides, and on the fourth for J. H., *or vacant*, there being no evidence given that the line on that side was run, it was not error for the court to charge the jury that the return was equivocal, or indicated nothing more than that the line on that side was left open or undecided upon by the surveyor.—*Id.*
3. Where a question existed whether the larger part of a tract of land lay in Centre or Clearfield county, which were there bounded by the Mushannon Creek, it being the usage to tax lands in the county in which the greater part of the tract was situate, the official book of the treasurer of Centre county was evidence to show that the tract in question was *not* returned for taxation in Centre county, although other tracts in the same lot of surveys were so returned, the taxes on the tract in question having been paid by the claimant in the county of Clearfield; and especially, when taken in connection with the deposition of the treasurer of Centre county, that the present claimant had furnished to him a list of his lands *in Centre county*, in which the tract in question did *not* appear.—*Id.*

WIDOW. See ADMINISTRATION.
WILL. See DEVISE.
WITNESS.
1. One who was counsel for the plaintiff at the time of the admissions of defendant made before the institution of the suit, but not counsel in the suit, and having no interest in the result of it, was a competent witness for the plaintiff to prove admissions by defendant as to the contract on which the suit was founded, and which were made at an interview had in consequence of a note from the counsel.—*Edwards* v. *Goldsmith*, 43.
2. If the interest of a witness in the event of the cause be *doubtful*, the court should receive his testimony and refer it to the jury to decide whether he has such an interest or not. But whether the question of interest be determined by the court or tried by the jury, and the witness is not examined on his *voir dire*, but evidence is adduced to show his incompetency, the testimony of the witness himself, in support of his own competency, should not be received.—*Gordon* v. *Bowers*, 226.

THE END

KFP45
.P45
v.16

Check Out More Titles From HardPress Classics Series In this collection we are offering thousands of classic and hard to find books. This series spans a vast array of subjects – so you are bound to find something of interest to enjoy reading and learning about.

Subjects:
Architecture
Art
Biography & Autobiography
Body, Mind &Spirit
Children & Young Adult
Dramas
Education
Fiction
History
Language Arts & Disciplines
Law
Literary Collections
Music
Poetry
Psychology
Science
…and many more.

Visit us at www.hardpress.net

Im The Story
personalised classic books

"Beautiful gift, lovely finish.
My Niece loves it, so precious!"

Helen R Brumfieldon

★ ★ ★ ★ ★

UNIQUE GIFT

FOR KIDS, PARTNERS
AND FRIENDS

Timeless books such as:

Kids

Alice in Wonderland · The Jungle Book · The Wonderful Wizard of Oz
Peter and Wendy · Robin Hood · The Prince and The Pauper
The Railway Children · Treasure Island · A Christmas Carol

Adults

Romeo and Juliet · Dracula

Highly Customisable · **Change** Books Title · **Replace** Characters Names with yours · **Upload** Photo for front page · **Add** Inscriptions

Visit
Im The Story .com
and order yours today!

CPSIA information can be obtained
at www.ICGtesting.com
Printed in the USA
BVHW061246160819
556068BV00020B/1831/P